USAMARU FURUYA

When I spend a lot of time drawing manga, sometimes a 13- to 17-year-old version of me stands behind me and watches.

He appears when I'm tired, and it makes me feel like I'm drawing what he wants to read.

From *Jump Square*, February to September 2009, plus *Jump SQ II*, volume 3.

USAMARU FURUYA made a splash with his 1994 manga debut in the legendary "underground" manga magazine *Garo* with his innovative four-panel series *Palepoli*, which was excerpted in the English-language anthology *Secret Comics Japan*. He also created a gag series called *Short Cuts* for *Young Sunday* magazine, which was later serialized in the English-language manga magazine *Pulp* and then published by VIZ. His other works include *Jisatsu Circle*, a manga adaptation of the film *Suicide Club*; *The Chronicles of the Clueless Age*, a collaboration with the writer Otsuichi; and *Happiness*, a series of shorts that ran in *IKKI* magazine. *Genkaku Picasso* is Furuya's first series for *Jump SQ*.

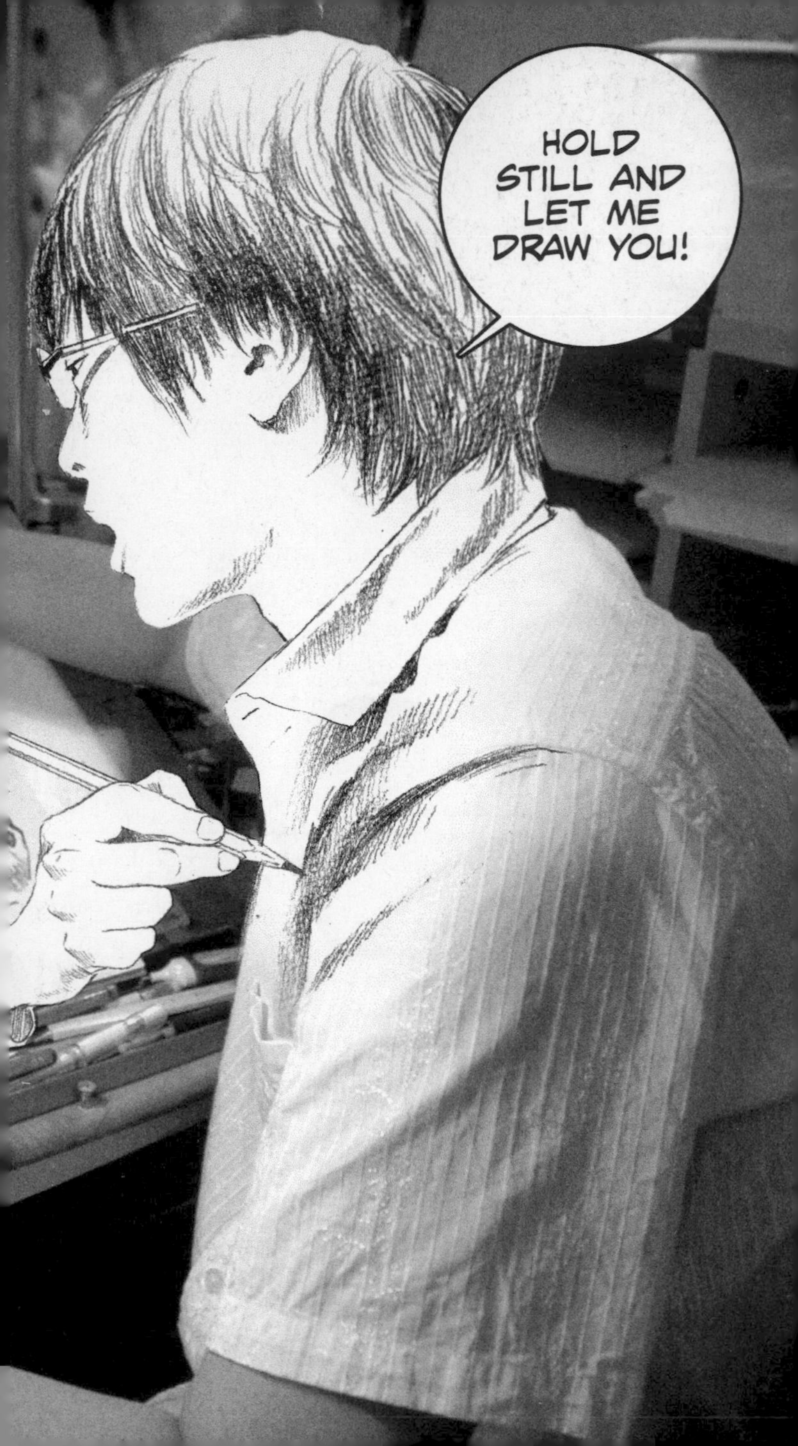
HOLD STILL AND LET ME DRAW YOU!

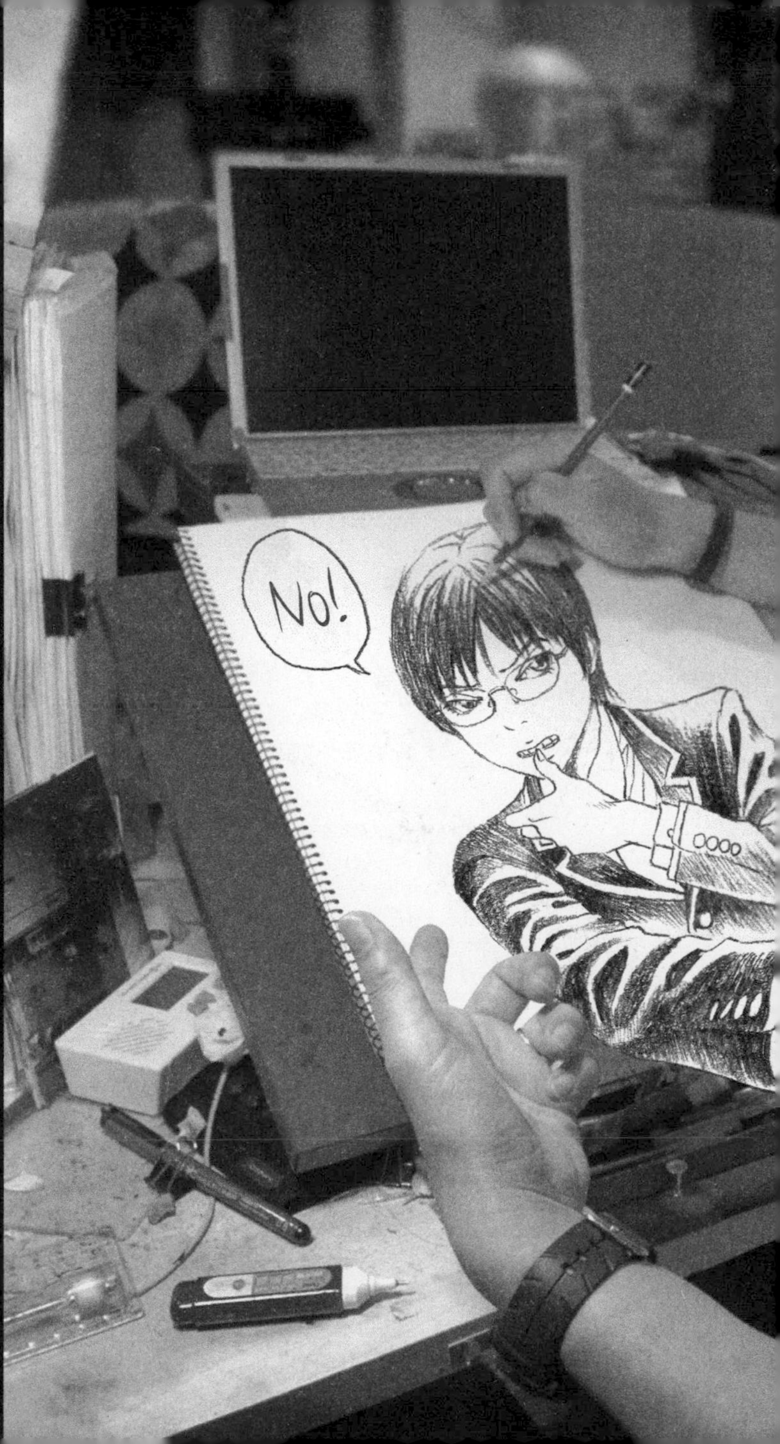
No!

GENKAKU PICASSO
VOL. 2

SHONEN JUMP Manga Edition

STORY AND ART BY **USAMARU FURUYA**

Translation – John Werry
Lettering – Bill Schuch
Design – Fawn Lau
Editors – Daniel Gillespie, Jann Jones

Printed in the U.S.A.

Published by VIZ Media, LLC
P.O. Box 77010
San Francisco, CA 94107

10 9 8 7 6 5 4 3 2 1
First printing, February 2011

www.viz.com

www.shonenjump.com

SHONEN JUMP MANGA

GENKAKU PICASSO

2

USAMARU FURUYA

GENKAKU PICASSO CHARACTERS

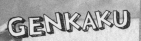

CHIAKI YAMAMOTO

She knows a lot about psychology and understands Picasso. Did an accident turn her into a fairy? Currently she lives in Picasso's breast pocket.

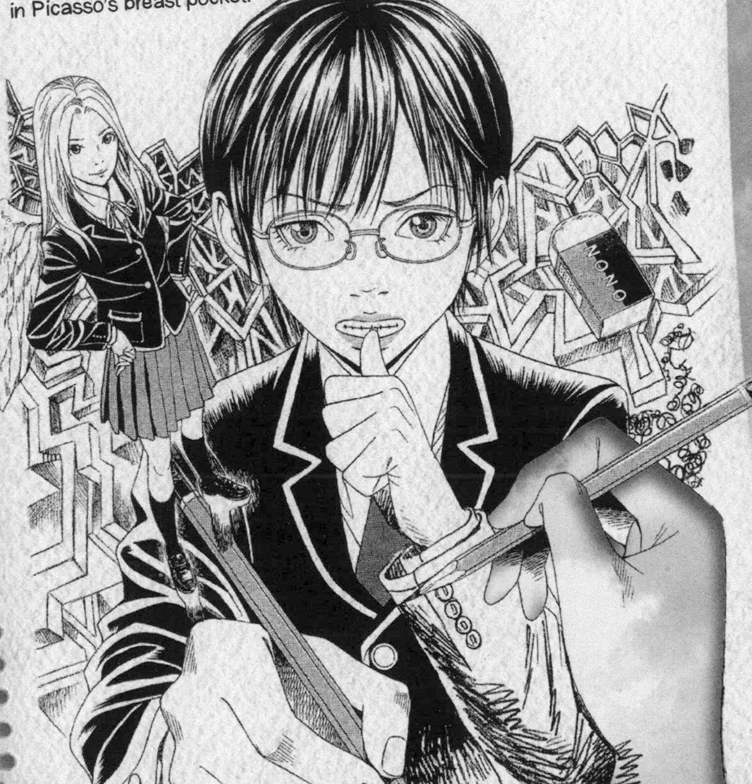

HIKARI "PICASSO" HAMURA

An introverted and slightly creepy aspiring artist. After an accident, he gained a strange power and now if he doesn't help people, his body will rot!!

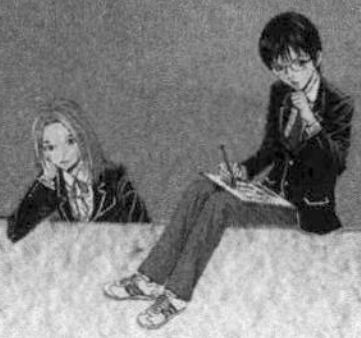

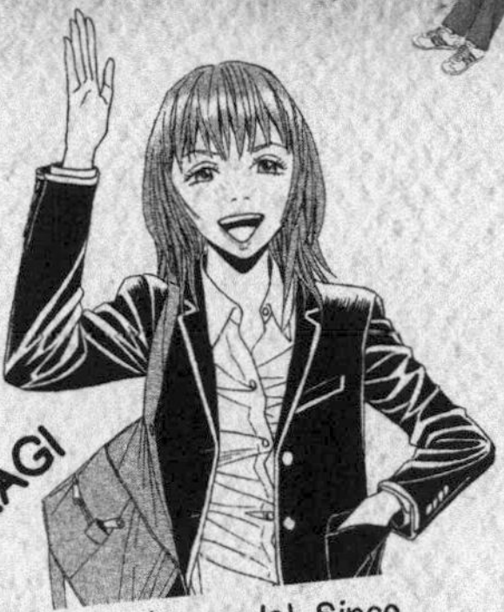

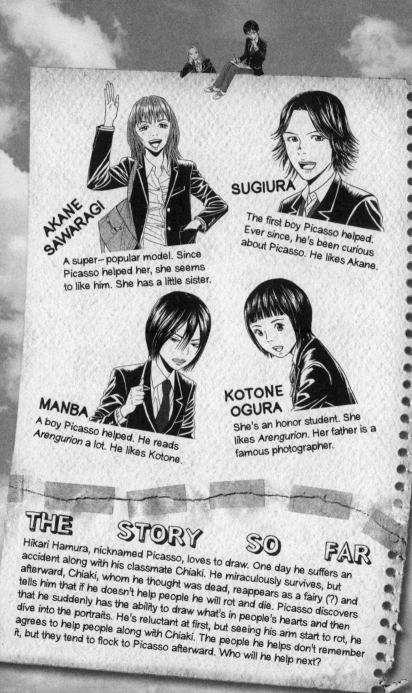

AKANE SAWARAGI

A super-popular model. Since Picasso helped her, she seems to like him. She has a little sister.

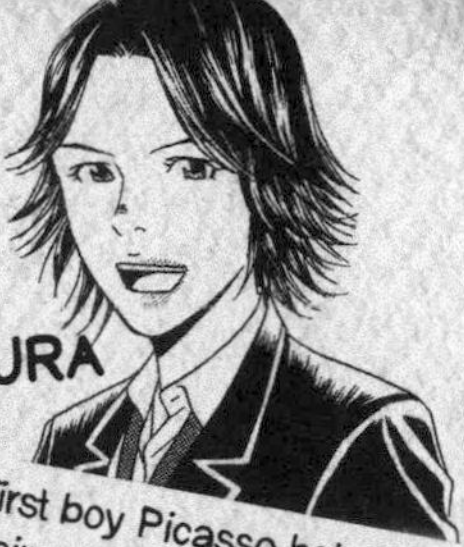

SUGIURA

The first boy Picasso helped. Ever since, he's been curious about Picasso. He likes Akane.

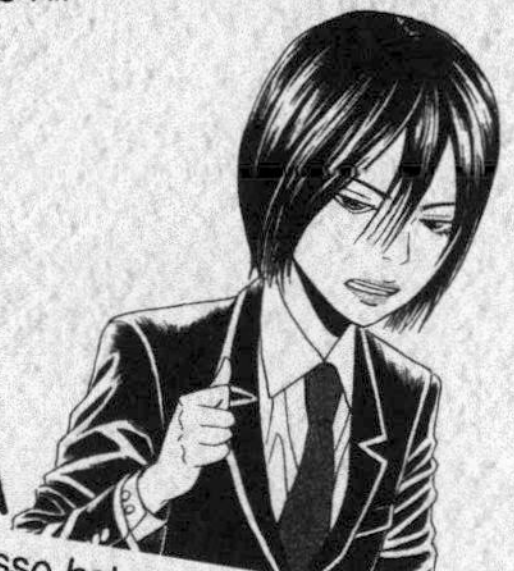

MANBA

A boy Picasso helped. He reads *Arengurion* a lot. He likes Kotone.

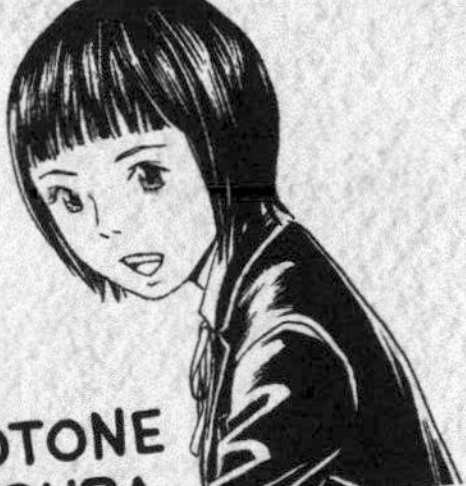

KOTONE OGURA

She's an honor student. She likes *Arengurion*. Her father is a famous photographer.

THE STORY SO FAR

Hikari Hamura, nicknamed Picasso, loves to draw. One day he suffers an accident along with his classmate Chiaki. He miraculously survives, but afterward, Chiaki, whom he thought was dead, reappears as a fairy (?) and tells him that if he doesn't help people he will rot and die. Picasso discovers that he suddenly has the ability to draw what's in people's hearts and then dive into the portraits. He's reluctant at first, but seeing his arm start to rot, he agrees to help people along with Chiaki. The people he helps don't remember it, but they tend to flock to Picasso afterward. Who will he help next?

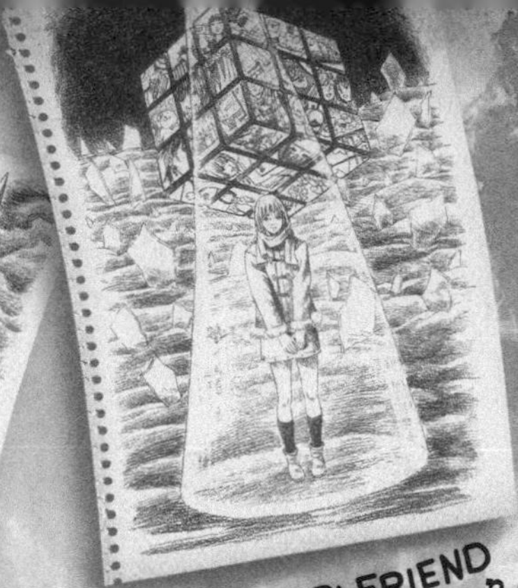

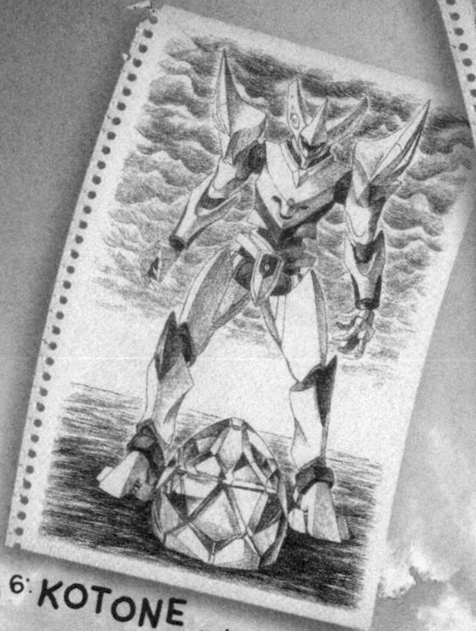

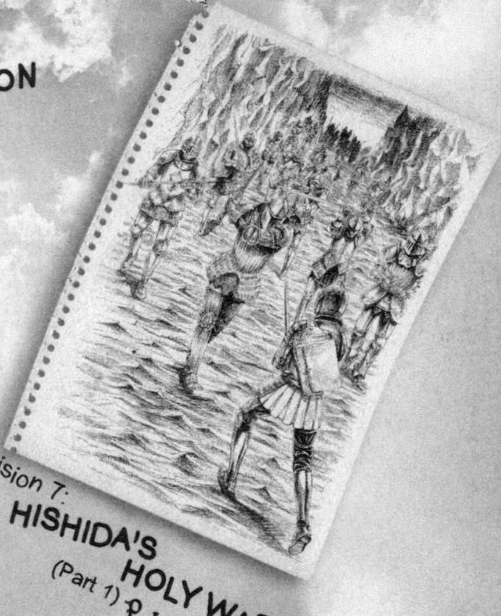

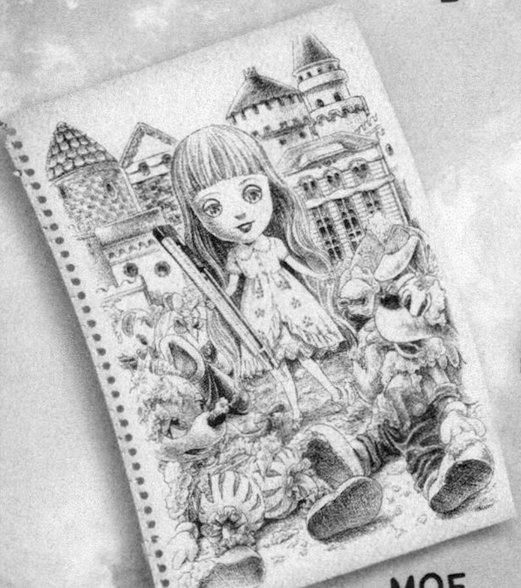

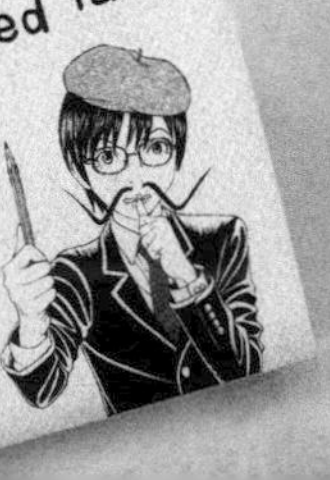

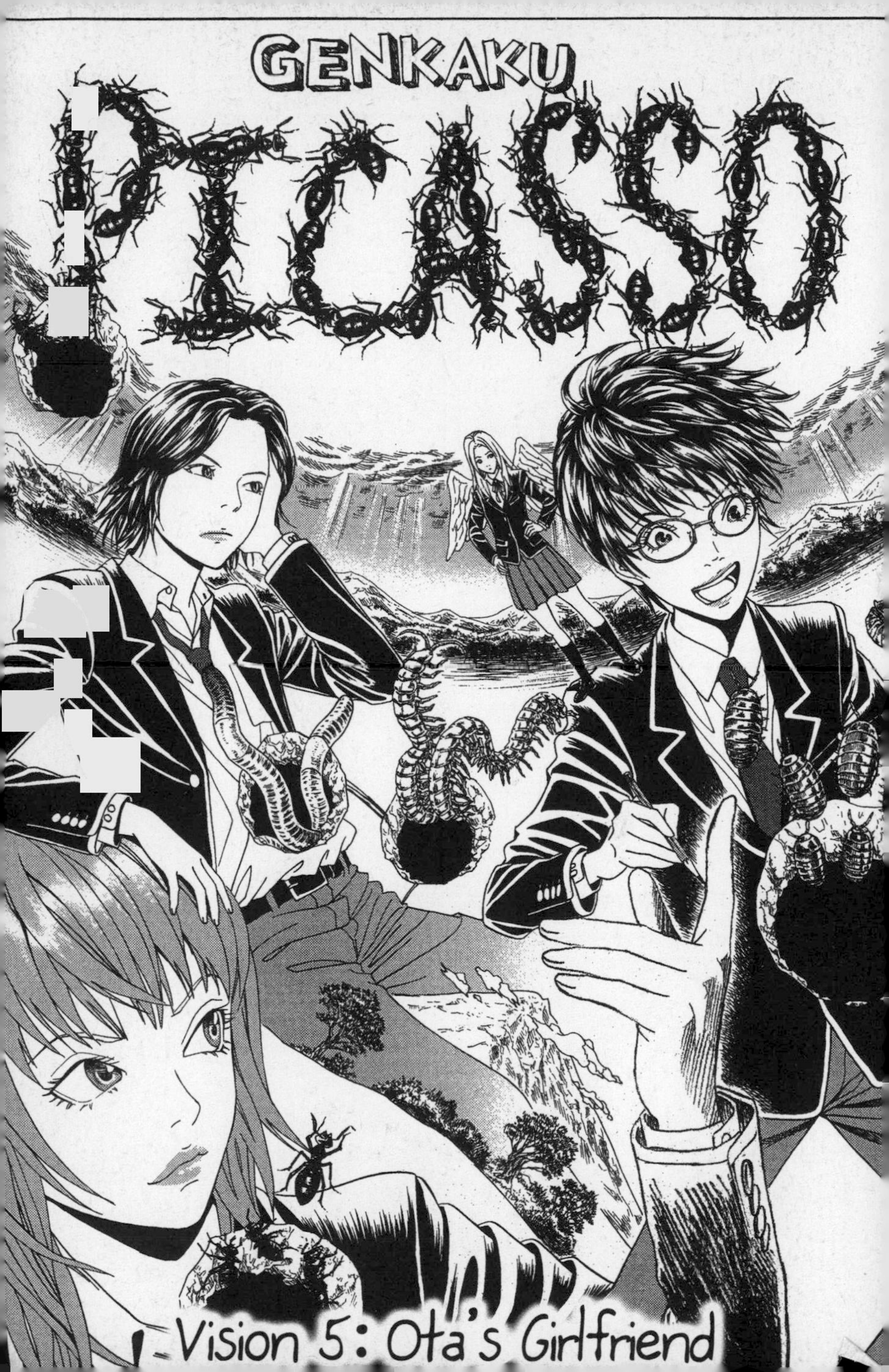
GENKAKU PICASSO
Vision 5: Ota's Girlfriend

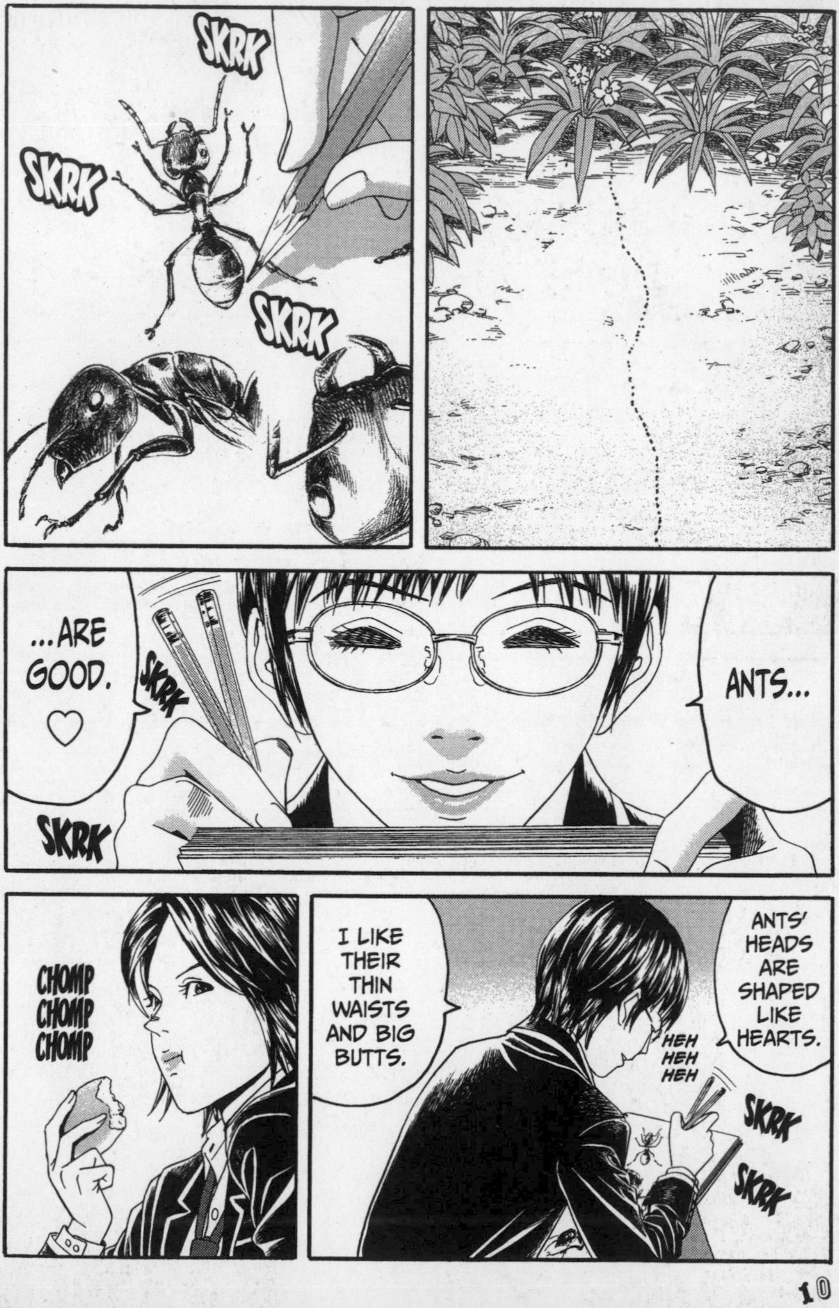
SKRK
SKRK
SKRK
ANTS...
...ARE GOOD. ♡
SKRK
SKRK
ANTS' HEADS ARE SHAPED LIKE HEARTS.
I LIKE THEIR THIN WAISTS AND BIG BUTTS.
HEH HEH HEH
SKRK
SKRK
CHOMP CHOMP CHOMP

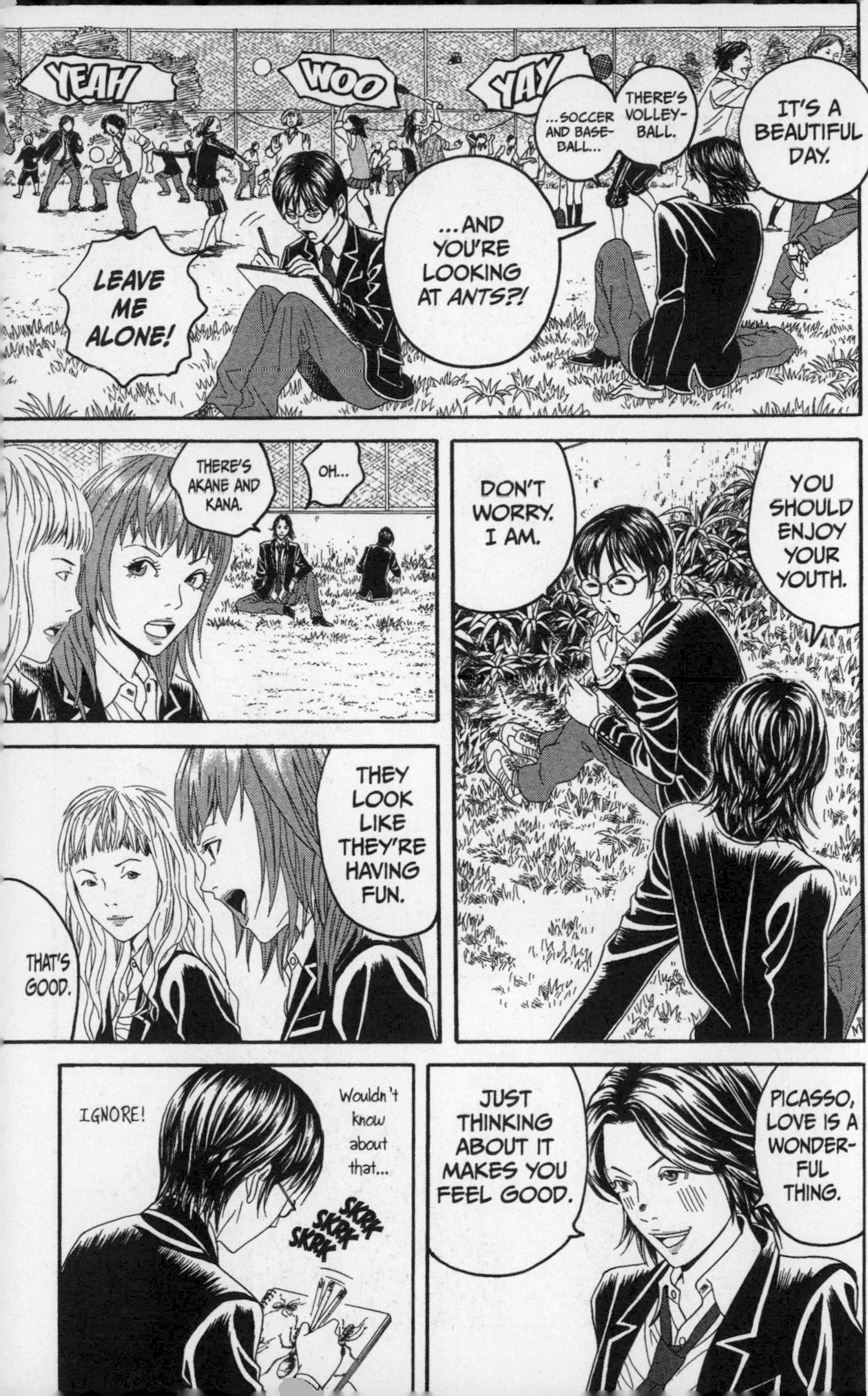
YAY
WOO
YEAH
IT'S A BEAUTIFUL DAY.
THERE'S VOLLEY-BALL.
...SOCCER AND BASE-BALL...
...AND YOU'RE LOOKING AT ANTS?!
LEAVE ME ALONE!
YOU SHOULD ENJOY YOUR YOUTH.
DON'T WORRY. I AM.
OH...
THERE'S AKANE AND KANA.
THEY LOOK LIKE THEY'RE HAVING FUN.
THAT'S GOOD.
PICASSO, LOVE IS A WONDER-FUL THING.
JUST THINKING ABOUT IT MAKES YOU FEEL GOOD.
Wouldn't know about that...
IGNORE!
SKRK SKRK SKRK

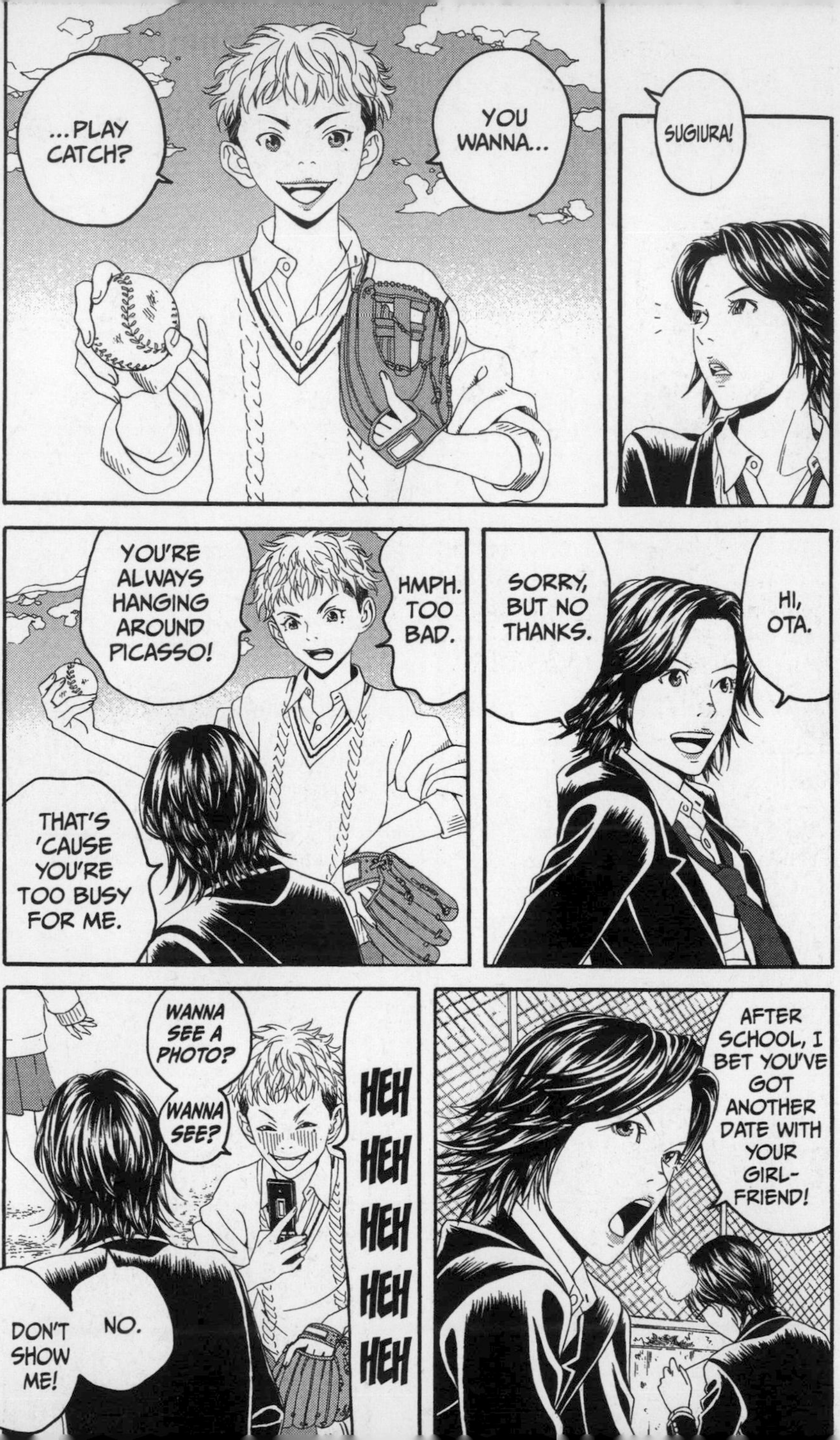
SUGIURA!
YOU WANNA...
...PLAY CATCH?
HI, OTA.
SORRY, BUT NO THANKS.
HMPH. TOO BAD.
YOU'RE ALWAYS HANGING AROUND PICASSO!
THAT'S 'CAUSE YOU'RE TOO BUSY FOR ME.
AFTER SCHOOL, I BET YOU'VE GOT ANOTHER DATE WITH YOUR GIRL-FRIEND!
HEH HEH HEH HEH HEH HEH
WANNA SEE A PHOTO?
WANNA SEE?
NO.
DON'T SHOW ME!

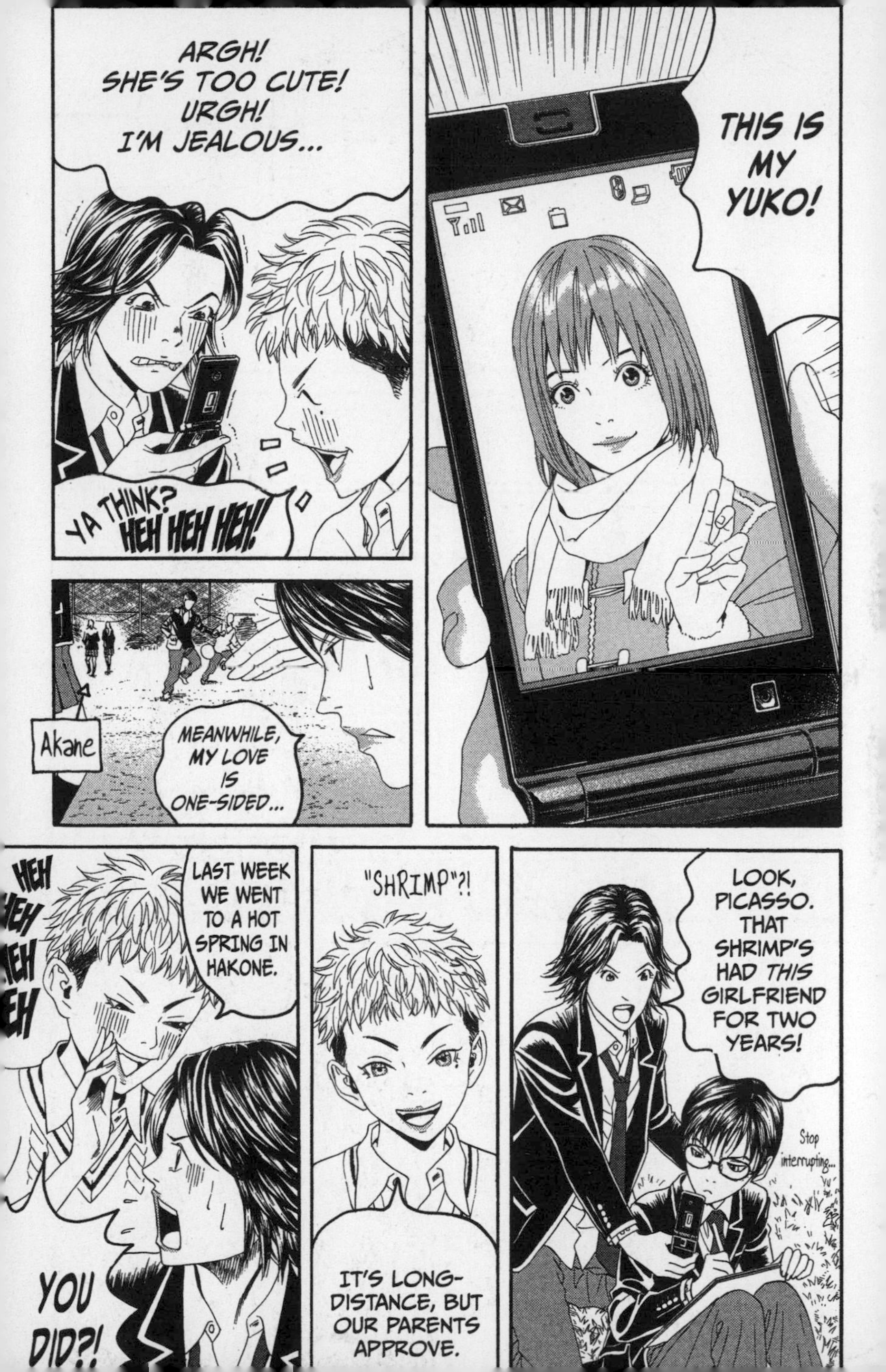
THIS IS MY YUKO!
ARGH! SHE'S TOO CUTE! URGH! I'M JEALOUS...
YA THINK? HEH HEH HEH!
Akane
MEANWHILE, MY LOVE IS ONE-SIDED...
LOOK, PICASSO. THAT SHRIMP'S HAD *THIS* GIRLFRIEND FOR TWO YEARS!
Stop interrupting...
"SHRIMP"?!
IT'S LONG-DISTANCE, BUT OUR PARENTS APPROVE.
HEH HEH HEH HEH
LAST WEEK WE WENT TO A HOT SPRING IN HAKONE.
YOU DID?!

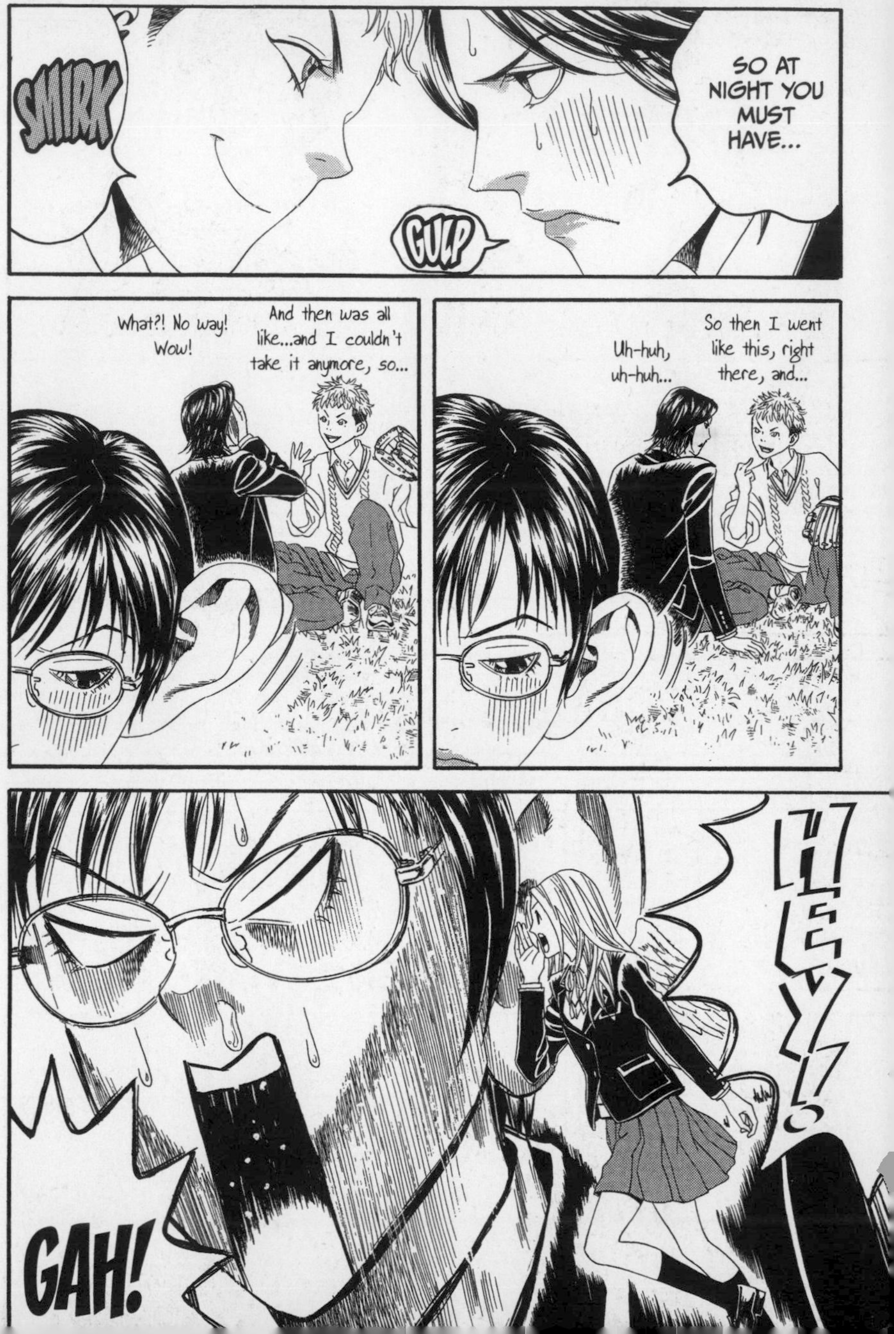
SO AT NIGHT YOU MUST HAVE...
SMIRK
GULP
So then I went like this, right there, and...
Uh-huh, uh-huh...
And then was all like...and I couldn't take it anymore, so...
What?! No way! Wow!
HEY!!
GAH!

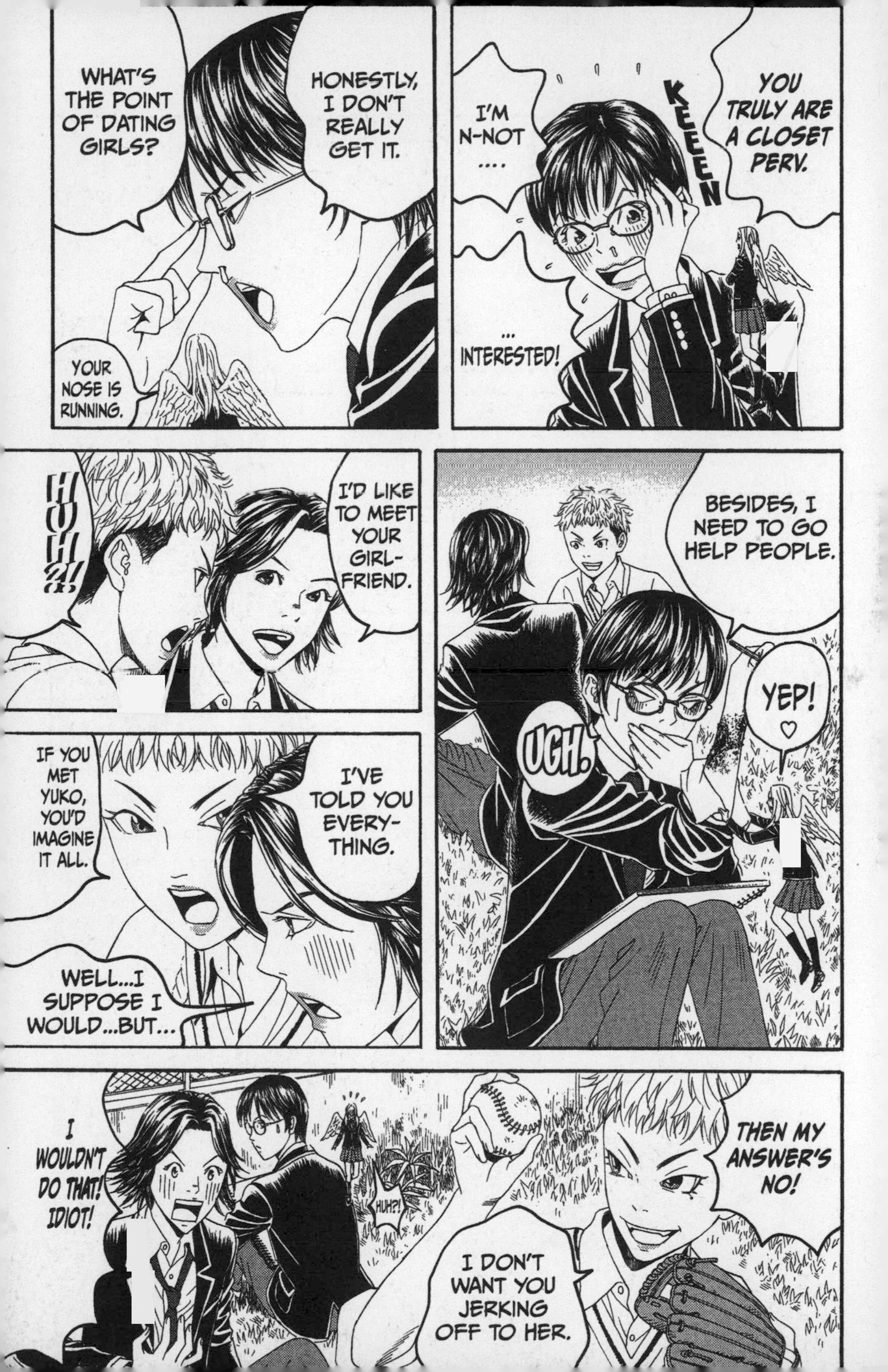
YOU TRULY ARE A CLOSET PERV.
KEEEN
I'M N-NOT ....
... INTERESTED!
HONESTLY, I DON'T REALLY GET IT.
WHAT'S THE POINT OF DATING GIRLS?
YOUR NOSE IS RUNNING.
BESIDES, I NEED TO GO HELP PEOPLE.
YEP! ♡
UGH.
I'D LIKE TO MEET YOUR GIRL-FRIEND.
HUH?!
I'VE TOLD YOU EVERY-THING.
IF YOU MET YUKO, YOU'D IMAGINE IT ALL.
WELL...I SUPPOSE I WOULD...BUT...
THEN MY ANSWER'S NO!
I DON'T WANT YOU JERKING OFF TO HER.
HUH?!
I WOULDN'T DO THAT! IDIOT!

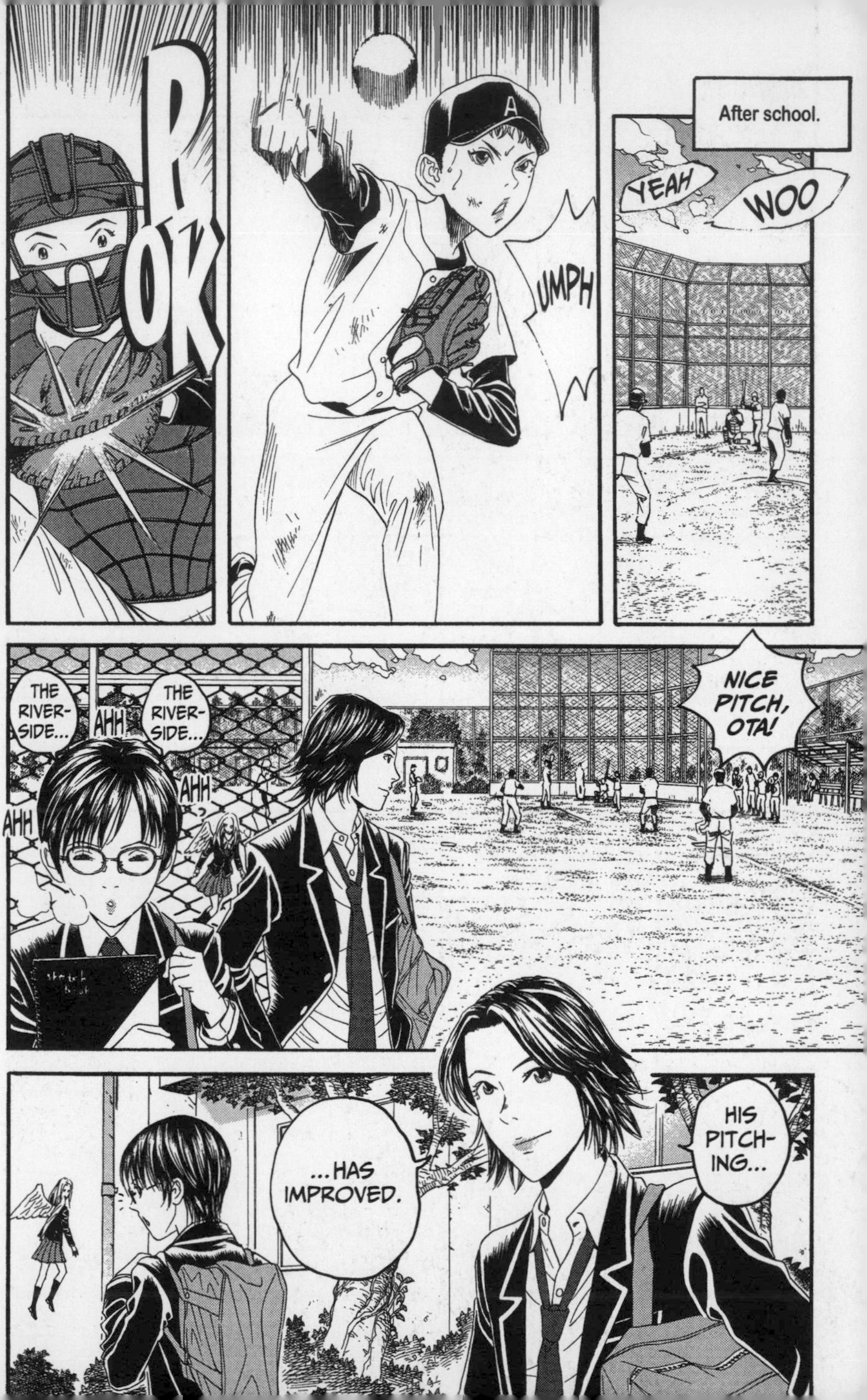
After school.
WOO
YEAH
UMPH
POK
NICE PITCH, OTA!
THE RIVER-SIDE...
AHH
THE RIVER-SIDE...
AHH
AHH
HIS PITCH-ING...
...HAS IMPROVED.

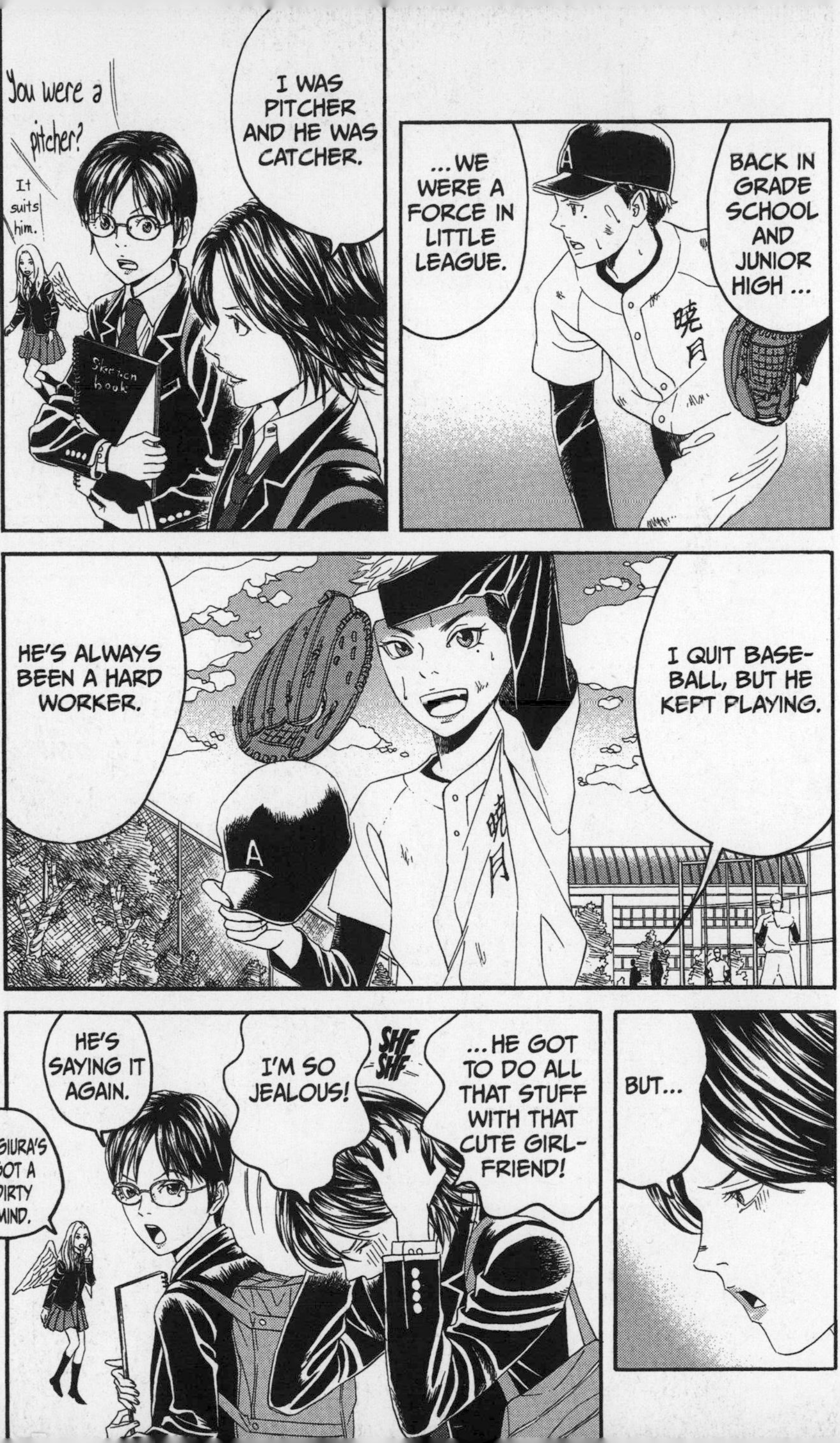
BACK IN GRADE SCHOOL AND JUNIOR HIGH ...
...WE WERE A FORCE IN LITTLE LEAGUE.
I WAS PITCHER AND HE WAS CATCHER.
You were a pitcher?
It suits him.
I QUIT BASEBALL, BUT HE KEPT PLAYING.
HE'S ALWAYS BEEN A HARD WORKER.
BUT...
...HE GOT TO DO ALL THAT STUFF WITH THAT CUTE GIRLFRIEND!
SHF SHF
I'M SO JEALOUS!
HE'S SAYING IT AGAIN.
SUGIURA'S GOT A DIRTY MIND.

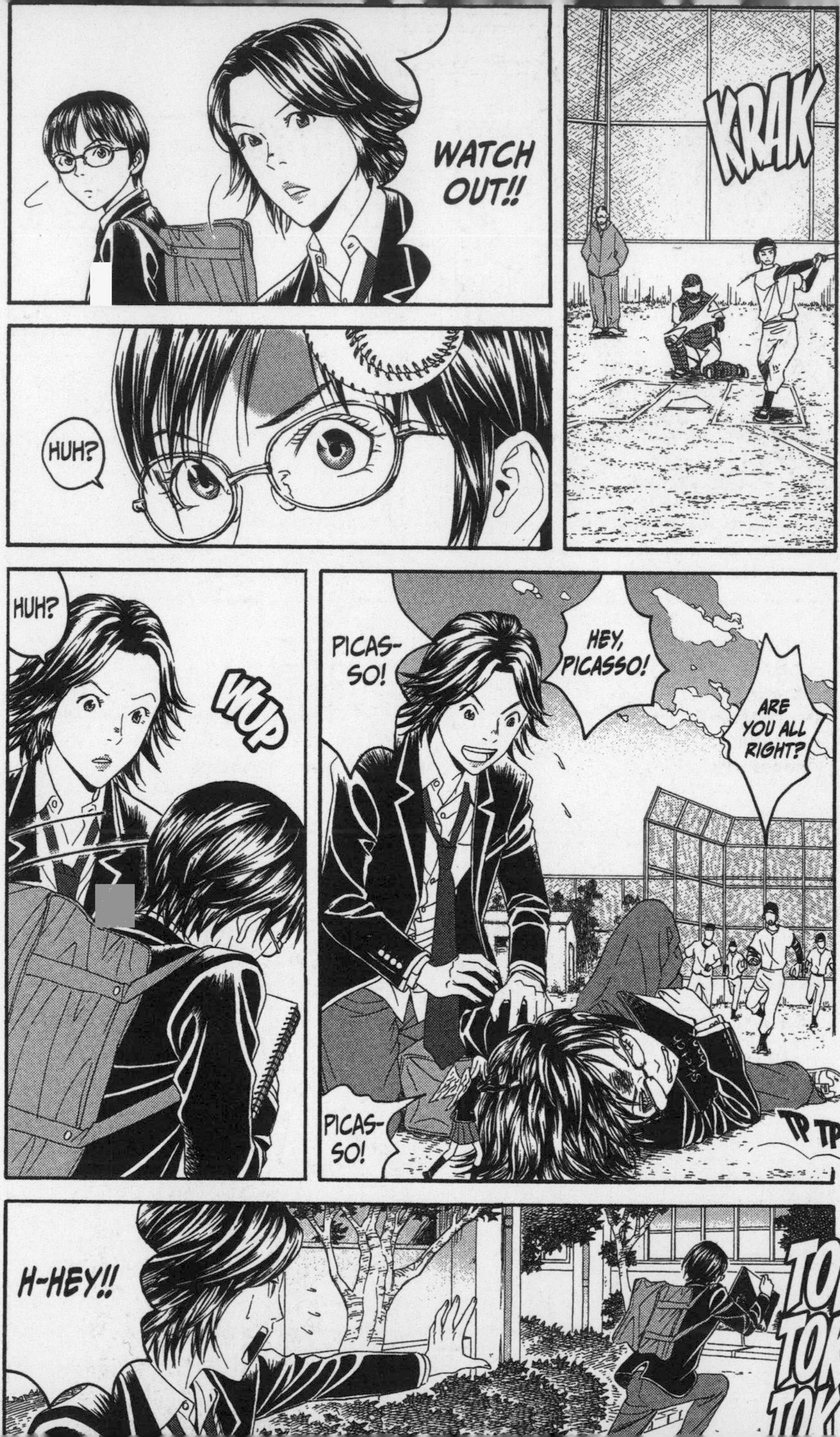
KRAK
WATCH OUT!!
HUH?
ARE YOU ALL RIGHT?
HEY, PICASSO!
PICAS-SO!
TP TP TP
PICAS-SO!
WUP
HUH?
TOK TOK TOK
H-HEY!!

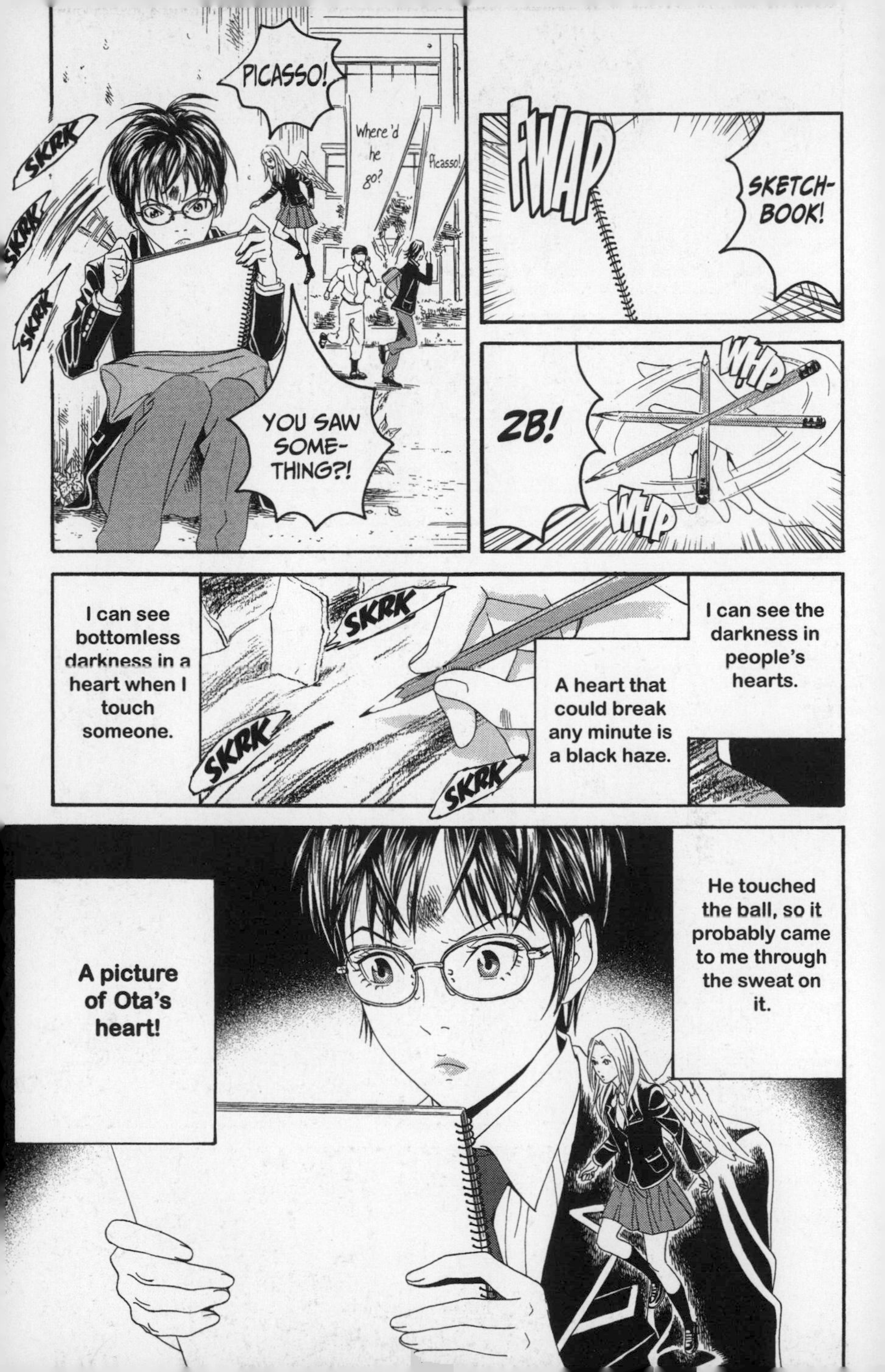
FWAP
SKETCH-BOOK!
WHP
2B!
WHP
PICASSO!
Picasso!
Where'd he go?
YOU SAW SOME-THING?!
SKRK
SKRK
SKRK
I can see the darkness in people's hearts.
A heart that could break any minute is a black haze.
SKRK
SKRK
SKRK
I can see bottomless darkness in a heart when I touch someone.
He touched the ball, so it probably came to me through the sweat on it.
A picture of Ota's heart!

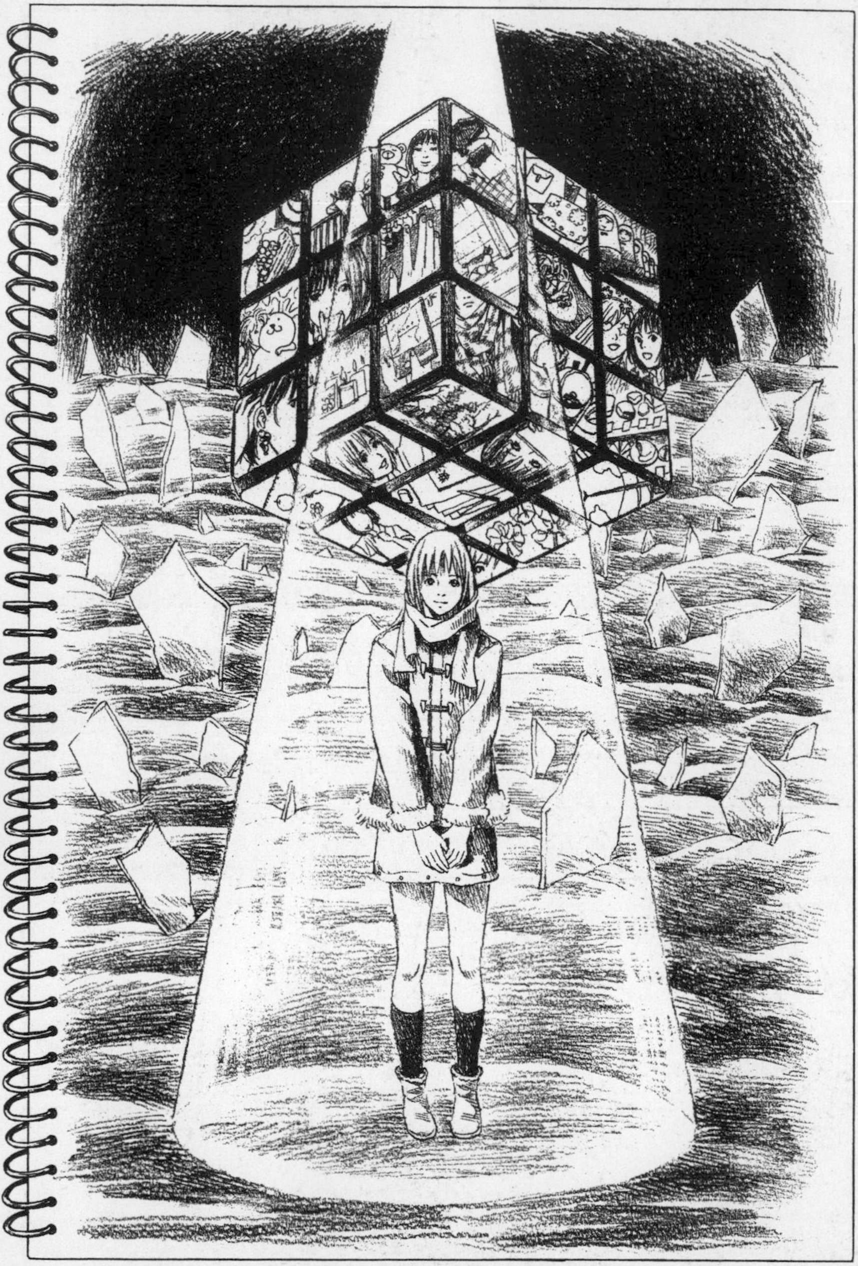

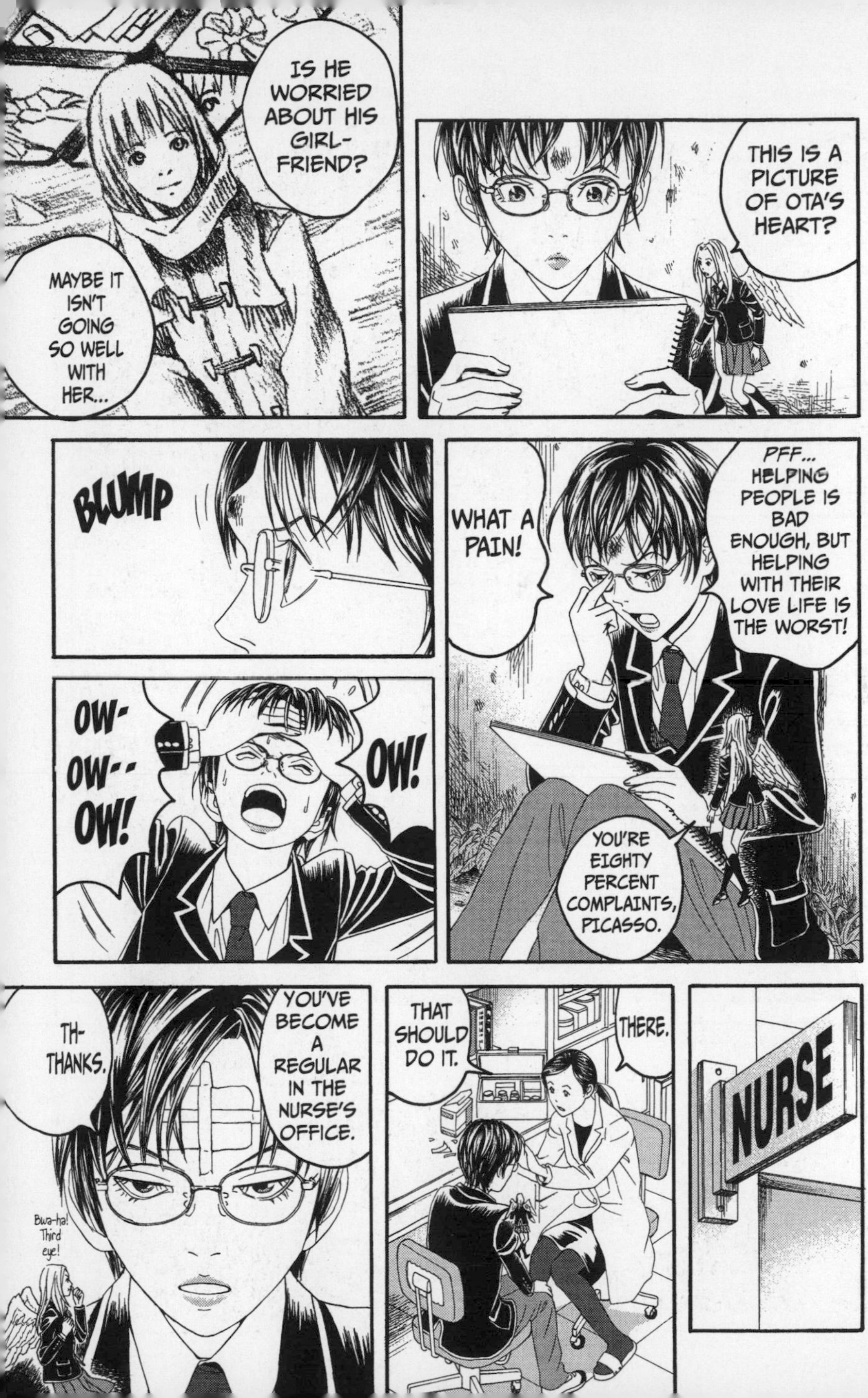
THIS IS A PICTURE OF OTA'S HEART?
IS HE WORRIED ABOUT HIS GIRL-FRIEND?
MAYBE IT ISN'T GOING SO WELL WITH HER...
PFF... HELPING PEOPLE IS BAD ENOUGH, BUT HELPING WITH THEIR LOVE LIFE IS THE WORST!
WHAT A PAIN!
YOU'RE EIGHTY PERCENT COMPLAINTS, PICASSO.
BLUMP
OW!
OW-OW--OW!
NURSE
THERE.
THAT SHOULD DO IT.
YOU'VE BECOME A REGULAR IN THE NURSE'S OFFICE.
TH-THANKS.
Bwa-ha! Third eye!

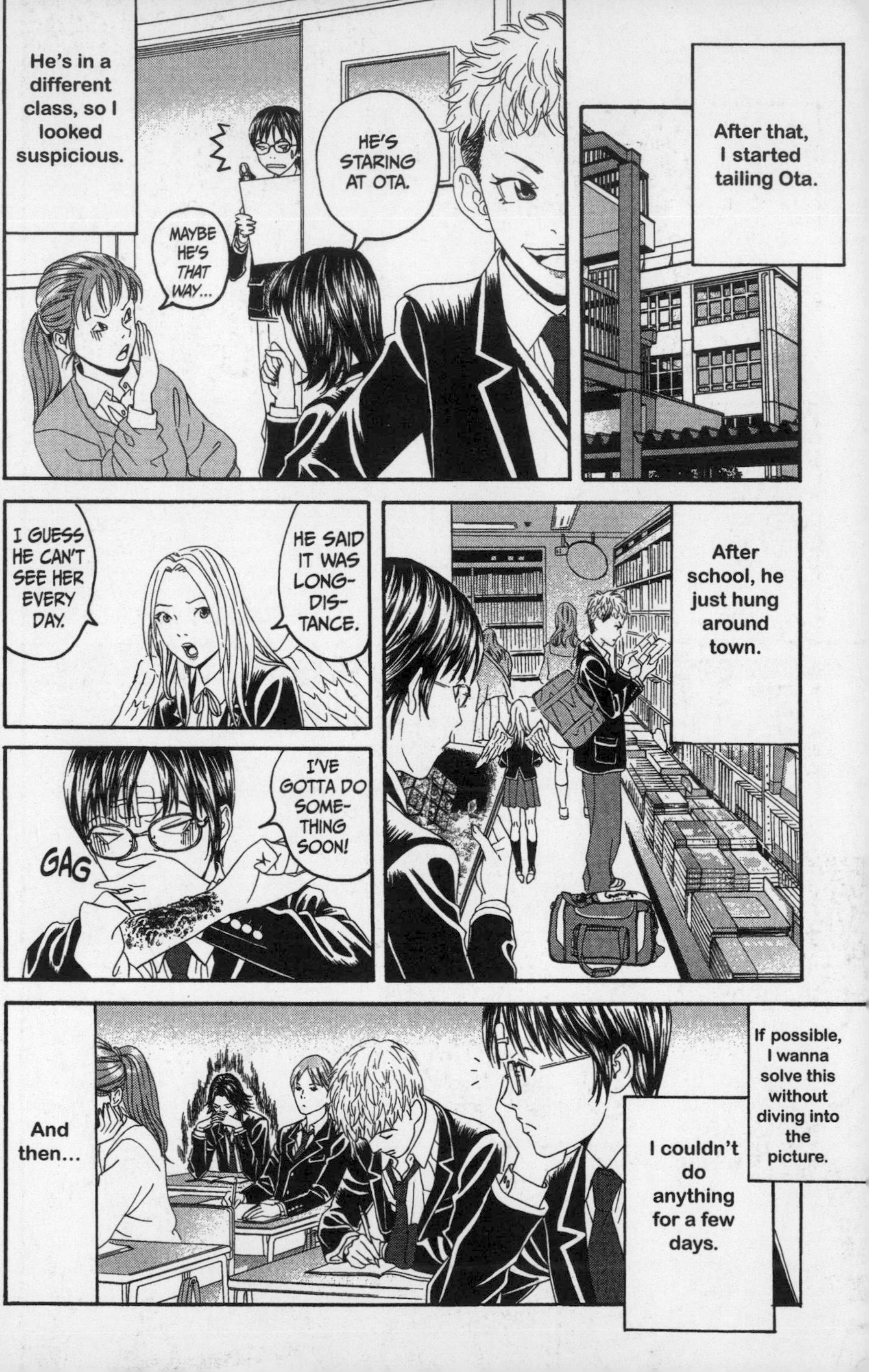
After that, I started tailing Ota.
HE'S STARING AT OTA.
He's in a different class, so I looked suspicious.
MAYBE HE'S THAT WAY...
After school, he just hung around town.
HE SAID IT WAS LONG-DISTANCE.
I GUESS HE CAN'T SEE HER EVERY DAY.
I'VE GOTTA DO SOMETHING SOON!
GAG
If possible, I wanna solve this without diving into the picture.
I couldn't do anything for a few days.
And then...

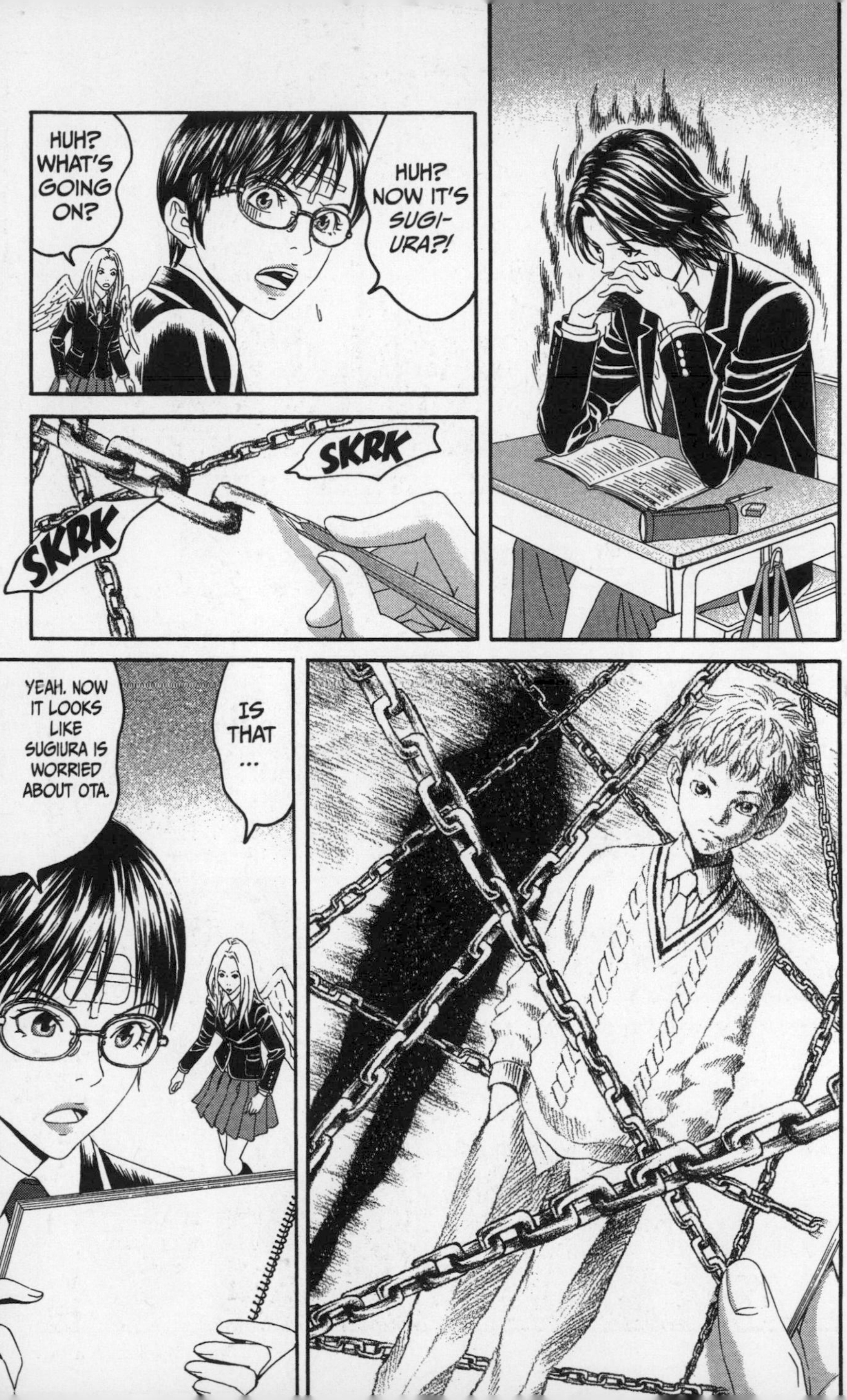
HUH? NOW IT'S SUGI-URA?!
HUH? WHAT'S GOING ON?
SKRK
SKRK
IS THAT ...
YEAH. NOW IT LOOKS LIKE SUGIURA IS WORRIED ABOUT OTA.

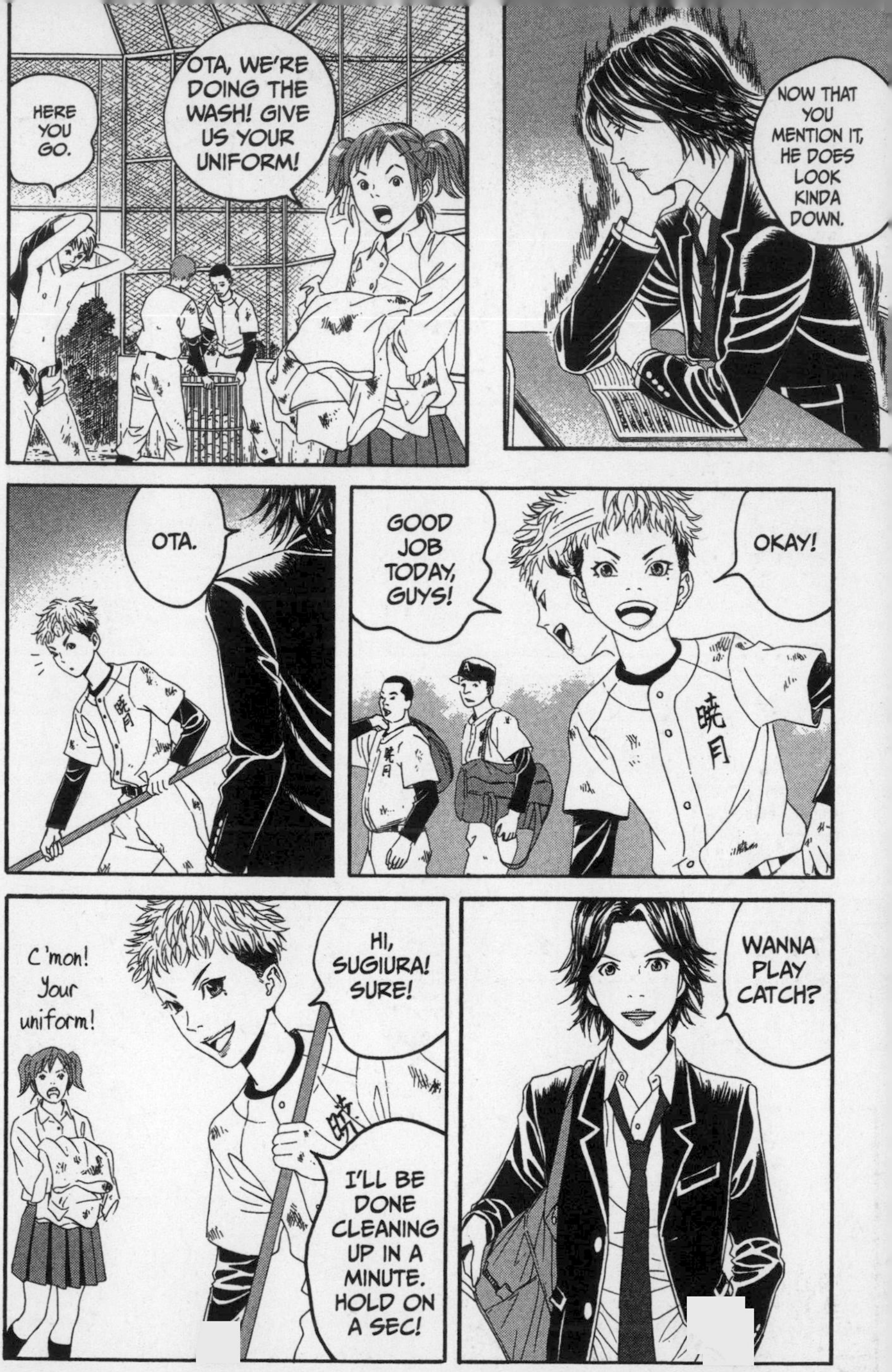
NOW THAT YOU MENTION IT, HE DOES LOOK KINDA DOWN.
OTA, WE'RE DOING THE WASH! GIVE US YOUR UNIFORM!
HERE YOU GO.
OKAY!
GOOD JOB TODAY, GUYS!
OTA.
WANNA PLAY CATCH?
HI, SUGIURA! SURE!
I'LL BE DONE CLEANING UP IN A MINUTE. HOLD ON A SEC!
C'mon! Your uniform!

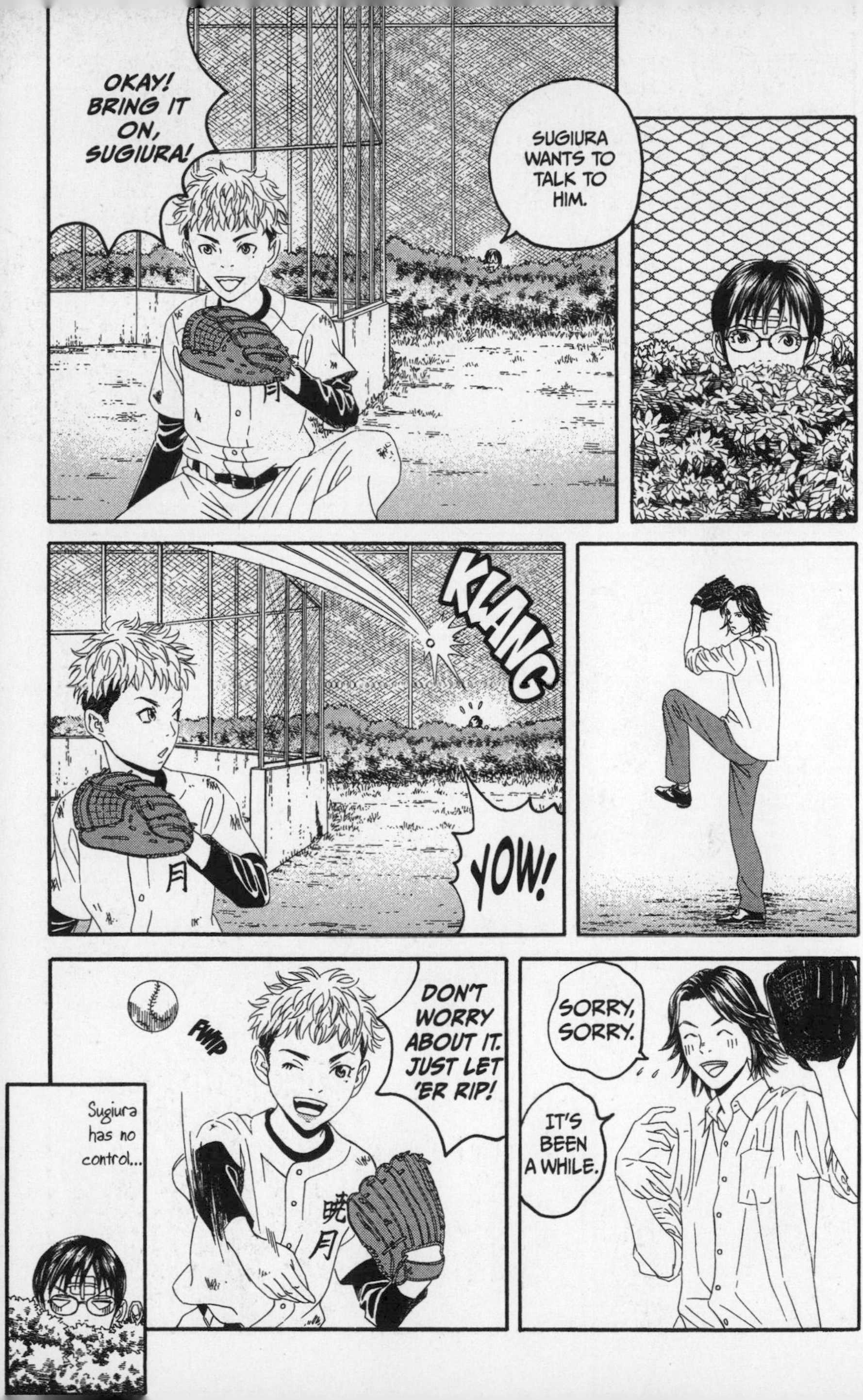
SUGIURA WANTS TO TALK TO HIM.
OKAY! BRING IT ON, SUGIURA!
KLANG
YOW!
SORRY, SORRY.
IT'S BEEN A WHILE.
DON'T WORRY ABOUT IT. JUST LET 'ER RIP!
FWIP
Sugiura has no control...

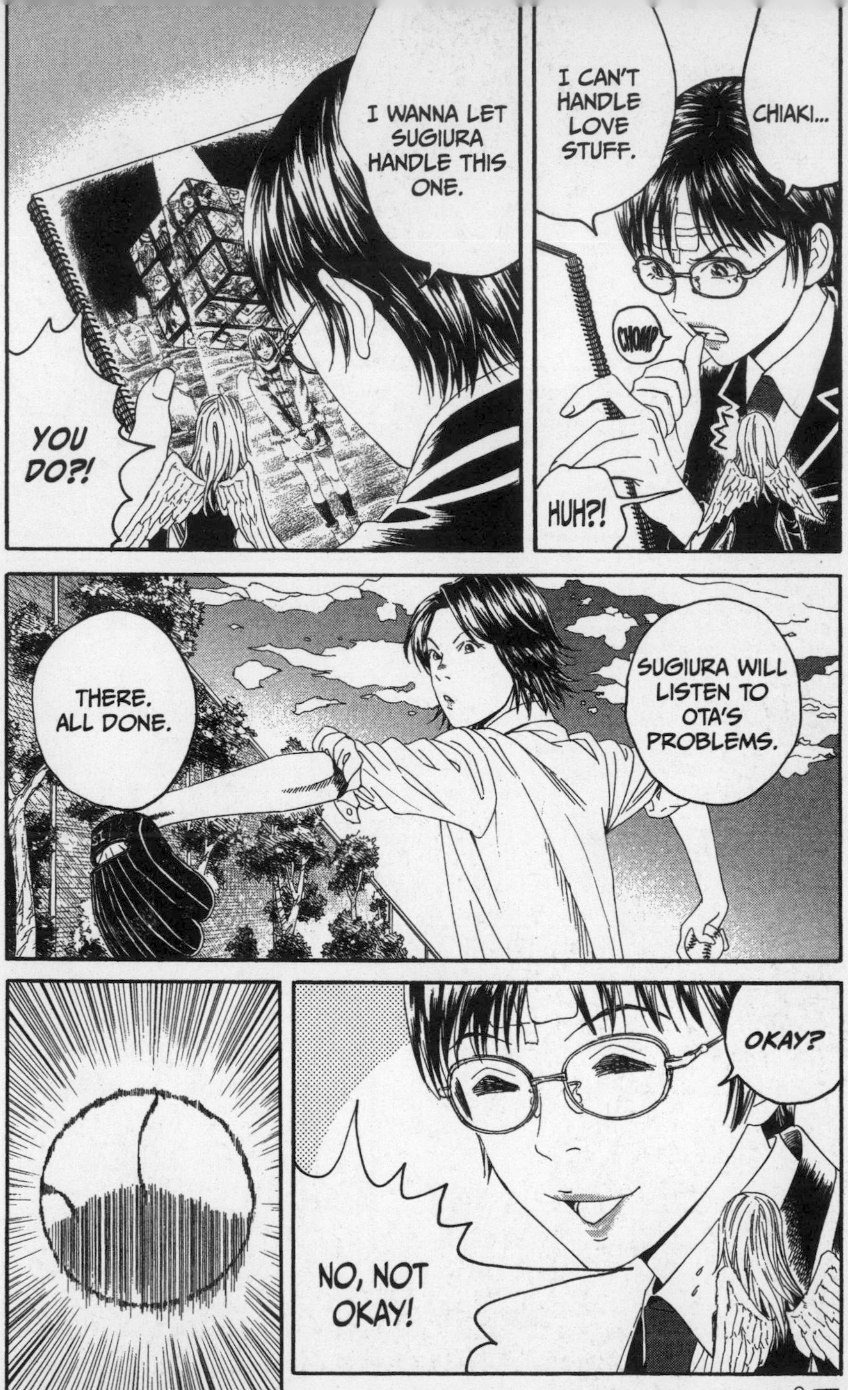
CHIAKI...
I CAN'T HANDLE LOVE STUFF.
CHOMP
HUH?!
I WANNA LET SUGIURA HANDLE THIS ONE.
YOU DO?!
SUGIURA WILL LISTEN TO OTA'S PROBLEMS.
THERE. ALL DONE.
OKAY?
NO, NOT OKAY!

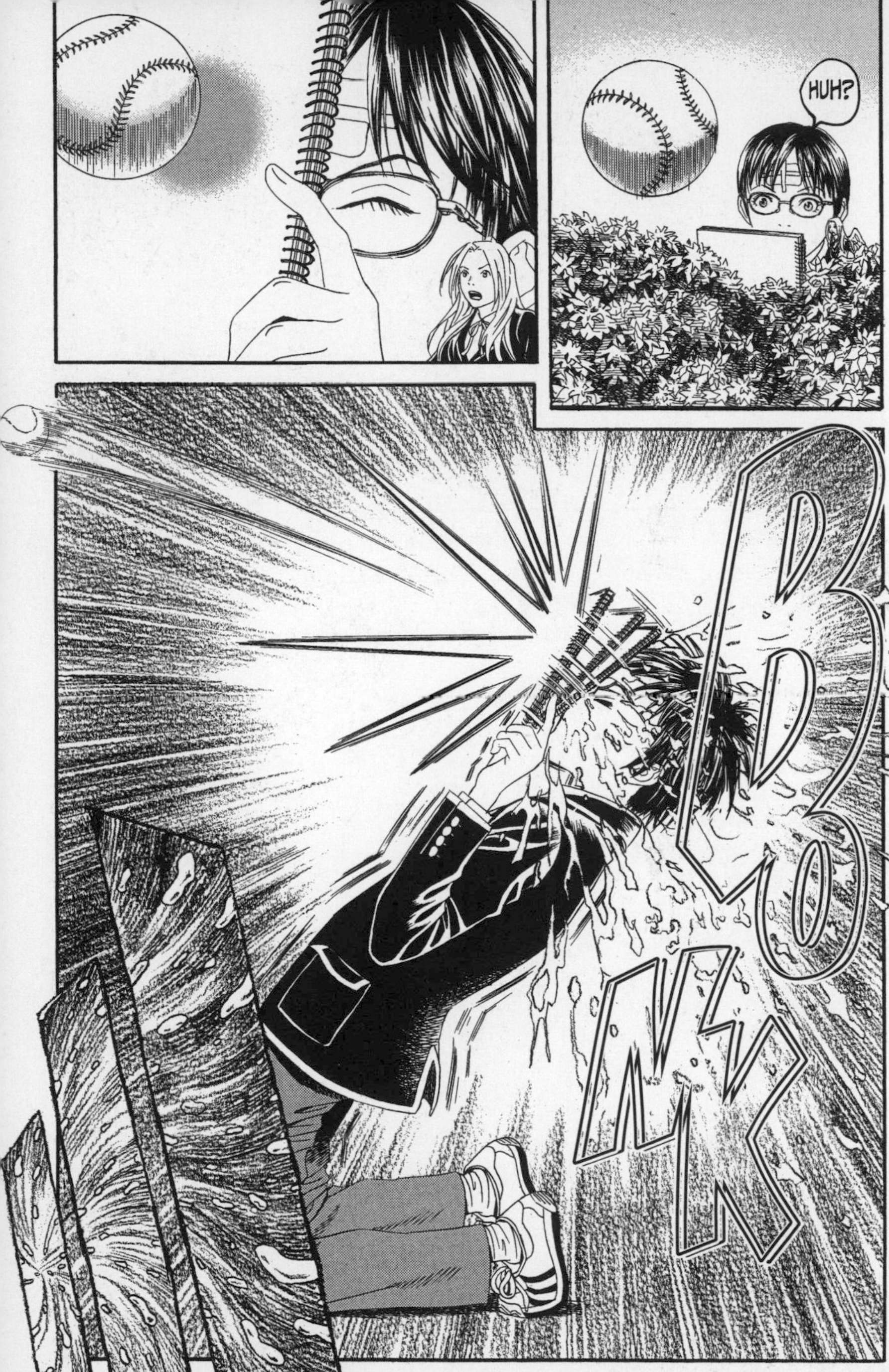
HUH?
BONK

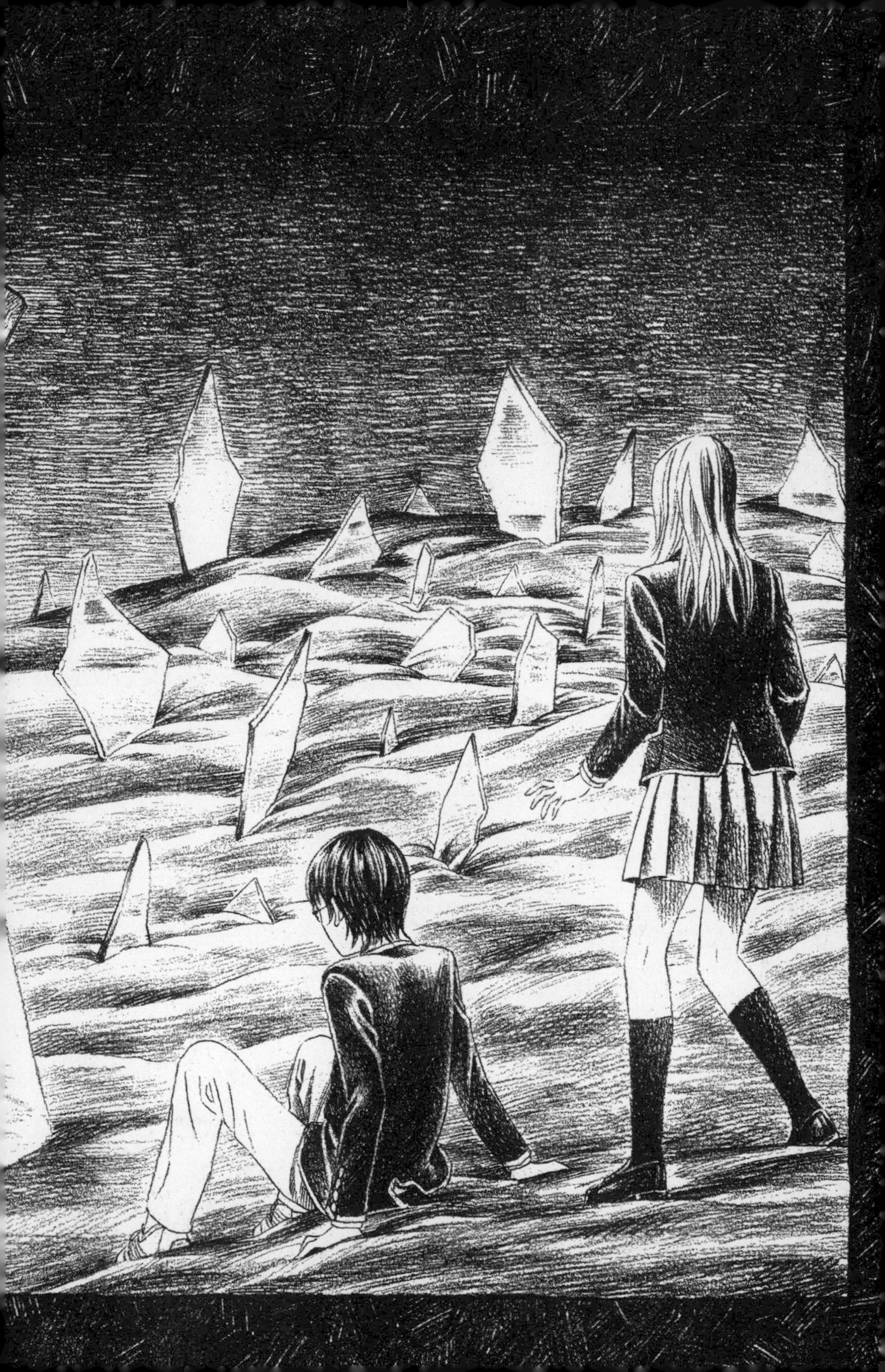

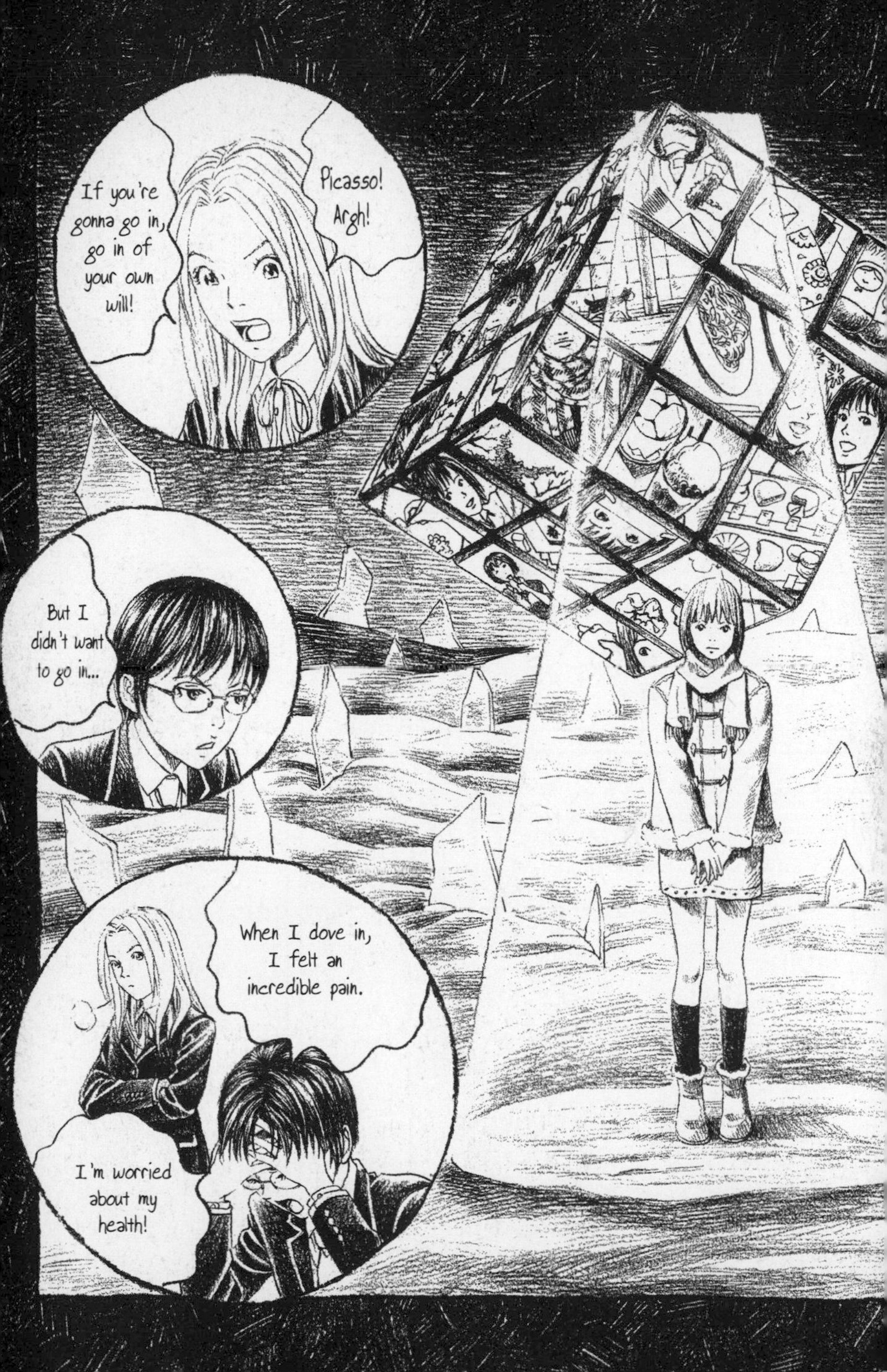
Picasso! Argh!
If you're gonna go in, go in of your own will!
But I didn't want to go in...
When I dove in, I felt an incredible pain.
I'm worried about my health!

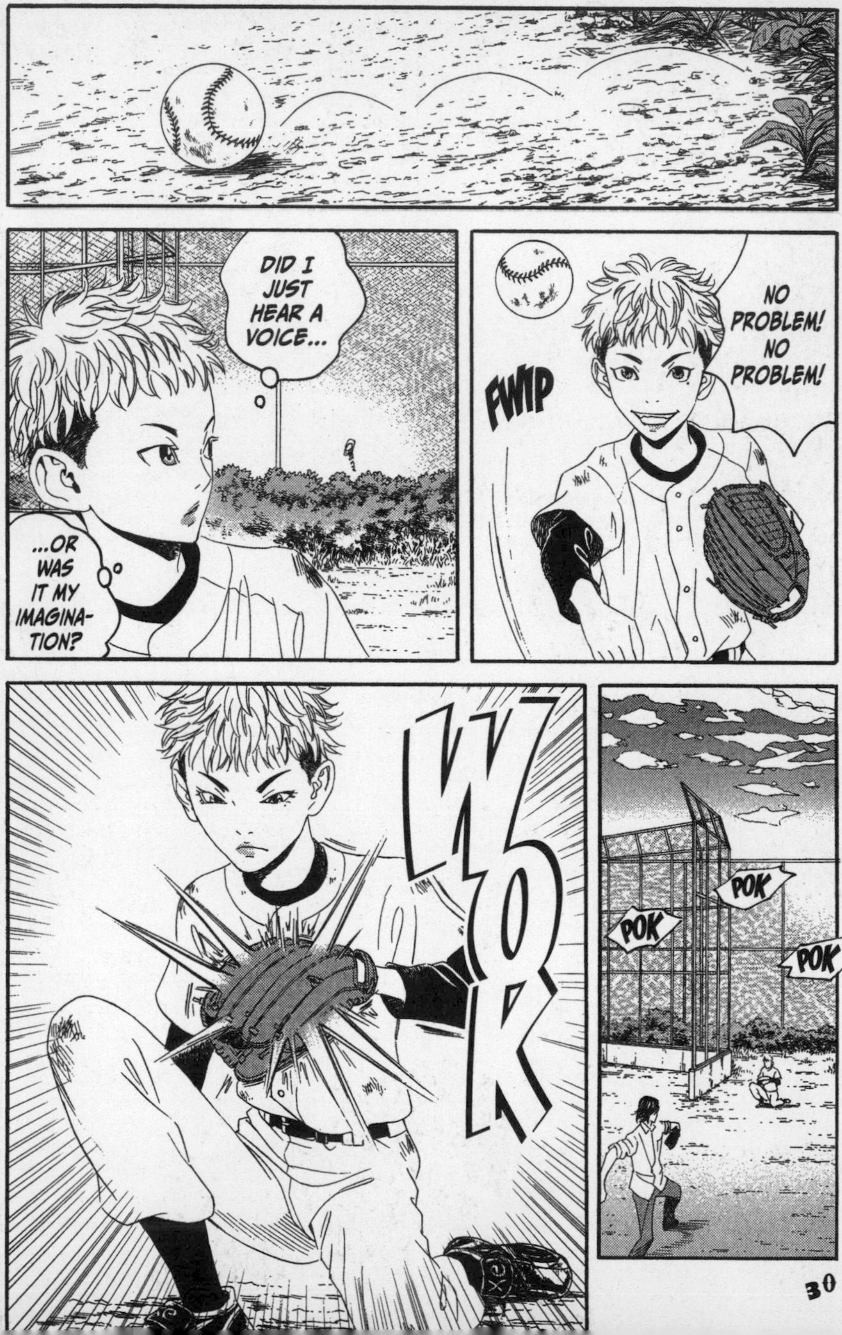
FWIP
NO PROBLEM! NO PROBLEM!
DID I JUST HEAR A VOICE...
...OR WAS IT MY IMAGINATION?
POK
POK
POK
WOK

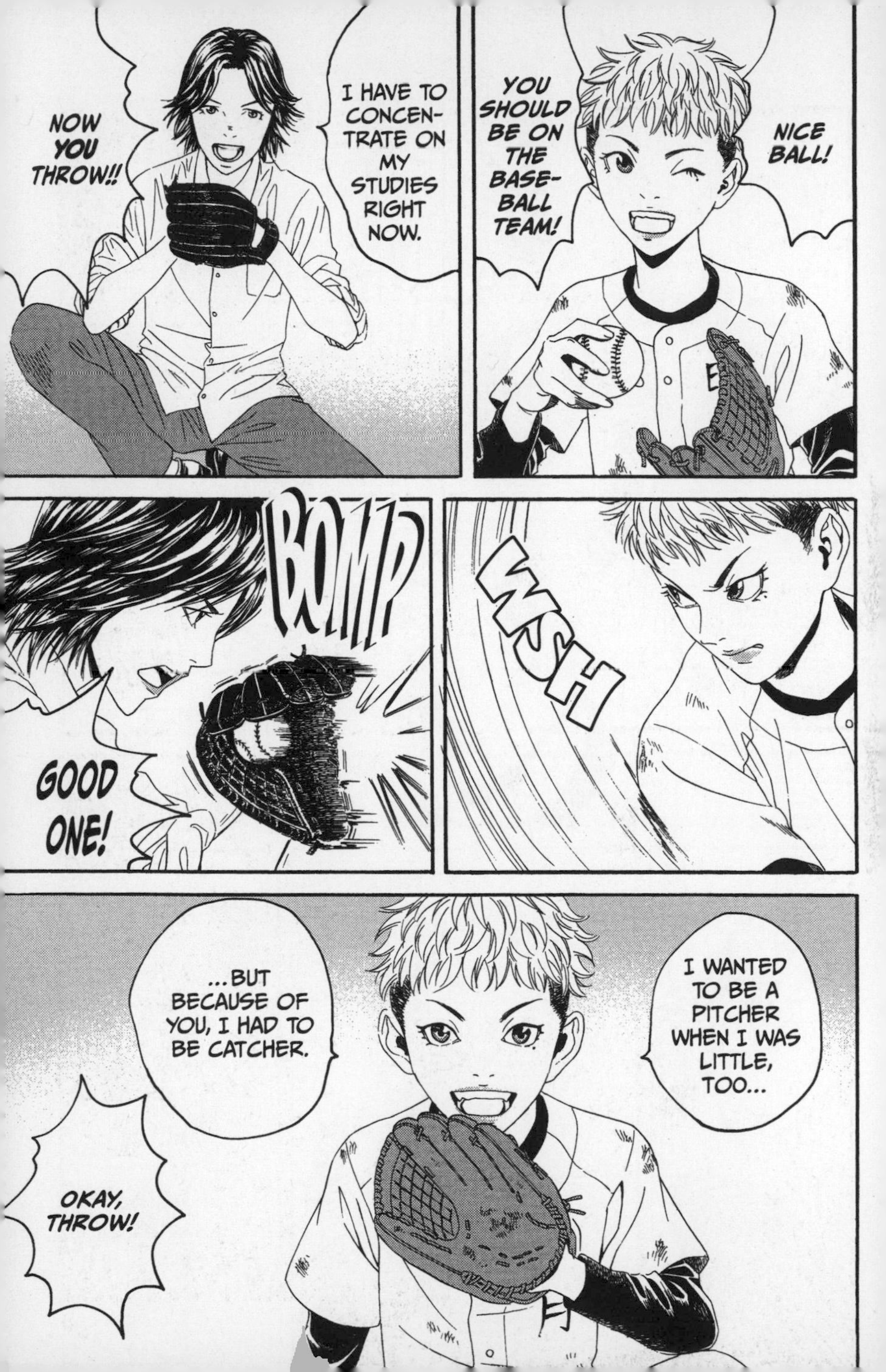
NICE BALL!
YOU SHOULD BE ON THE BASEBALL TEAM!
I HAVE TO CONCENTRATE ON MY STUDIES RIGHT NOW.
NOW YOU THROW!!
WSH
BOMP
GOOD ONE!
I WANTED TO BE A PITCHER WHEN I WAS LITTLE, TOO...
...BUT BECAUSE OF YOU, I HAD TO BE CATCHER.
OKAY, THROW!

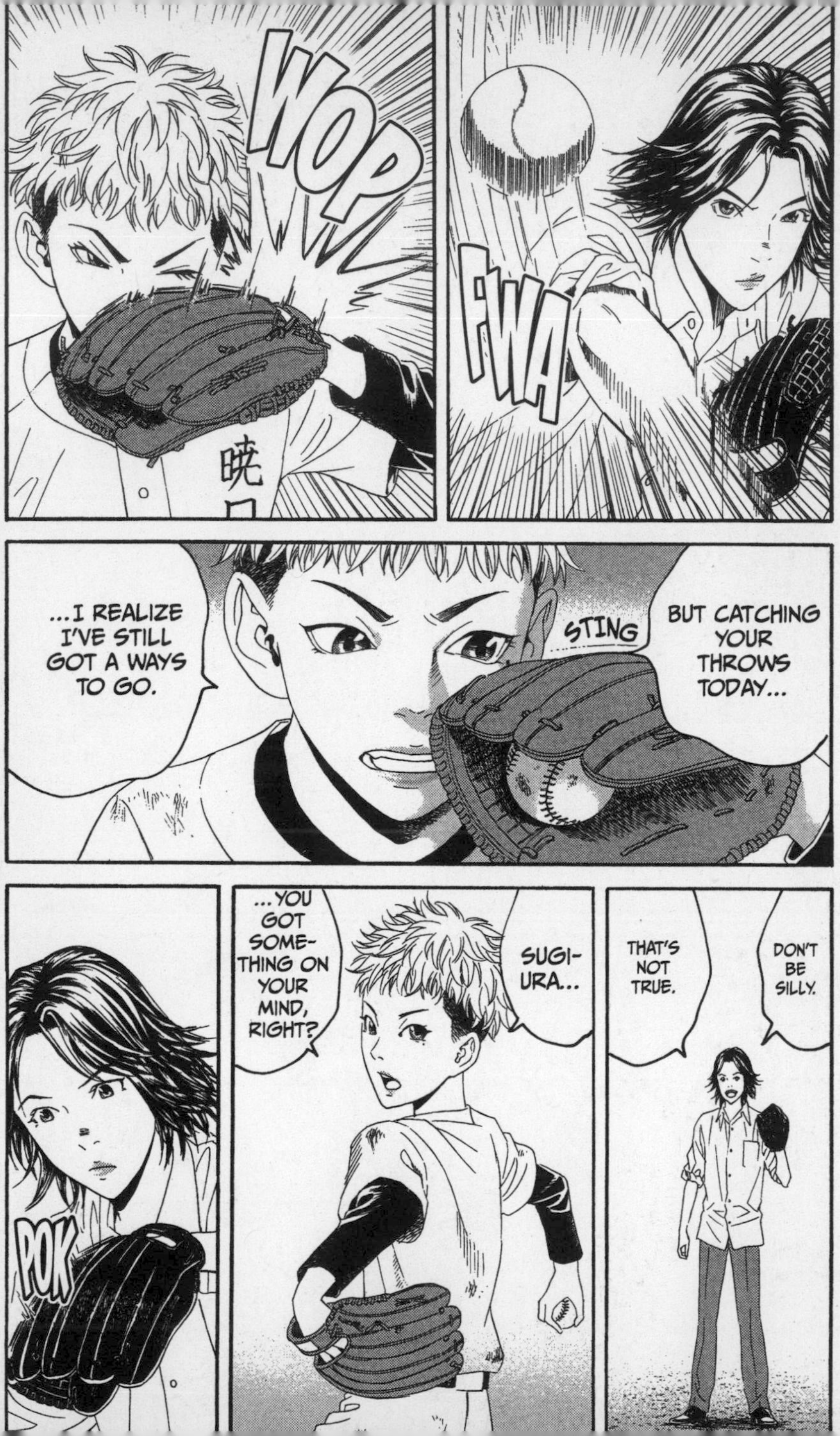
FWA
WOP
暁
BUT CATCHING YOUR THROWS TODAY...
STING
...I REALIZE I'VE STILL GOT A WAYS TO GO.
DON'T BE SILLY.
THAT'S NOT TRUE.
SUGI-URA...
...YOU GOT SOME-THING ON YOUR MIND, RIGHT?
POK

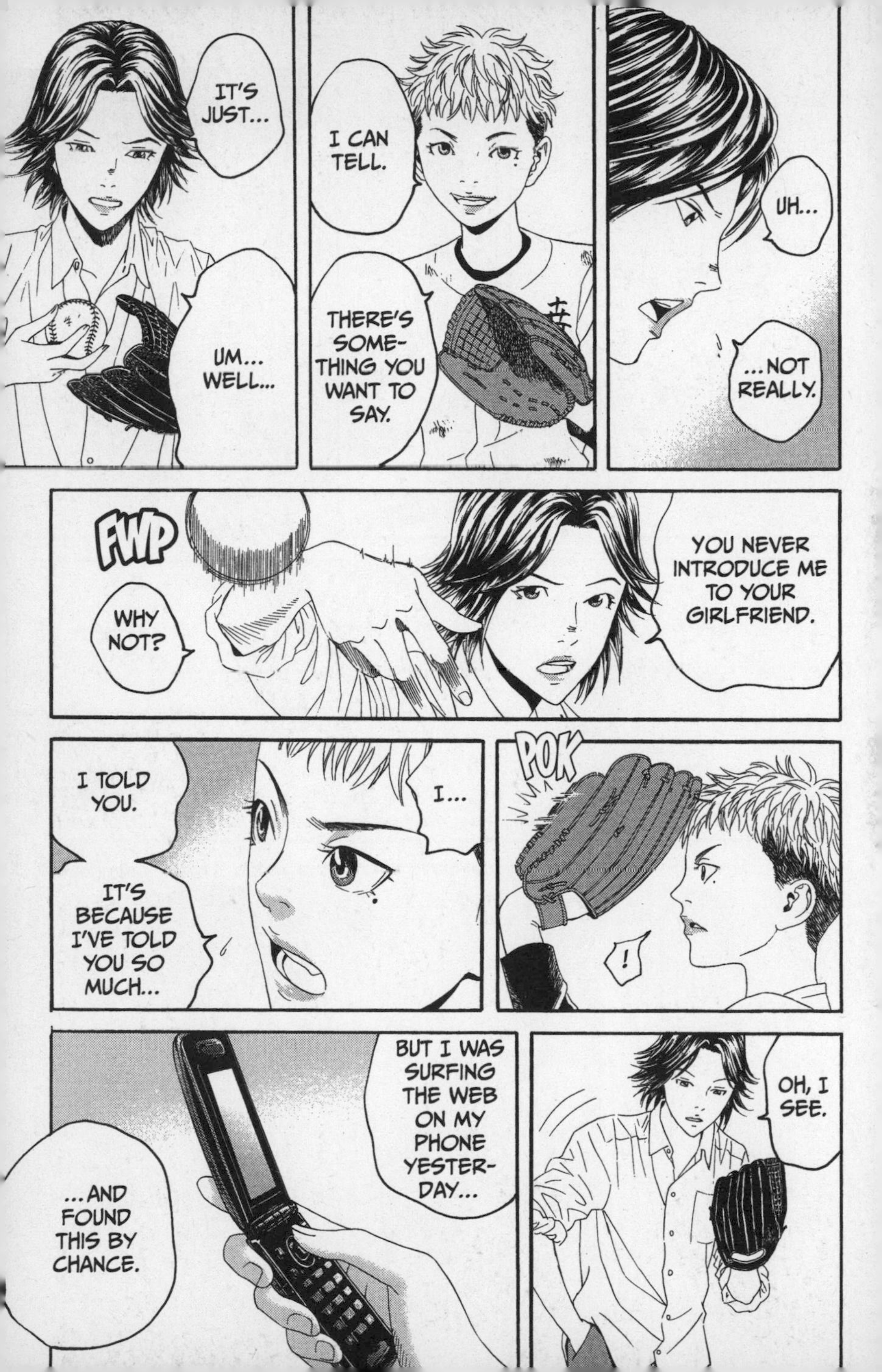
UH...
...NOT REALLY.
I CAN TELL.
THERE'S SOME-THING YOU WANT TO SAY.
IT'S JUST...
UM... WELL...
YOU NEVER INTRODUCE ME TO YOUR GIRLFRIEND.
FWP
WHY NOT?
POK
!
I...
I TOLD YOU.
IT'S BECAUSE I'VE TOLD YOU SO MUCH...
OH, I SEE.
BUT I WAS SURFING THE WEB ON MY PHONE YESTER-DAY...
...AND FOUND THIS BY CHANCE.

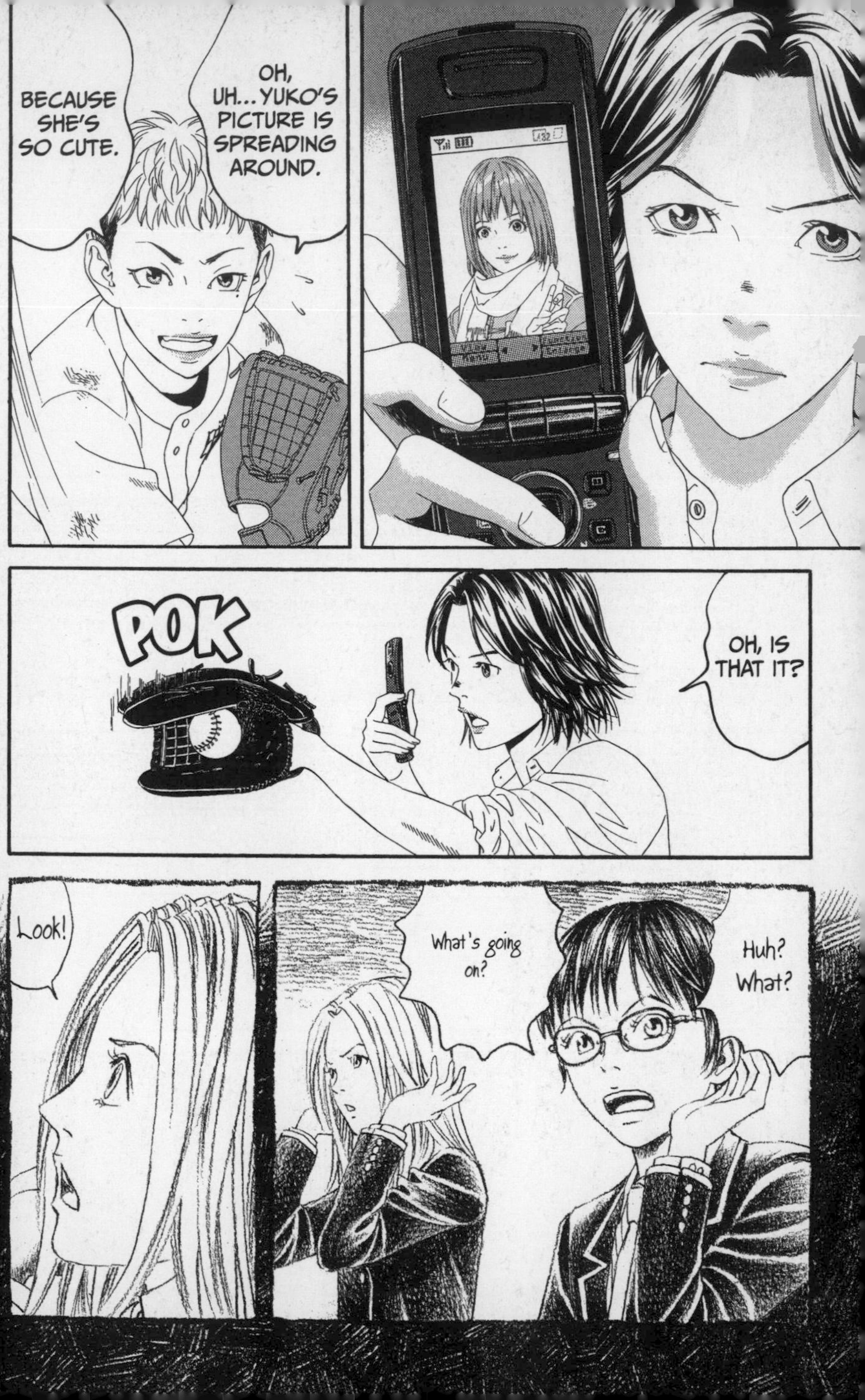
OH, UH...YUKO'S PICTURE IS SPREADING AROUND.
BECAUSE SHE'S SO CUTE.
OH, IS THAT IT?
POK
Huh? What?
What's going on?
Look!

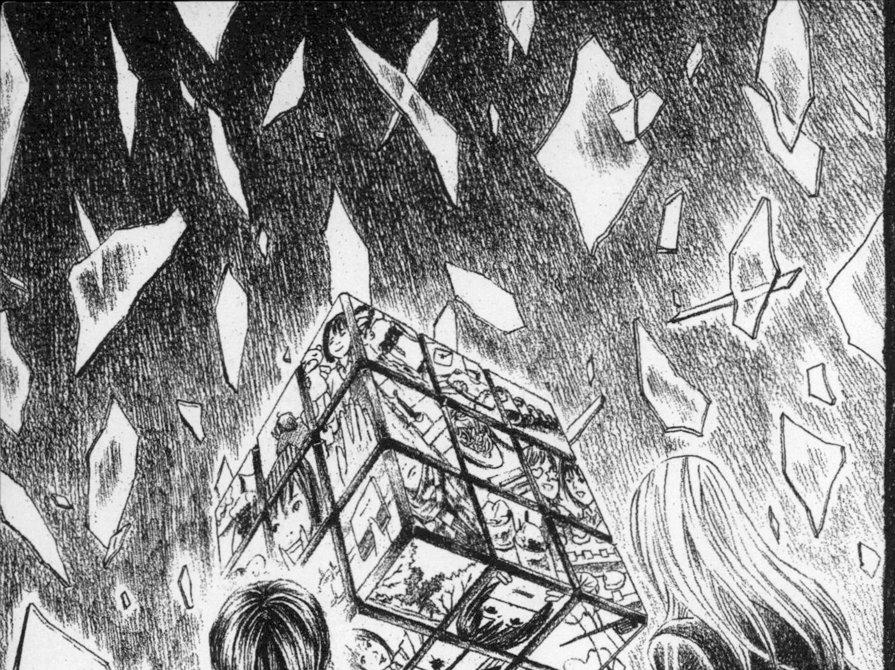

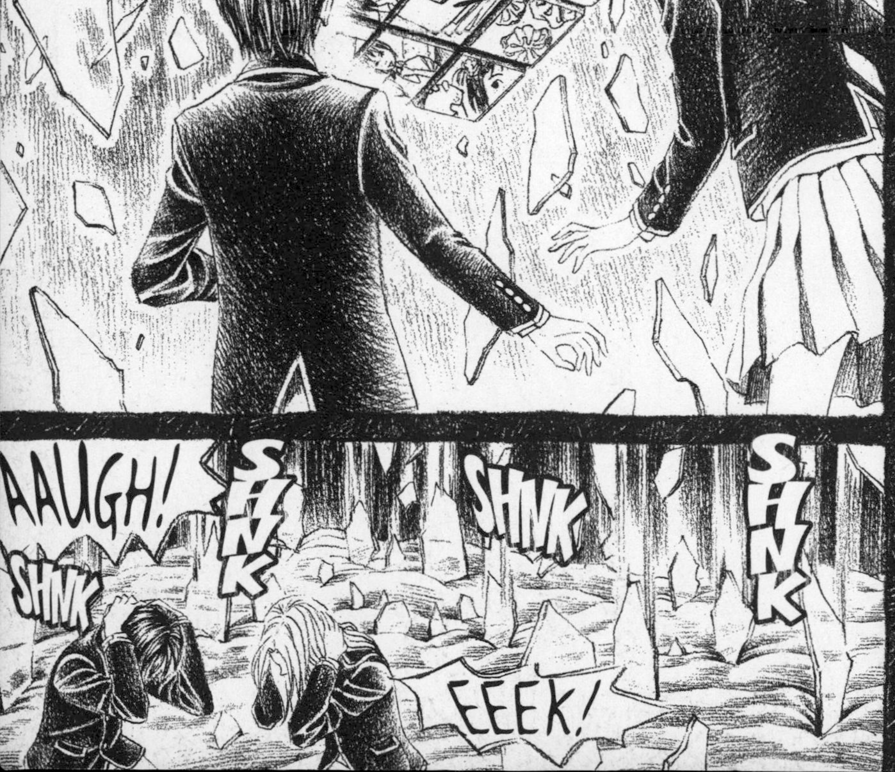
SHNK
SHNK
SHNK
AAUGH!
SHNK
EEEK!

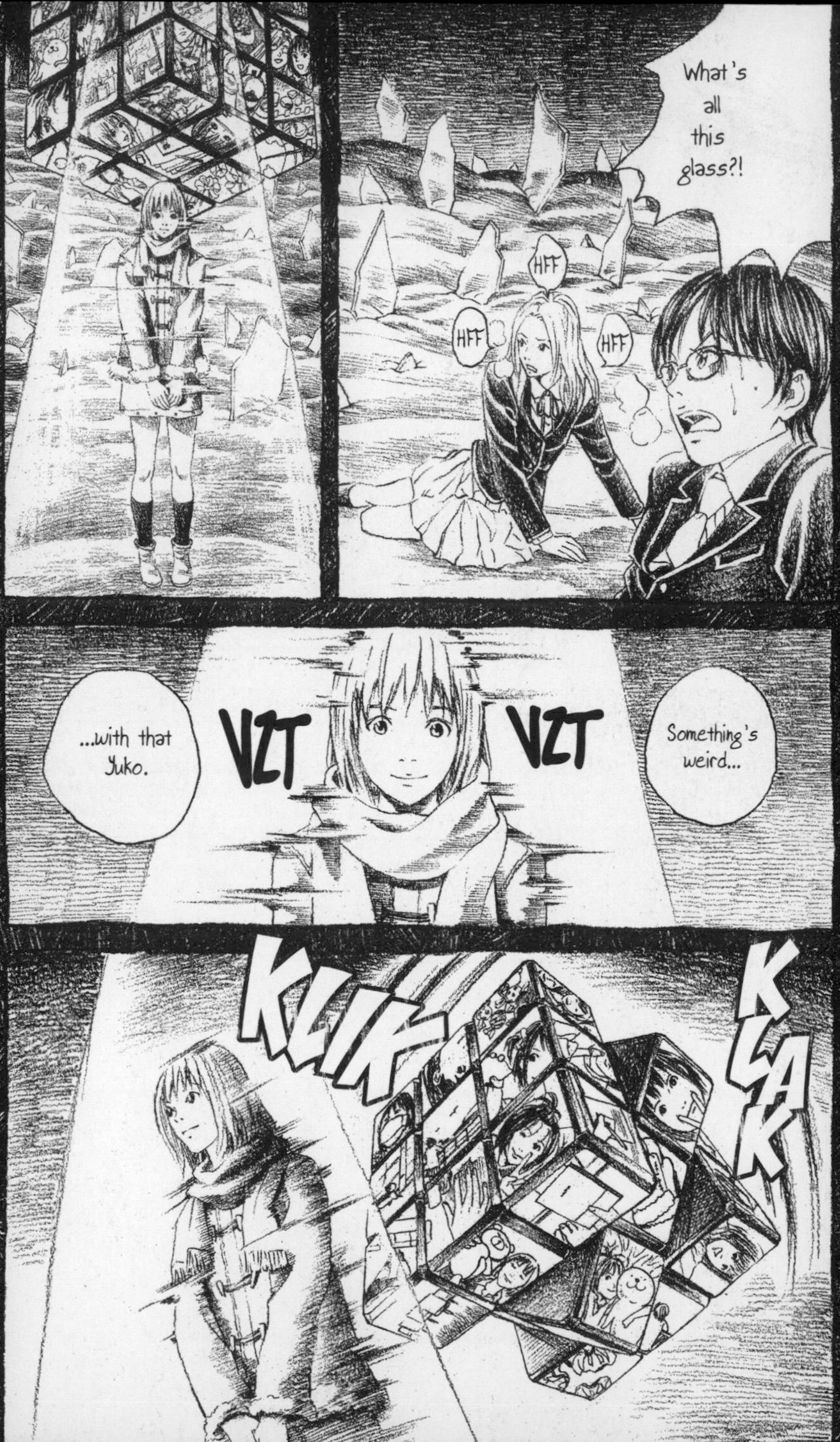
What's all this glass?!
HFF
HFF
HFF
Something's weird...
VZT
VZT
...with that Yuko.
KLAK
KLIK

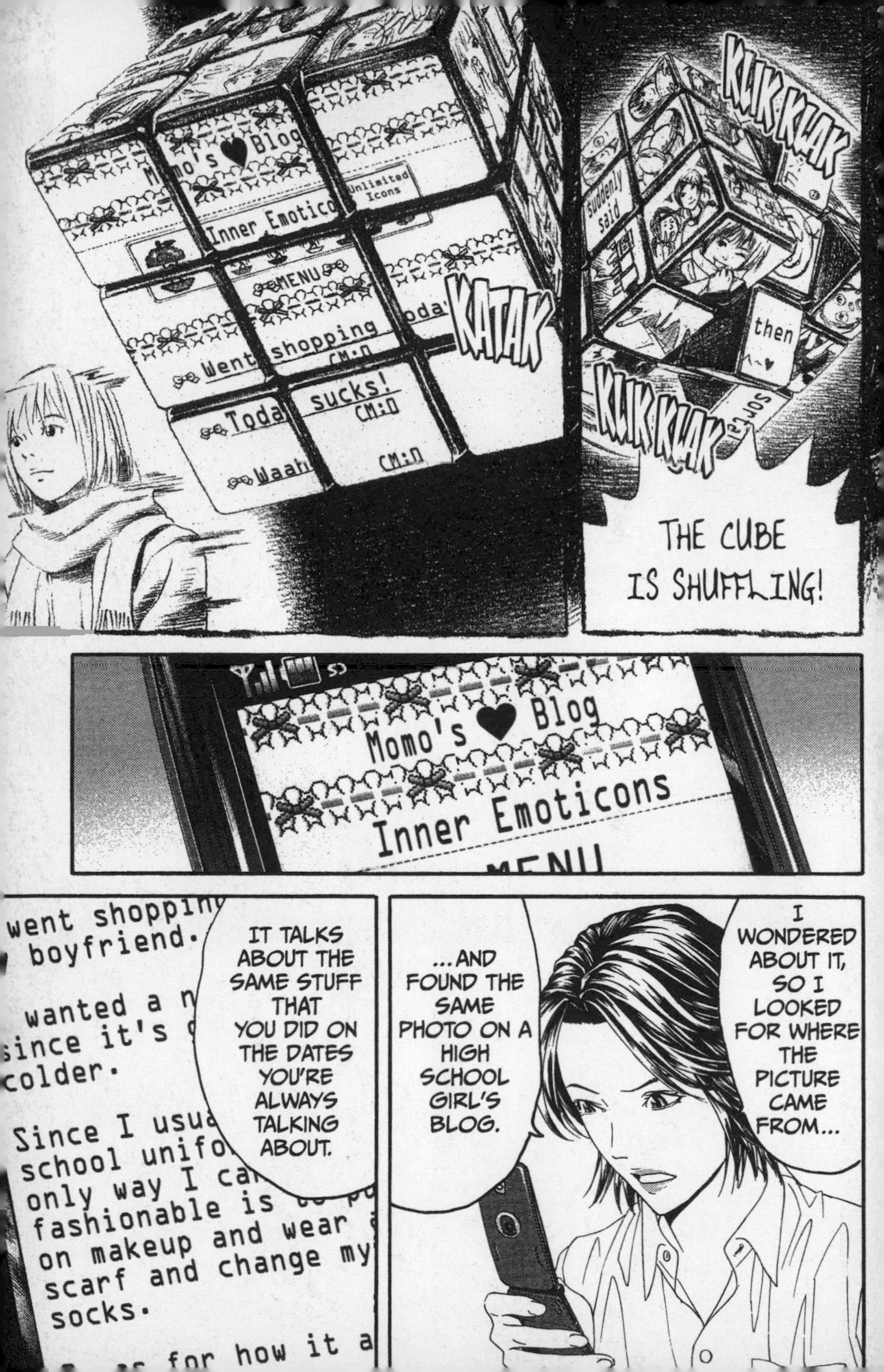
KLIK KLAK
suddenly said
then
KLIK KLAK
THE CUBE IS SHUFFLING!
Momo's ♥ Blog
Unlimited Icons
Inner Emotico
MENU
KATAK
Went shopping
Toda
sucks!
CM:D
Waah
Momo's ♥ Blog
Inner Emoticons
I WONDERED ABOUT IT, SO I LOOKED FOR WHERE THE PICTURE CAME FROM...
...AND FOUND THE SAME PHOTO ON A HIGH SCHOOL GIRL'S BLOG.
IT TALKS ABOUT THE SAME STUFF THAT YOU DID ON THE DATES YOU'RE ALWAYS TALKING ABOUT.
went shoppin
boyfriend.
wanted a n
since it's
colder.
Since I usua
school unifo
only way I ca
fashionable is
on makeup and wear
scarf and change my
socks.
for how it a

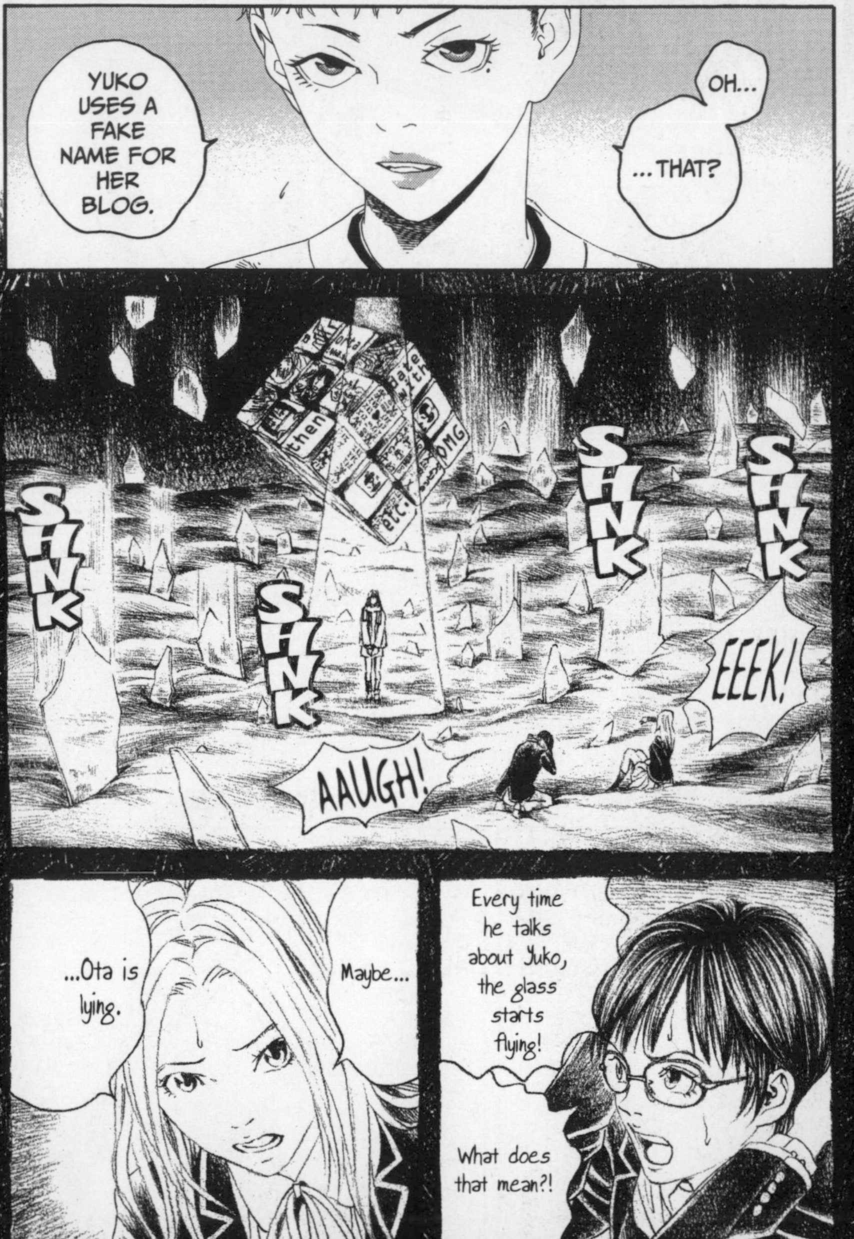
YUKO USES A FAKE NAME FOR HER BLOG.
OH...
...THAT?
SHNK
SHNK
EEEK!
SHNK
SHNK
AAUGH!
Every time he talks about Yuko, the glass starts flying!
What does that mean?!
Maybe...
...Ota is lying.

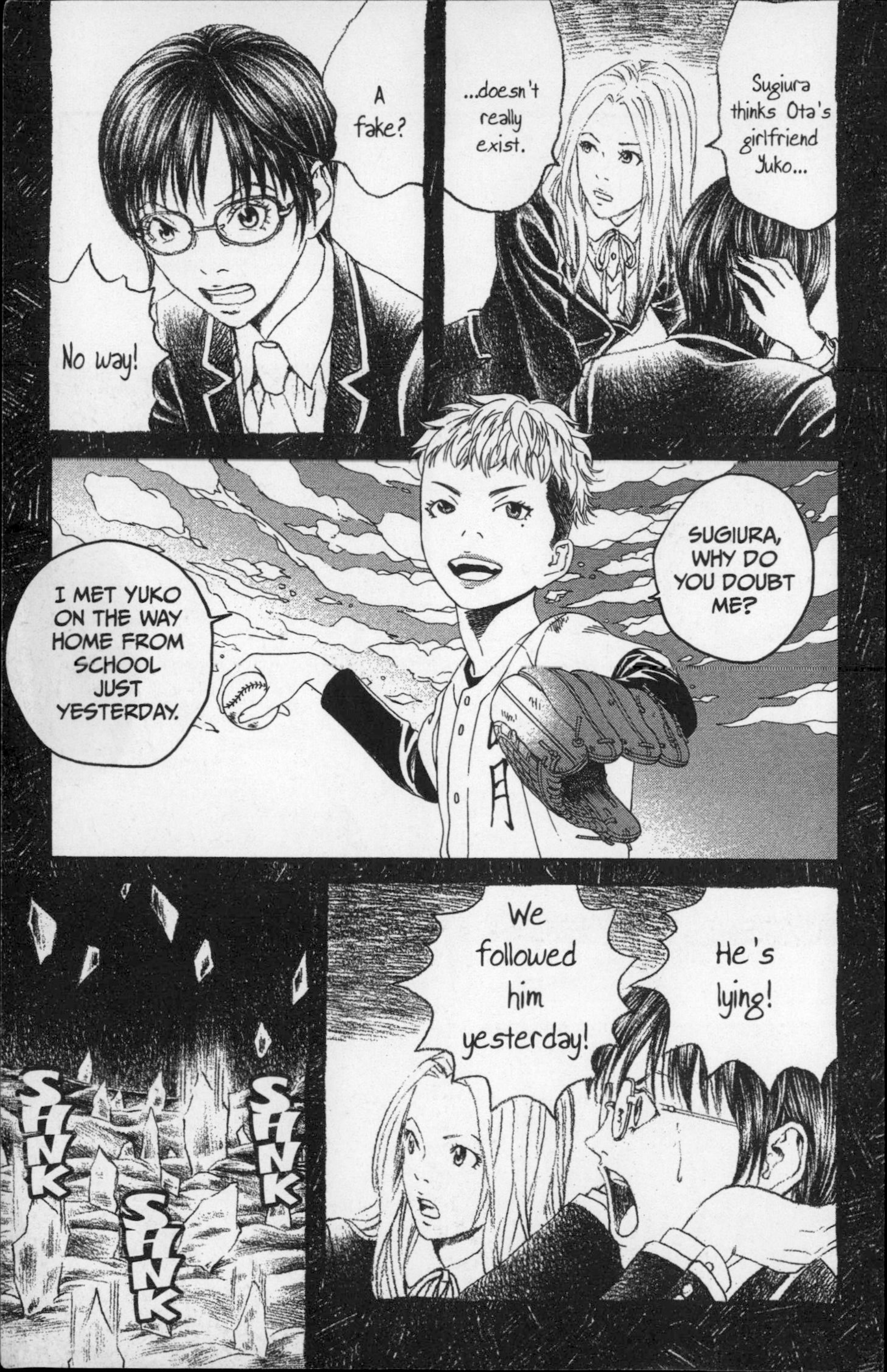
Sugiura thinks Ota's girlfriend Yuko...
...doesn't really exist.
A fake?
No way!
SUGIURA, WHY DO YOU DOUBT ME?
I MET YUKO ON THE WAY HOME FROM SCHOOL JUST YESTERDAY.
He's lying!
We followed him yesterday!
SHNK
SHNK
SHNK

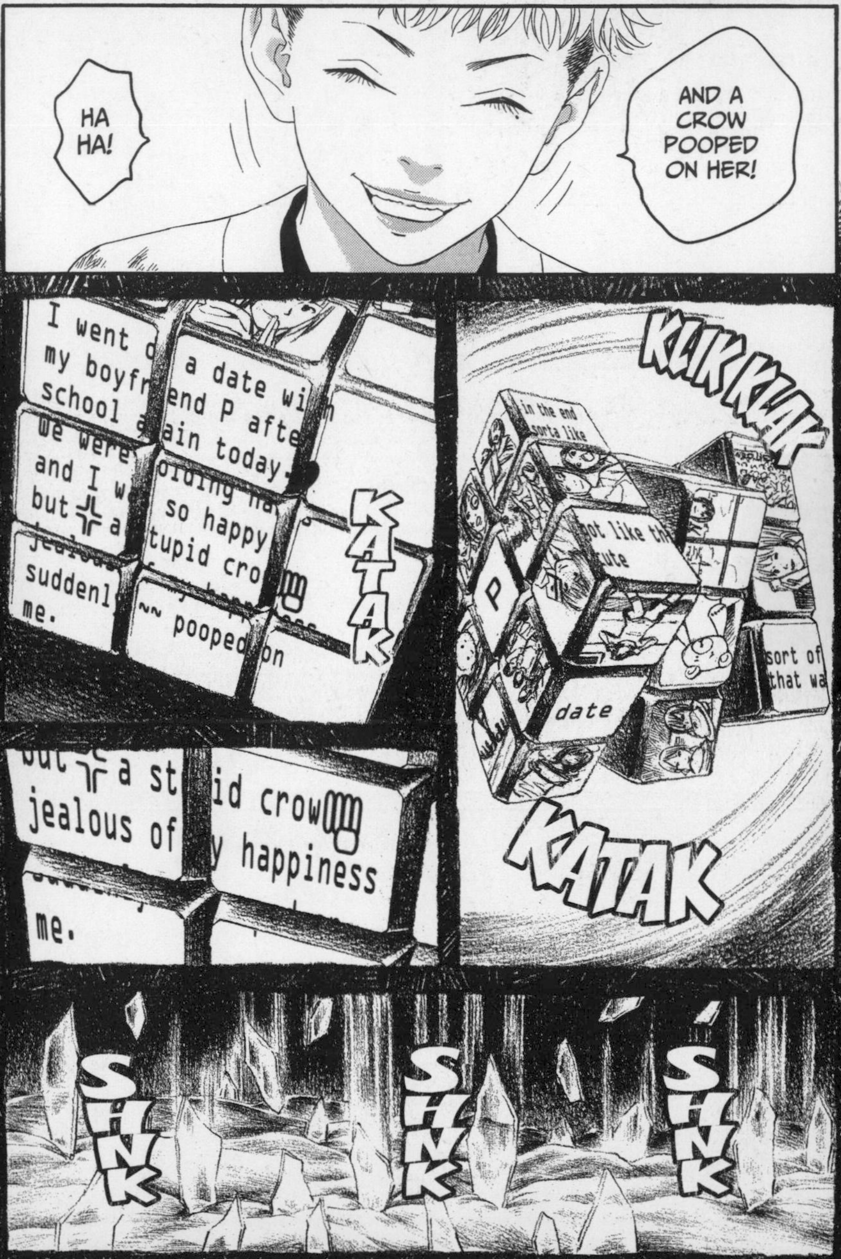
AND A CROW POOPED ON HER!
HA HA!
KLIK KLAK
in the end sorta like
P
date
sort of
KATAK
I went
a date with
my boyfr
end P afte
school
ain today.
so happy
tupid cro
sudden
me.
pooped on
KATAK
a st
id crow
jealous of
y happiness
me.
SHNK
SHNK
SHNK

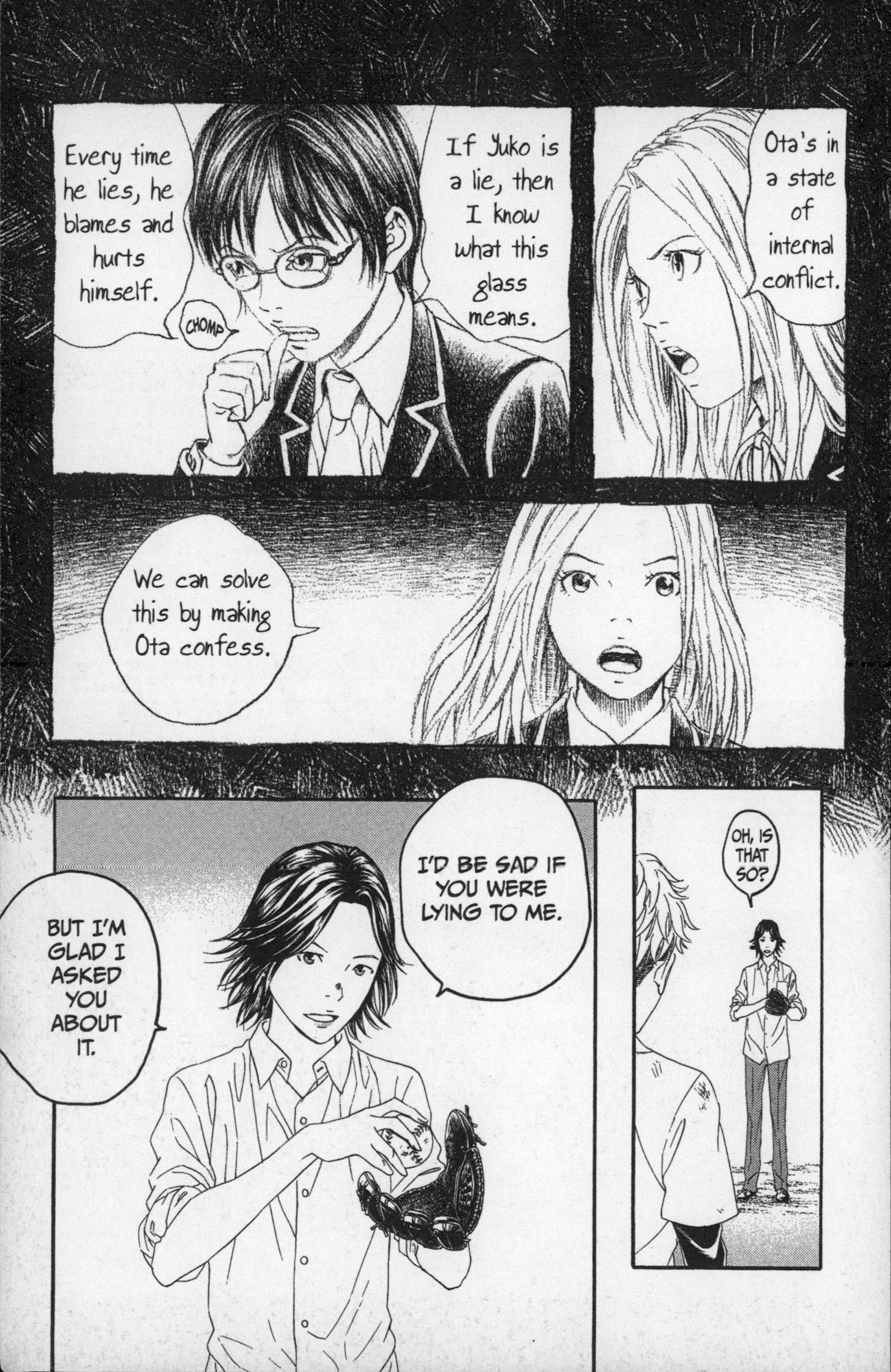

Ota's in a state of internal conflict.
If Yuko is a lie, then I know what this glass means.
Every time he lies, he blames and hurts himself.
CHOMP
We can solve this by making Ota confess.
OH, IS THAT SO?
I'D BE SAD IF YOU WERE LYING TO ME.
BUT I'M GLAD I ASKED YOU ABOUT IT.

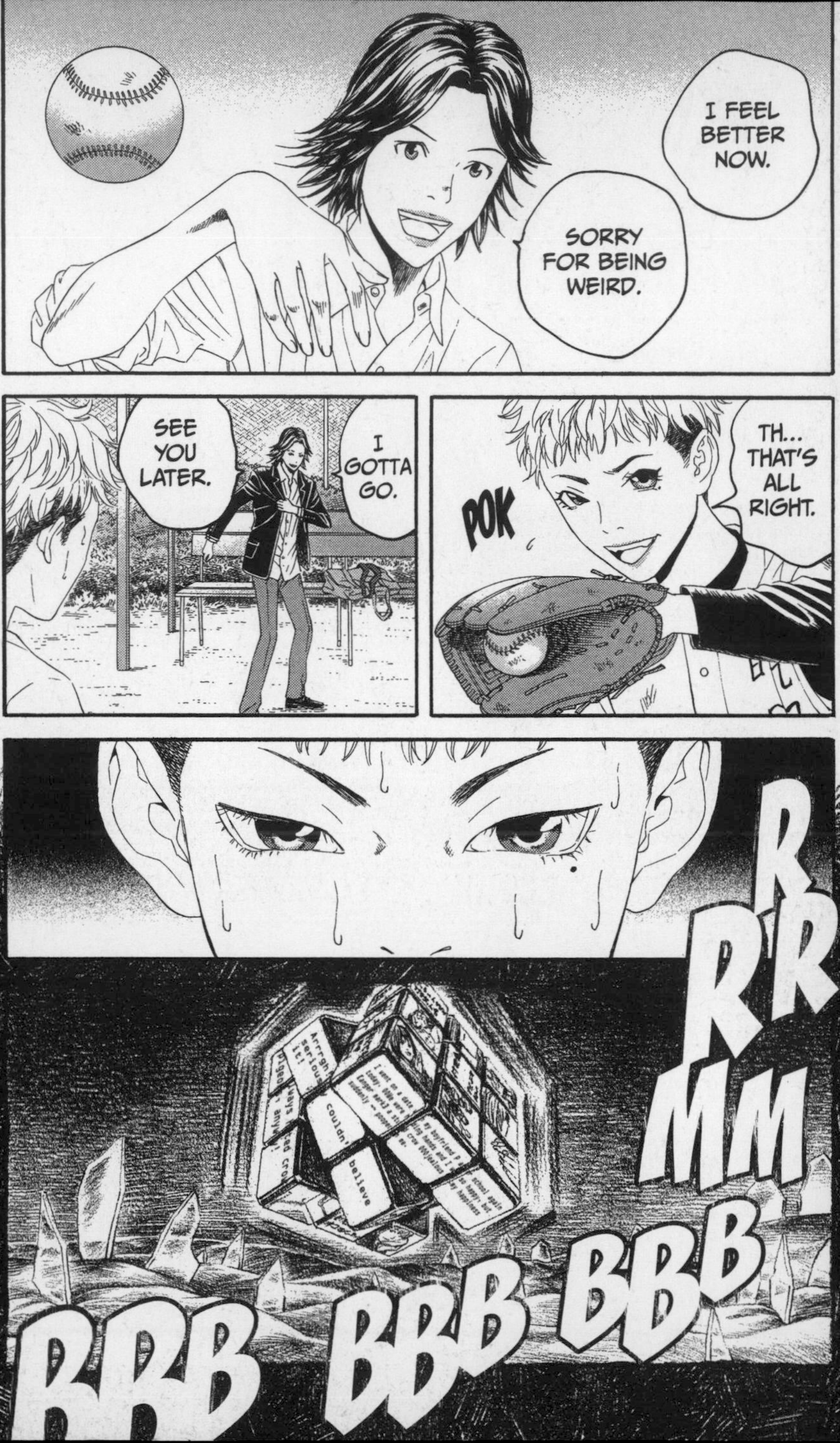
I FEEL BETTER NOW.
SORRY FOR BEING WEIRD.
TH... THAT'S ALL RIGHT.
POK
I GOTTA GO.
SEE YOU LATER.
RRRMM
BBB BBB BBB

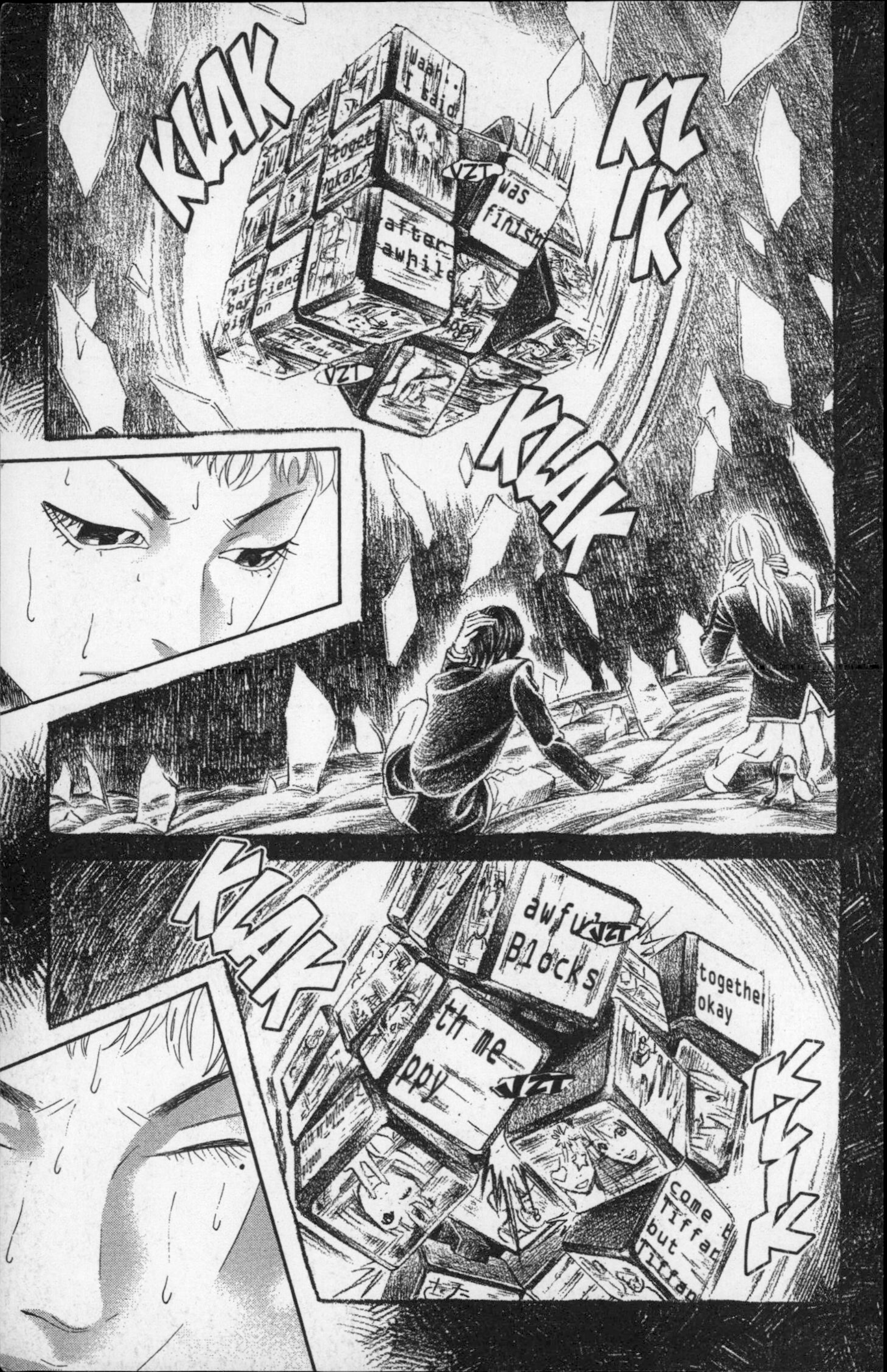
KLIK
KLAK
Waah.. I said
VZT
was finish
together okay
after awhile
with my boyfriend pigeon
VZT
KLAK
KLIK
KLAK
awful blocks
VZT
together okay
th me ppy
VZT
come Tiffan but Tiffan

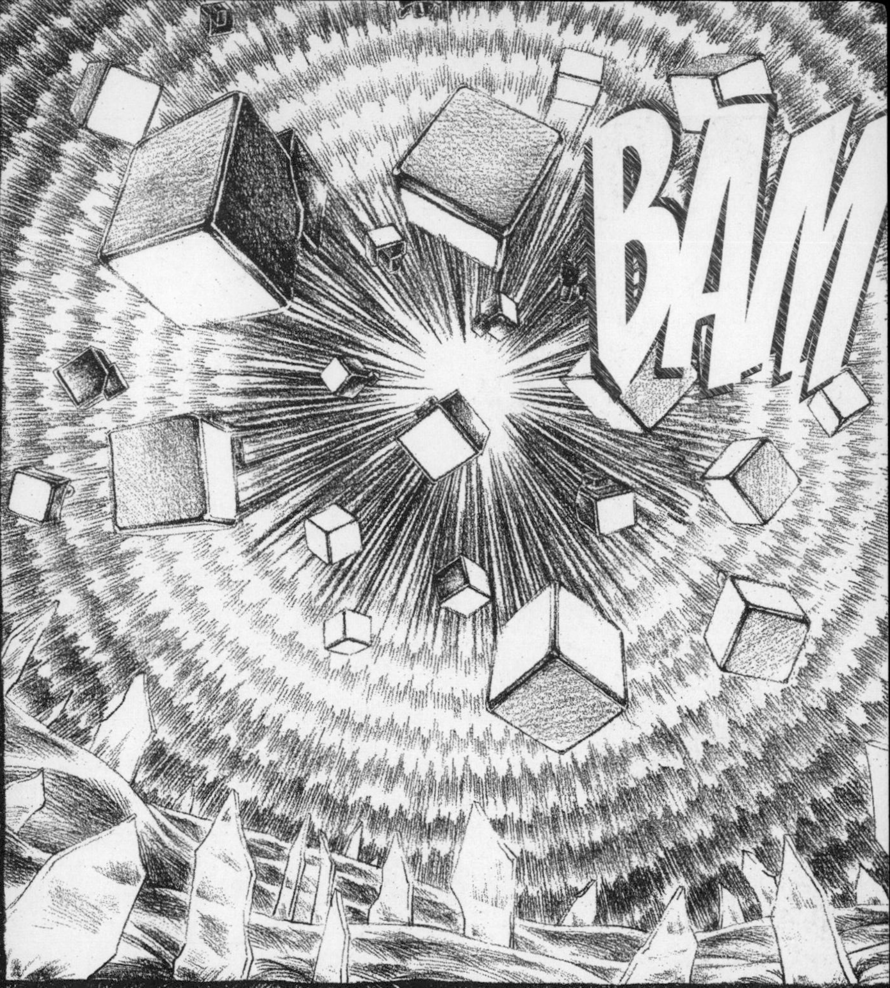
BAM

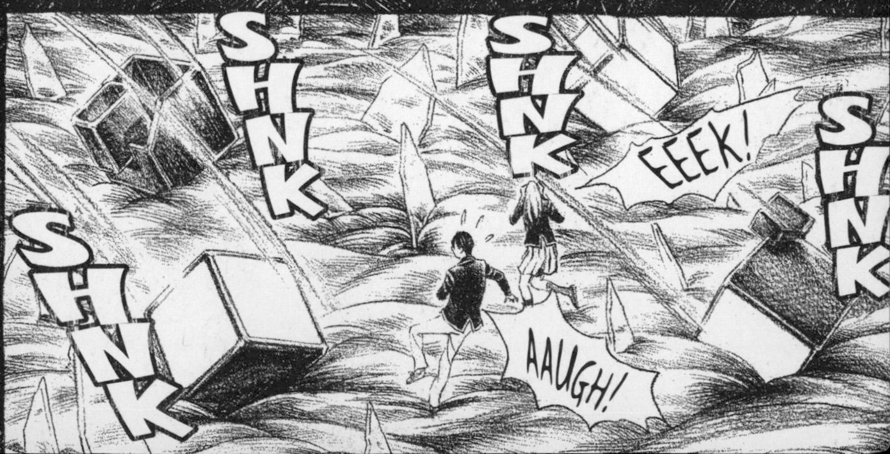
SHNK
EEEK!
SHNK
SHNK
AAUGH!
SHNK

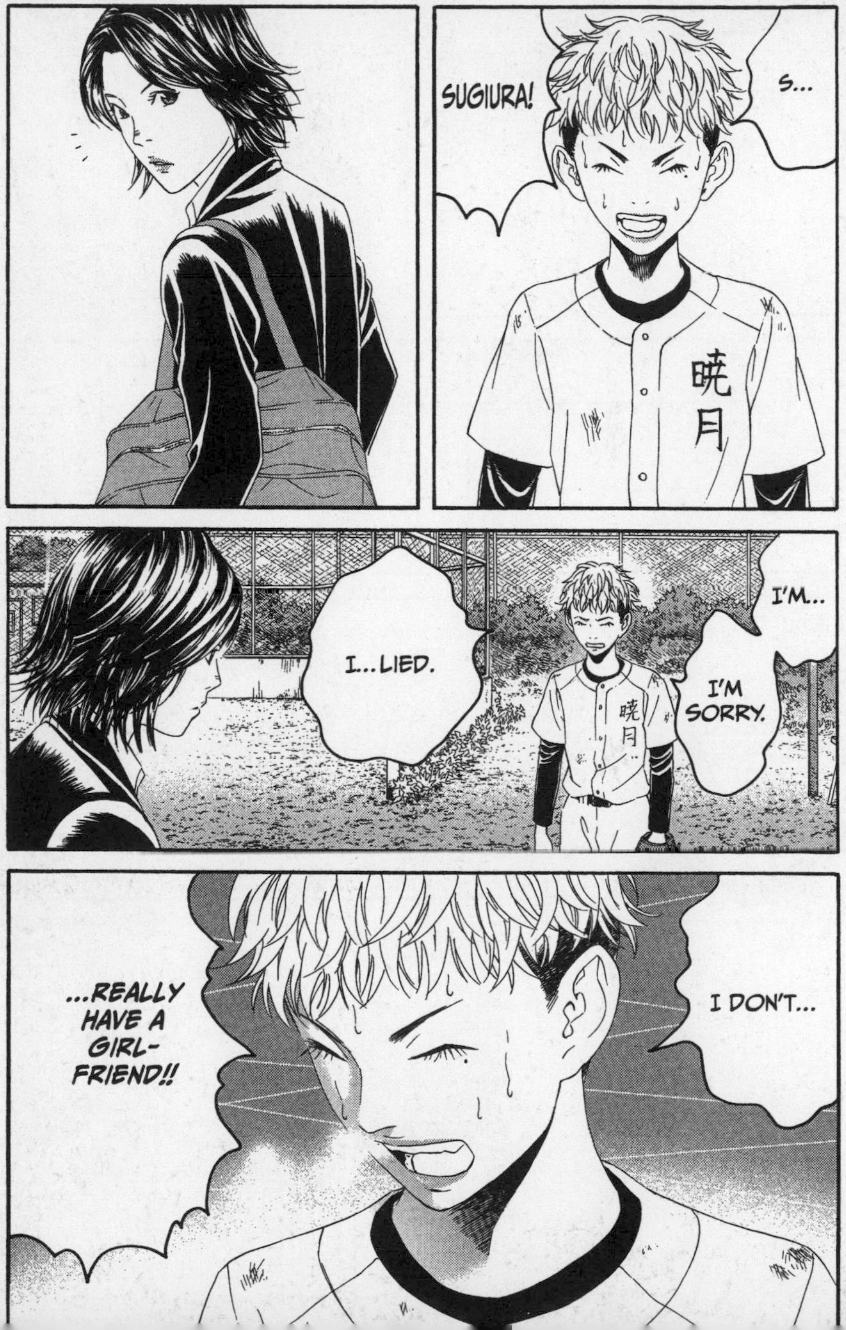
S...
SUGIURA!
暁月
I'M...
I'M SORRY.
I...LIED.
I DON'T...
...REALLY HAVE A GIRL-FRIEND!!

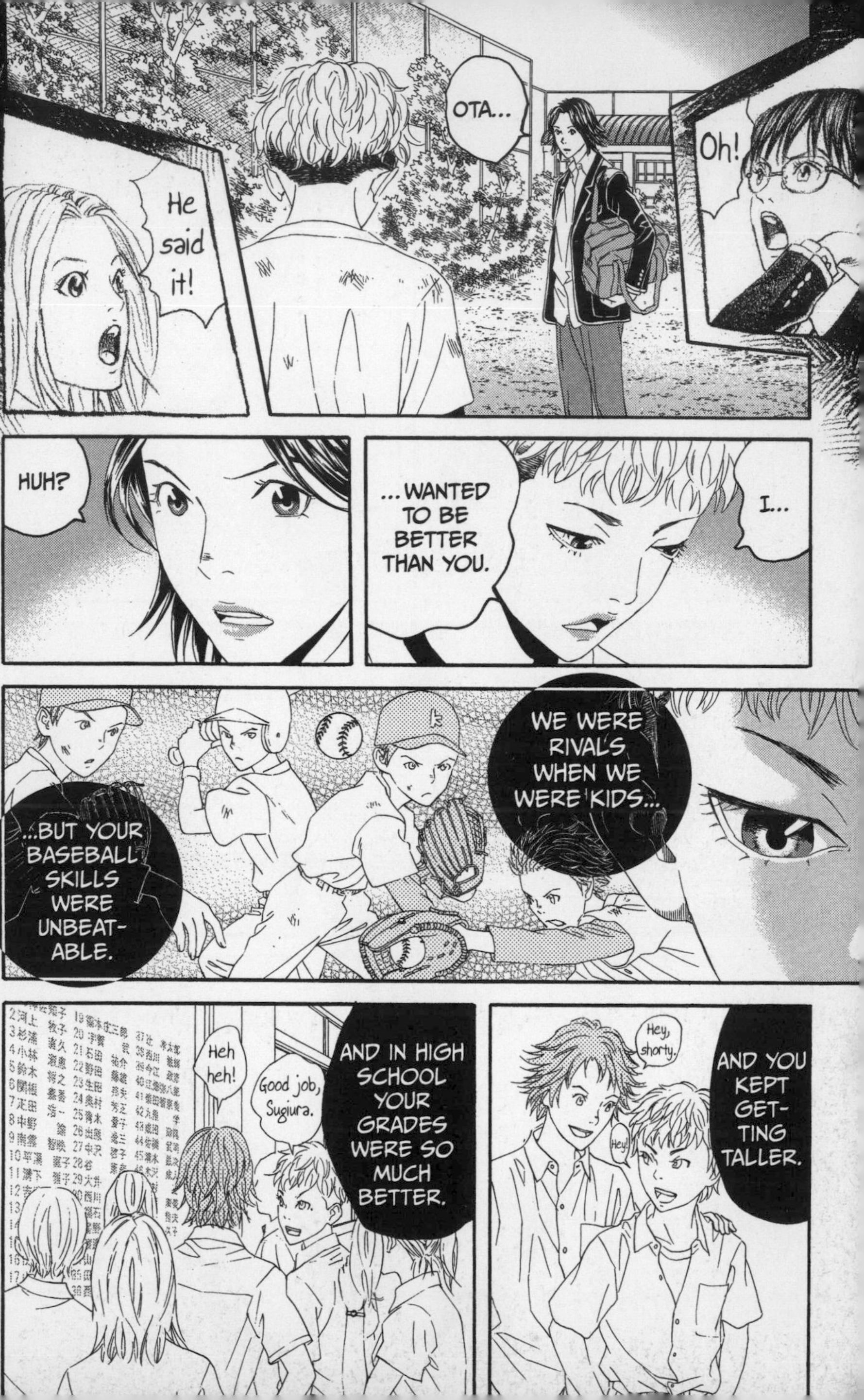
Oh!
OTA...
He said it!
I...
...WANTED TO BE BETTER THAN YOU.
HUH?
WE WERE RIVALS WHEN WE WERE KIDS...
...BUT YOUR BASEBALL SKILLS WERE UNBEAT-ABLE.
AND YOU KEPT GET-TING TALLER.
Hey, shorty.
Hey!
AND IN HIGH SCHOOL YOUR GRADES WERE SO MUCH BETTER.
Good job, Sugiura.
Heh heh!

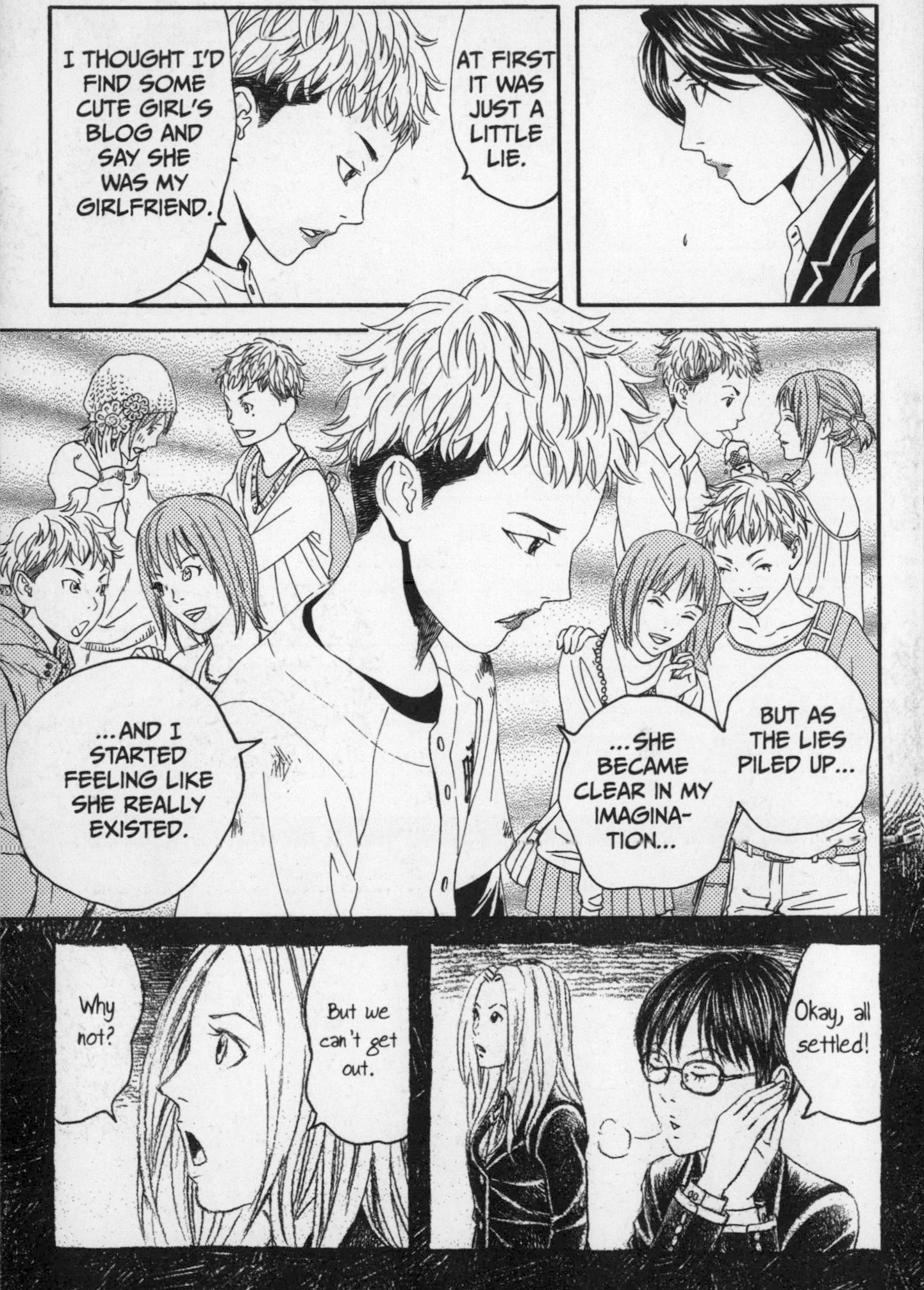
AT FIRST IT WAS JUST A LITTLE LIE.
I THOUGHT I'D FIND SOME CUTE GIRL'S BLOG AND SAY SHE WAS MY GIRLFRIEND.
BUT AS THE LIES PILED UP...
...SHE BECAME CLEAR IN MY IMAGINA-TION...
...AND I STARTED FEELING LIKE SHE REALLY EXISTED.
Okay, all settled!
But we can't get out.
Why not?

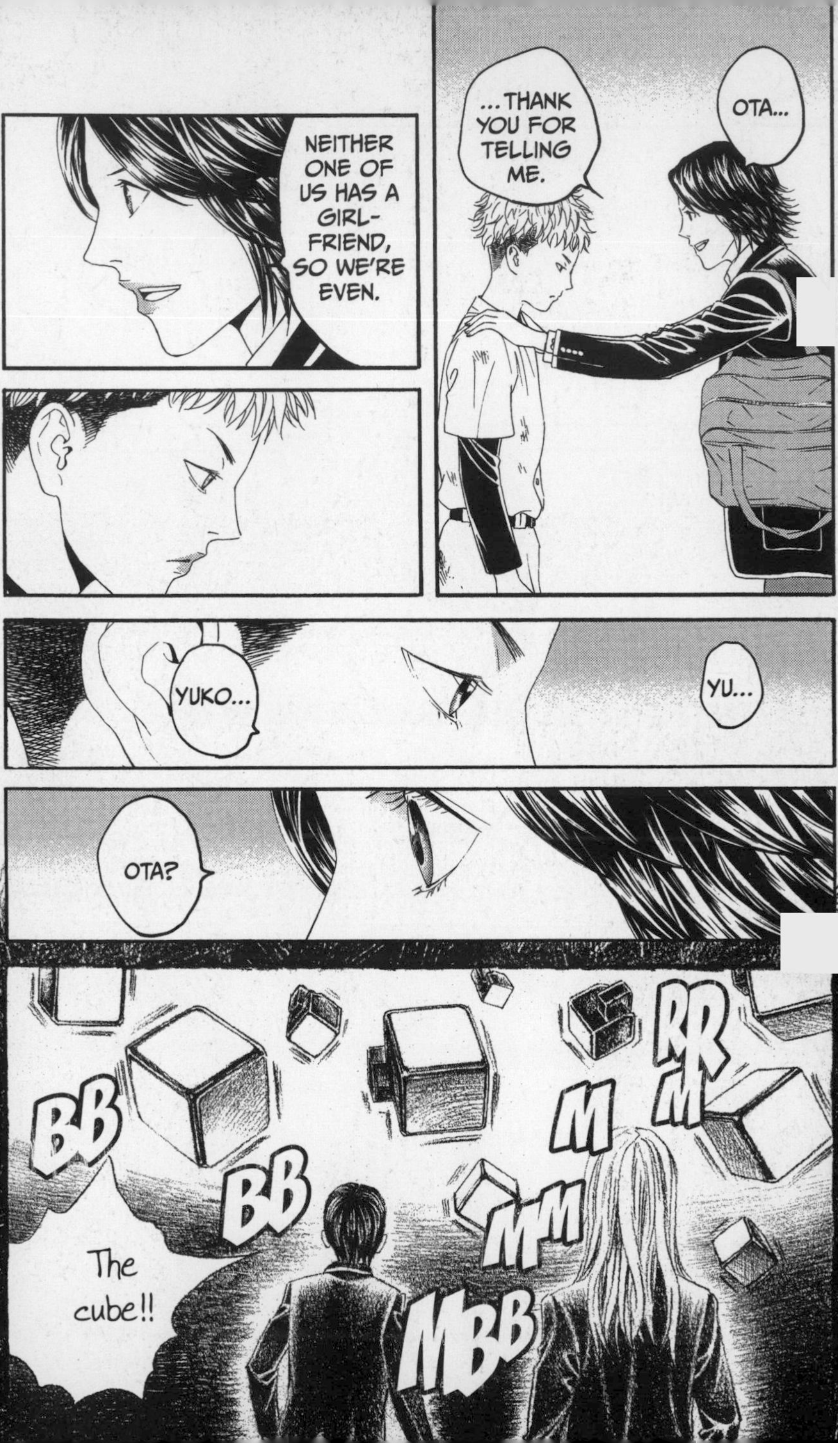
OTA...
...THANK YOU FOR TELLING ME.
NEITHER ONE OF US HAS A GIRL-FRIEND, SO WE'RE EVEN.
YU...
YUKO...
OTA?
RRM
M
MBB
MMM
BB
BB
The cube!!

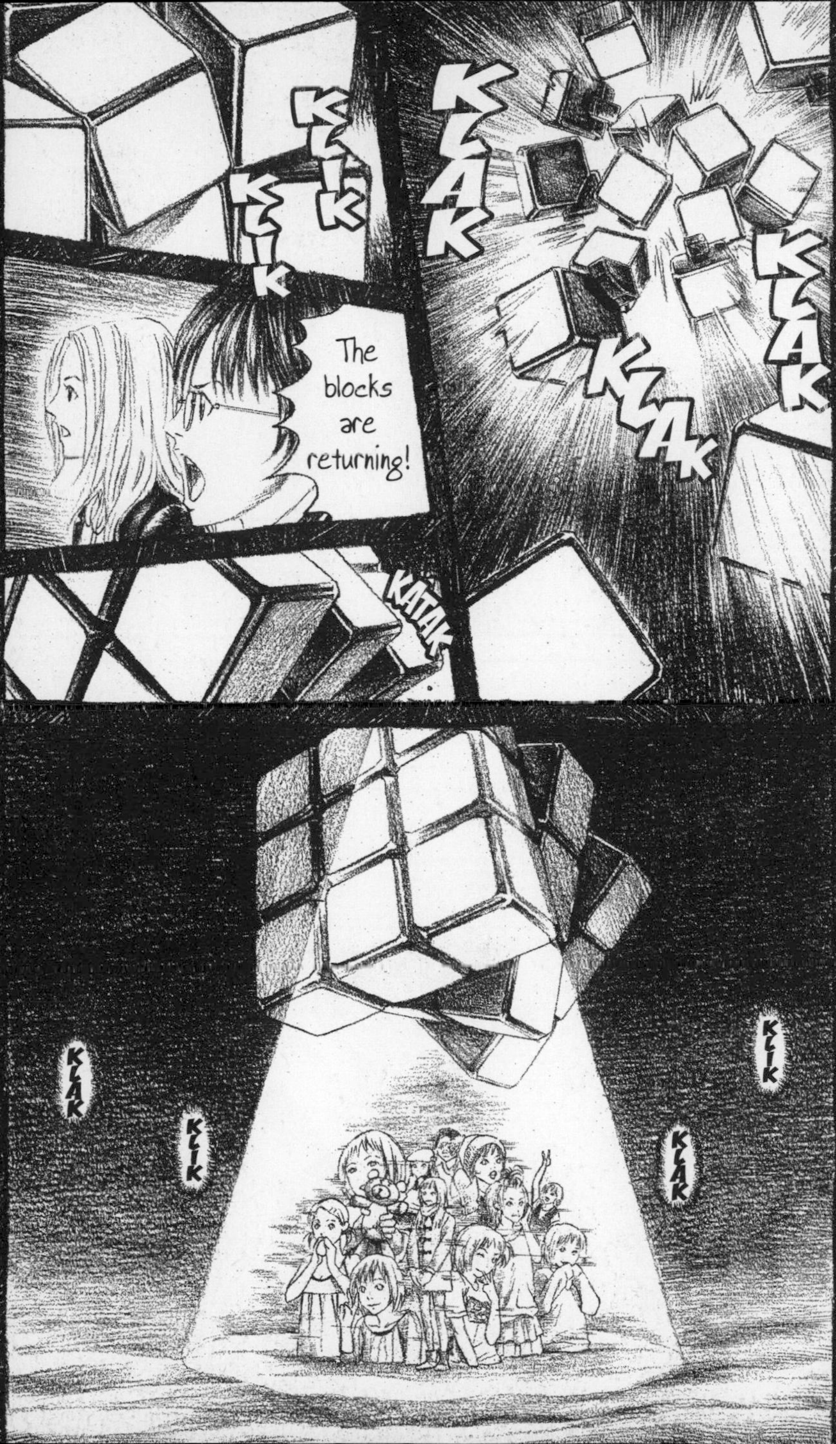
KLAK
KLAK
KLAK
KLIK
KLIK
The blocks are returning!
KATAK
KLIK
KLAK
KLIK
KLAK

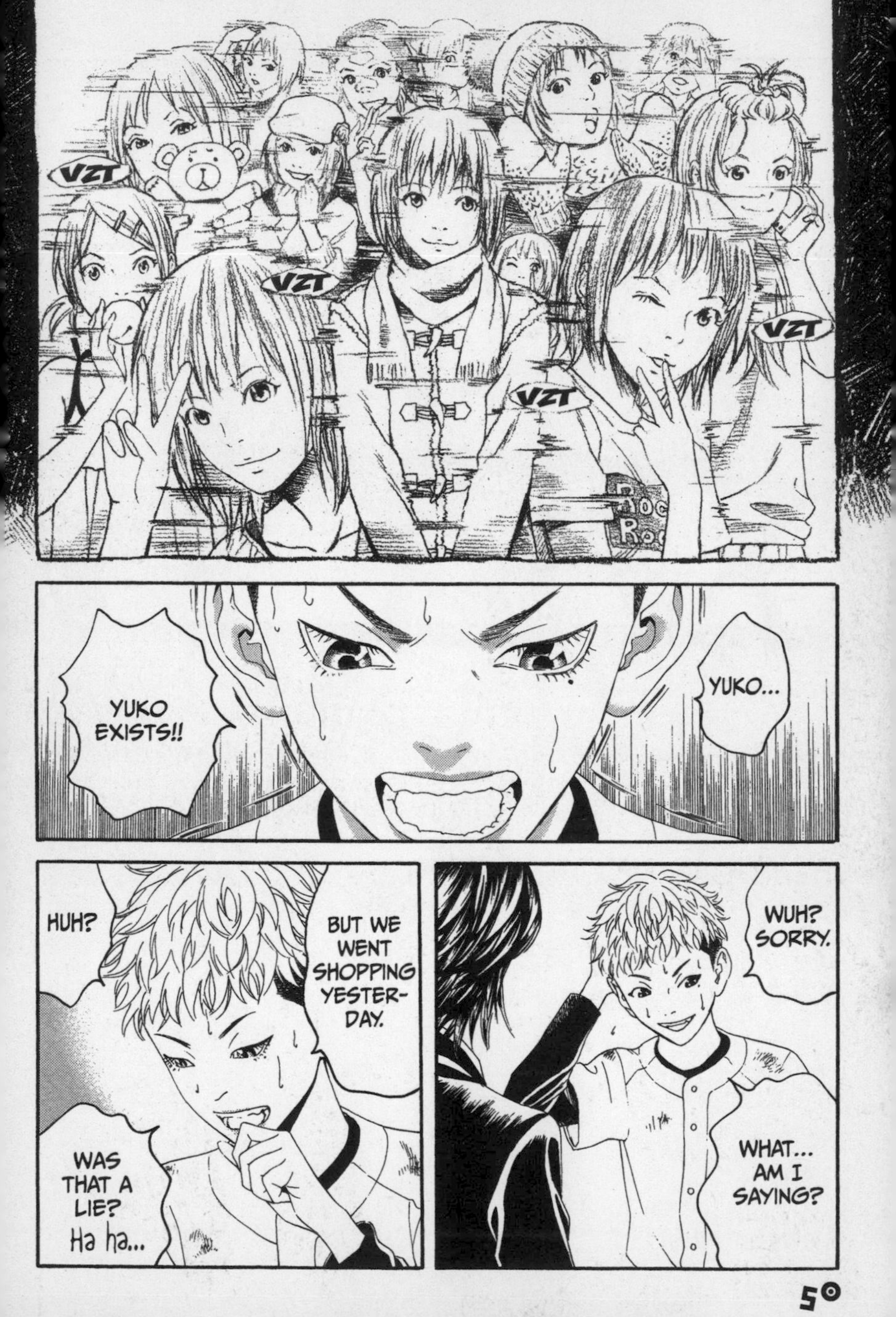
VZT
VZT
VZT
VZT
YUKO...
YUKO EXISTS!!
WUH? SORRY.
WHAT... AM I SAYING?
BUT WE WENT SHOPPING YESTER-DAY.
HUH?
WAS THAT A LIE?
Ha ha...

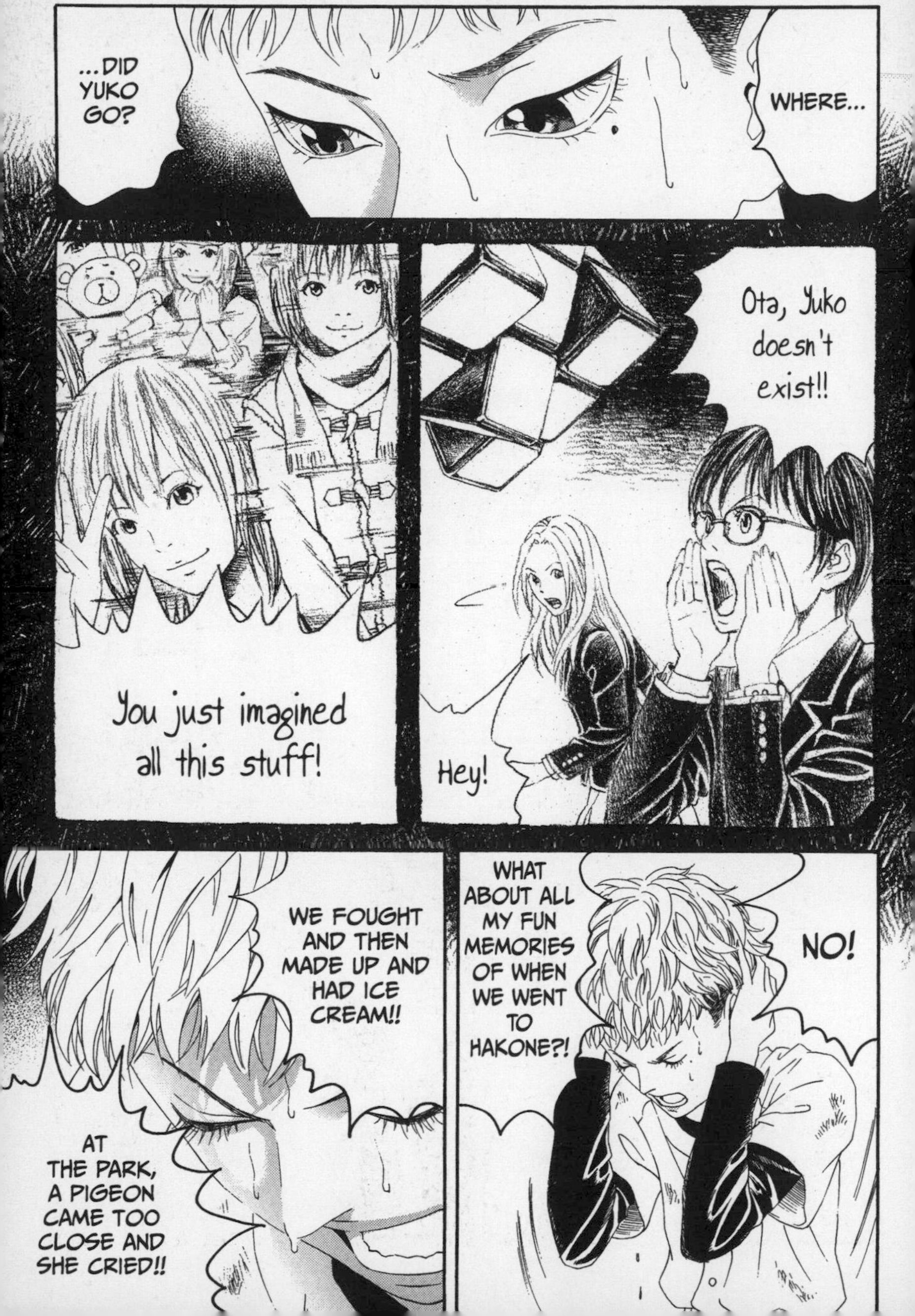
WHERE...
...DID YUKO GO?
Ota, Yuko doesn't exist!!
Hey!
You just imagined all this stuff!
NO!
WHAT ABOUT ALL MY FUN MEMORIES OF WHEN WE WENT TO HAKONE?!
WE FOUGHT AND THEN MADE UP AND HAD ICE CREAM!!
AT THE PARK, A PIGEON CAME TOO CLOSE AND SHE CRIED!!

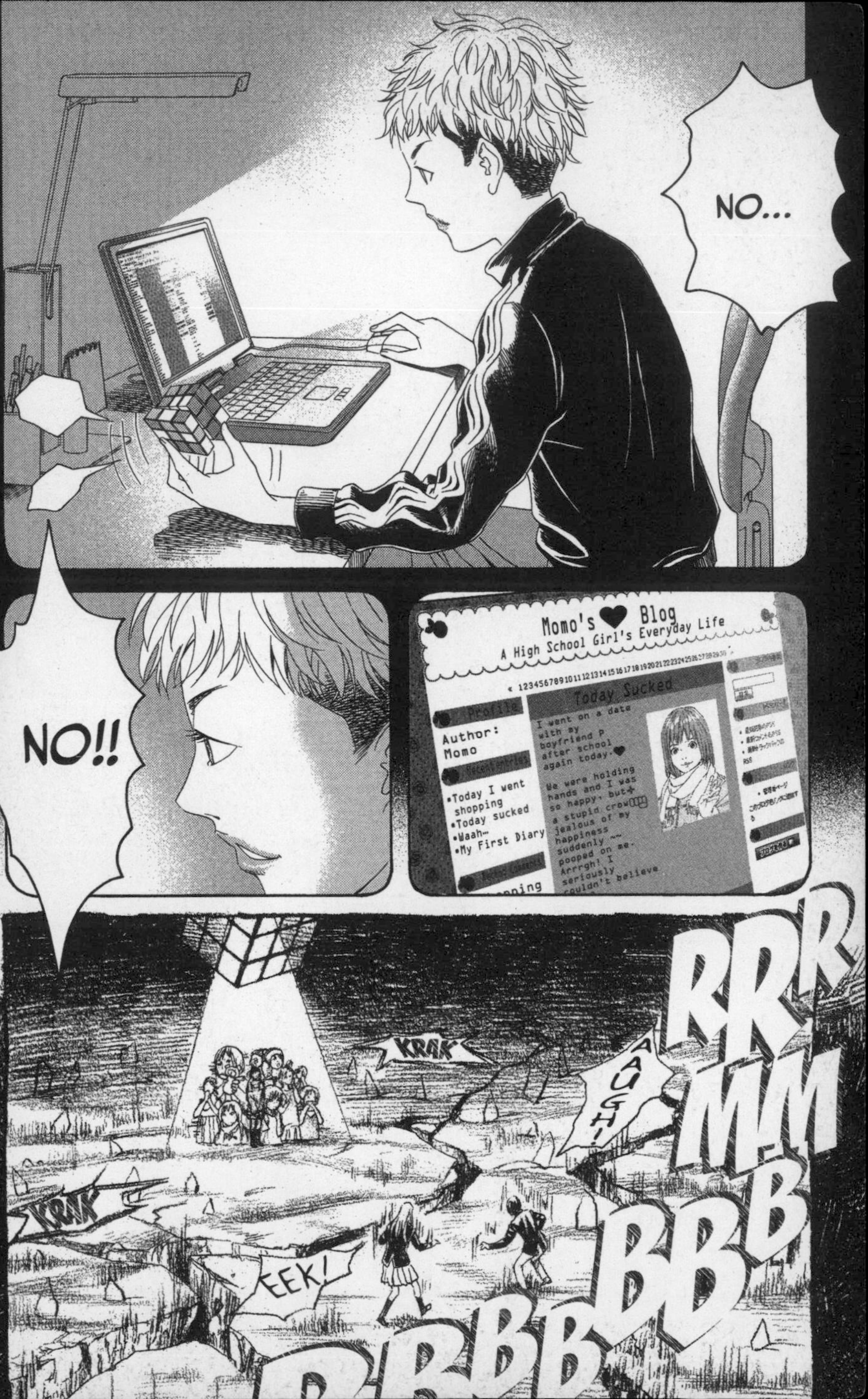
NO...
Momo's Blog
A High School Girl's Everyday Life
Today Sucked
Profile
Author: Momo
Recent entries
•Today I went shopping
•Today sucked
•Waah…
•My First Diary
I went on a date with my boyfriend after school again today.
We were holding hands and I was so happy, but a stupid crow jealous of my happiness suddenly ~~ pooped on me. Arrrgh! I seriously couldn't believe
NO!!
RRRMMMBBBBBB
AUGH!
KRAK
KRAK
EEK!

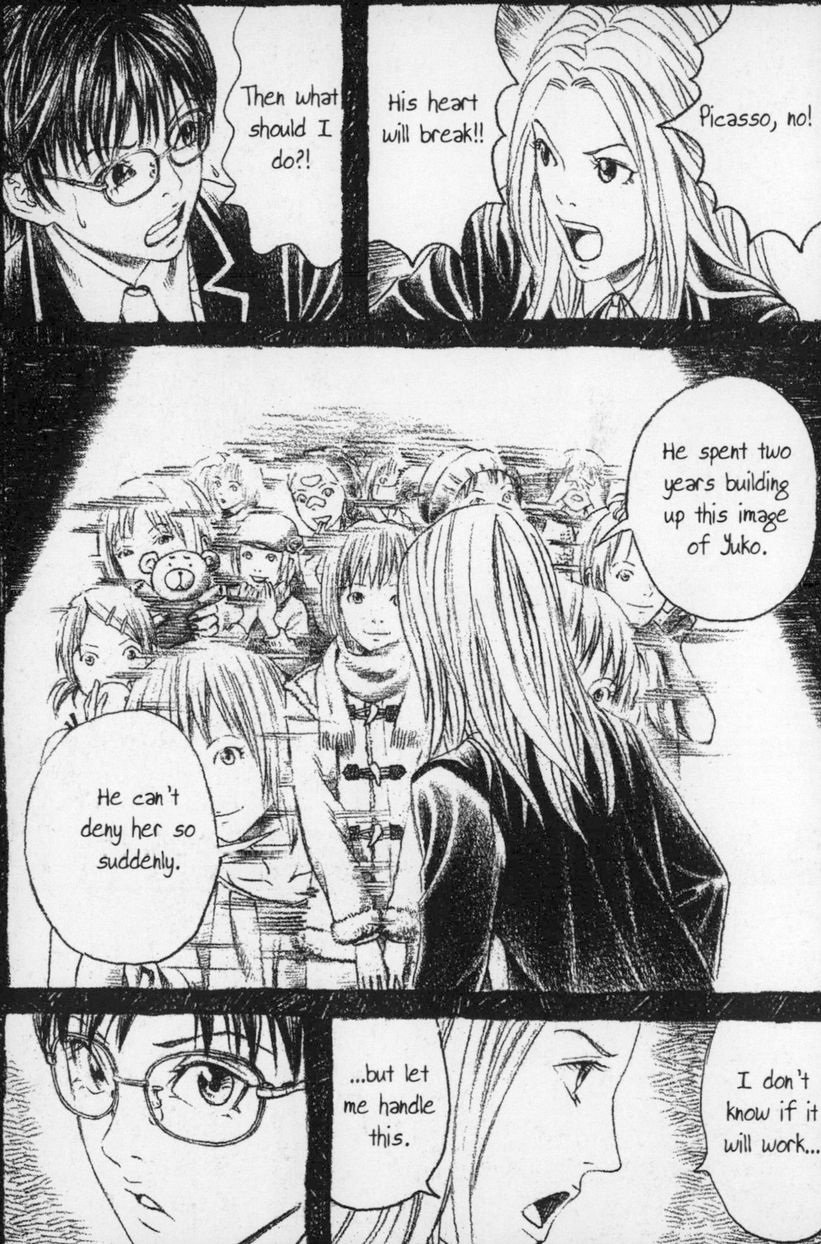
Picasso, no!
His heart will break!!
Then what should I do?!
He spent two years building up this image of Yuko.
He can't deny her so suddenly.
I don't know if it will work...
...but let me handle this.

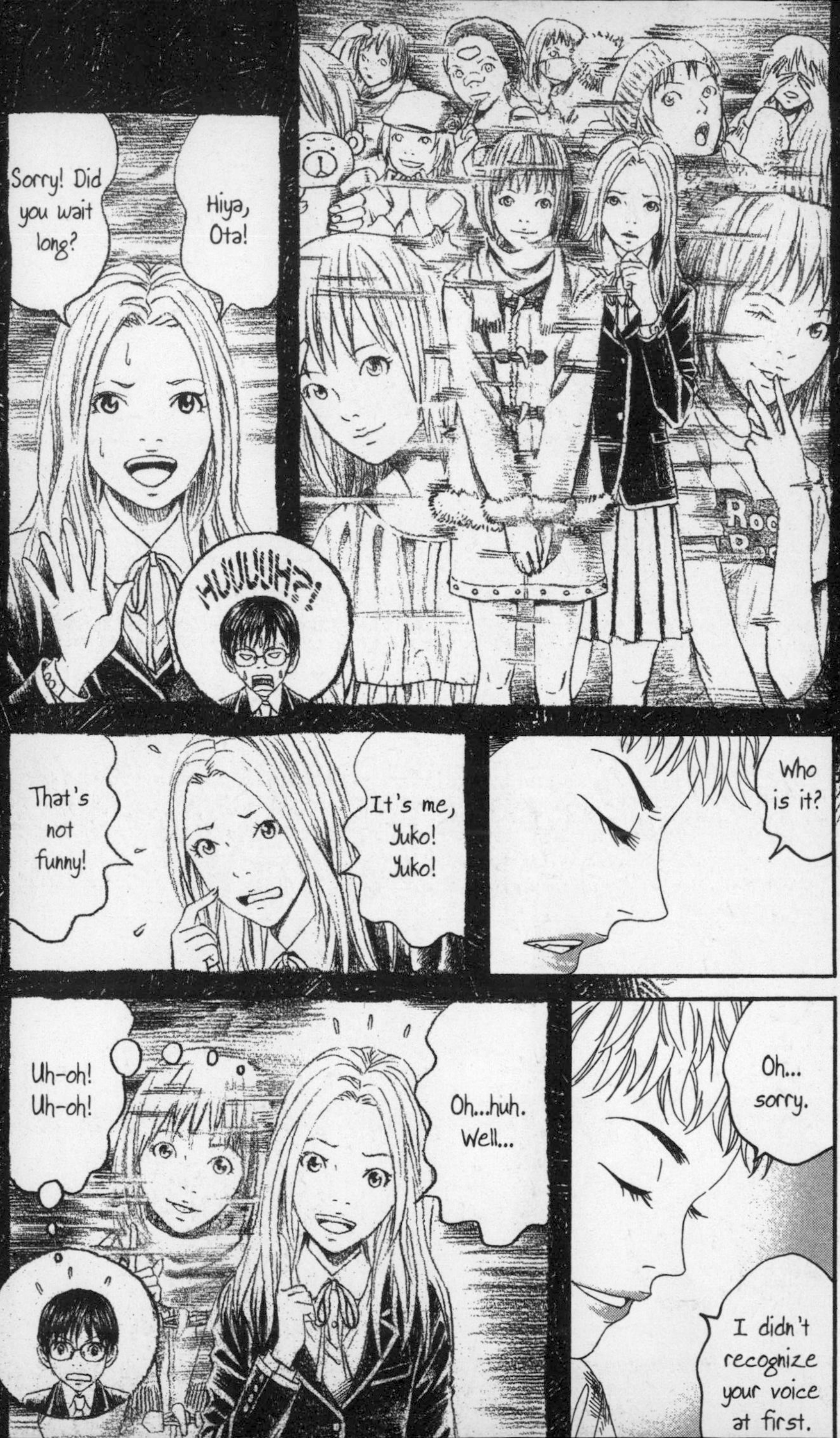
Hiya, Ota!
Sorry! Did you wait long?
HUUUUH?!
Who is it?
It's me, Yuko! Yuko!
That's not funny!
Oh... sorry.
I didn't recognize your voice at first.
Oh...huh. Well...
Uh-oh! Uh-oh!

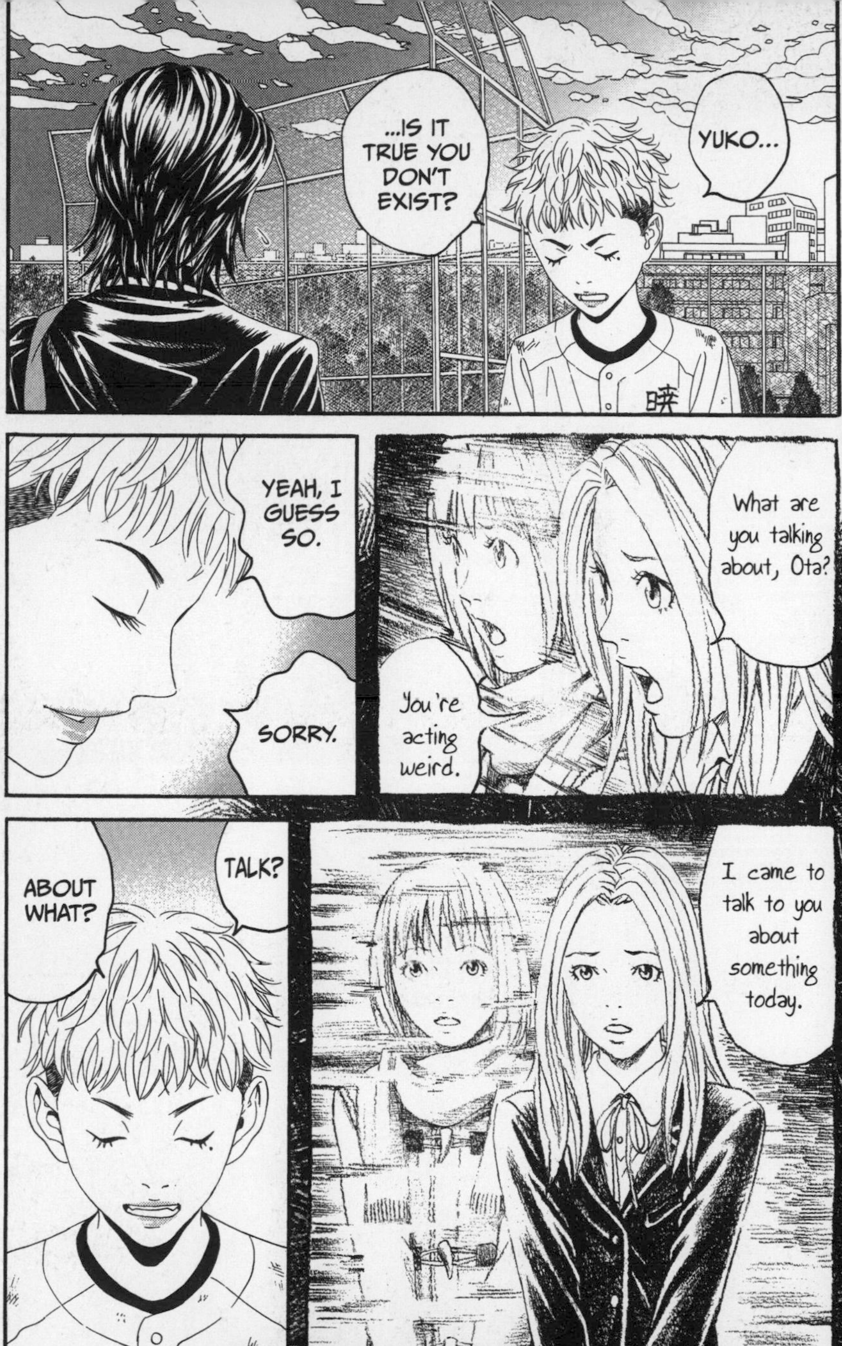
YUKO...
...IS IT TRUE YOU DON'T EXIST?
What are you talking about, Ota?
You're acting weird.
YEAH, I GUESS SO.
SORRY.
I came to talk to you about something today.
TALK?
ABOUT WHAT?

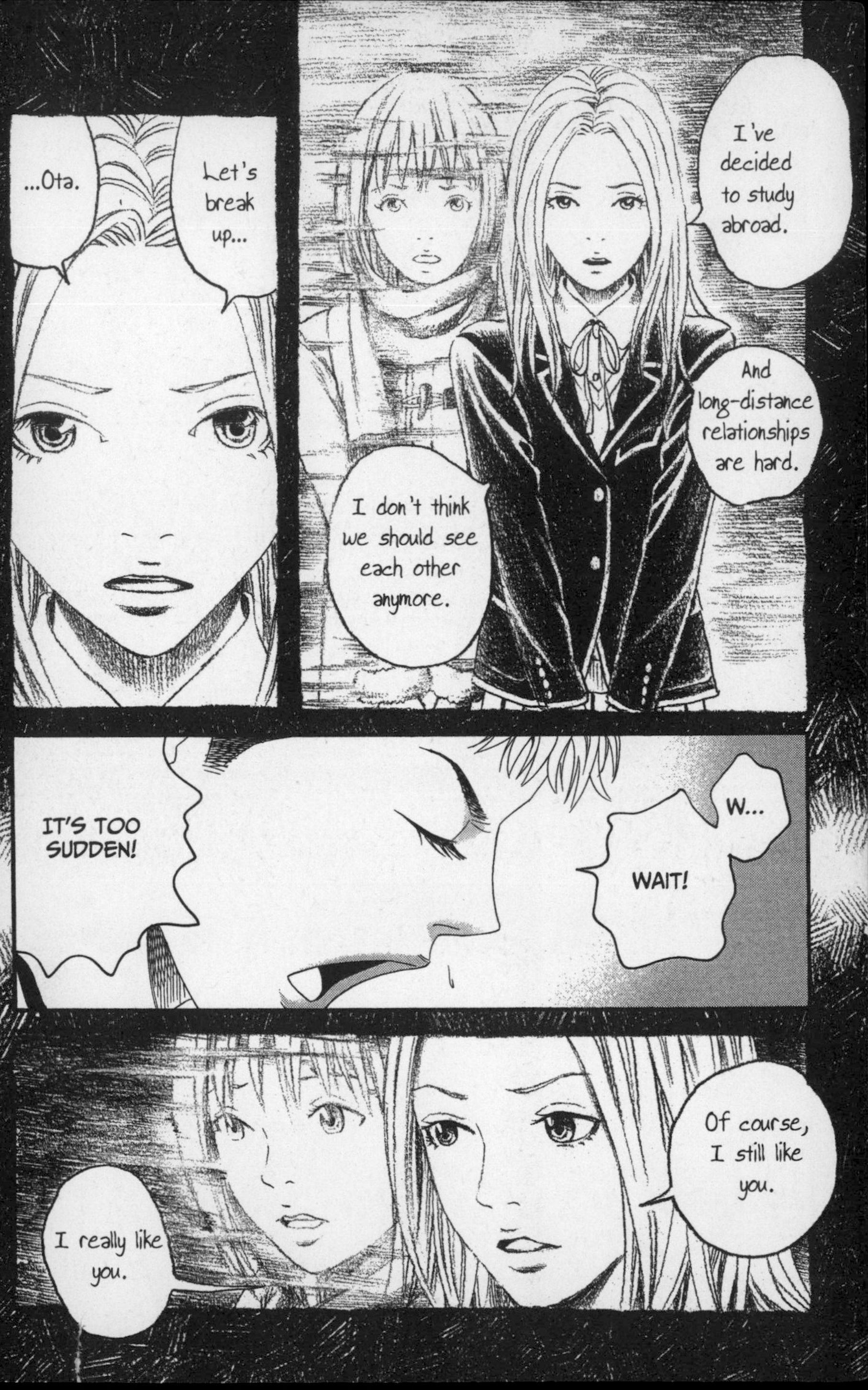
I've decided to study abroad.
And long-distance relationships are hard.
I don't think we should see each other anymore.
Let's break up...
...Ota.
W...
WAIT!
IT'S TOO SUDDEN!
Of course, I still like you.
I really like you.

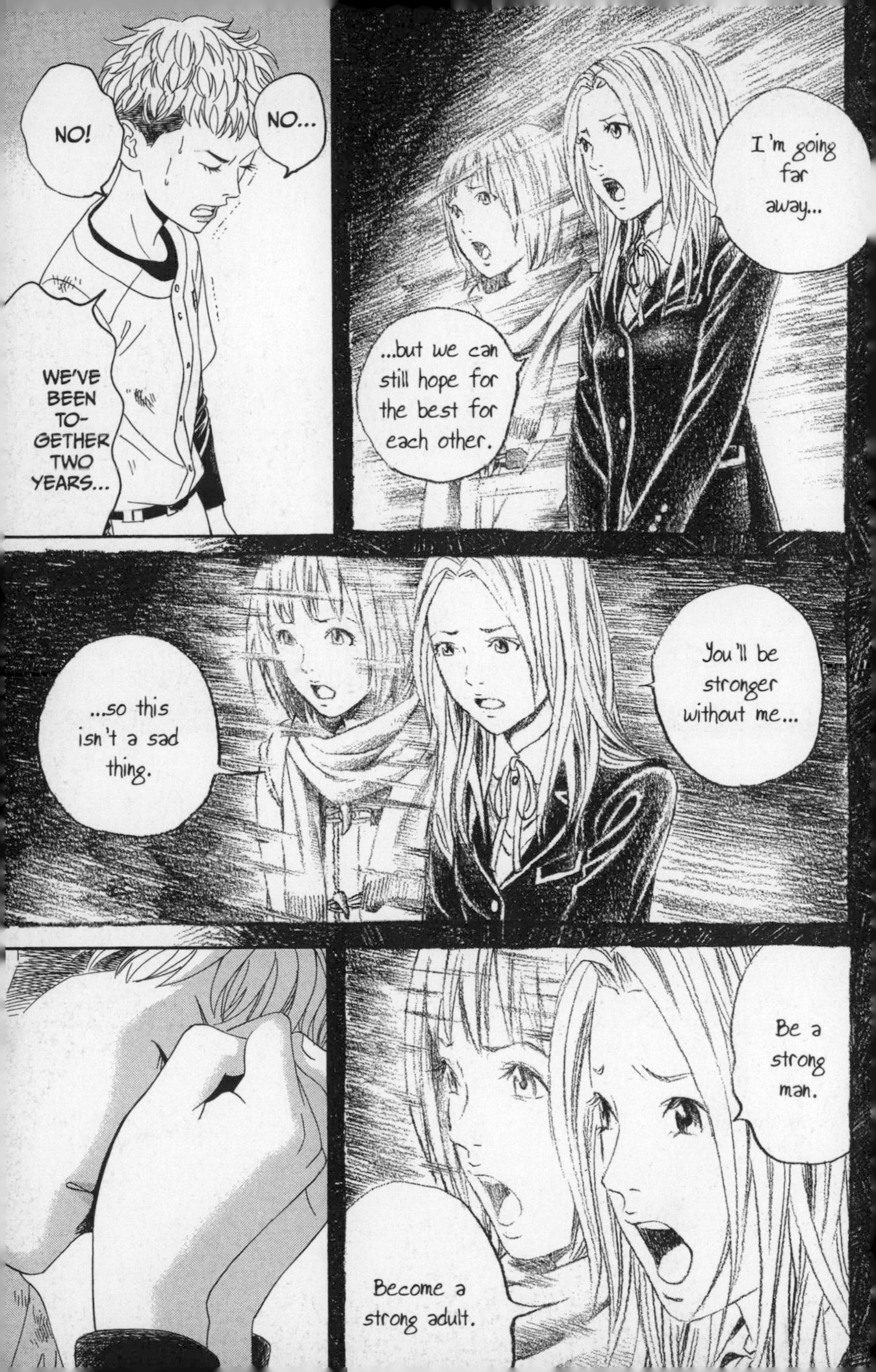
I'm going far away...
...but we can still hope for the best for each other.
NO...
NO!
WE'VE BEEN TO-GETHER TWO YEARS...
You'll be stronger without me...
...so this isn't a sad thing.
Be a strong man.
Become a strong adult.

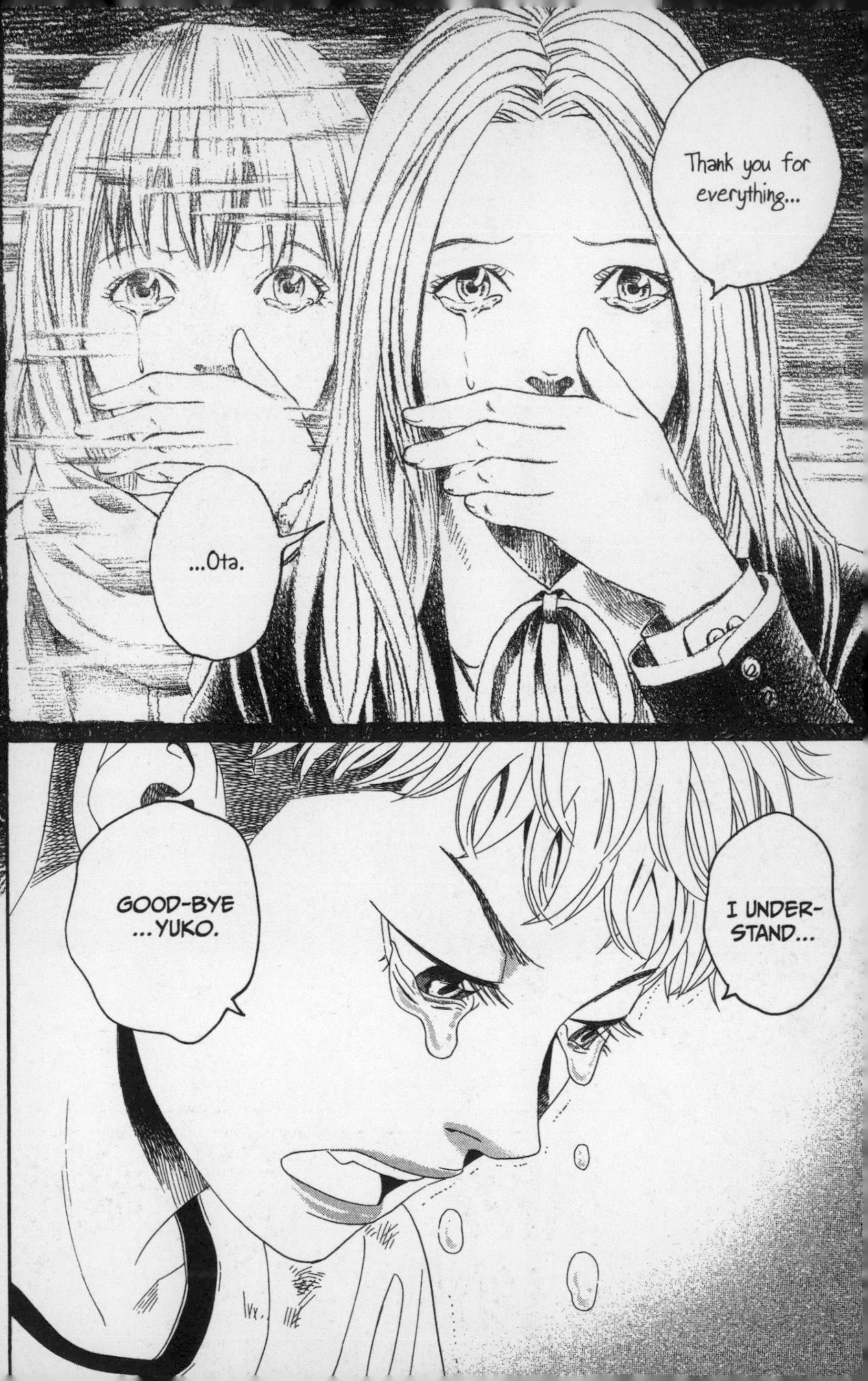
Thank you for everything...
...Ota.
I UNDER-STAND...
GOOD-BYE ...YUKO.

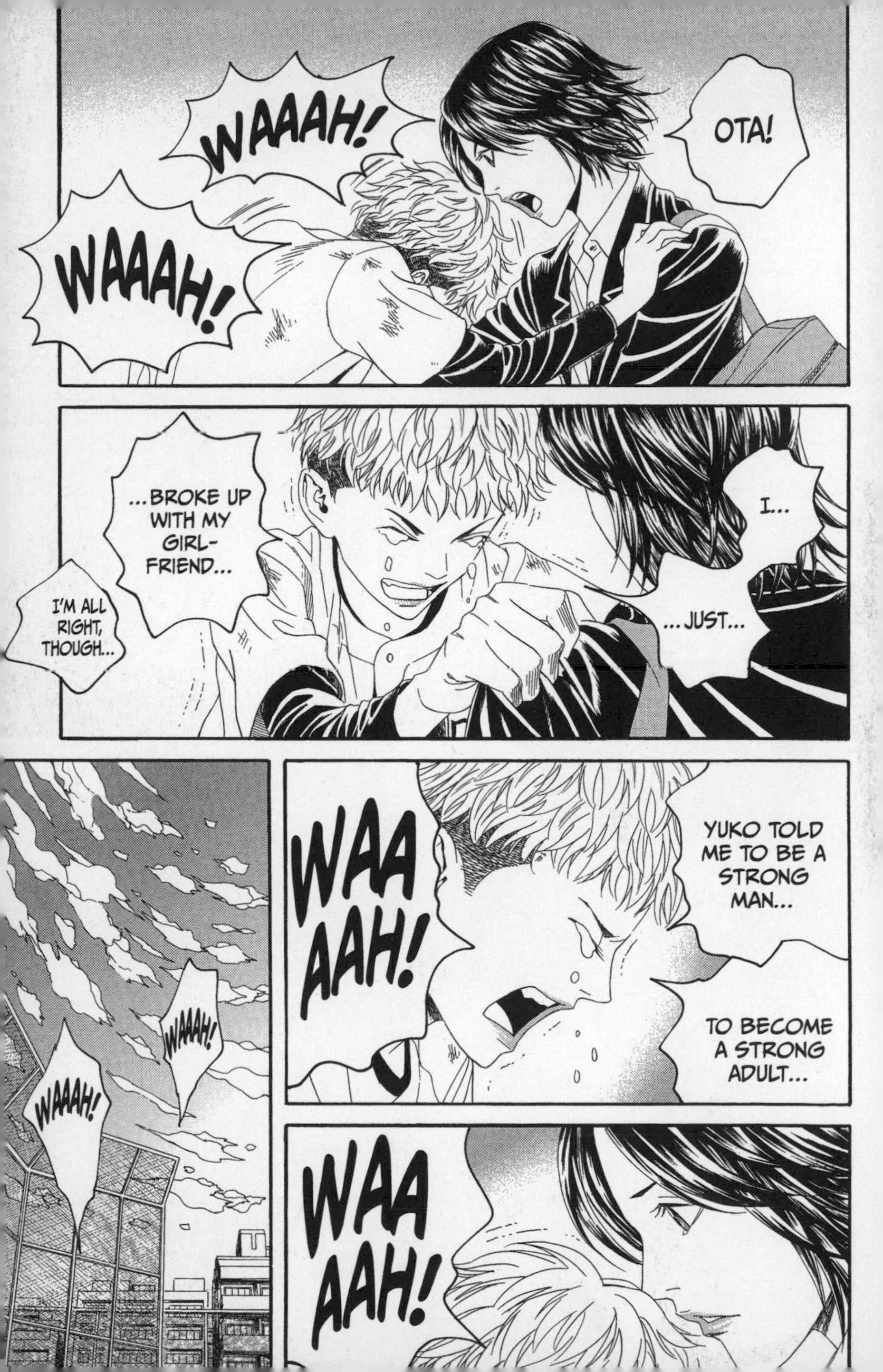
OTA!
WAAAH!
WAAAH!
I...
...JUST...
...BROKE UP WITH MY GIRL-FRIEND...
I'M ALL RIGHT, THOUGH...
YUKO TOLD ME TO BE A STRONG MAN...
TO BECOME A STRONG ADULT...
WAA AAH!
WAA AAH!
WAAAH!
WAAAH!

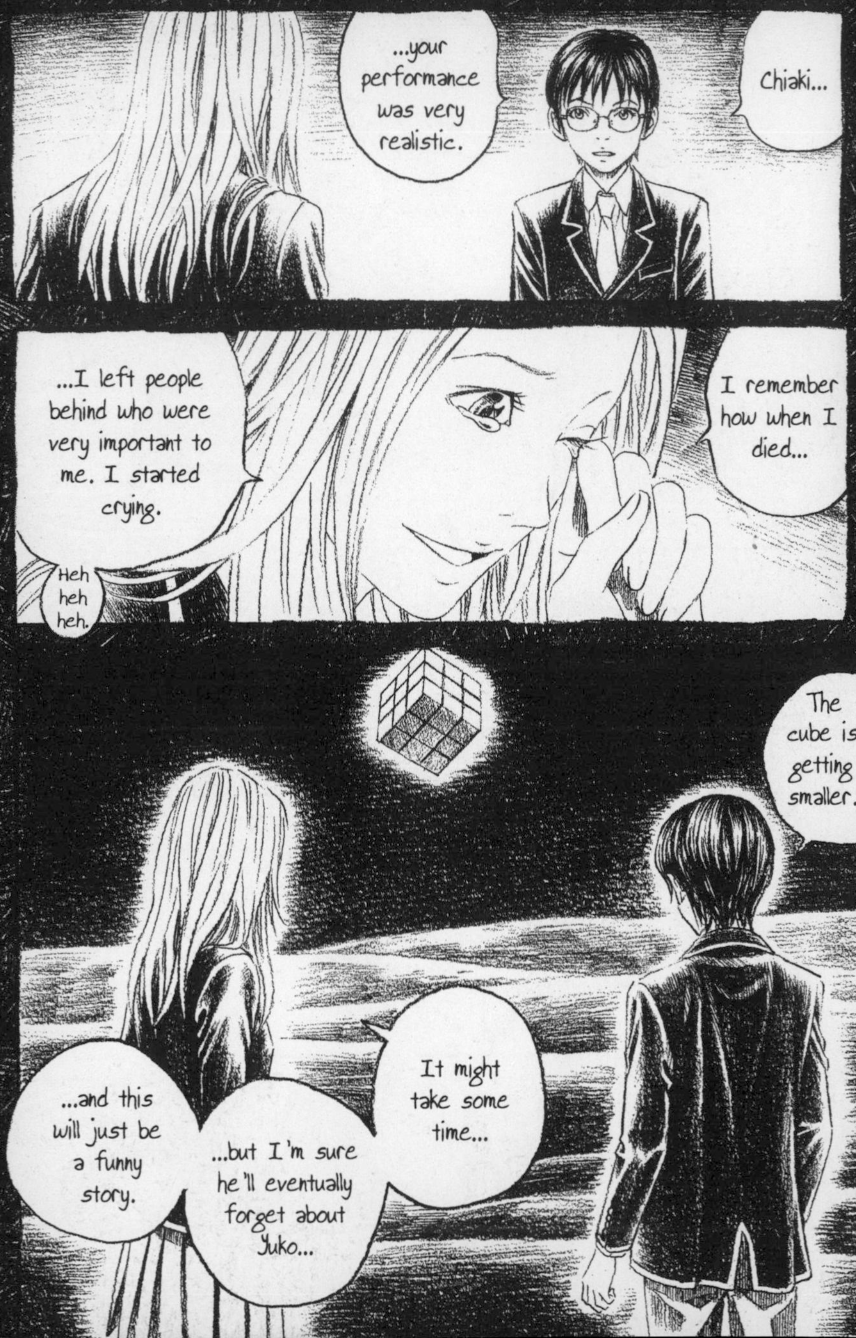
Chiaki...
...your performance was very realistic.
I remember how when I died...
...I left people behind who were very important to me. I started crying.
Heh heh heh.
The cube is getting smaller.
It might take some time...
...but I'm sure he'll eventually forget about Yuko...
...and this will just be a funny story.

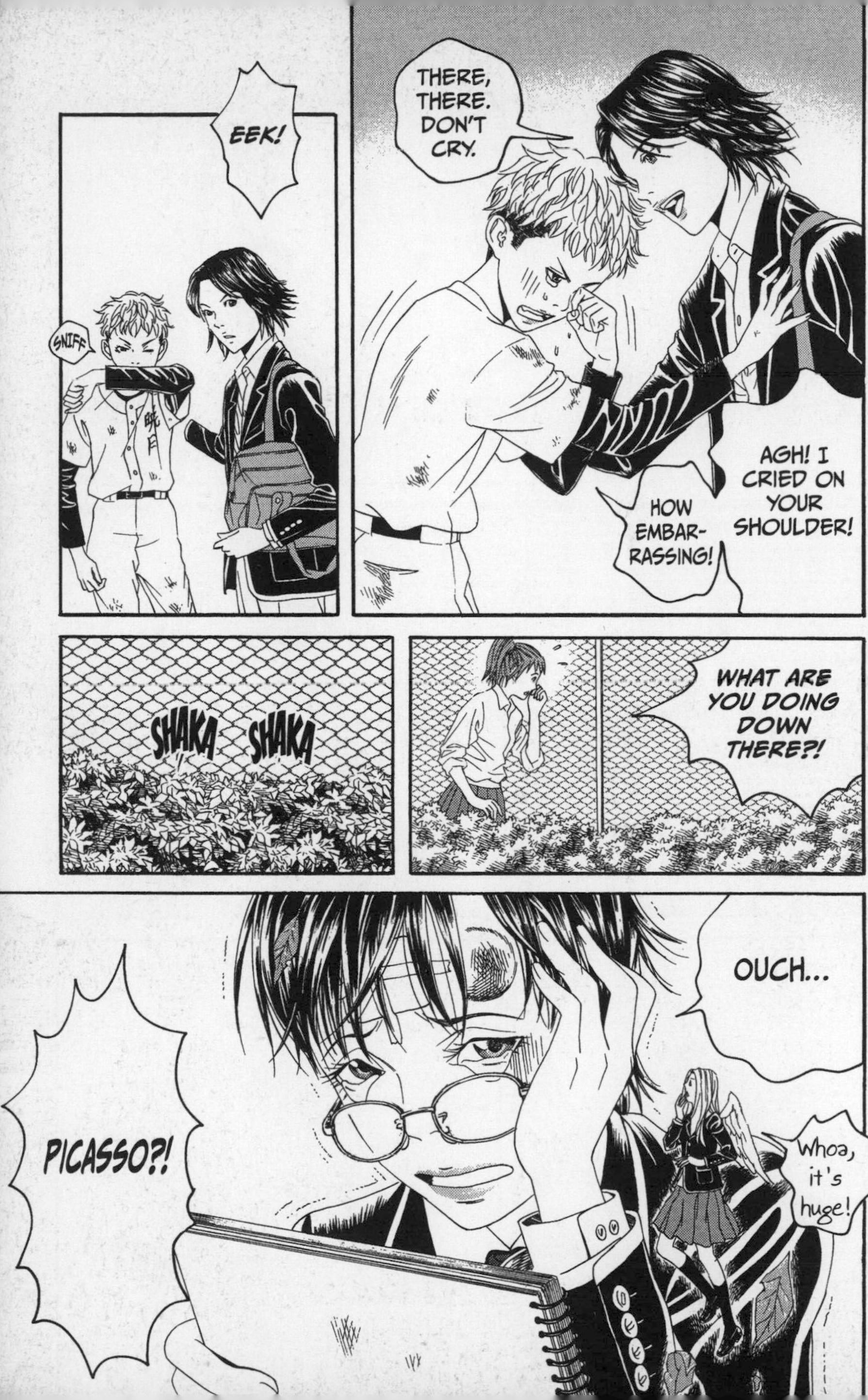
THERE, THERE. DON'T CRY.
AGH! I CRIED ON YOUR SHOULDER!
HOW EMBAR-RASSING!
EEK!
SNIFF
WHAT ARE YOU DOING DOWN THERE?!
SHAKA SHAKA
OUCH...
Whoa, it's huge!
PICASSO?!

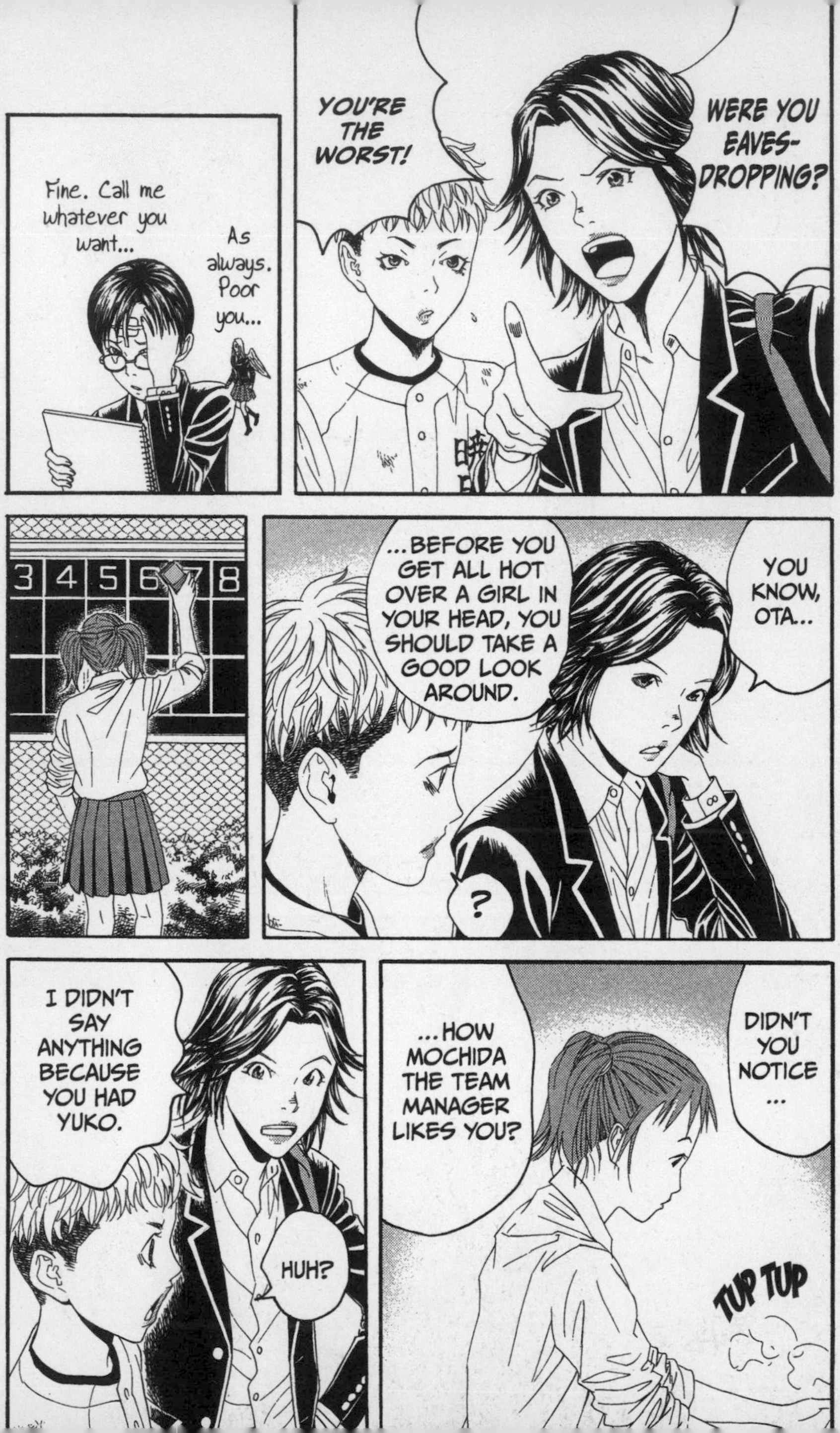
WERE YOU EAVES-DROPPING?
YOU'RE THE WORST!
Fine. Call me whatever you want...
As always. Poor you...
YOU KNOW, OTA...
...BEFORE YOU GET ALL HOT OVER A GIRL IN YOUR HEAD, YOU SHOULD TAKE A GOOD LOOK AROUND.
?
DIDN'T YOU NOTICE ...
...HOW MOCHIDA THE TEAM MANAGER LIKES YOU?
TUP TUP
I DIDN'T SAY ANYTHING BECAUSE YOU HAD YUKO.
HUH?

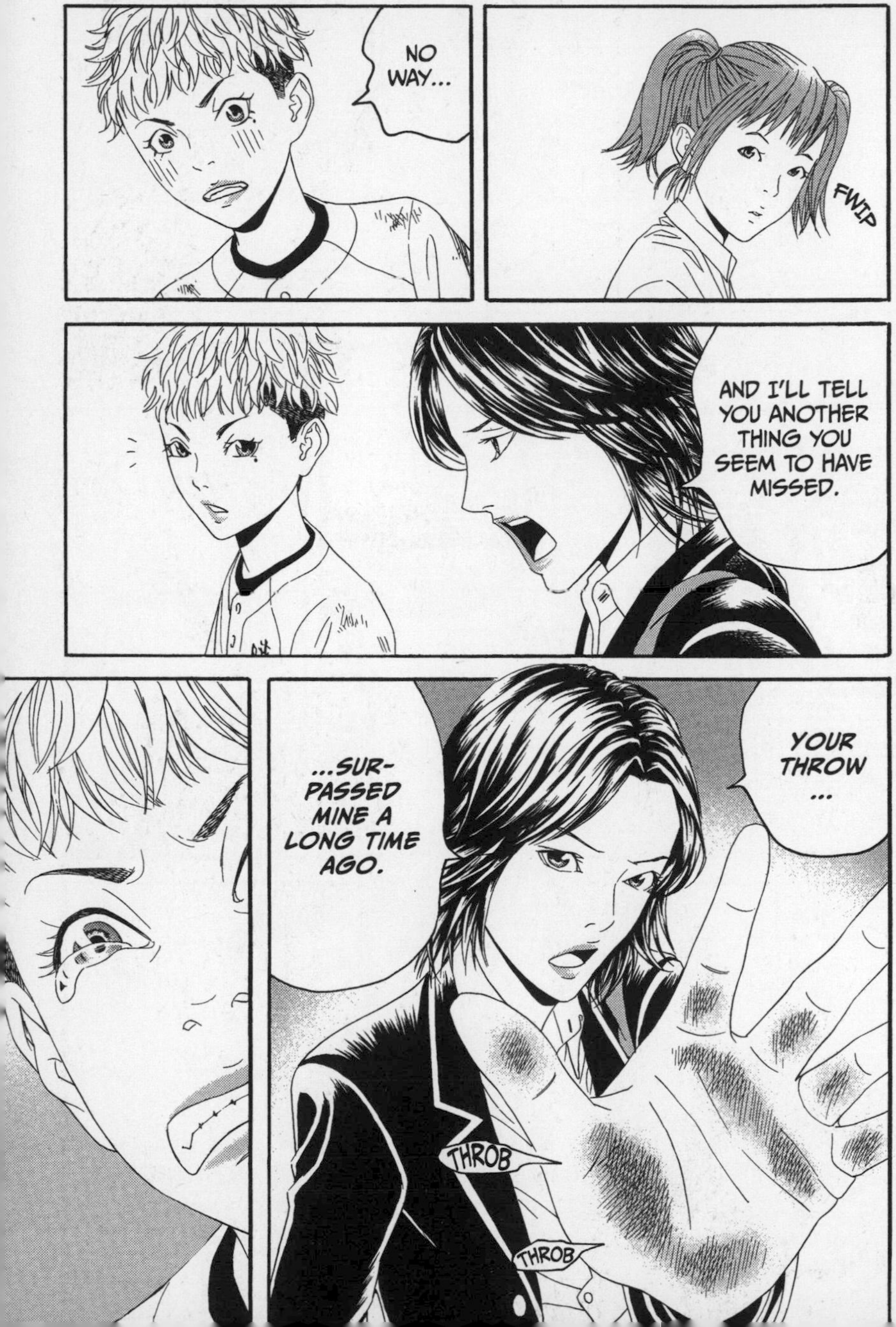
FWIP
NO WAY...
AND I'LL TELL YOU ANOTHER THING YOU SEEM TO HAVE MISSED.
YOUR THROW ...
...SUR-PASSED MINE A LONG TIME AGO.
THROB
THROB

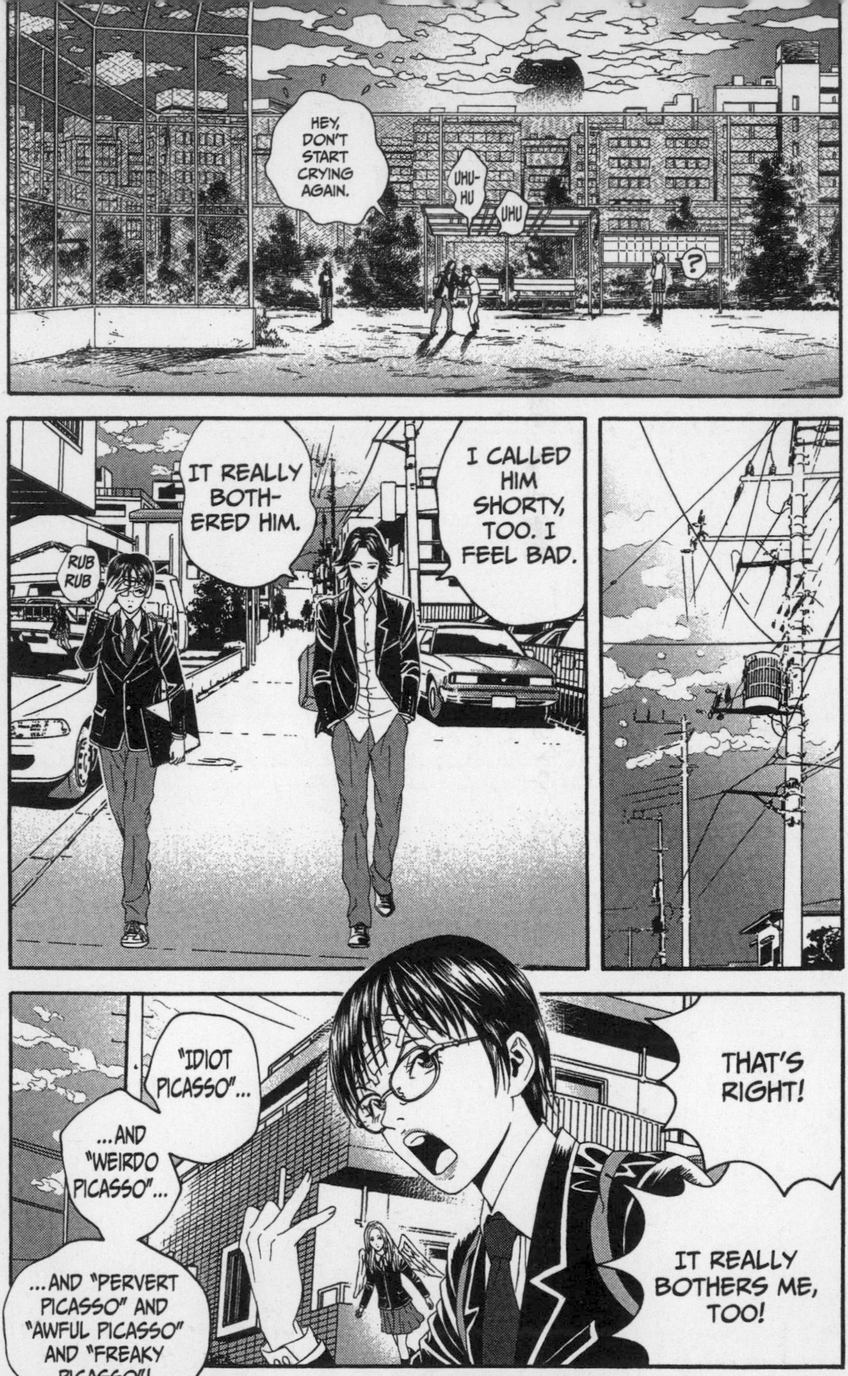
HEY, DON'T START CRYING AGAIN.
UHU-HU
UHU
?
I CALLED HIM SHORTY, TOO. I FEEL BAD.
IT REALLY BOTH-ERED HIM.
RUB RUB
THAT'S RIGHT!
IT REALLY BOTHERS ME, TOO!
"IDIOT PICASSO"...
...AND "WEIRDO PICASSO"...
...AND "PERVERT PICASSO" AND "AWFUL PICASSO" AND "FREAKY PICASSO"!

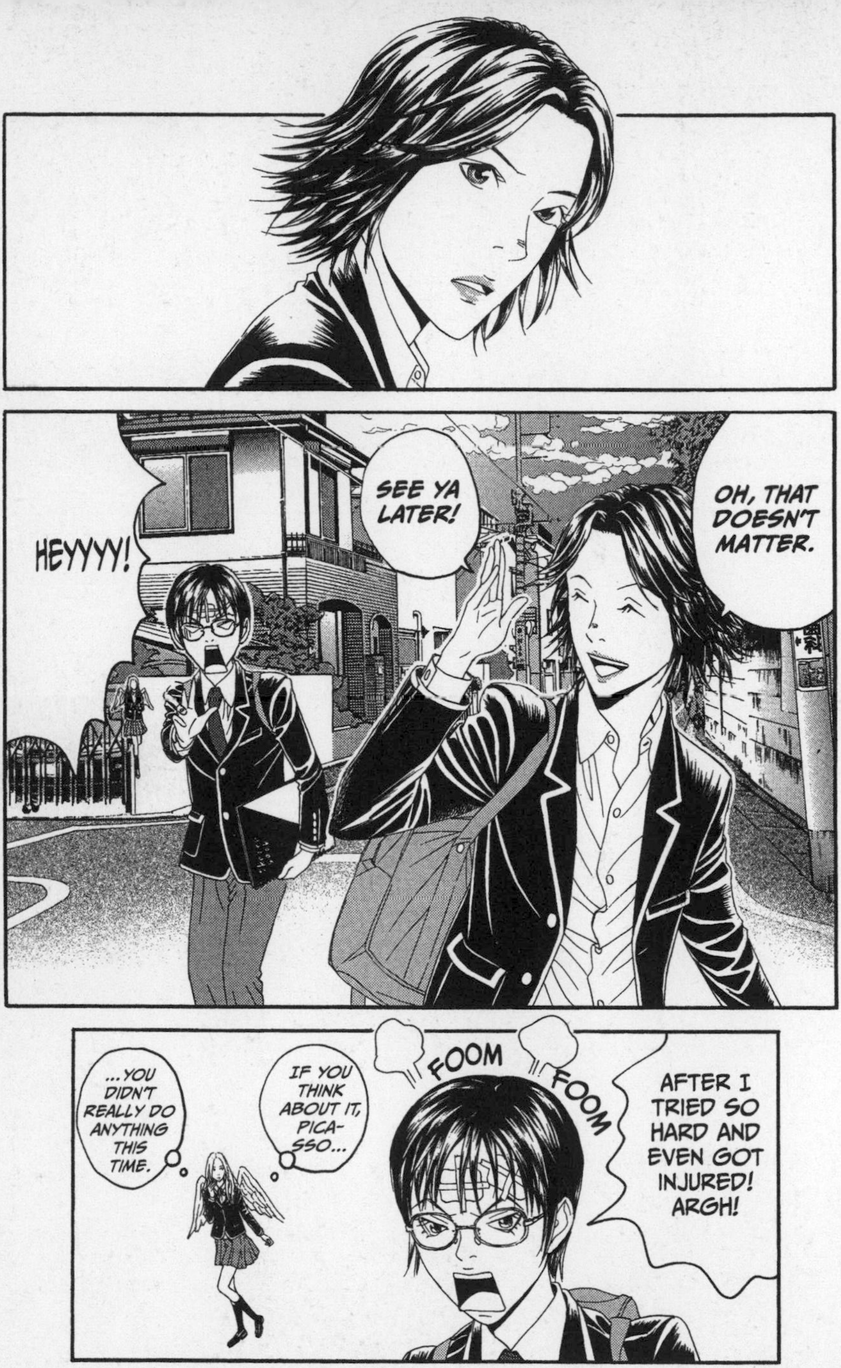
OH, THAT DOESN'T MATTER.
SEE YA LATER!
HEYYYY!
AFTER I TRIED SO HARD AND EVEN GOT INJURED! ARGH!
FOOM FOOM
IF YOU THINK ABOUT IT, PICA-SSO...
...YOU DIDN'T REALLY DO ANYTHING THIS TIME.

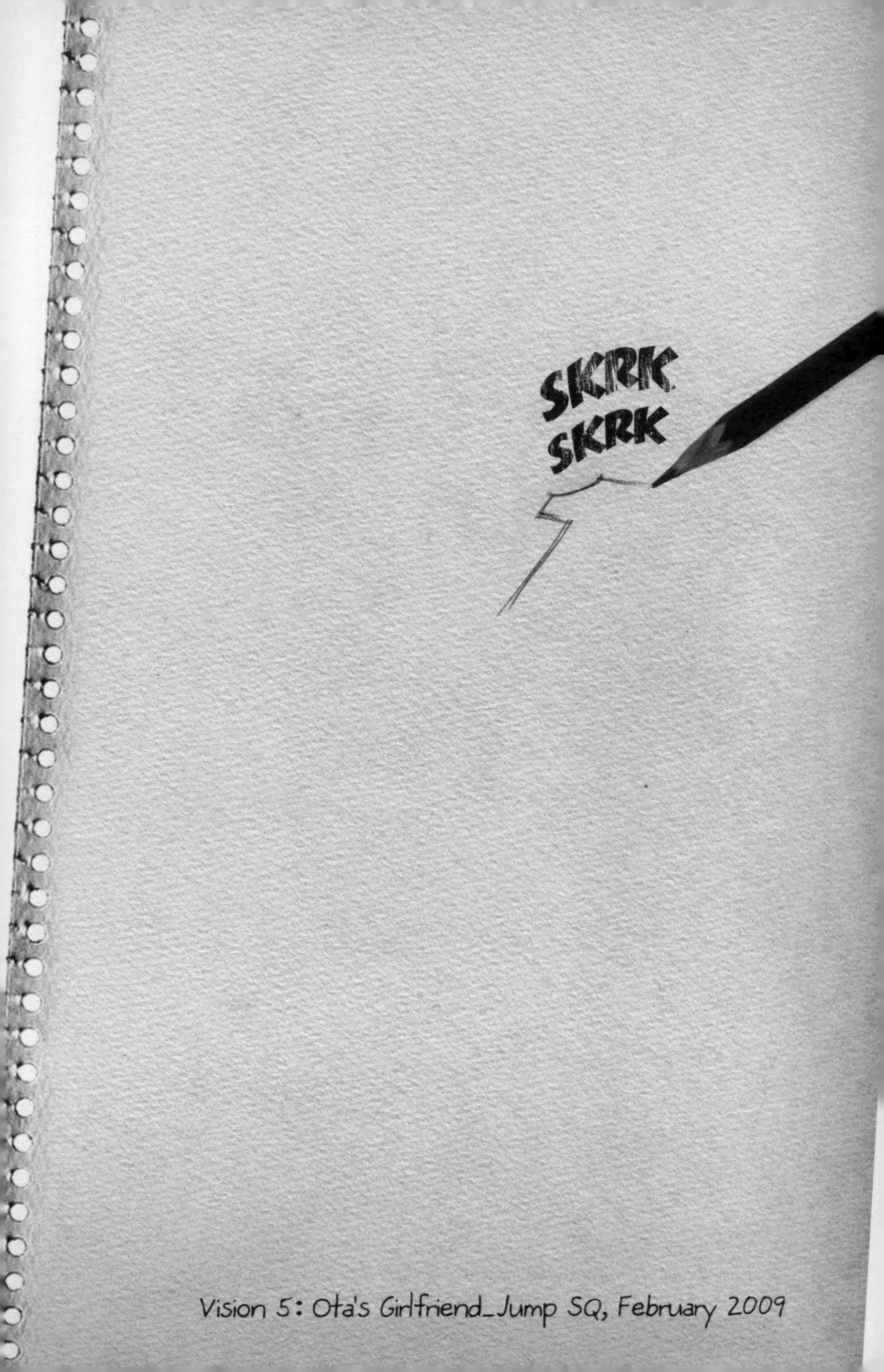
SKRK
SKRK

Vision 5: Ota's Girlfriend_Jump SQ, February 2009

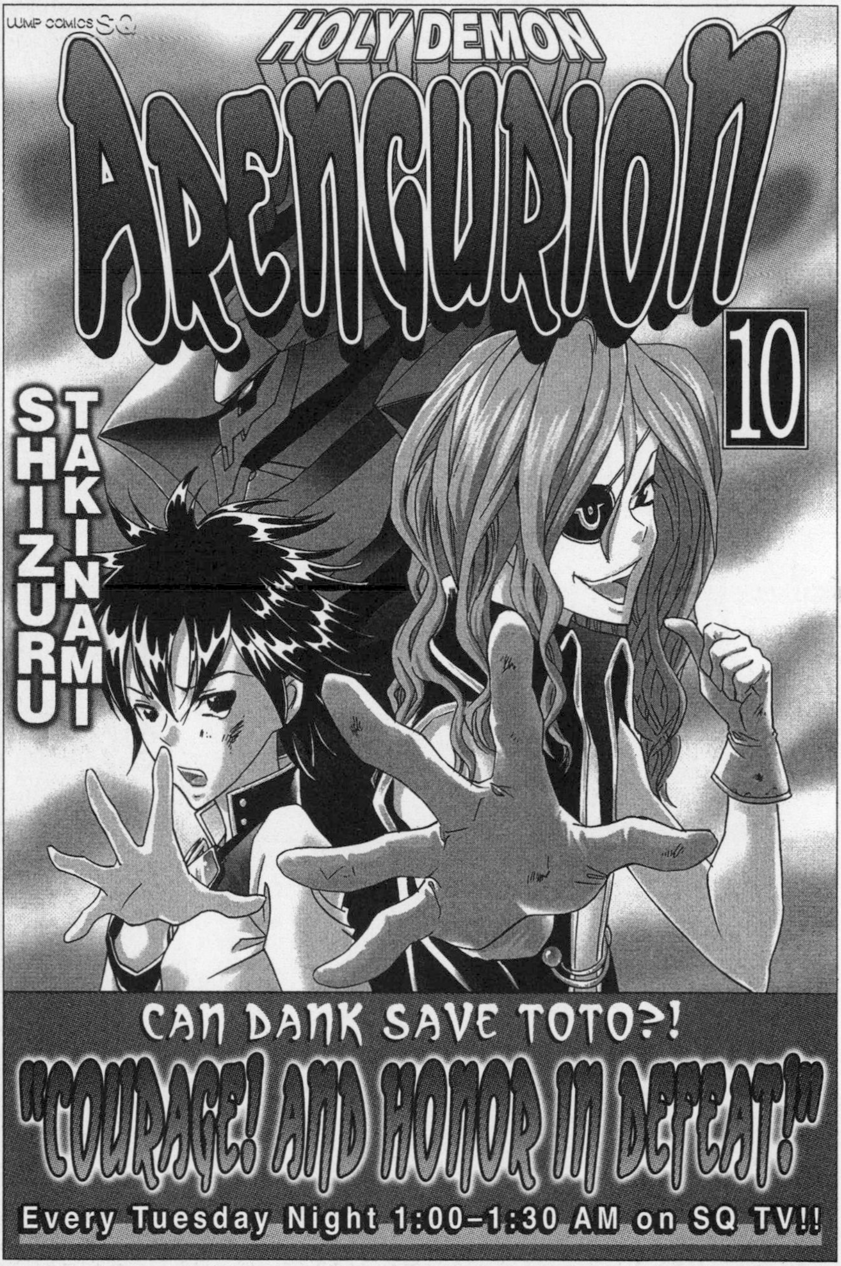
HOLY DEMON
ARENGURION
10
SHIZURU TAKINAMI
CAN DANK SAVE TOTO?!
"COURAGE! AND HONOR IN DEFEAT!"
Every Tuesday Night 1:00–1:30 AM on SQ TV!!

Vision 6: Kotone and Arengurion (Part I)

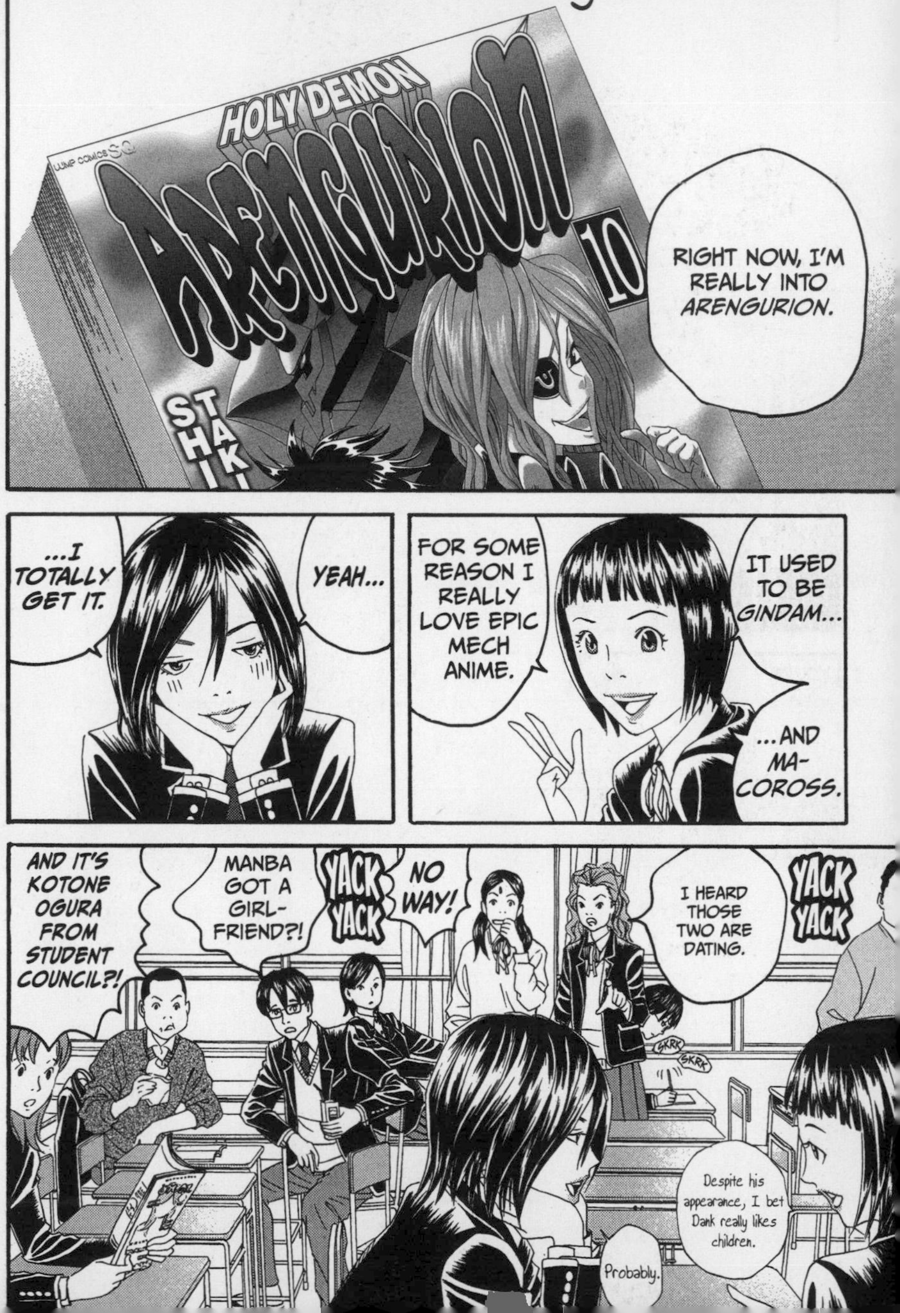
HOLY DEMON
ARENGURION
10
RIGHT NOW, I'M REALLY INTO ARENGURION.
IT USED TO BE GINDAM...
FOR SOME REASON I REALLY LOVE EPIC MECH ANIME.
...AND MA-COROSS.
YEAH...
...I TOTALLY GET IT.
YACK YACK
I HEARD THOSE TWO ARE DATING.
NO WAY!
YACK YACK
MANBA GOT A GIRL-FRIEND?!
AND IT'S KOTONE OGURA FROM STUDENT COUNCIL?!
SKRK
SKRK
Despite his appearance, I bet Dank really likes children.
Probably.

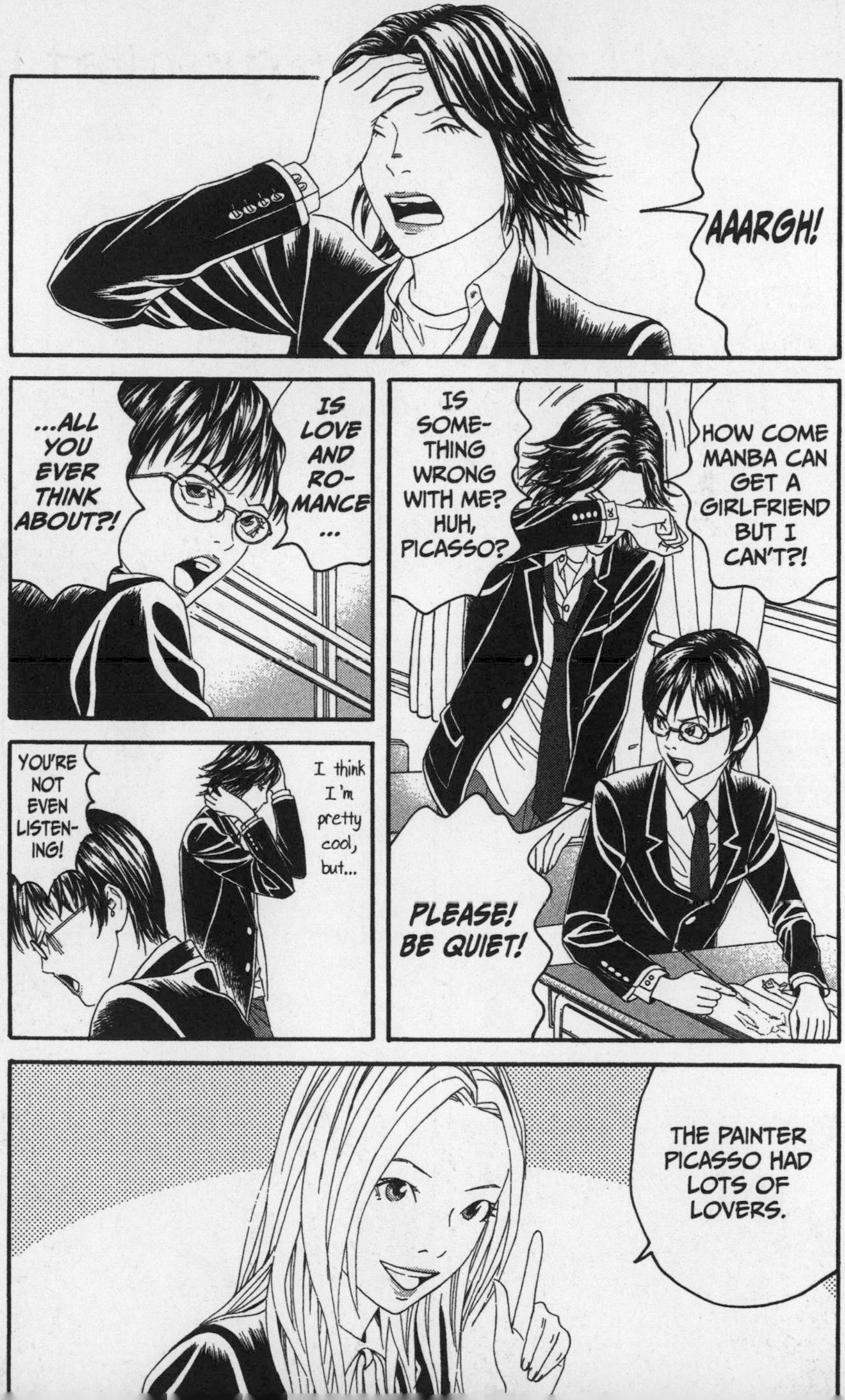
AAARGH!
HOW COME MANBA CAN GET A GIRLFRIEND BUT I CAN'T?!
IS SOME-THING WRONG WITH ME? HUH, PICASSO?
PLEASE! BE QUIET!
IS LOVE AND RO-MANCE...
...ALL YOU EVER THINK ABOUT?!
I think I'm pretty cool, but...
YOU'RE NOT EVEN LISTEN-ING!
THE PAINTER PICASSO HAD LOTS OF LOVERS.

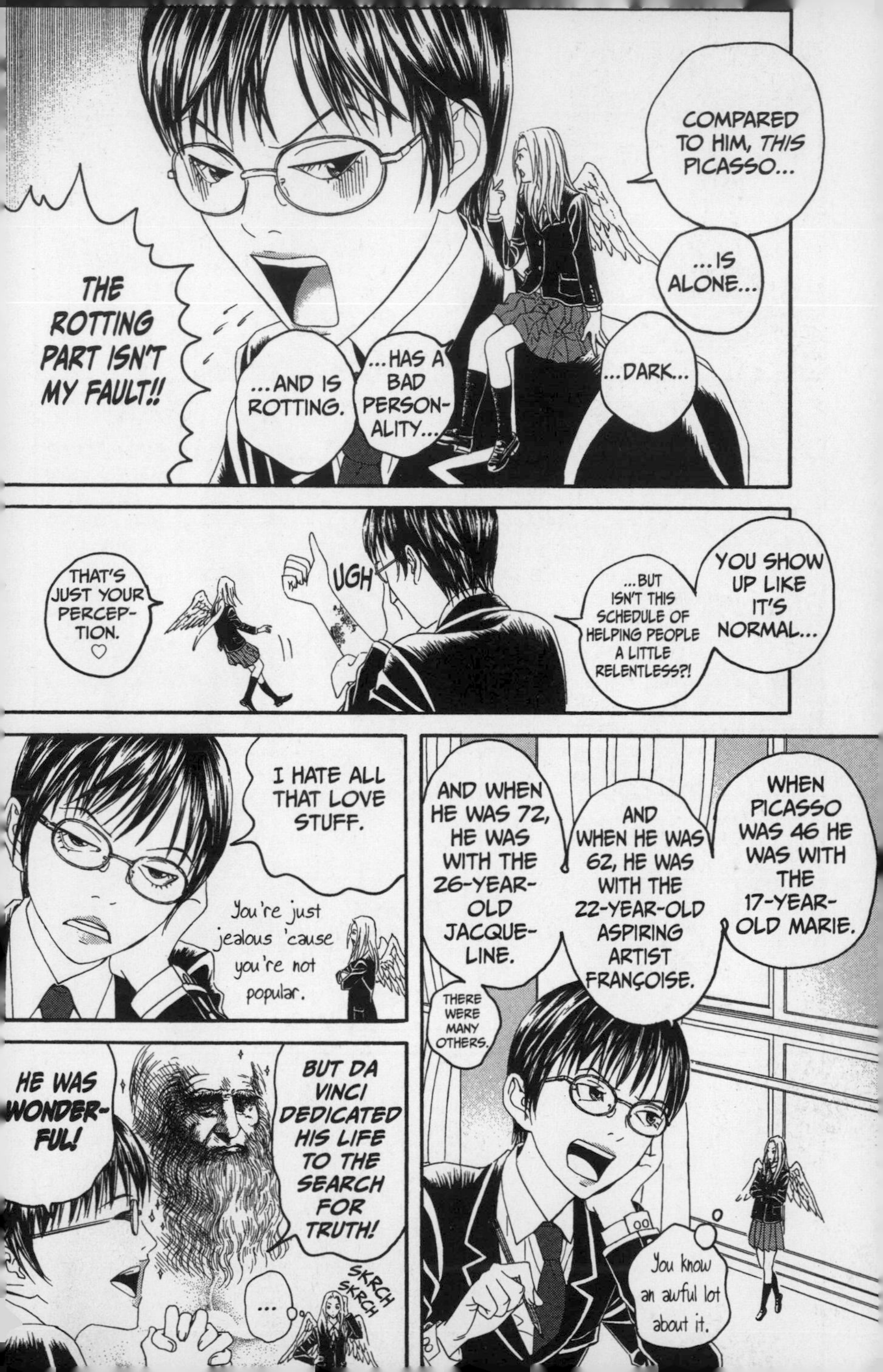
COMPARED TO HIM, THIS PICASSO...
...IS ALONE...
...DARK...
...HAS A BAD PERSON-ALITY...
...AND IS ROTTING.
THE ROTTING PART ISN'T MY FAULT!!
YOU SHOW UP LIKE IT'S NORMAL...
...BUT ISN'T THIS SCHEDULE OF HELPING PEOPLE A LITTLE RELENTLESS?!
UGH
THAT'S JUST YOUR PERCEP-TION. ♡
WHEN PICASSO WAS 46 HE WAS WITH THE 17-YEAR-OLD MARIE.
AND WHEN HE WAS 62, HE WAS WITH THE 22-YEAR-OLD ASPIRING ARTIST FRANÇOISE.
AND WHEN HE WAS 72, HE WAS WITH THE 26-YEAR-OLD JACQUE-LINE.
THERE WERE MANY OTHERS.
You know an awful lot about it.
I HATE ALL THAT LOVE STUFF.
You're just jealous 'cause you're not popular.
BUT DA VINCI DEDICATED HIS LIFE TO THE SEARCH FOR TRUTH!
HE WAS WONDER-FUL!
...
SKRCH SKRCH

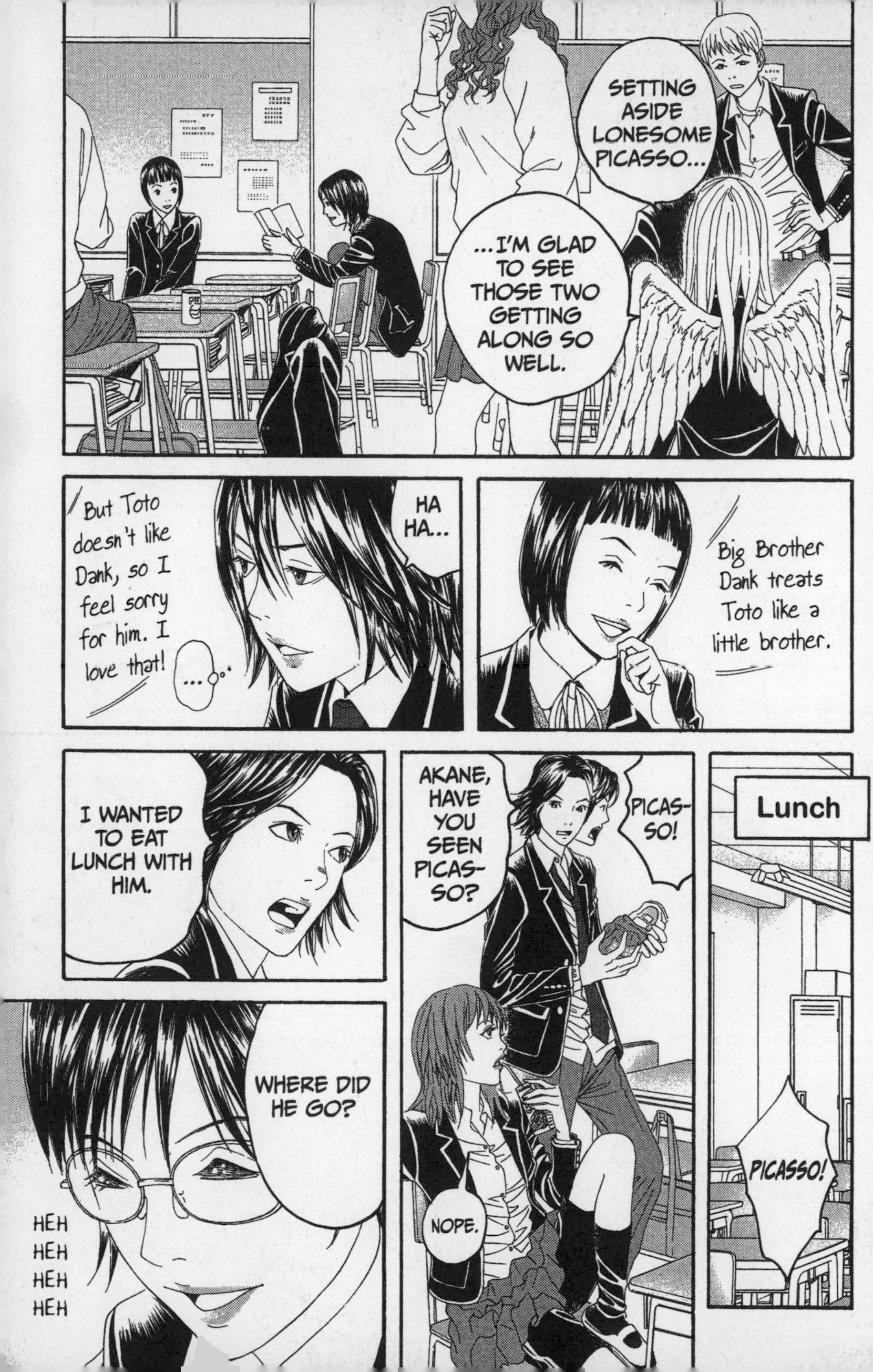
SETTING ASIDE LONESOME PICASSO...
...I'M GLAD TO SEE THOSE TWO GETTING ALONG SO WELL.
Big Brother Dank treats Toto like a little brother.
HA HA...
But Toto doesn't like Dank, so I feel sorry for him. I love that!
...
Lunch
PICASSO!
PICAS-SO!
AKANE, HAVE YOU SEEN PICAS-SO?
NOPE.
I WANTED TO EAT LUNCH WITH HIM.
WHERE DID HE GO?
HEH HEH HEH HEH

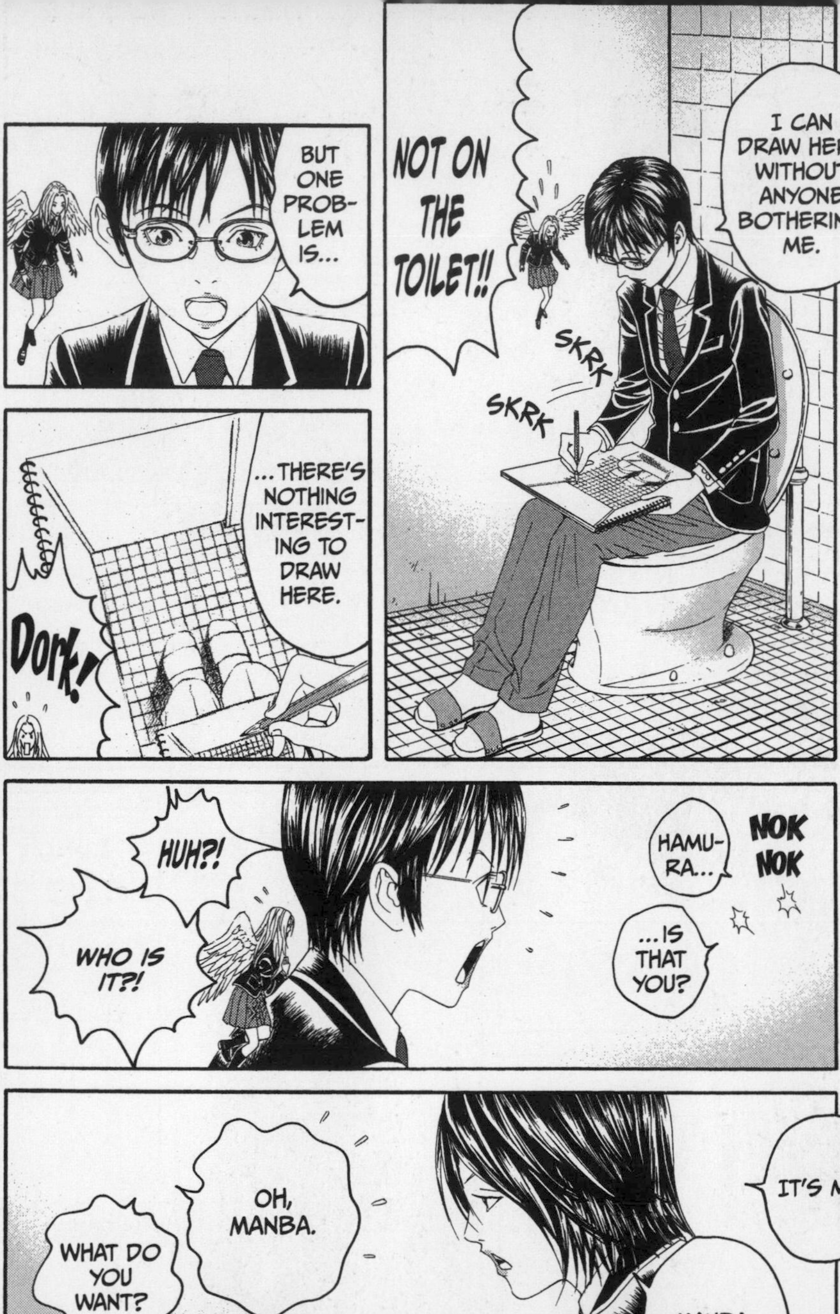
I CAN DRAW HERE WITHOUT ANYONE BOTHERING ME.
SKRK
SKRK
NOT ON THE TOILET!!
BUT ONE PROB-LEM IS...
...THERE'S NOTHING INTERESTING TO DRAW HERE.
Dork!
NOK NOK
HAMU-RA...
...IS THAT YOU?
HUH?!
WHO IS IT?!
IT'S ME.
MANBA.
OH, MANBA.
WHAT DO YOU WANT?

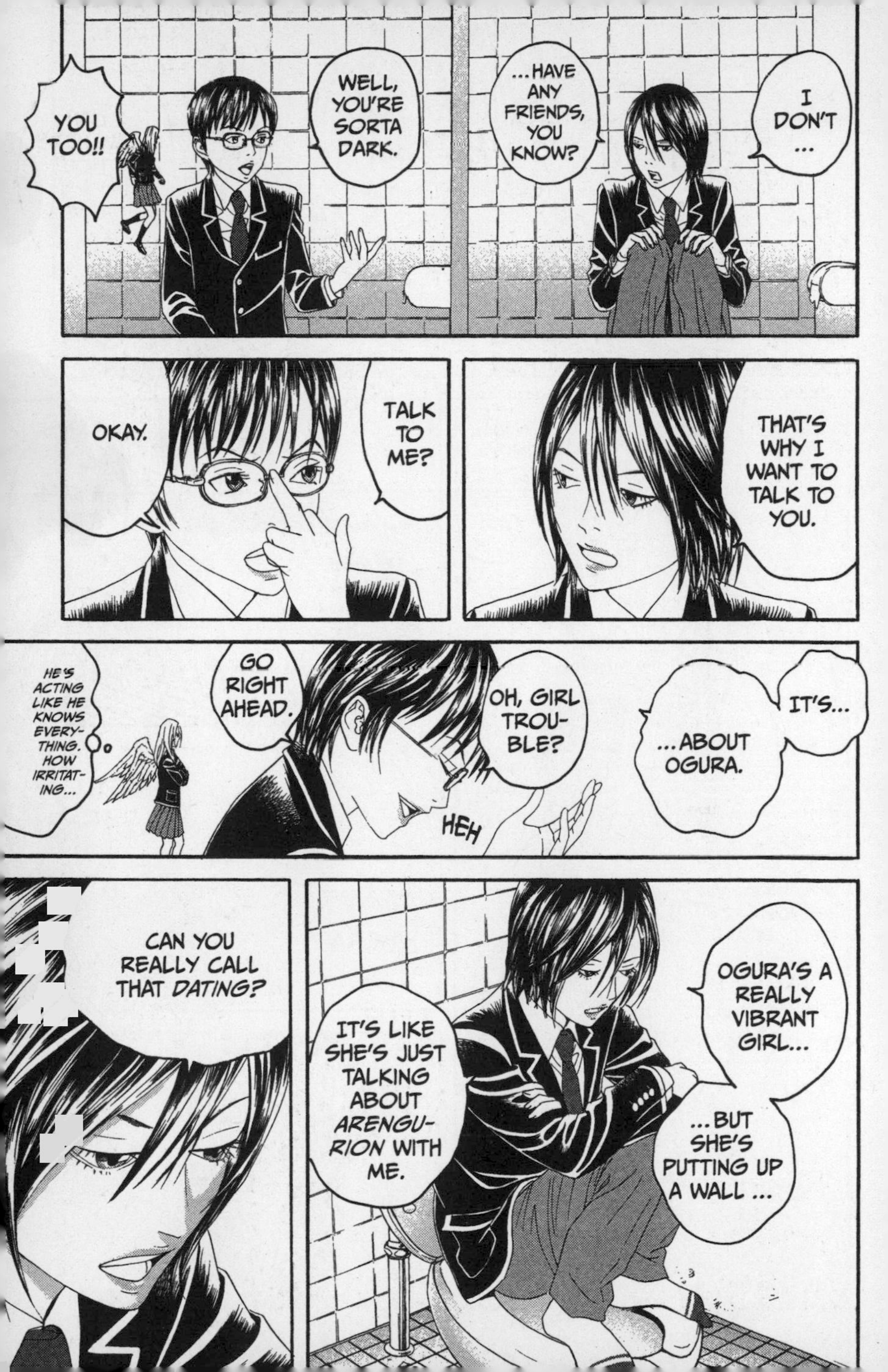
I DON'T ...
...HAVE ANY FRIENDS, YOU KNOW?
WELL, YOU'RE SORTA DARK.
YOU TOO!!
THAT'S WHY I WANT TO TALK TO YOU.
TALK TO ME?
OKAY.
IT'S...
...ABOUT OGURA.
OH, GIRL TROUBLE?
HEH
GO RIGHT AHEAD.
HE'S ACTING LIKE HE KNOWS EVERYTHING. HOW IRRITATING...
OGURA'S A REALLY VIBRANT GIRL...
...BUT SHE'S PUTTING UP A WALL ...
IT'S LIKE SHE'S JUST TALKING ABOUT *ARENGURION* WITH ME.
CAN YOU REALLY CALL THAT *DATING*?

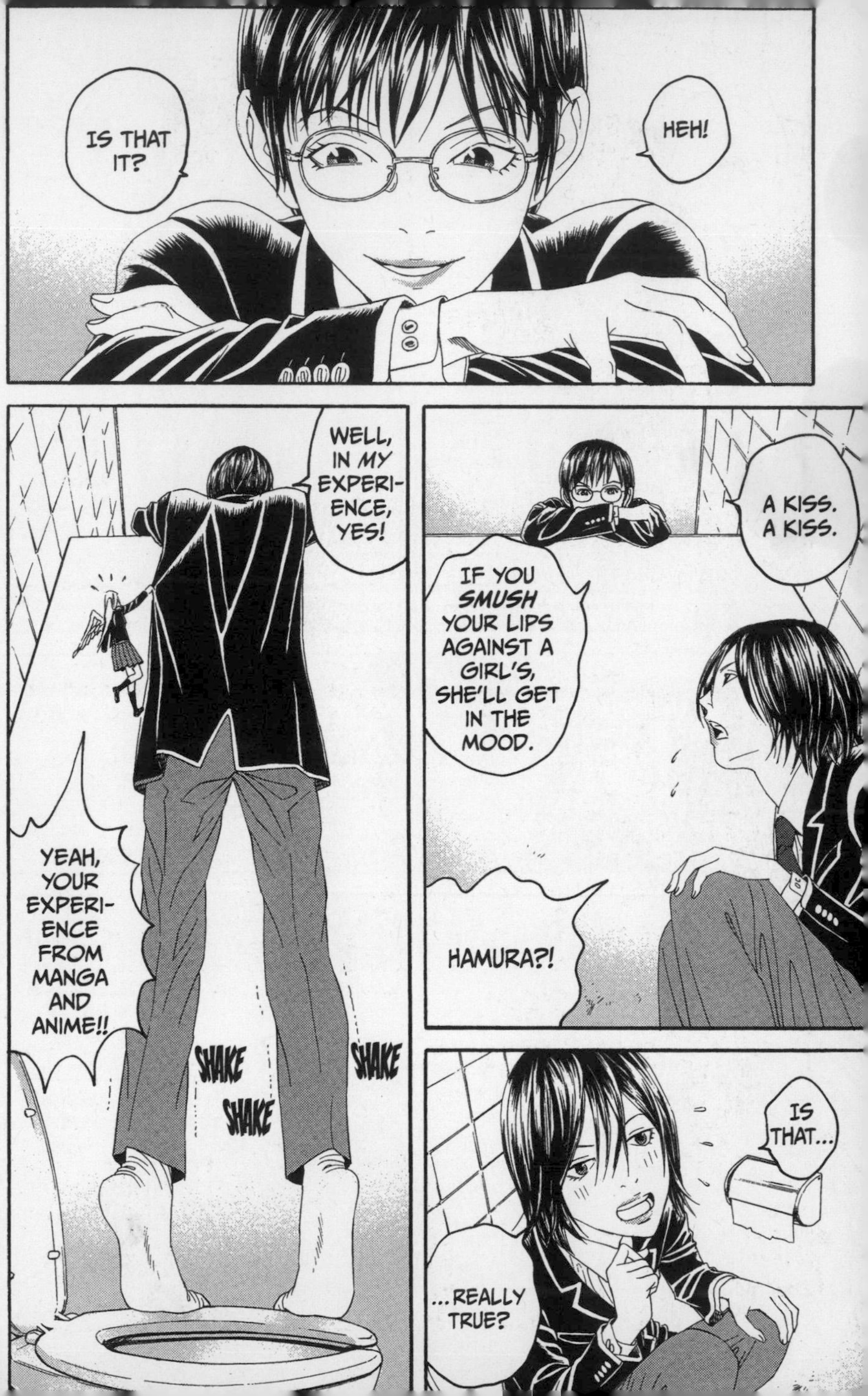
HEH!
IS THAT IT?
A KISS. A KISS.
IF YOU SMUSH YOUR LIPS AGAINST A GIRL'S, SHE'LL GET IN THE MOOD.
HAMURA?!
IS THAT...
...REALLY TRUE?
WELL, IN MY EXPERIENCE, YES!
YEAH, YOUR EXPERIENCE FROM MANGA AND ANIME!!
SHAKE
SHAKE
SHAKE

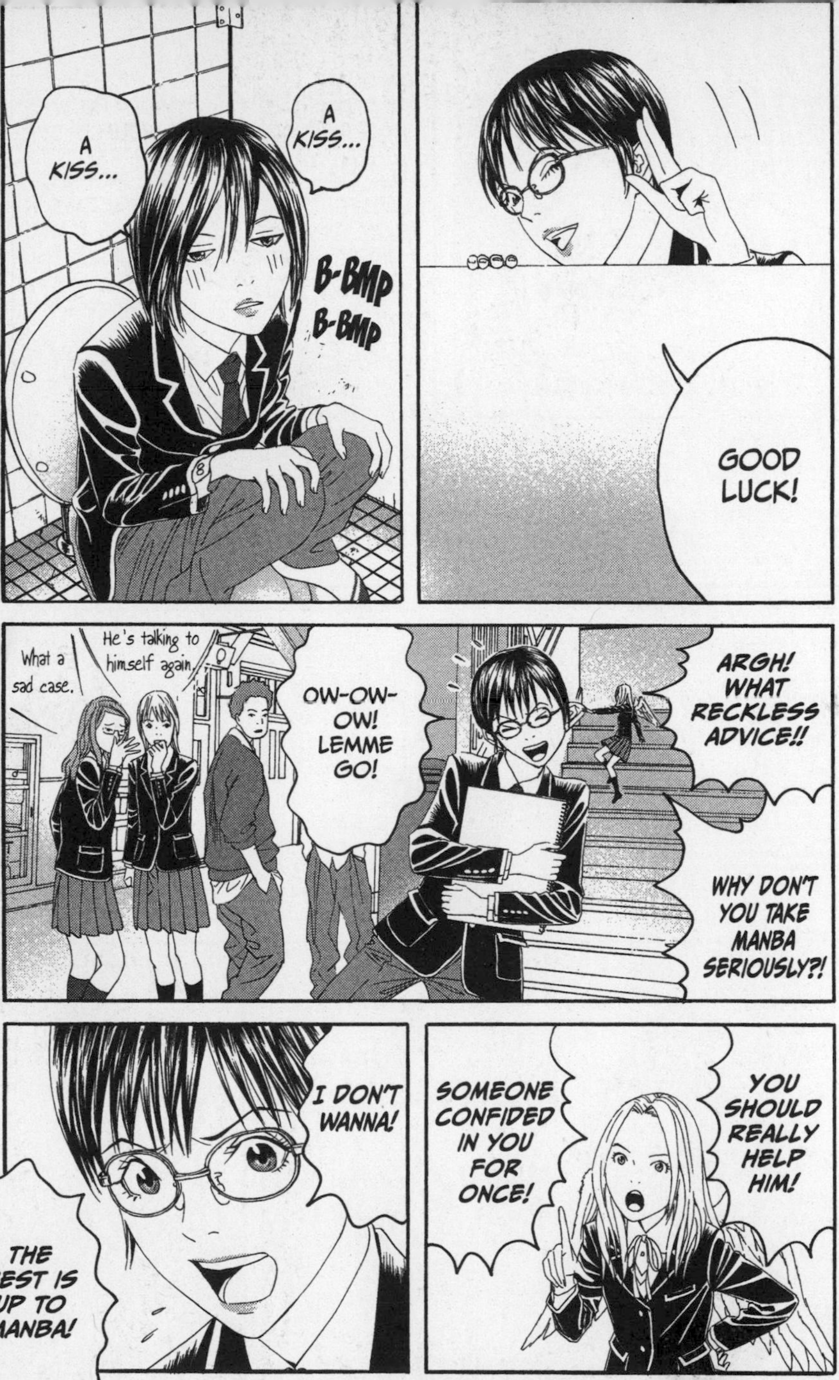
GOOD LUCK!
A KISS...
A KISS...
B-BMP
B-BMP
ARGH! WHAT RECKLESS ADVICE!!
WHY DON'T YOU TAKE MANBA SERIOUSLY?!
OW-OW-OW! LEMME GO!
He's talking to himself again.
What a sad case.
YOU SHOULD REALLY HELP HIM!
SOMEONE CONFIDED IN YOU FOR ONCE!
I DON'T WANNA!
THE REST IS UP TO MANBA!

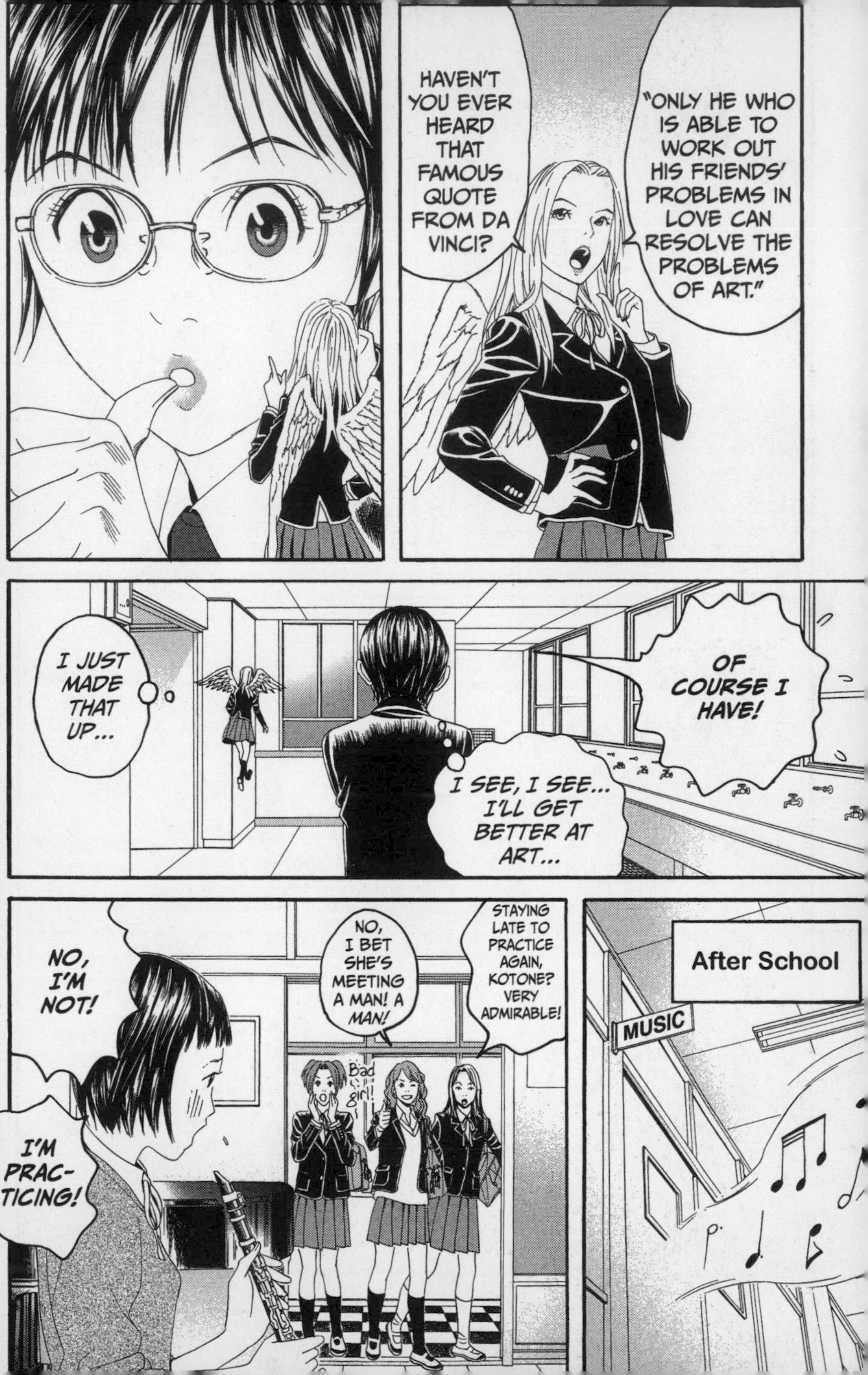
HAVEN'T YOU EVER HEARD THAT FAMOUS QUOTE FROM DA VINCI?
"ONLY HE WHO IS ABLE TO WORK OUT HIS FRIENDS' PROBLEMS IN LOVE CAN RESOLVE THE PROBLEMS OF ART."
OF COURSE I HAVE!
I SEE, I SEE... I'LL GET BETTER AT ART...
I JUST MADE THAT UP...
After School
MUSIC
STAYING LATE TO PRACTICE AGAIN, KOTONE? VERY ADMIRABLE!
NO, I BET SHE'S MEETING A MAN! A MAN!
Bad girl!
NO, I'M NOT!
I'M PRAC-TICING!

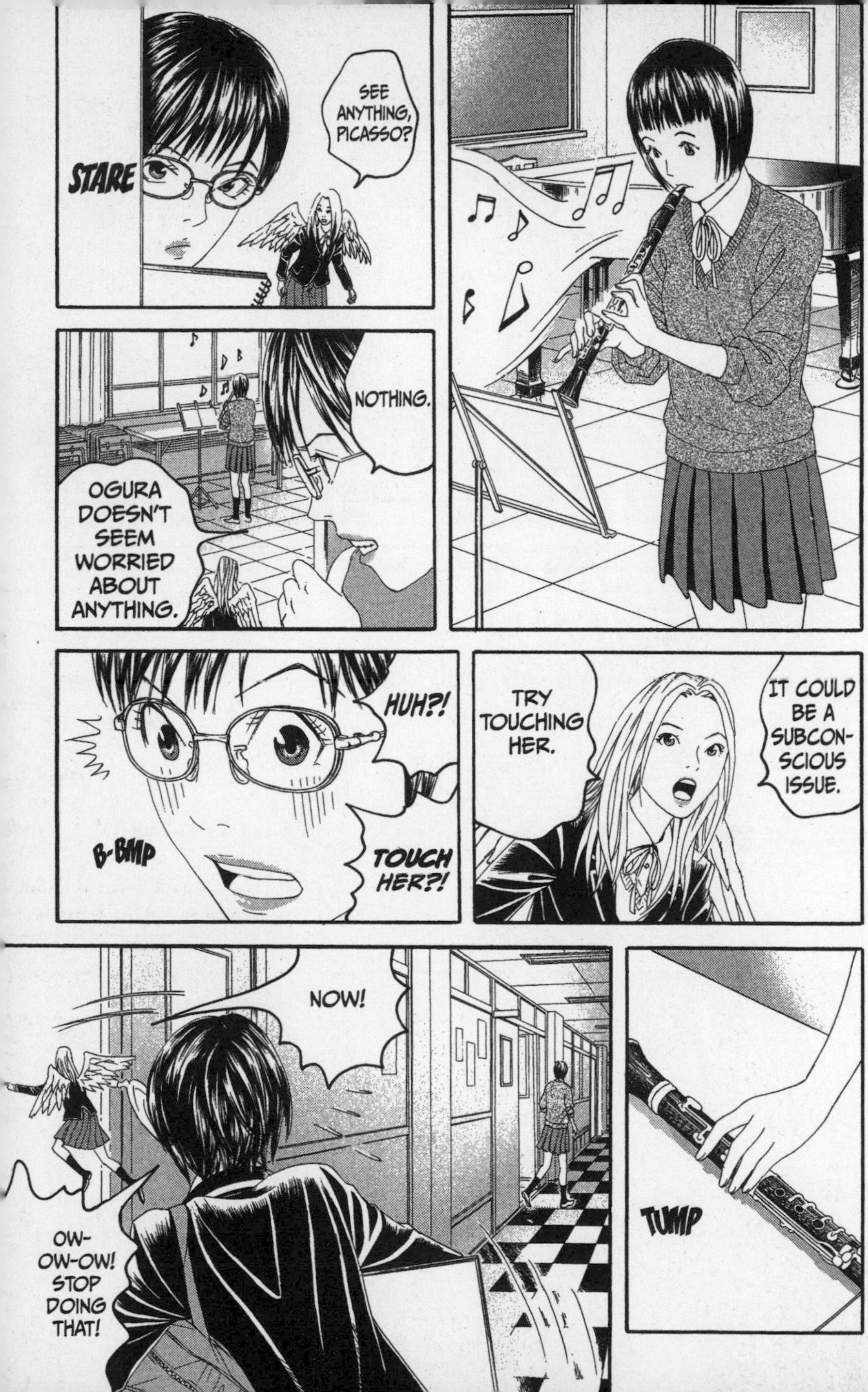
SEE ANYTHING, PICASSO?
STARE
NOTHING.
OGURA DOESN'T SEEM WORRIED ABOUT ANYTHING.
IT COULD BE A SUBCON-SCIOUS ISSUE.
TRY TOUCHING HER.
HUH?!
TOUCH HER?!
B-BMP
TUMP
NOW!
OW-OW-OW! STOP DOING THAT!

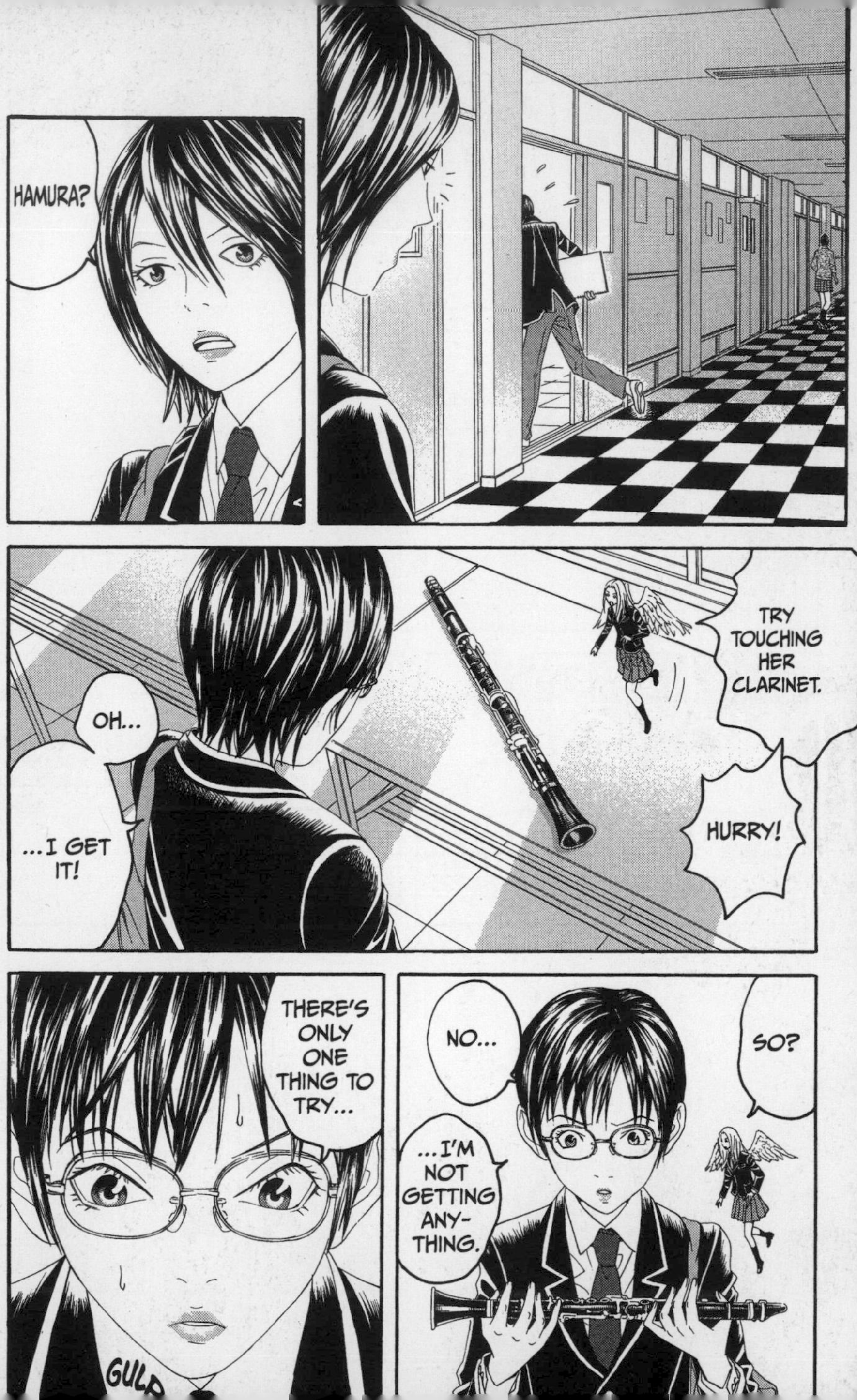
HAMURA?
TRY TOUCHING HER CLARINET.
HURRY!
OH...
...I GET IT!
SO?
NO...
...I'M NOT GETTING ANY-THING.
THERE'S ONLY ONE THING TO TRY...
GULP

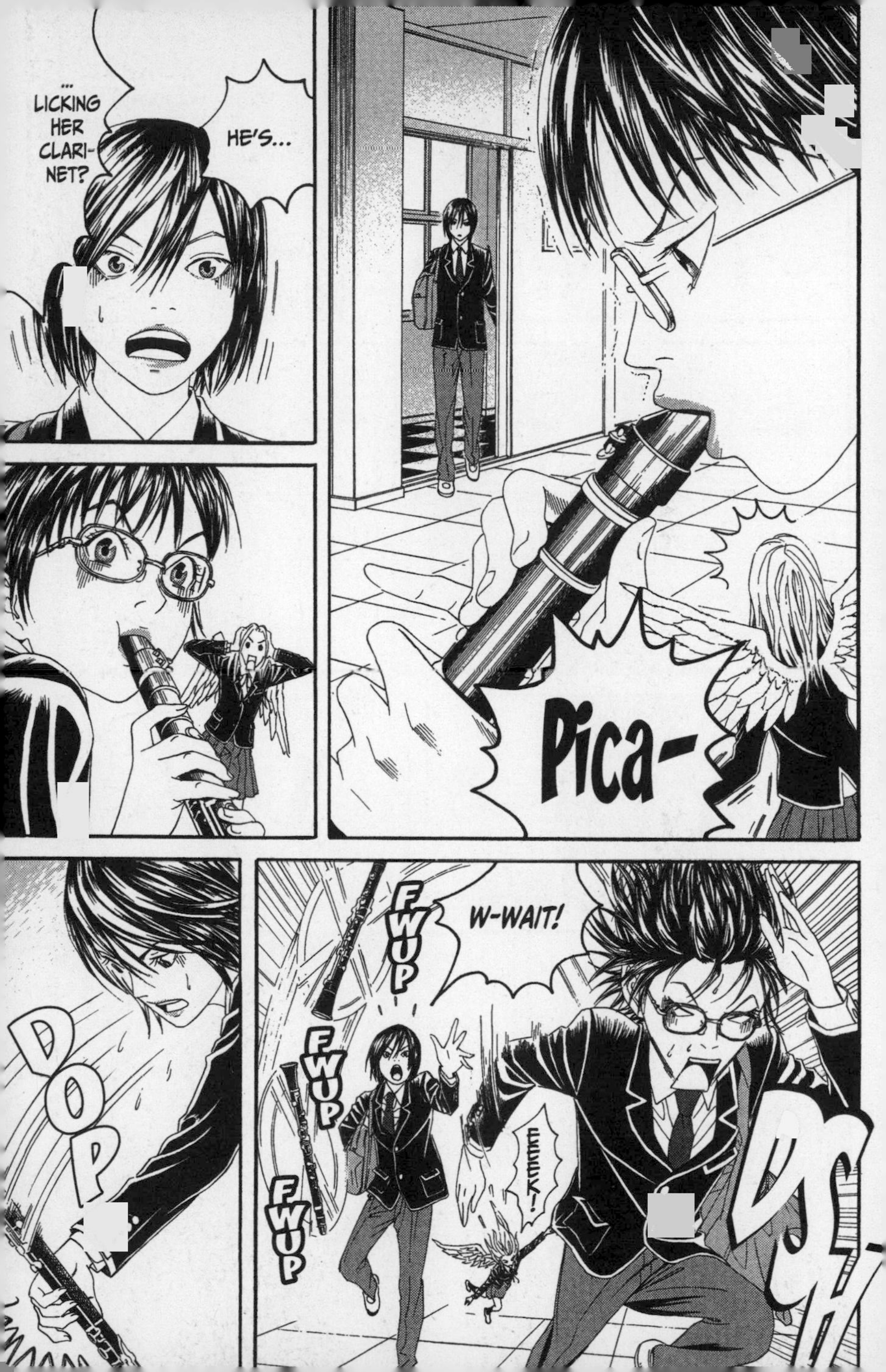
Pica-
HE'S...
... LICKING HER CLARI- NET?
W-WAIT!
FWUP
FWUP
FWUP
EEEEK!
DOP

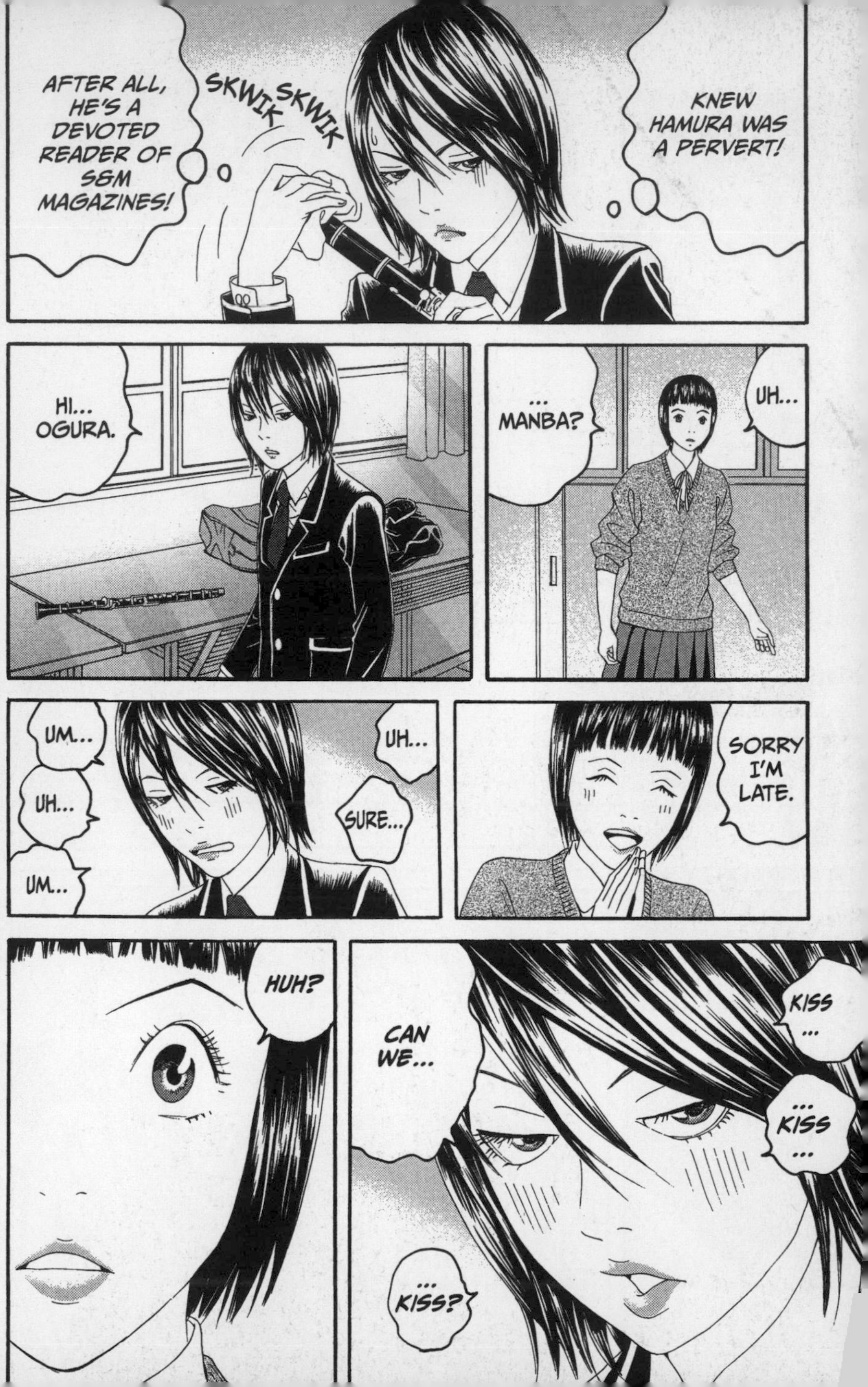
KNEW HAMURA WAS A PERVERT!
SKWIK SKWIK
AFTER ALL, HE'S A DEVOTED READER OF S&M MAGAZINES!
UH...
... MANBA?
HI... OGURA.
SORRY I'M LATE.
UH...
SURE...
UM...
UH...
UM...
KISS ...
... KISS ...
CAN WE...
... KISS?
HUH?

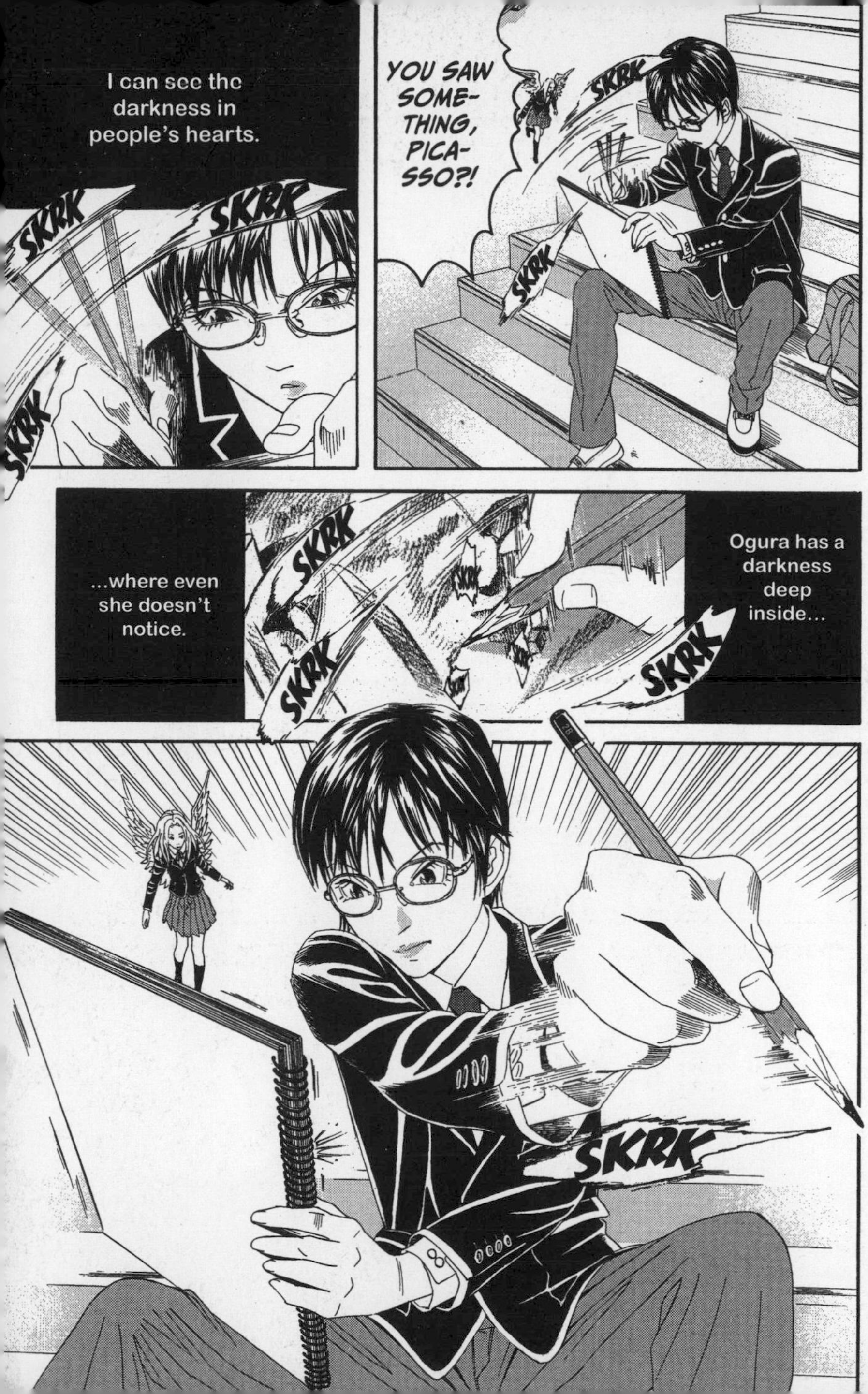
YOU SAW SOME-THING, PICA-SSO?!
SKRK
SKRK
I can see the darkness in people's hearts.
SKRK
SKRK
SKRK
Ogura has a darkness deep inside...
SKRK
SKRK
SKRK
...where even she doesn't notice.
SKRK

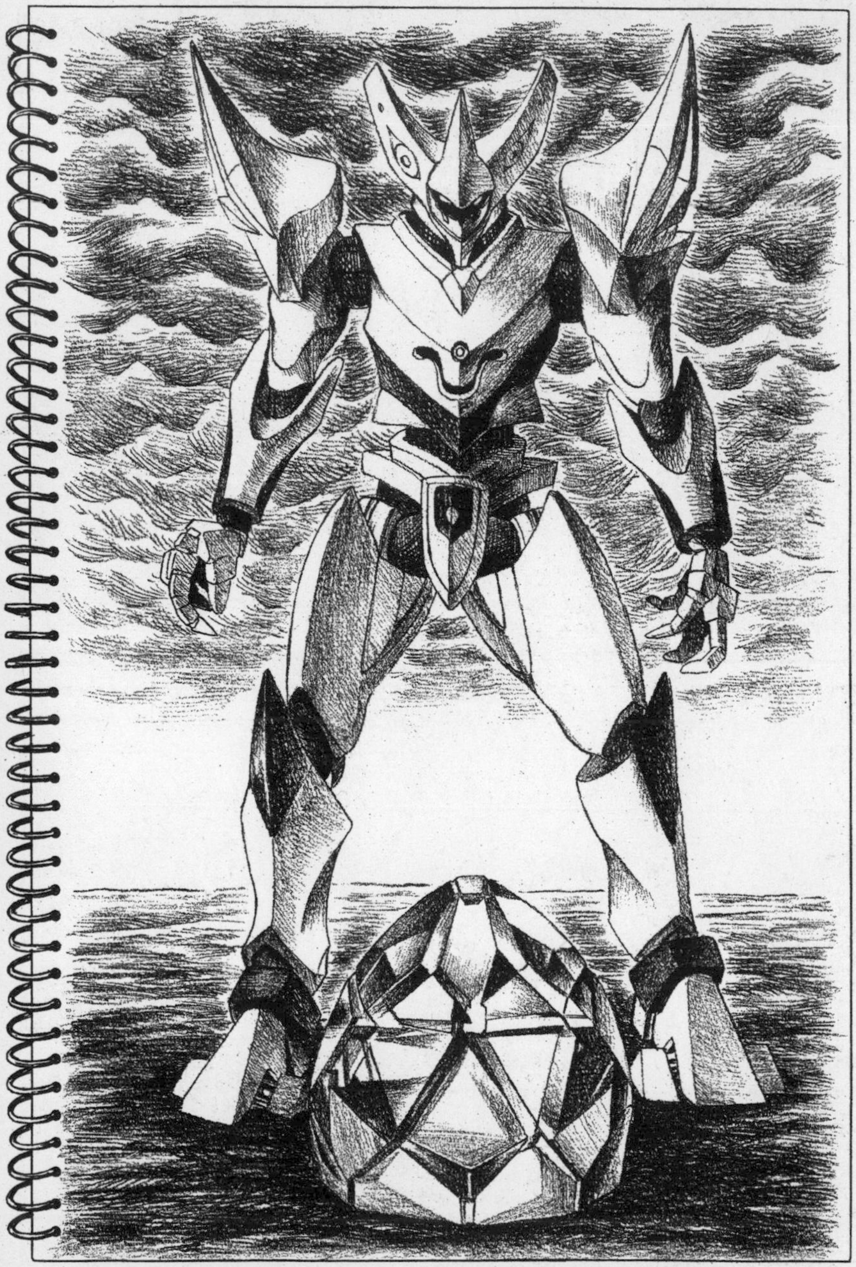

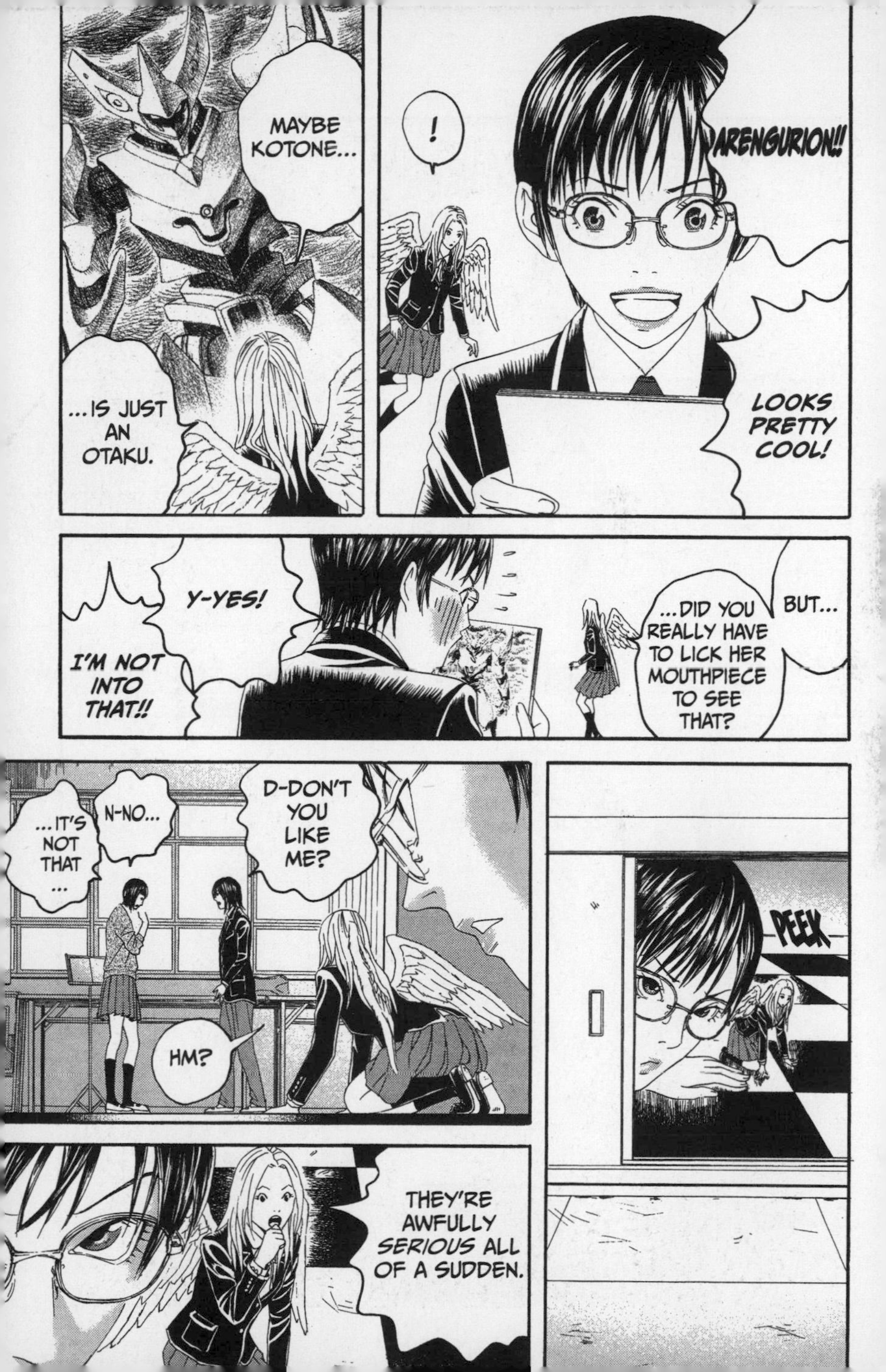
ARENGURION!!
LOOKS PRETTY COOL!
!
MAYBE KOTONE...
...IS JUST AN OTAKU.
BUT...
...DID YOU REALLY HAVE TO LICK HER MOUTHPIECE TO SEE THAT?
Y-YES!
I'M NOT INTO THAT!!
PEEK
D-DON'T YOU LIKE ME?
N-NO...
...IT'S NOT THAT ...
HM?
THEY'RE AWFULLY SERIOUS ALL OF A SUDDEN.

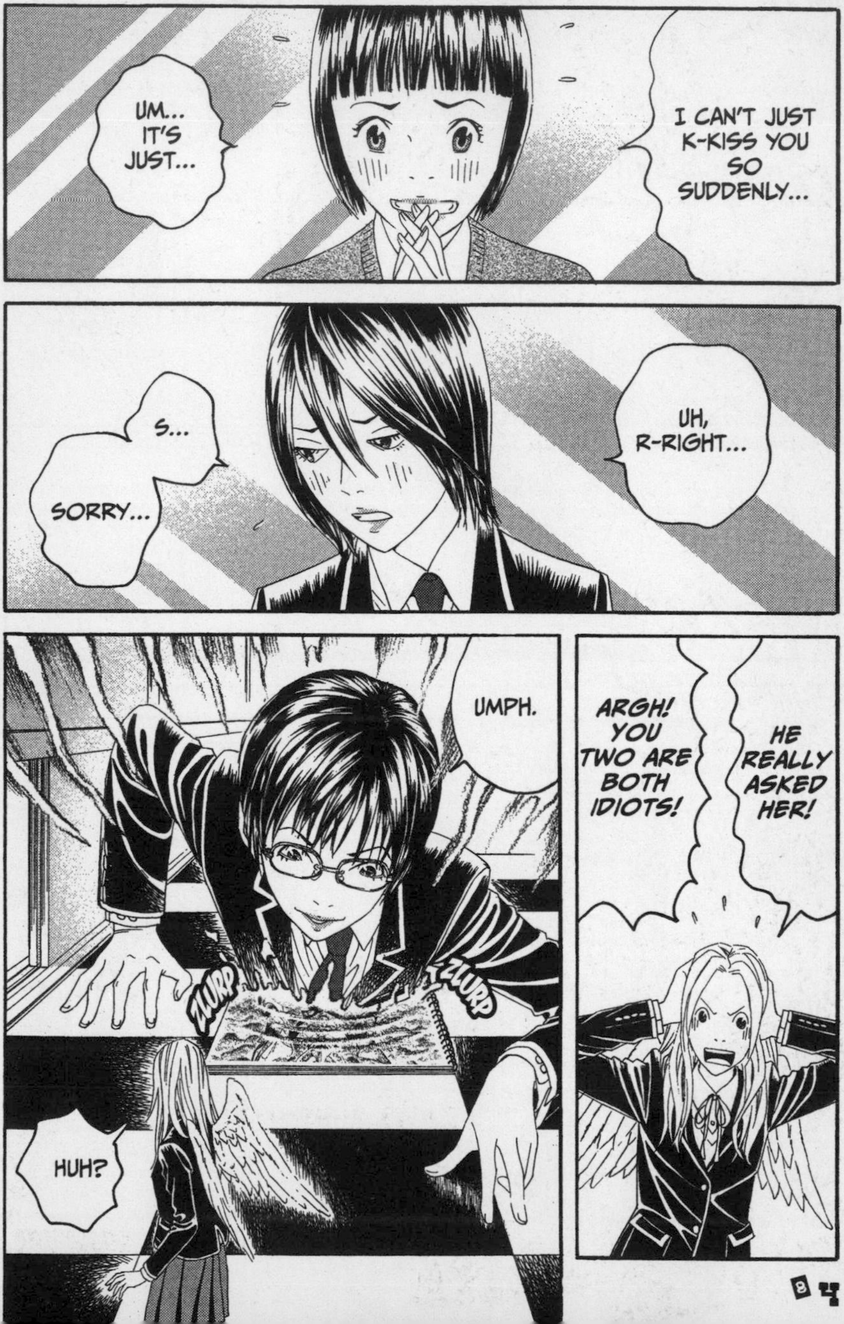
I CAN'T JUST K-KISS YOU SO SUDDENLY...
UM... IT'S JUST...
UH, R-RIGHT...
S...
SORRY...
HE REALLY ASKED HER!
ARGH! YOU TWO ARE BOTH IDIOTS!
UMPH.
ZLURP
ZLURP
HUH?

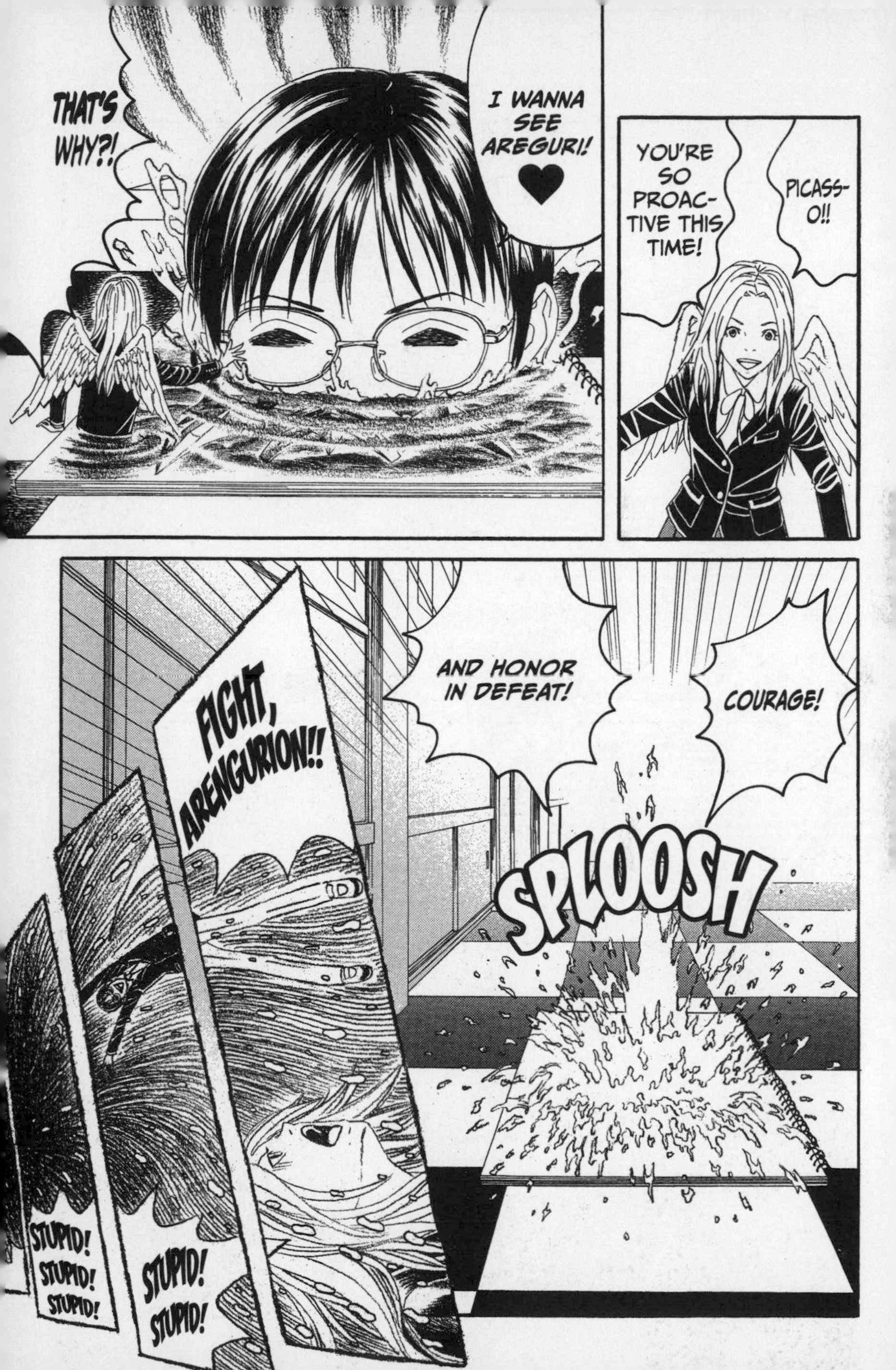
PICASS-O!!
YOU'RE SO PROACTIVE THIS TIME!
I WANNA SEE AREGURI! ♥
THAT'S WHY?!
COURAGE!
AND HONOR IN DEFEAT!
SPLOOSH
FIGHT, ARENGURION!!
STUPID! STUPID!
STUPID! STUPID! STUPID!

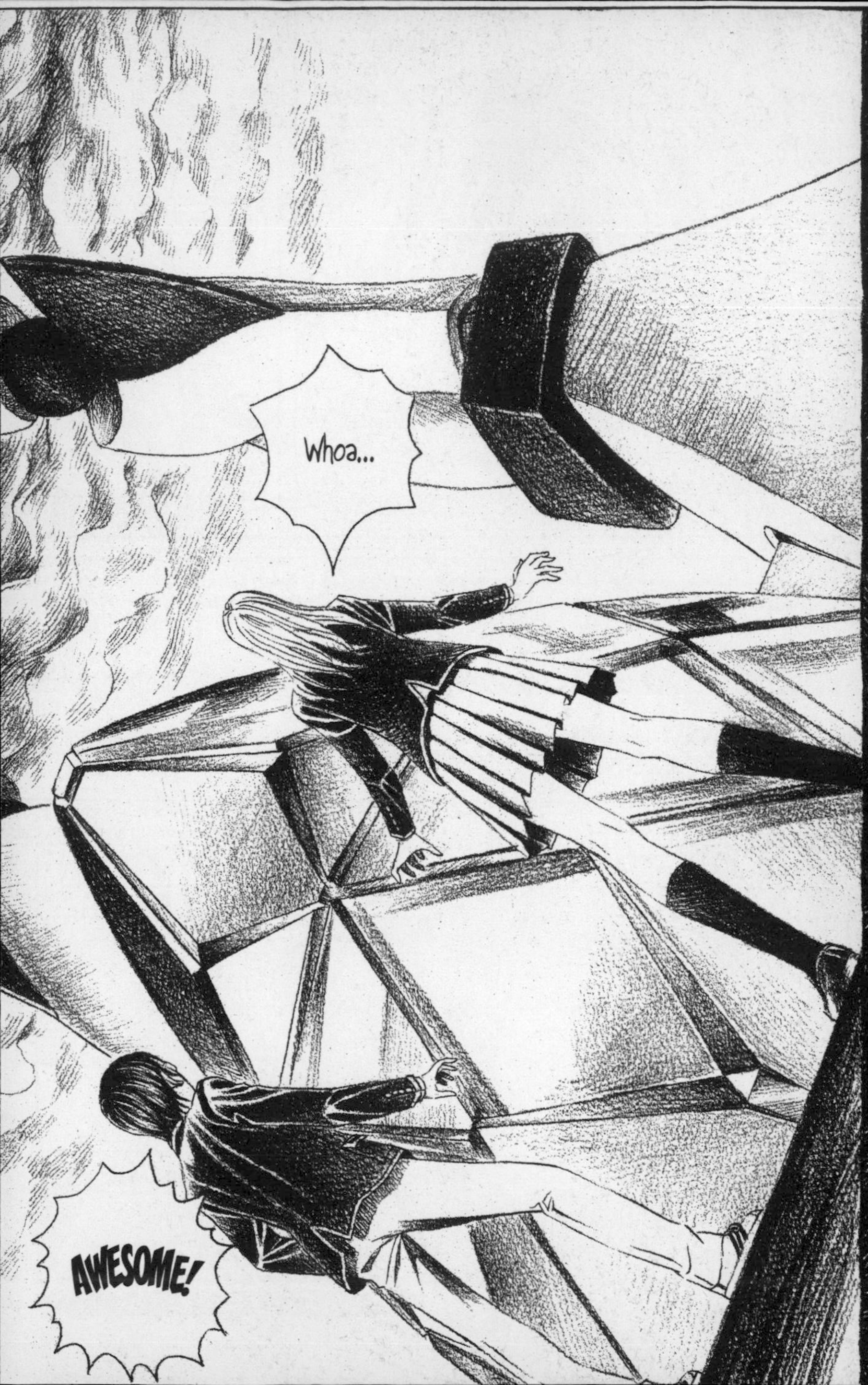
Whoa...
AWESOME!

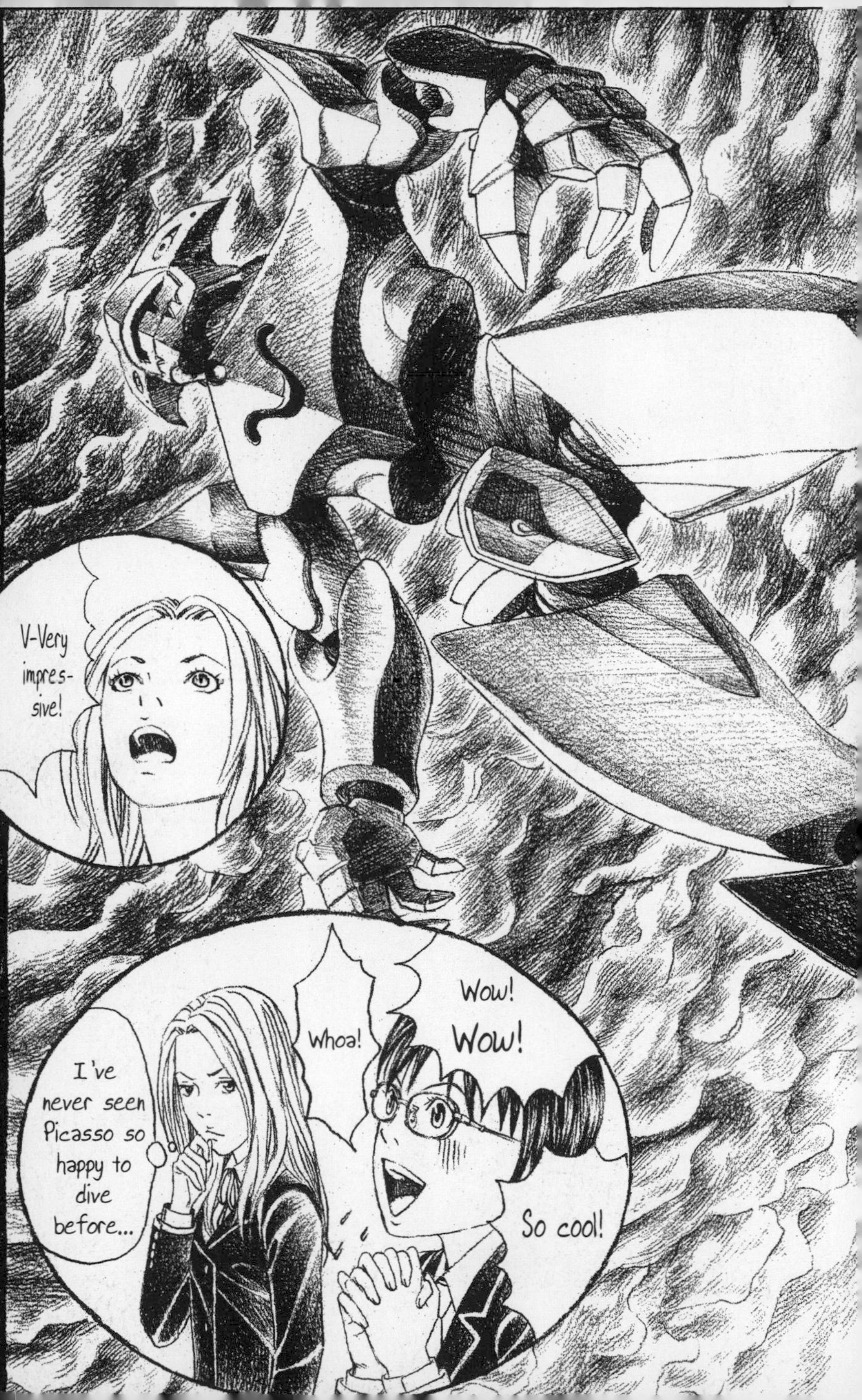
V-Very impres-sive!
Wow! Wow!
Whoa!
So cool!
I've never seen Picasso so happy to dive before...

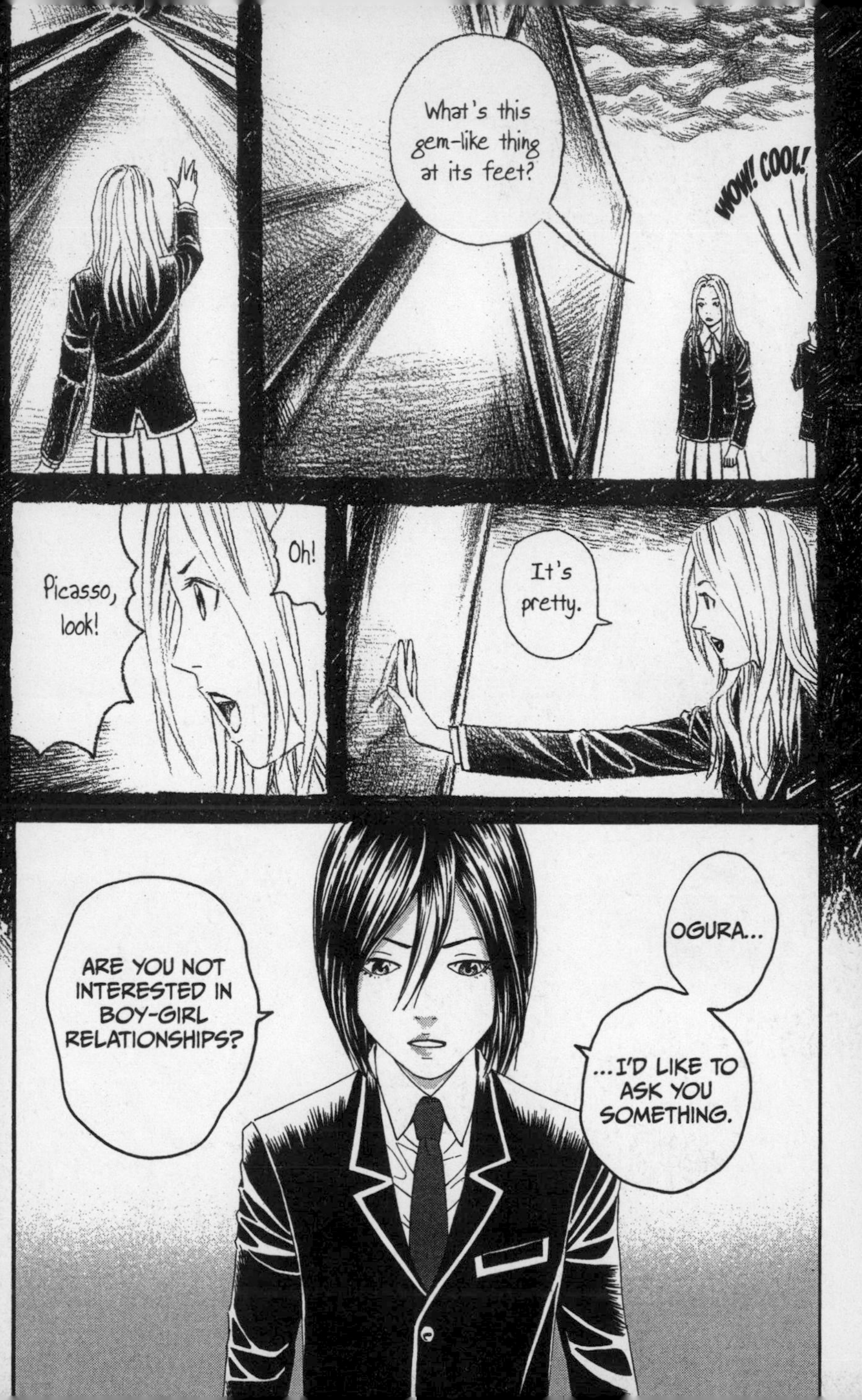
WOW! COOL!
What's this gem-like thing at its feet?
It's pretty.
Oh!
Picasso, look!
OGURA...
...I'D LIKE TO ASK YOU SOMETHING.
ARE YOU NOT INTERESTED IN BOY-GIRL RELATIONSHIPS?

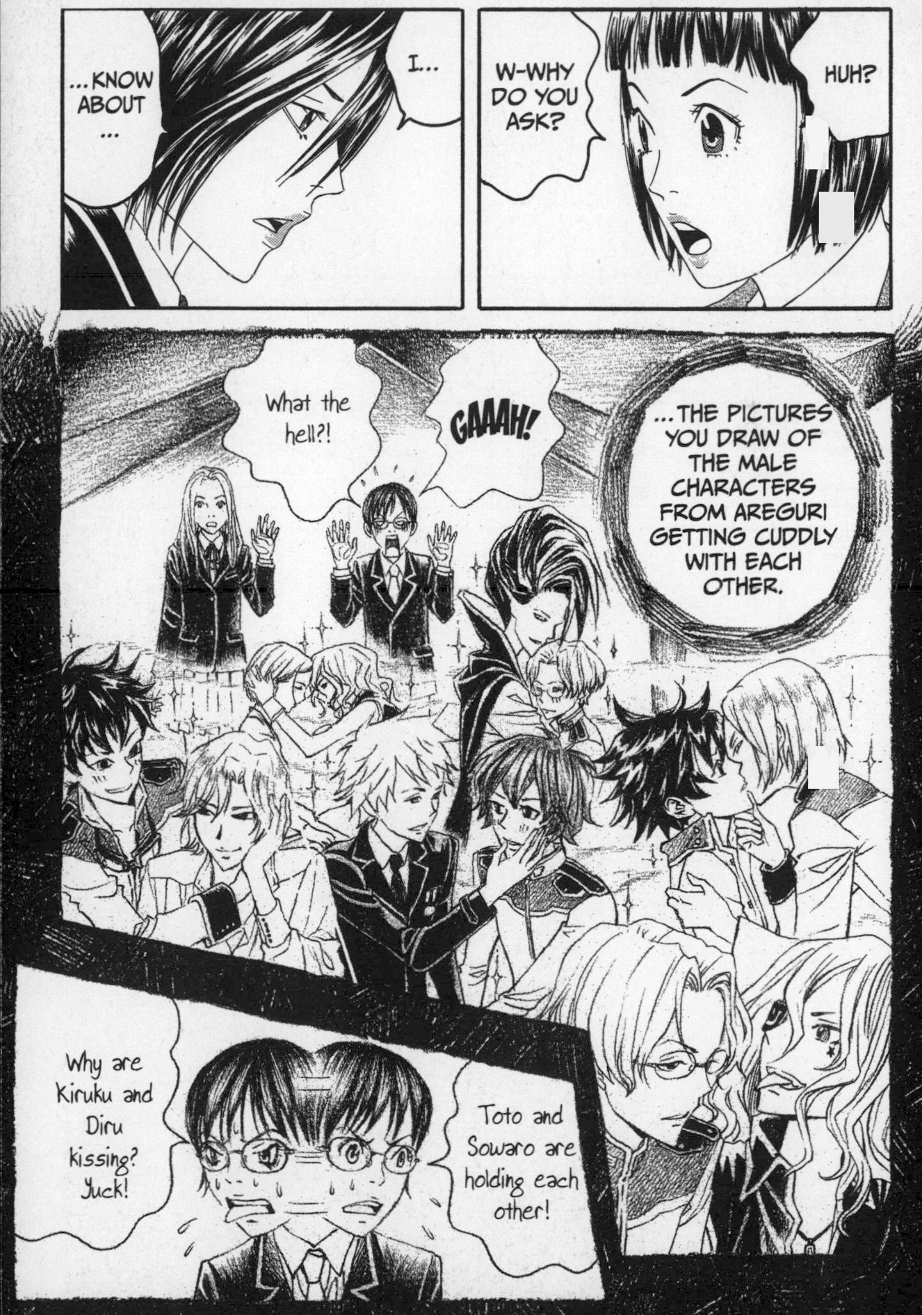
HUH?
W-WHY DO YOU ASK?
I...
...KNOW ABOUT ...
...THE PICTURES YOU DRAW OF THE MALE CHARACTERS FROM AREGURI GETTING CUDDLY WITH EACH OTHER.
GAAAH!
What the hell?!
Toto and Sowaro are holding each other!
Why are Kiruku and Diru kissing? Yuck!

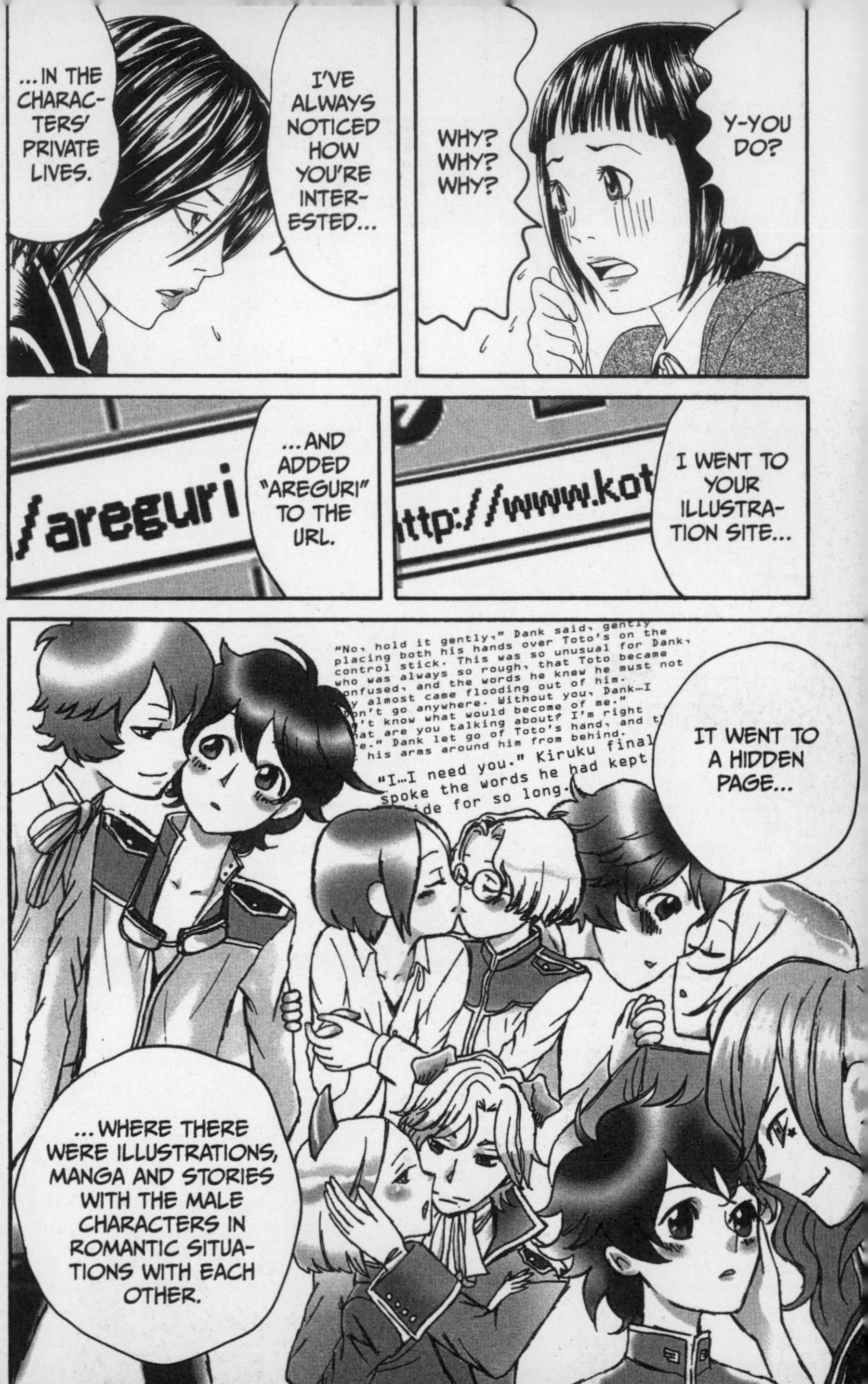
Y-YOU DO?
WHY? WHY? WHY?
I'VE ALWAYS NOTICED HOW YOU'RE INTERESTED...
...IN THE CHARACTERS' PRIVATE LIVES.
I WENT TO YOUR ILLUSTRATION SITE...
http://www.kot
...AND ADDED "AREGURI" TO THE URL.
/areguri
IT WENT TO A HIDDEN PAGE...
"No, hold it gently," Dank said, gently
placing both his hands over Toto's on the
control stick. This was so unusual for Dank,
who was always so rough, that Toto became
onfused, and the words he knew he must not
y almost came flooding out of him.
on't go anywhere. Without you, Dank...I
't know what would become of me."
at are you talking about? I'm right
e." Dank let go of Toto's hand, and t
his arms around him from behind.
"I...I need you." Kiruku final
spoke the words he had kept
ide for so long.
...WHERE THERE WERE ILLUSTRATIONS, MANGA AND STORIES WITH THE MALE CHARACTERS IN ROMANTIC SITUATIONS WITH EACH OTHER.

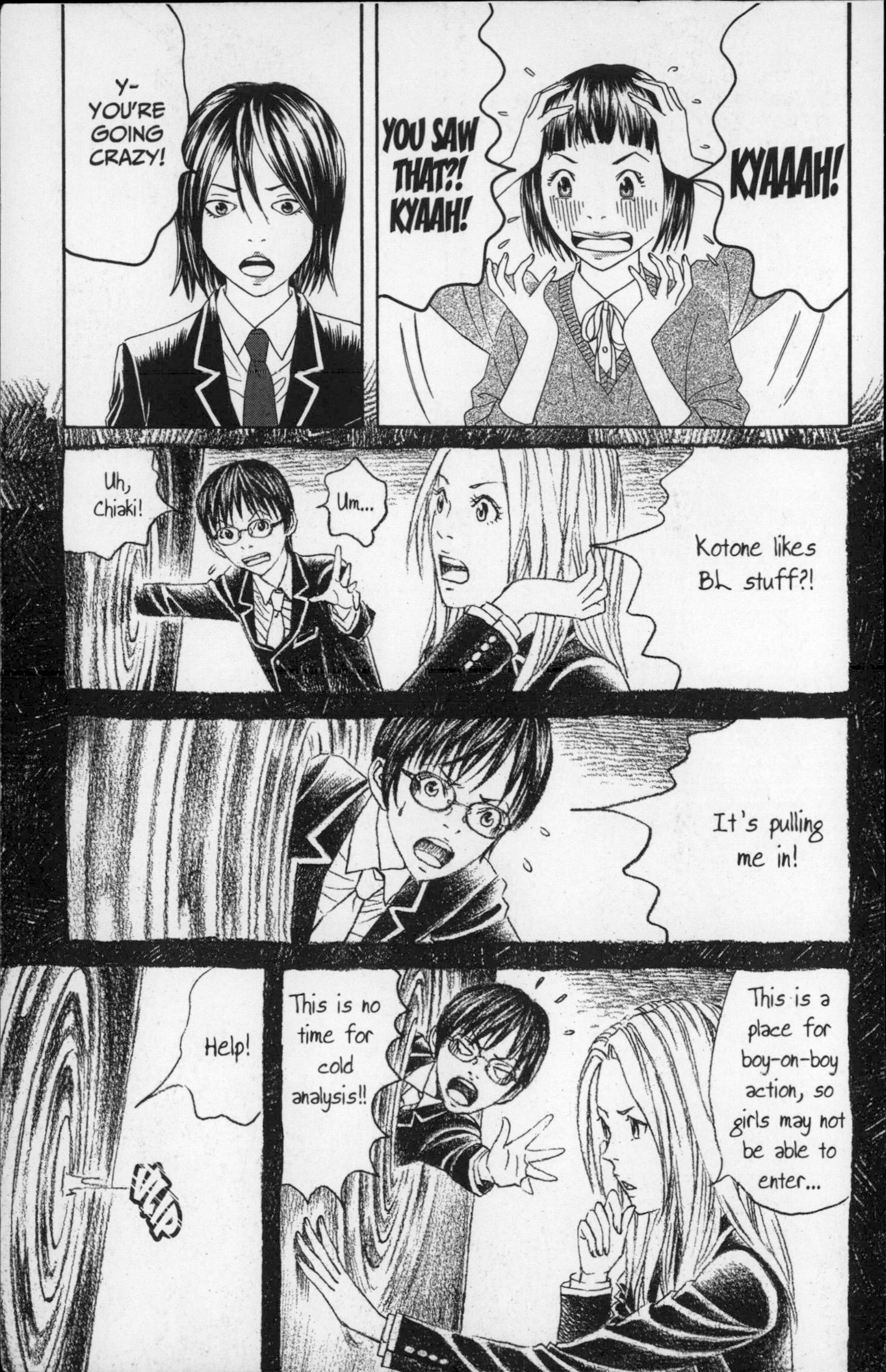
YOU SAW THAT?! KYAAH!
KYAAAH!
Y-YOU'RE GOING CRAZY!
Kotone likes BL stuff?!
Um...
Uh, Chiaki!
It's pulling me in!
This is a place for boy-on-boy action, so girls may not be able to enter...
This is no time for cold analysis!!
Help!

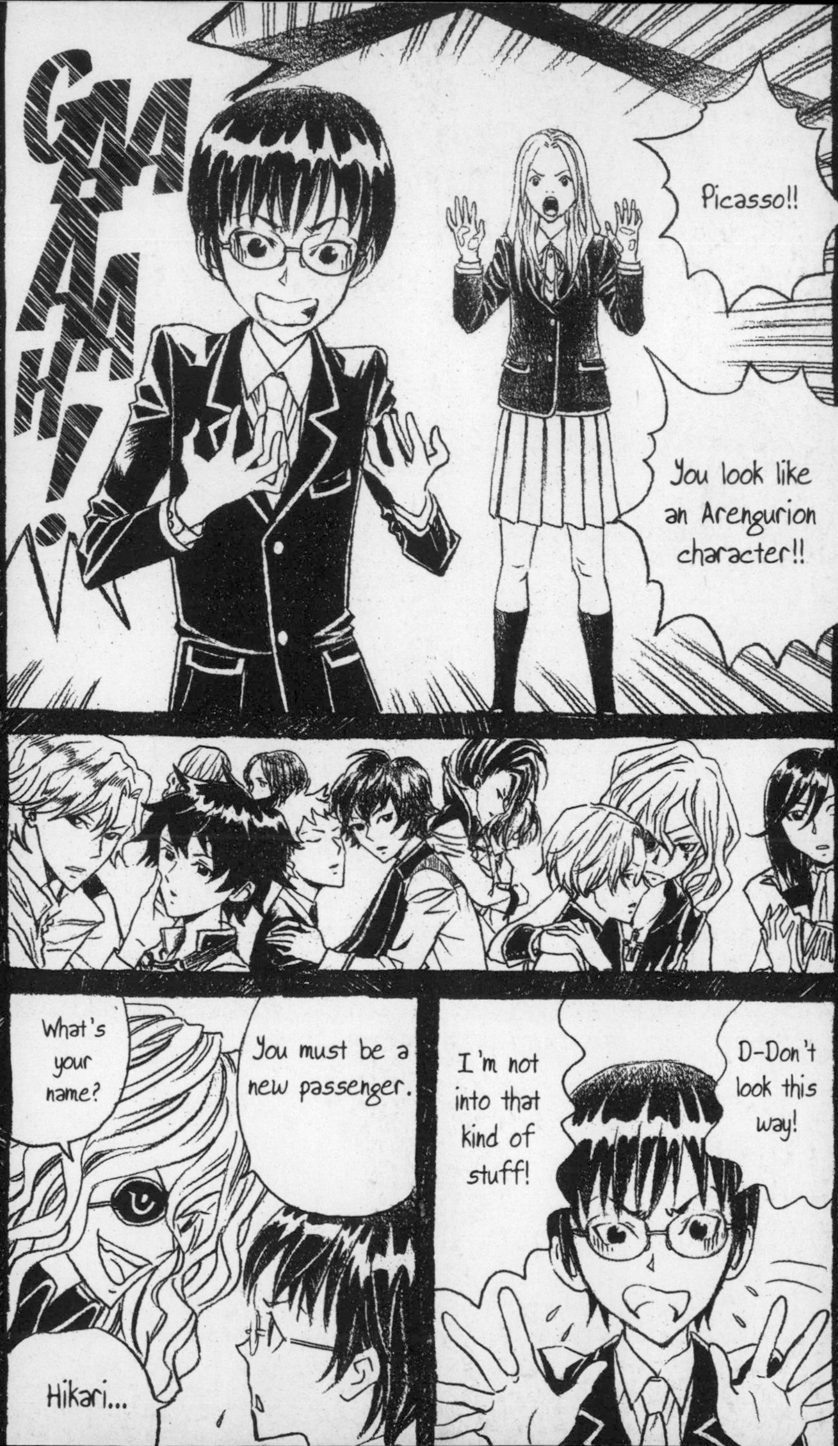
Picasso!!
You look like an Arengurion character!!
GAAAHH!
D-Don't look this way!
I'm not into that kind of stuff!
You must be a new passenger.
What's your name?
Hikari...

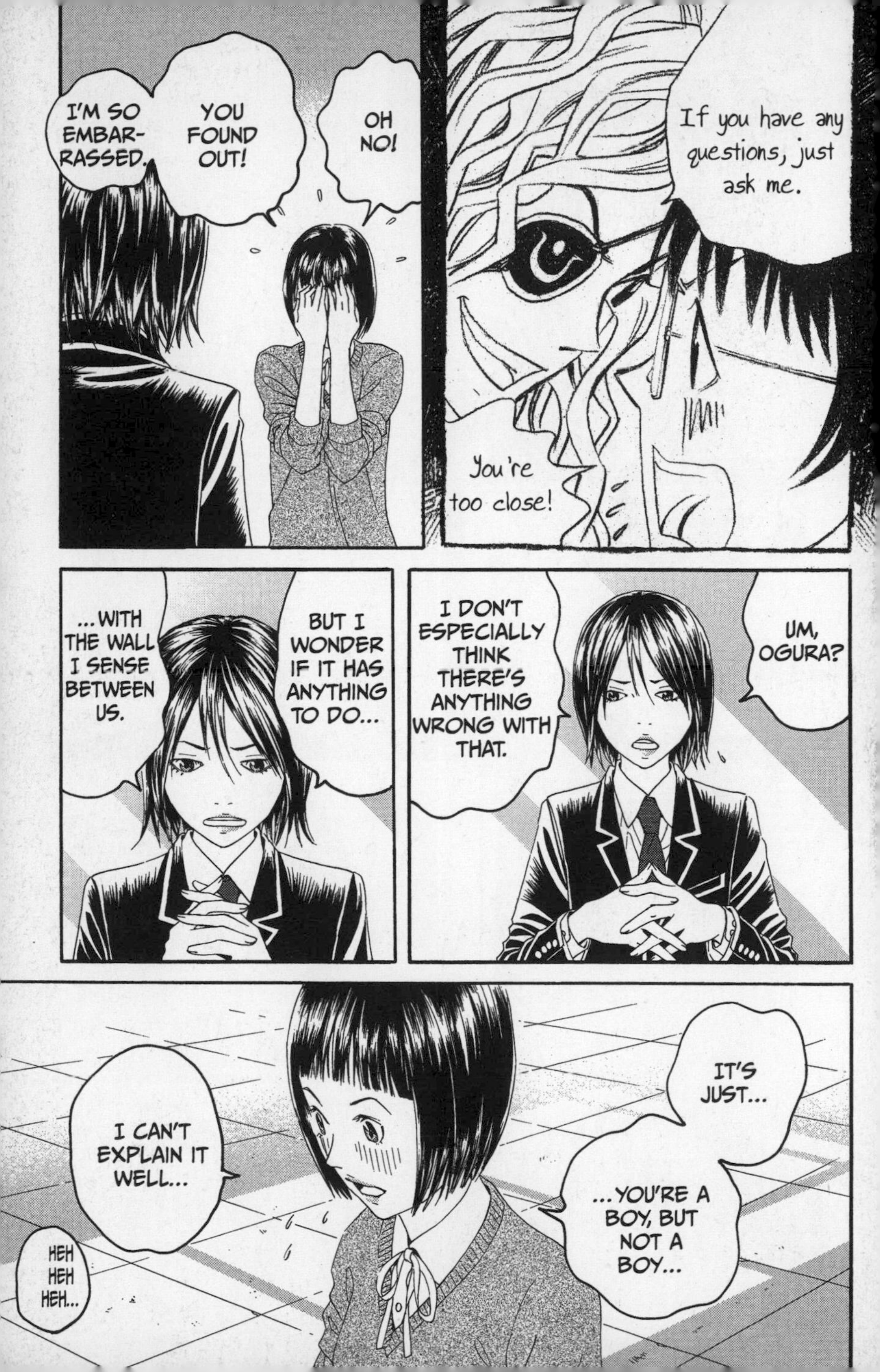
If you have any questions, just ask me.
You're too close!
OH NO!
YOU FOUND OUT!
I'M SO EMBARRASSED.
UM, OGURA?
I DON'T ESPECIALLY THINK THERE'S ANYTHING WRONG WITH THAT.
BUT I WONDER IF IT HAS ANYTHING TO DO...
...WITH THE WALL I SENSE BETWEEN US.
IT'S JUST...
...YOU'RE A BOY, BUT NOT A BOY...
I CAN'T EXPLAIN IT WELL...
HEH HEH HEH...

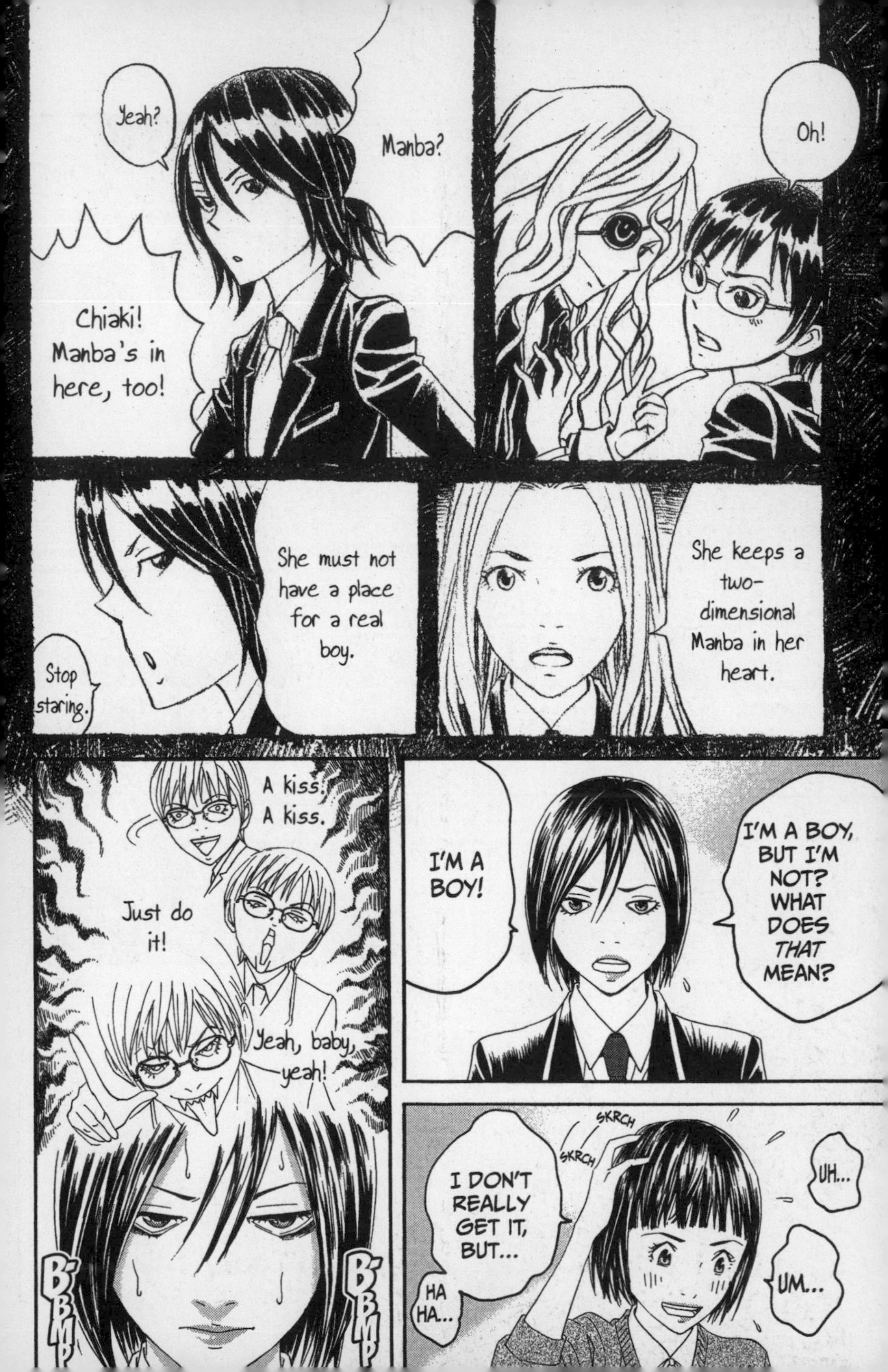
Oh!
Chiaki! Manba's in here, too!
Manba?
Yeah?
She keeps a two-dimensional Manba in her heart.
She must not have a place for a real boy.
Stop staring.
I'M A BOY, BUT I'M NOT? WHAT DOES *THAT* MEAN?
I'M A BOY!
UH...
UM...
SKRCH
SKRCH
I DON'T REALLY GET IT, BUT...
HA HA...
A kiss. A kiss.
Just do it!
Yeah, baby, yeah!
B-BMP
B-BMP

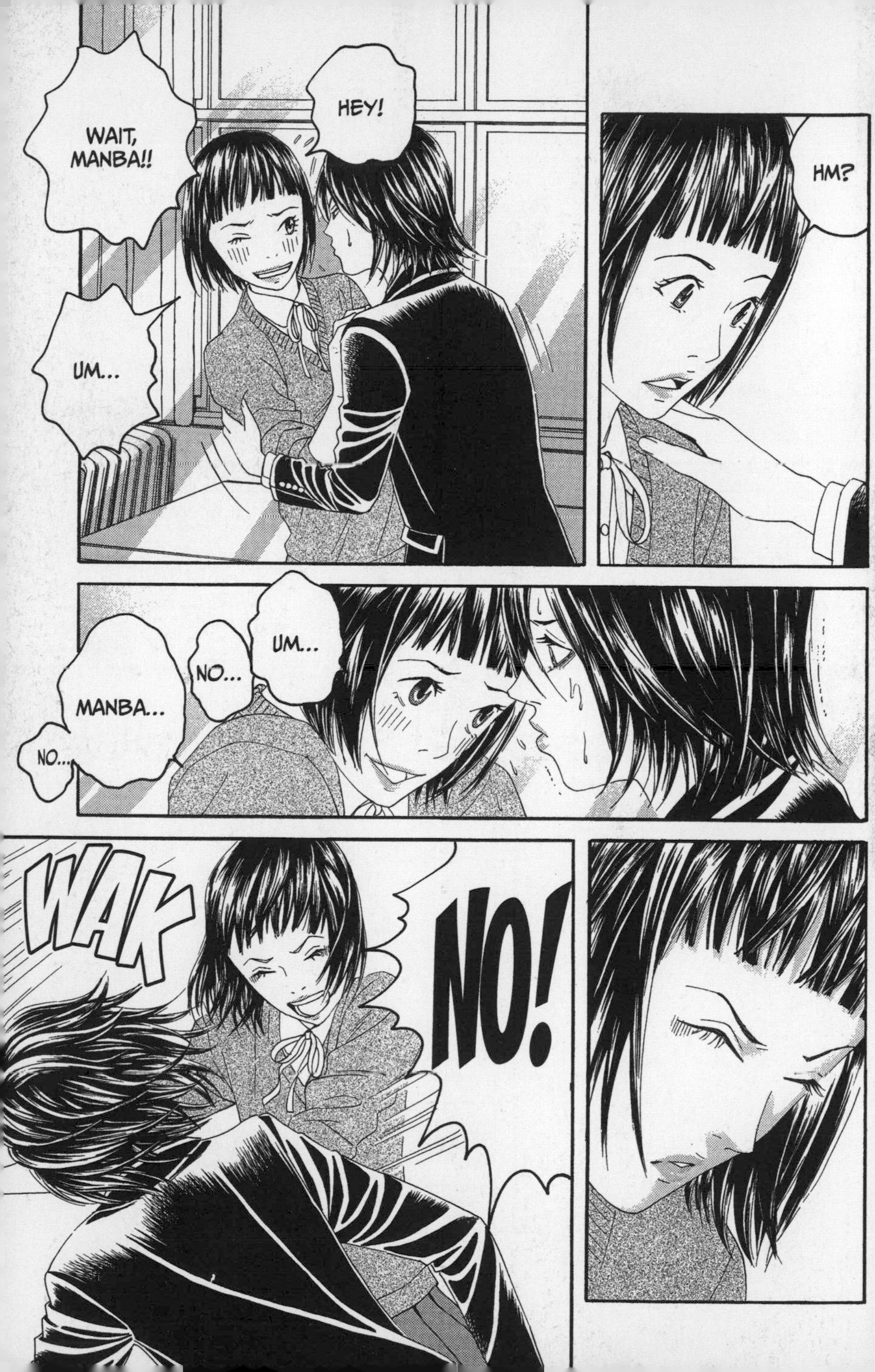
HM?
HEY!
WAIT, MANBA!!
UM...
UM...
NO...
MANBA...
NO...
NO!
WAK

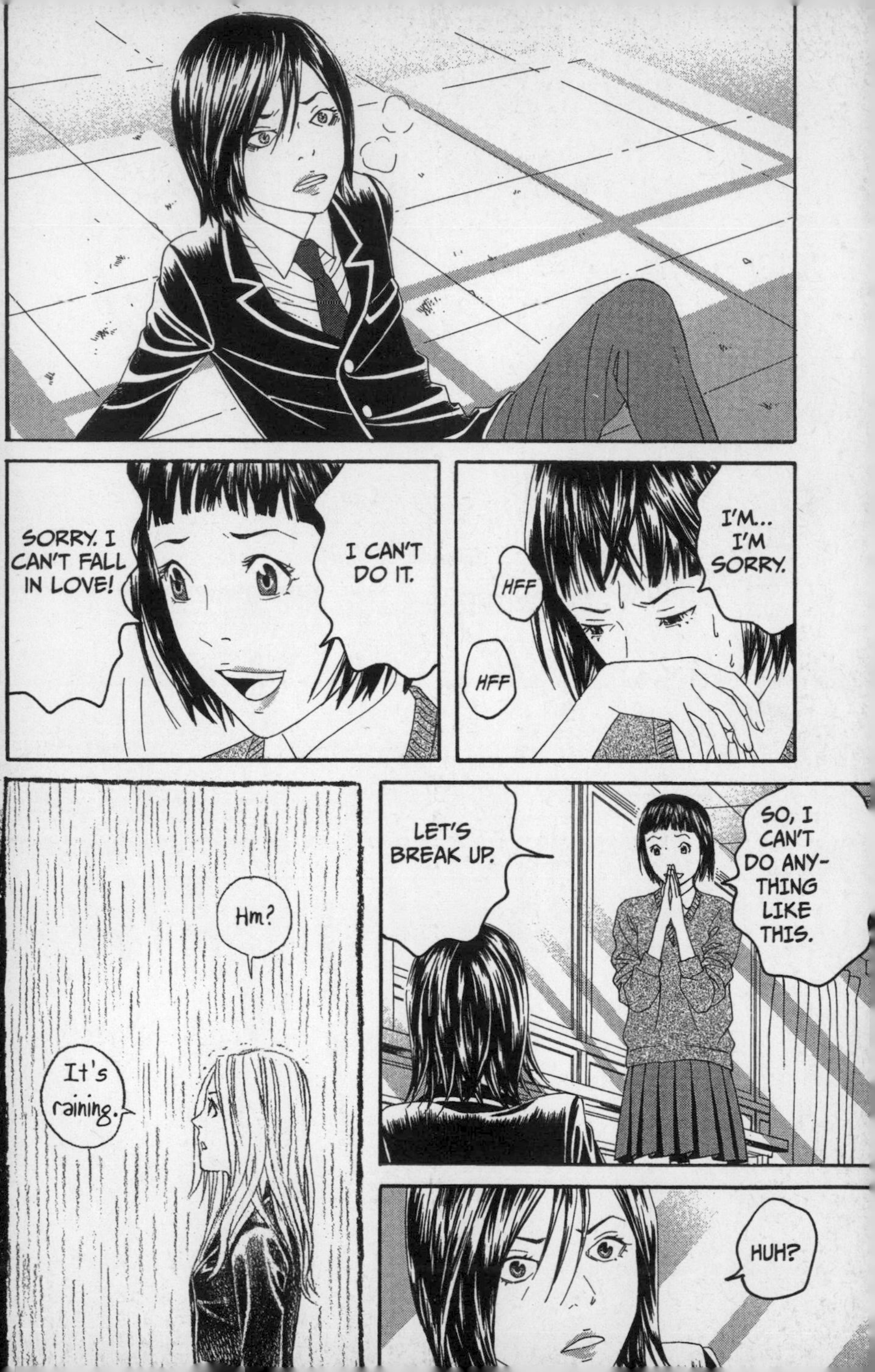
I'M... I'M SORRY.
HFF
HFF
I CAN'T DO IT.
SORRY. I CAN'T FALL IN LOVE!
SO, I CAN'T DO ANY-THING LIKE THIS.
LET'S BREAK UP.
HUH?
Hm?
It's raining.

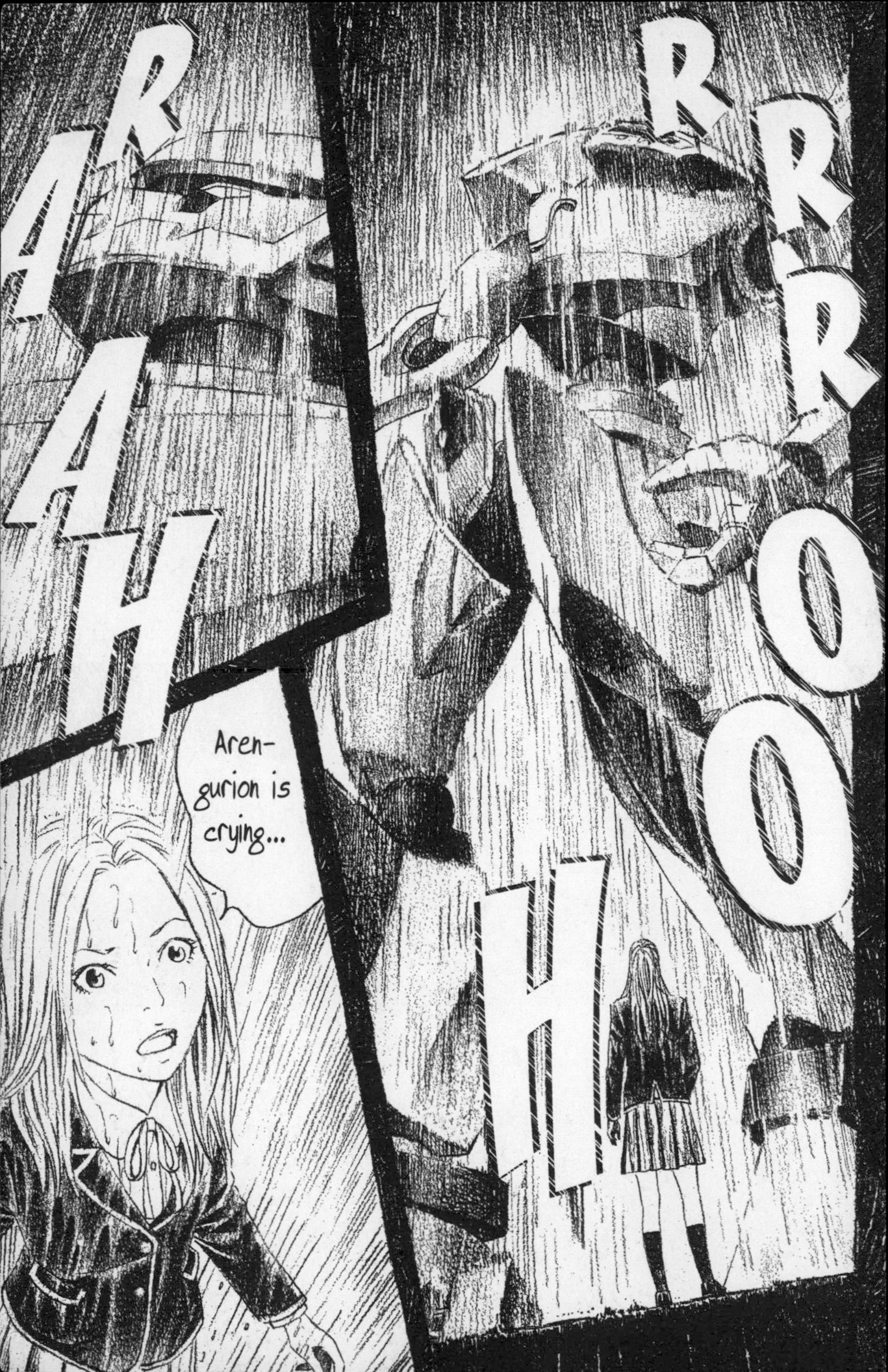
RRRROOH
RAAAH
Aren-gurion is crying...

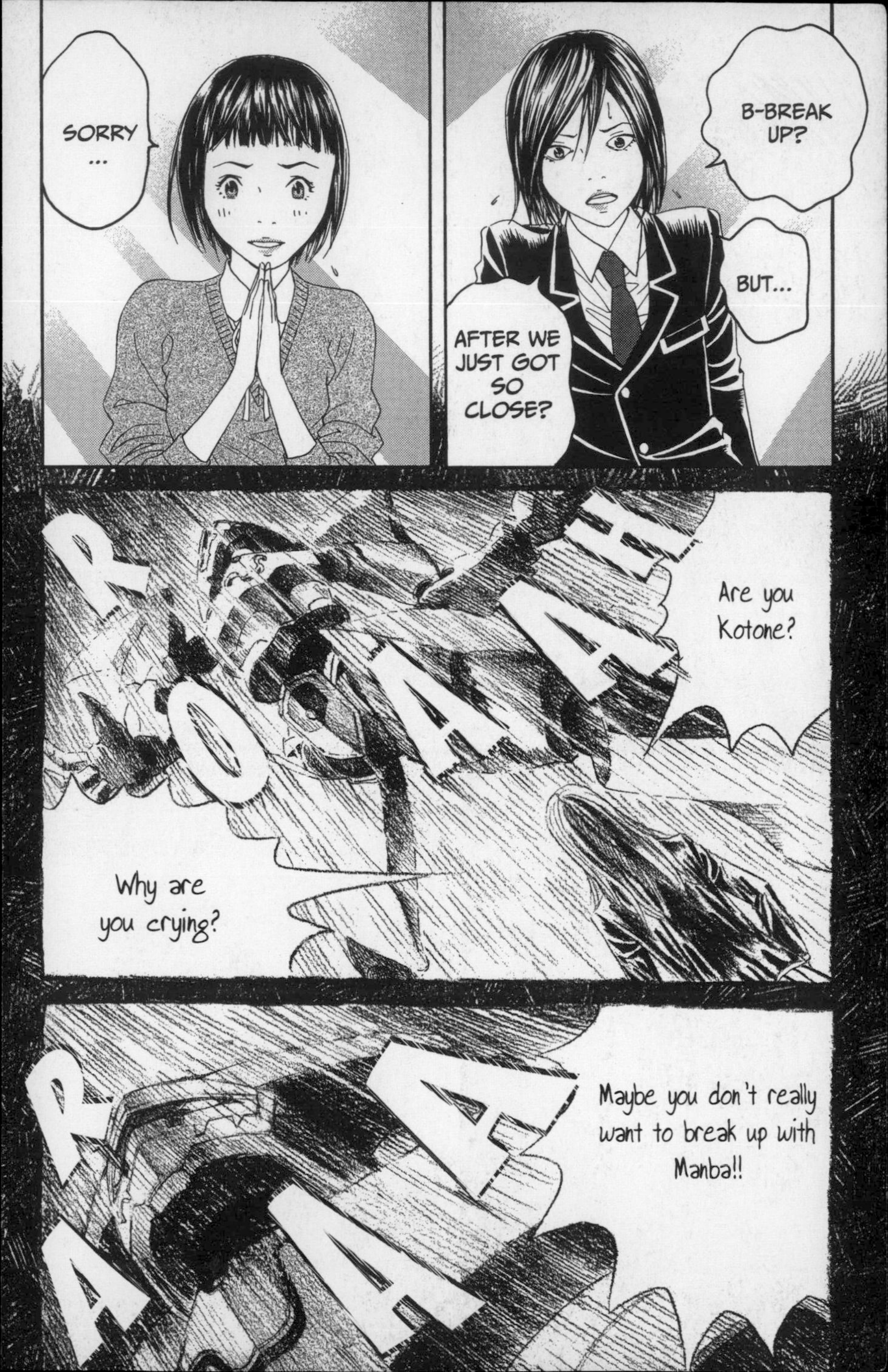
B-BREAK UP?
BUT...
AFTER WE JUST GOT SO CLOSE?
SORRY ...
ROAAAH
Are you Kotone?
Why are you crying?
RAAAA
Maybe you don't really want to break up with Manba!!

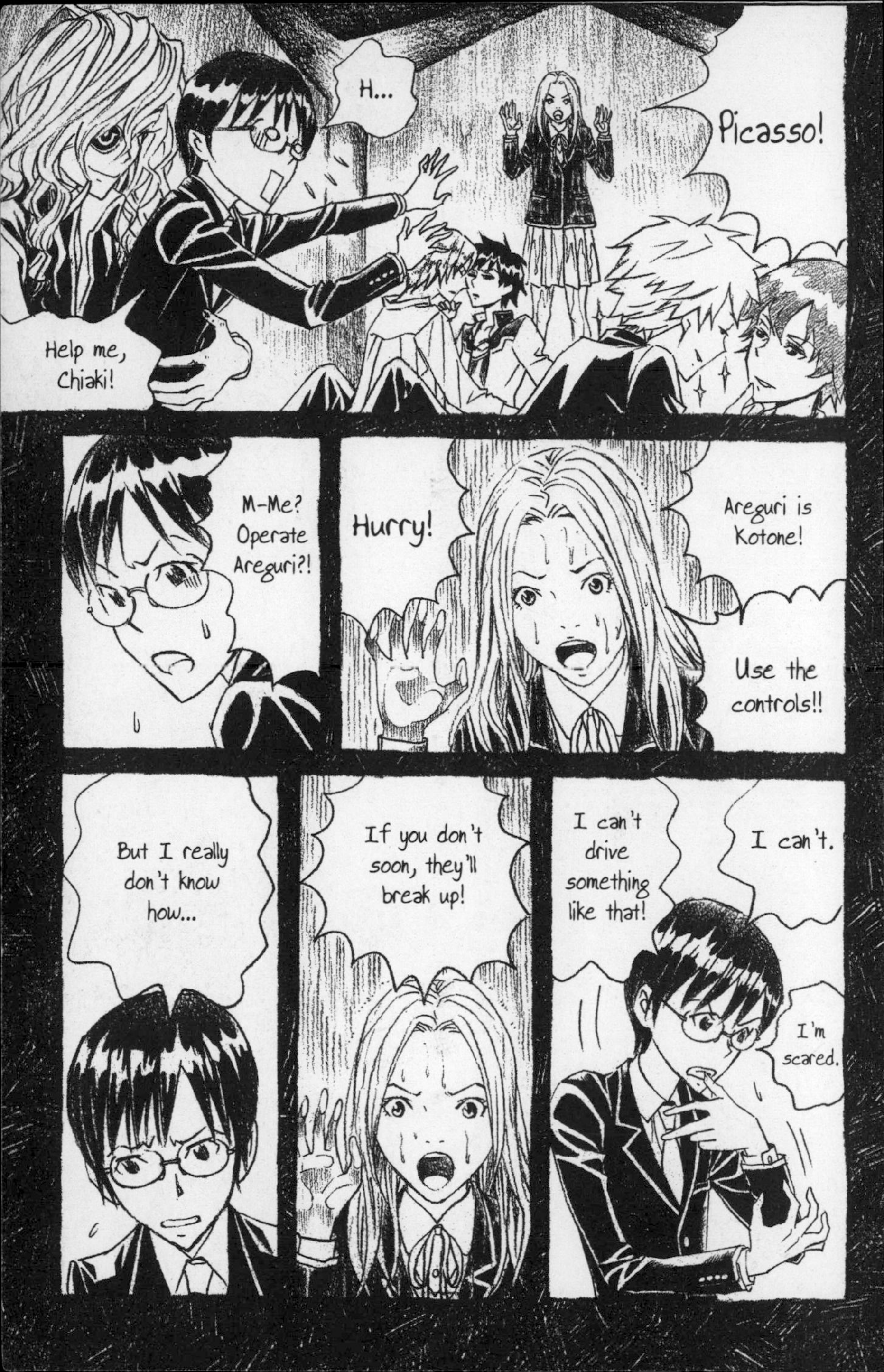
Picasso!
H...
Help me, Chiaki!
Areguri is Kotone!
Use the controls!!
Hurry!
M-Me? Operate Areguri?!
I can't.
I can't drive something like that!
I'm scared.
If you don't soon, they'll break up!
But I really don't know how...

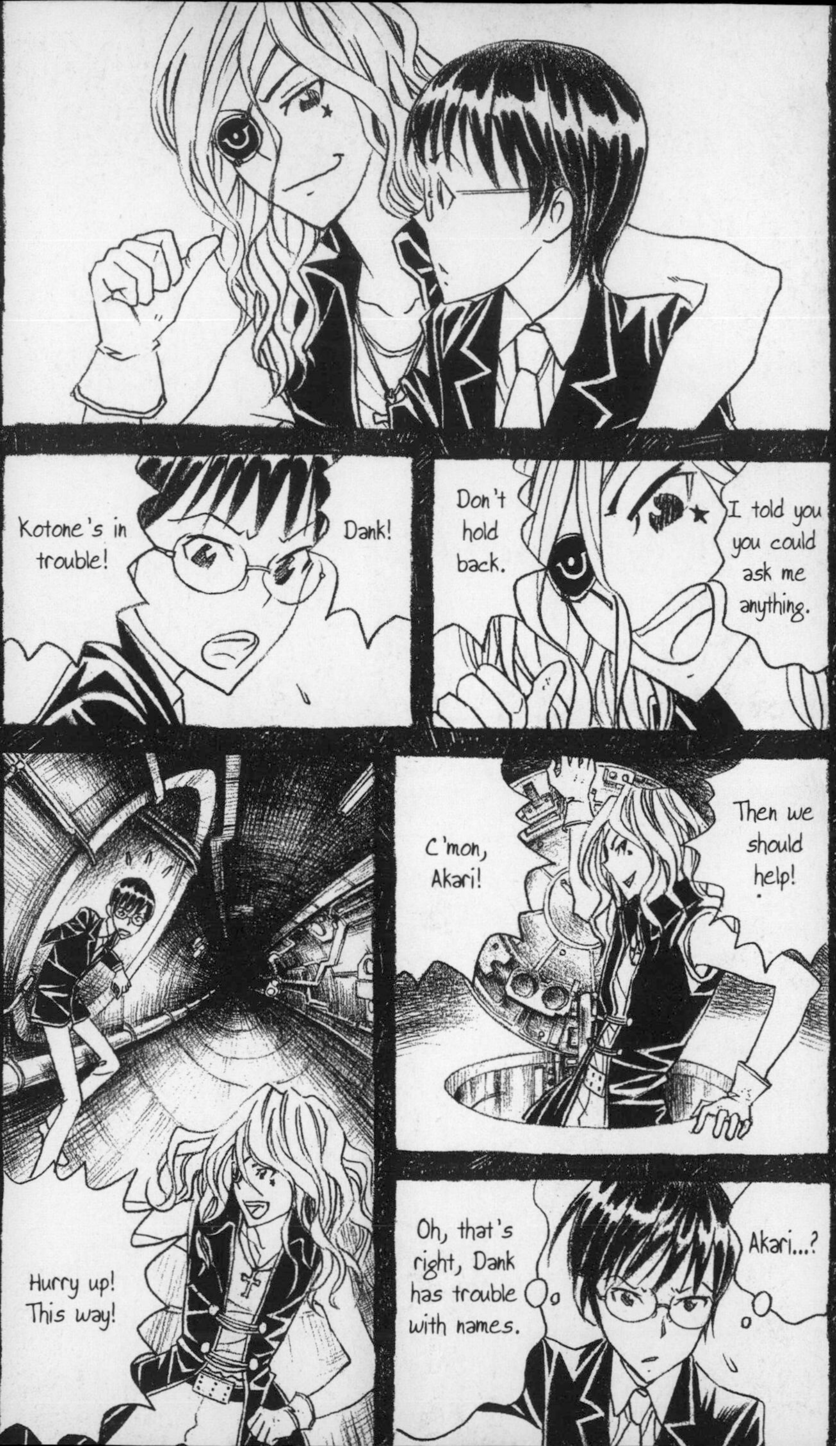
I told you you could ask me anything.
Don't hold back.
Dank!
Kotone's in trouble!
Then we should help!
C'mon, Akari!
Akari...?
Oh, that's right, Dank has trouble with names.
Hurry up! This way!

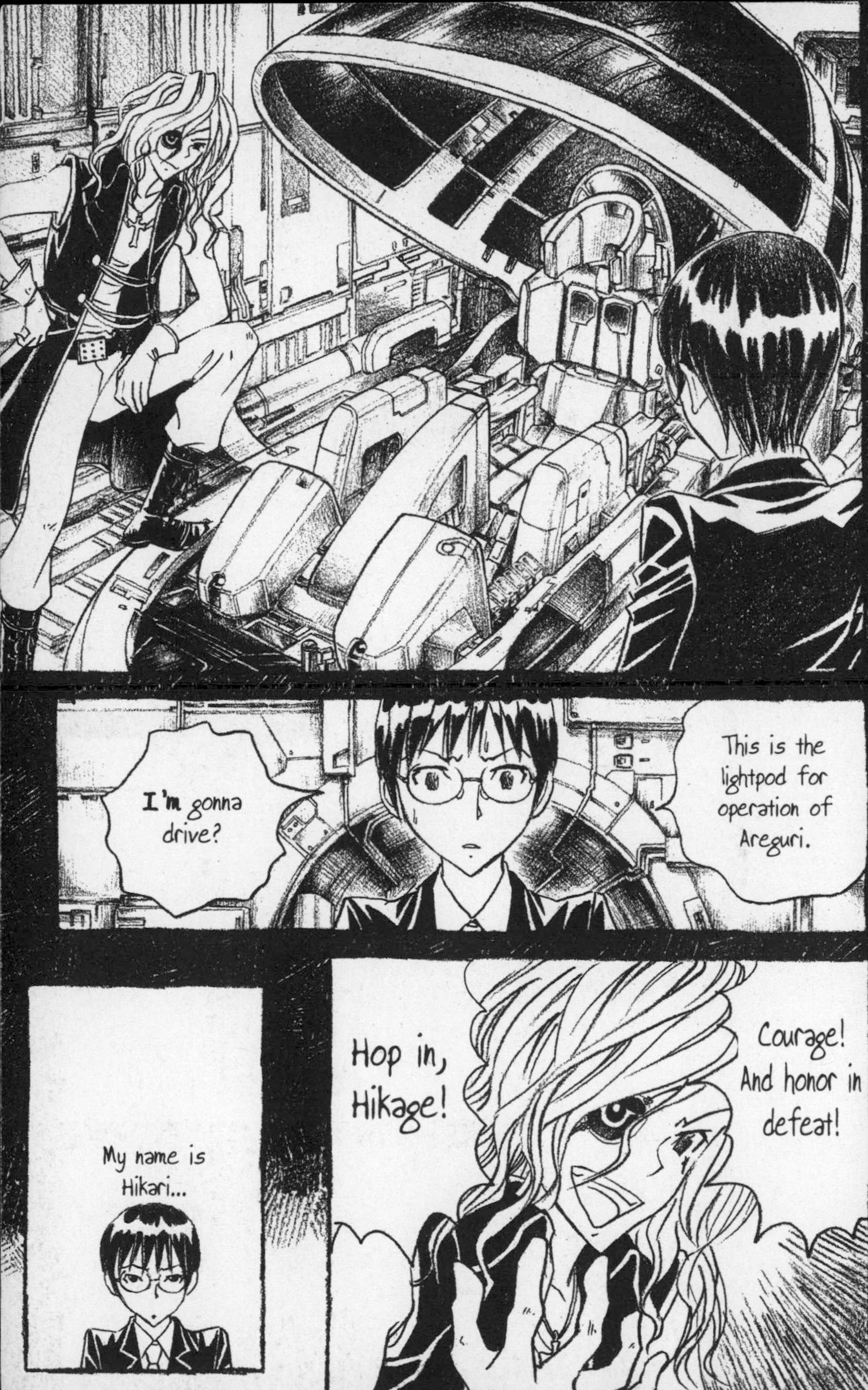
This is the lightpod for operation of Areguri.
I'm gonna drive?
Courage! And honor in defeat!
Hop in, Hikage!
My name is Hikari...

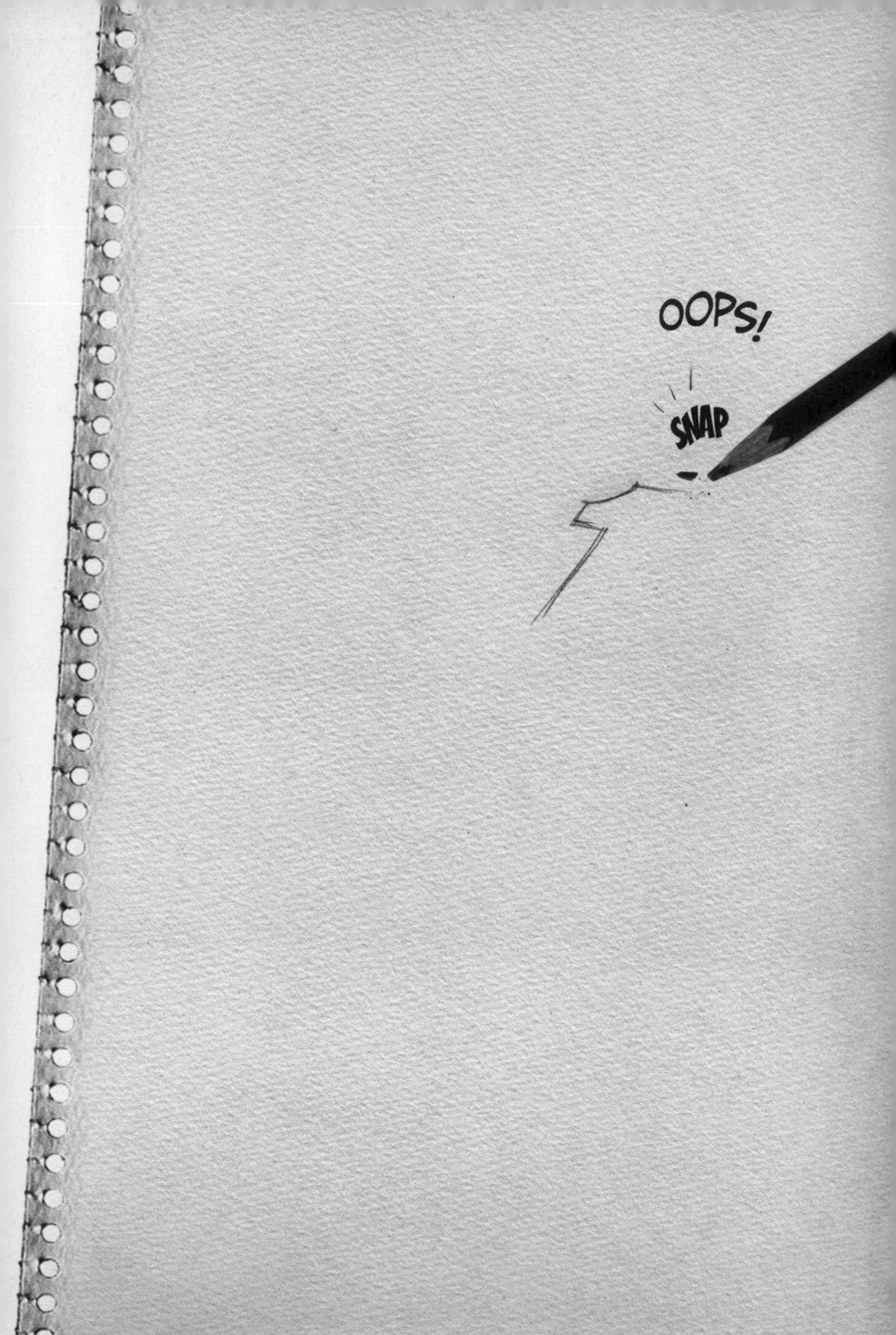
OOPS!
SNAP

Vision 6: Kotone and Arengurion (Part 1)_Jump SQ, March 2009

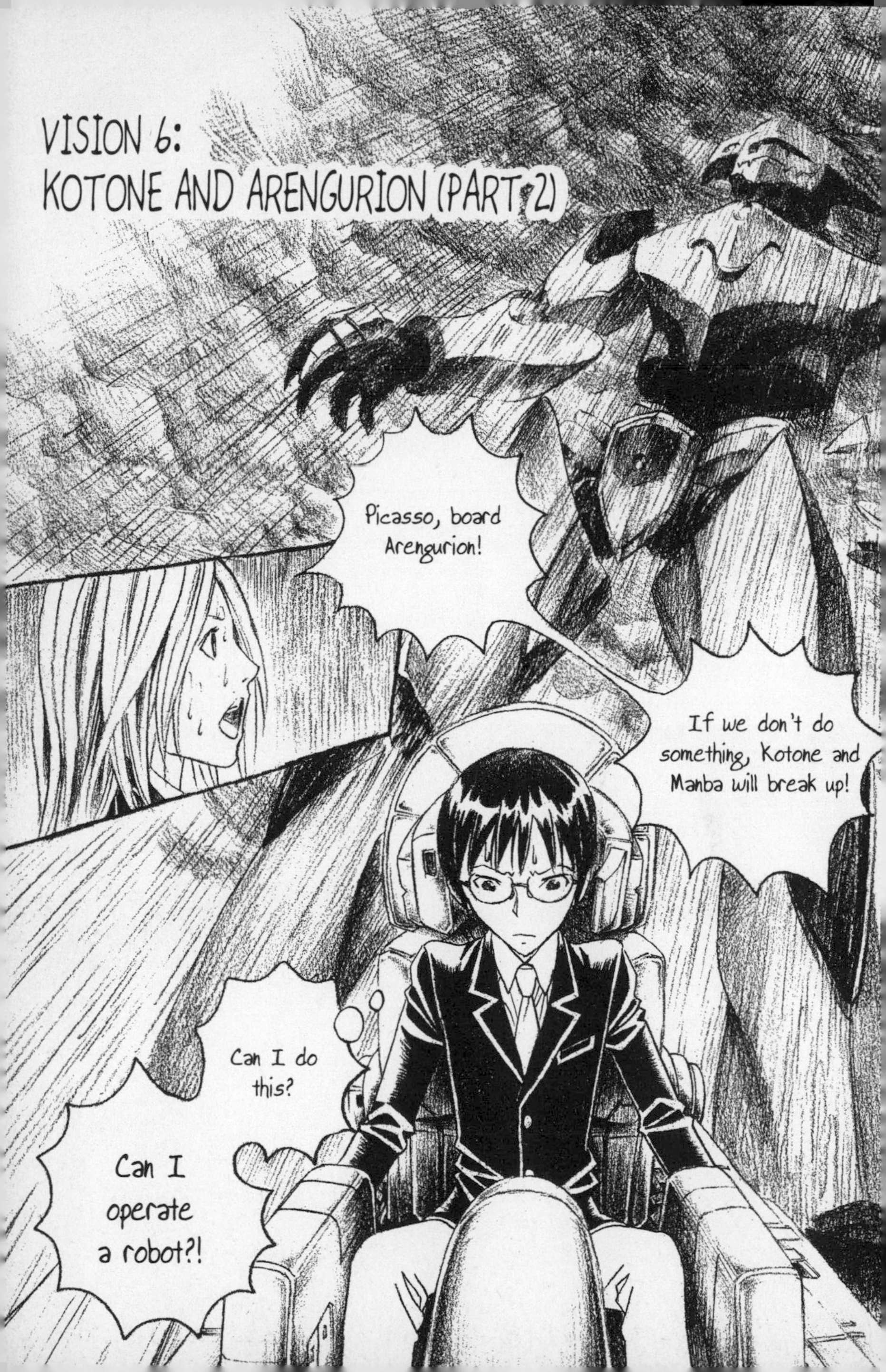
VISION 6: KOTONE AND ARENGURION (PART 2)
Picasso, board Arengurion!
If we don't do something, Kotone and Manba will break up!
Can I do this?
Can I operate a robot?!

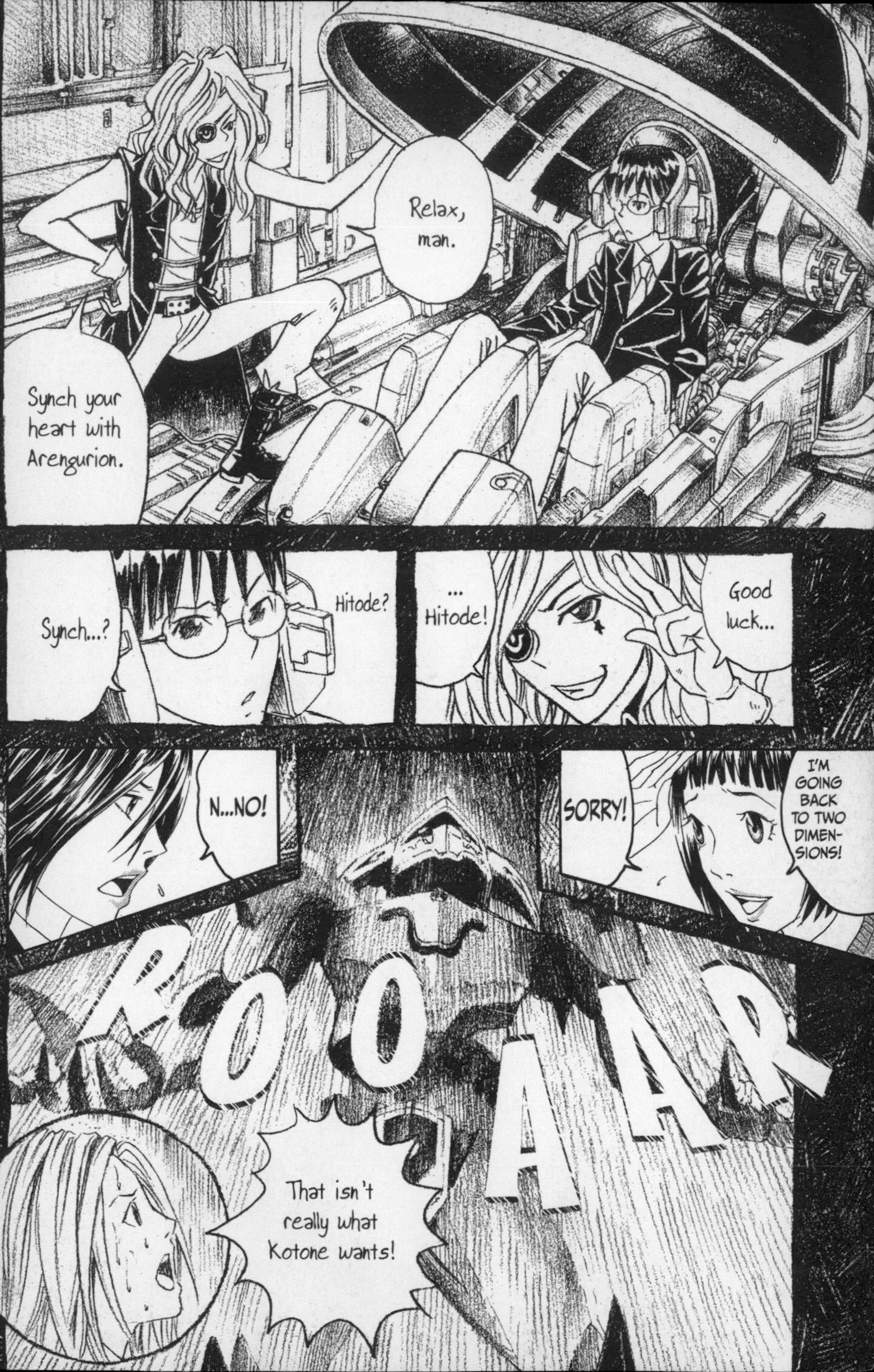
Relax, man.
Synch your heart with Arengurion.
Good luck...
... Hitode!
Hitode?
Synch...?
I'M GOING BACK TO TWO DIMENSIONS!
SORRY!
N...NO!
ROOAAR
That isn't really what Kotone wants!

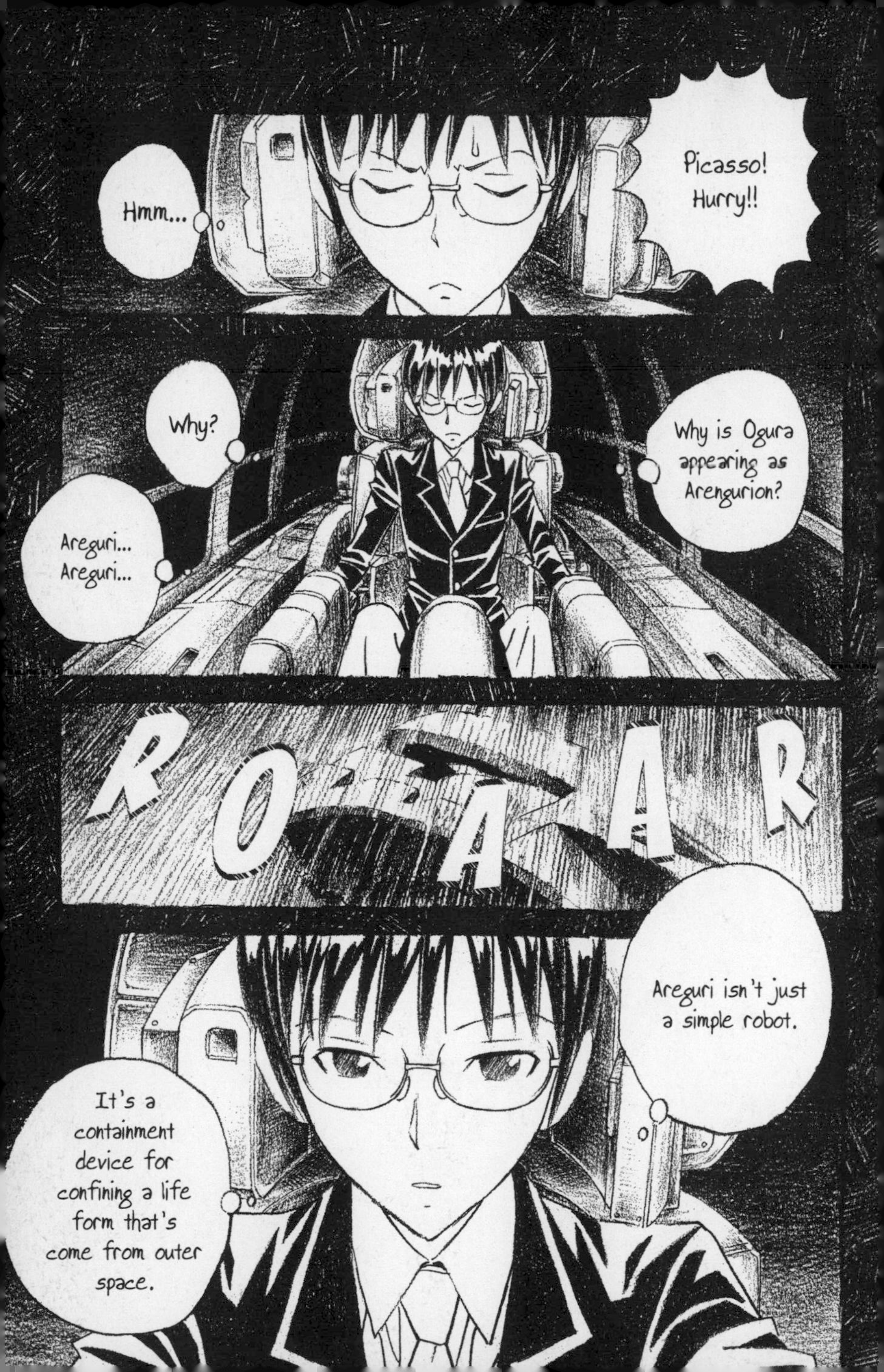
Picasso! Hurry!!
Hmm...
Why is Ogura appearing as Arengurion?
Why?
Areguri... Areguri...
ROAAR
Areguri isn't just a simple robot.
It's a containment device for confining a life form that's come from outer space.

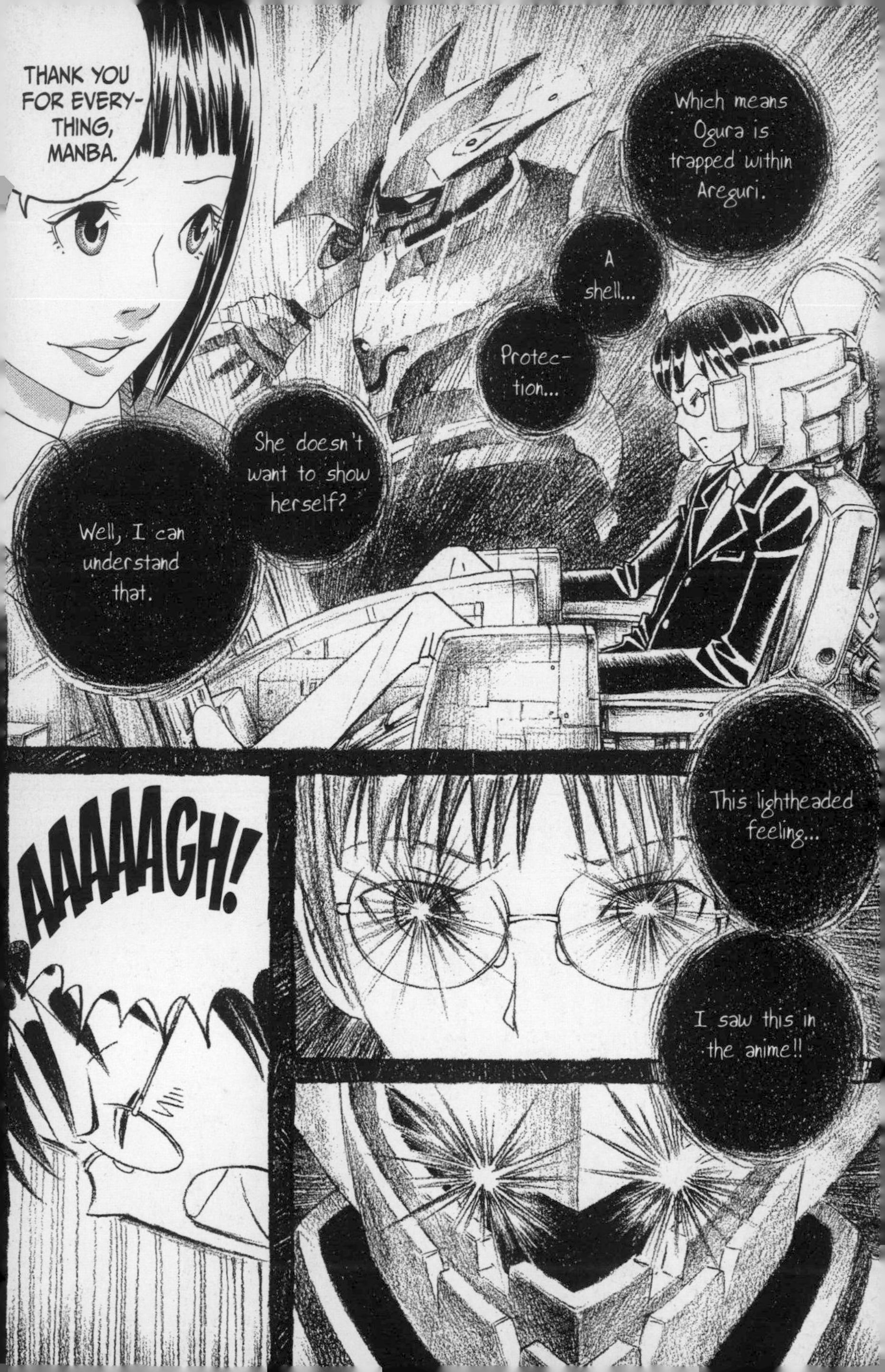
Which means Ogura is trapped within Areguri.
A shell...
Protection...
She doesn't want to show herself?
Well, I can understand that.
THANK YOU FOR EVERYTHING, MANBA.
This lightheaded feeling...
I saw this in the anime!!
AAAAAGH!

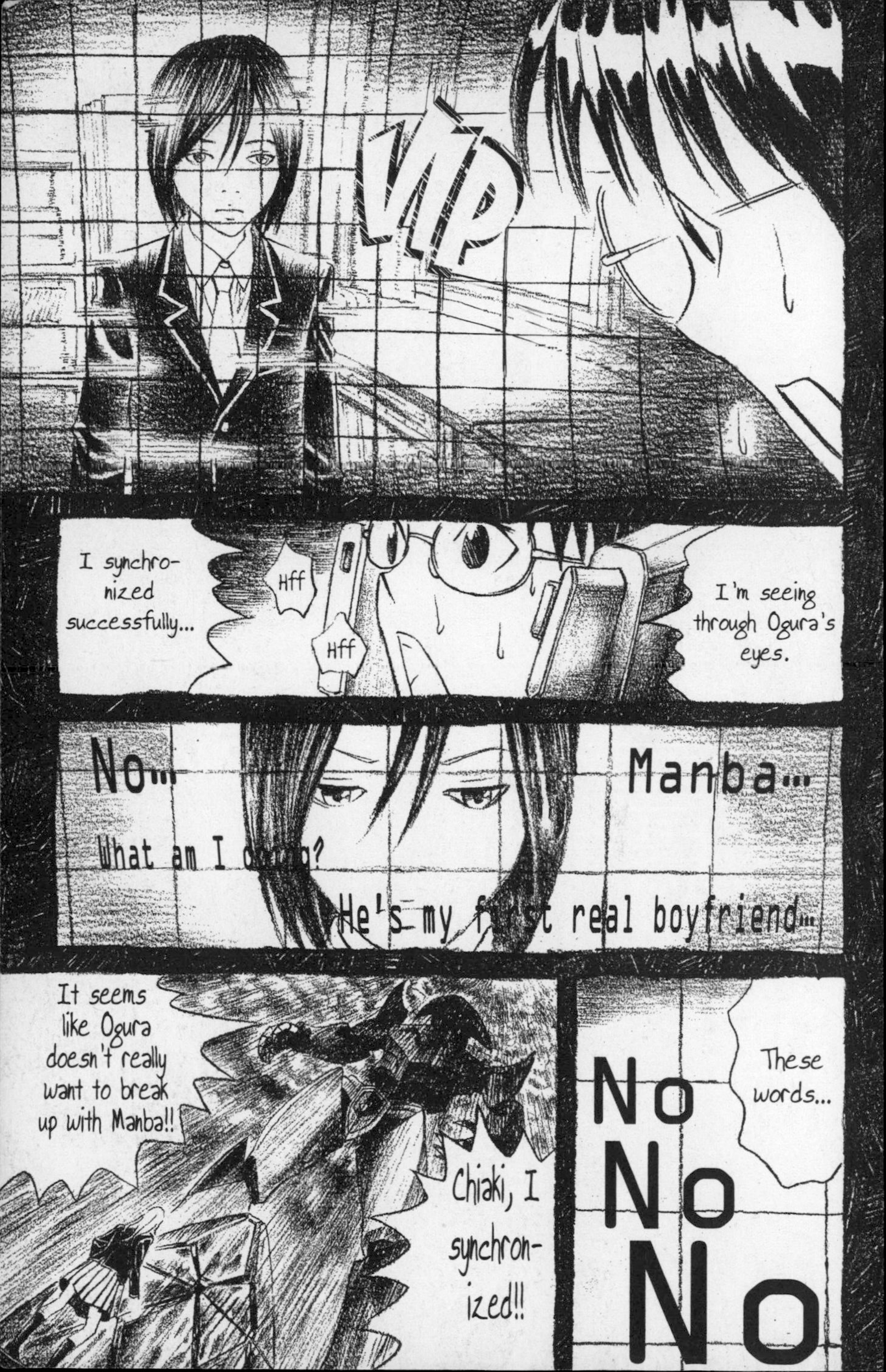
VIP
I'm seeing through Ogura's eyes.
Hff
Hff
I synchronized successfully...
Manba...
No...
What am I doing?
He's my first real boyfriend...
These words...
No No No
Chiaki, I synchronized!!
It seems like Ogura doesn't really want to break up with Manba!!

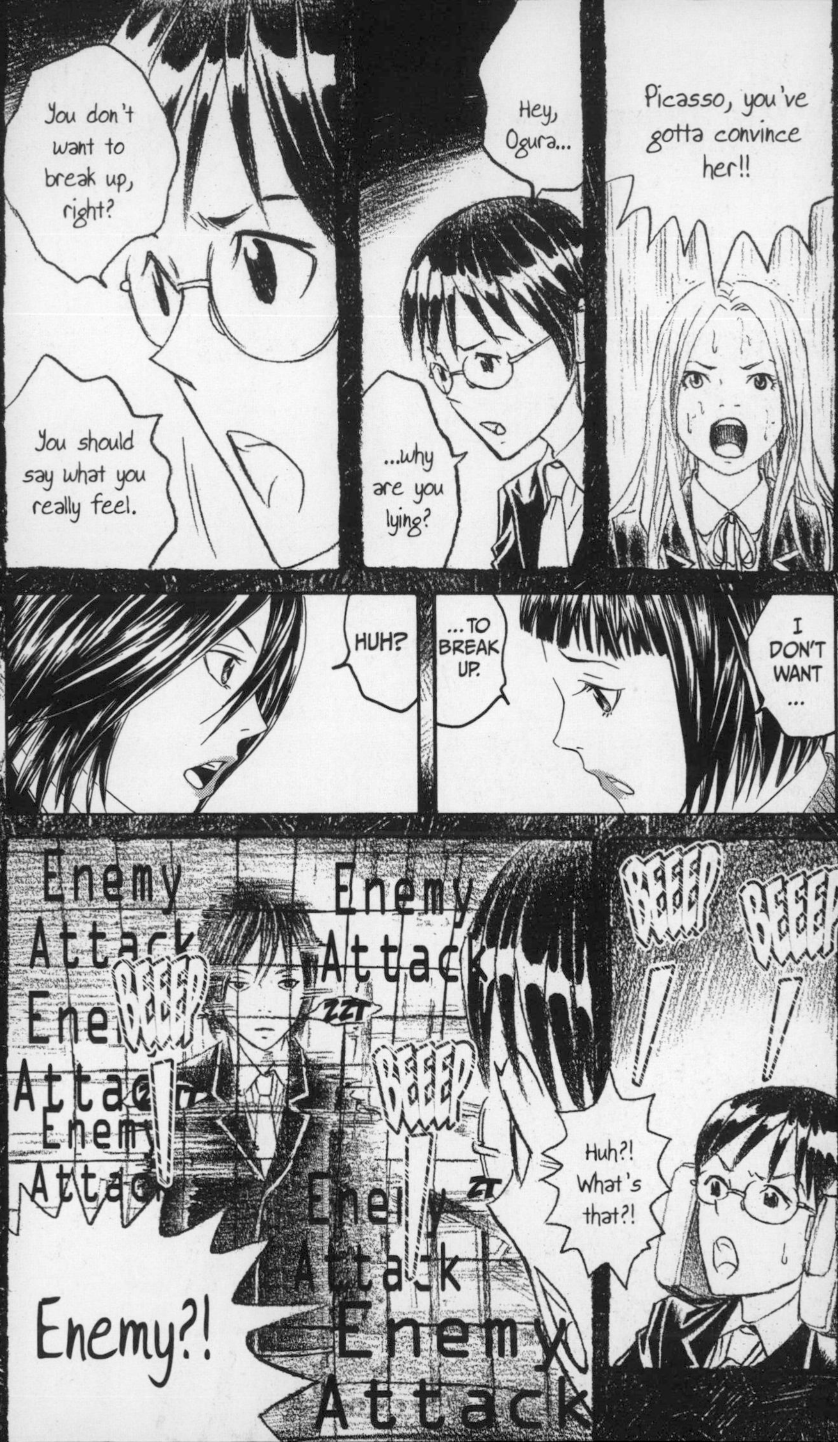
Picasso, you've gotta convince her!!
Hey, Ogura...
...why are you lying?
You don't want to break up, right?
You should say what you really feel.
I DON'T WANT ...
...TO BREAK UP.
HUH?
BEEP
BEEP
Huh?! What's that?!
Enemy Attack
Enemy Attack
BEEP
ZZT
BEEP
ZT
Enemy Attack
Enemy?!

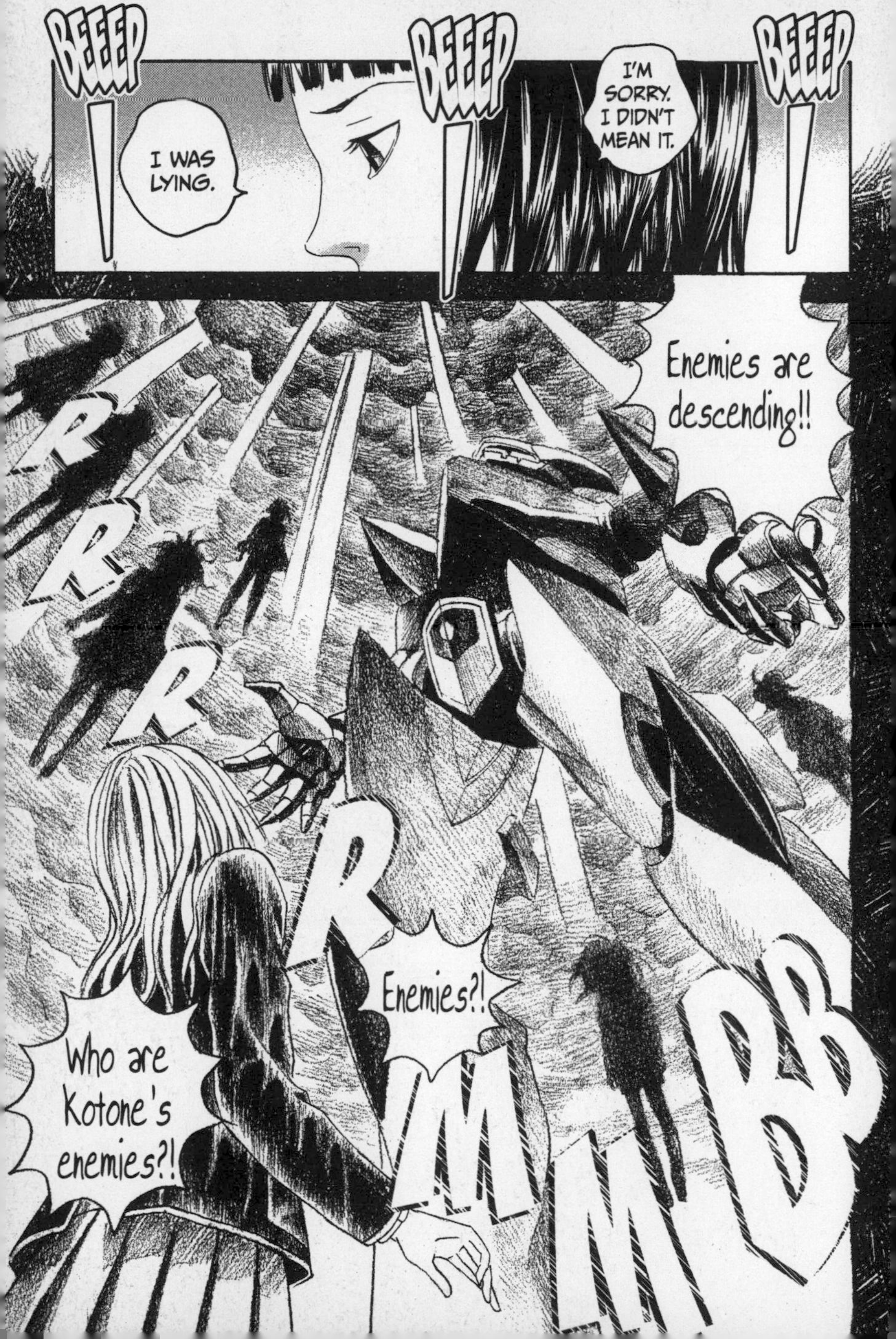
BEEEP
I'M SORRY. I DIDN'T MEAN IT.
BEEEP
I WAS LYING.
BEEEP
Enemies are descending!!
RRRRMMBB
Enemies?!
Who are Kotone's enemies?!

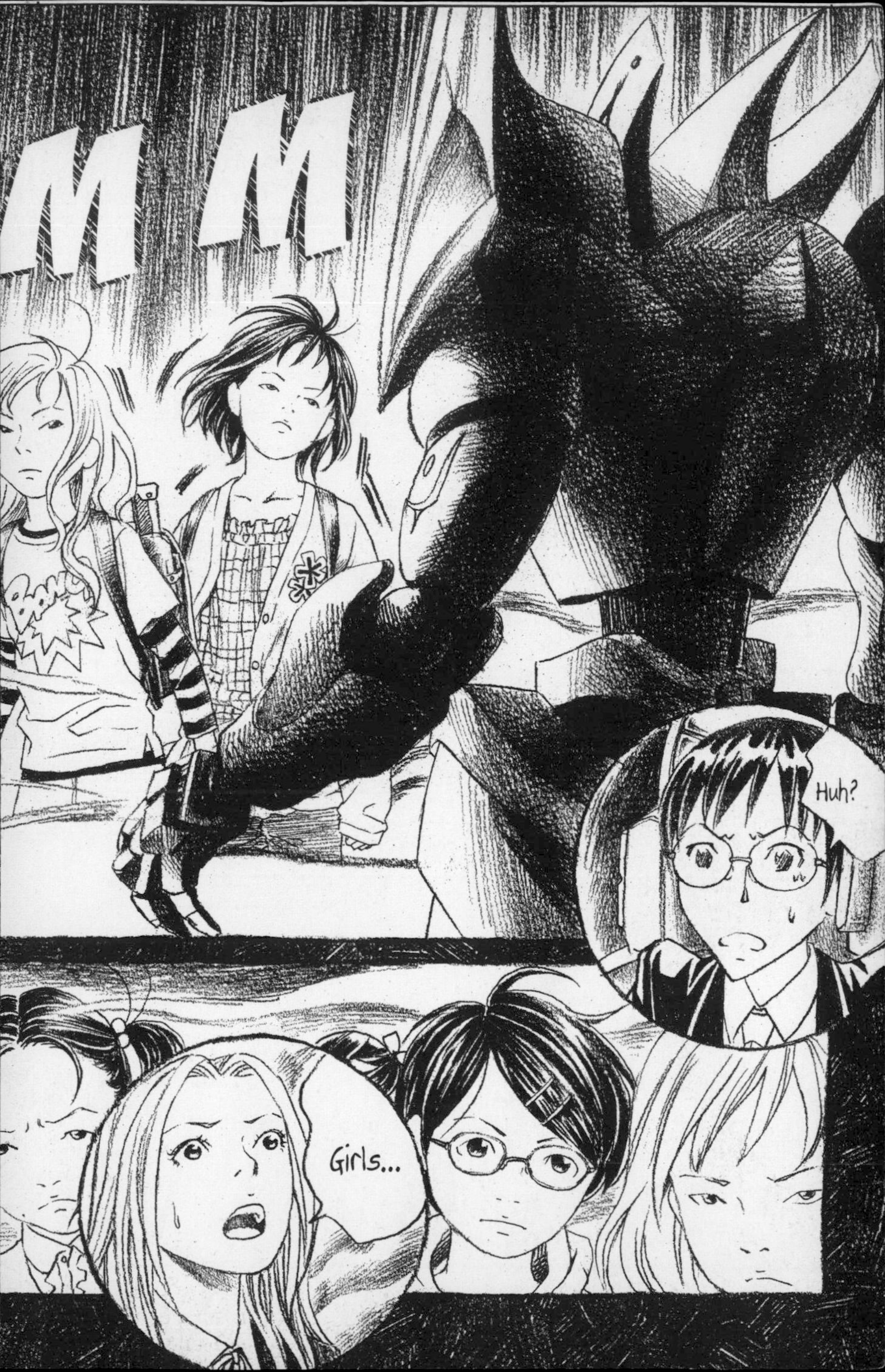
M M
Huh?
Girls...

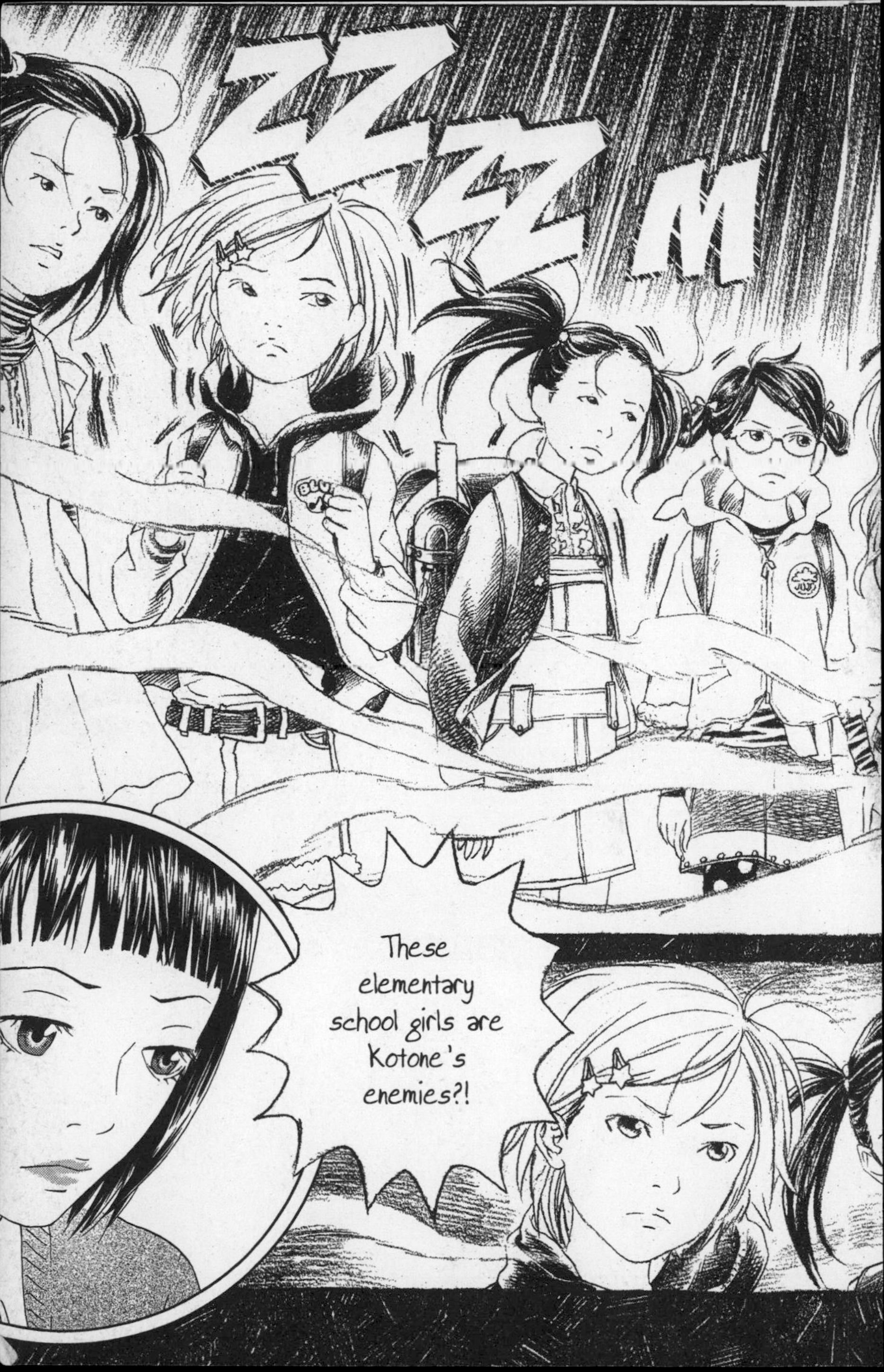
ZZZZM
These elementary school girls are Kotone's enemies?!

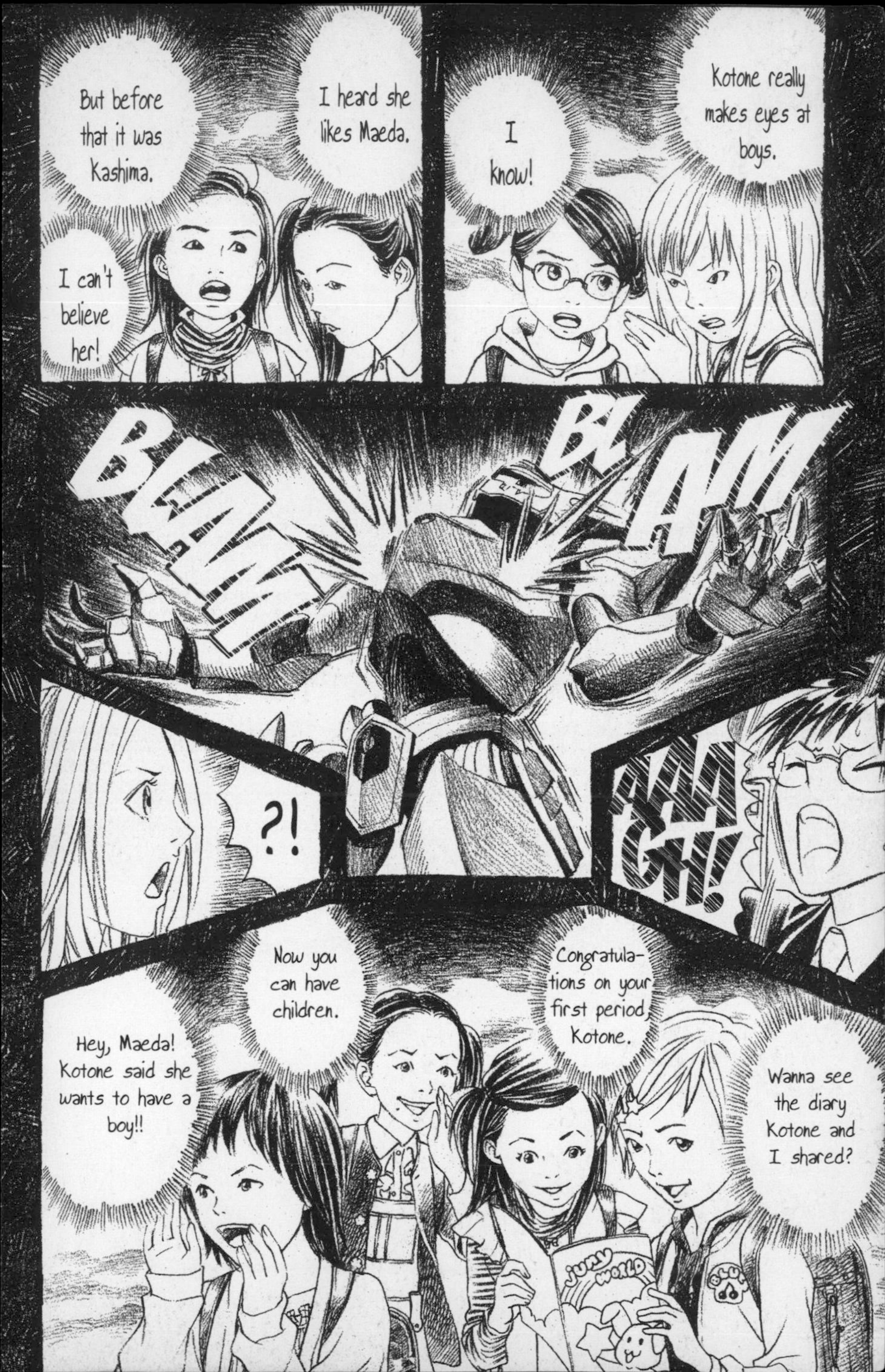
Kotone really makes eyes at boys.
I know!
I heard she likes Maeda.
But before that it was Kashima.
I can't believe her!
BLAM
BLAM
AAAGH!
?!
Wanna see the diary Kotone and I shared?
Congratula-tions on your first period, Kotone.
Now you can have children.
Hey, Maeda! Kotone said she wants to have a boy!!
JUNY WORLD

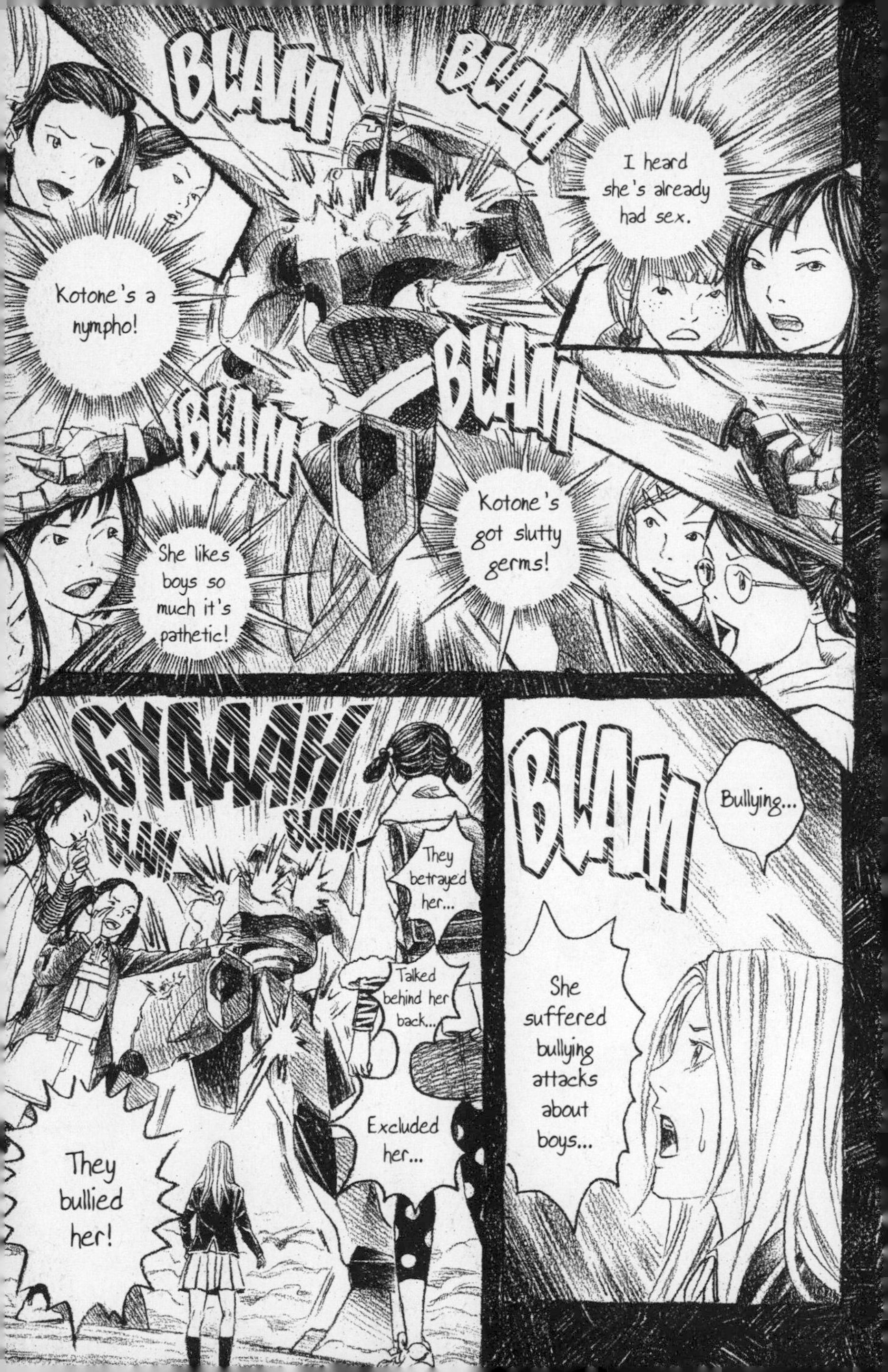

BLAM
BLAM
I heard she's already had sex.
Kotone's a nympho!
BLAM
BLAM
Kotone's got slutty germs!
She likes boys so much it's pathetic!
BLAM
Bullying...
She suffered bullying attacks about boys...
GYAAAH!
They betrayed her...
Talked behind her back...
Excluded her...
They bullied her!

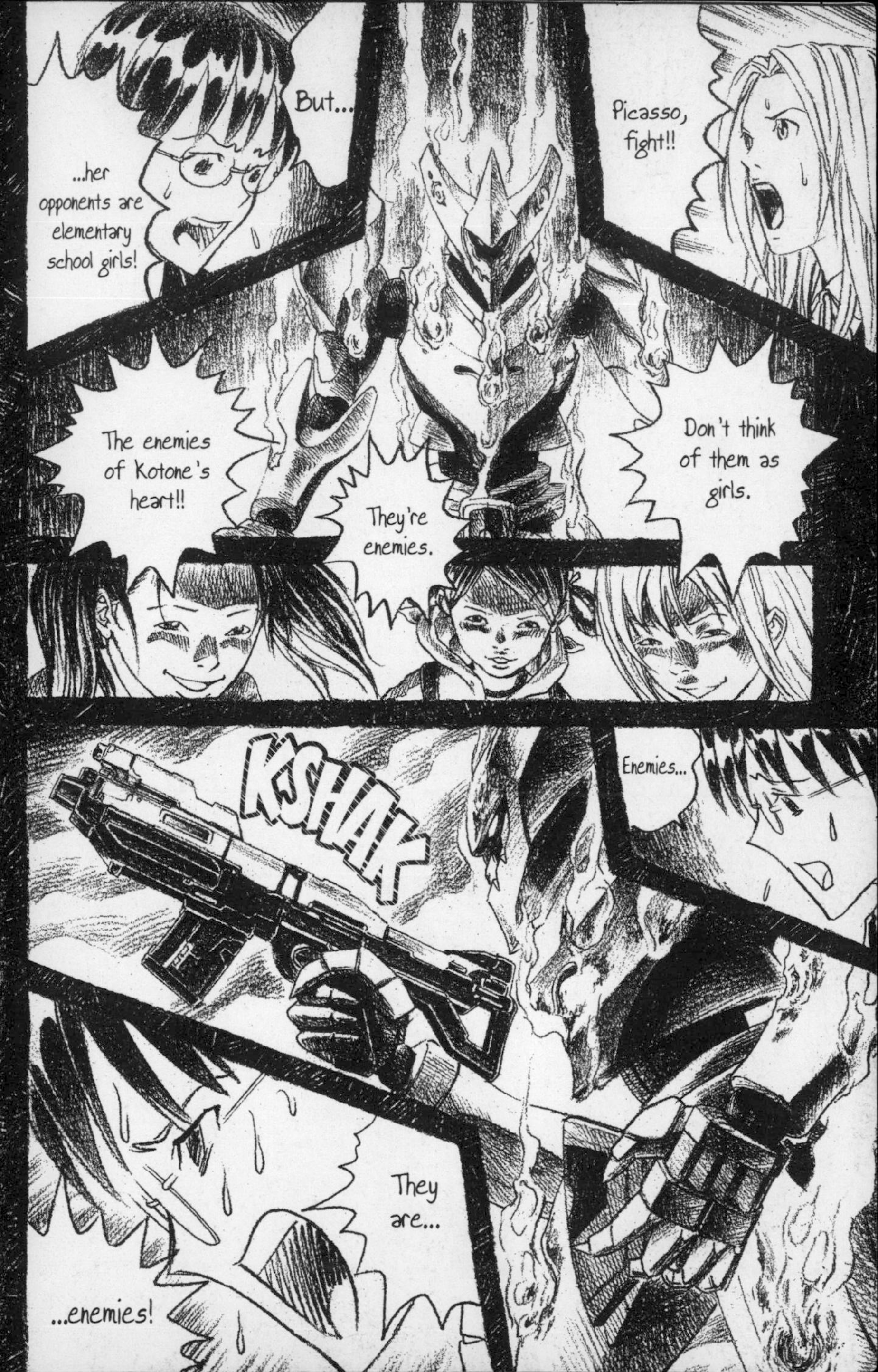
Picasso, fight!!
But...
...her opponents are elementary school girls!
Don't think of them as girls.
They're enemies.
The enemies of Kotone's heart!!
Enemies...
KSHAK
They are...
...enemies!

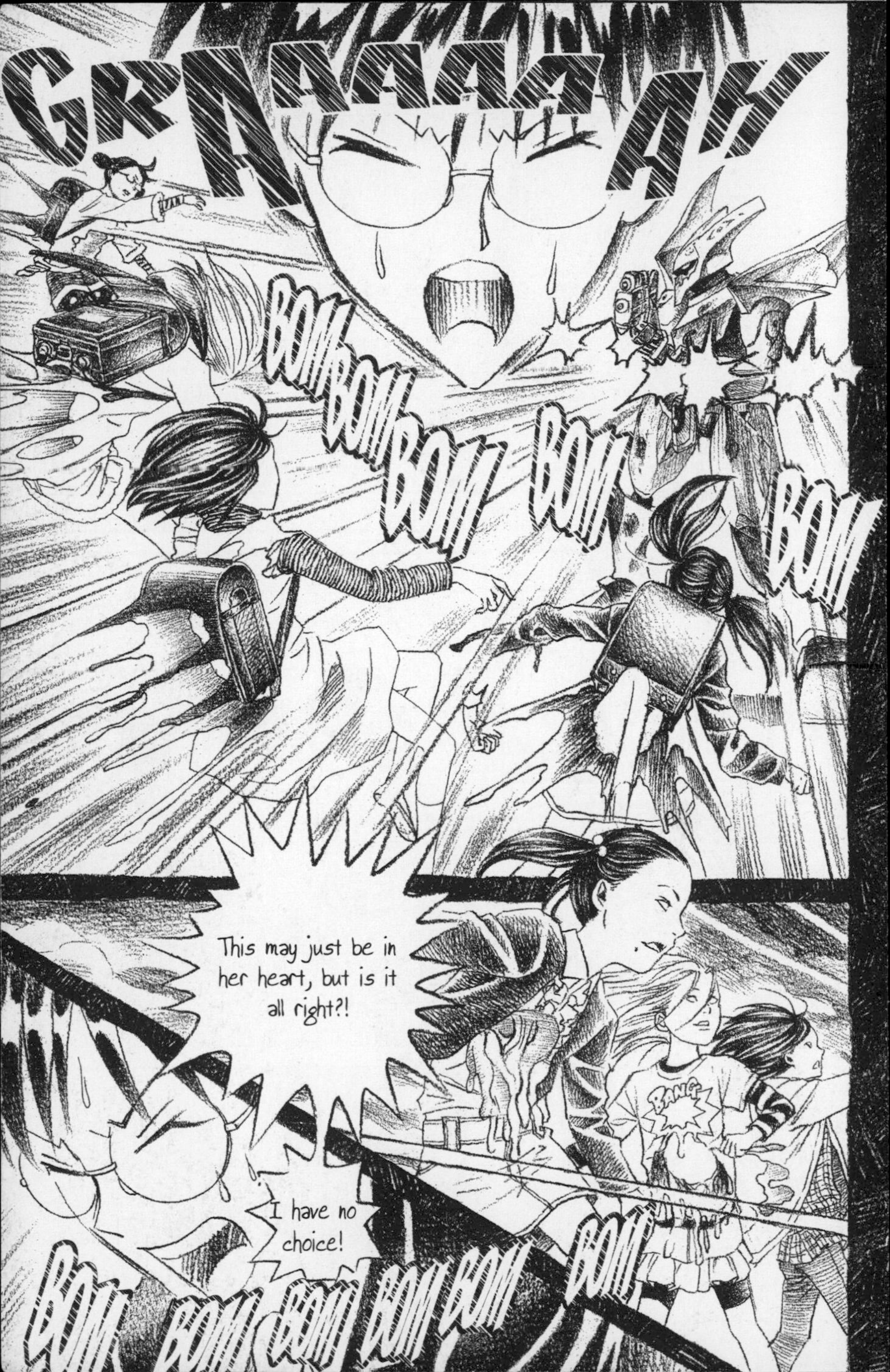
GRAAAAAAAH
BOM BOM BOM
BOM
BOM
This may just be in her heart, but is it all right?!
BANG
I have no choice!
BOM
BOM BOM BOM
BOM BOM

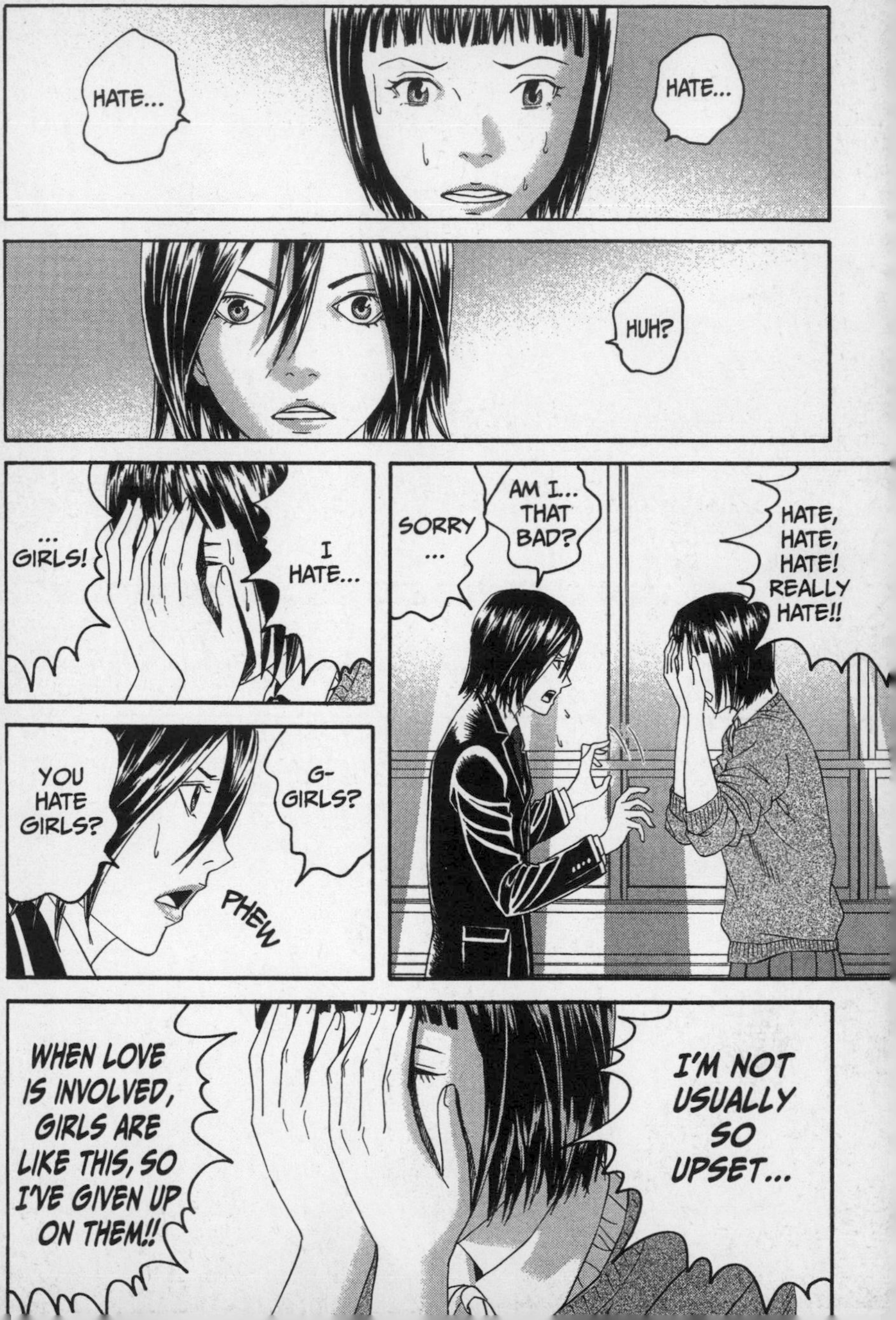
HATE...
HATE...
HUH?
HATE, HATE, HATE! REALLY HATE!!
AM I... THAT BAD?
SORRY ...
I HATE...
... GIRLS!
G-GIRLS?
YOU HATE GIRLS?
PHEW
I'M NOT USUALLY SO UPSET...
WHEN LOVE IS INVOLVED, GIRLS ARE LIKE THIS, SO I'VE GIVEN UP ON THEM!!

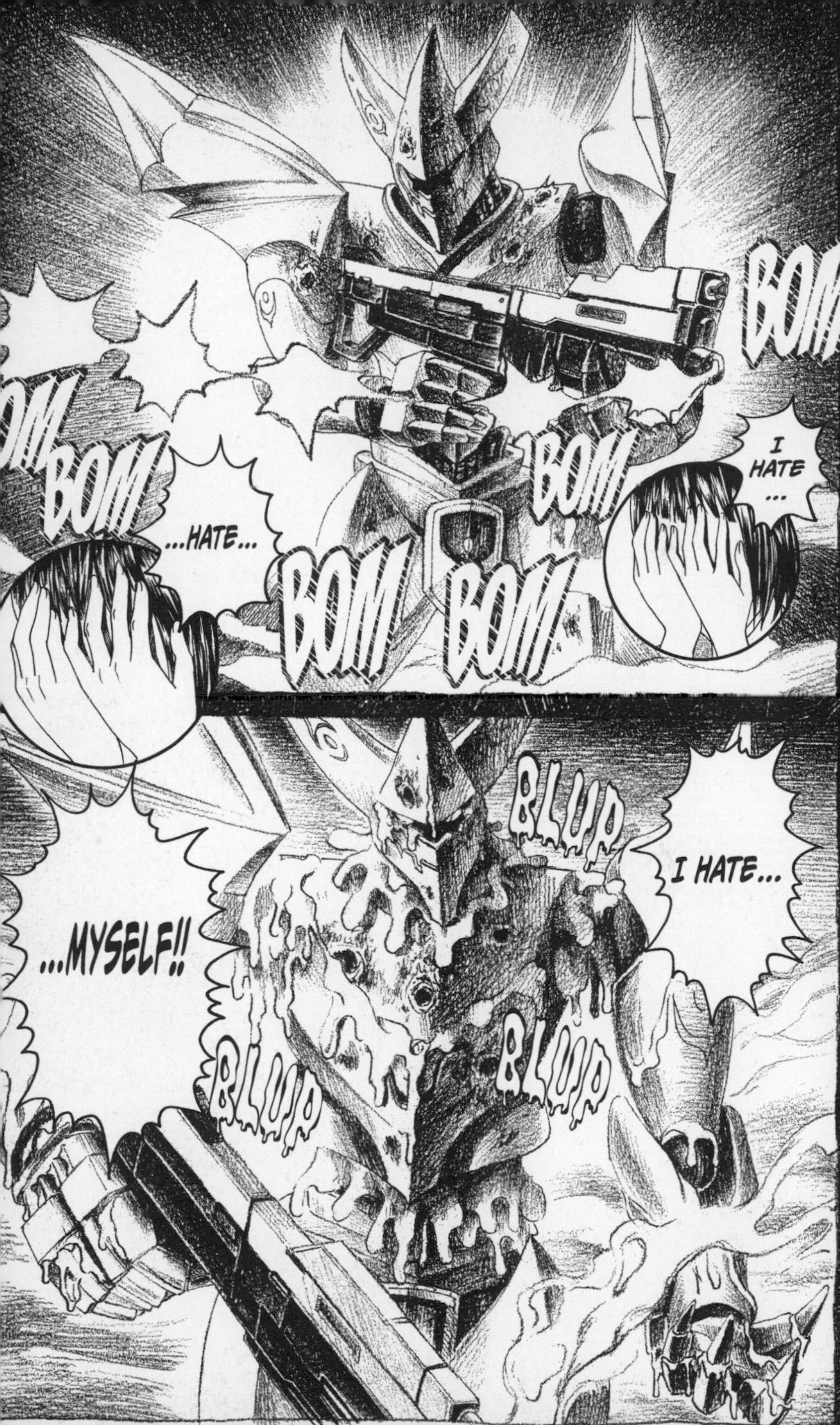
BOM
I HATE ...
BOM
BOM
BOM
...HATE...
BOM
I HATE...
BLUP
BLUP
BLUP
...MYSELF!!

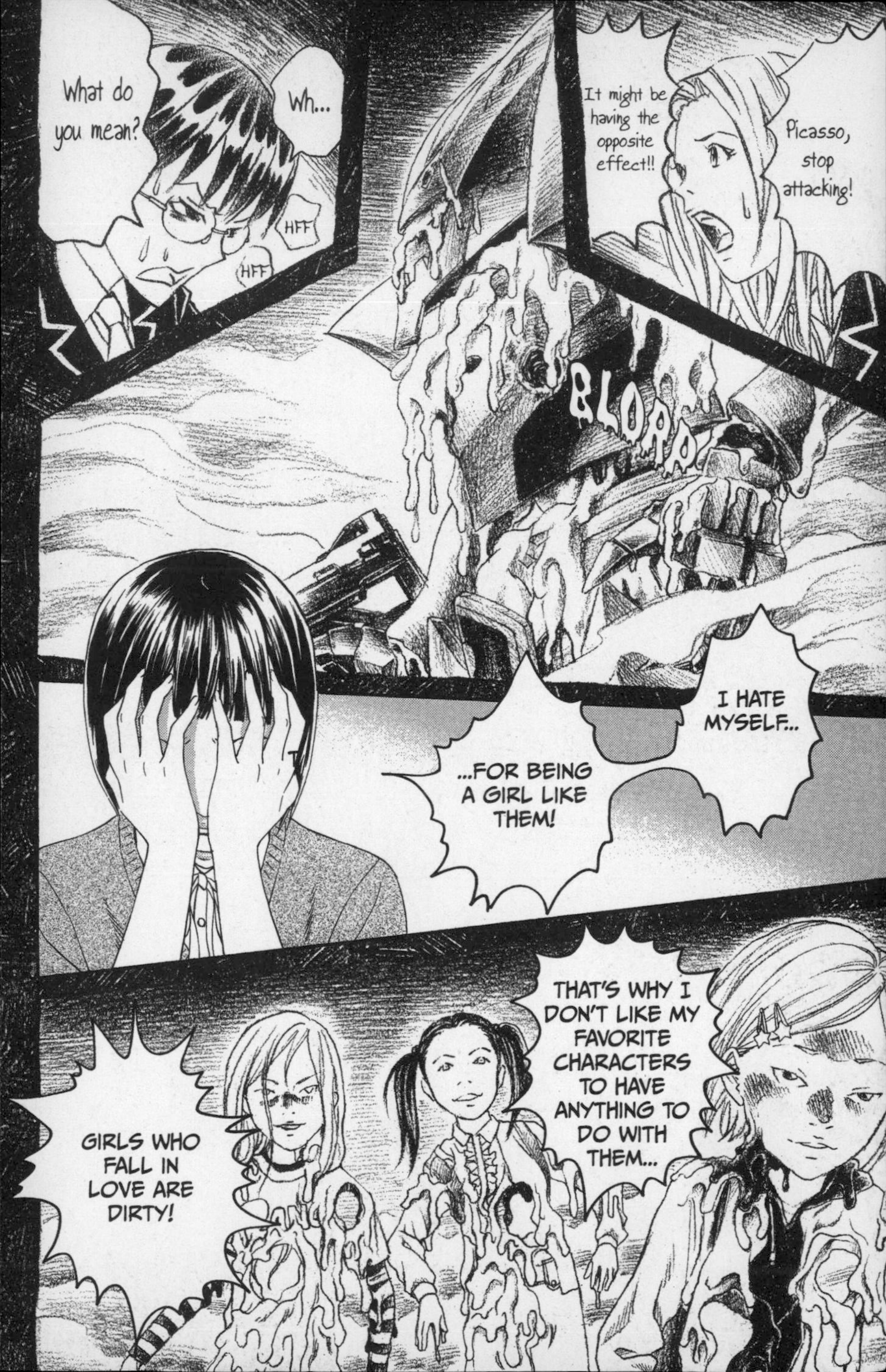

Picasso, stop attacking!
It might be having the opposite effect!!
Wh...
What do you mean?
HFF
HFF
BLORP
I HATE MYSELF...
...FOR BEING A GIRL LIKE THEM!
THAT'S WHY I DON'T LIKE MY FAVORITE CHARACTERS TO HAVE ANYTHING TO DO WITH THEM...
GIRLS WHO FALL IN LOVE ARE DIRTY!

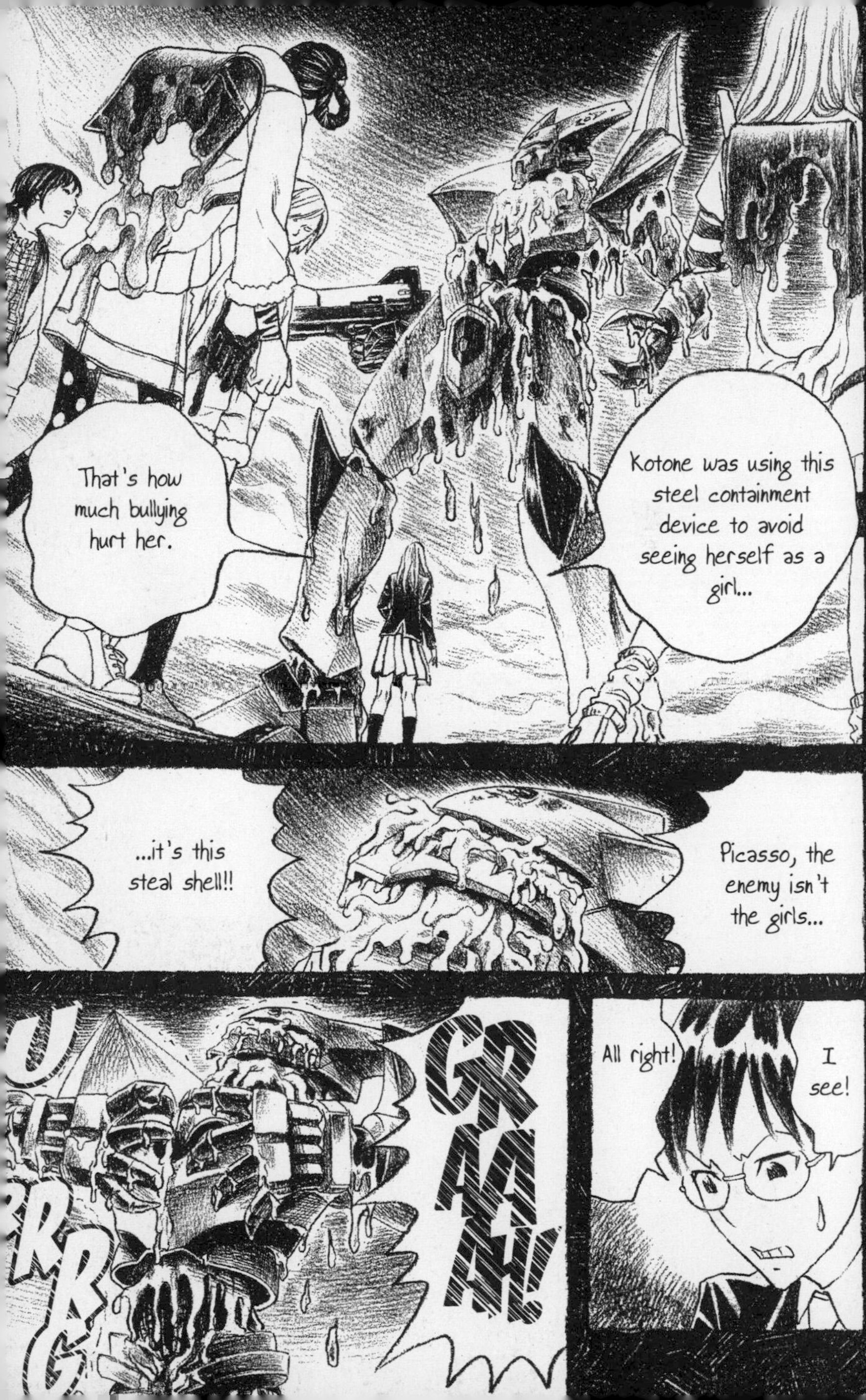
Kotone was using this steel containment device to avoid seeing herself as a girl...
That's how much bullying hurt her.
Picasso, the enemy isn't the girls...
...it's this steal shell!!
I see!
All right!
GRAAAH!
URRBG

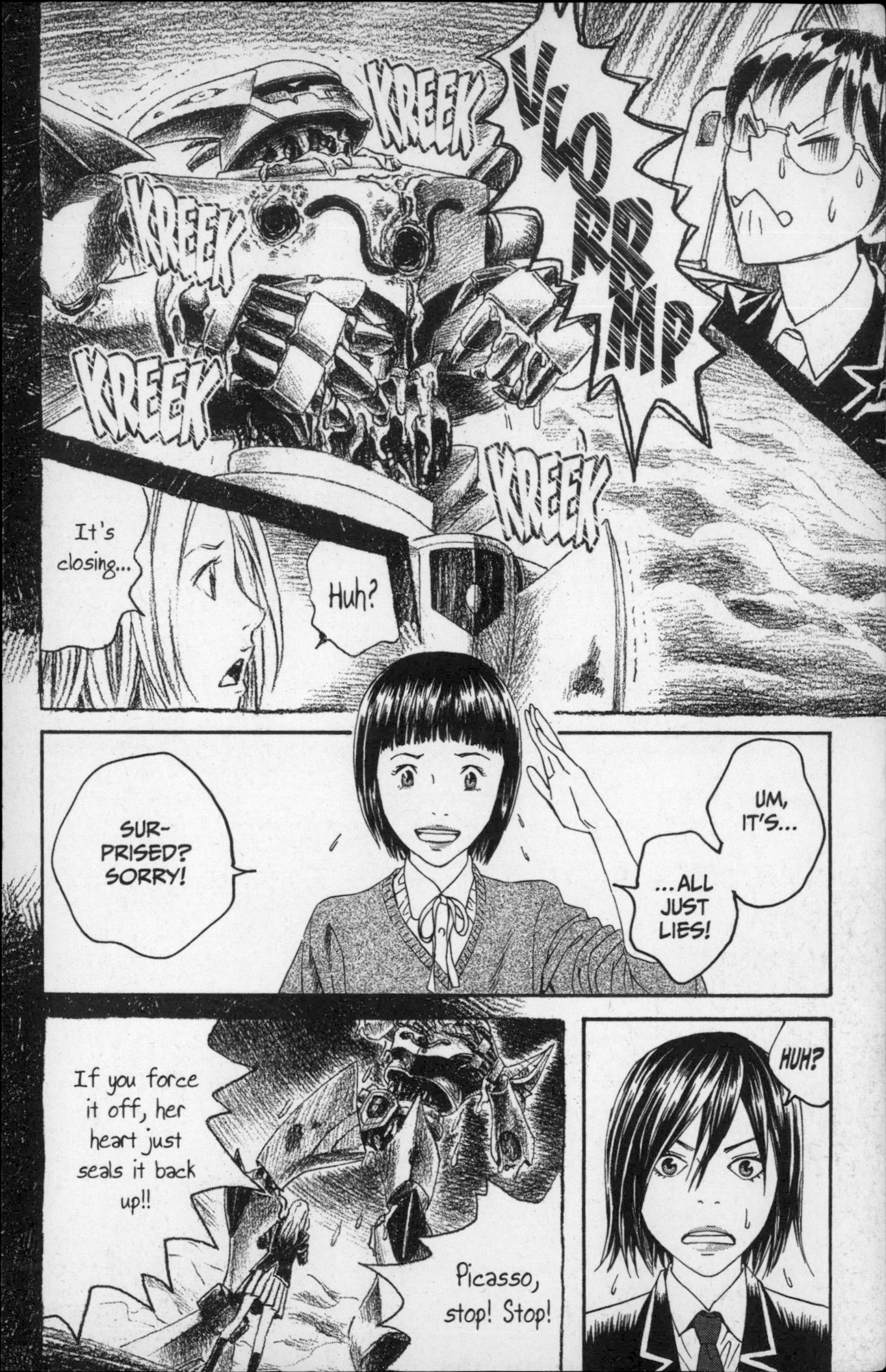
VLORRMP
KREEK
KREEK
KREEK
KREEK
It's closing...
Huh?
UM, IT'S...
...ALL JUST LIES!
SUR-PRISED? SORRY!
HUH?
Picasso, stop! Stop!
If you force it off, her heart just seals it back up!!

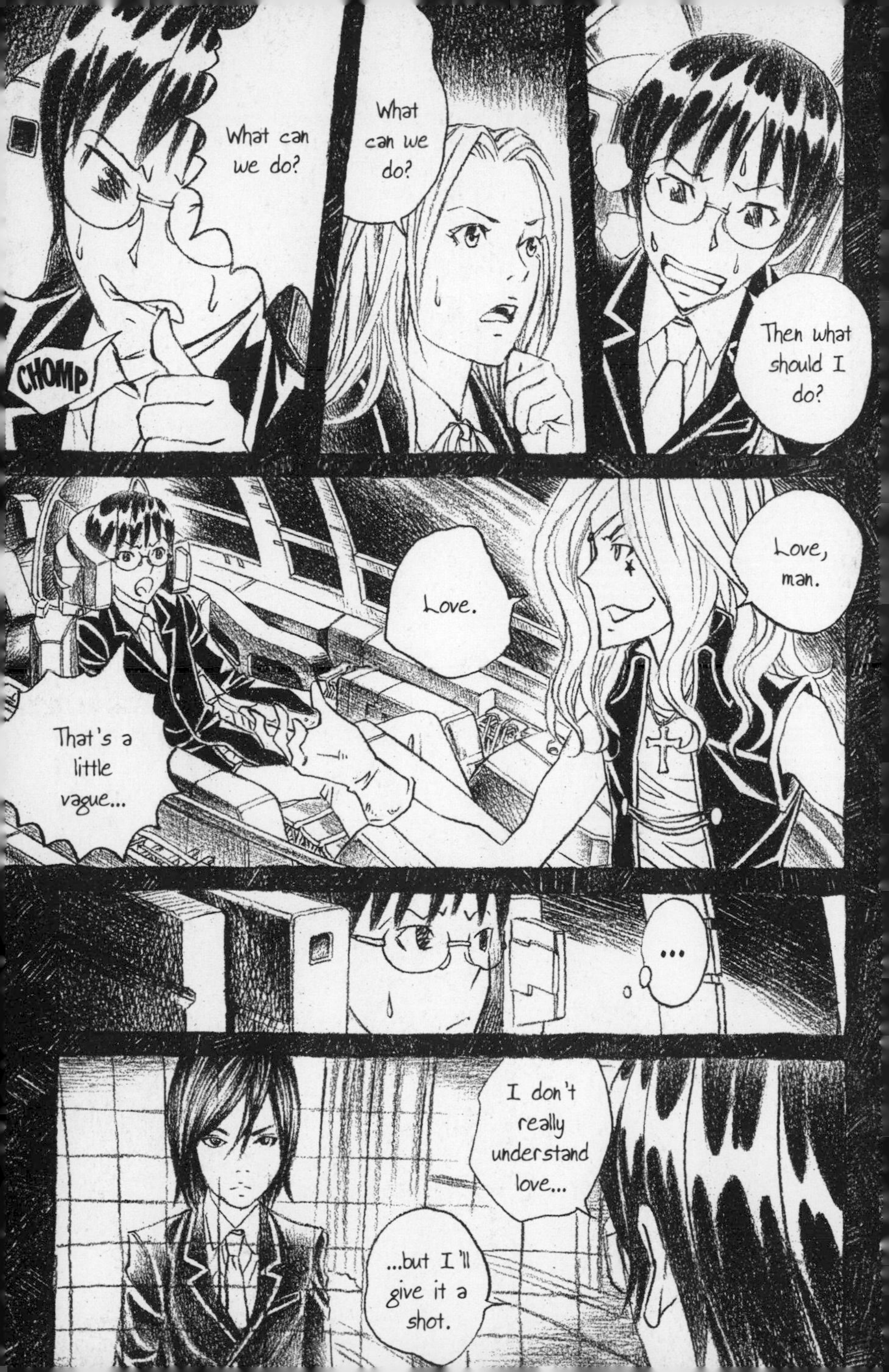
Then what should I do?
What can we do?
What can we do?
CHOMP
Love, man.
Love.
That's a little vague...
...
I don't really understand love...
...but I'll give it a shot.

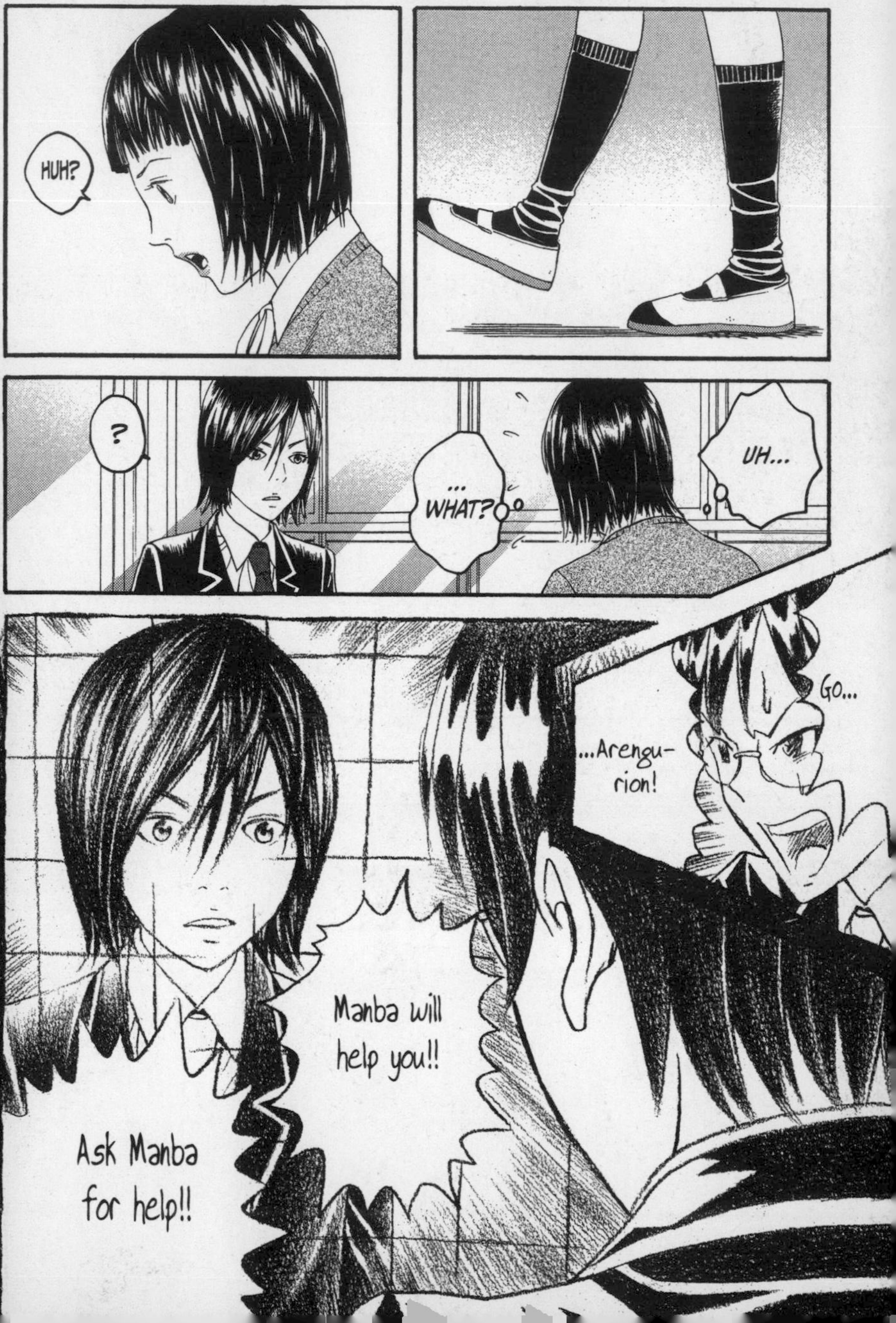
HUH?
UH...
... WHAT?
?
GO...
...Arengu-rion!
Manba will help you!!
Ask Manba for help!!

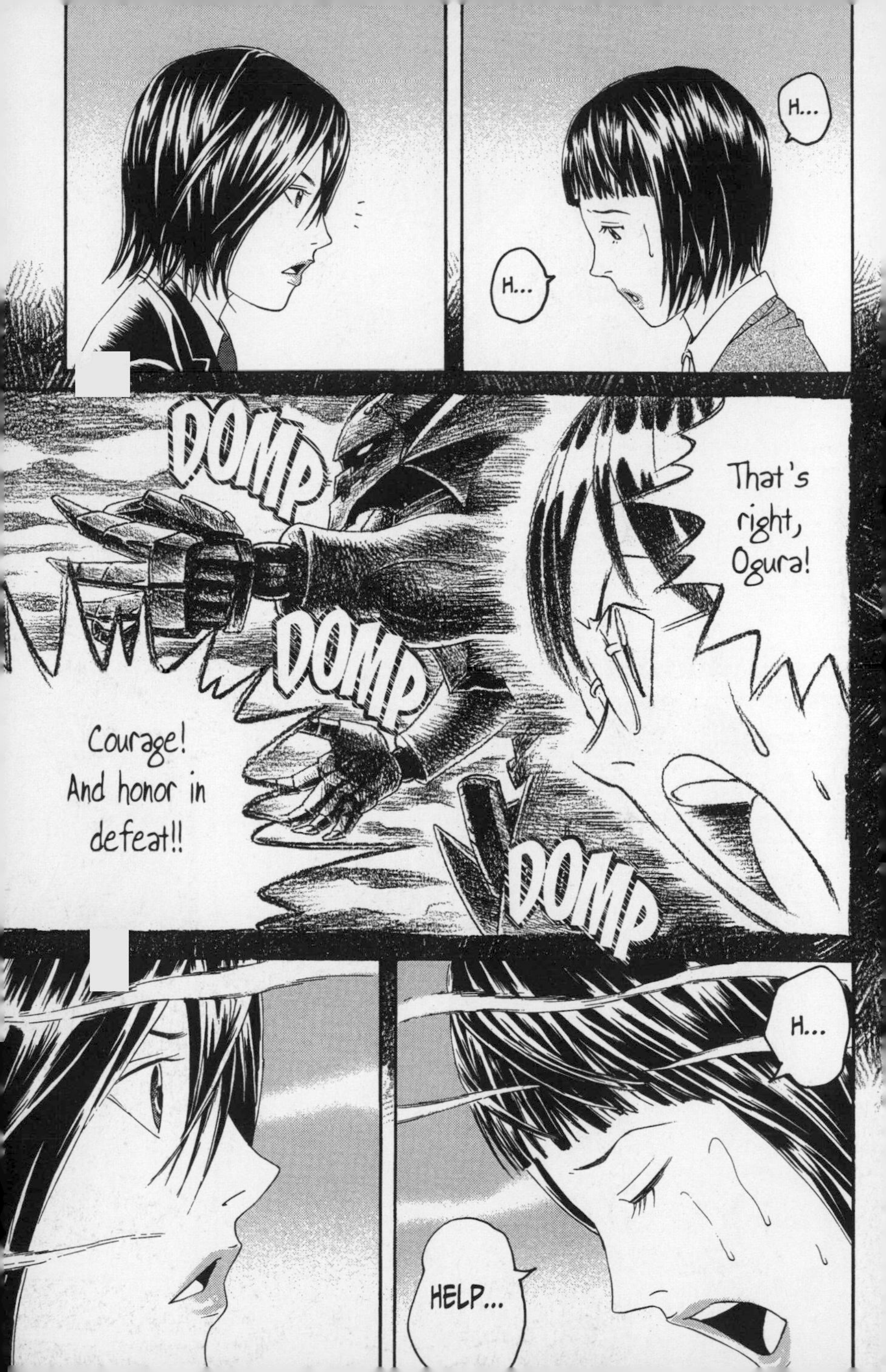
H...
H...
That's right, Ogura!
DOMP
DOMP
DOMP
Courage! And honor in defeat!!
H...
HELP...

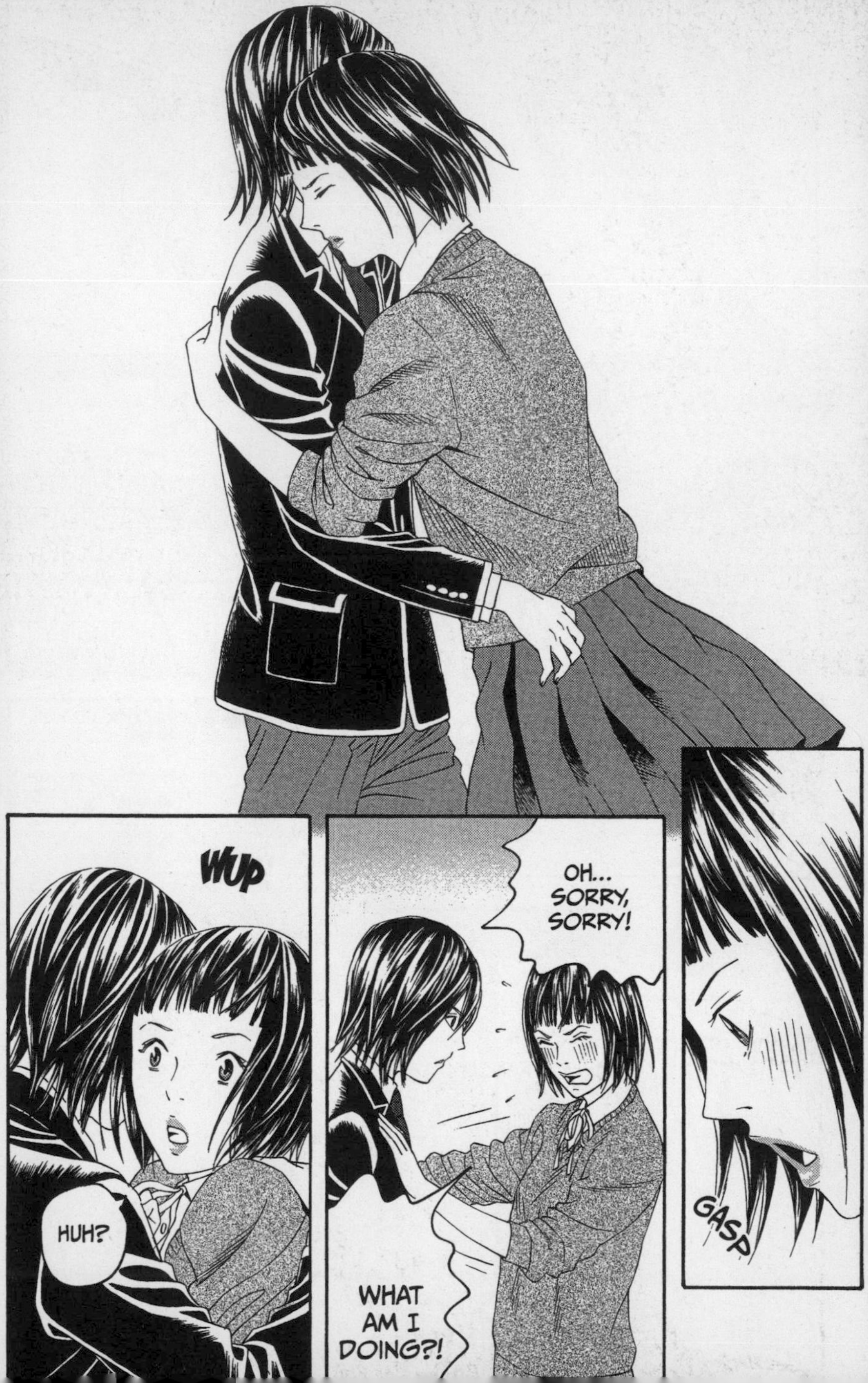
GASP
OH... SORRY, SORRY!
WHAT AM I DOING?!
WUP
HUH?

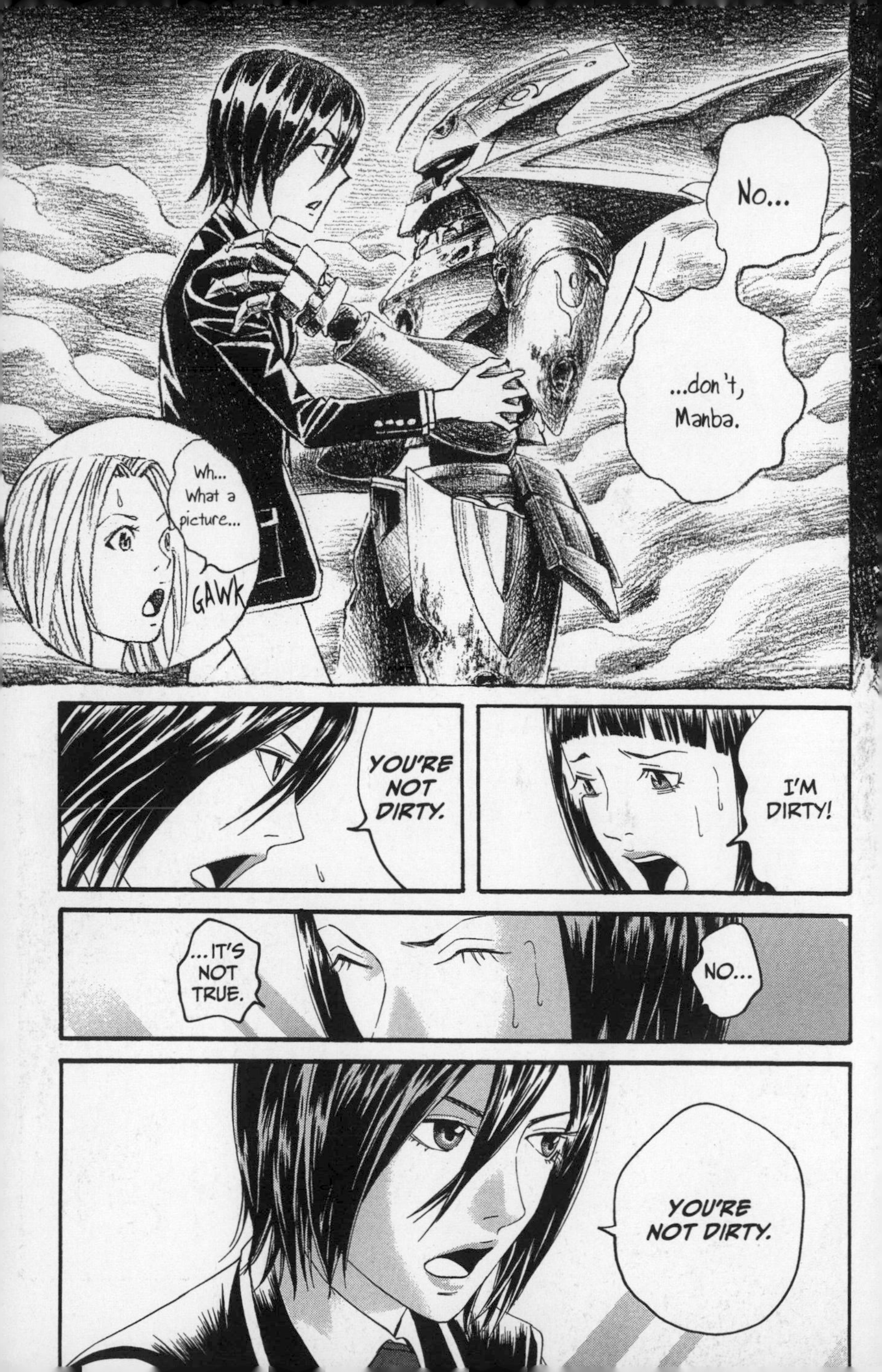
No...
...don't, Manba.
Wh... What a picture...
GAWK
I'M DIRTY!
YOU'RE NOT DIRTY.
NO...
...IT'S NOT TRUE.
YOU'RE NOT DIRTY.

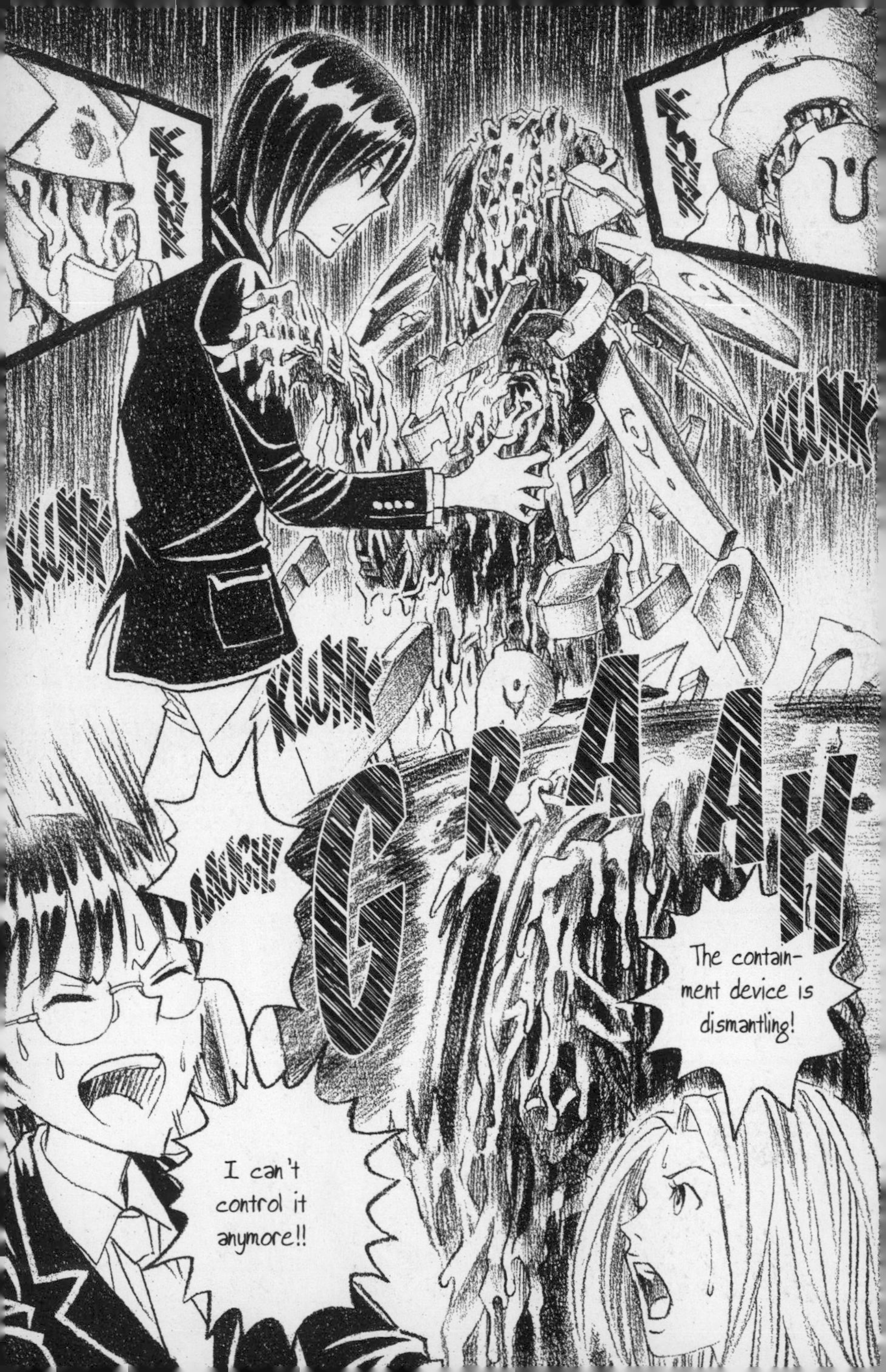
KRK
KRK
KLUNK
KLUNK
KLUNK
GRAAH
The contain-
ment device is
dismantling!
I can't
control it
anymore!!

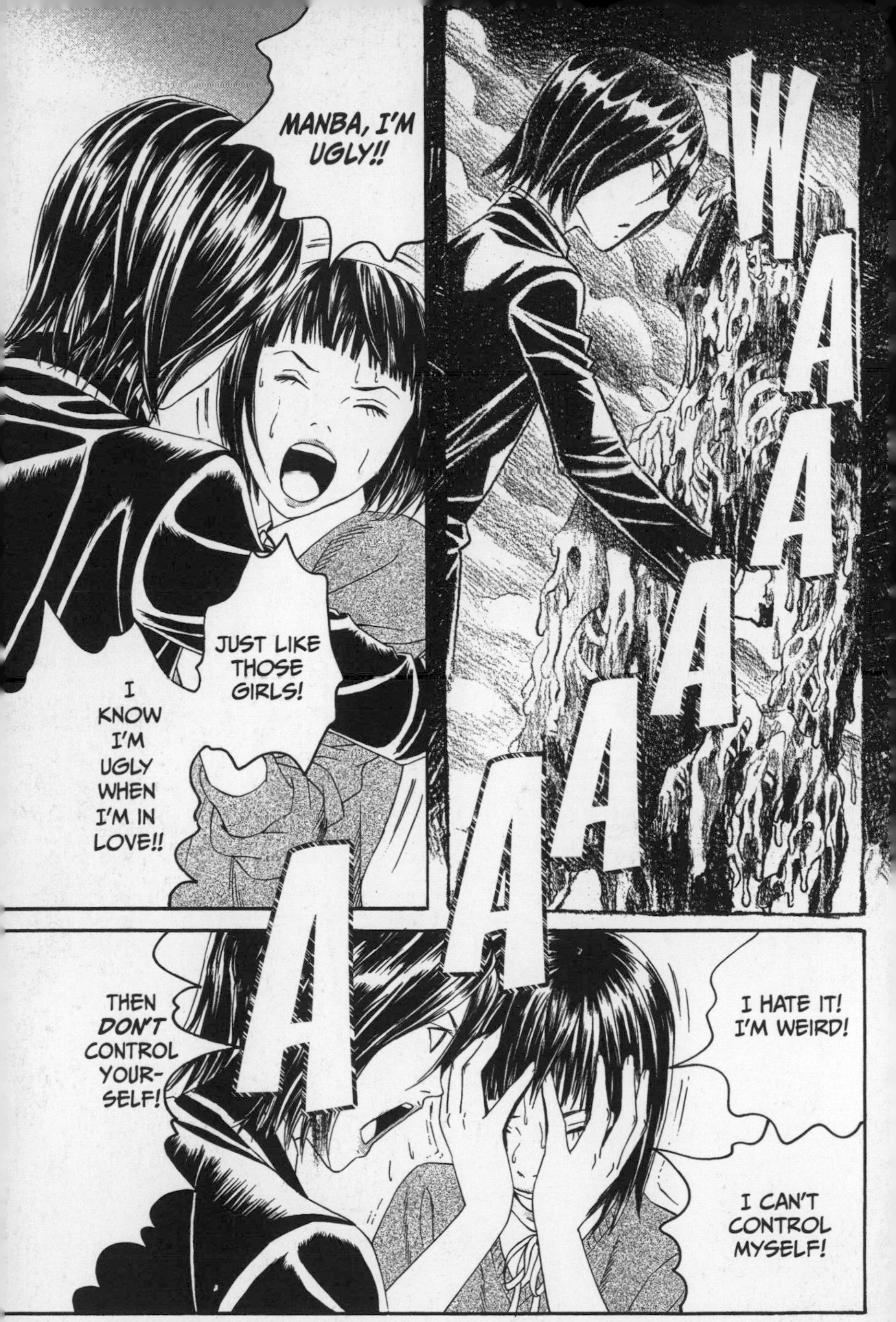
WAAAAAAAAA
MANBA, I'M UGLY!!
JUST LIKE THOSE GIRLS!
I KNOW I'M UGLY WHEN I'M IN LOVE!!
I HATE IT! I'M WEIRD!
I CAN'T CONTROL MYSELF!
THEN *DON'T* CONTROL YOUR-SELF!

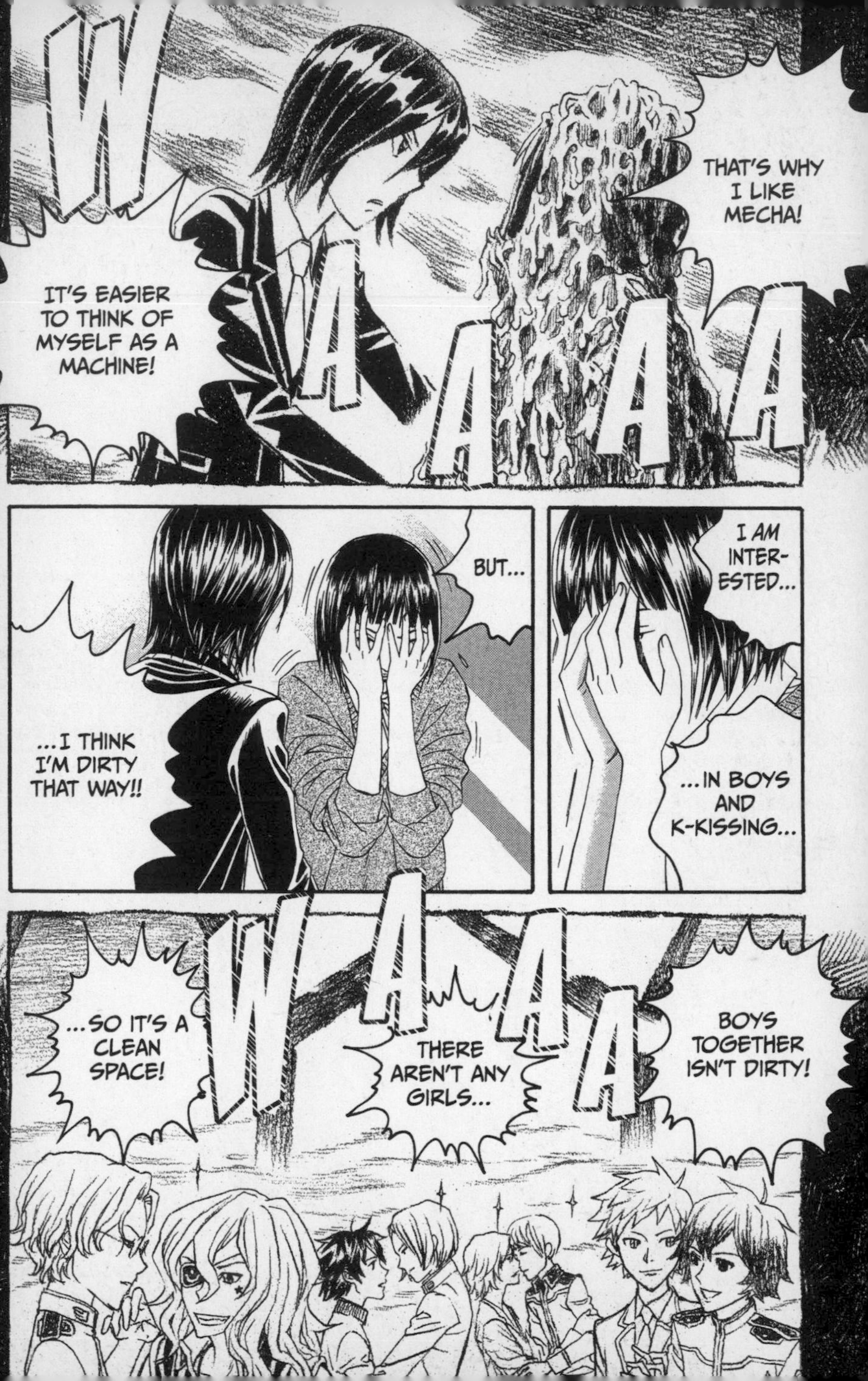
THAT'S WHY I LIKE MECHA!
IT'S EASIER TO THINK OF MYSELF AS A MACHINE!
WAAAAA
I AM INTER-ESTED...
...IN BOYS AND K-KISSING...
BUT...
...I THINK I'M DIRTY THAT WAY!!
BOYS TOGETHER ISN'T DIRTY!
THERE AREN'T ANY GIRLS...
...SO IT'S A CLEAN SPACE!
WAAAA

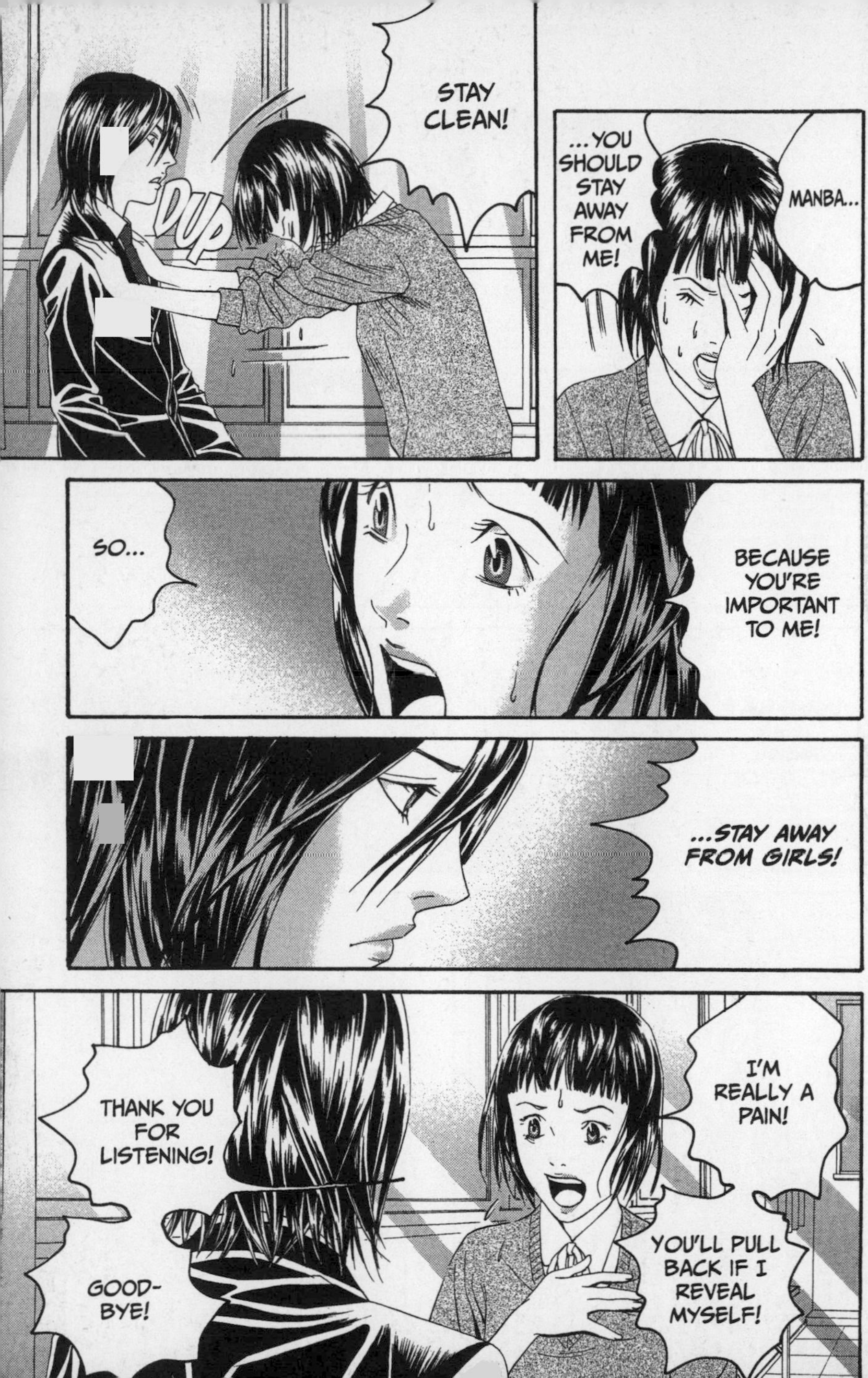
MANBA...
...YOU SHOULD STAY AWAY FROM ME!
STAY CLEAN!
DUP
BECAUSE YOU'RE IMPORTANT TO ME!
SO...
...STAY AWAY FROM GIRLS!
I'M REALLY A PAIN!
YOU'LL PULL BACK IF I REVEAL MYSELF!
THANK YOU FOR LISTENING!
GOOD-BYE!

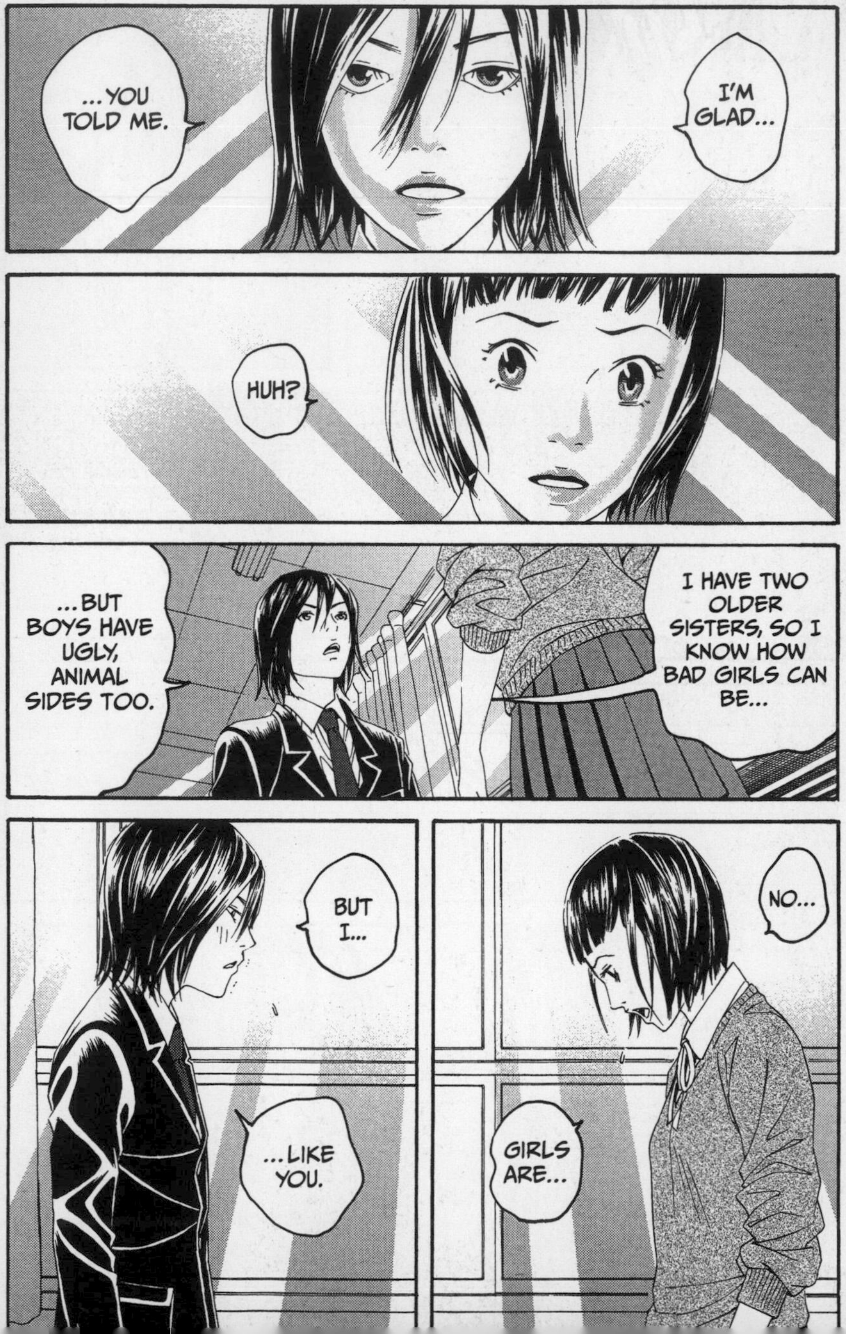
I'M GLAD...
...YOU TOLD ME.
HUH?
I HAVE TWO OLDER SISTERS, SO I KNOW HOW BAD GIRLS CAN BE...
...BUT BOYS HAVE UGLY, ANIMAL SIDES TOO.
NO...
GIRLS ARE...
BUT I...
...LIKE YOU.

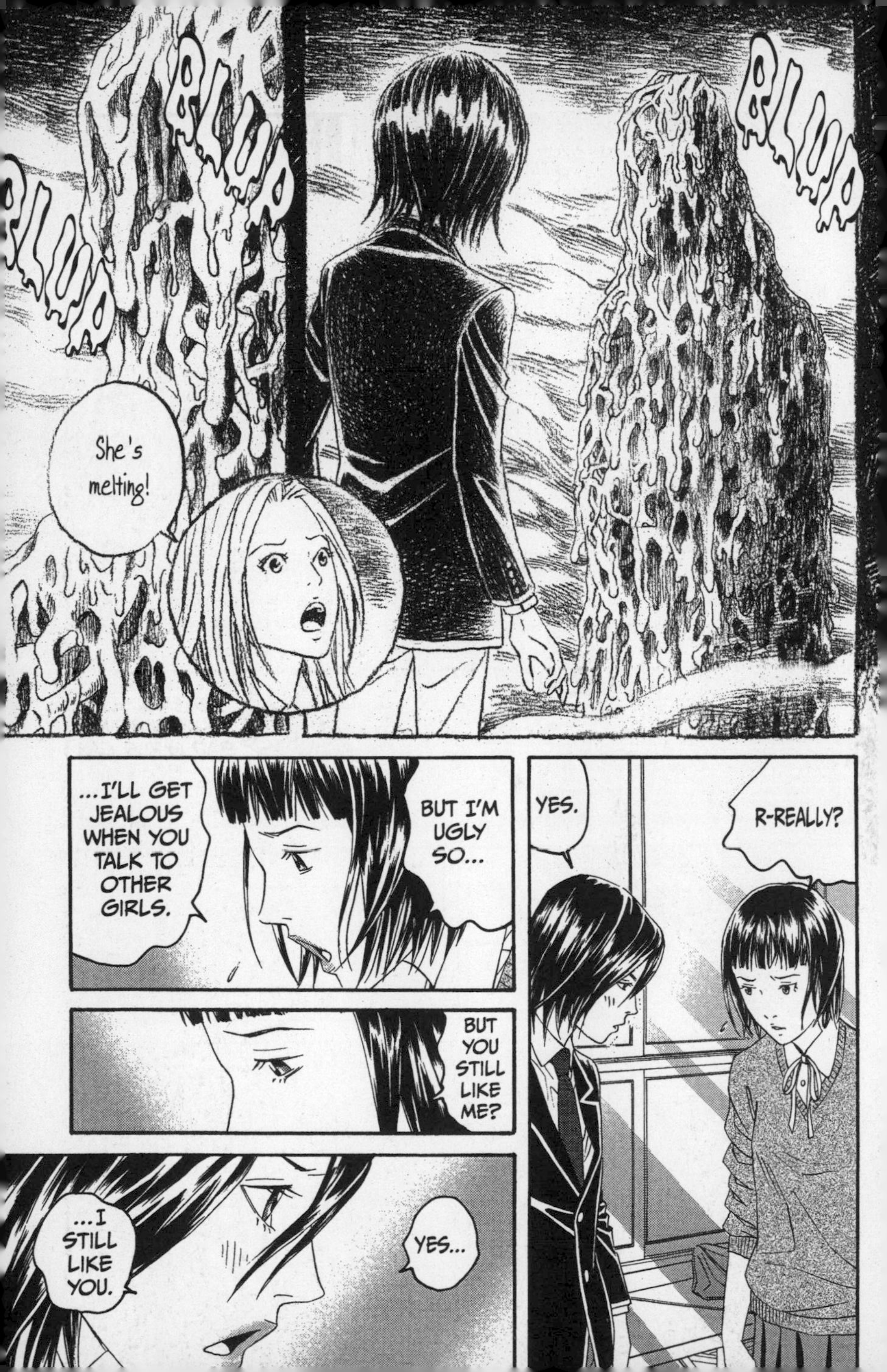
BLUUP
BLUUP
BLUUP
She's melting!
R-REALLY?
YES.
BUT I'M UGLY SO...
...I'LL GET JEALOUS WHEN YOU TALK TO OTHER GIRLS.
BUT YOU STILL LIKE ME?
YES...
...I STILL LIKE YOU.

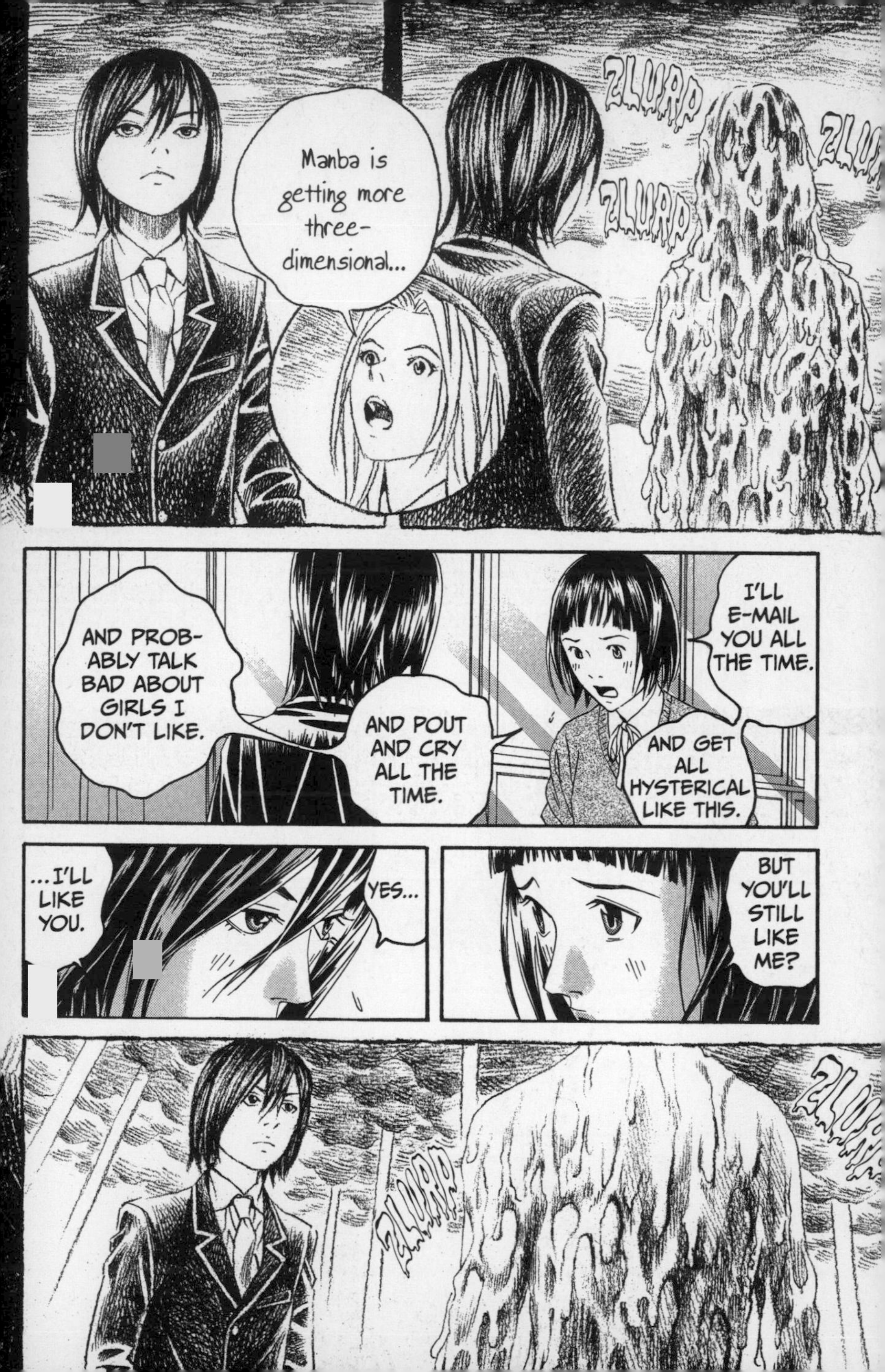
ZLURP
ZLURP
Manba is getting more three-dimensional...
I'LL E-MAIL YOU ALL THE TIME.
AND GET ALL HYSTERICAL LIKE THIS.
AND POUT AND CRY ALL THE TIME.
AND PROB-ABLY TALK BAD ABOUT GIRLS I DON'T LIKE.
BUT YOU'LL STILL LIKE ME?
YES...
...I'LL LIKE YOU.
ZLURP

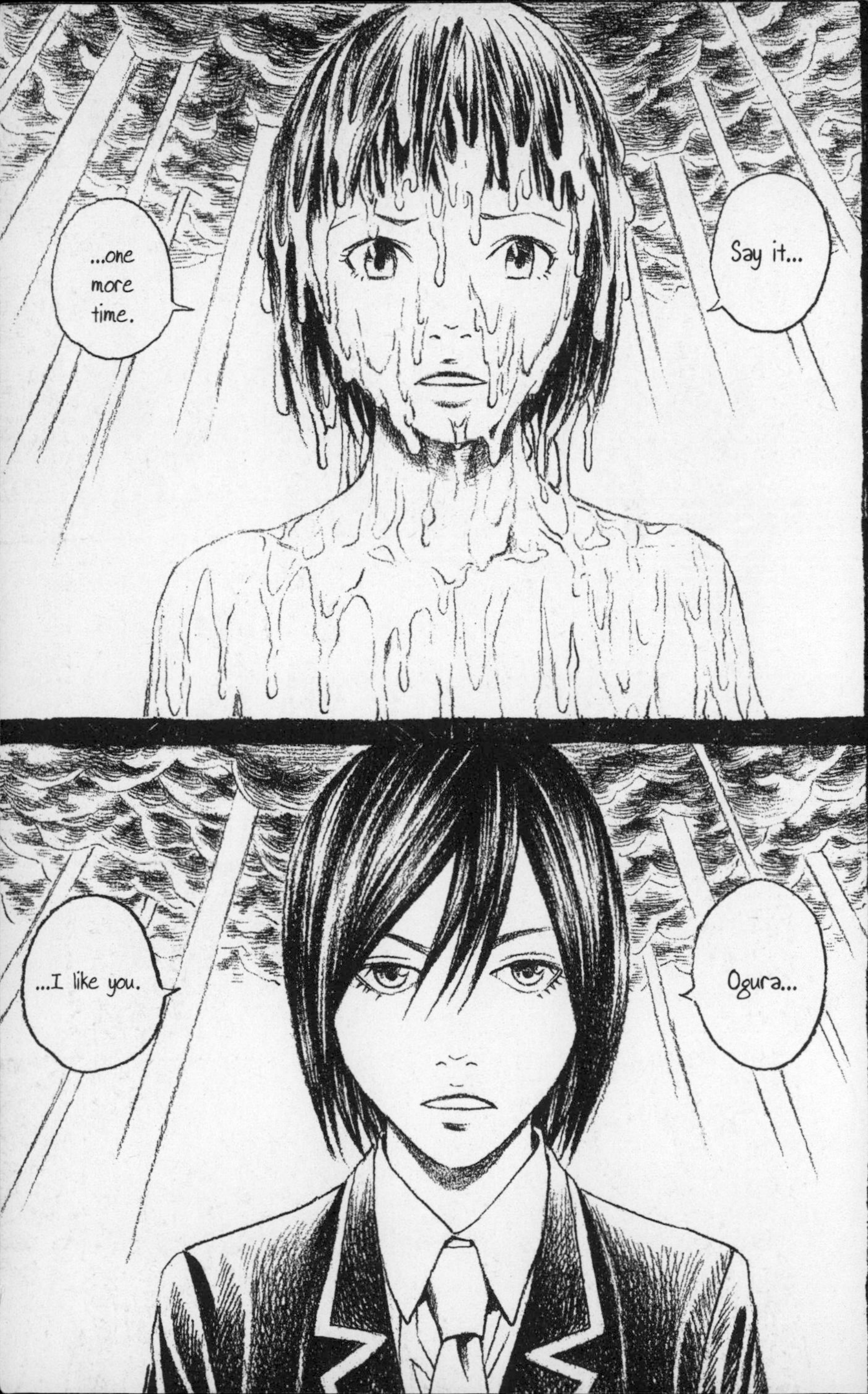
Say it...
...one more time.
Ogura...
...I like you.

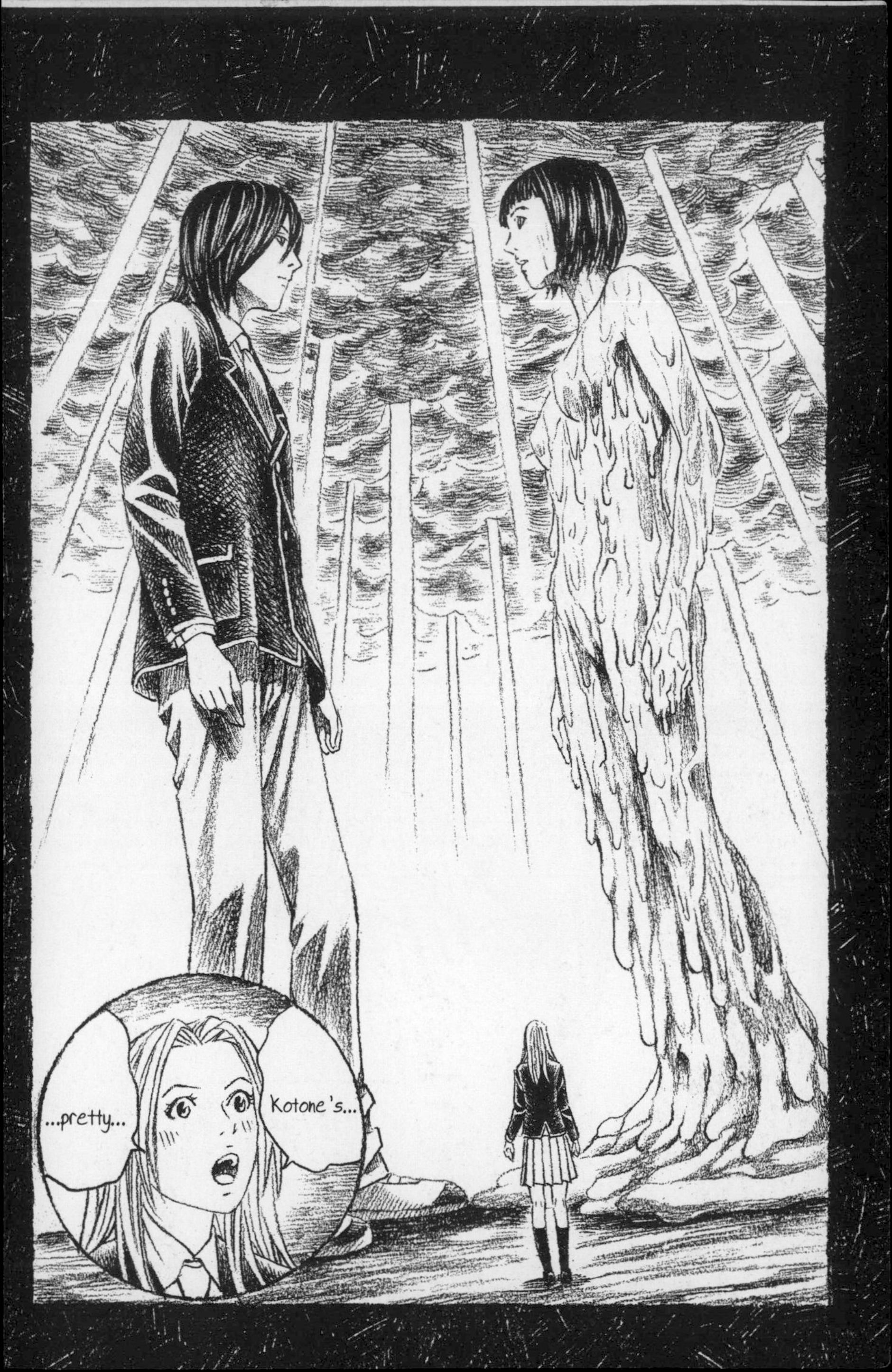
Kotone's...
...pretty...

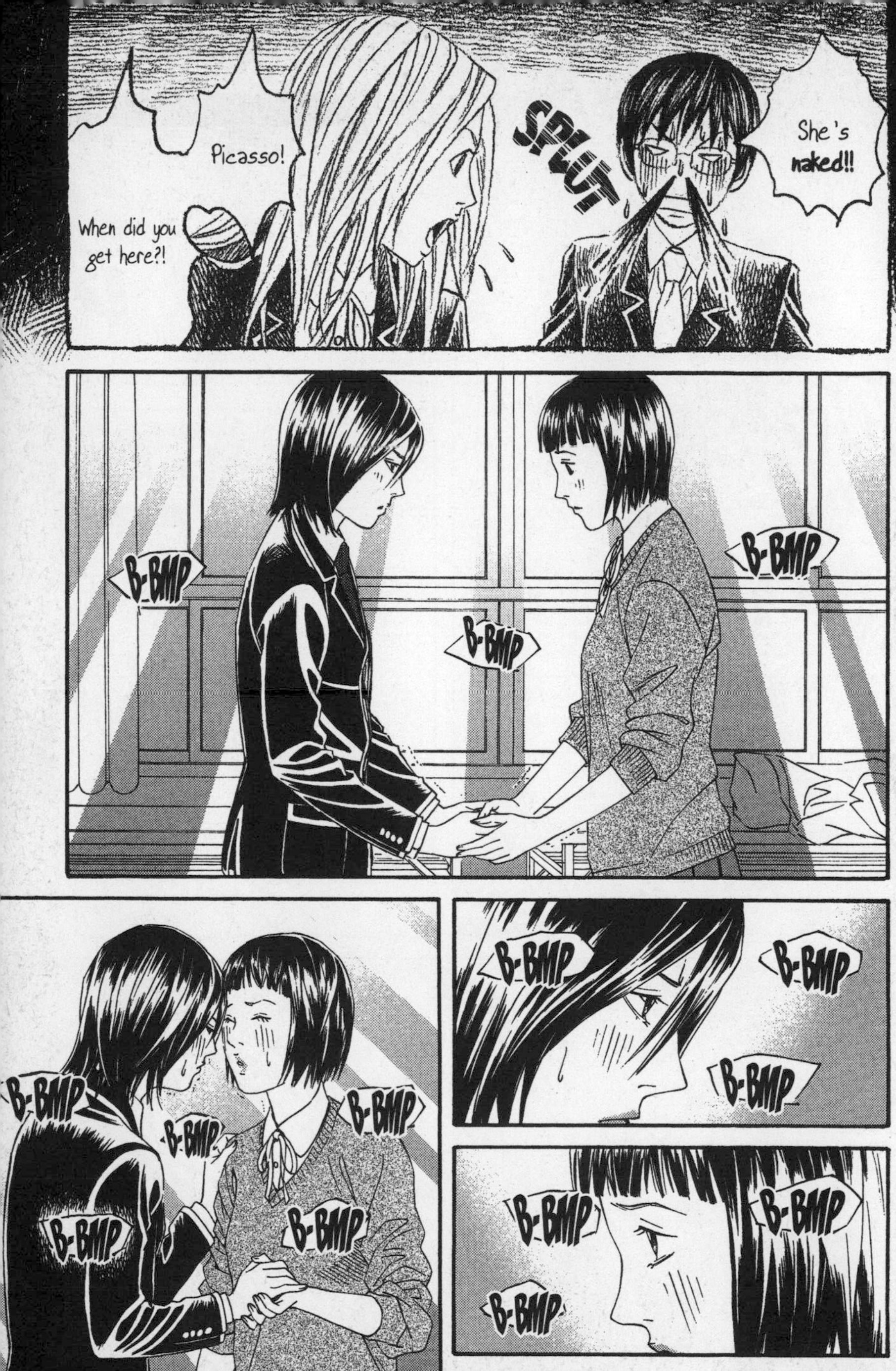
She's **naked!!**
SPLUT
Picasso!
When did you get here?!
B-BMP
B-BMP
B-BMP
B-BMP
B-BMP
B-BMP
B-BMP
B-BMP
B-BMP
B-BMP
B-BMP
B-BMP
B-BMP
B-BMP

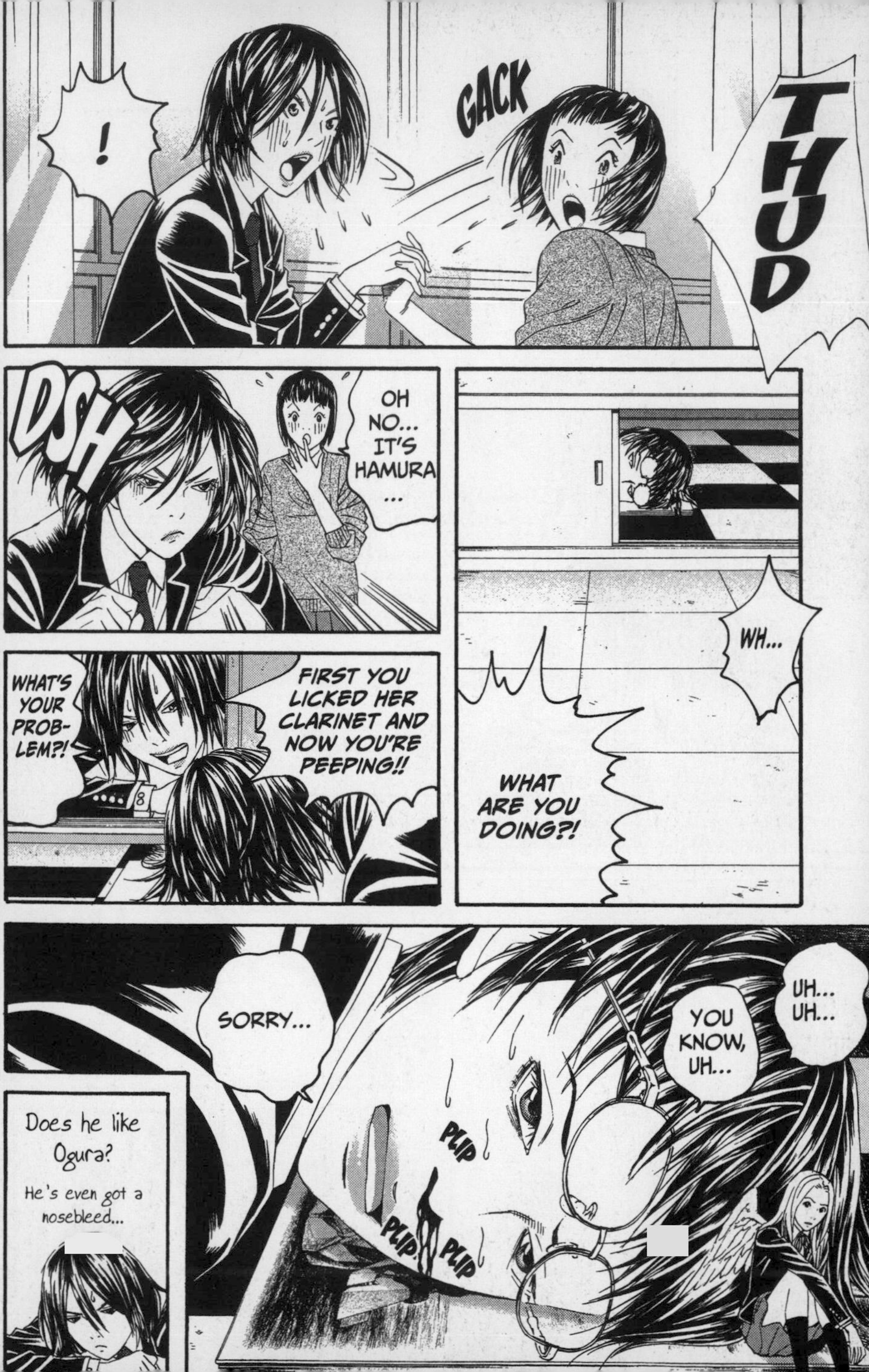
THUD
GACK
!
WH...
WHAT ARE YOU DOING?!
OH NO... IT'S HAMURA ...
DSH
FIRST YOU LICKED HER CLARINET AND NOW YOU'RE PEEPING!!
WHAT'S YOUR PROB-LEM?!
UH... UH...
YOU KNOW, UH...
SORRY...
PLIP
PLIP
PLIP
Does he like Ogura?
He's even got a nosebleed...

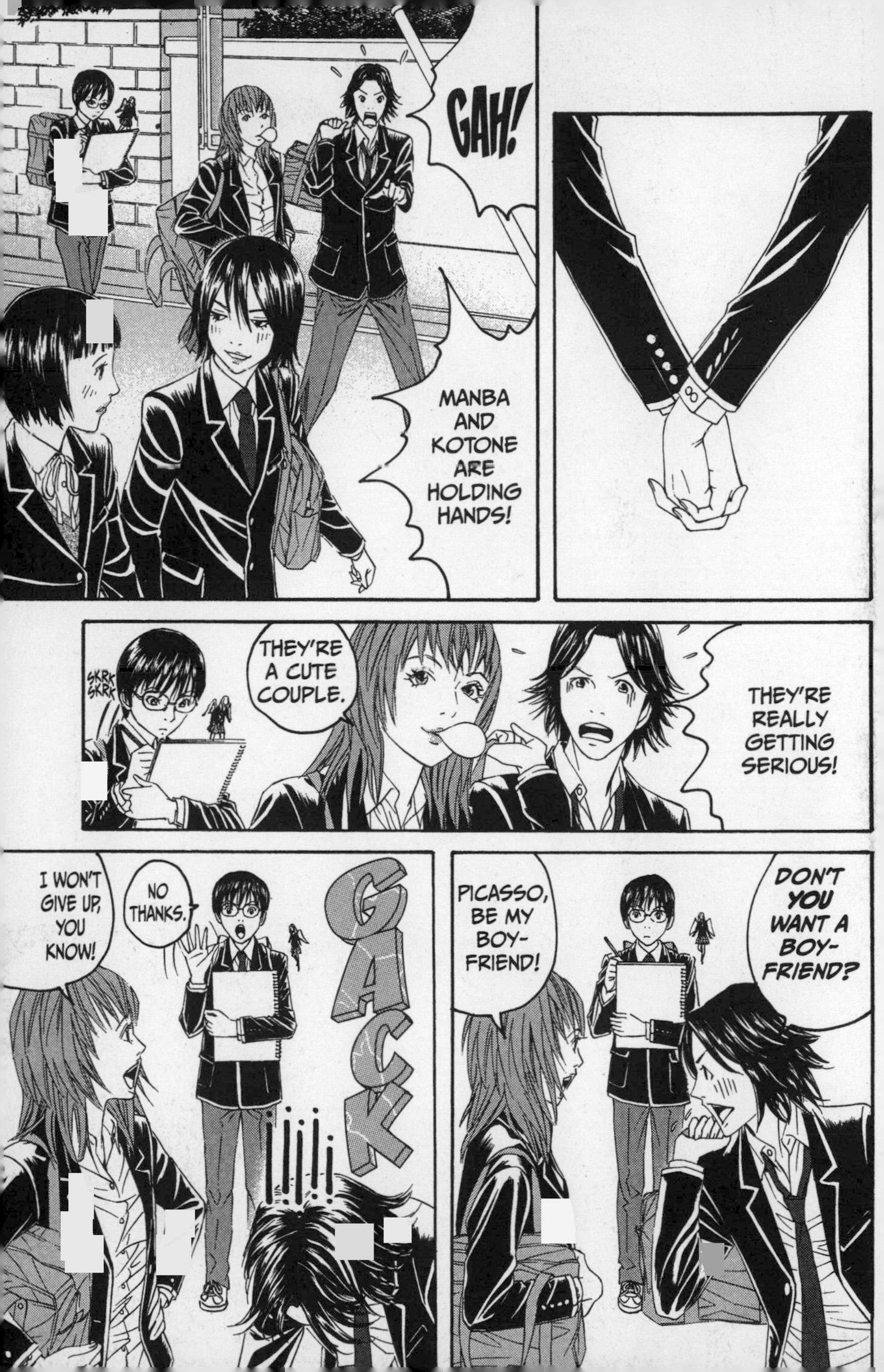
GAH!
MANBA AND KOTONE ARE HOLDING HANDS!
THEY'RE REALLY GETTING SERIOUS!
THEY'RE A CUTE COUPLE.
SKRK SKRK
DON'T YOU WANT A BOY-FRIEND?
PICASSO, BE MY BOY-FRIEND!
GACK
NO THANKS.
I WON'T GIVE UP, YOU KNOW!

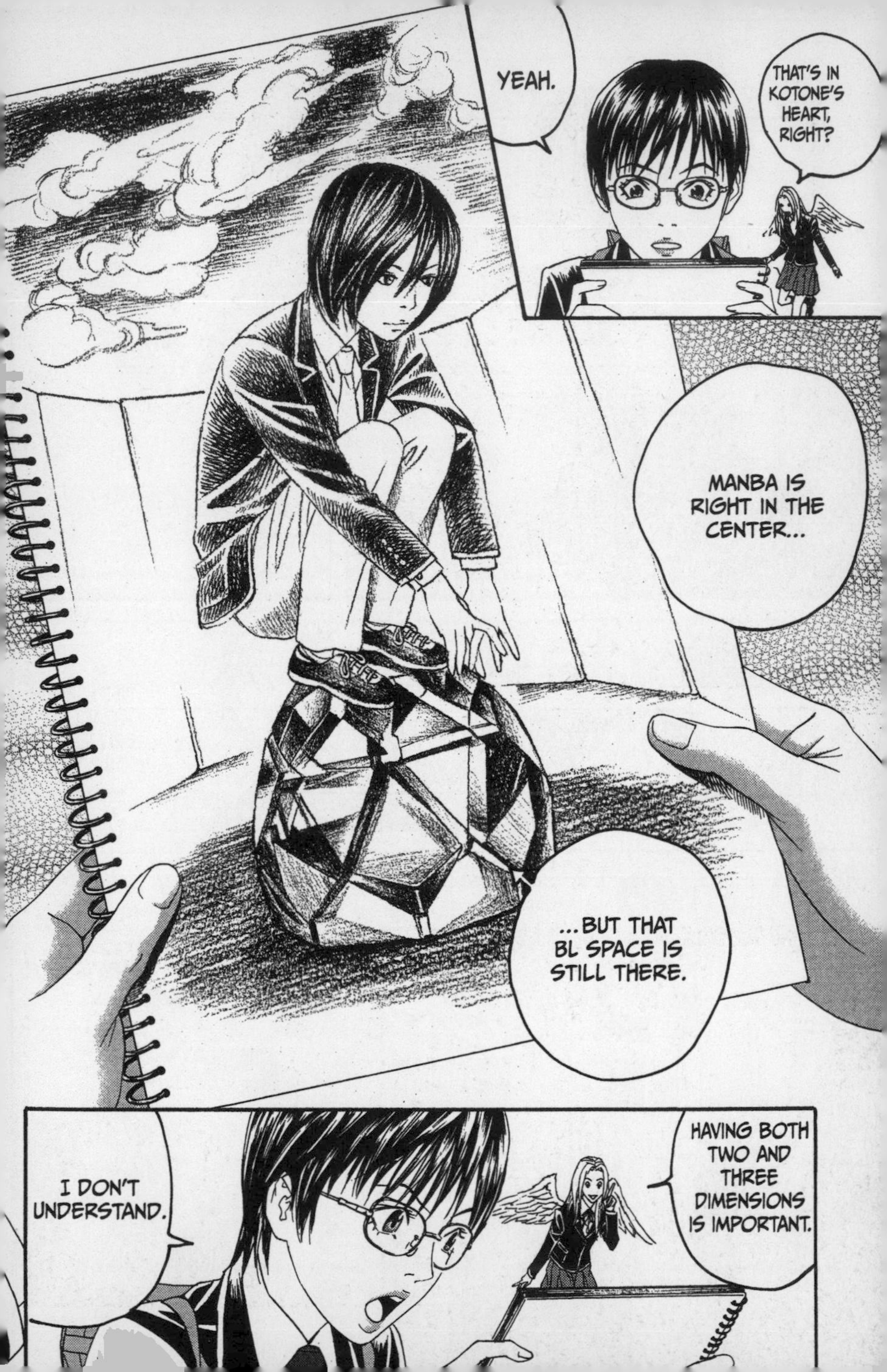
THAT'S IN KOTONE'S HEART, RIGHT?
YEAH.
MANBA IS RIGHT IN THE CENTER...
...BUT THAT BL SPACE IS STILL THERE.
HAVING BOTH TWO AND THREE DIMENSIONS IS IMPORTANT.
I DON'T UNDERSTAND.

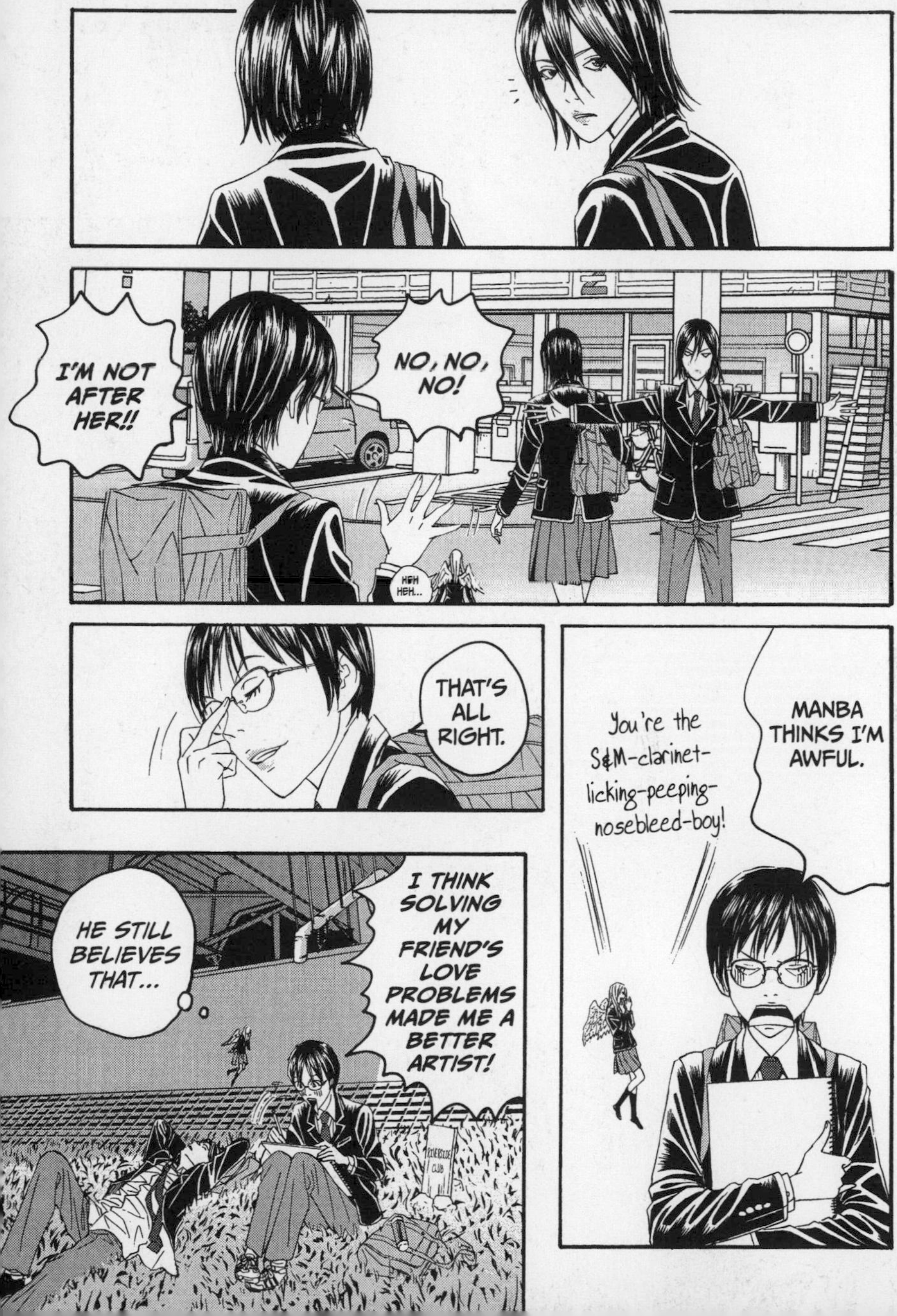
NO, NO, NO!
I'M NOT AFTER HER!!
HEH HEH...
MANBA THINKS I'M AWFUL.
You're the S&M-clarinet-licking-peeping-nosebleed-boy!
THAT'S ALL RIGHT.
I THINK SOLVING MY FRIEND'S LOVE PROBLEMS MADE ME A BETTER ARTIST!
HE STILL BELIEVES THAT...

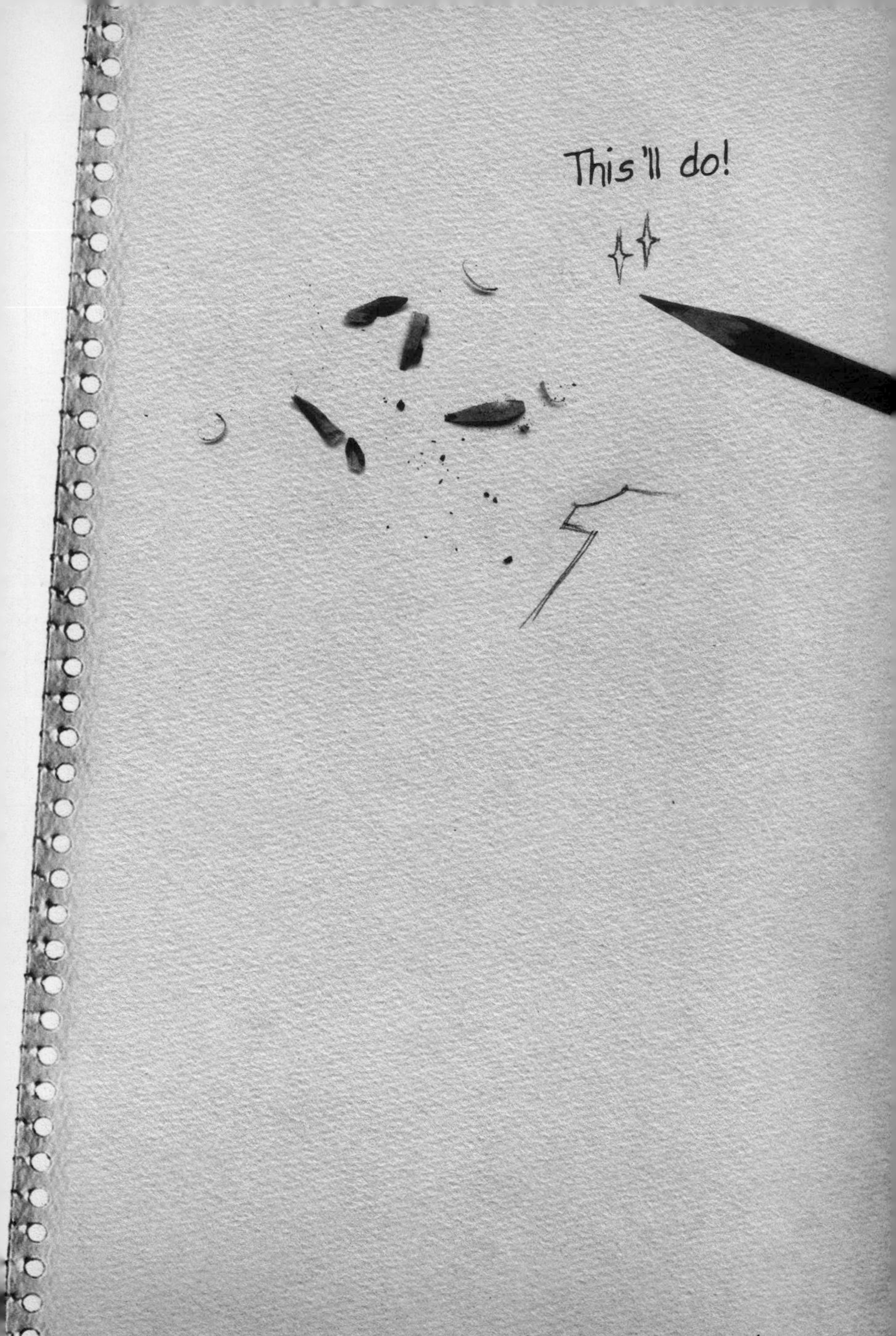
This'll do!

Vision6: Kotone and Arengurion (Part 2)_Jump SQ, April 2009

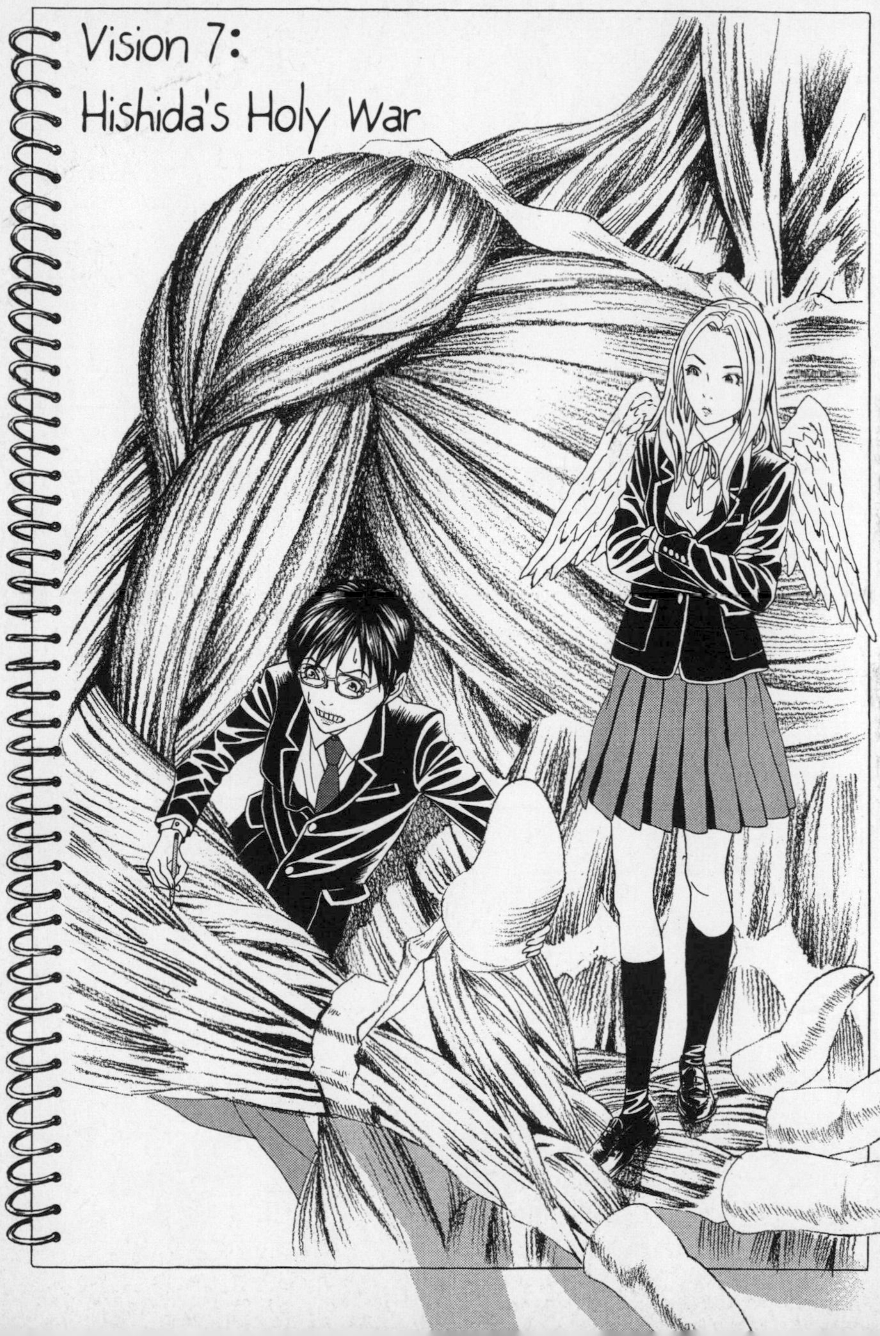
Vision 7:
Hishida's Holy War

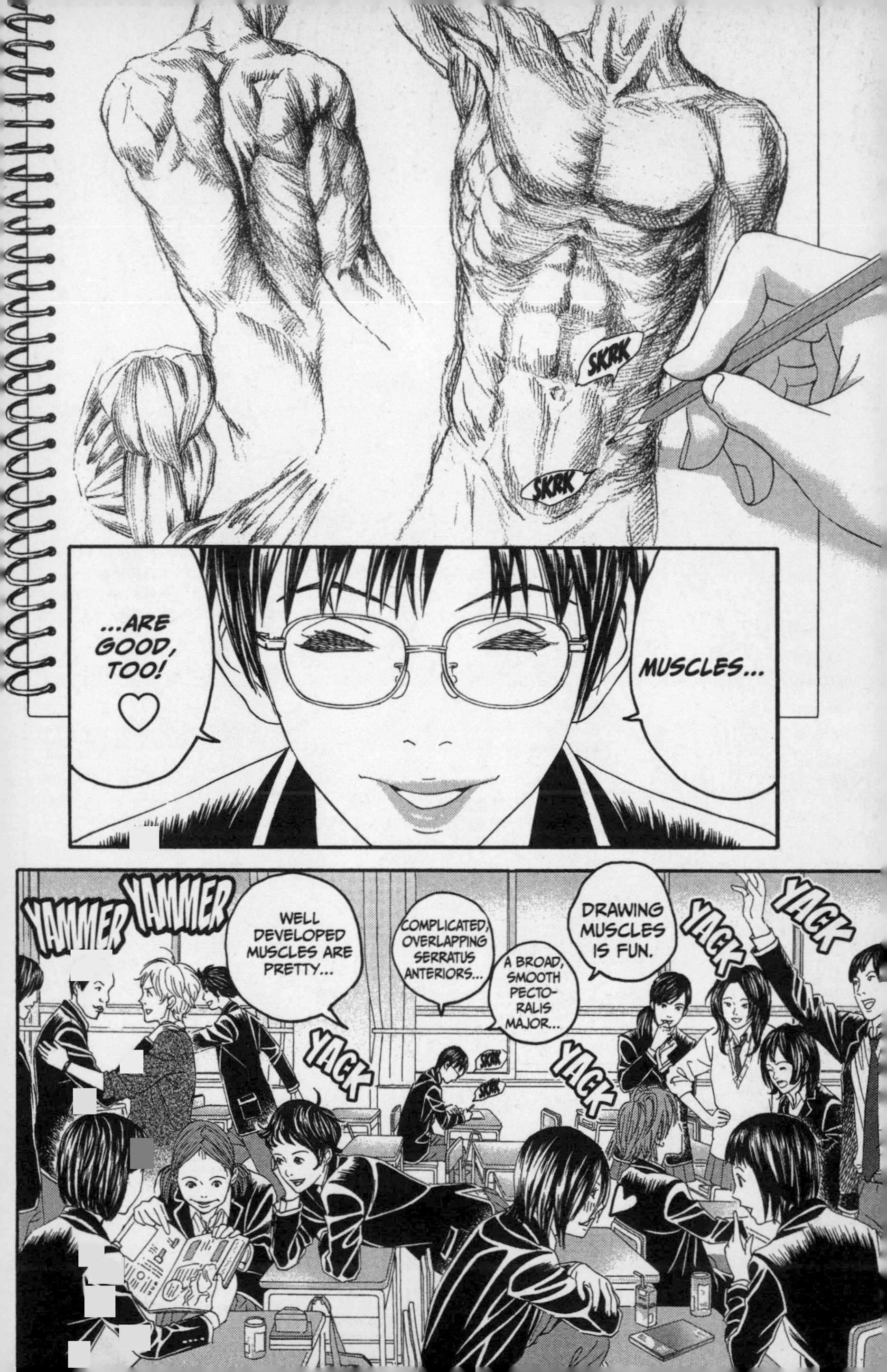
SKRK
SKRK
MUSCLES...
...ARE GOOD, TOO! ♥
YACK
YACK
DRAWING MUSCLES IS FUN.
A BROAD, SMOOTH PECTO-RALIS MAJOR...
COMPLICATED, OVERLAPPING SERRATUS ANTERIORS...
YACK
WELL DEVELOPED MUSCLES ARE PRETTY...
SKRK
SKRK
YACK
YAMMER
YAMMER

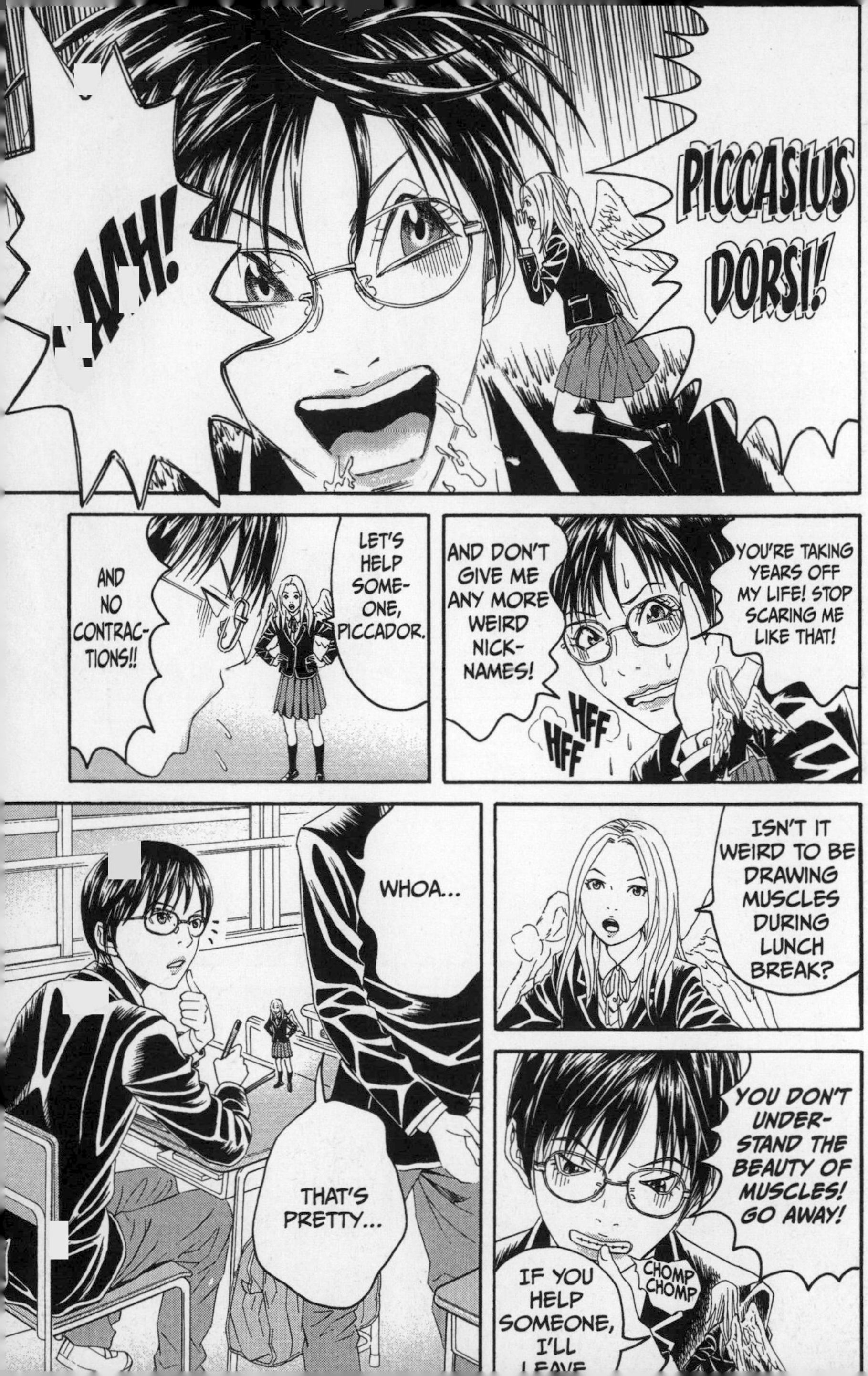
PICCASIUS DORSI!
AAH!
YOU'RE TAKING YEARS OFF MY LIFE! STOP SCARING ME LIKE THAT!
AND DON'T GIVE ME ANY MORE WEIRD NICK-NAMES!
HFF HFF
LET'S HELP SOME-ONE, PICCADOR.
AND NO CONTRAC-TIONS!!
ISN'T IT WEIRD TO BE DRAWING MUSCLES DURING LUNCH BREAK?
YOU DON'T UNDER-STAND THE BEAUTY OF MUSCLES! GO AWAY!
CHOMP CHOMP
IF YOU HELP SOMEONE, I'LL
WHOA...
THAT'S PRETTY...

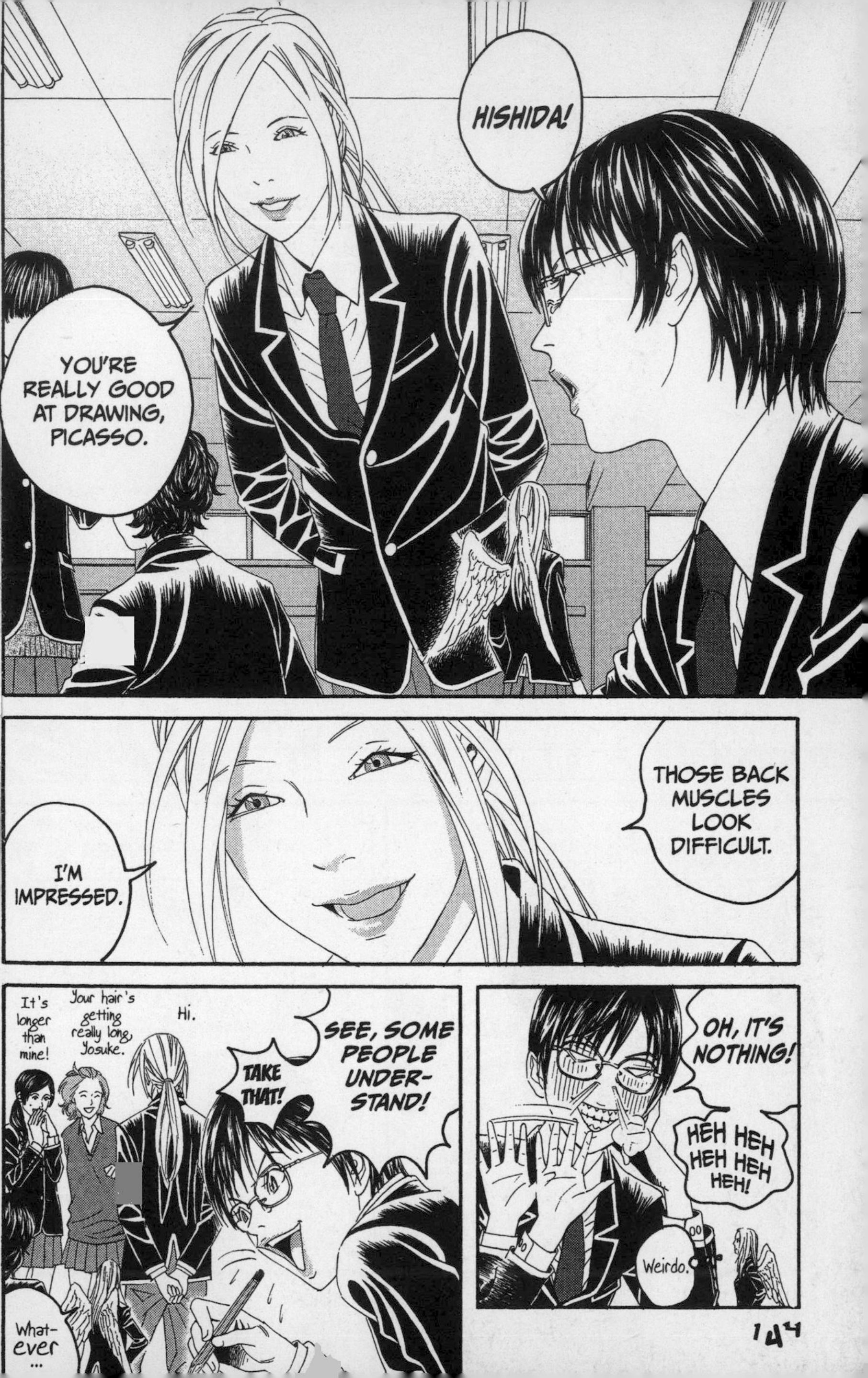
HISHIDA!
YOU'RE REALLY GOOD AT DRAWING, PICASSO.
THOSE BACK MUSCLES LOOK DIFFICULT.
I'M IMPRESSED.
OH, IT'S NOTHING!
HEH HEH HEH HEH HEH!
Weirdo.
SEE, SOME PEOPLE UNDER-STAND!
TAKE THAT!
Hi.
Your hair's getting really long, Yosuke.
It's longer than mine!
What-ever...

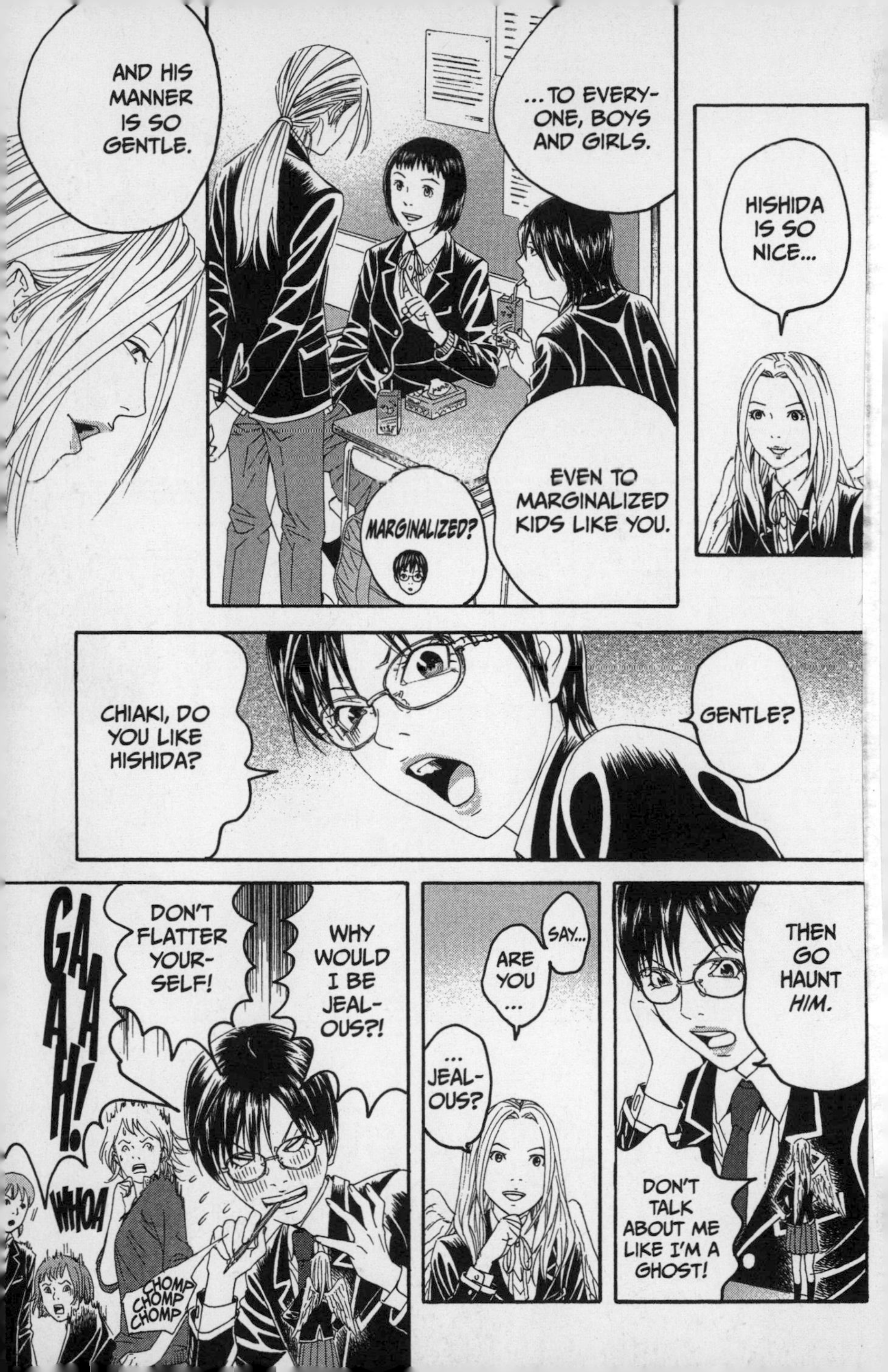
HISHIDA IS SO NICE...
...TO EVERY-ONE, BOYS AND GIRLS.
EVEN TO MARGINALIZED KIDS LIKE YOU.
MARGINALIZED?
AND HIS MANNER IS SO GENTLE.
GENTLE?
CHIAKI, DO YOU LIKE HISHIDA?
THEN GO HAUNT *HIM.*
DON'T TALK ABOUT ME LIKE I'M A GHOST!
SAY...
ARE YOU ...
... JEAL-OUS?
WHY WOULD I BE JEAL-OUS?!
DON'T FLATTER YOUR-SELF!
GAAAH!
WHOA
CHOMP CHOMP CHOMP

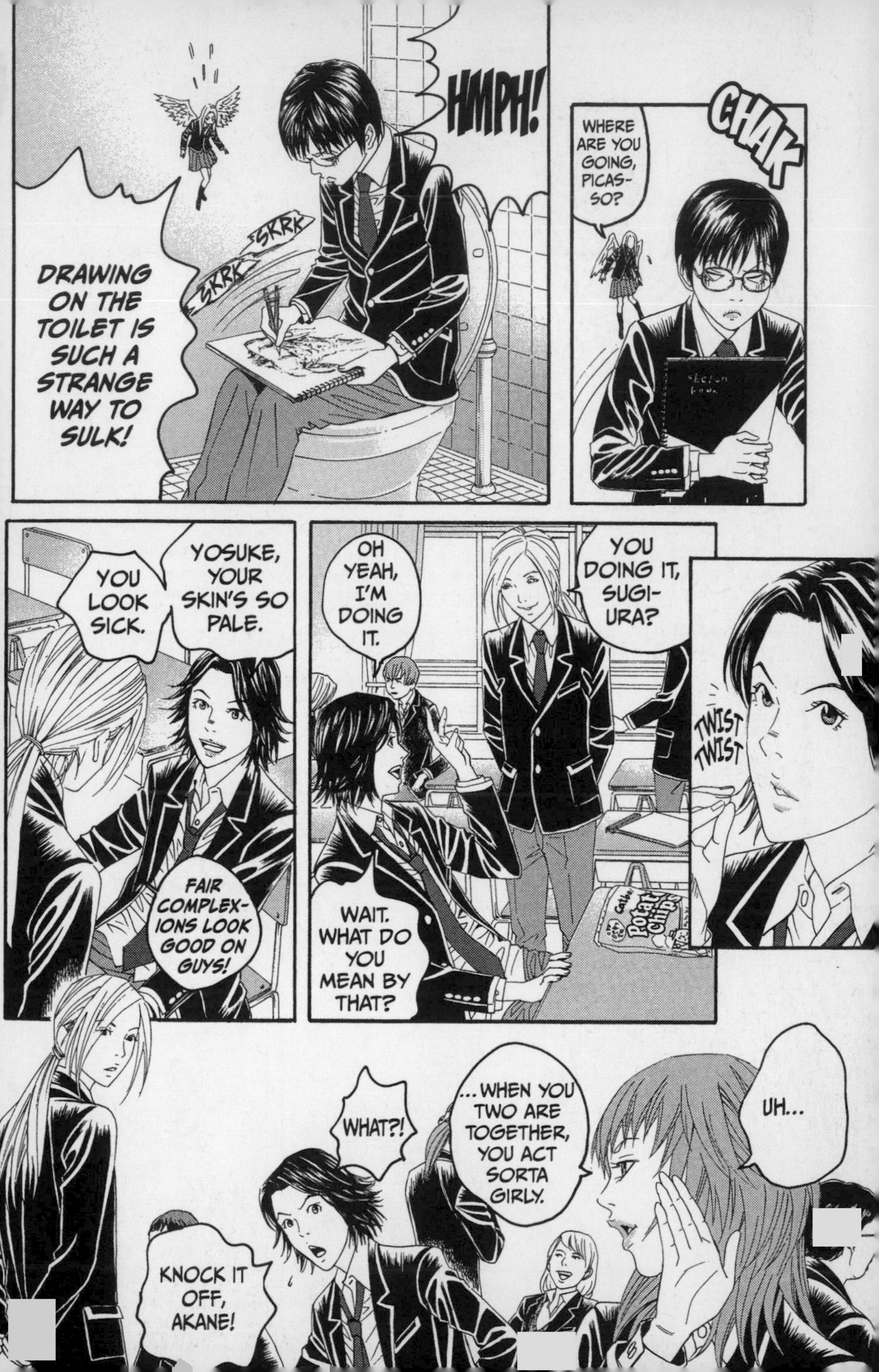
CHAK
WHERE ARE YOU GOING, PICAS-SO?
HMPH!
SKRK
SKRK
DRAWING ON THE TOILET IS SUCH A STRANGE WAY TO SULK!
TWIST TWIST
YOU DOING IT, SUGI-URA?
OH YEAH, I'M DOING IT.
WAIT. WHAT DO YOU MEAN BY THAT?
YOSUKE, YOUR SKIN'S SO PALE.
YOU LOOK SICK.
FAIR COMPLEX-IONS LOOK GOOD ON GUYS!
UH...
...WHEN YOU TWO ARE TOGETHER, YOU ACT SORTA GIRLY.
WHAT?!
KNOCK IT OFF, AKANE!

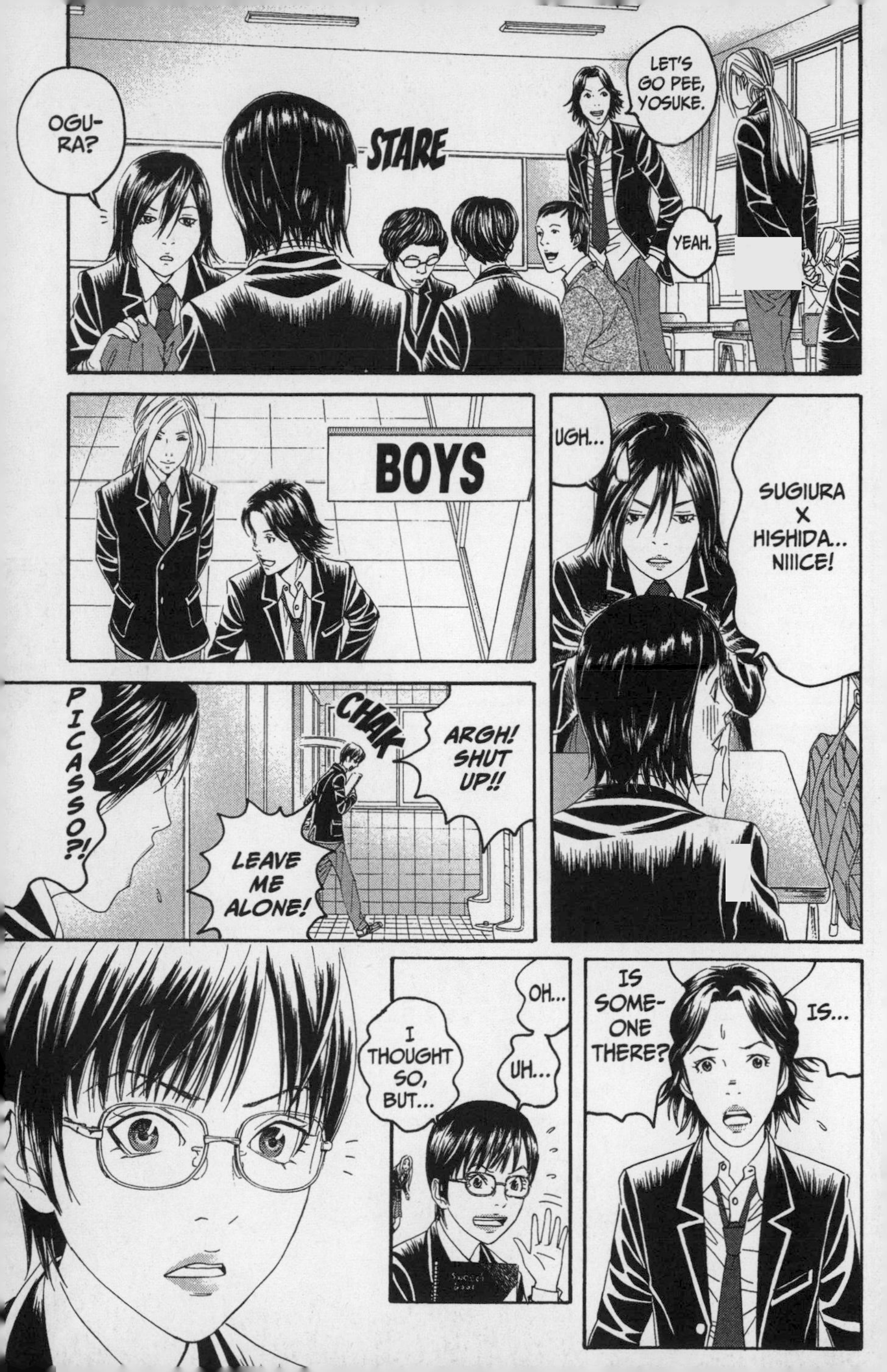
LET'S GO PEE, YOSUKE.
YEAH.
STARE
OGU-RA?
SUGIURA X HISHIDA... NIIICE!
UGH...
BOYS
ARGH! SHUT UP!!
CHAK
LEAVE ME ALONE!
PICASSO?!
IS...
IS SOME-ONE THERE?
OH...
UH...
I THOUGHT SO, BUT...

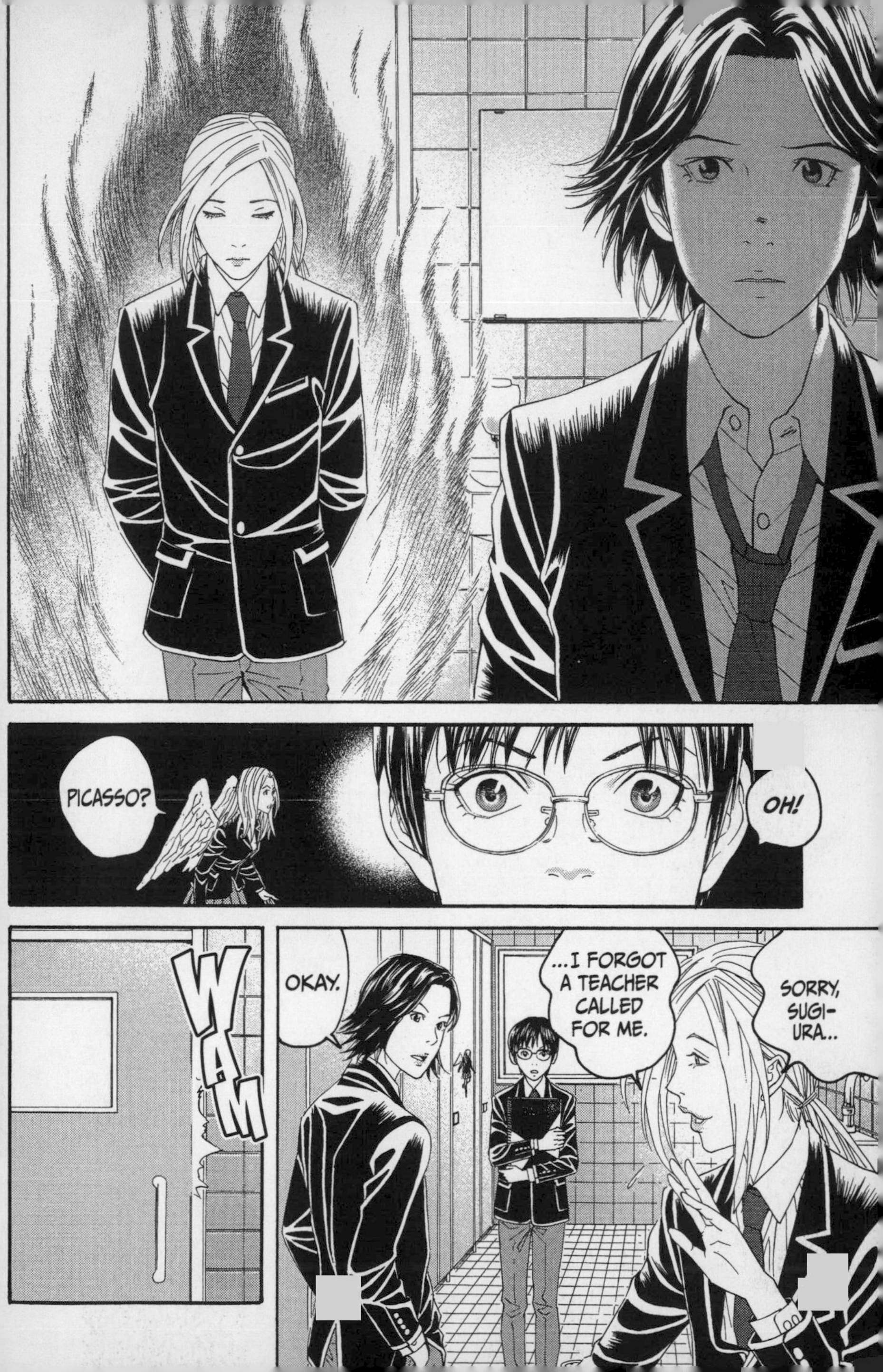
OH!
PICASSO?
SORRY, SUGI-URA...
...I FORGOT A TEACHER CALLED FOR ME.
OKAY.
WAM

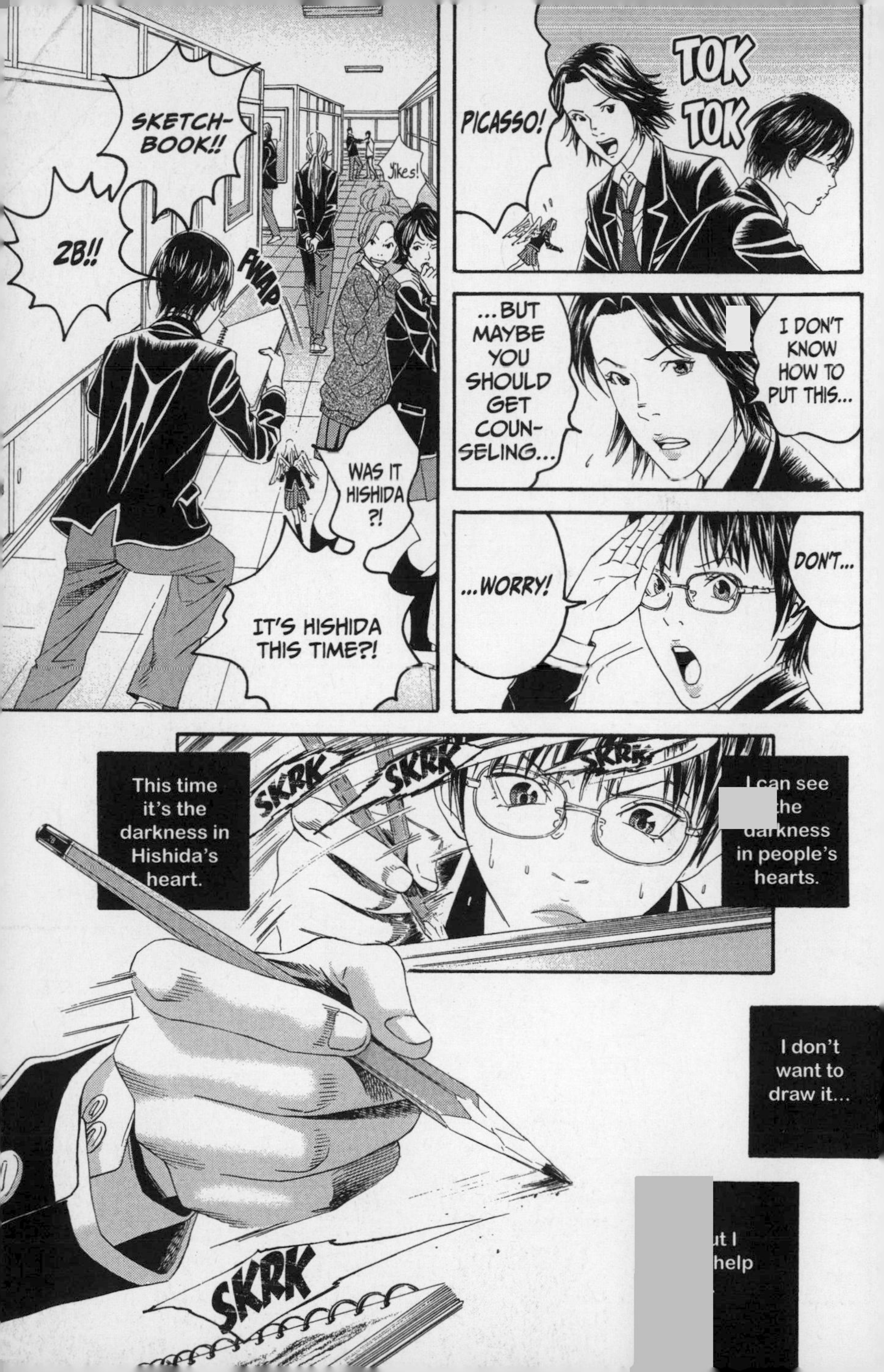
TOK TOK
PICASSO!
I DON'T KNOW HOW TO PUT THIS...
...BUT MAYBE YOU SHOULD GET COUN-SELING...
DON'T...
...WORRY!
SKETCH-BOOK!!
ZB!!
FWAP
Yikes!
WAS IT HISHIDA ?!
IT'S HISHIDA THIS TIME?!
can see the darkness in people's hearts.
SKRK SKRK SKRK
This time it's the darkness in Hishida's heart.
I don't want to draw it...
ut I
help
SKRK

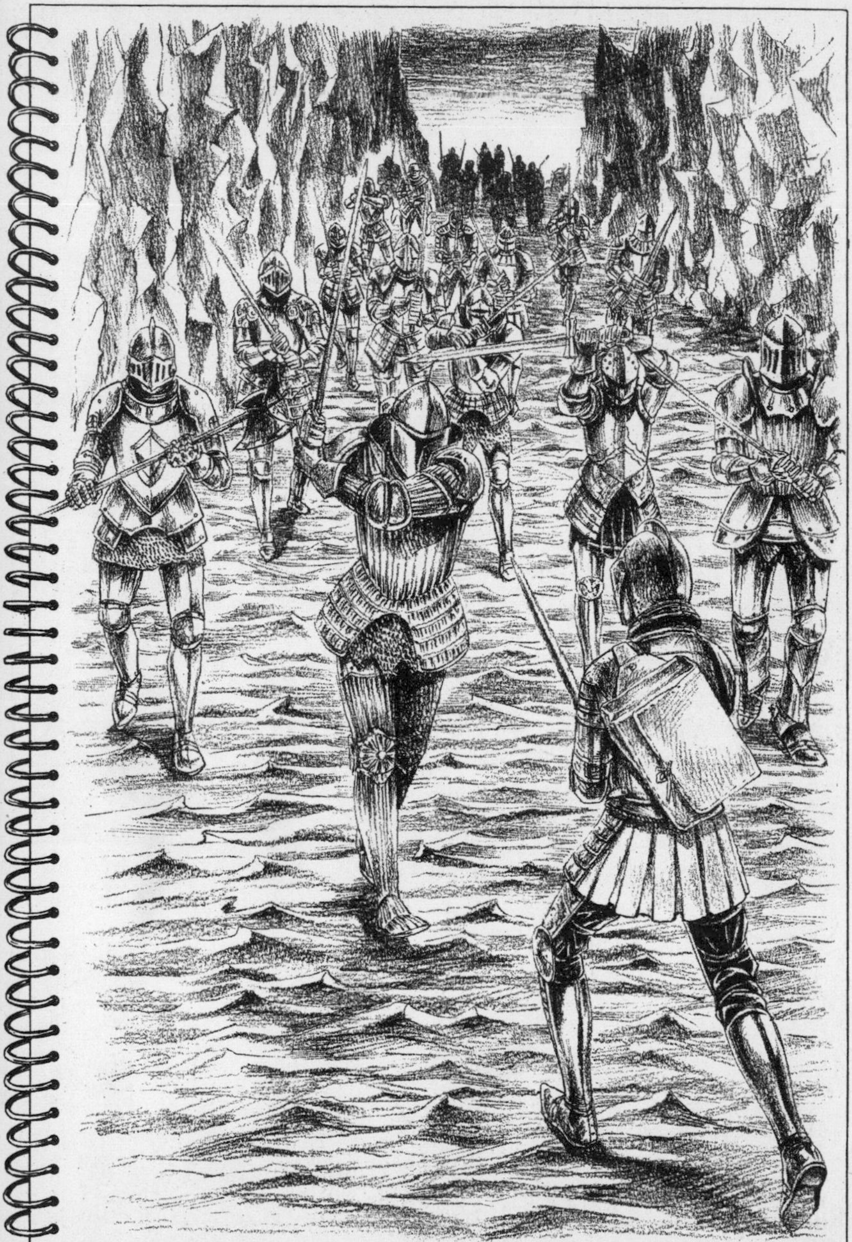

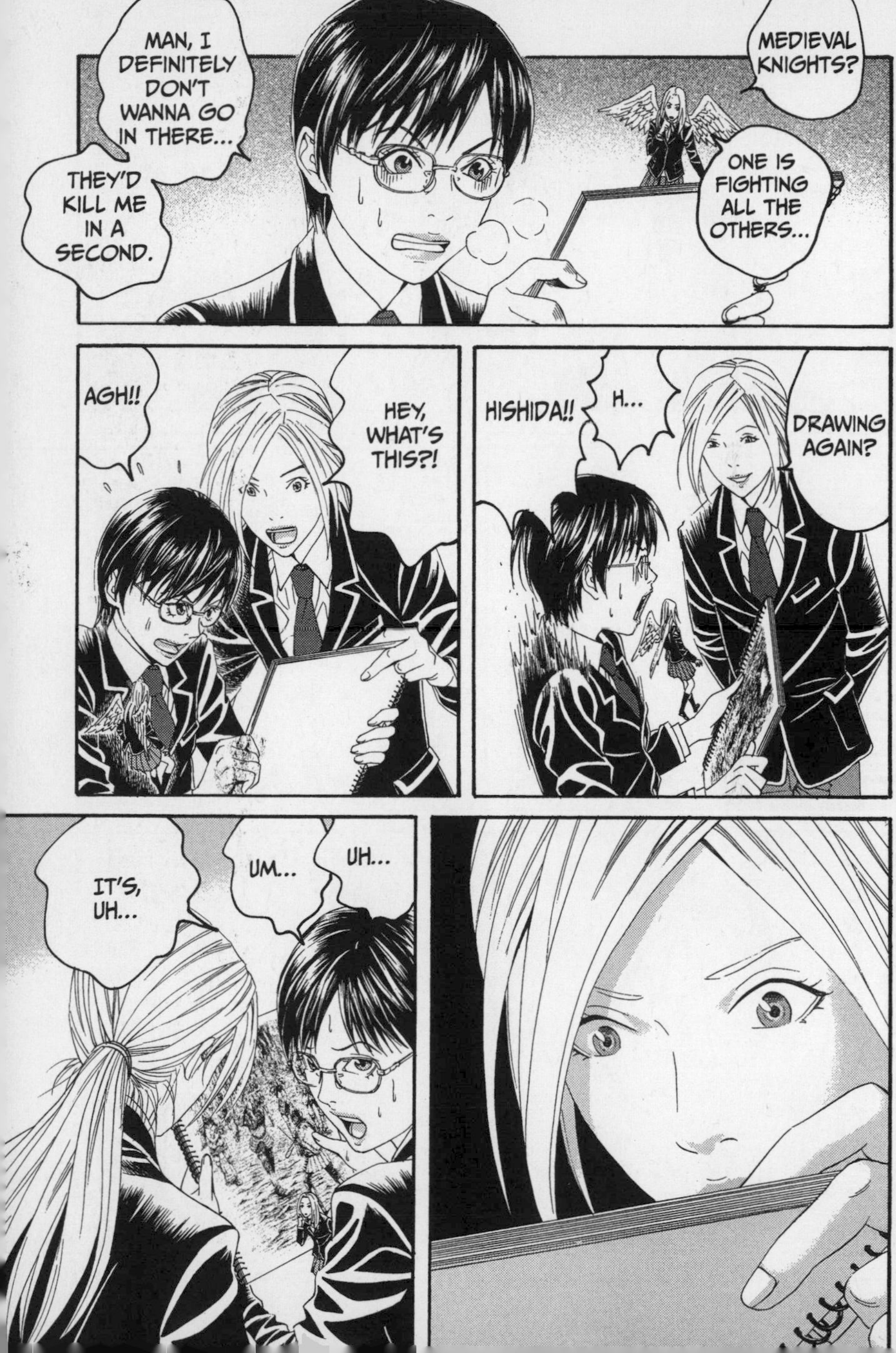
MEDIEVAL KNIGHTS?
ONE IS FIGHTING ALL THE OTHERS...
MAN, I DEFINITELY DON'T WANNA GO IN THERE...
THEY'D KILL ME IN A SECOND.
DRAWING AGAIN?
H...
HISHIDA!!
HEY, WHAT'S THIS?!
AGH!!
UH...
UM...
IT'S, UH...

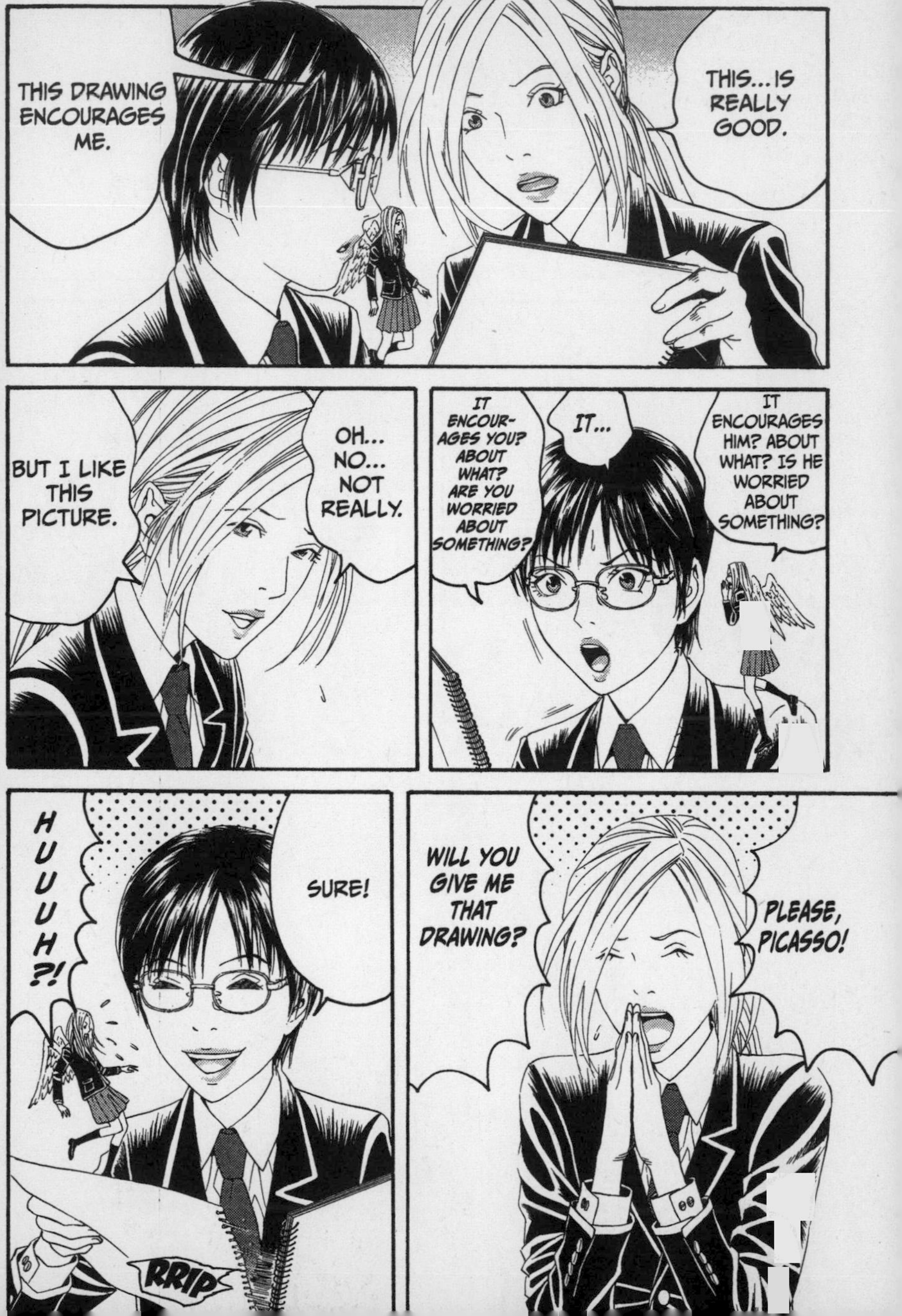
THIS...IS REALLY GOOD.
THIS DRAWING ENCOURAGES ME.
IT ENCOURAGES HIM? ABOUT WHAT? IS HE WORRIED ABOUT SOMETHING?
IT...
IT ENCOUR-AGES YOU? ABOUT WHAT? ARE YOU WORRIED ABOUT SOMETHING?
OH... NO... NOT REALLY.
BUT I LIKE THIS PICTURE.
PLEASE, PICASSO!
WILL YOU GIVE ME THAT DRAWING?
SURE!
HUUUUH?!
RRIP

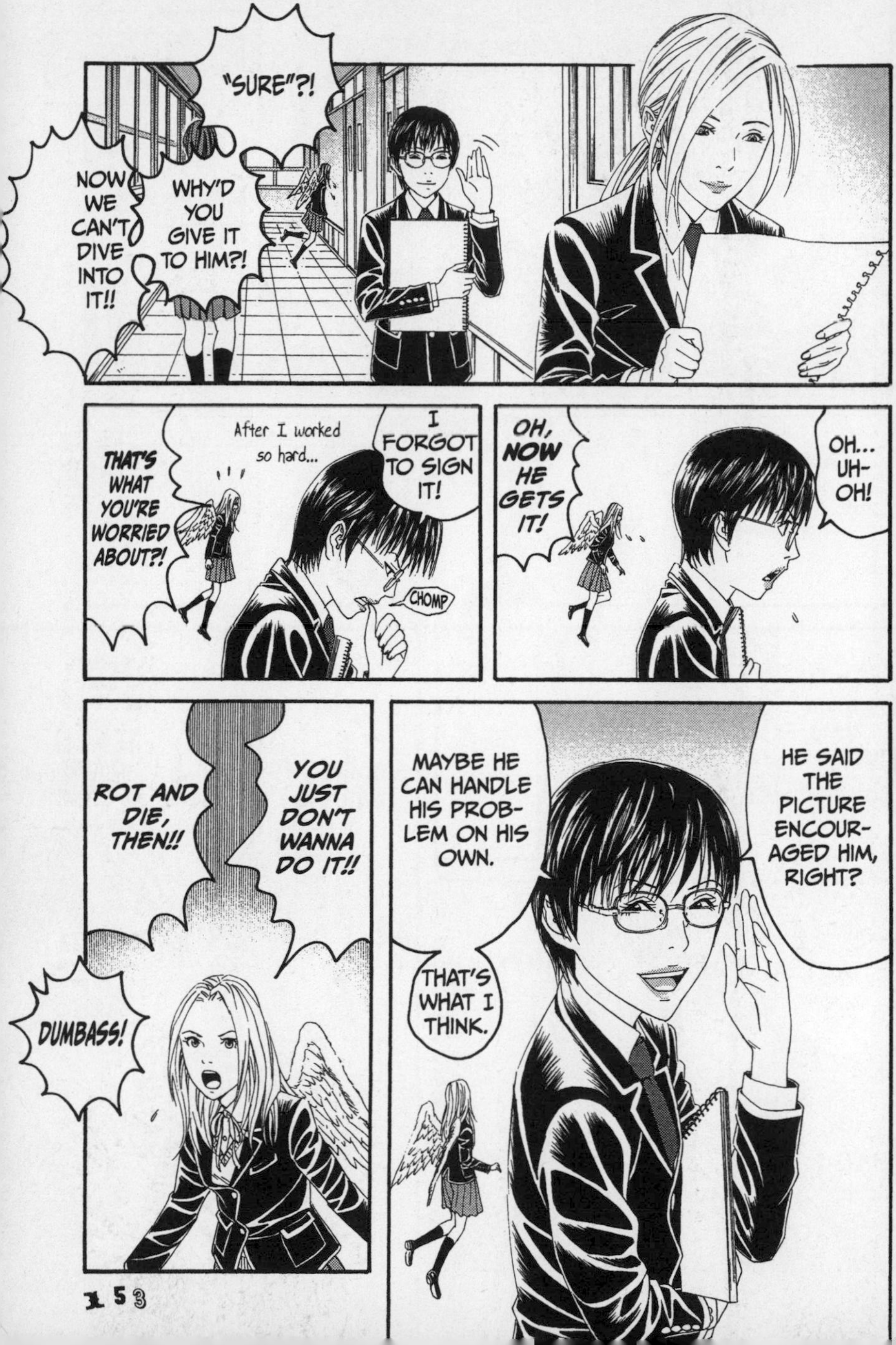
"SURE"?!
WHY'D YOU GIVE IT TO HIM?!
NOW WE CAN'T DIVE INTO IT!!
OH... UH-OH!
OH, NOW HE GETS IT!
I FORGOT TO SIGN IT!
CHOMP
After I worked so hard...
THAT'S WHAT YOU'RE WORRIED ABOUT?!
HE SAID THE PICTURE ENCOURAGED HIM, RIGHT?
MAYBE HE CAN HANDLE HIS PROBLEM ON HIS OWN.
THAT'S WHAT I THINK.
YOU JUST DON'T WANNA DO IT!!
ROT AND DIE, THEN!!
DUMBASS!

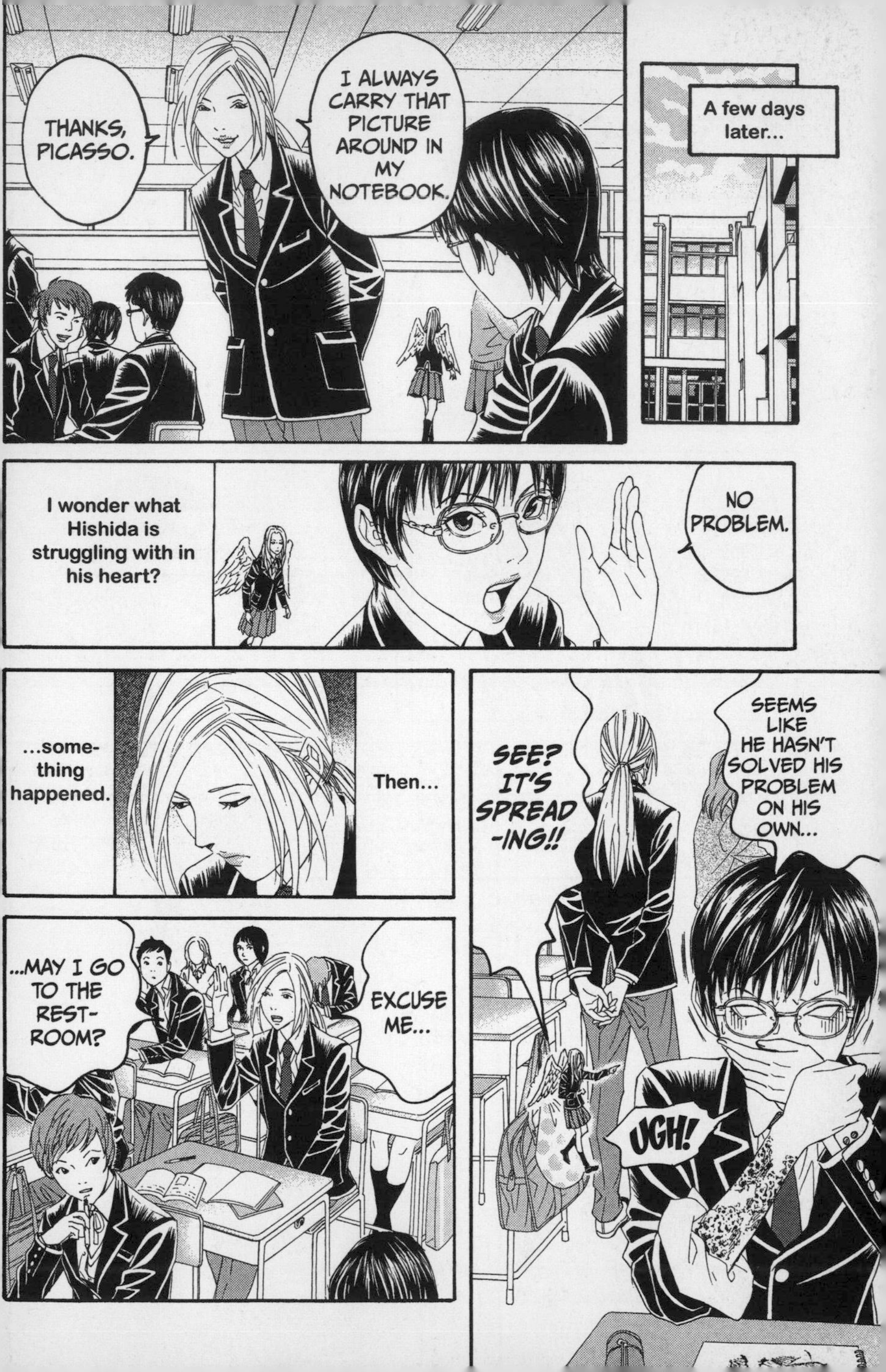
A few days later...
I ALWAYS CARRY THAT PICTURE AROUND IN MY NOTEBOOK.
THANKS, PICASSO.
NO PROBLEM.
I wonder what Hishida is struggling with in his heart?
SEEMS LIKE HE HASN'T SOLVED HIS PROBLEM ON HIS OWN...
SEE? IT'S SPREAD-ING!!
UGH!
Then...
...some-thing happened.
EXCUSE ME...
...MAY I GO TO THE REST-ROOM?

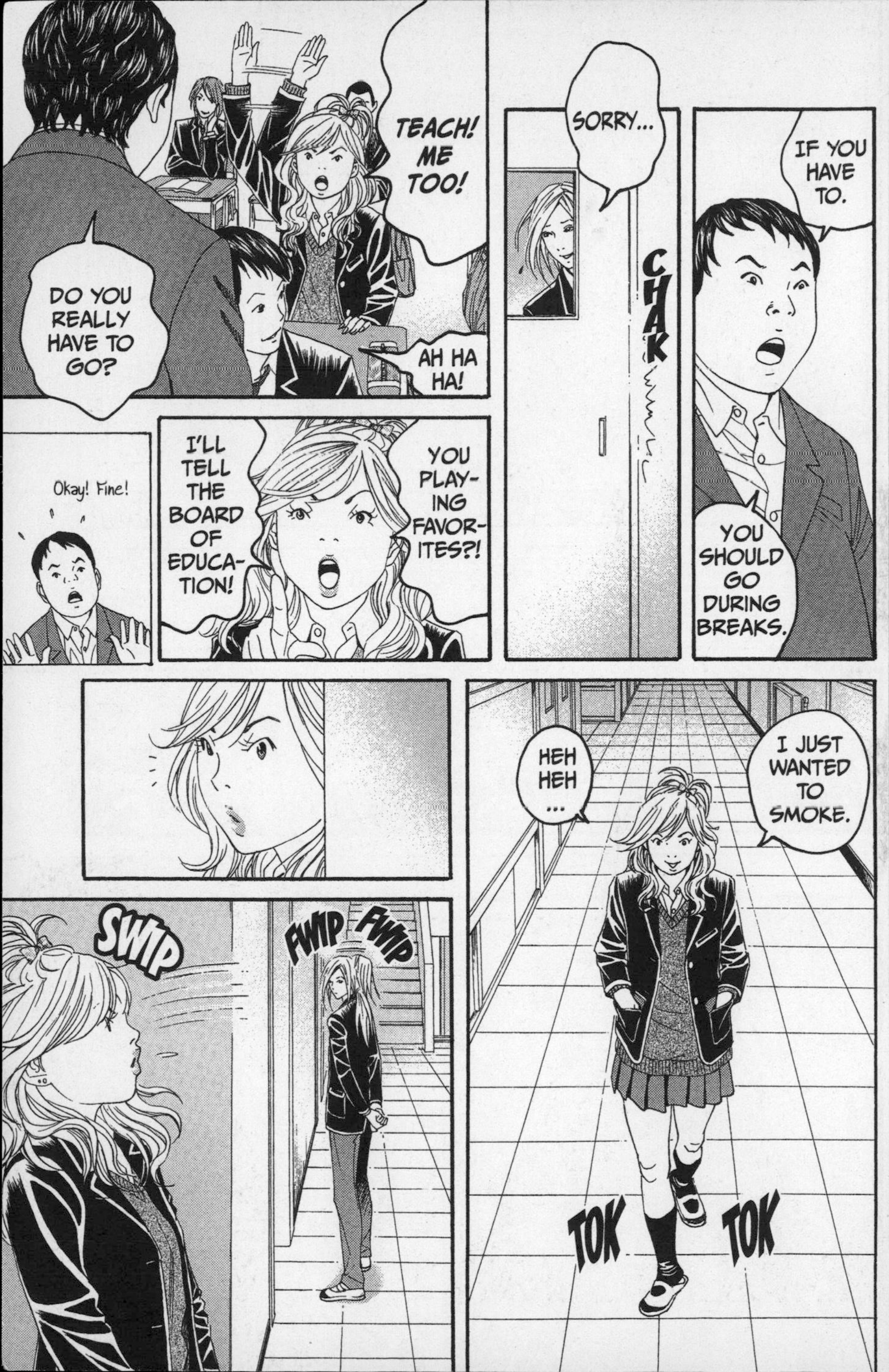
IF YOU HAVE TO.
YOU SHOULD GO DURING BREAKS.
SORRY...
CHAK
TEACH! ME TOO!
AH HA HA!
DO YOU REALLY HAVE TO GO?
YOU PLAYING FAVORITES?!
I'LL TELL THE BOARD OF EDUCATION!
Okay! Fine!
I JUST WANTED TO SMOKE.
HEH HEH ...
TOK
TOK
SWIP
FWIP FWIP

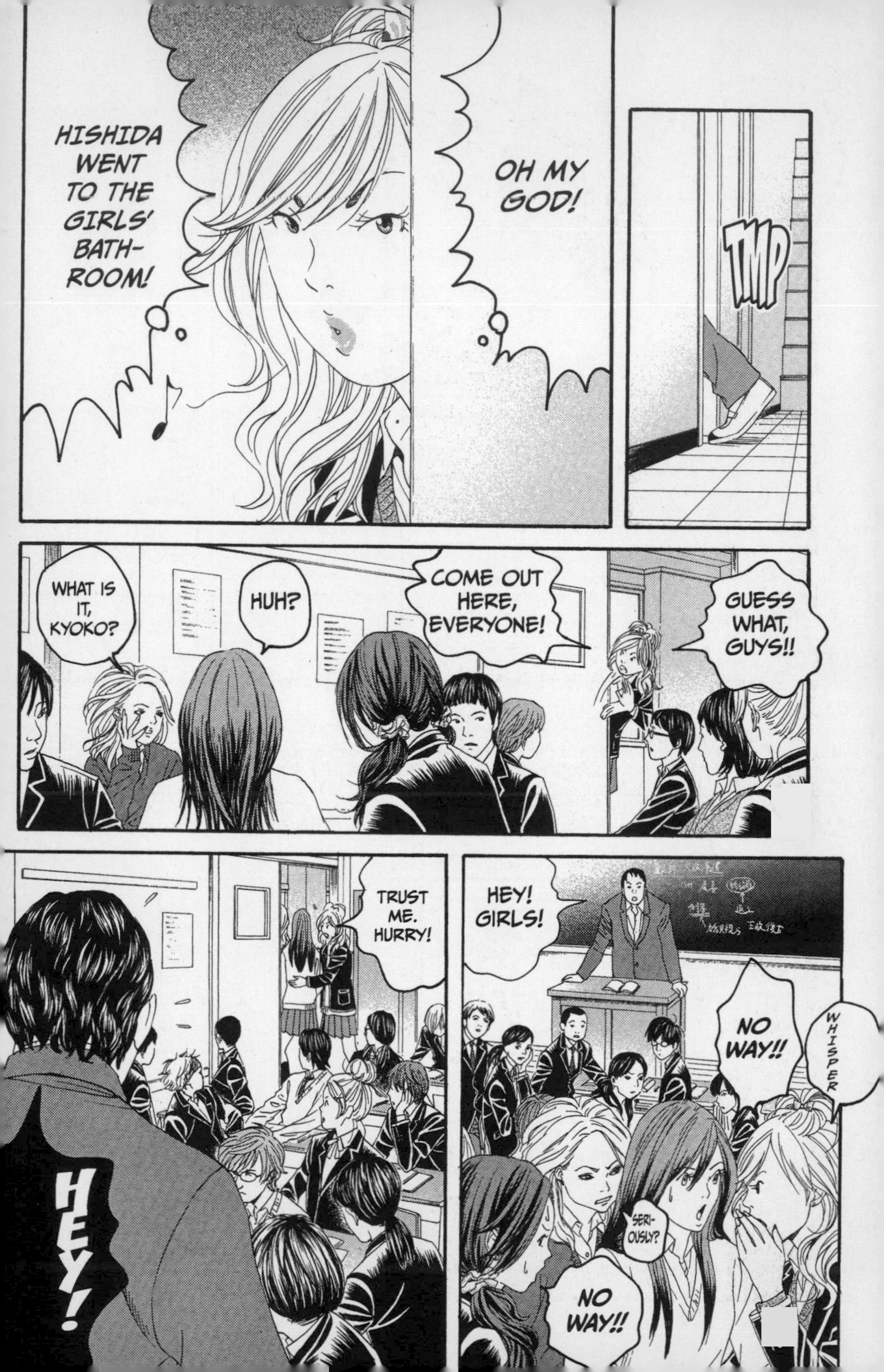
TMP
OH MY GOD!
HISHIDA WENT TO THE GIRLS' BATH-ROOM!
GUESS WHAT, GUYS!!
COME OUT HERE, EVERYONE!
HUH?
WHAT IS IT, KYOKO?
WHISPER
NO WAY!!
HEY! GIRLS!
SERI-OUSLY?
NO WAY!!
TRUST ME. HURRY!
HEY!

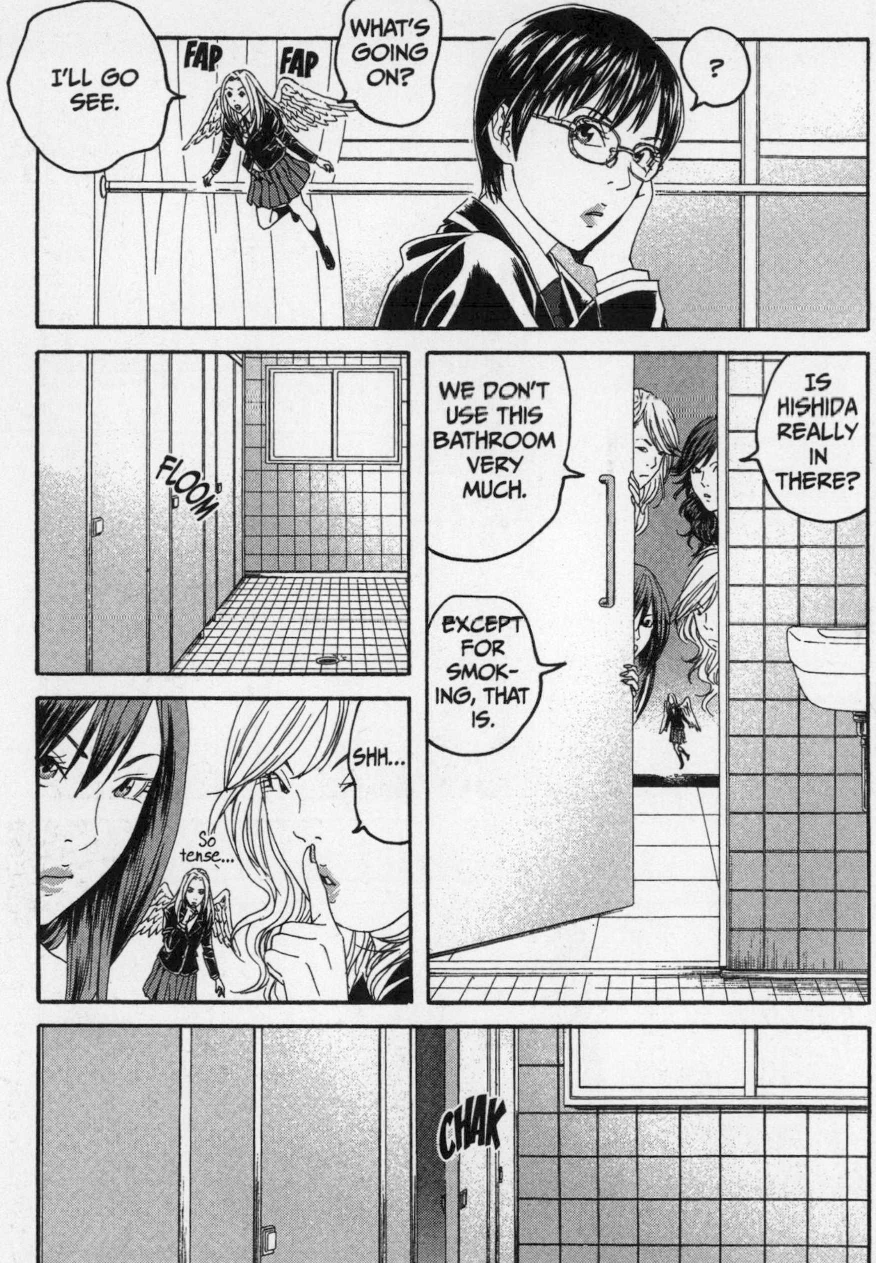
?
WHAT'S GOING ON?
FAP
FAP
I'LL GO SEE.
IS HISHIDA REALLY IN THERE?
WE DON'T USE THIS BATHROOM VERY MUCH.
EXCEPT FOR SMOK-ING, THAT IS.
FLOOM
SHH...
So tense...
CHAK

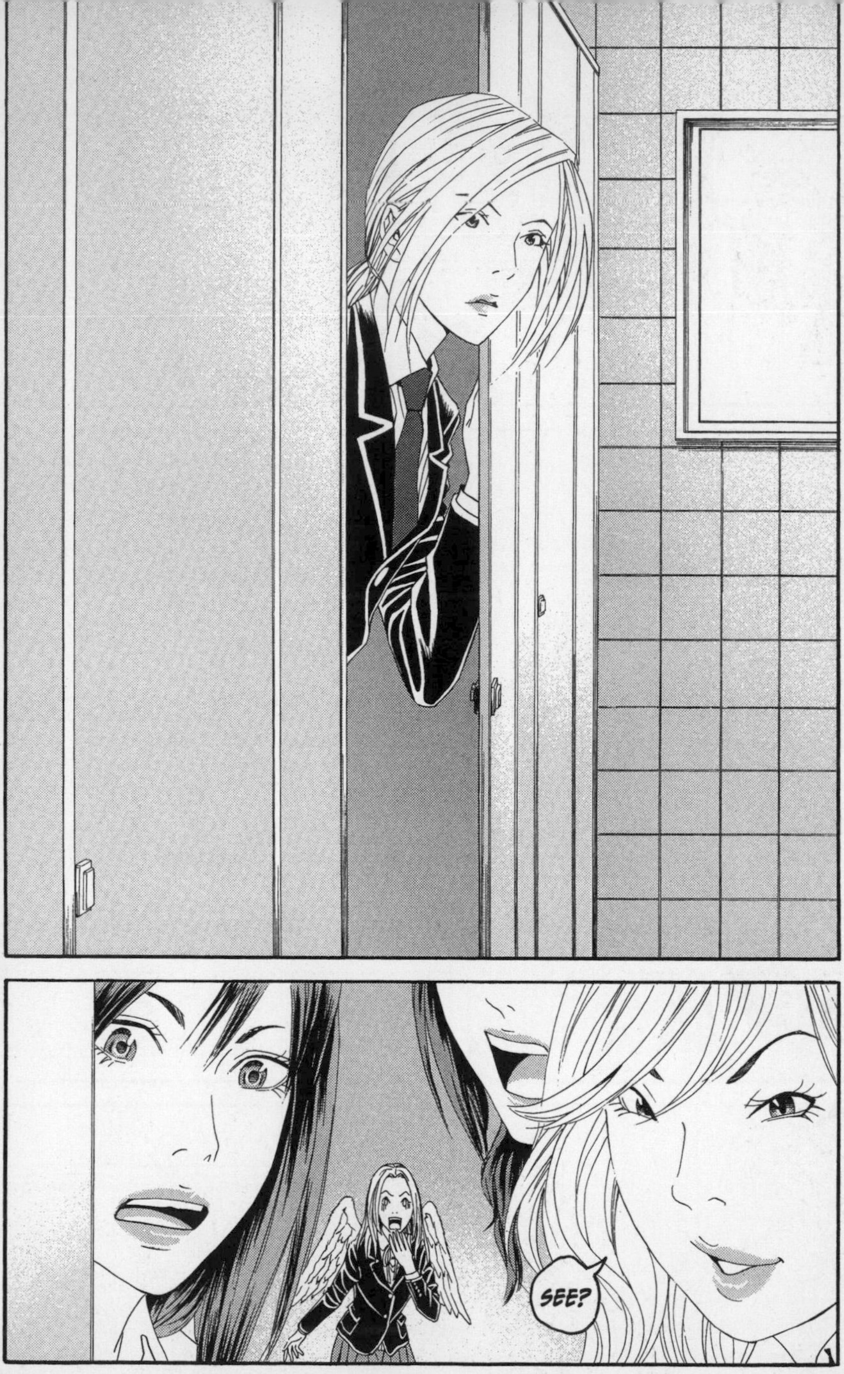
SEE?

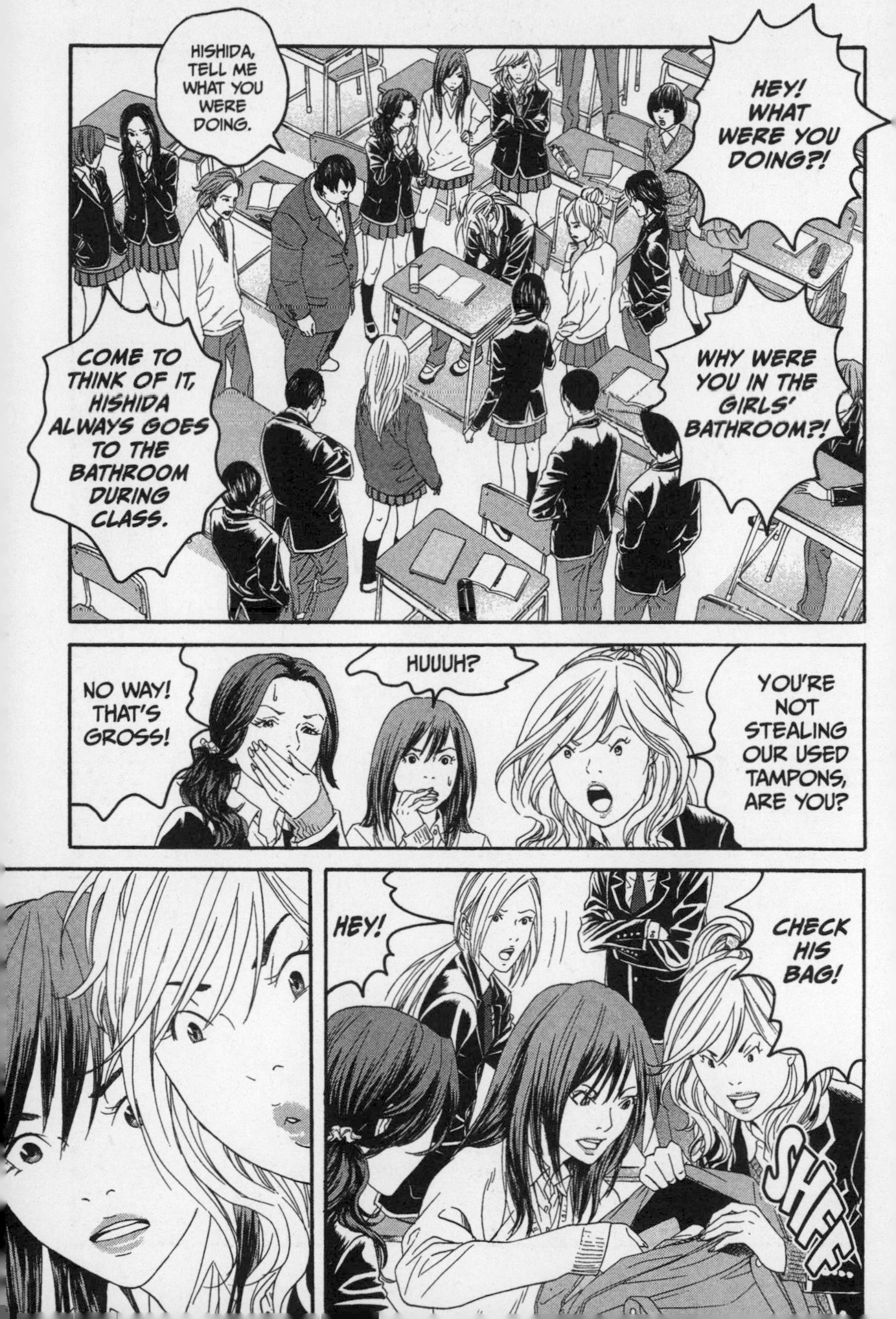
HEY! WHAT WERE YOU DOING?!
HISHIDA, TELL ME WHAT YOU WERE DOING.
WHY WERE YOU IN THE GIRLS' BATHROOM?!
COME TO THINK OF IT, HISHIDA ALWAYS GOES TO THE BATHROOM DURING CLASS.
YOU'RE NOT STEALING OUR USED TAMPONS, ARE YOU?
HUUUH?
NO WAY! THAT'S GROSS!
CHECK HIS BAG!
HEY!
SHFF...

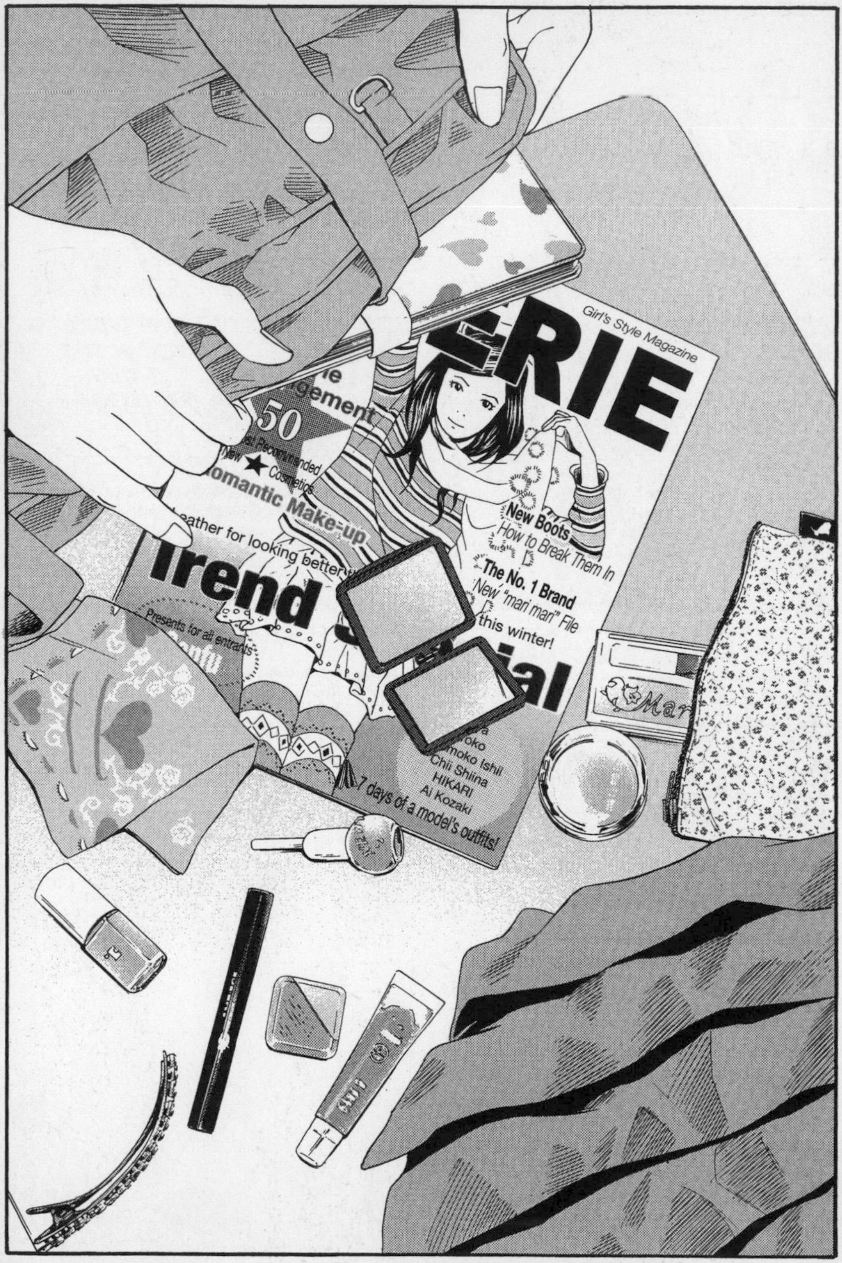
Girl's Style Magazine
ERIE
50
New ★ Cosmetics
Trend
Presents for all entrants
New Boots
How to Break Them In
The No. 1 Brand
New "mari mari" File
this winter!
Chii Shiina
HIKARI
Ai Kozaki
7 days of a model's outfits!

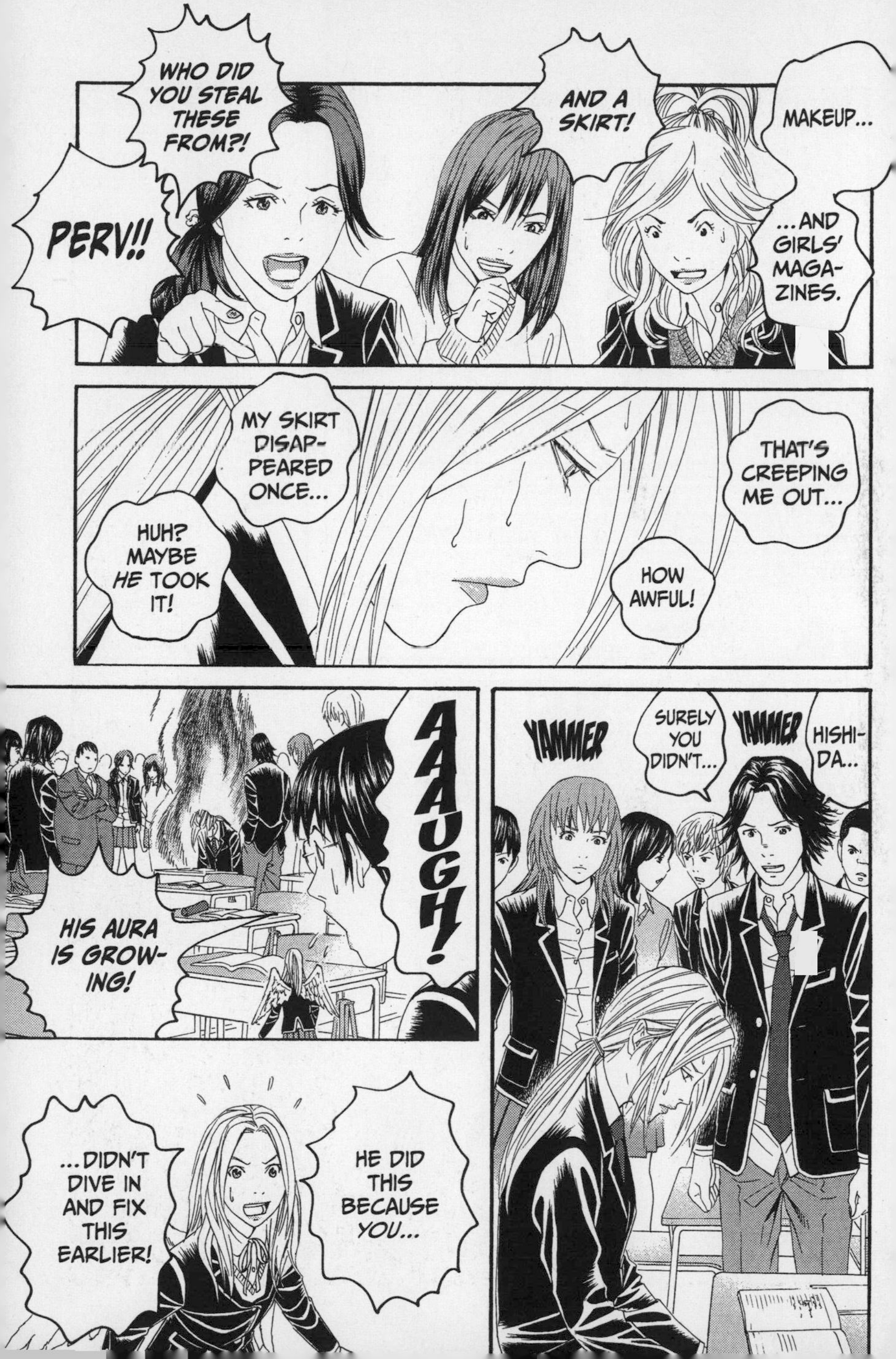
MAKEUP...
...AND GIRLS' MAGAZINES.
AND A SKIRT!
WHO DID YOU STEAL THESE FROM?!
PERV!!
THAT'S CREEPING ME OUT...
HOW AWFUL!
MY SKIRT DISAPPEARED ONCE...
HUH? MAYBE HE TOOK IT!
HISHIDA...
YAMMER
SURELY YOU DIDN'T...
YAMMER
AAAUGH!
HIS AURA IS GROWING!
HE DID THIS BECAUSE YOU...
...DIDN'T DIVE IN AND FIX THIS EARLIER!

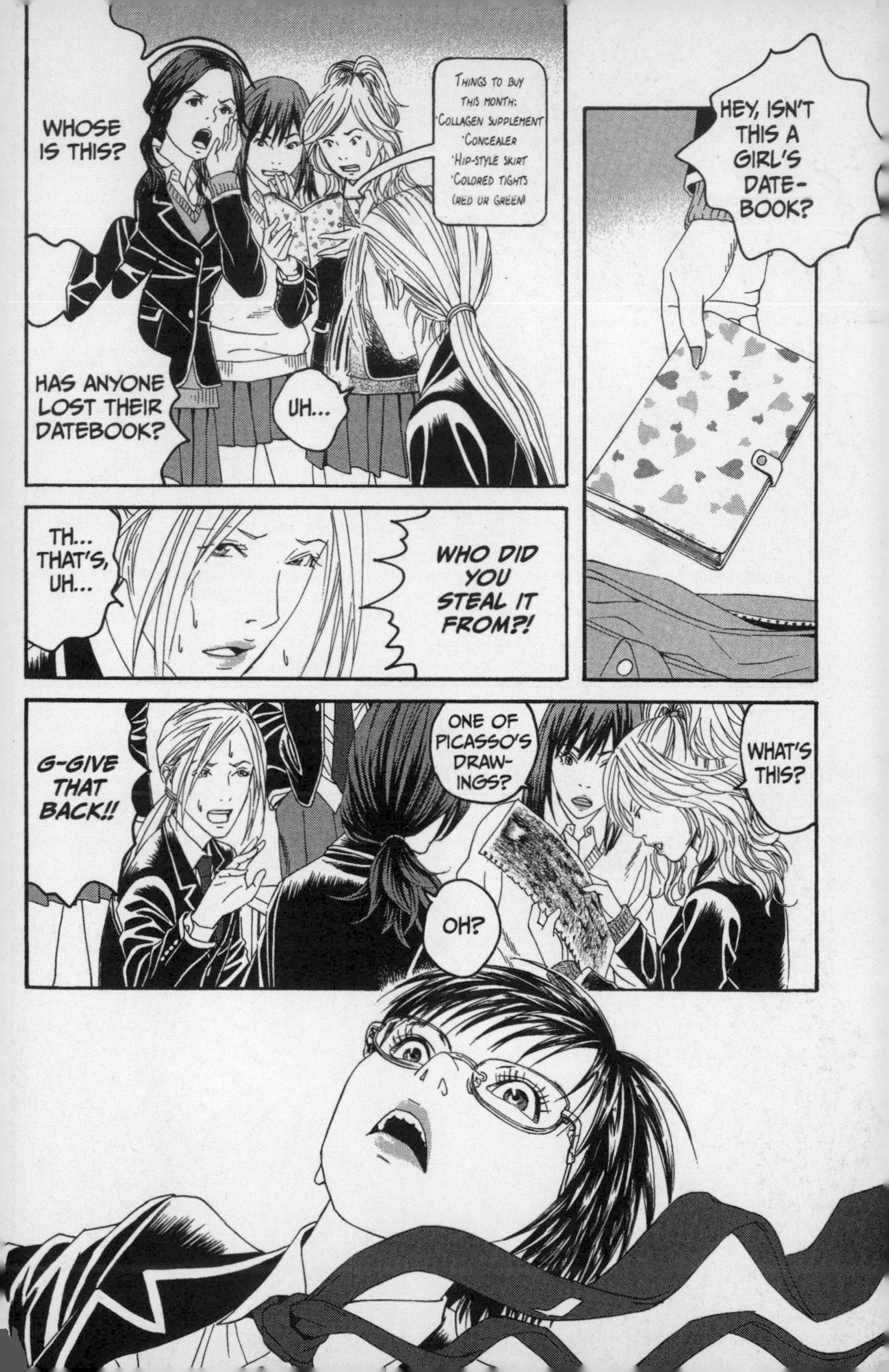
HEY, ISN'T THIS A GIRL'S DATE-BOOK?
THINGS TO BUY THIS MONTH: ·COLLAGEN SUPPLEMENT ·CONCEALER ·HIP-STYLE SKIRT ·COLORED TIGHTS (RED OR GREEN)
WHOSE IS THIS?
UH...
HAS ANYONE LOST THEIR DATEBOOK?
WHO DID YOU STEAL IT FROM?!
TH... THAT'S, UH...
WHAT'S THIS?
ONE OF PICASSO'S DRAW-INGS?
OH?
G-GIVE THAT BACK!!

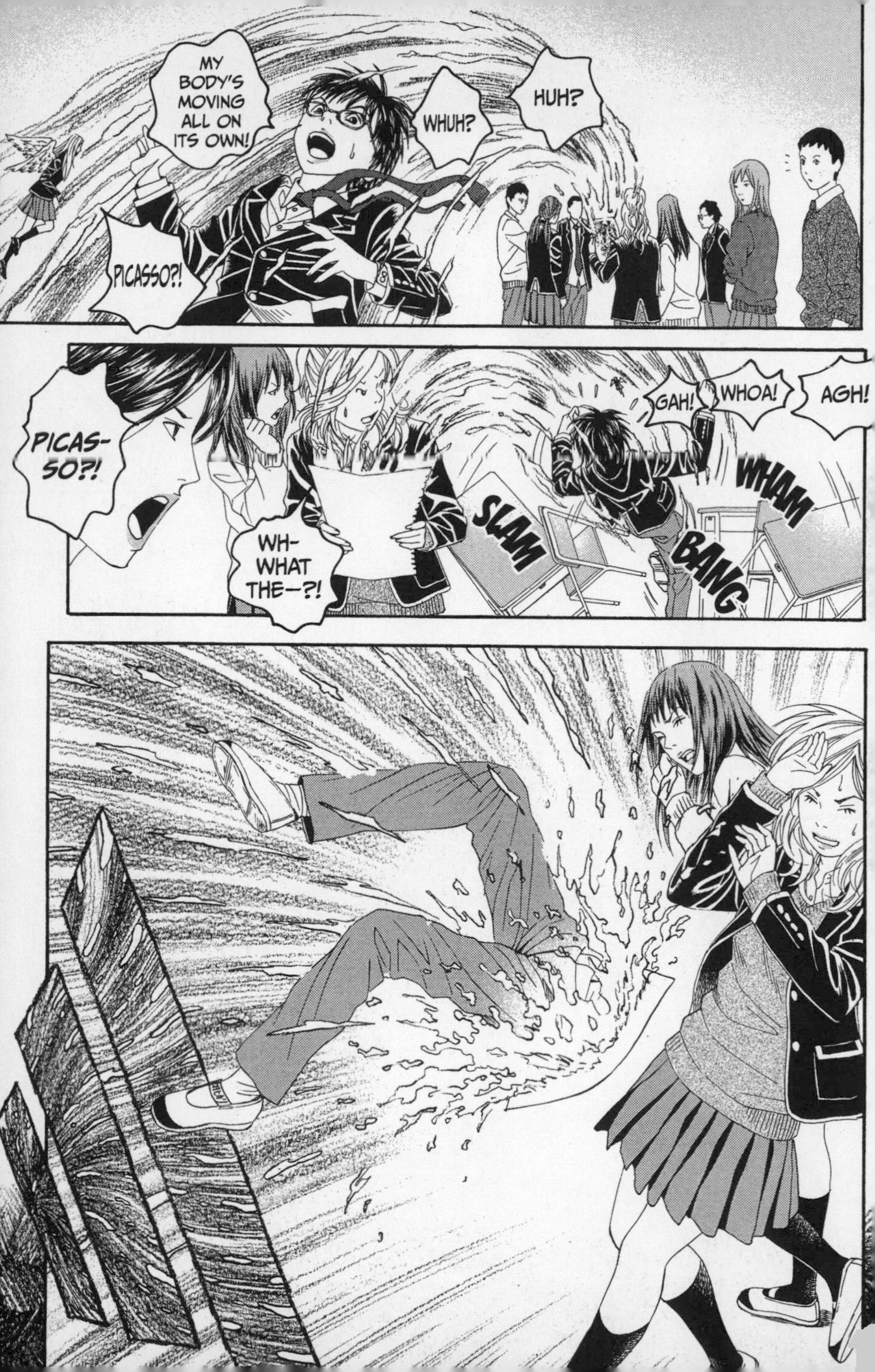
HUH?
WHUH?
MY BODY'S MOVING ALL ON ITS OWN!
PICASSO?!
AGH!
WHOA!
GAH!
WHAM
BANG
SLAM
WH-WHAT THE--?!
PICAS-SO?!

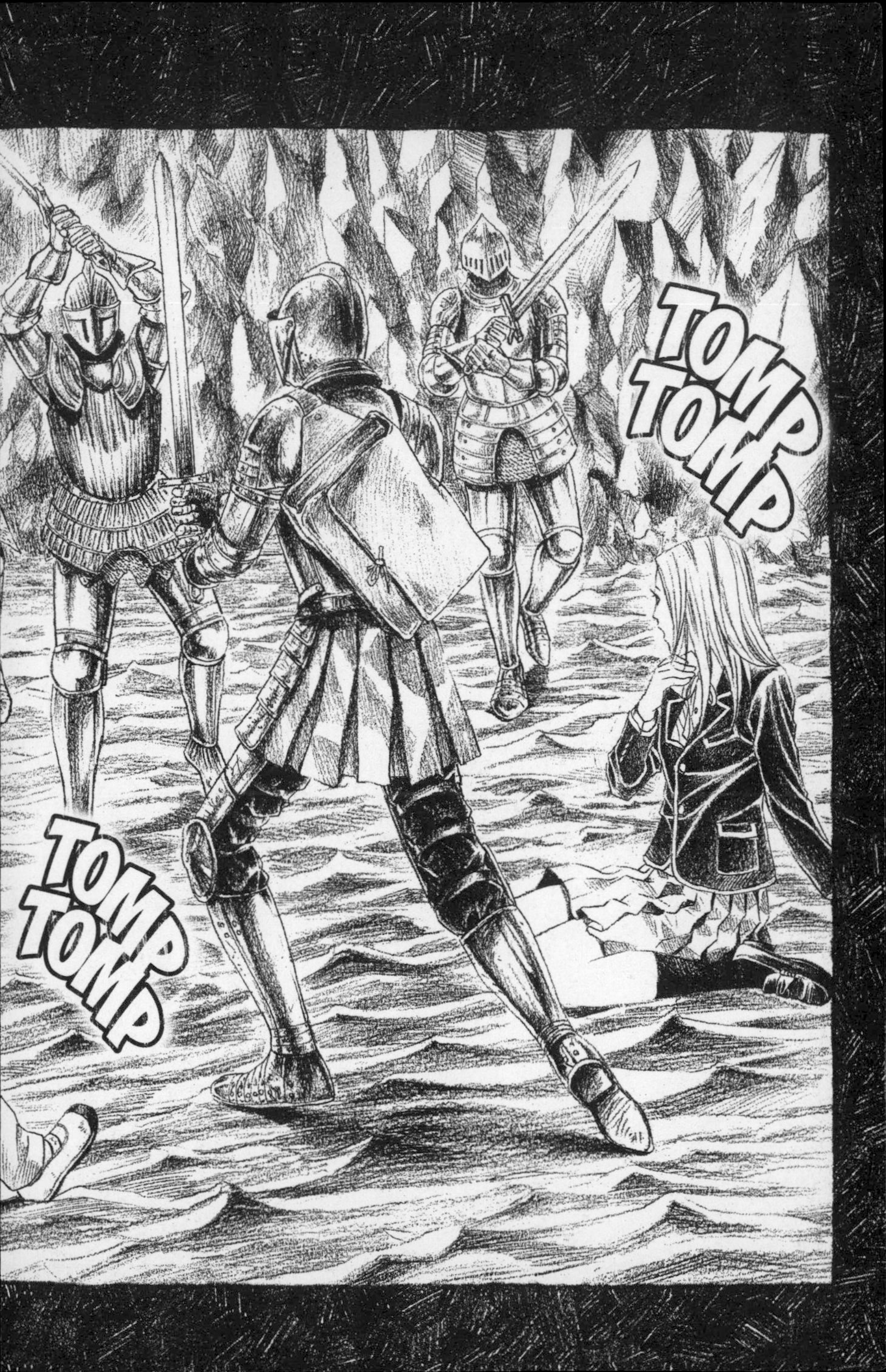
TOMP
TOMP
TOMP
TOMP

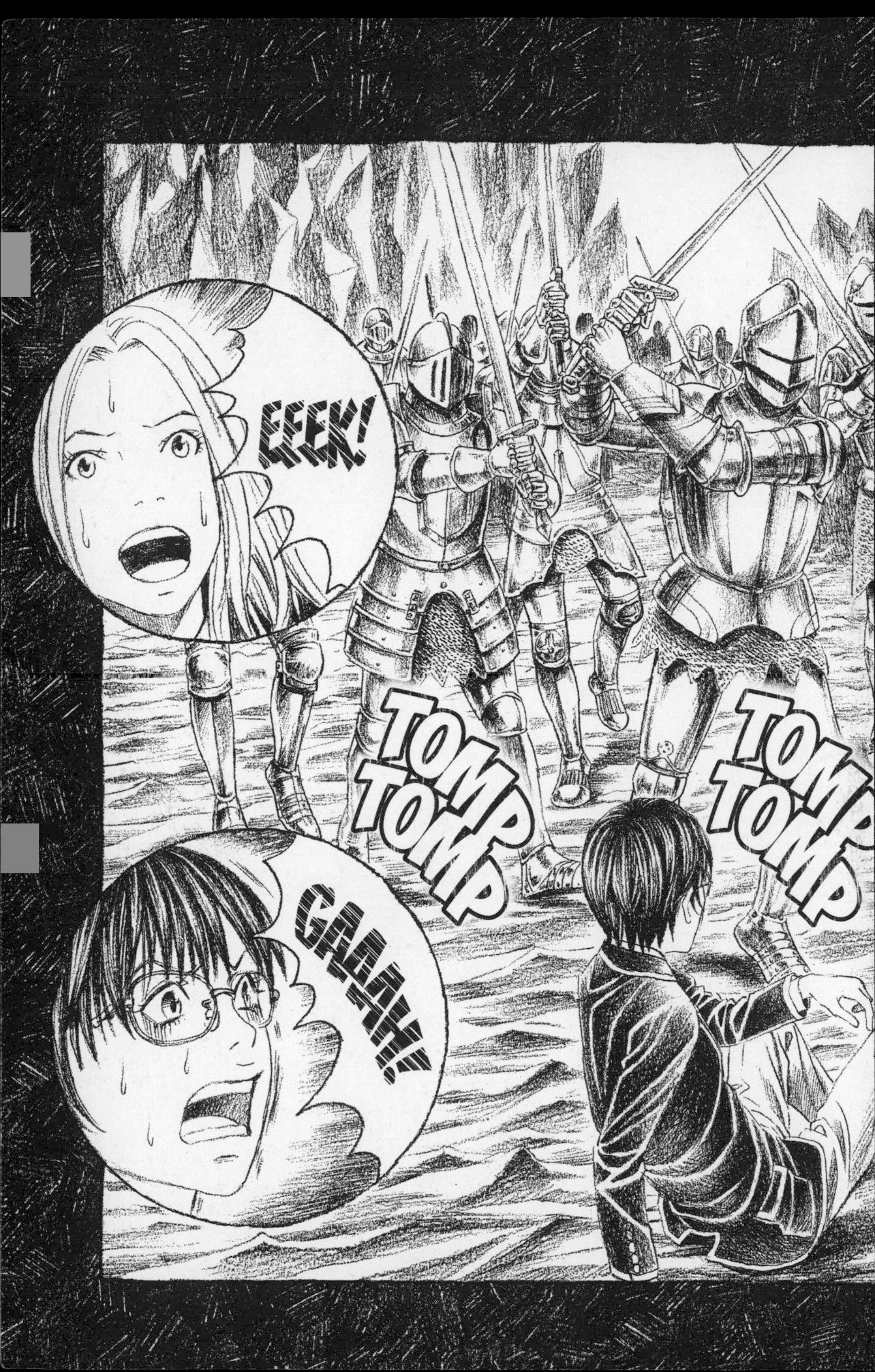
EEEK!
TOMP TOMP
TOMP TOMP
GAAAH!!

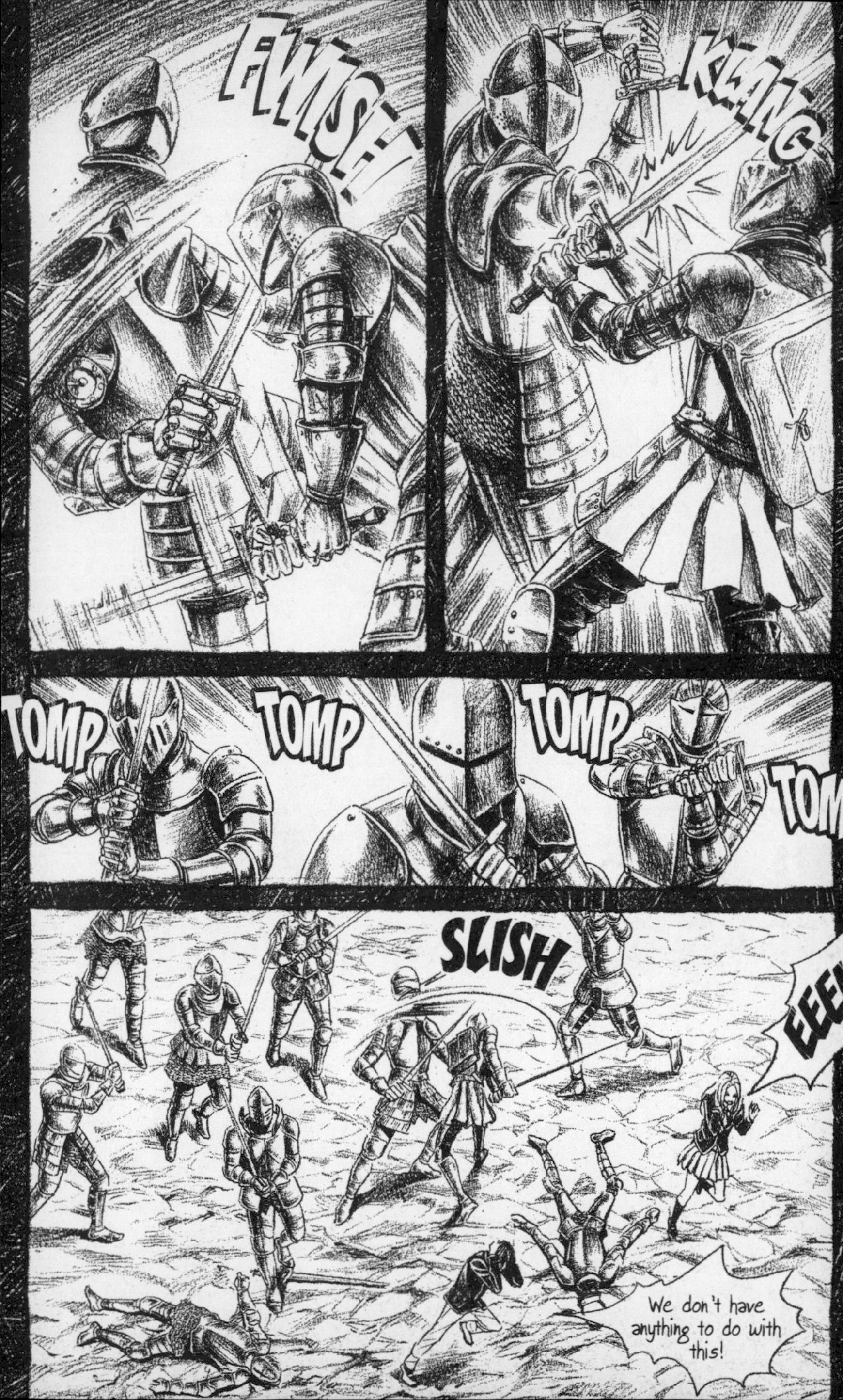
KLANG
FWISH!!
TOMP
TOMP
TOMP
TOMP
EEEK!
SLISH
We don't have anything to do with this!

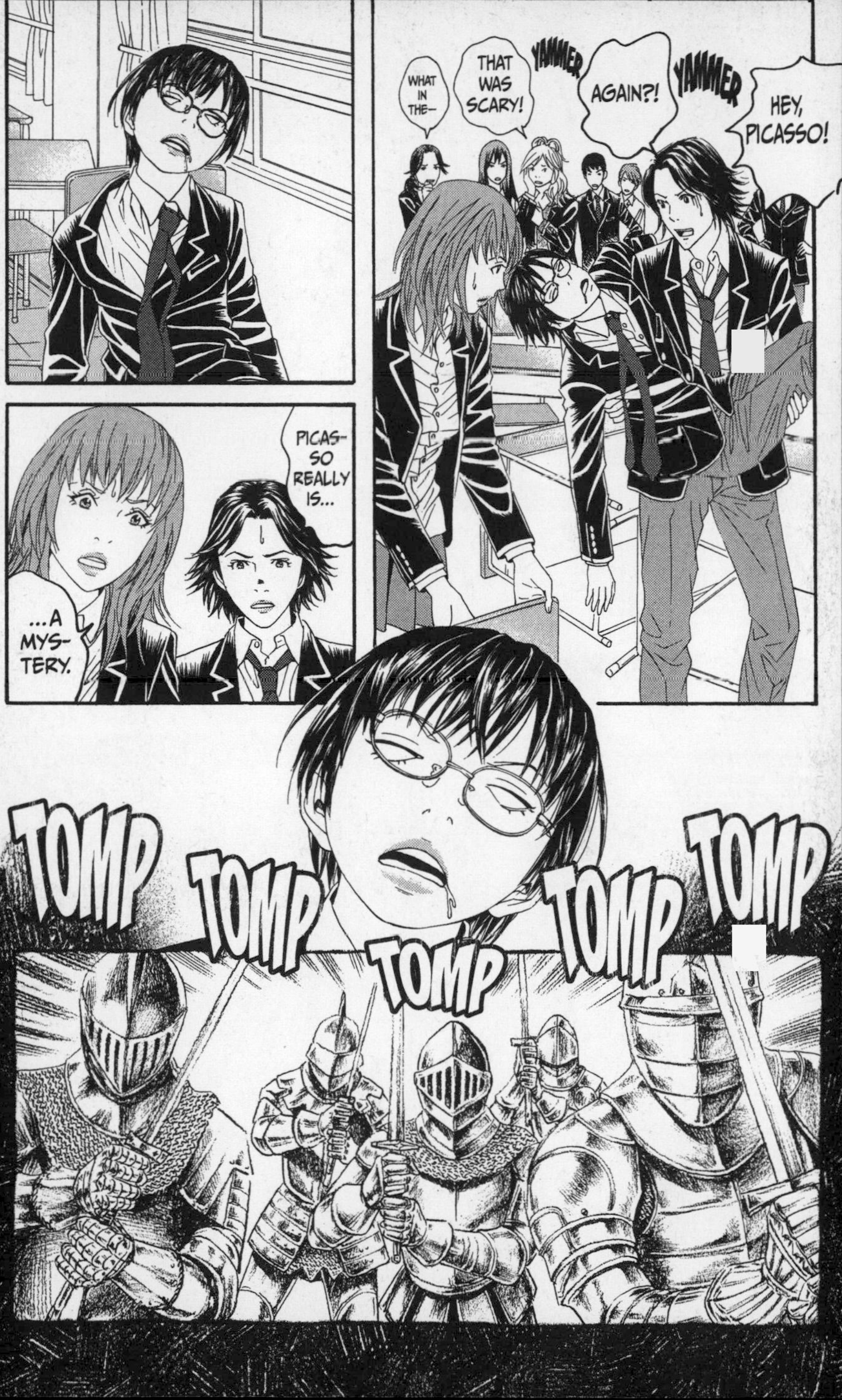
HEY, PICASSO!
YAMMER
AGAIN?!
YAMMER
THAT WAS SCARY!
WHAT IN THE—
PICAS-SO REALLY IS...
...A MYS-TERY.
TOMP
TOMP
TOMP
TOMP
TOMP

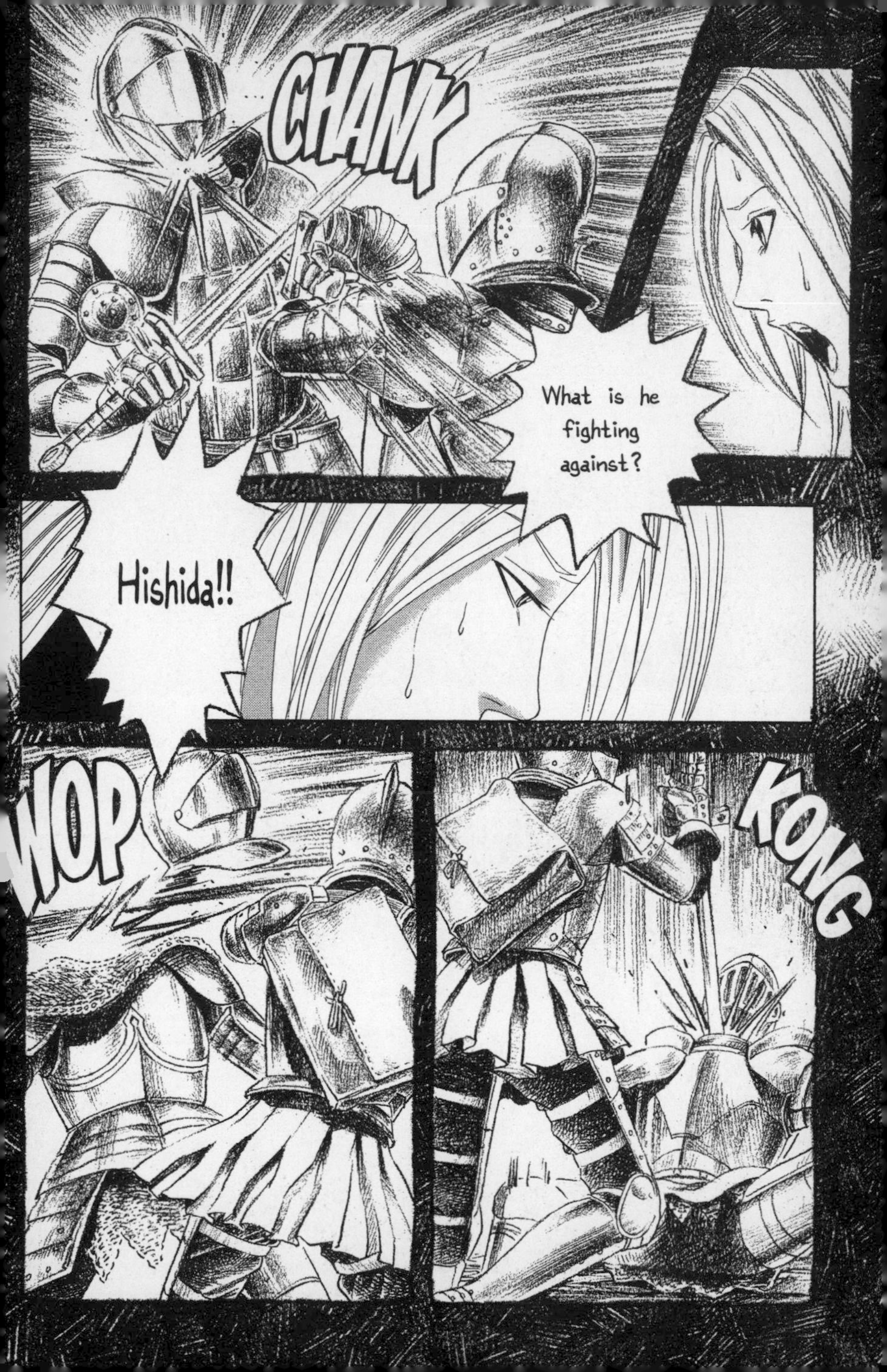
What is he fighting against?
CHANK
Hishida!!
KONG
WOP

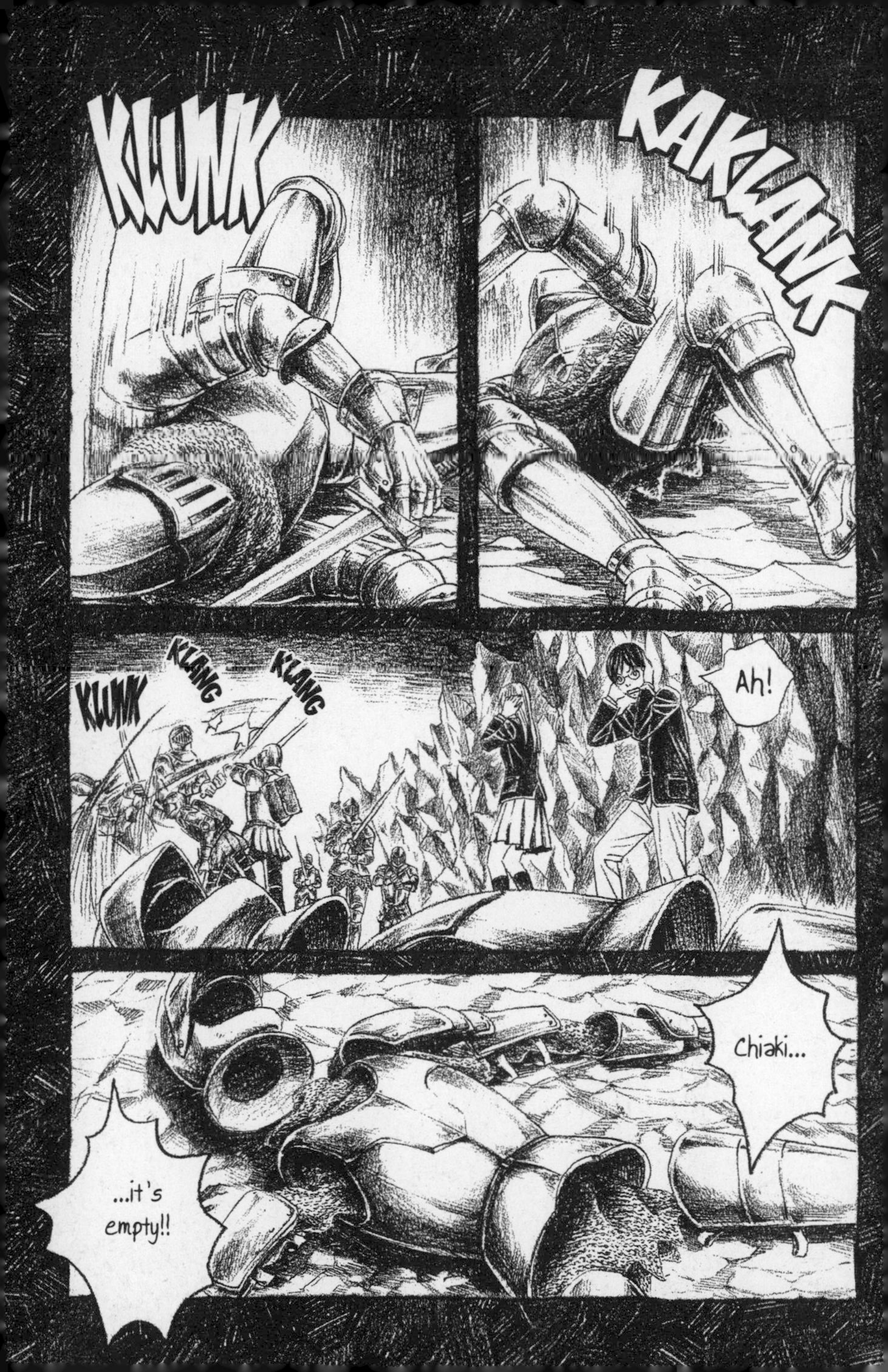

KAKWANK
KLUNK
Ah!
KLANG
KLANG
KLUNK
Chiaki...
...it's empty!!

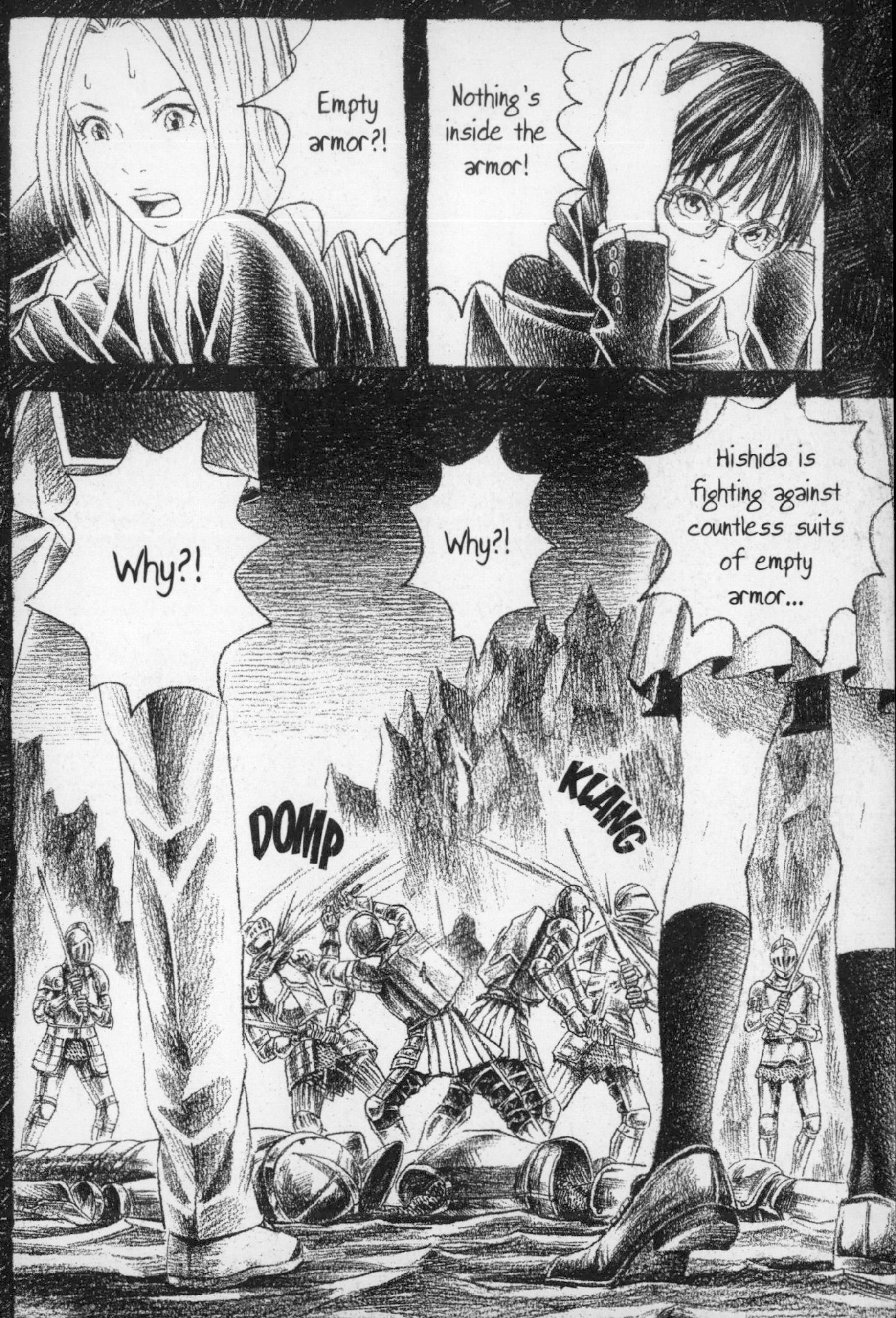
Nothing's inside the armor!
Empty armor?!
Hishida is fighting against countless suits of empty armor...
Why?!
Why?!
KLANG
DOMP

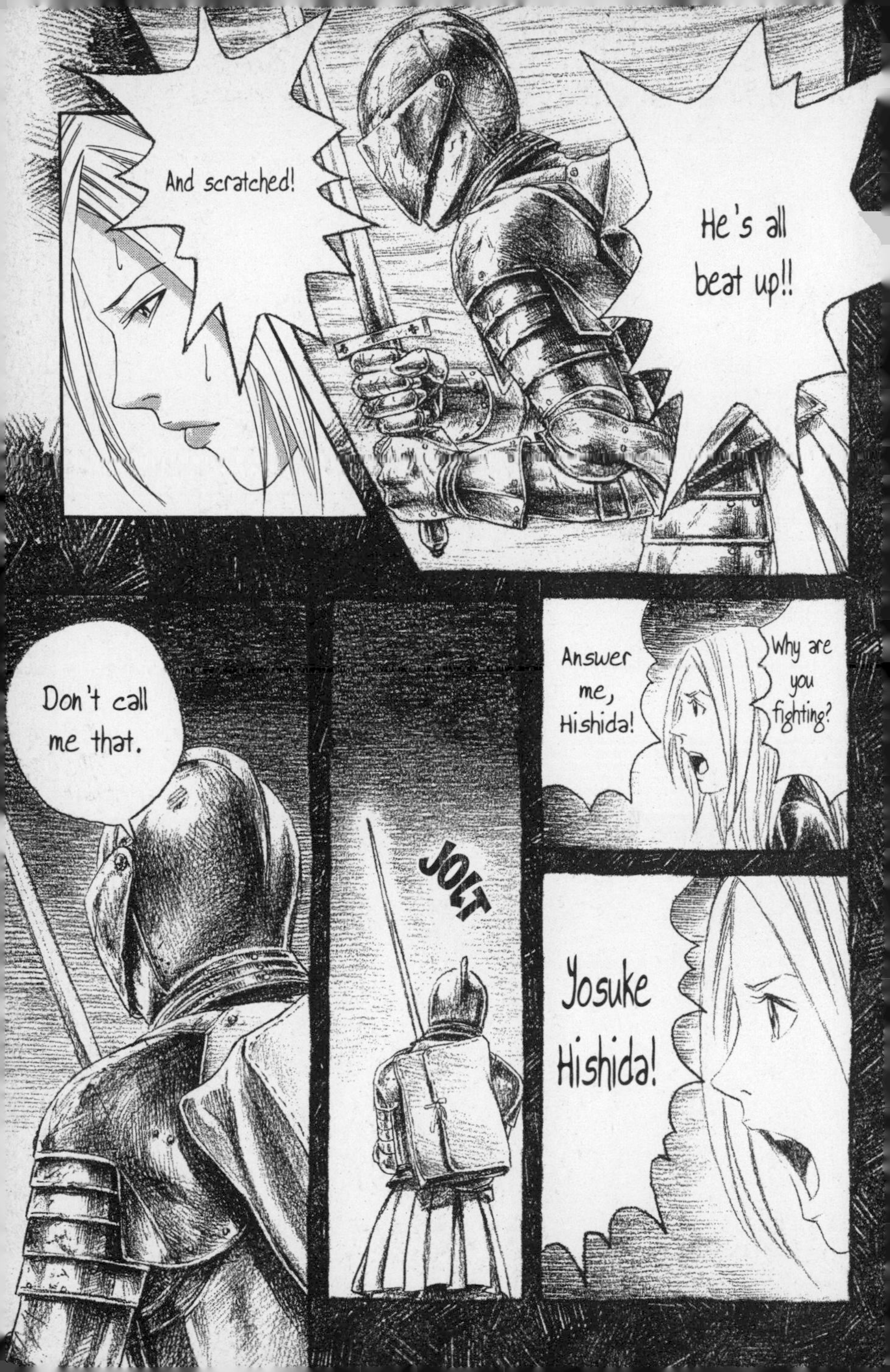
He's all beat up!!
And scratched!
Why are you fighting?
Answer me, Hishida!
Yosuke Hishida!
JOLT
Don't call me that.

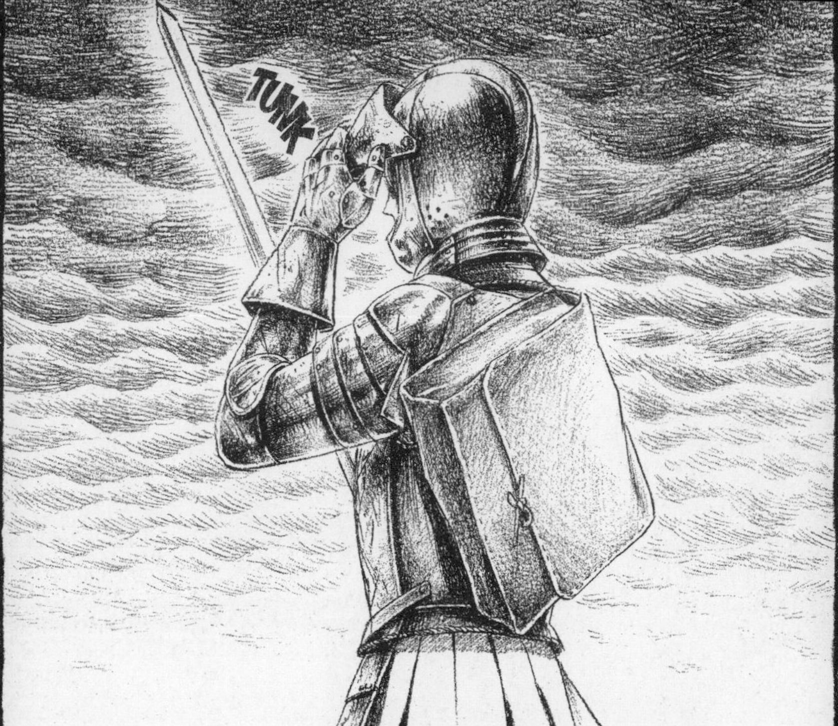
TUNK
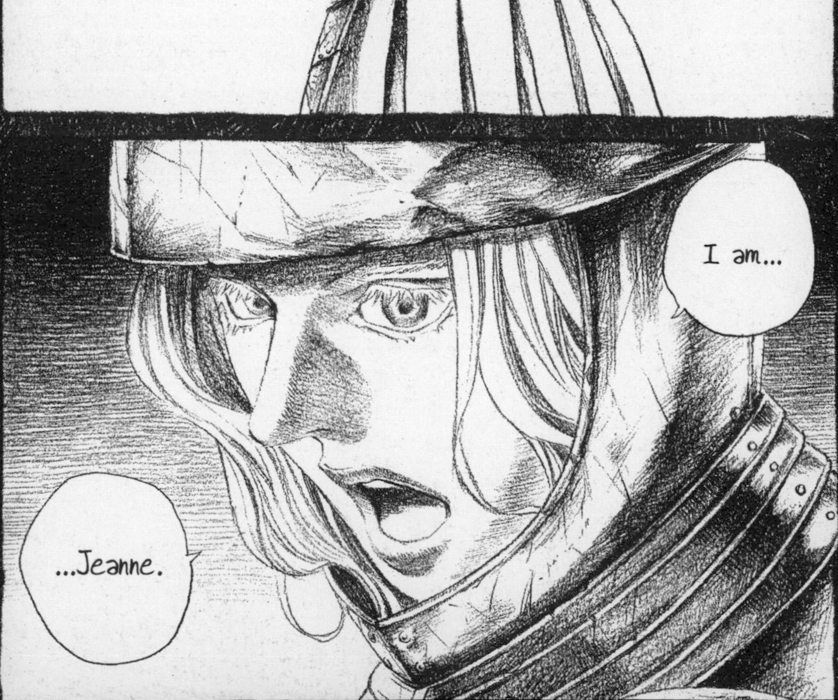
I am...
...Jeanne.

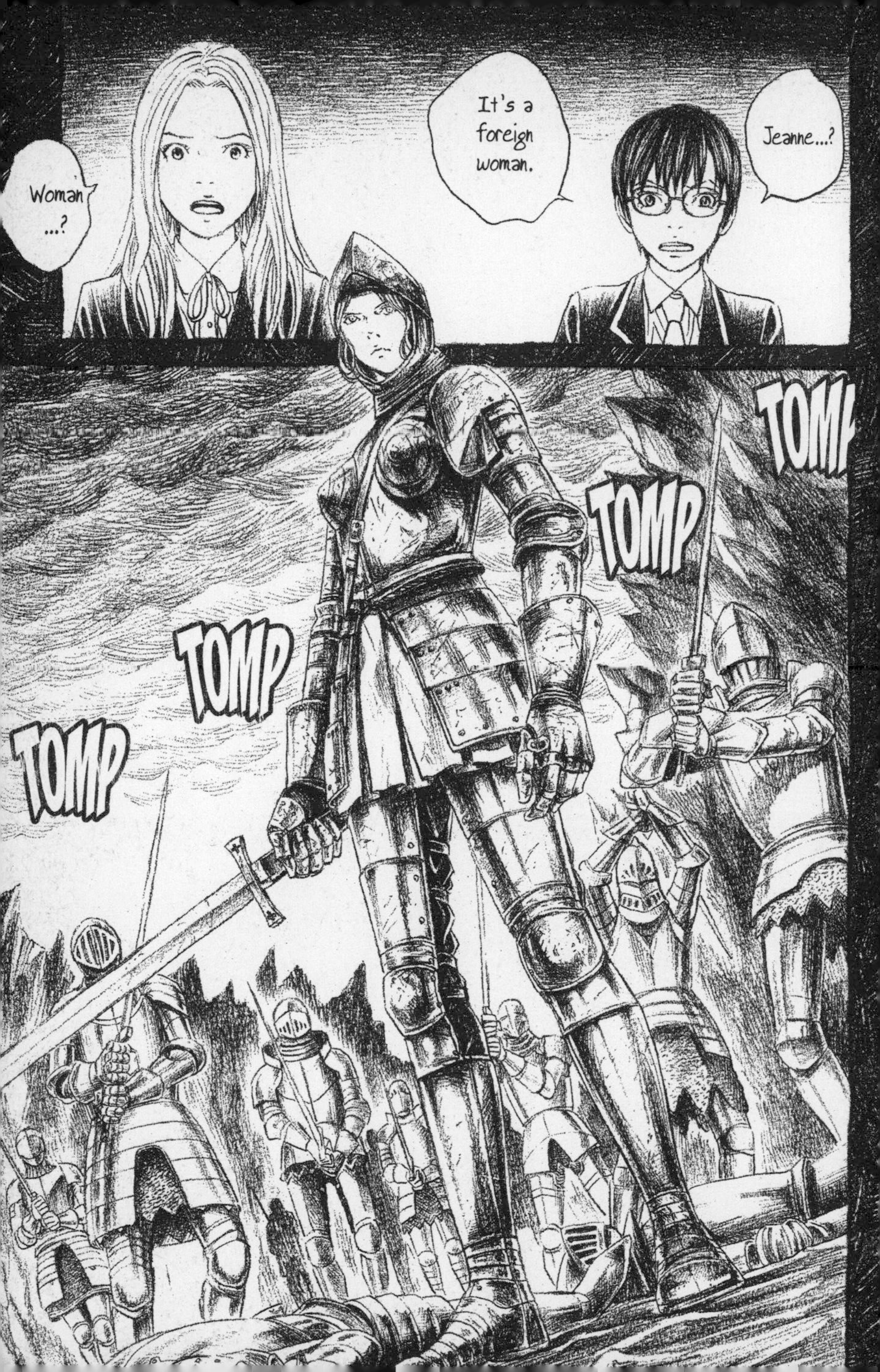
Jeanne...?
It's a foreign woman.
Woman ...?
TOMP
TOMP
TOMP
TOMP

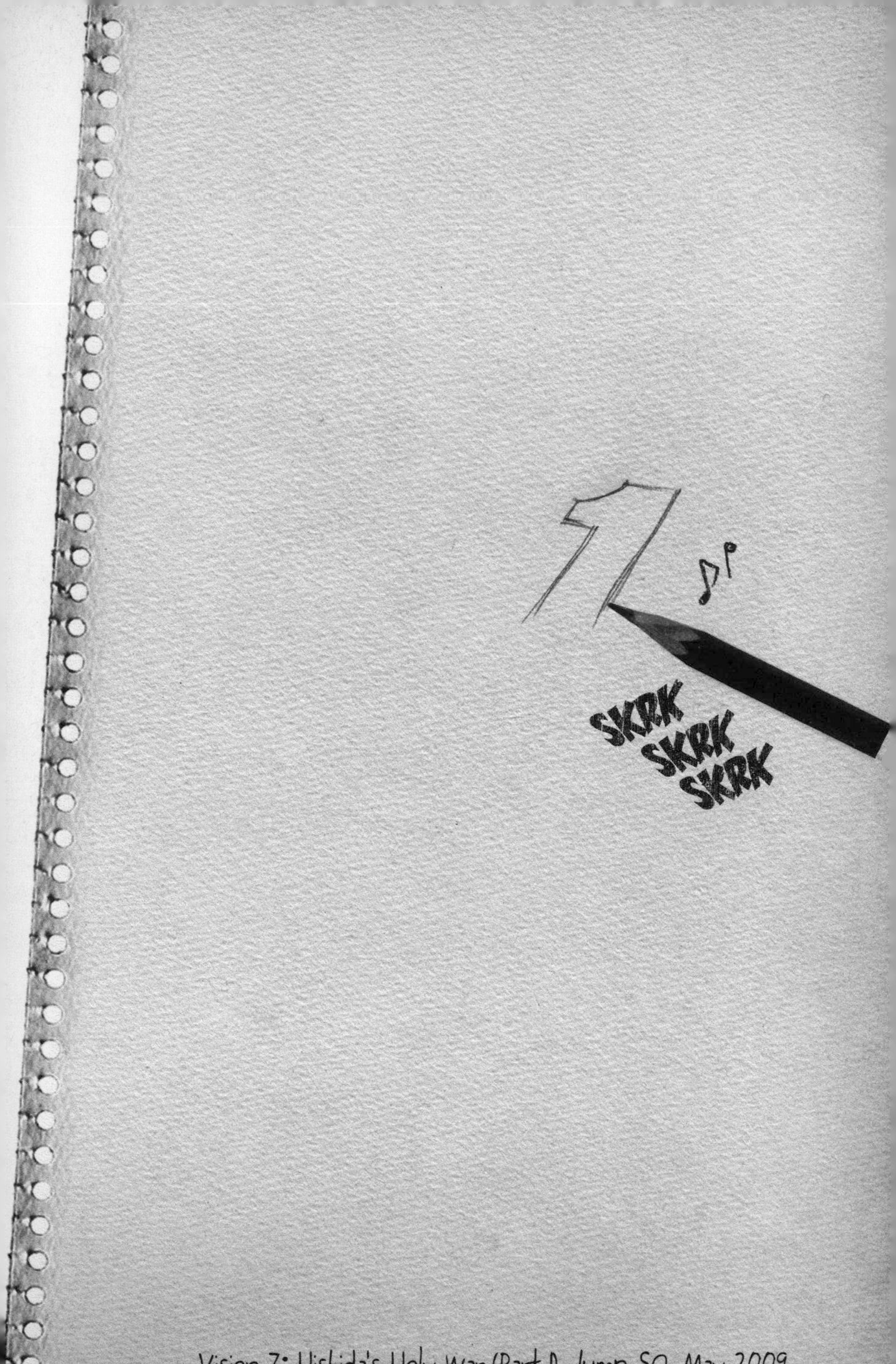
SKRK
SKRK
SKRK

Vision 7: Hishida's Holy War (Part 1)_Jump SQ, May 2009

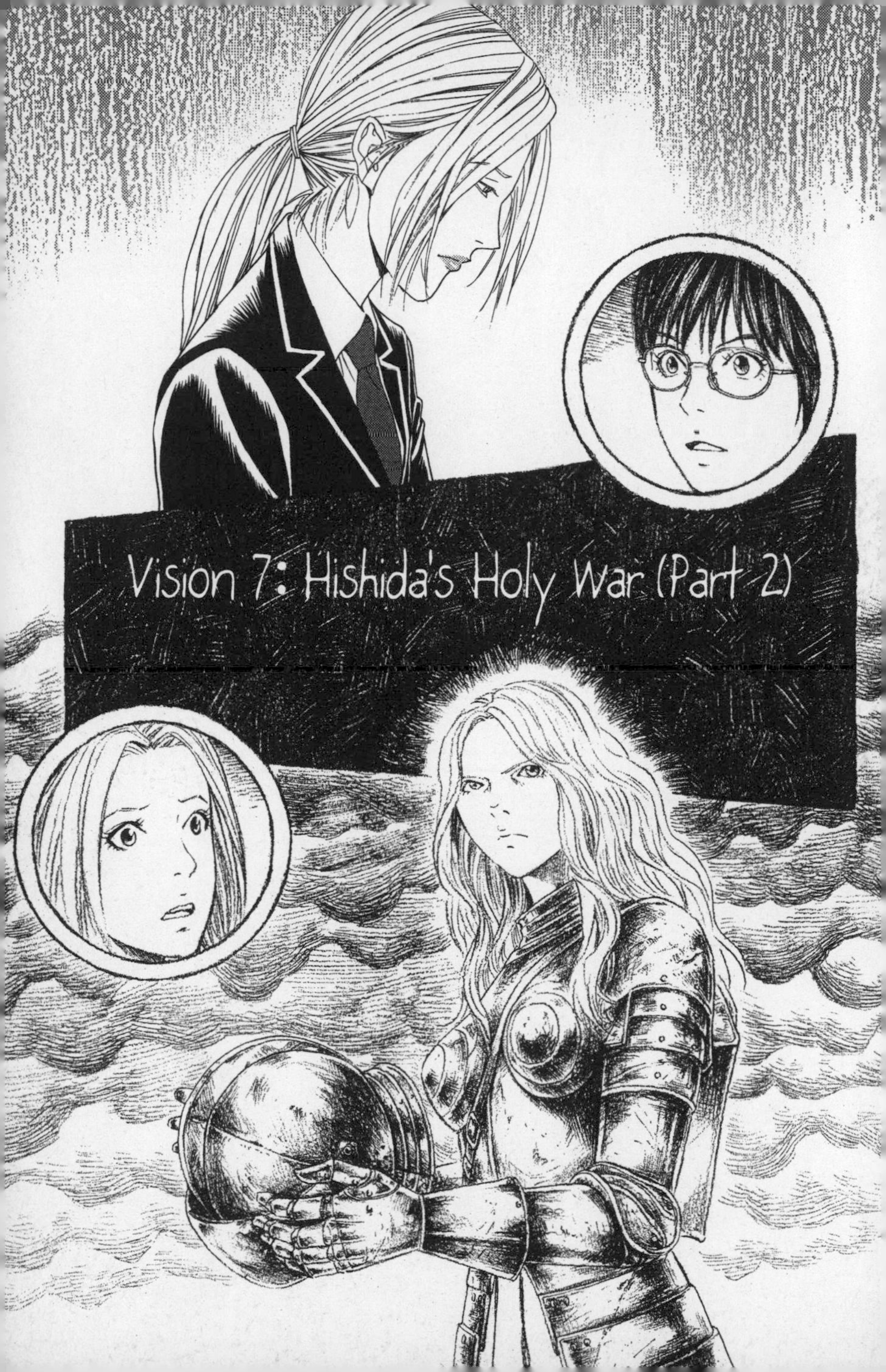
Vision 7: Hishida's Holy War (Part 2)

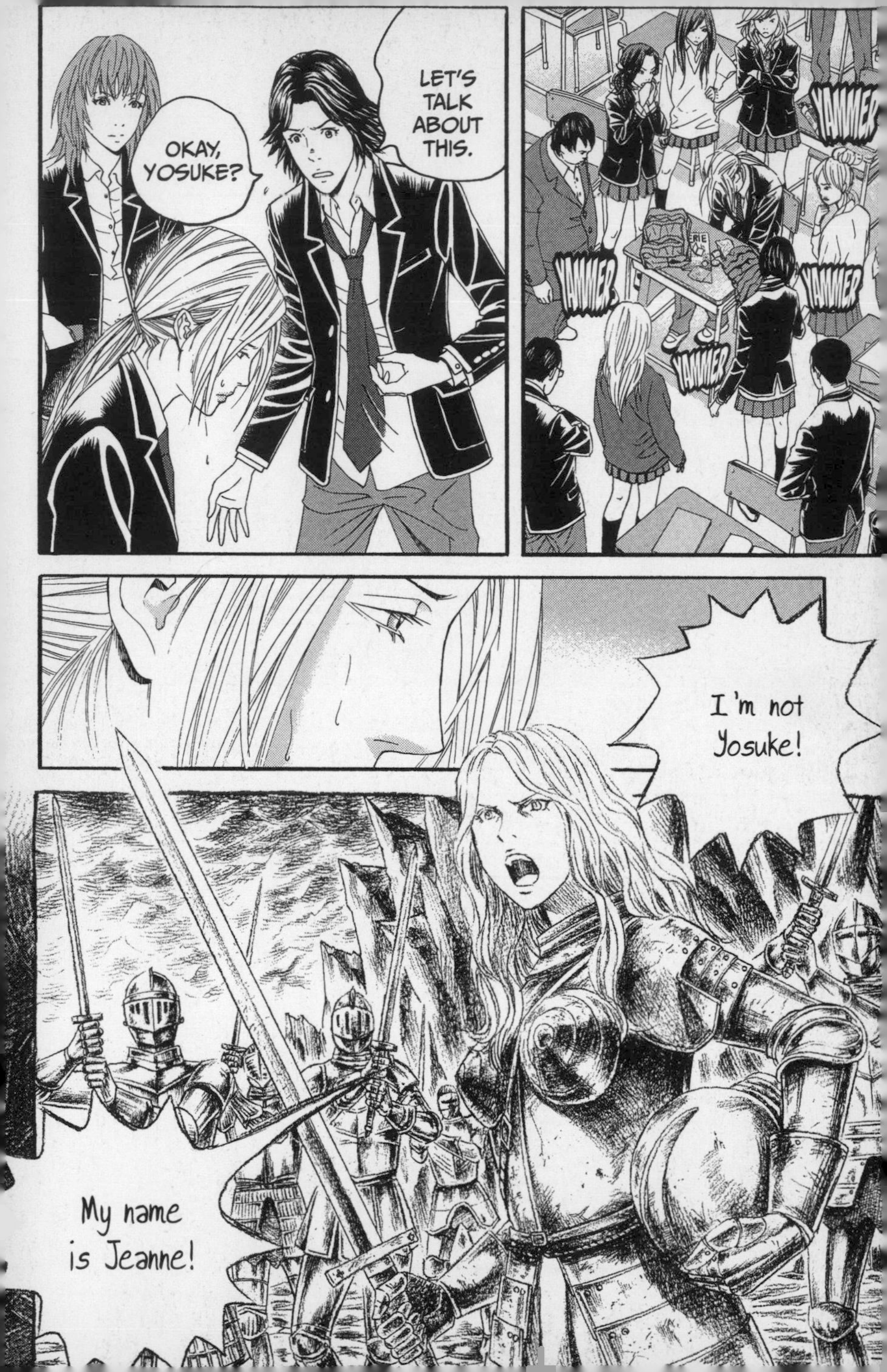
YAMMER
YAMMER
YAMMER
YAMMER
LET'S TALK ABOUT THIS.
OKAY, YOSUKE?
I'm not Yosuke!
My name is Jeanne!

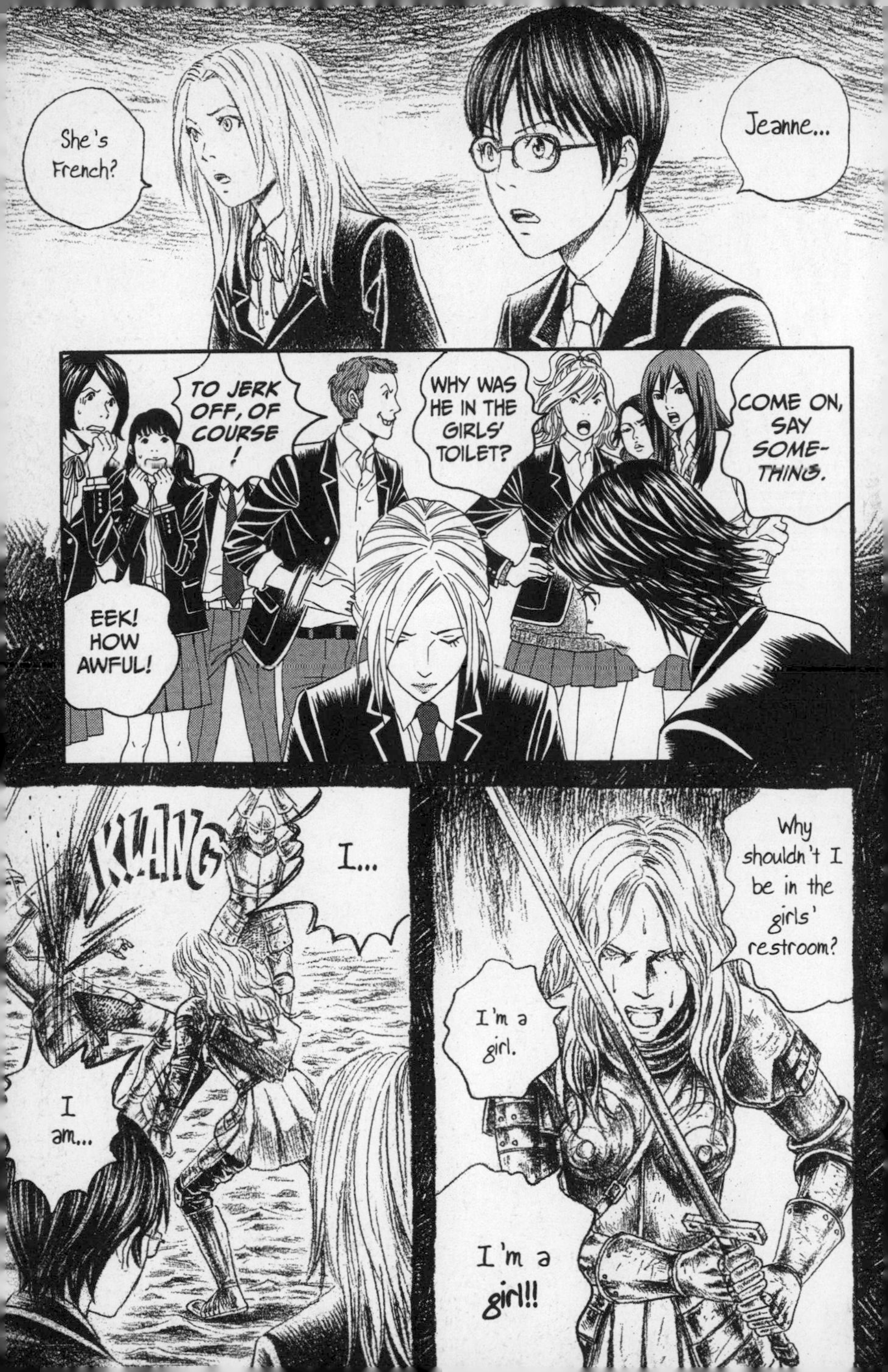
Jeanne...
She's French?
COME ON, SAY SOME-THING.
WHY WAS HE IN THE GIRLS' TOILET?
TO JERK OFF, OF COURSE!
EEK! HOW AWFUL!
Why shouldn't I be in the girls' restroom?
I'm a girl.
I'm a girl!!
KLANG
I...
I am...

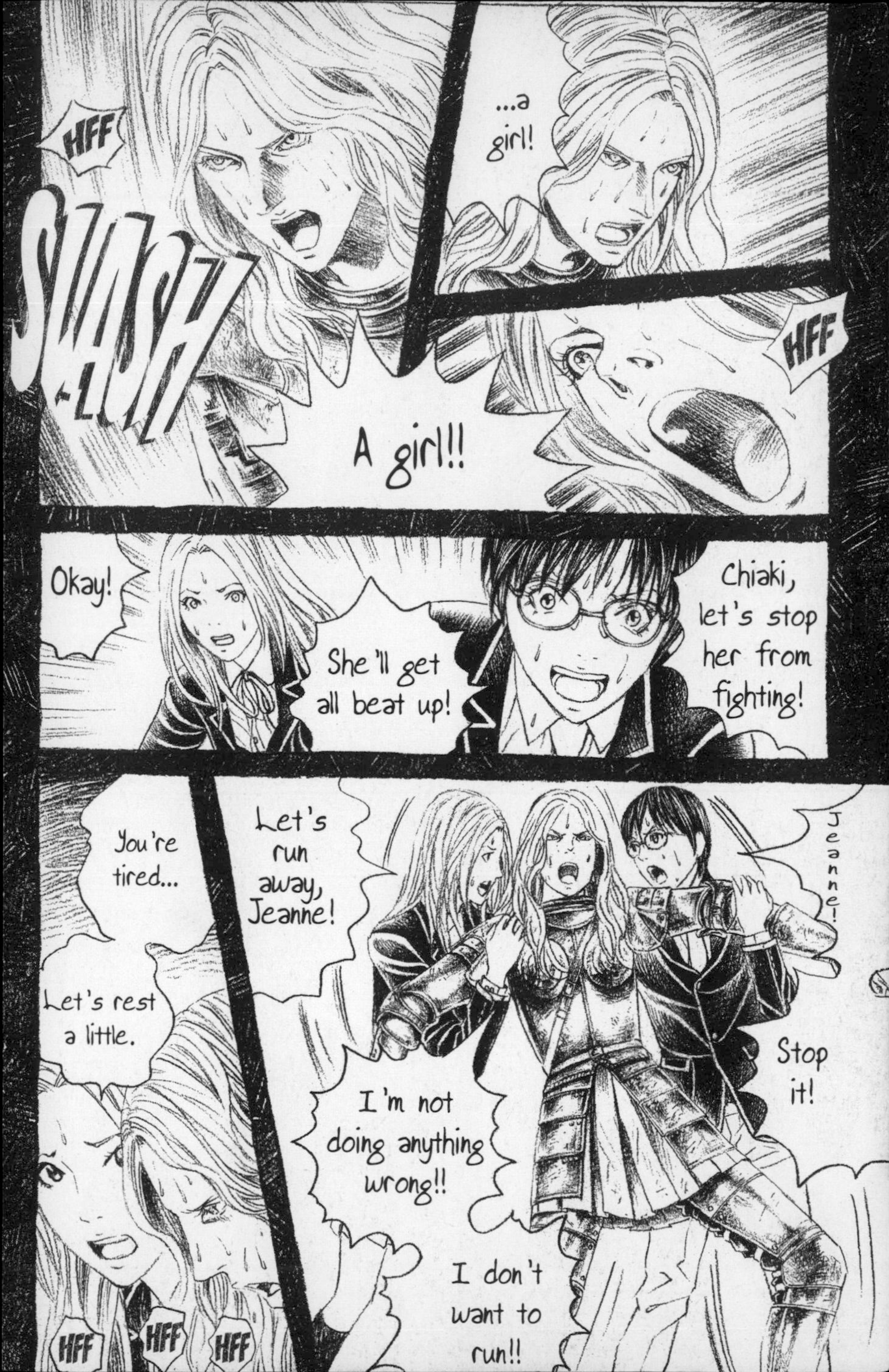
...a girl!
HFF
A girl!!
HFF
SLASH
Chiaki, let's stop her from fighting!
She'll get all beat up!
Okay!
Jeanne!
Let's run away, Jeanne!
Stop it!
I'm not doing anything wrong!!
I don't want to run!!
You're tired...
Let's rest a little.
HFF
HFF
HFF

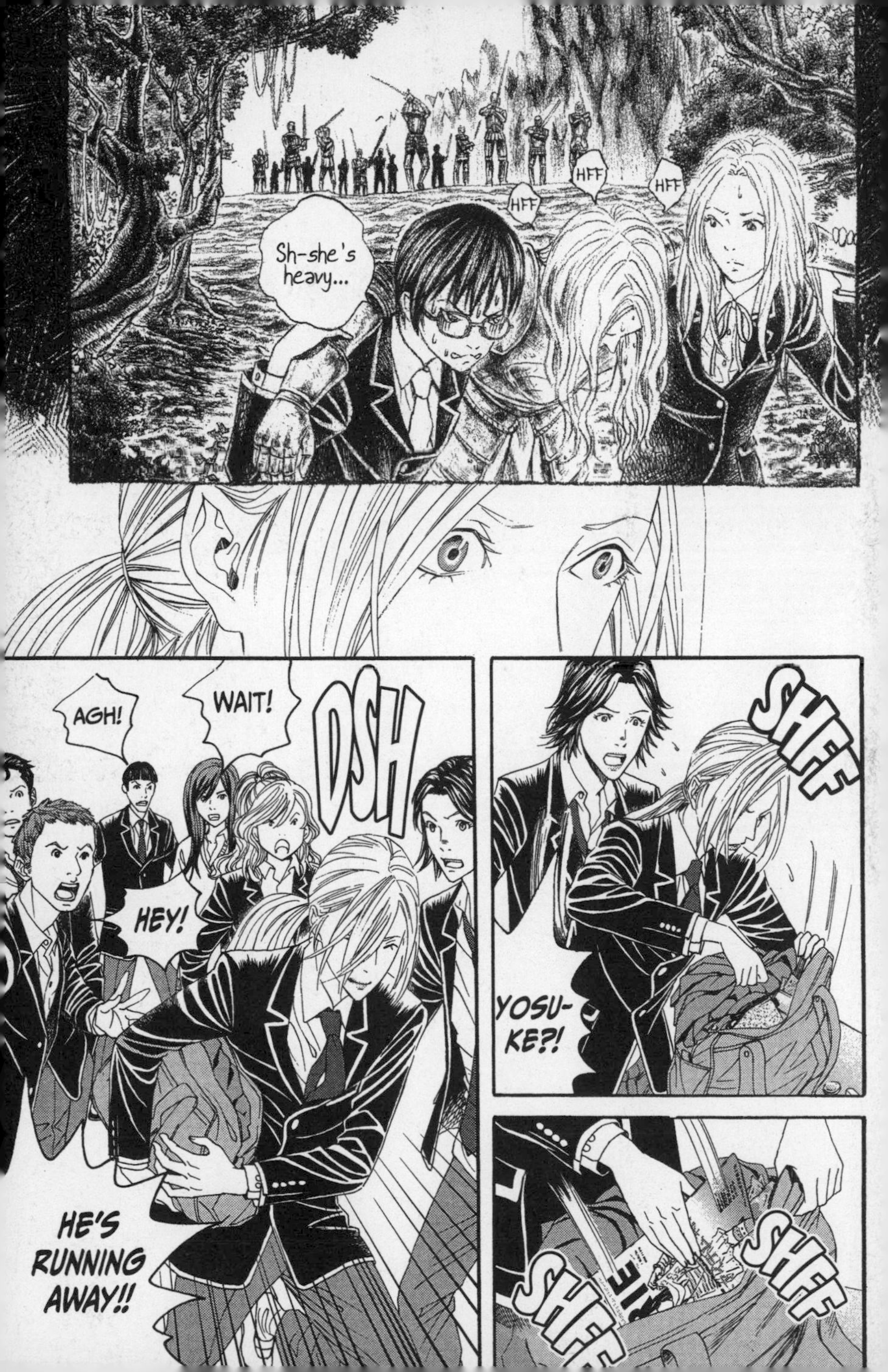
HFF
HFF
HFF
Sh-she's heavy...
SHFF
YOSU-KE?!
SHFF
SHFF
OSH
WAIT!
AGH!
HEY!
HE'S RUNNING AWAY!!

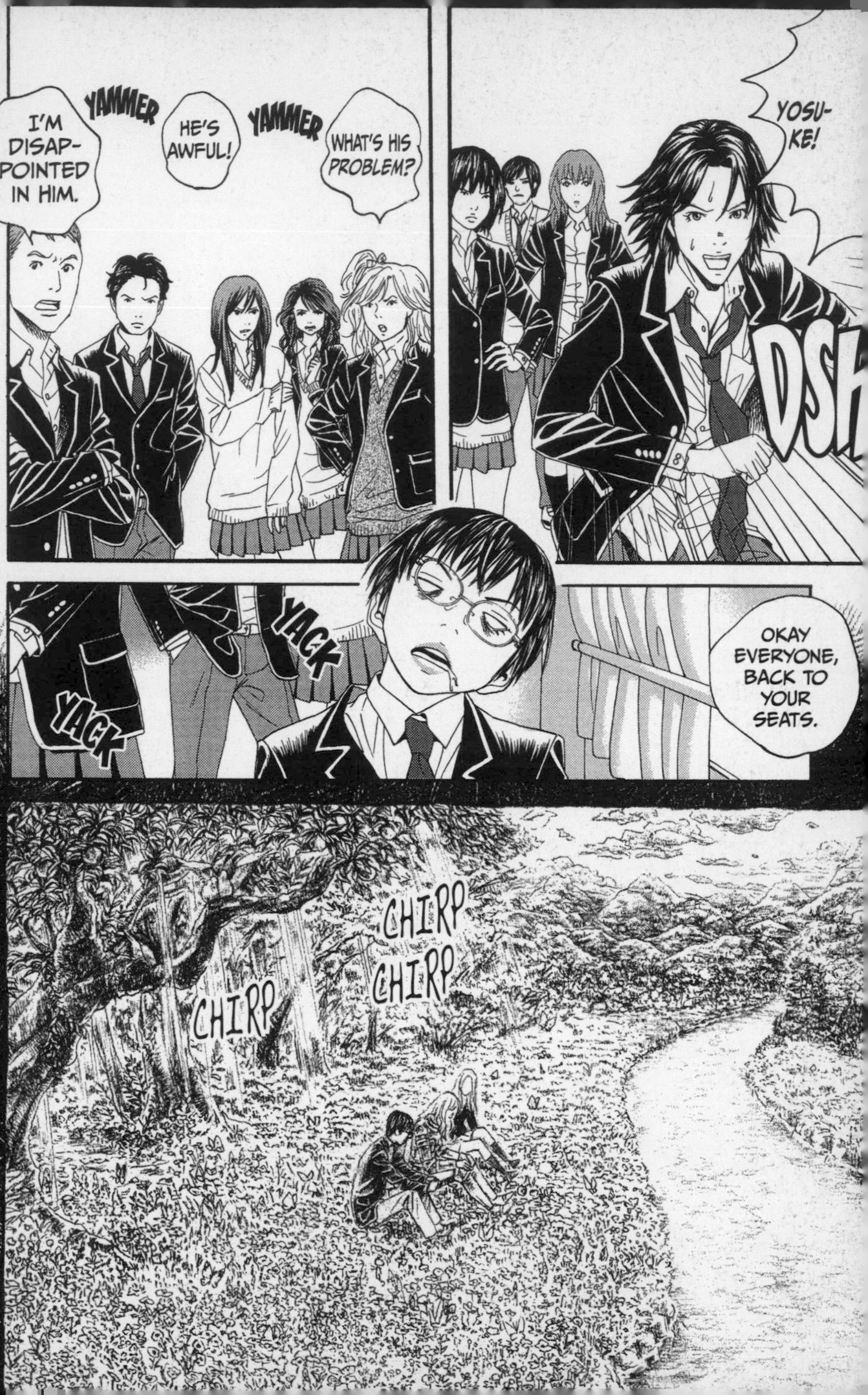
YOSU-KE!
DSH
WHAT'S HIS PROBLEM?
YAMMER
HE'S AWFUL!
YAMMER
I'M DISAP-POINTED IN HIM.
OKAY EVERYONE, BACK TO YOUR SEATS.
YACK
YACK
CHIRP
CHIRP
CHIRP

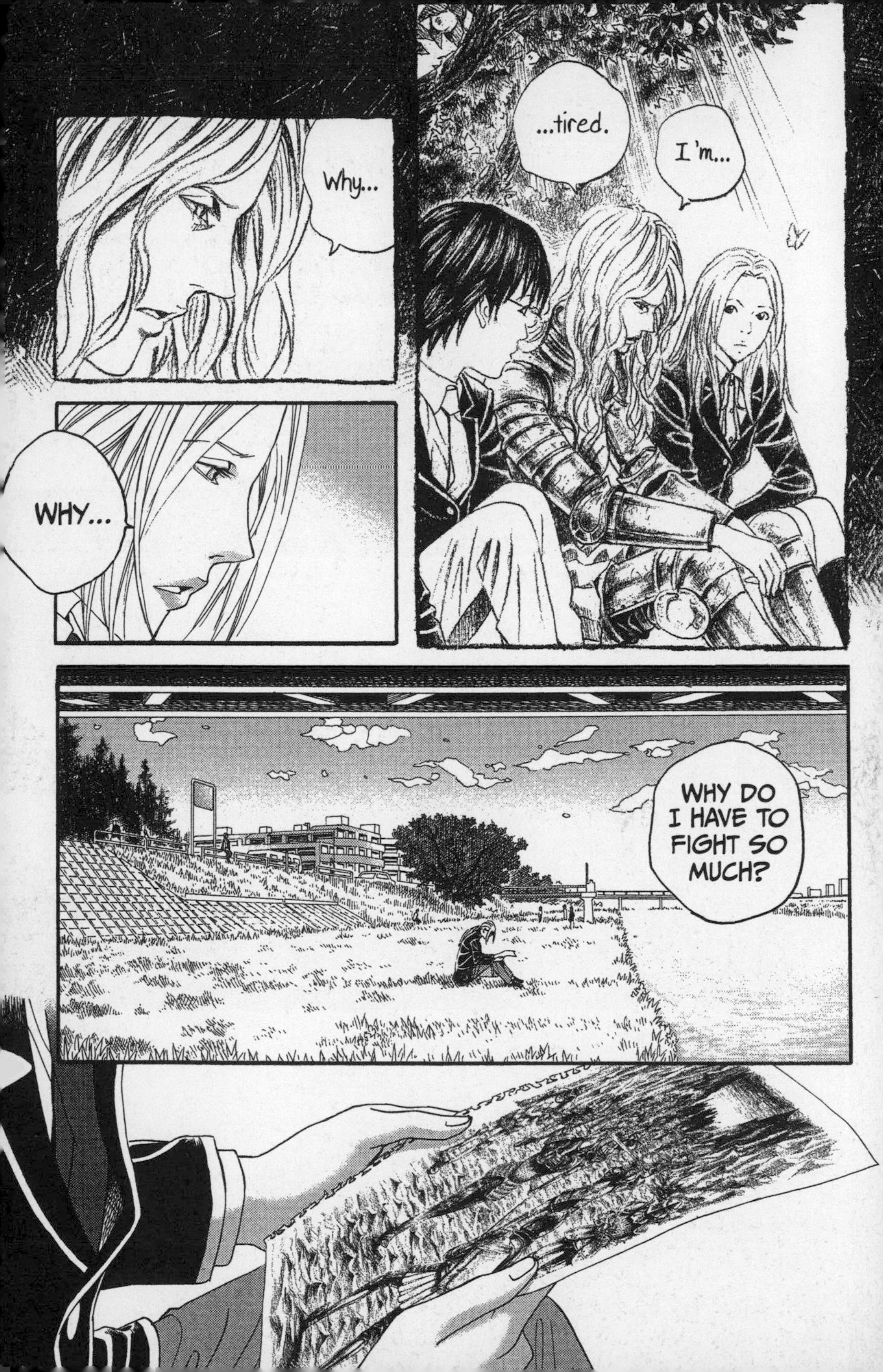
I'm...
...tired.
Why...
WHY...
WHY DO I HAVE TO FIGHT SO MUCH?

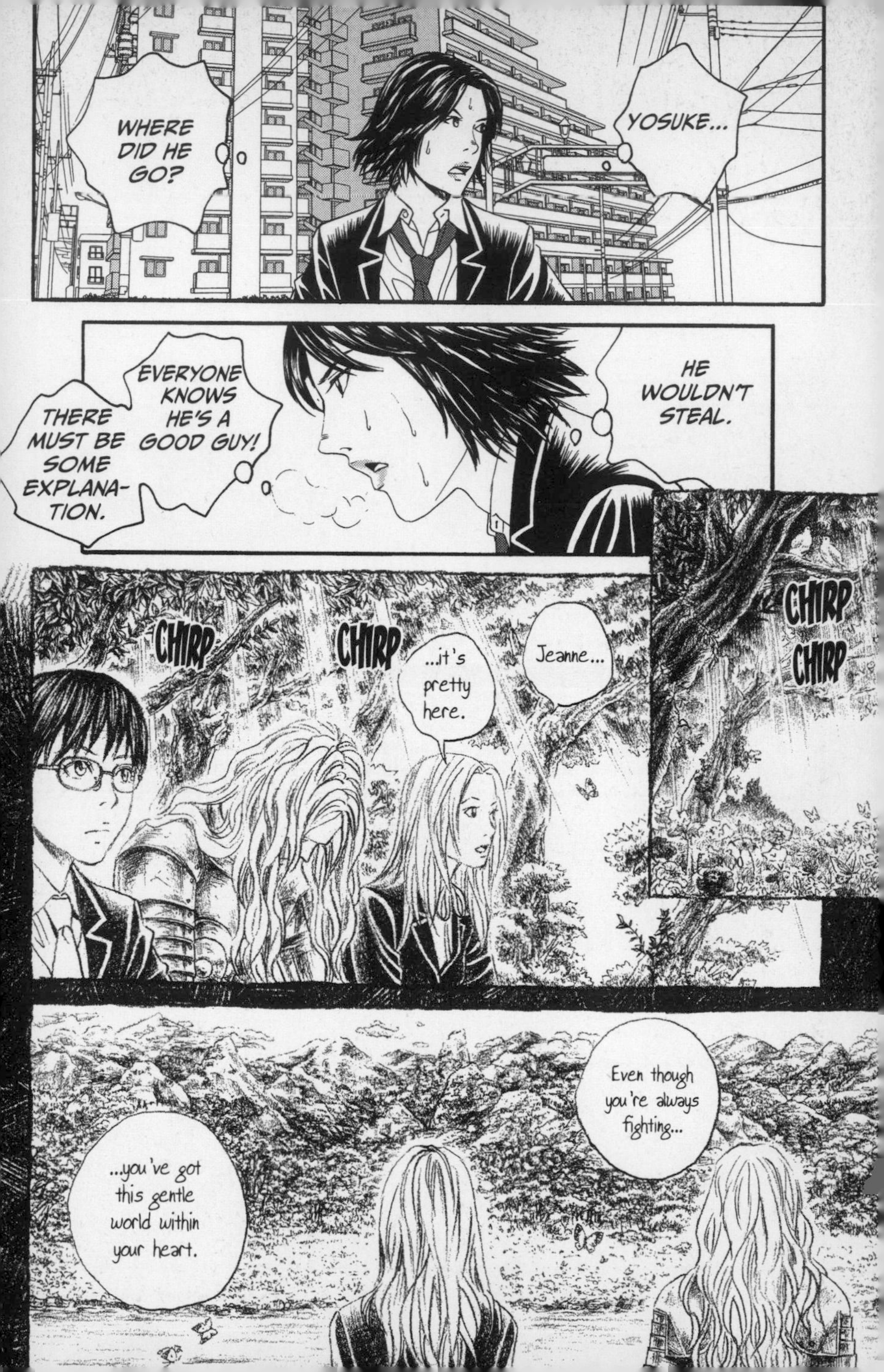
YOSUKE...
WHERE DID HE GO?
HE WOULDN'T STEAL.
EVERYONE KNOWS HE'S A GOOD GUY!
THERE MUST BE SOME EXPLANATION.
CHIRP CHIRP
Jeanne...
...it's pretty here.
CHIRP
CHIRP
Even though you're always fighting...
...you've got this gentle world within your heart.

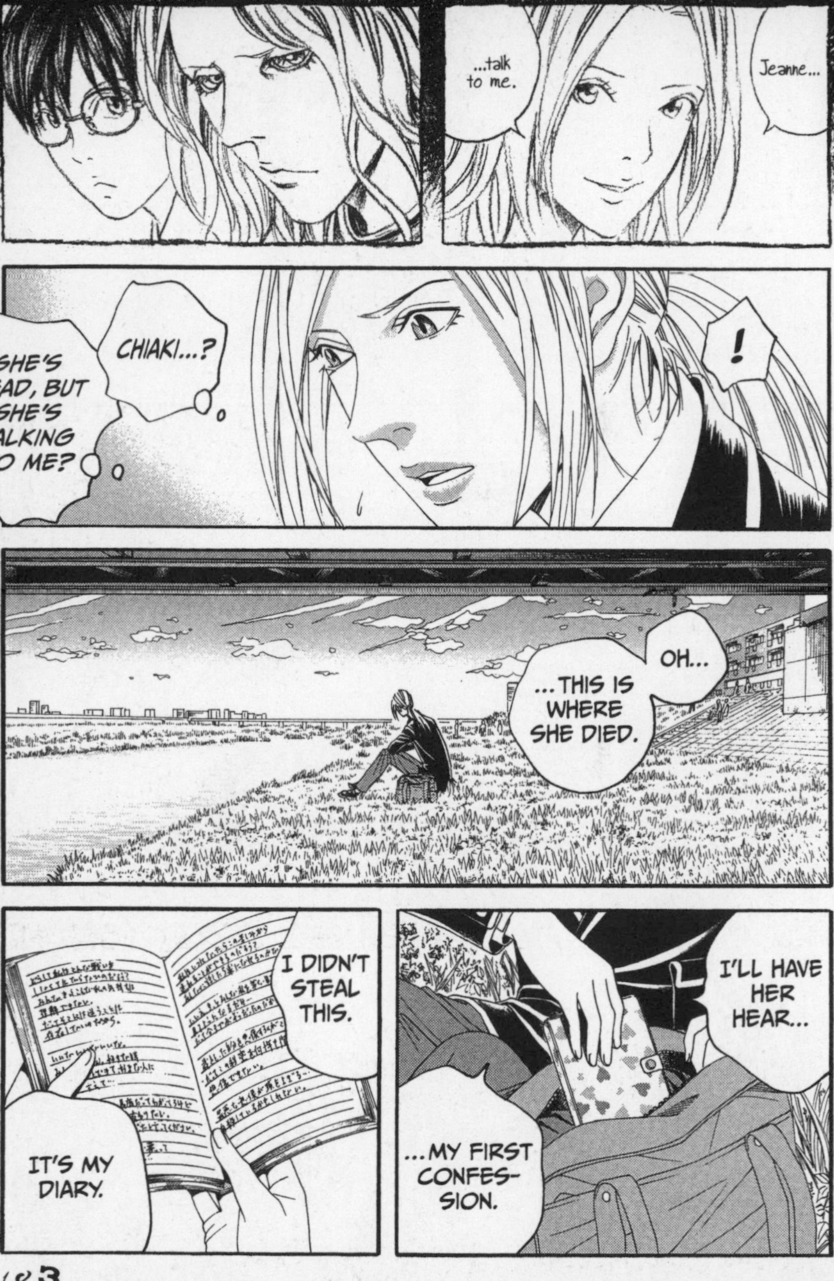
Jeanne...
...talk to me.
!
CHIAKI...?
SHE'S DEAD, BUT SHE'S TALKING TO ME?
OH...
...THIS IS WHERE SHE DIED.
I'LL HAVE HER HEAR...
...MY FIRST CONFES-SION.
I DIDN'T STEAL THIS.
IT'S MY DIARY.

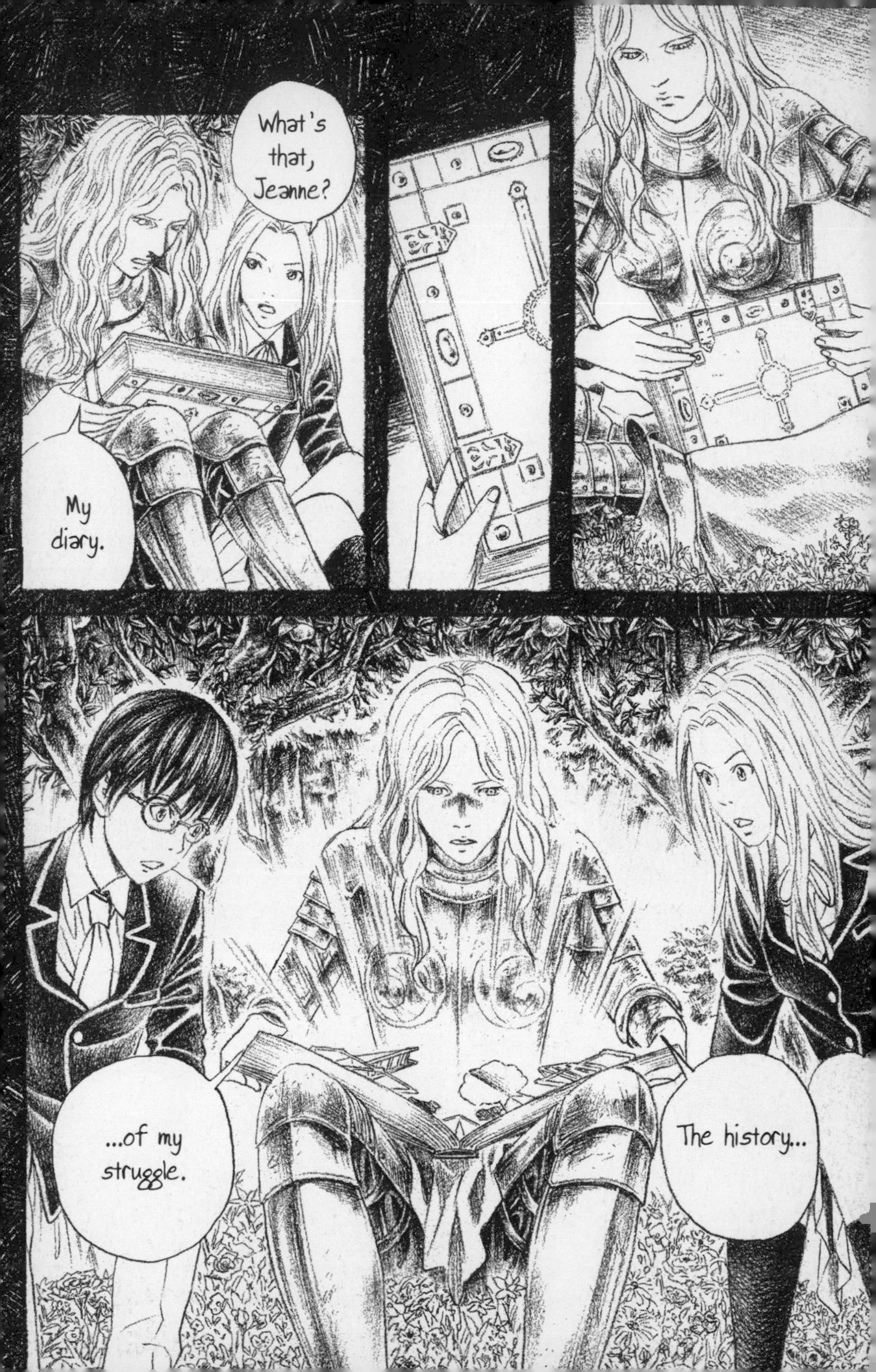
What's that, Jeanne?
My diary.
The history...
...of my struggle.

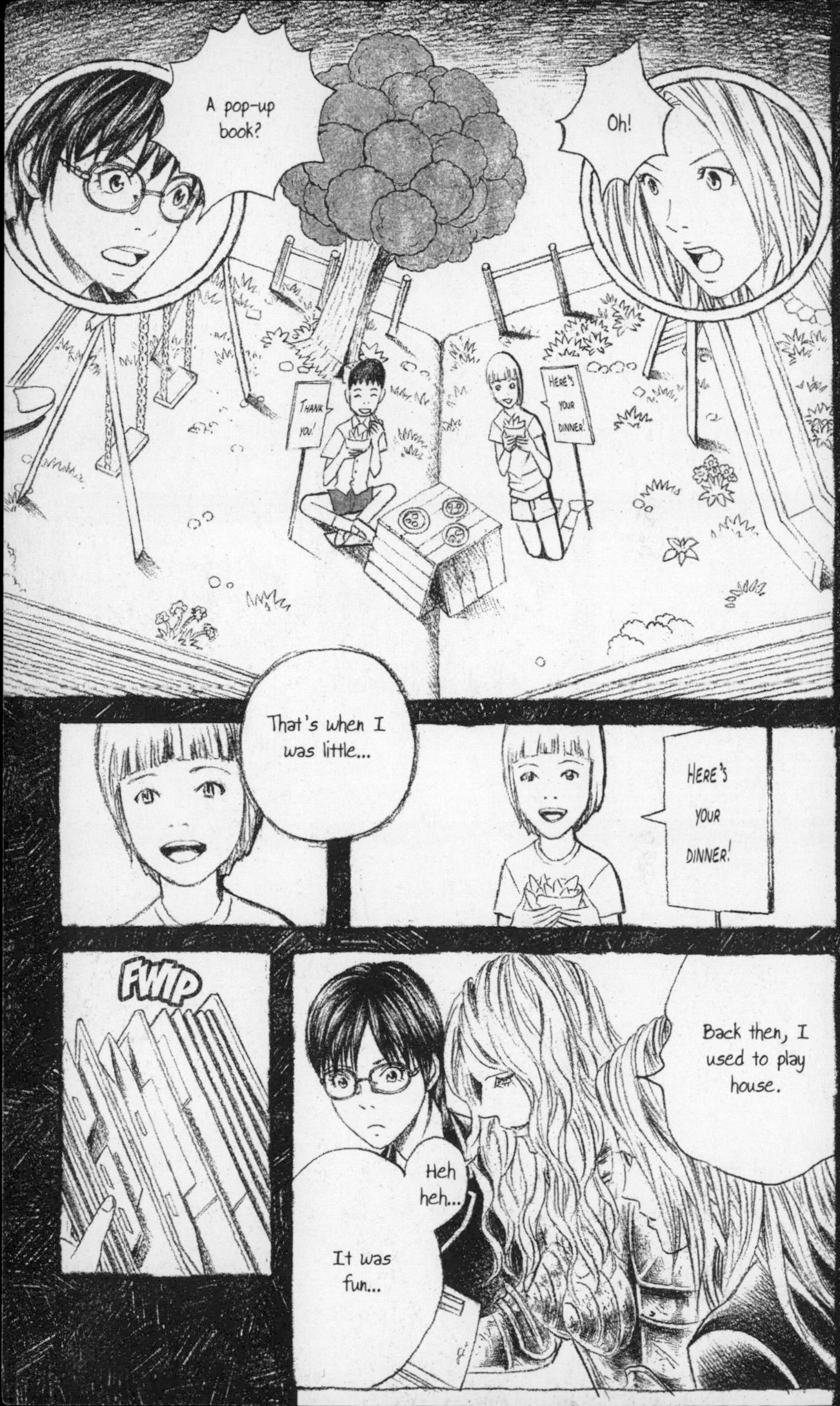
Oh!
A pop-up book?
HERE'S YOUR DINNER!
THANK YOU!
HERE'S YOUR DINNER!
That's when I was little...
Back then, I used to play house.
Heh heh...
It was fun...
FWIP

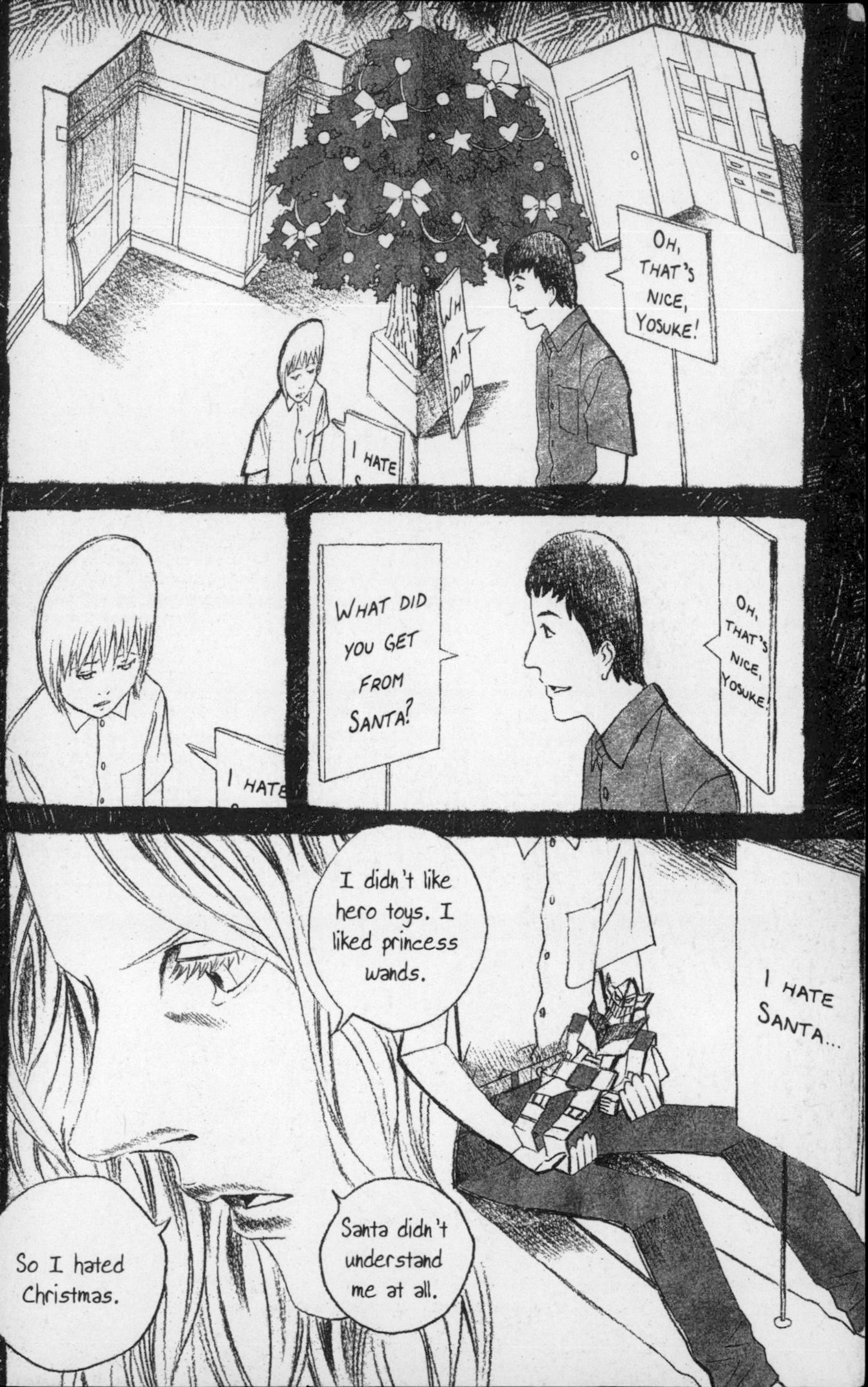
OH, THAT'S NICE, YOSUKE!
WH AT DID
I HATE
OH, THAT'S NICE, YOSUKE!
WHAT DID YOU GET FROM SANTA?
I HATE
I HATE SANTA...
I didn't like hero toys. I liked princess wands.
Santa didn't understand me at all.
So I hated Christmas.

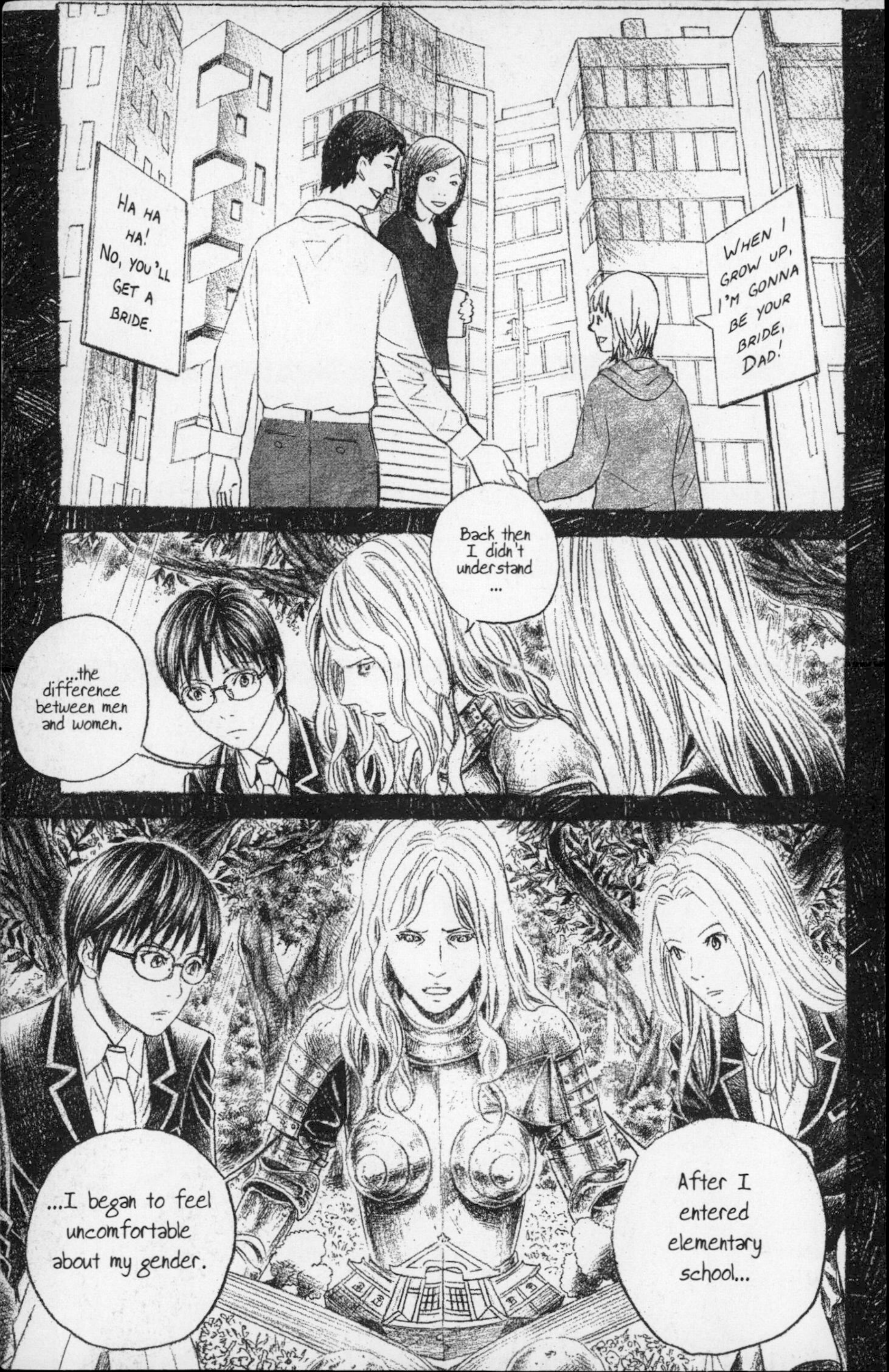
WHEN I GROW UP, I'M GONNA BE YOUR BRIDE, DAD!
HA HA HA! NO, YOU'LL GET A BRIDE.
Back then I didn't understand ...
...the difference between men and women.
After I entered elementary school...
...I began to feel uncomfortable about my gender.

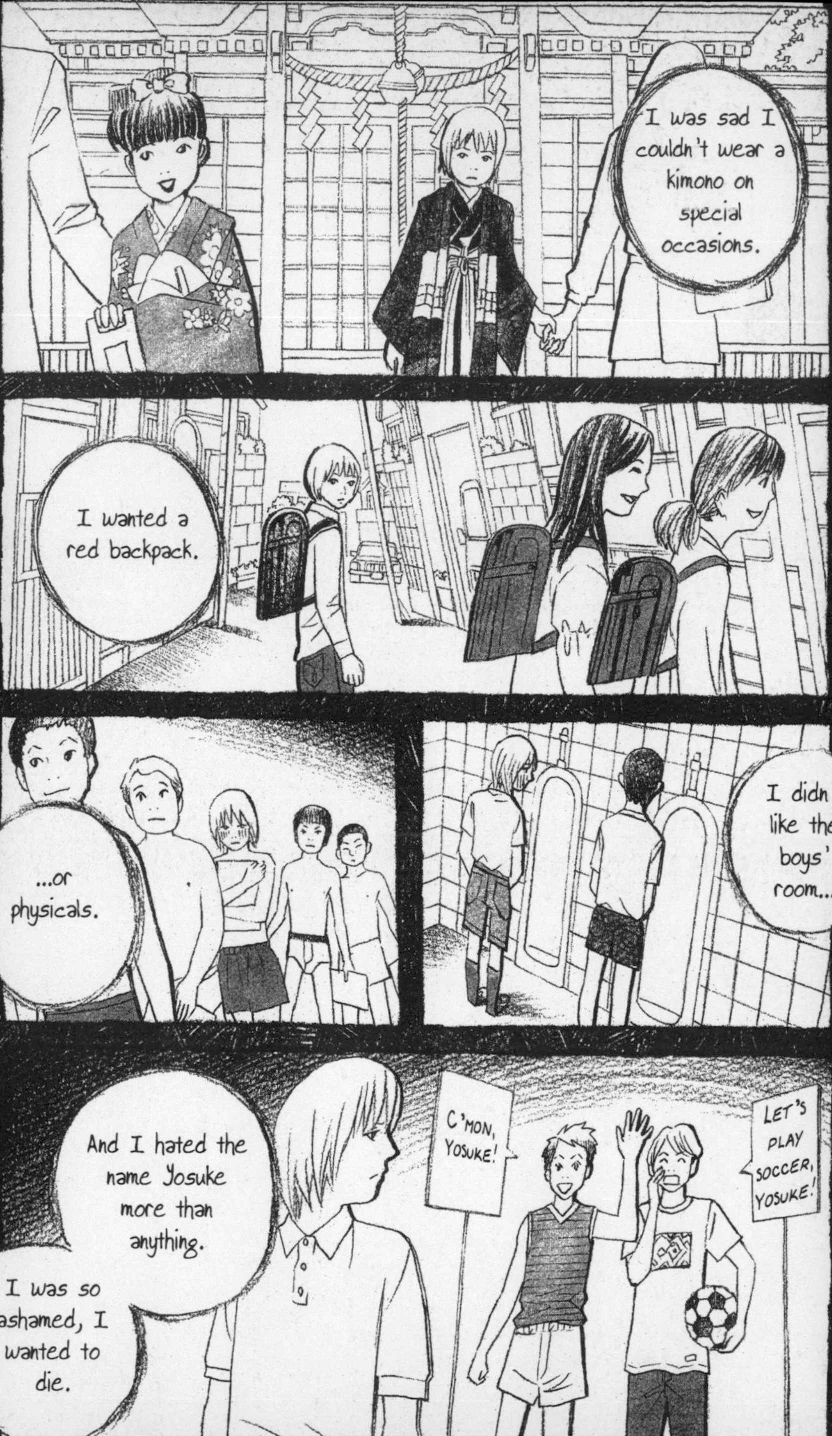
I was sad I couldn't wear a kimono on special occasions.
I wanted a red backpack.
I didn't like the boys' room...
...or physicals.
LET'S PLAY SOCCER, YOSUKE!
C'MON, YOSUKE!
And I hated the name Yosuke more than anything.
I was so ashamed, I wanted to die.

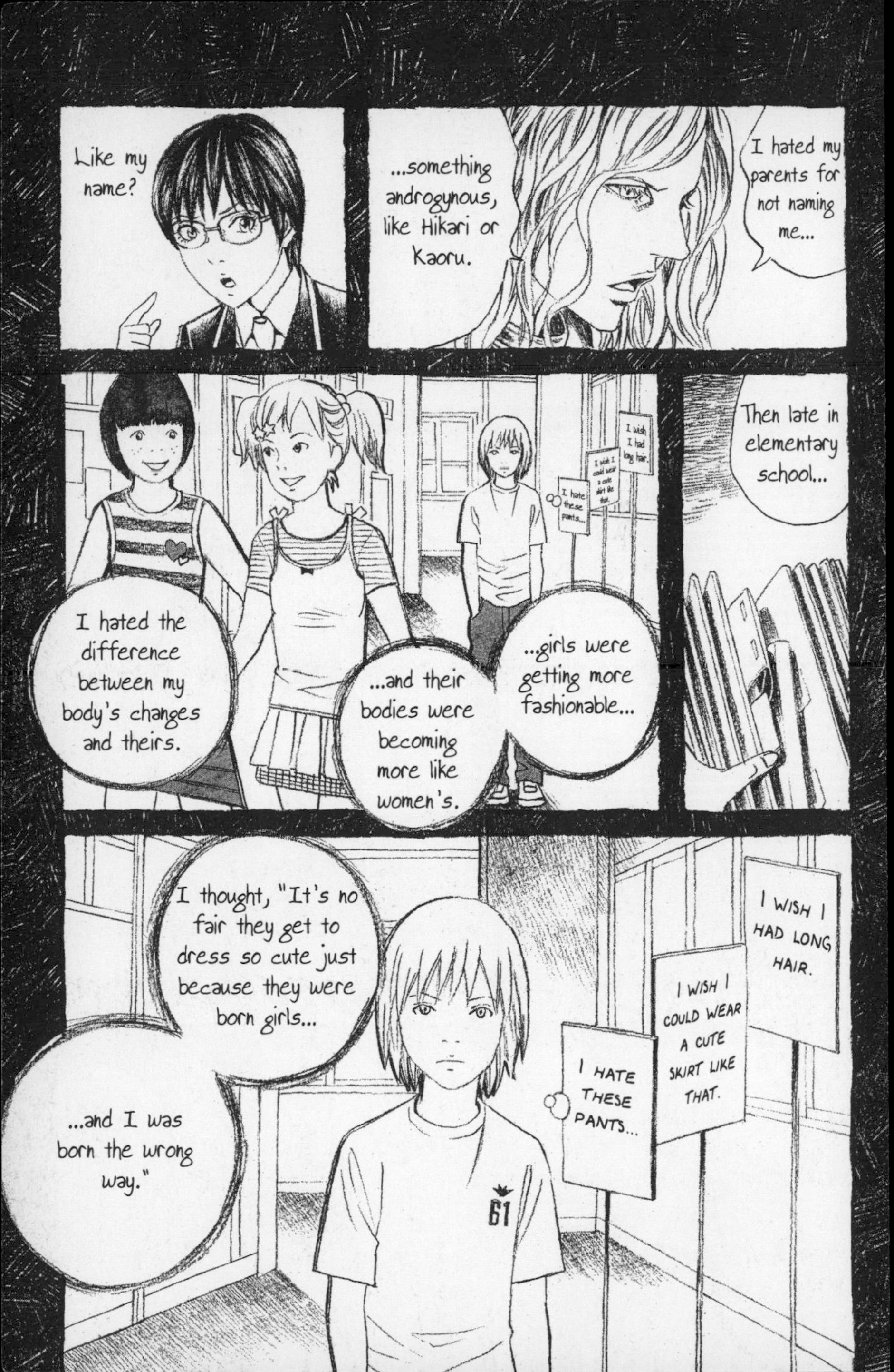
I hated my parents for not naming me...
...something androgynous, like Hikari or Kaoru.
Like my name?
Then late in elementary school...
I wish I had long hair.
I wish I could wear a cute skirt like that.
I hate these pants...
...girls were getting more fashionable...
...and their bodies were becoming more like women's.
I hated the difference between my body's changes and theirs.
I WISH I HAD LONG HAIR.
I WISH I COULD WEAR A CUTE SKIRT LIKE THAT.
I HATE THESE PANTS...
I thought, "It's no fair they get to dress so cute just because they were born girls...
...and I was born the wrong way."

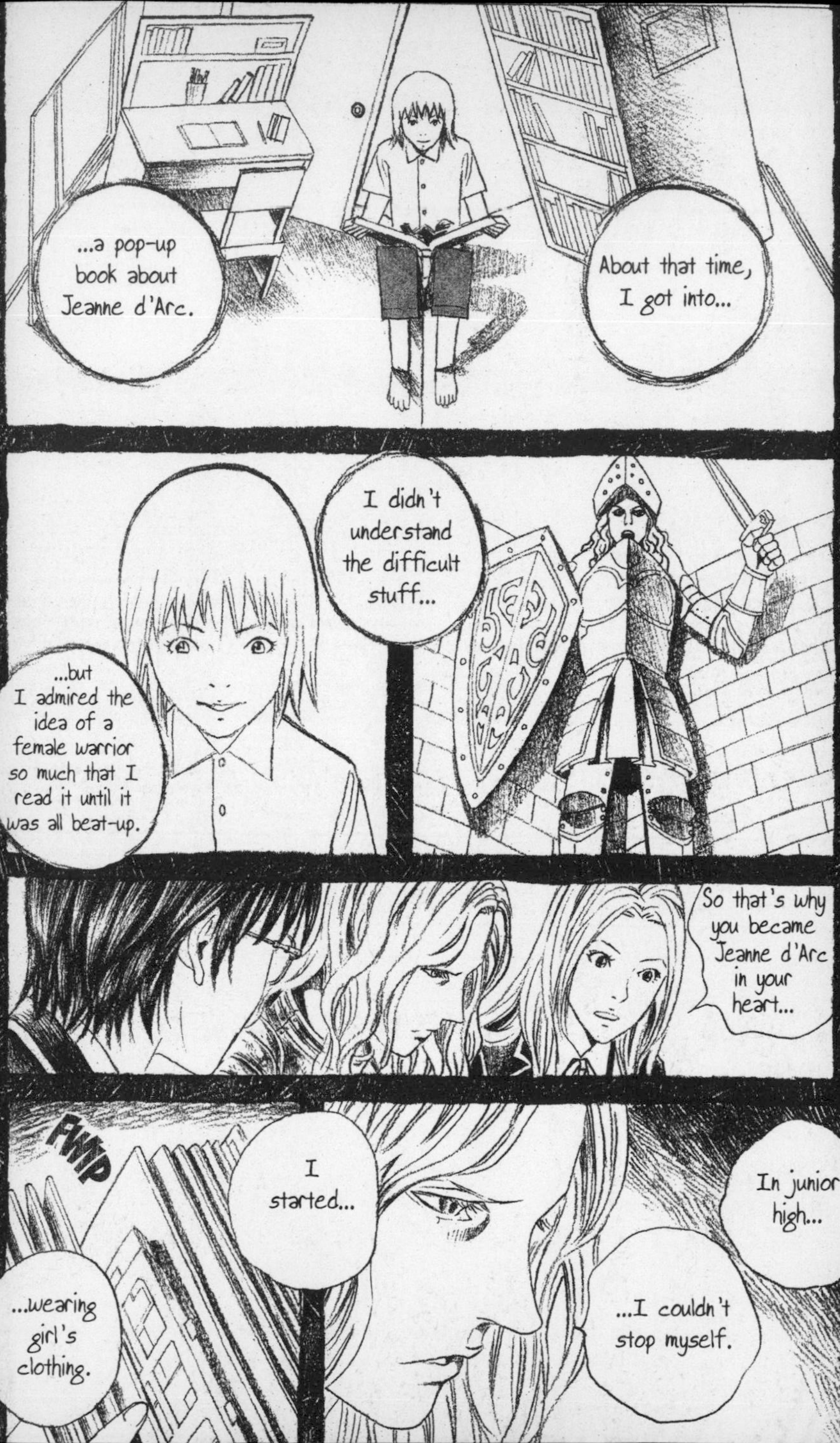
About that time, I got into...
...a pop-up book about Jeanne d'Arc.
I didn't understand the difficult stuff...
...but I admired the idea of a female warrior so much that I read it until it was all beat-up.
So that's why you became Jeanne d'Arc in your heart...
FWMP
In junior high...
...I couldn't stop myself.
I started...
...wearing girl's clothing.

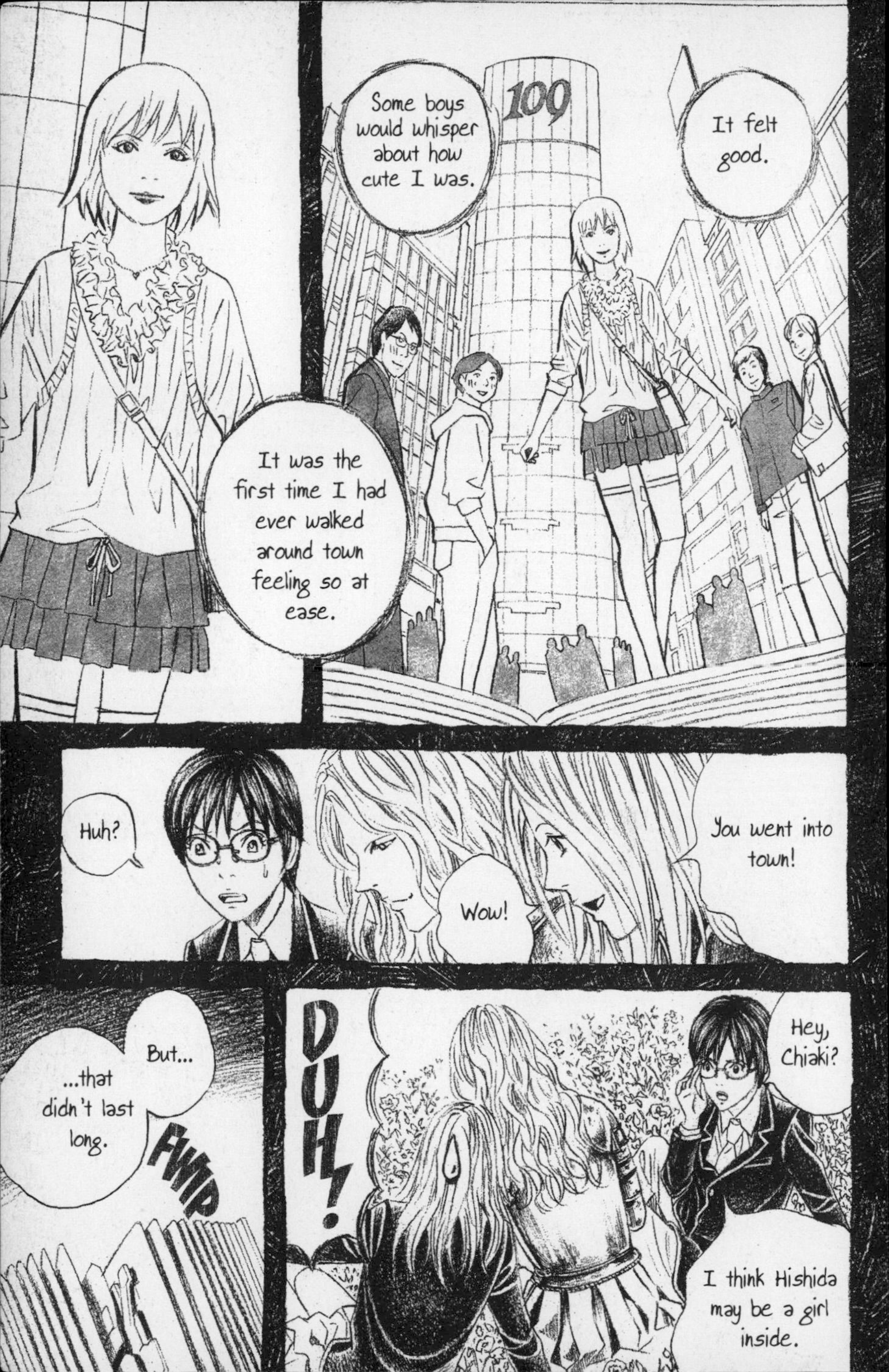
It felt good.
Some boys would whisper about how cute I was.
109
It was the first time I had ever walked around town feeling so at ease.
You went into town!
Wow!
Huh?
Hey, Chiaki?
DUHS!
I think Hishida may be a girl inside.
But...
...that didn't last long.
FWIP

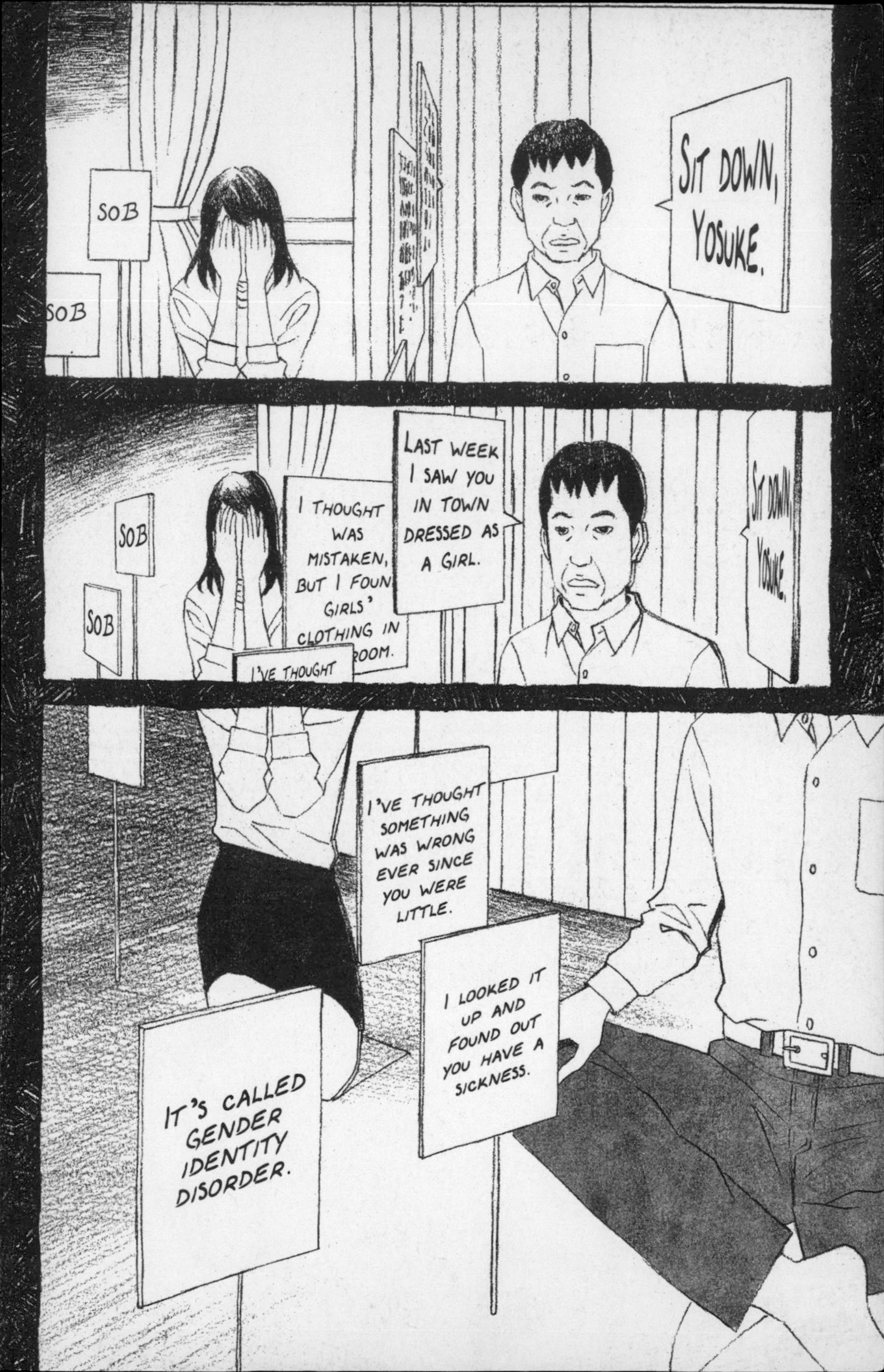
SIT DOWN, YOSUKE.
SOB
SOB
SIT DOWN, YOSUKE.
LAST WEEK I SAW YOU IN TOWN DRESSED AS A GIRL.
I THOUGHT WAS MISTAKEN, BUT I FOUN GIRLS' CLOTHING IN ROOM.
SOB
SOB
I'VE THOUGHT
I'VE THOUGHT SOMETHING WAS WRONG EVER SINCE YOU WERE LITTLE.
I LOOKED IT UP AND FOUND OUT YOU HAVE A SICKNESS.
IT'S CALLED GENDER IDENTITY DISORDER.

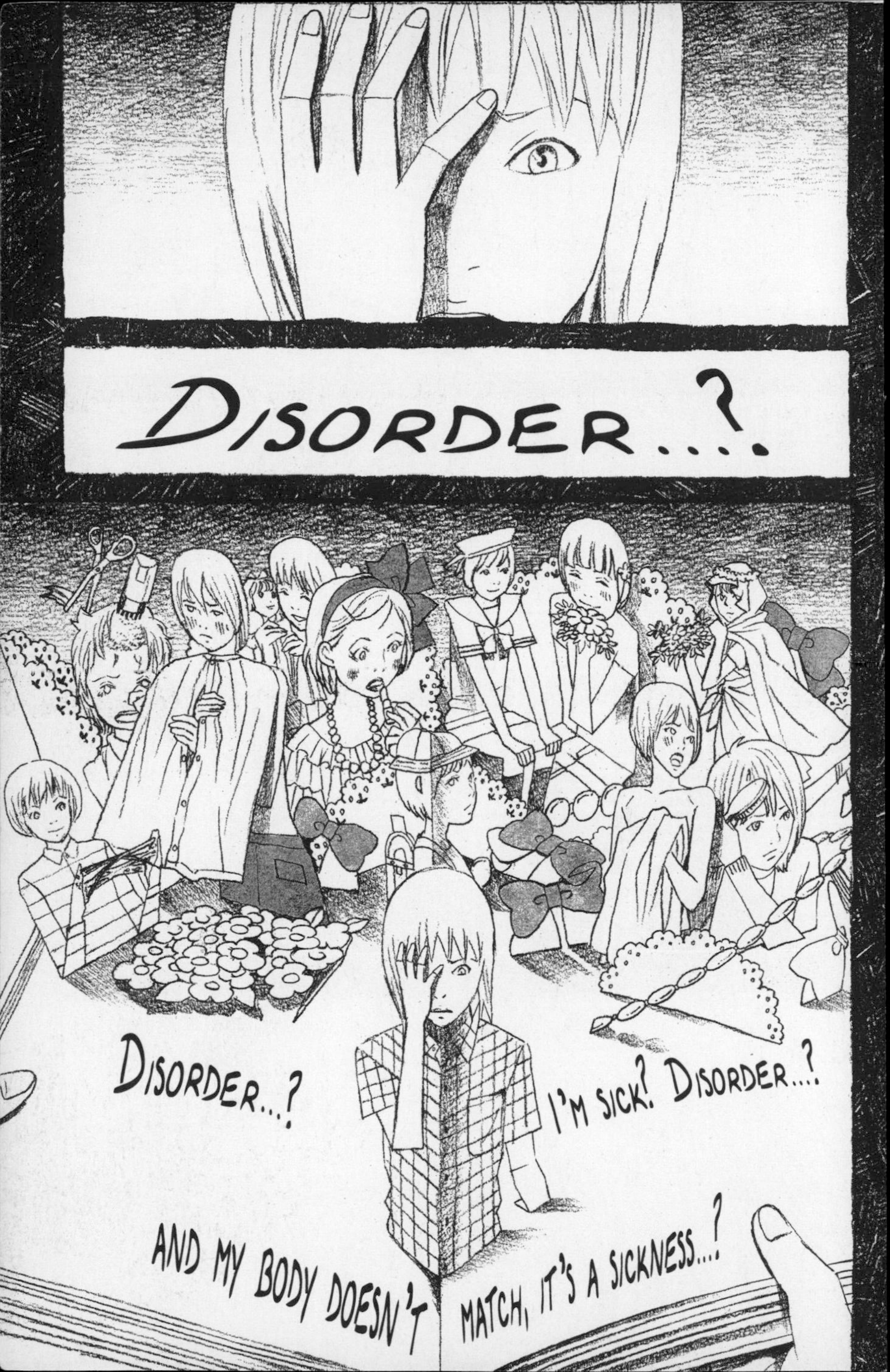
DISORDER...?
I'M SICK? DISORDER...?
DISORDER...?
AND MY BODY DOESN'T MATCH, IT'S A SICKNESS...?

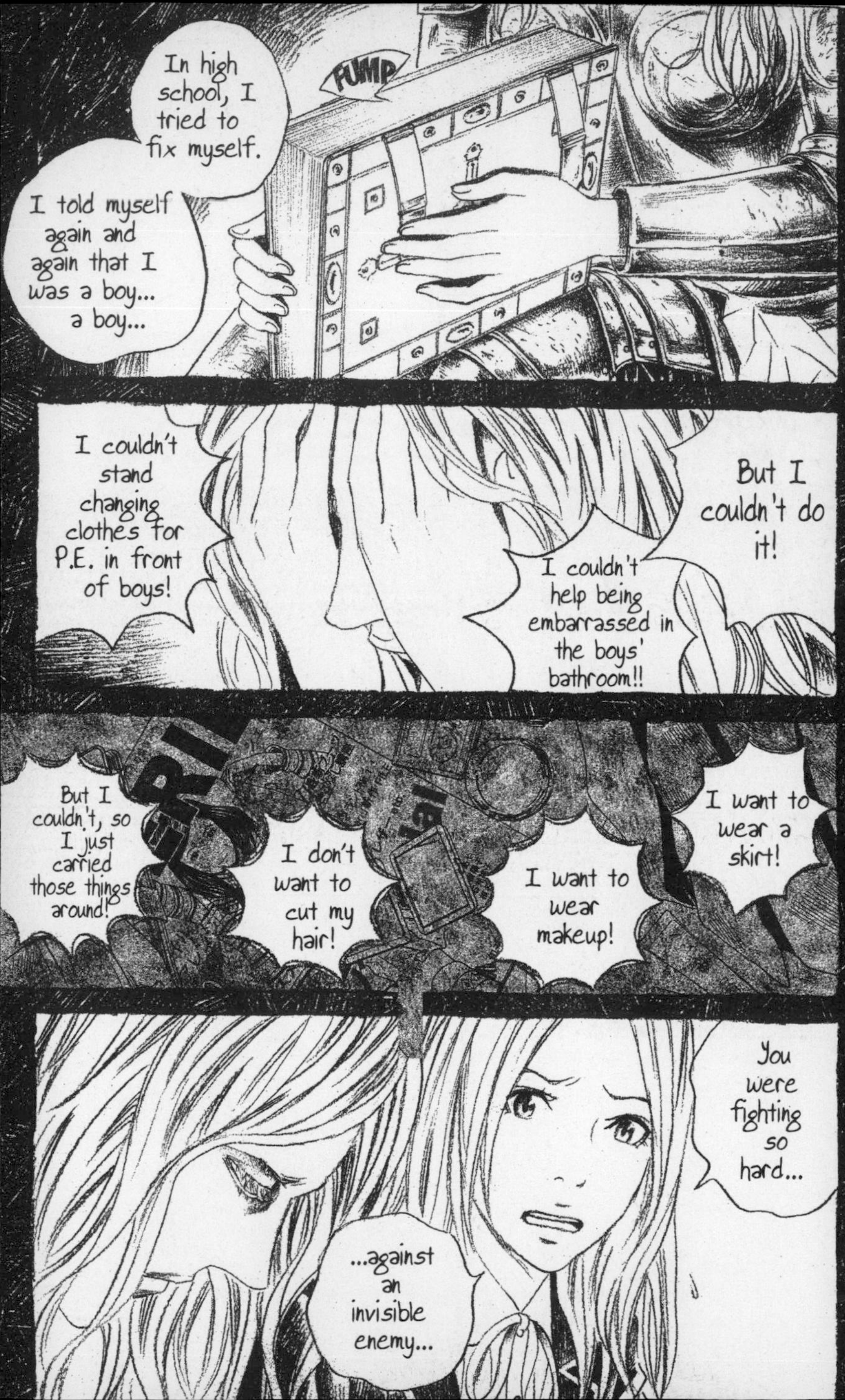

In high school, I tried to fix myself.
I told myself again and again that I was a boy... a boy...
FUMP
But I couldn't do it!
I couldn't help being embarrassed in the boys' bathroom!!
I couldn't stand changing clothes for P.E. in front of boys!
I want to wear a skirt!
I want to wear makeup!
I don't want to cut my hair!
But I couldn't, so I just carried those things around!
You were fighting so hard...
...against an invisible enemy...

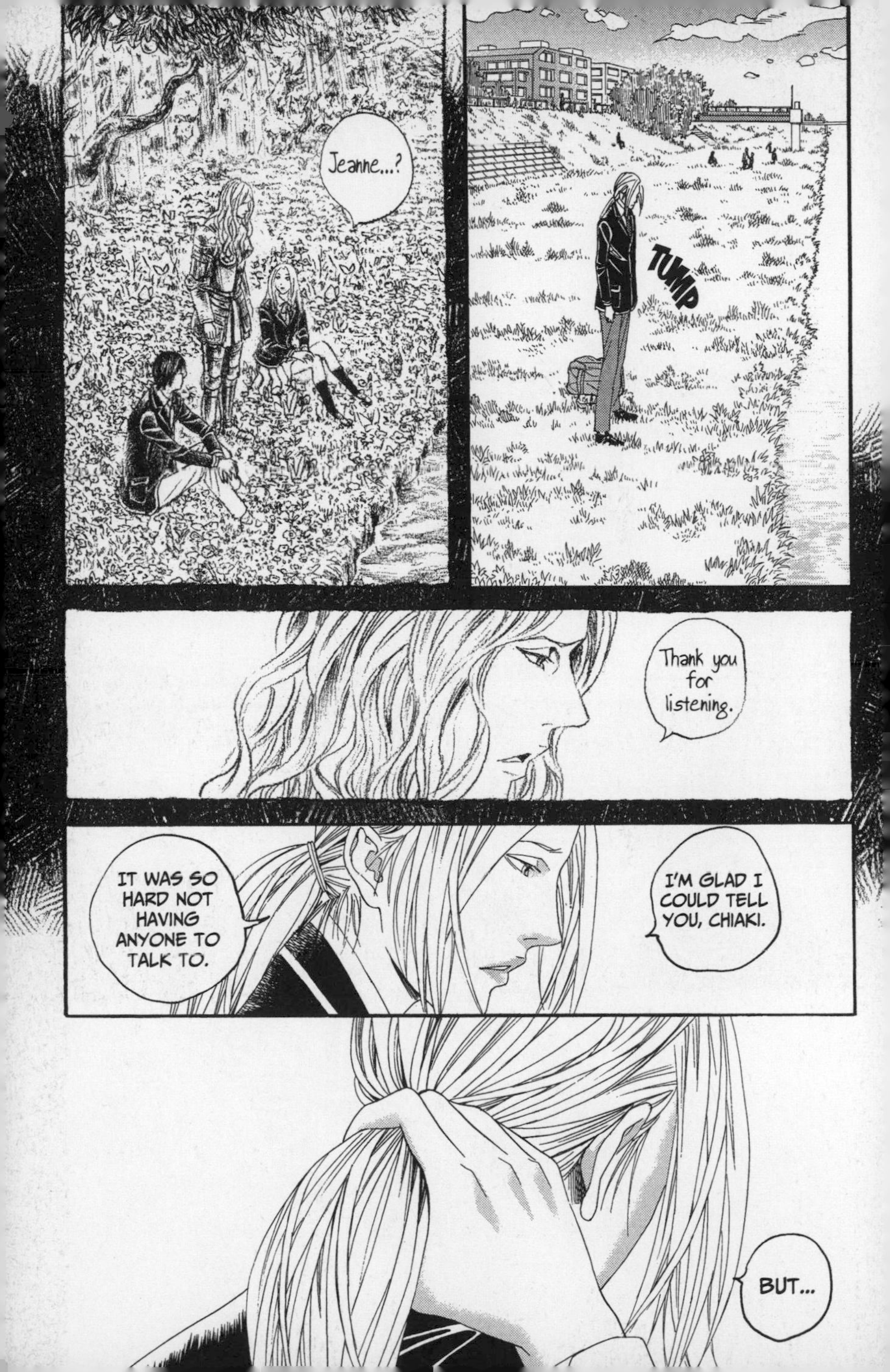
TUMP
Jeanne...?
Thank you for listening.
I'M GLAD I COULD TELL YOU, CHIAKI.
IT WAS SO HARD NOT HAVING ANYONE TO TALK TO.
BUT...

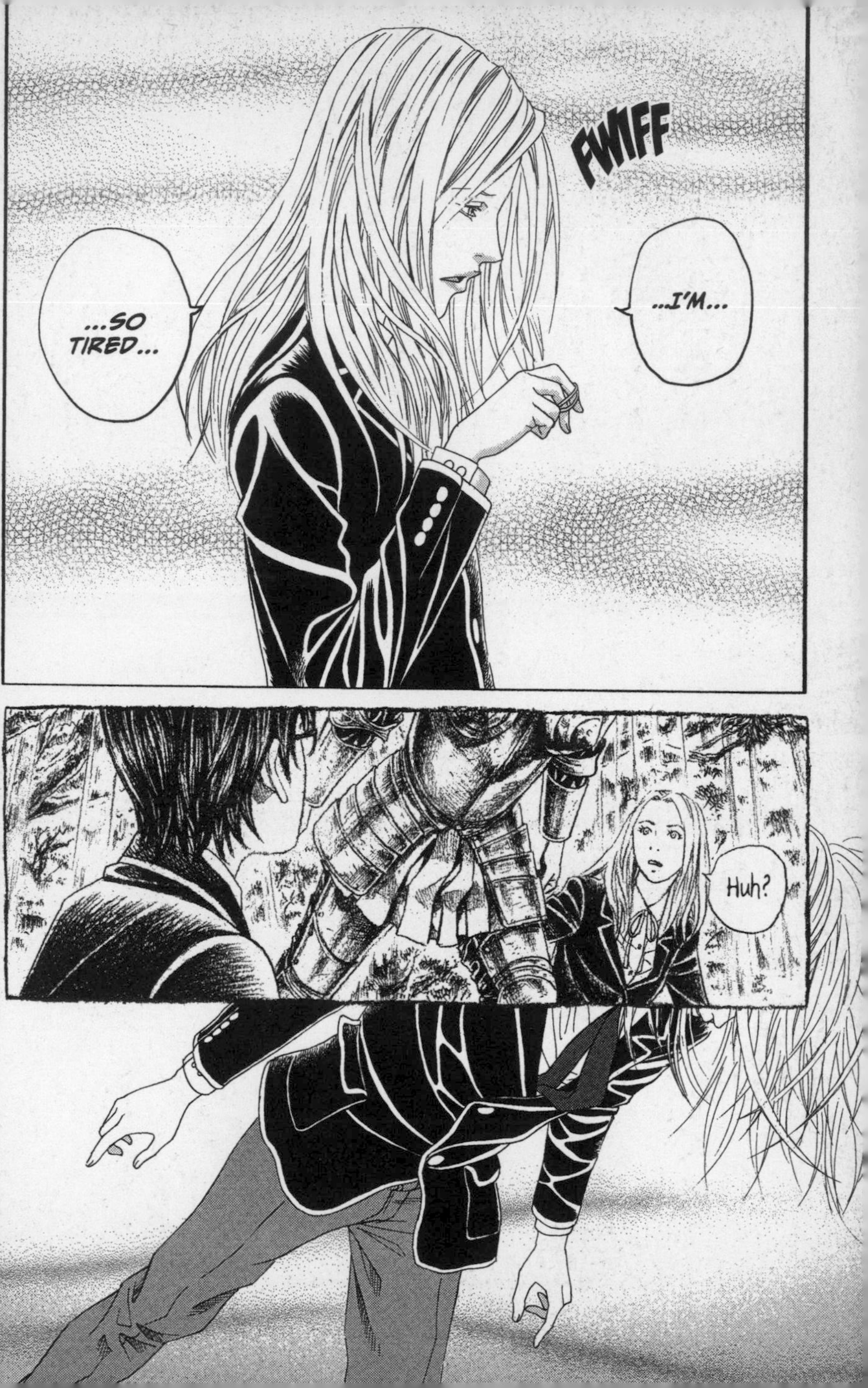
FWIFF
...I'M...
...SO TIRED...
Huh?

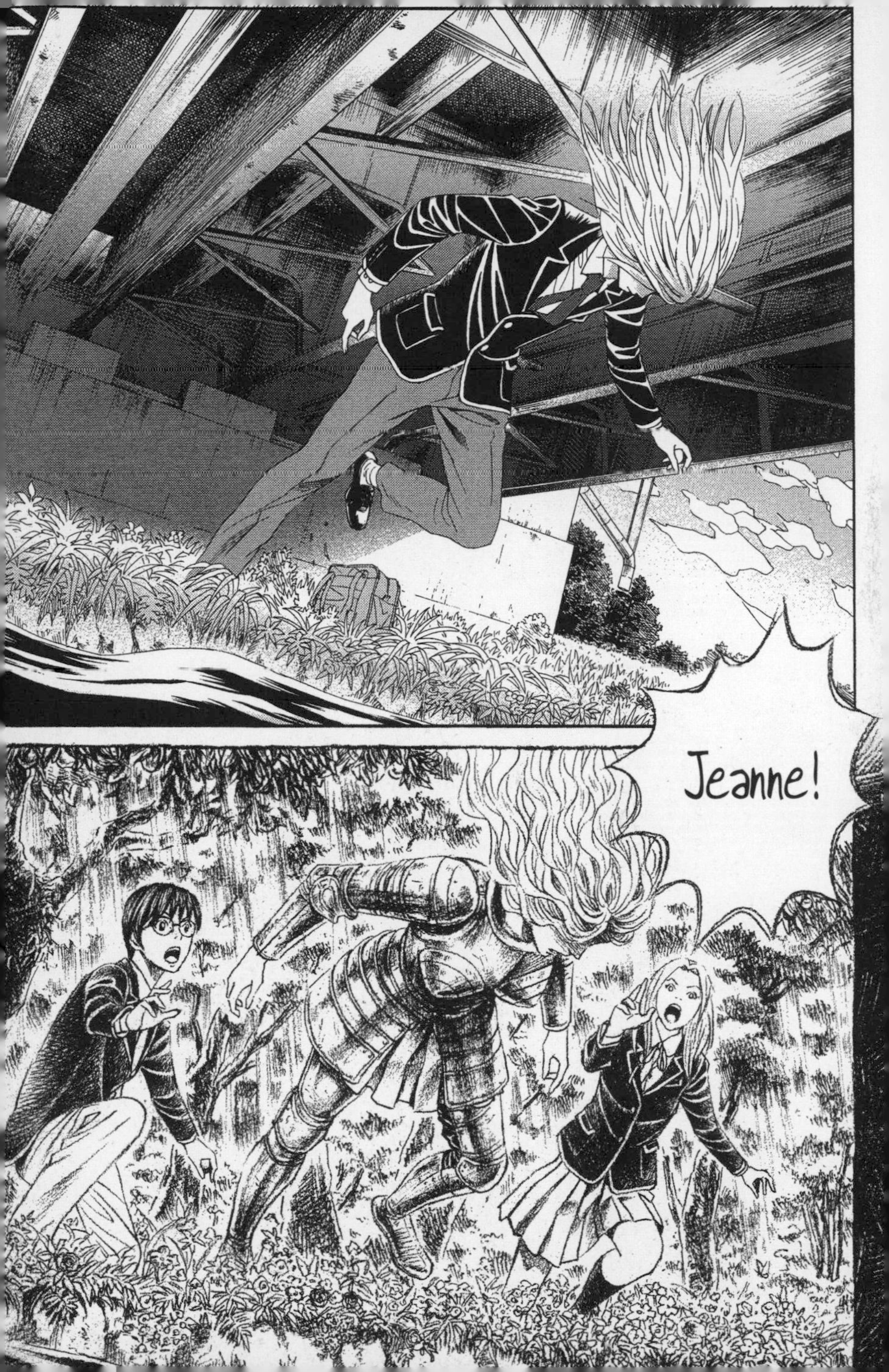
Jeanne!

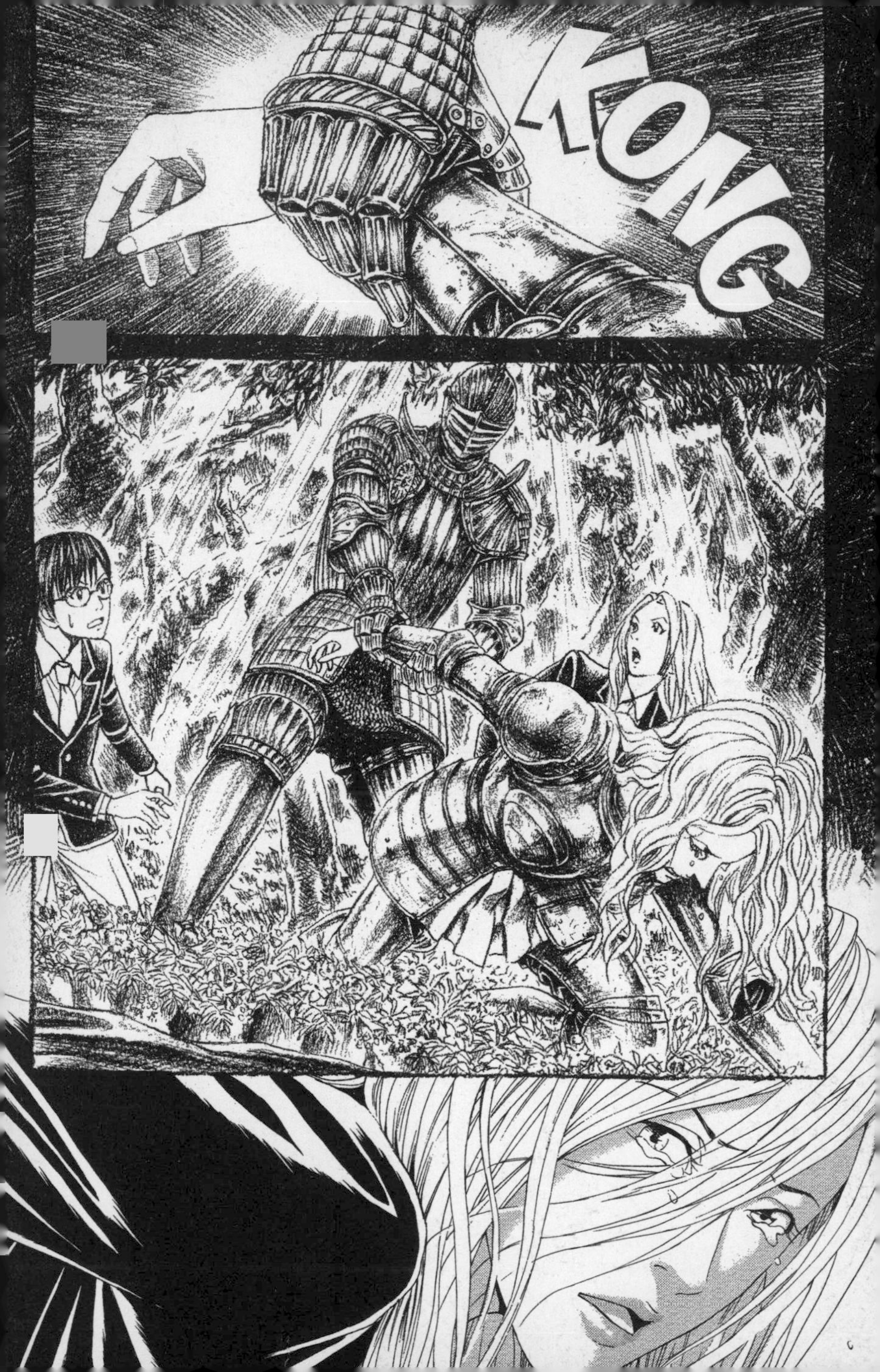
KONG

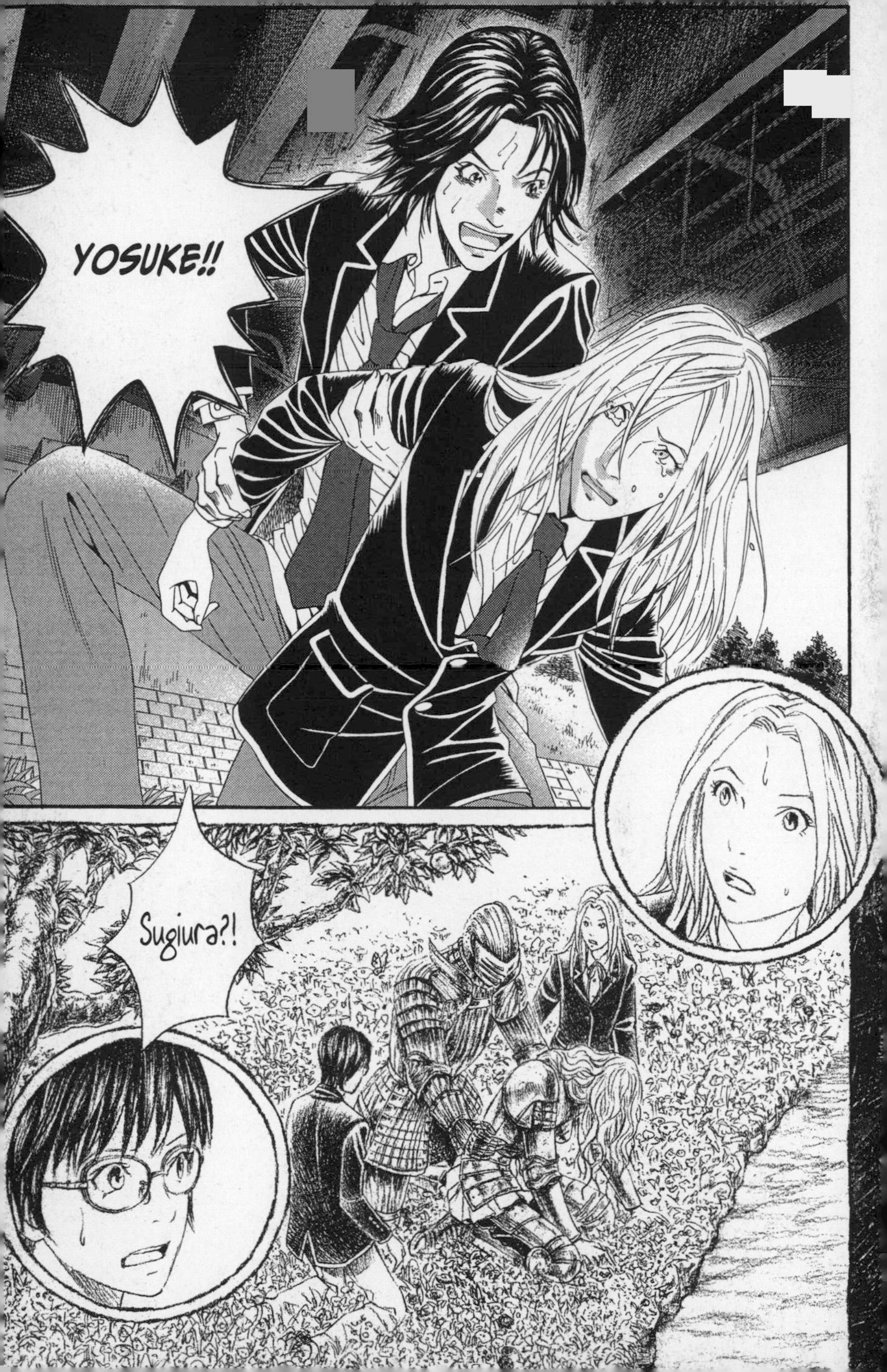
YOSUKE!!
Sugiura?!

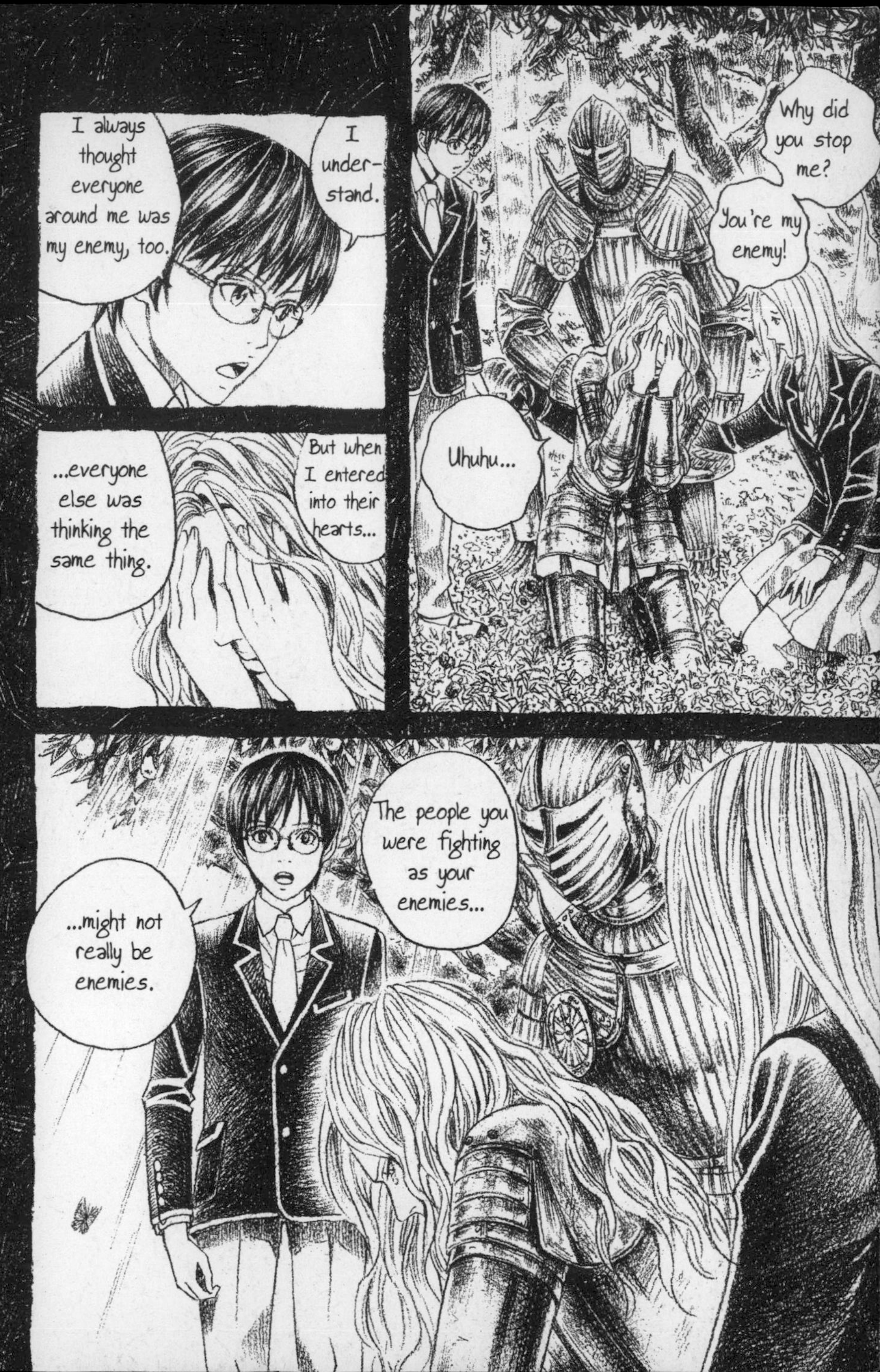
Why did you stop me?
You're my enemy!
Uhuhu...
I understand.
I always thought everyone around me was my enemy, too.
But when I entered into their hearts...
...everyone else was thinking the same thing.
The people you were fighting as your enemies...
...might not really be enemies.

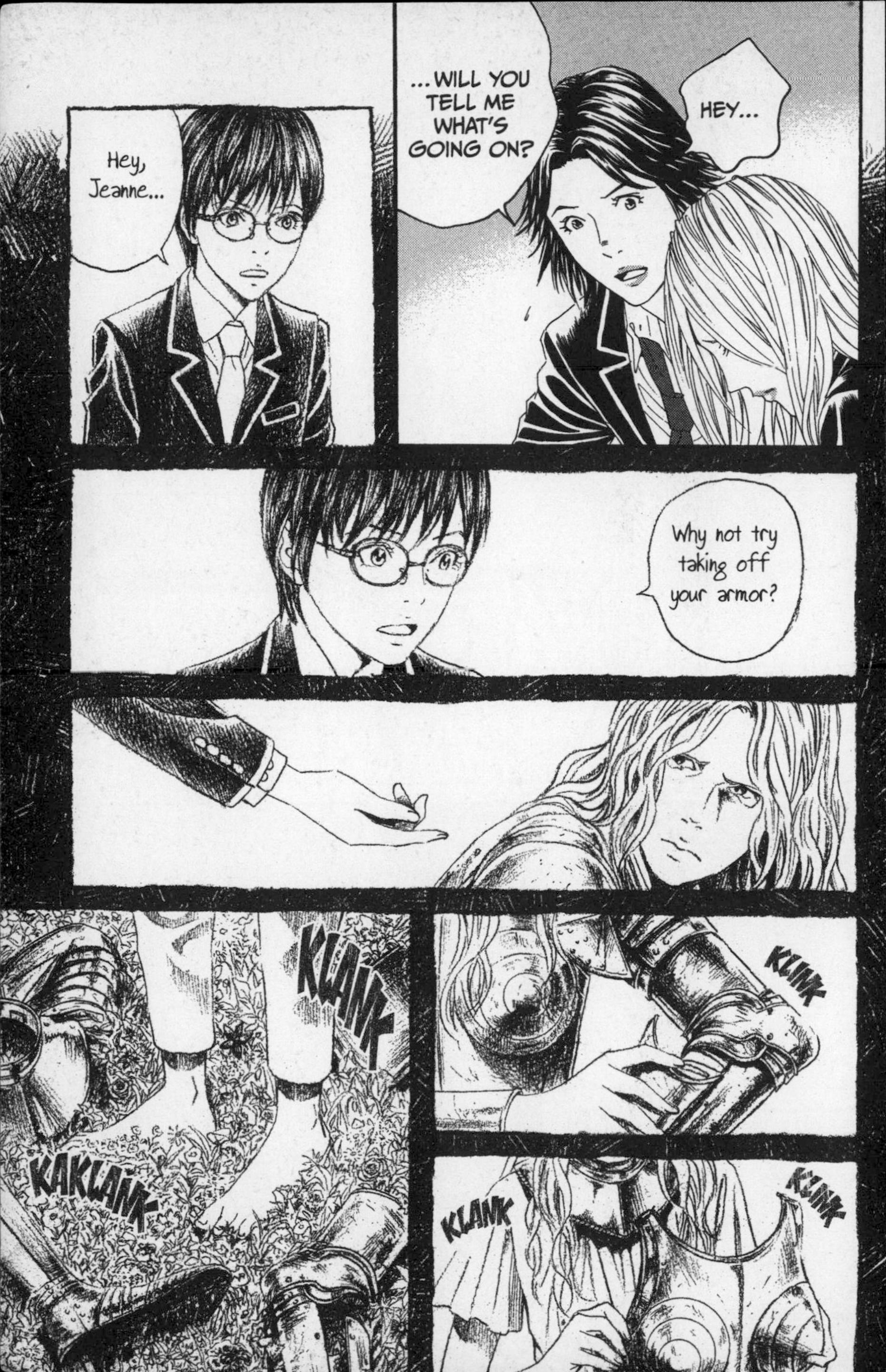
HEY...
...WILL YOU TELL ME WHAT'S GOING ON?
Hey, Jeanne...
Why not try taking off your armor?
KLINK
KLINK
KLANK
KLANK
KAKLANK

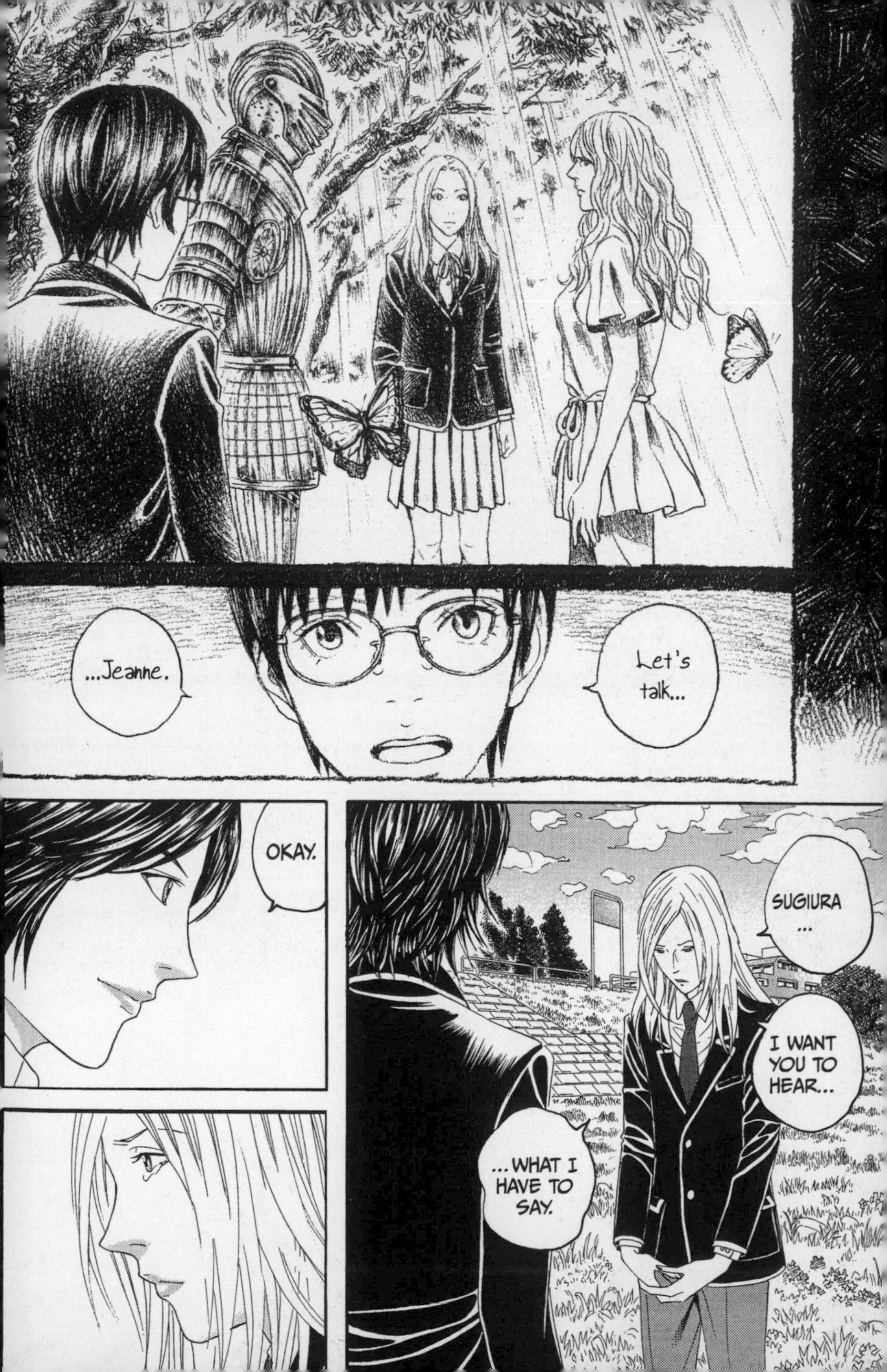
Let's talk...
...Jeanne.
SUGIURA ...
I WANT YOU TO HEAR...
...WHAT I HAVE TO SAY.
OKAY.

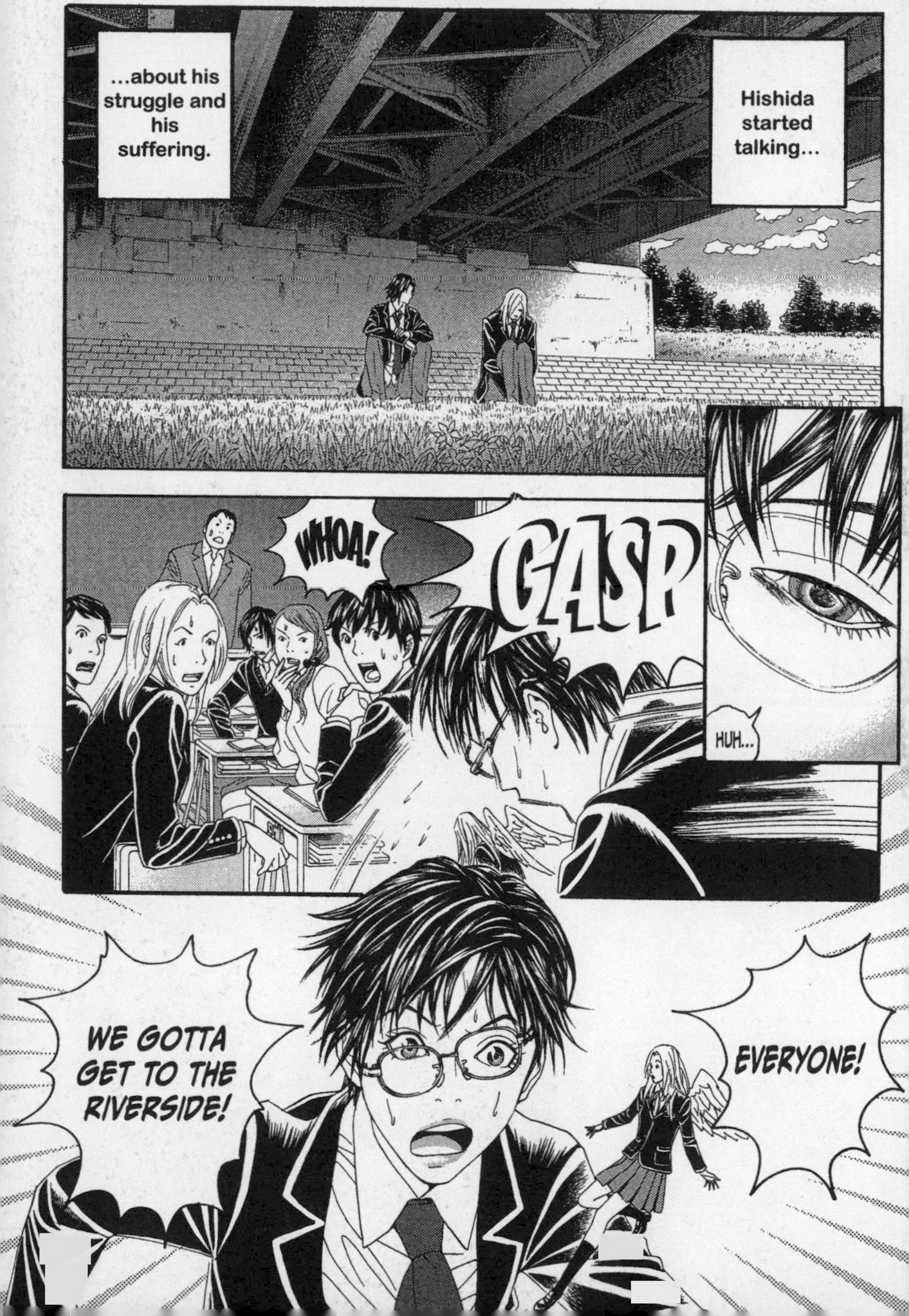
Hishida started talking...
...about his struggle and his suffering.
HUH...
GASP
WHOA!
EVERYONE!
WE GOTTA GET TO THE RIVERSIDE!

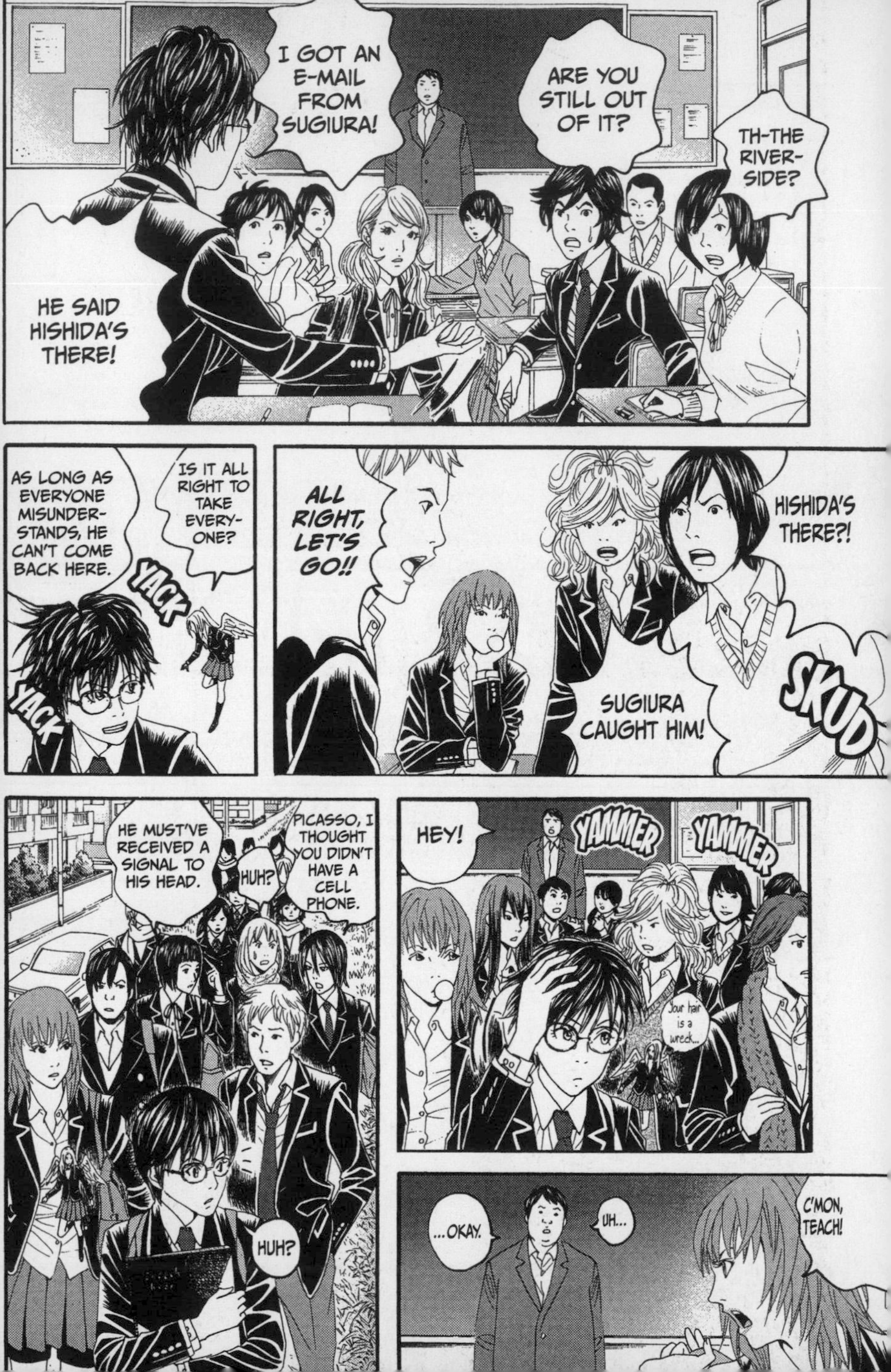
TH-THE RIVER-SIDE?
ARE YOU STILL OUT OF IT?
I GOT AN E-MAIL FROM SUGIURA!
HE SAID HISHIDA'S THERE!
HISHIDA'S THERE?!
SKUD
SUGIURA CAUGHT HIM!
ALL RIGHT, LET'S GO!!
IS IT ALL RIGHT TO TAKE EVERYONE?
AS LONG AS EVERYONE MISUNDERSTANDS, HE CAN'T COME BACK HERE.
YACK
YACK
YAMMER
YAMMER
HEY!
Your hair is a wreck...
C'MON, TEACH!
UH...
...OKAY.
PICASSO, I THOUGHT YOU DIDN'T HAVE A CELL PHONE.
HUH?
HE MUST'VE RECEIVED A SIGNAL TO HIS HEAD.
HUH?

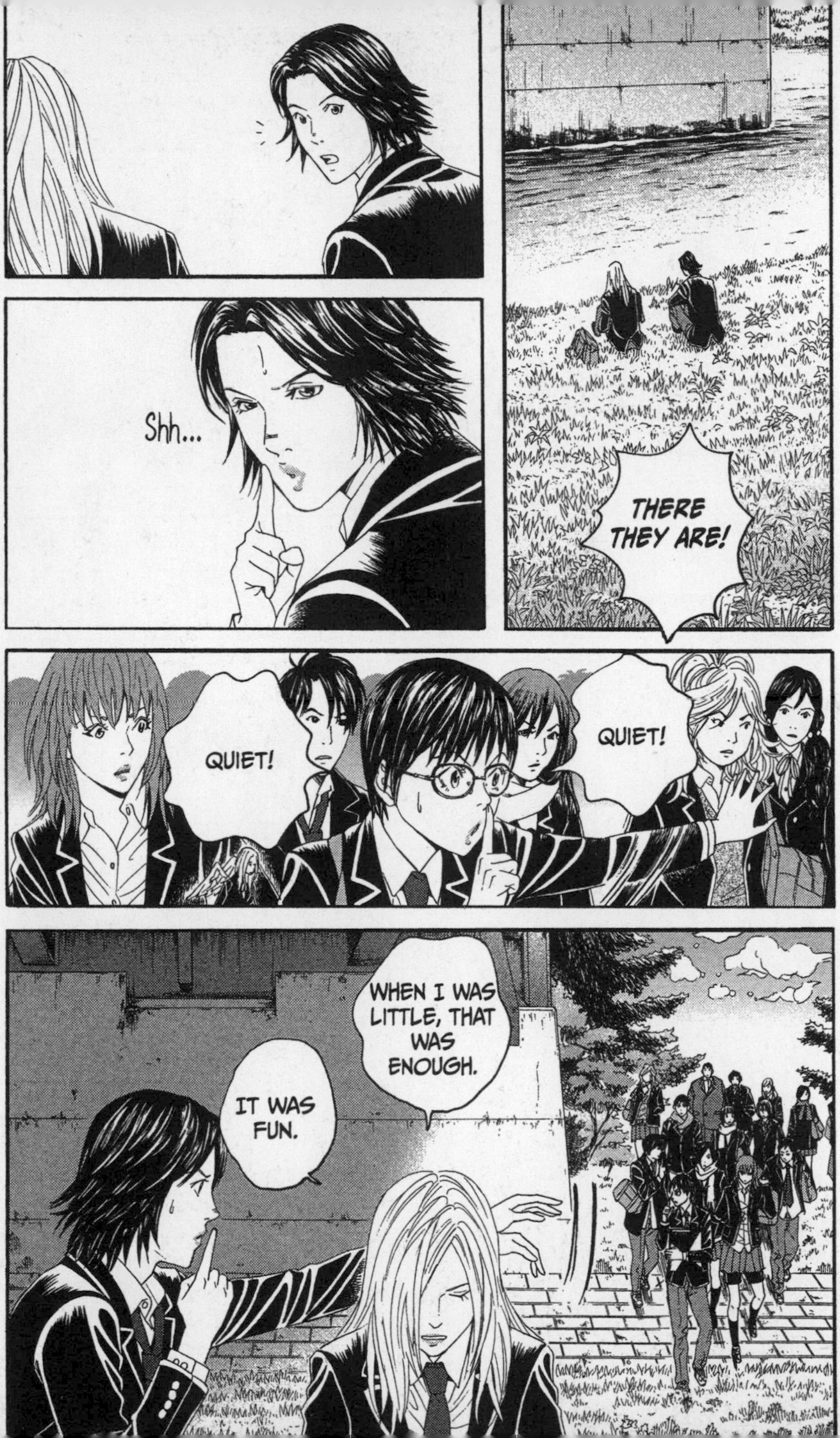
THERE THEY ARE!
Shh...
QUIET!
QUIET!
WHEN I WAS LITTLE, THAT WAS ENOUGH.
IT WAS FUN.

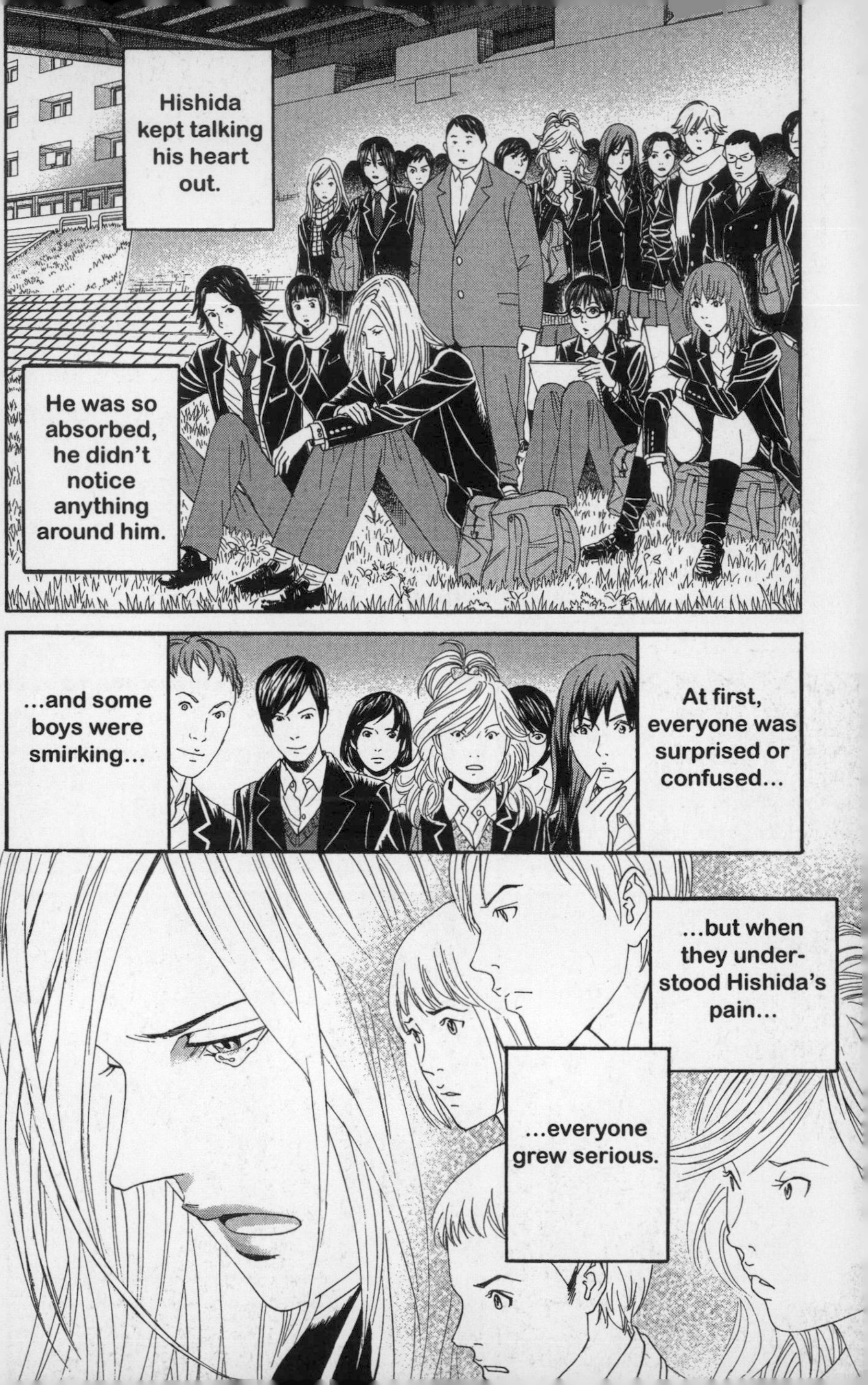
Hishida kept talking his heart out.
He was so absorbed, he didn't notice anything around him.
At first, everyone was surprised or confused...
...and some boys were smirking...
...but when they understood Hishida's pain...
...everyone grew serious.

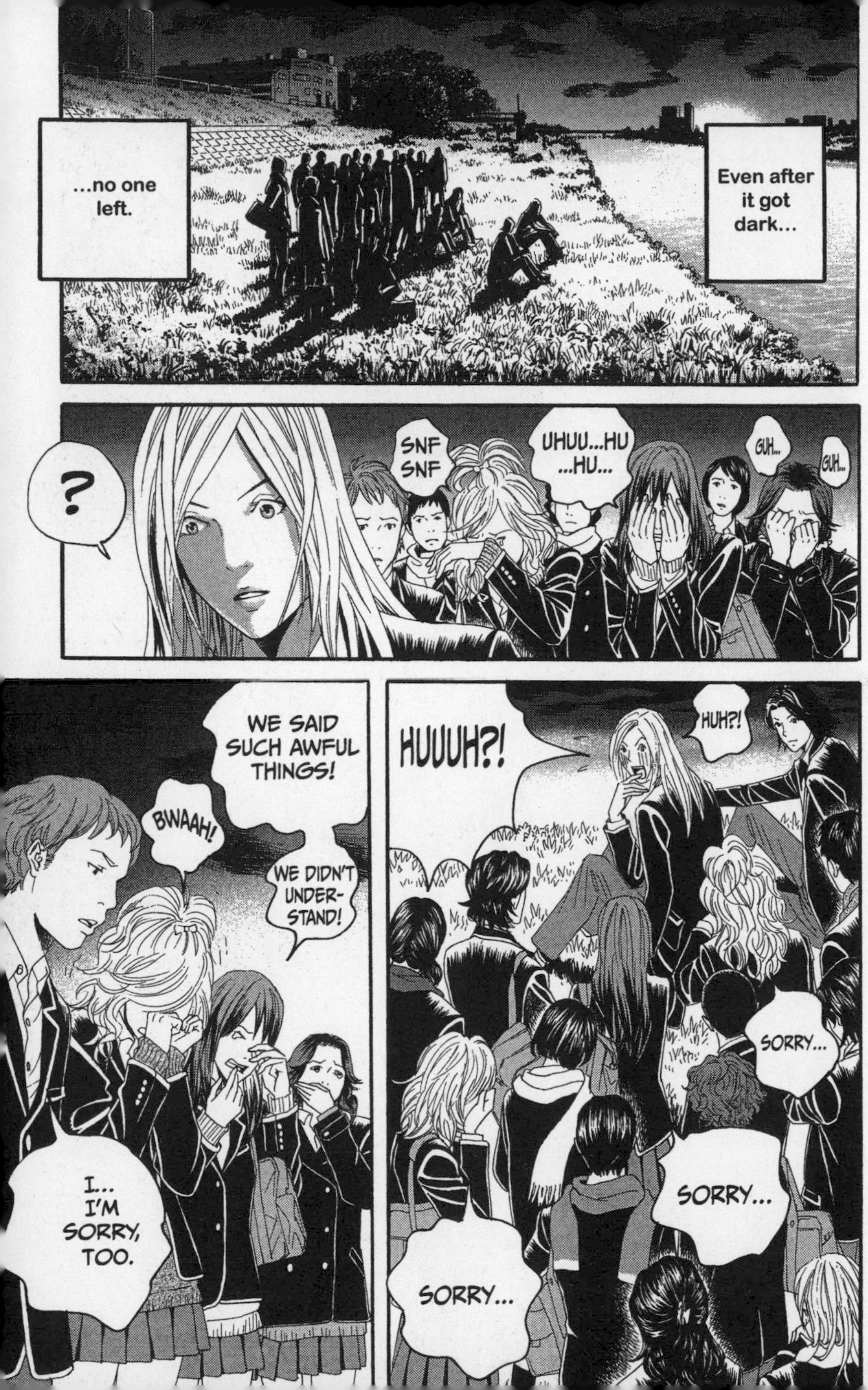
Even after it got dark...
...no one left.
GUH...
GUH...
UHUU...HU ...HU...
SNF SNF
?
HUH?!
HUUUH?!
SORRY...
SORRY...
SORRY...
WE SAID SUCH AWFUL THINGS!
BWAAH!
WE DIDN'T UNDER-STAND!
I... I'M SORRY, TOO.

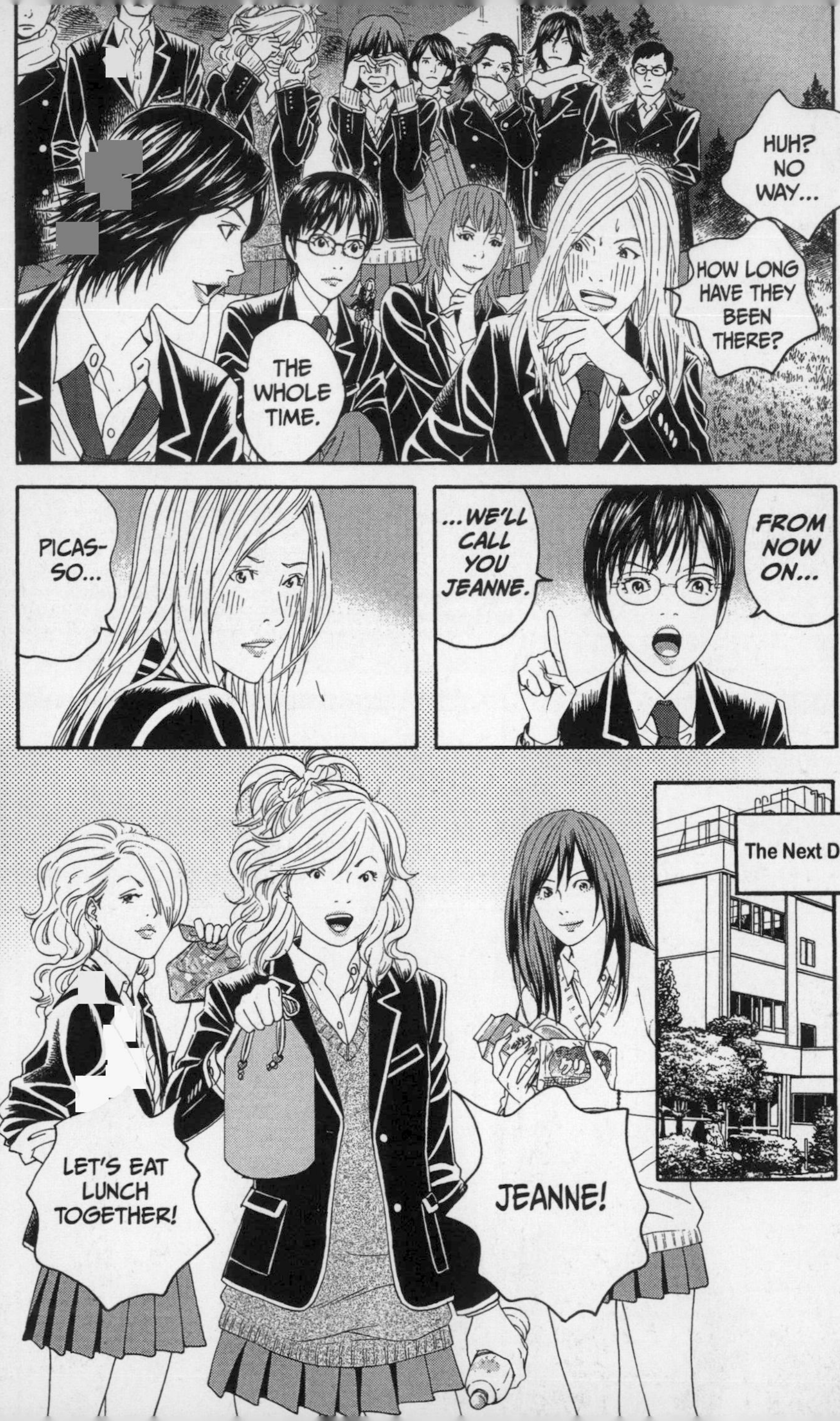
HUH? NO WAY...
HOW LONG HAVE THEY BEEN THERE?
THE WHOLE TIME.
FROM NOW ON...
...WE'LL CALL YOU JEANNE.
PICAS-SO...
The Next Day
JEANNE!
LET'S EAT LUNCH TOGETHER!

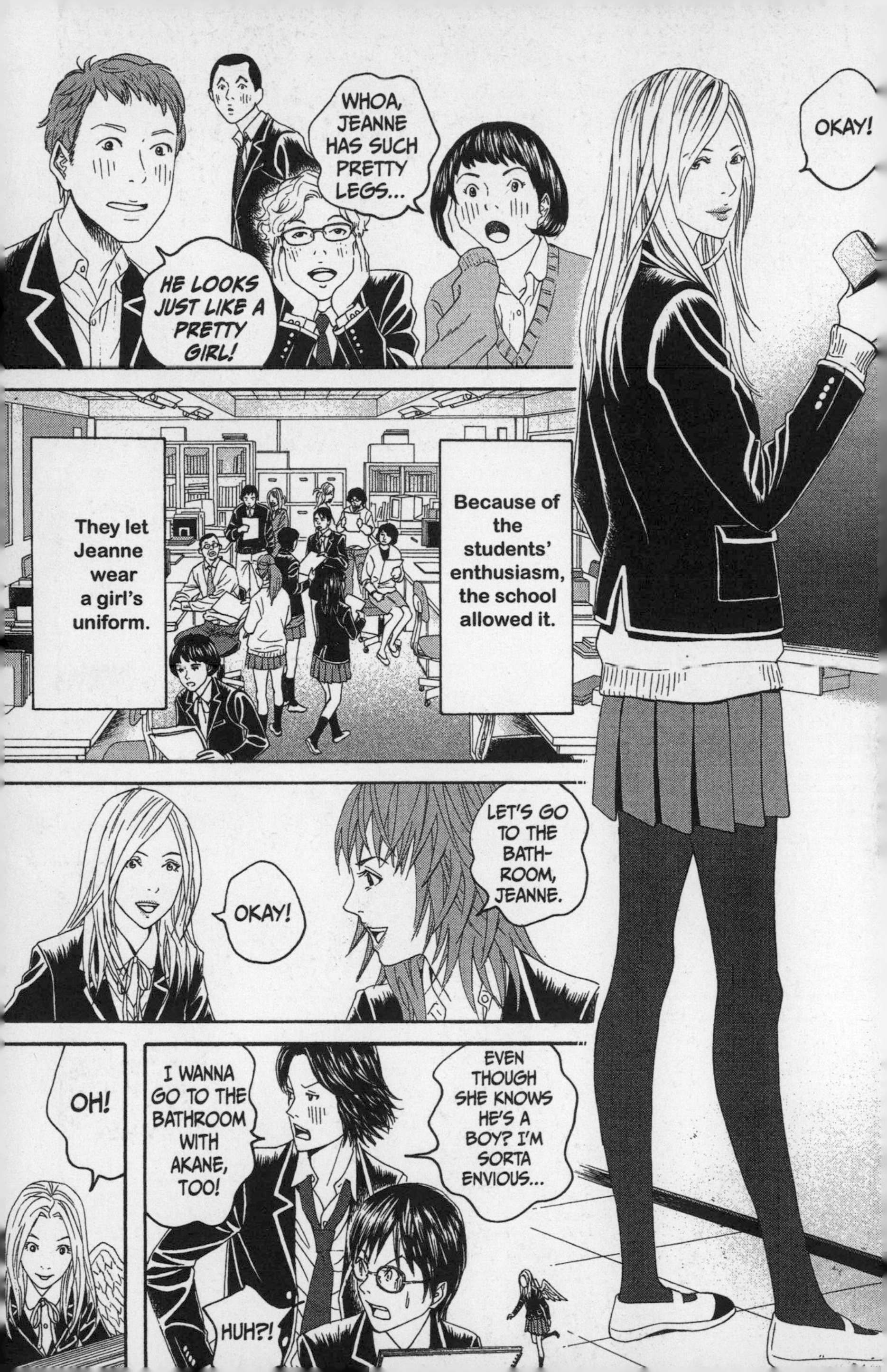
OKAY!
WHOA, JEANNE HAS SUCH PRETTY LEGS...
HE LOOKS JUST LIKE A PRETTY GIRL!
Because of the students' enthusiasm, the school allowed it.
They let Jeanne wear a girl's uniform.
LET'S GO TO THE BATH-ROOM, JEANNE.
OKAY!
EVEN THOUGH SHE KNOWS HE'S A BOY? I'M SORTA ENVIOUS...
I WANNA GO TO THE BATHROOM WITH AKANE, TOO!
HUH?!
OH!

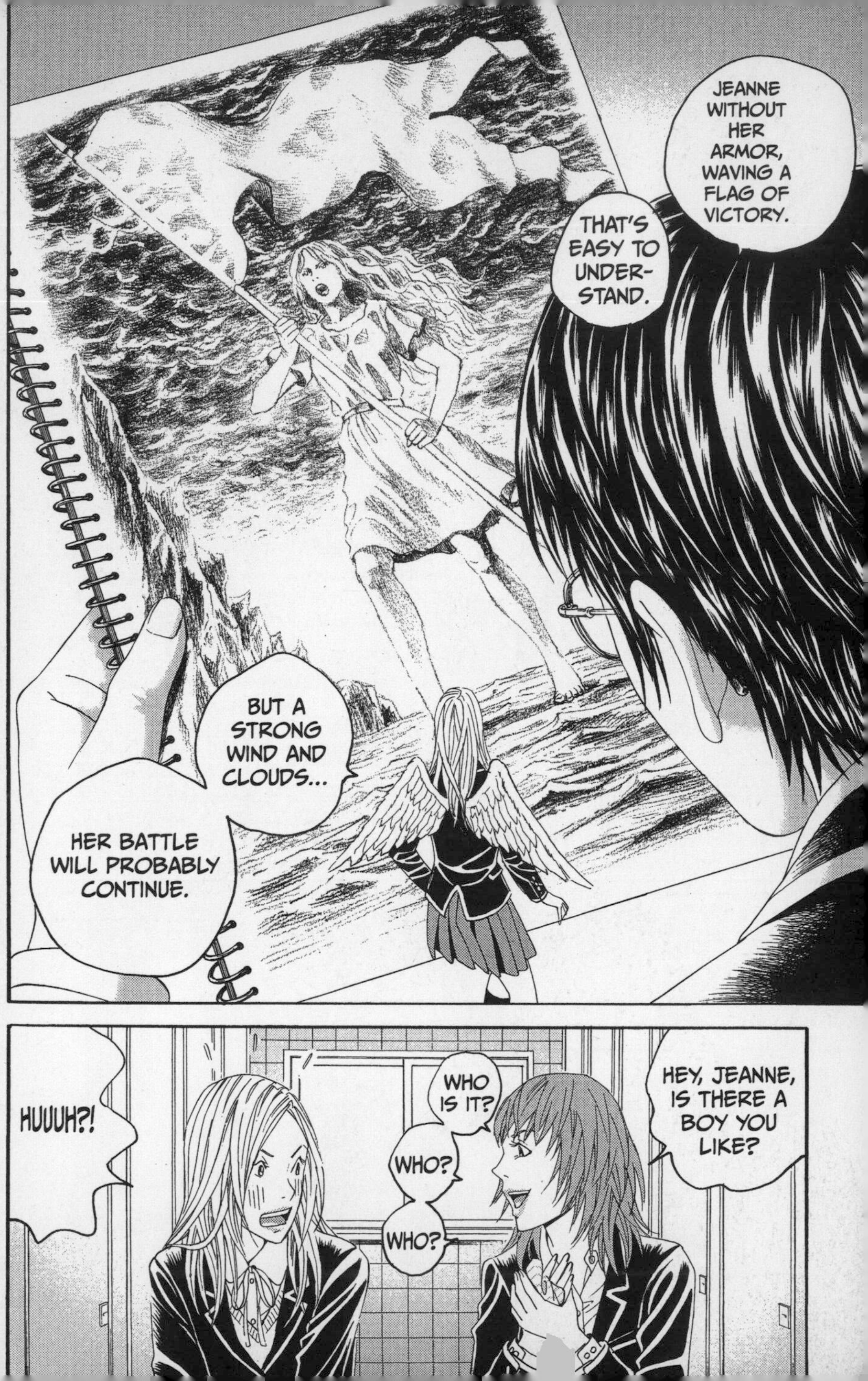
JEANNE WITHOUT HER ARMOR, WAVING A FLAG OF VICTORY.
THAT'S EASY TO UNDER-STAND.
BUT A STRONG WIND AND CLOUDS...
HER BATTLE WILL PROBABLY CONTINUE.
HEY, JEANNE, IS THERE A BOY YOU LIKE?
WHO IS IT?
WHO?
WHO?
HUUUH?!

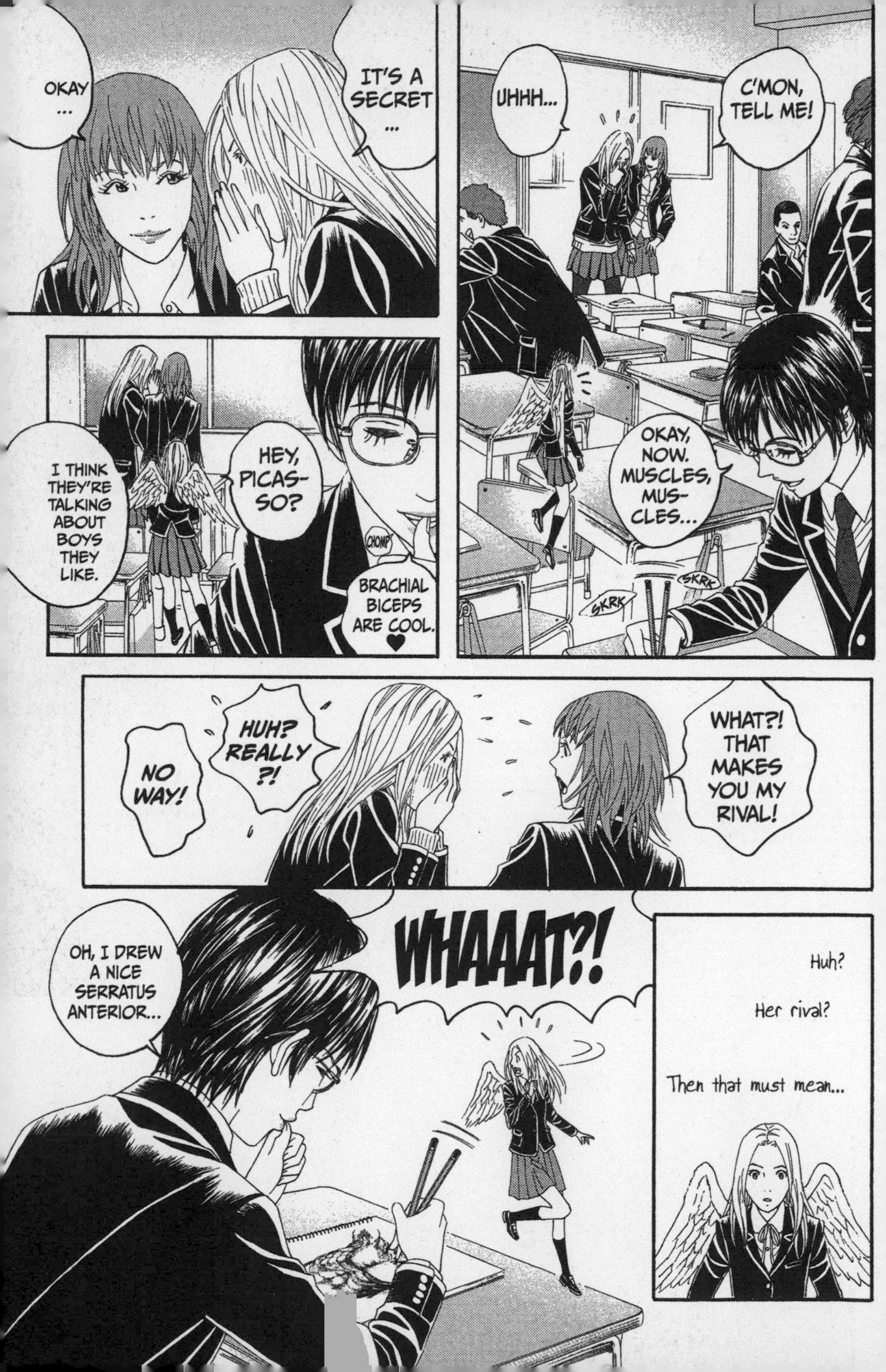
C'MON, TELL ME!
UHHH...
OKAY, NOW. MUSCLES, MUS-CLES...
SKRK
SKRK
IT'S A SECRET ...
OKAY ...
HEY, PICAS-SO?
I THINK THEY'RE TALKING ABOUT BOYS THEY LIKE.
CHOMP
BRACHIAL BICEPS ARE COOL. ♥
WHAT?! THAT MAKES YOU MY RIVAL!
HUH? REALLY ?!
NO WAY!
Huh?
Her rival?
Then that must mean...
WHAAAT?!
OH, I DREW A NICE SERRATUS ANTERIOR...

SKRK SKRK SKRK

Vision 7: Hishida's Holy War (Part 2)_Jump SQ, July 2009

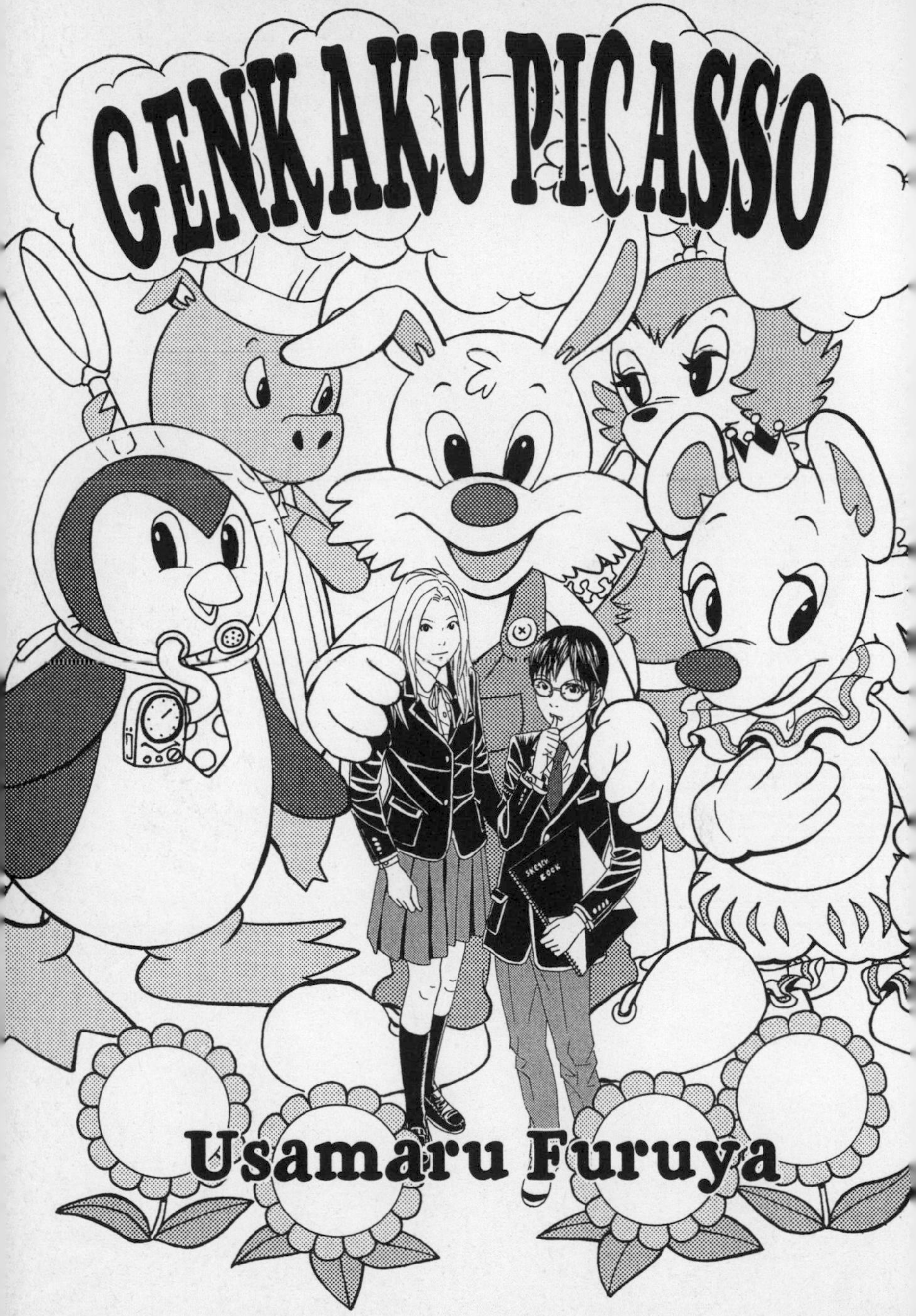
GENKAKU PICASSO
SKETCH BOOK
Usamaru Furuya

Vision 8: Borise World and Moe (Part 1)

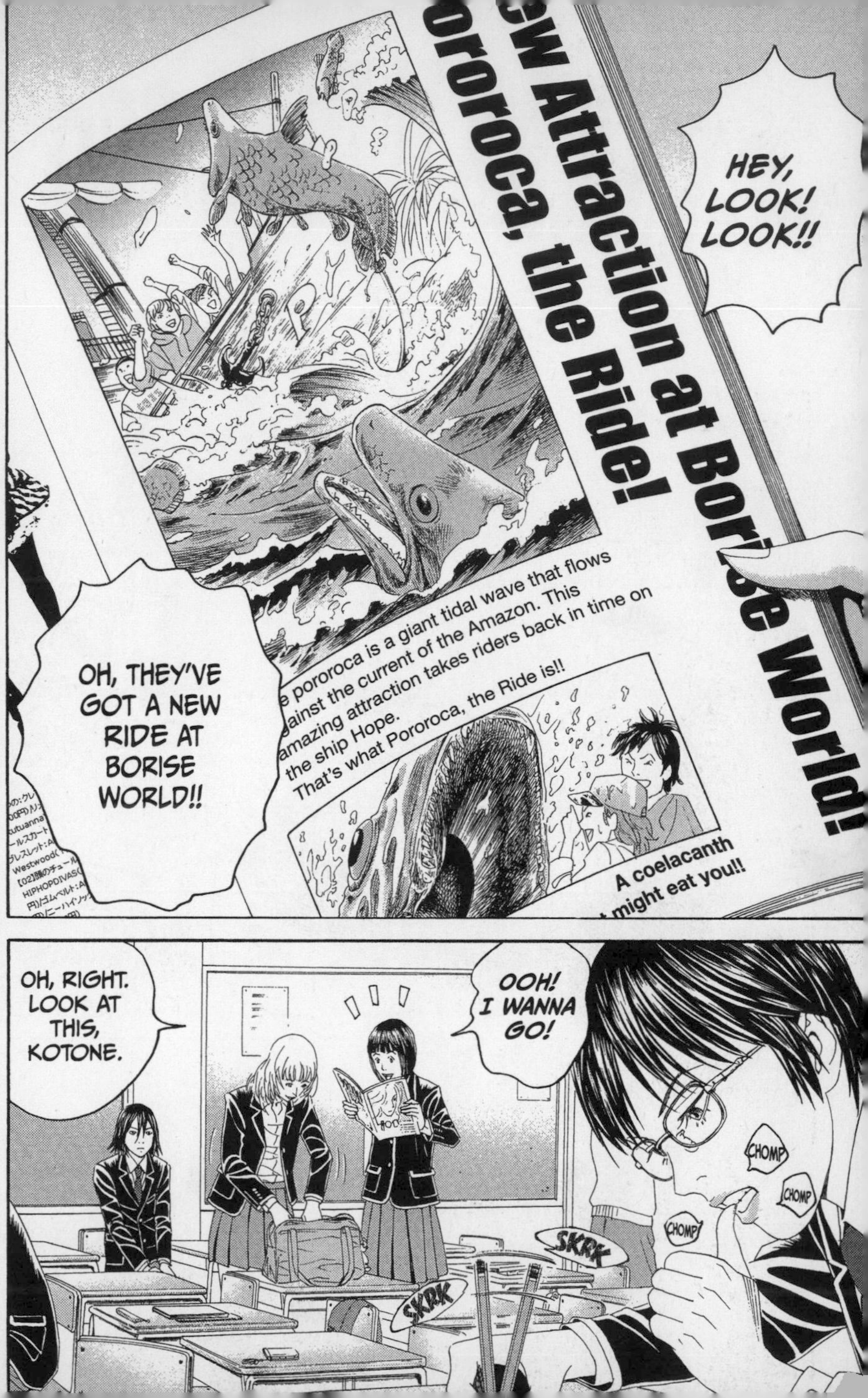
HEY, LOOK! LOOK!!
ew Attraction at Bor
se World!
Pororoca, the Ride!
e pororoca is a giant tidal wave that flows gainst the current of the Amazon. This amazing attraction takes riders back in time on the ship Hope.
That's what Pororoca, the Ride is!!
A coelacanth
might eat you!!
OH, THEY'VE GOT A NEW RIDE AT BORISE WORLD!!
CHOMP
CHOMP
CHOMP
OOH! I WANNA GO!
SKRK
SKRK
OH, RIGHT. LOOK AT THIS, KOTONE.

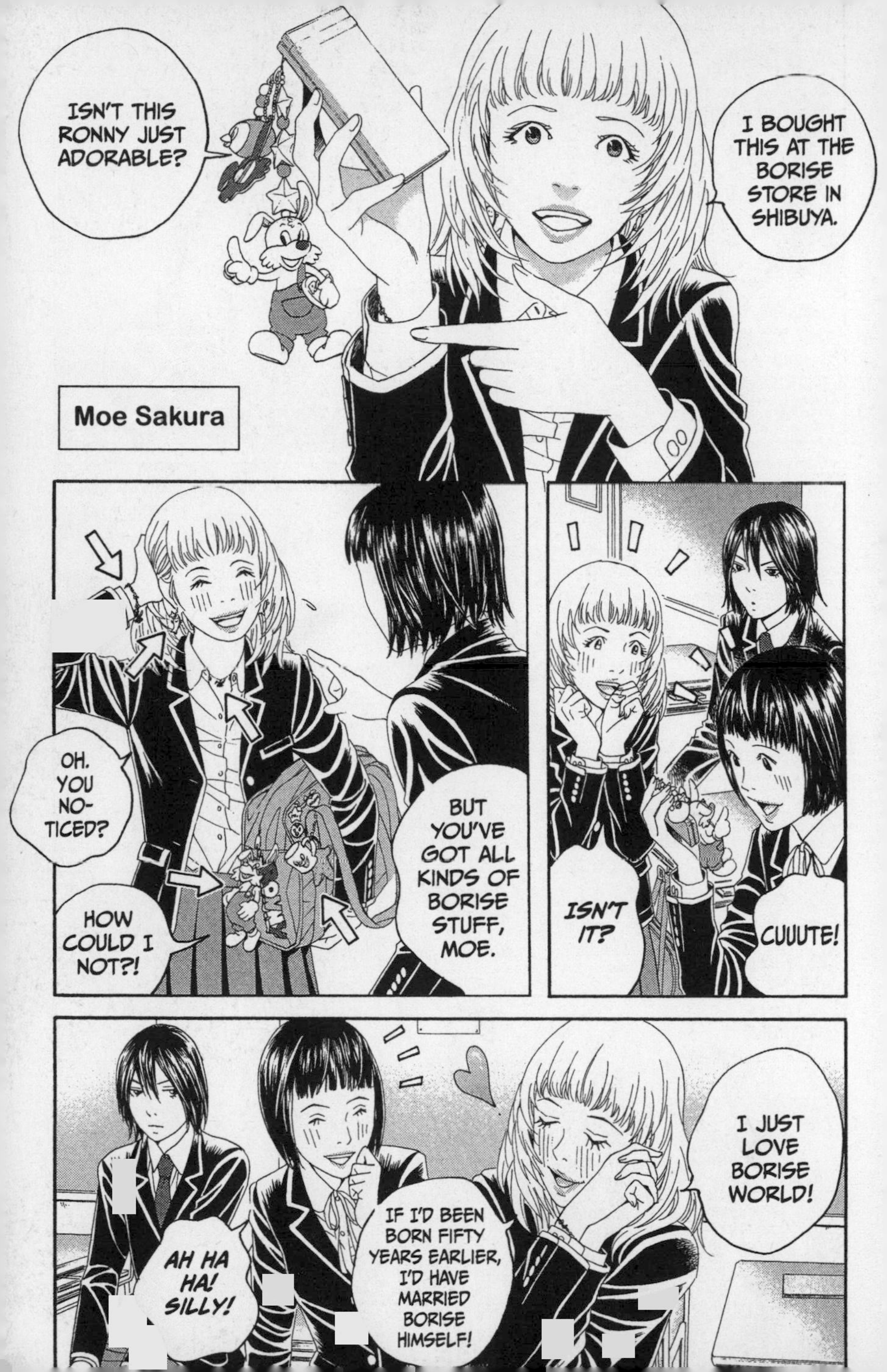
I BOUGHT THIS AT THE BORISE STORE IN SHIBUYA.
ISN'T THIS RONNY JUST ADORABLE?
Moe Sakura
CUUUTE!
ISN'T IT?
BUT YOU'VE GOT ALL KINDS OF BORISE STUFF, MOE.
OH. YOU NO-TICED?
HOW COULD I NOT?!
I JUST LOVE BORISE WORLD!
IF I'D BEEN BORN FIFTY YEARS EARLIER, I'D HAVE MARRIED BORISE HIMSELF!
AH HA HA! SILLY!

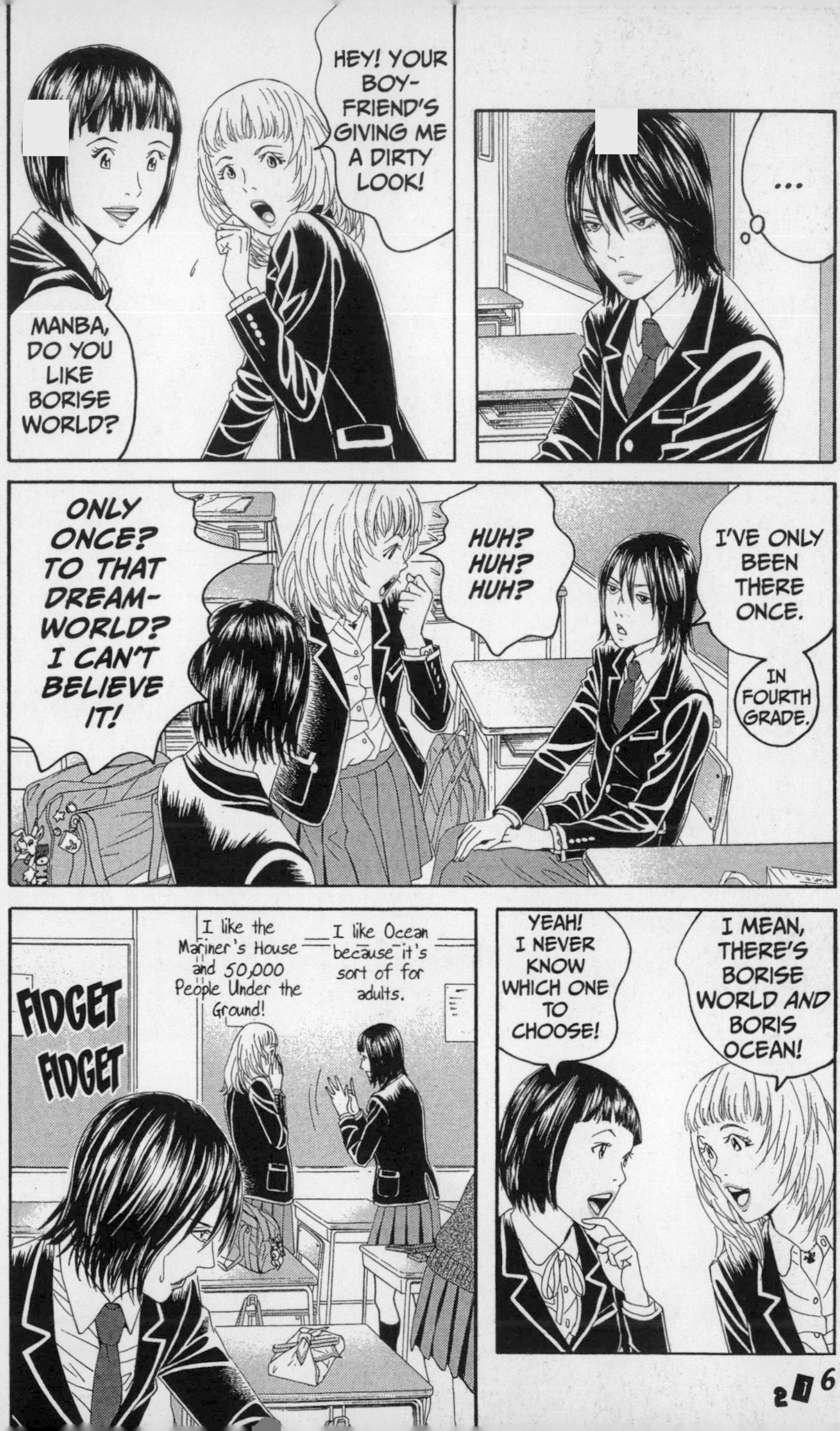
...
HEY! YOUR BOY-FRIEND'S GIVING ME A DIRTY LOOK!
MANBA, DO YOU LIKE BORISE WORLD?
I'VE ONLY BEEN THERE ONCE.
IN FOURTH GRADE.
HUH? HUH? HUH?
ONLY ONCE? TO THAT DREAM-WORLD? I CAN'T BELIEVE IT!
I MEAN, THERE'S BORISE WORLD AND BORIS OCEAN!
YEAH! I NEVER KNOW WHICH ONE TO CHOOSE!
I like Ocean because it's sort of for adults.
I like the Mariner's House and 50,000 People Under the Ground!
FIDGET FIDGET

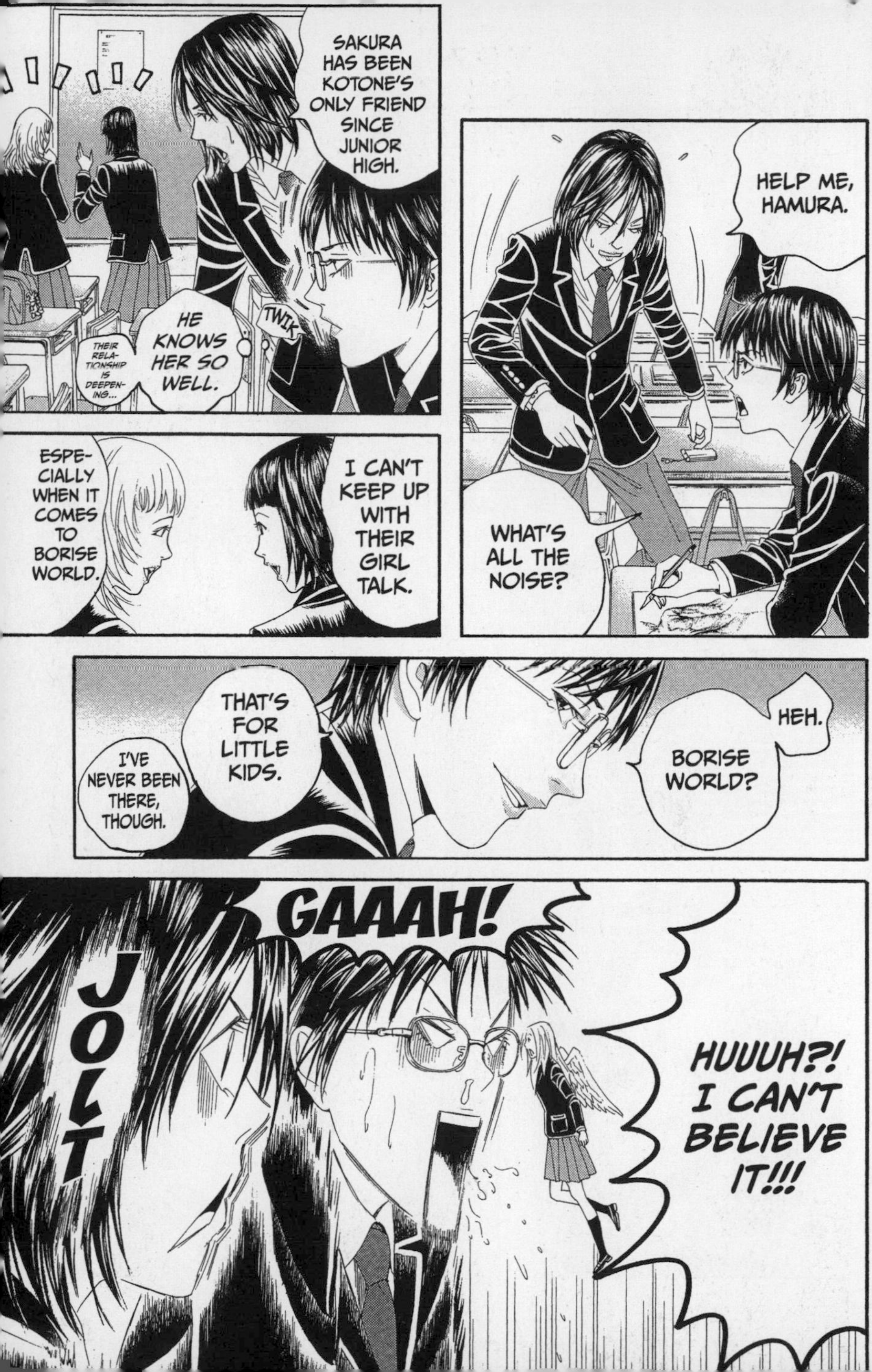

HELP ME, HAMURA.
WHAT'S ALL THE NOISE?
SAKURA HAS BEEN KOTONE'S ONLY FRIEND SINCE JUNIOR HIGH.
TWIK
HE KNOWS HER SO WELL.
THEIR RELATIONSHIP IS DEEPENING...
I CAN'T KEEP UP WITH THEIR GIRL TALK.
ESPECIALLY WHEN IT COMES TO BORISE WORLD.
HEH.
BORISE WORLD?
THAT'S FOR LITTLE KIDS.
I'VE NEVER BEEN THERE, THOUGH.
HUUUH?! I CAN'T BELIEVE IT!!!
GAAAH!
JOLT

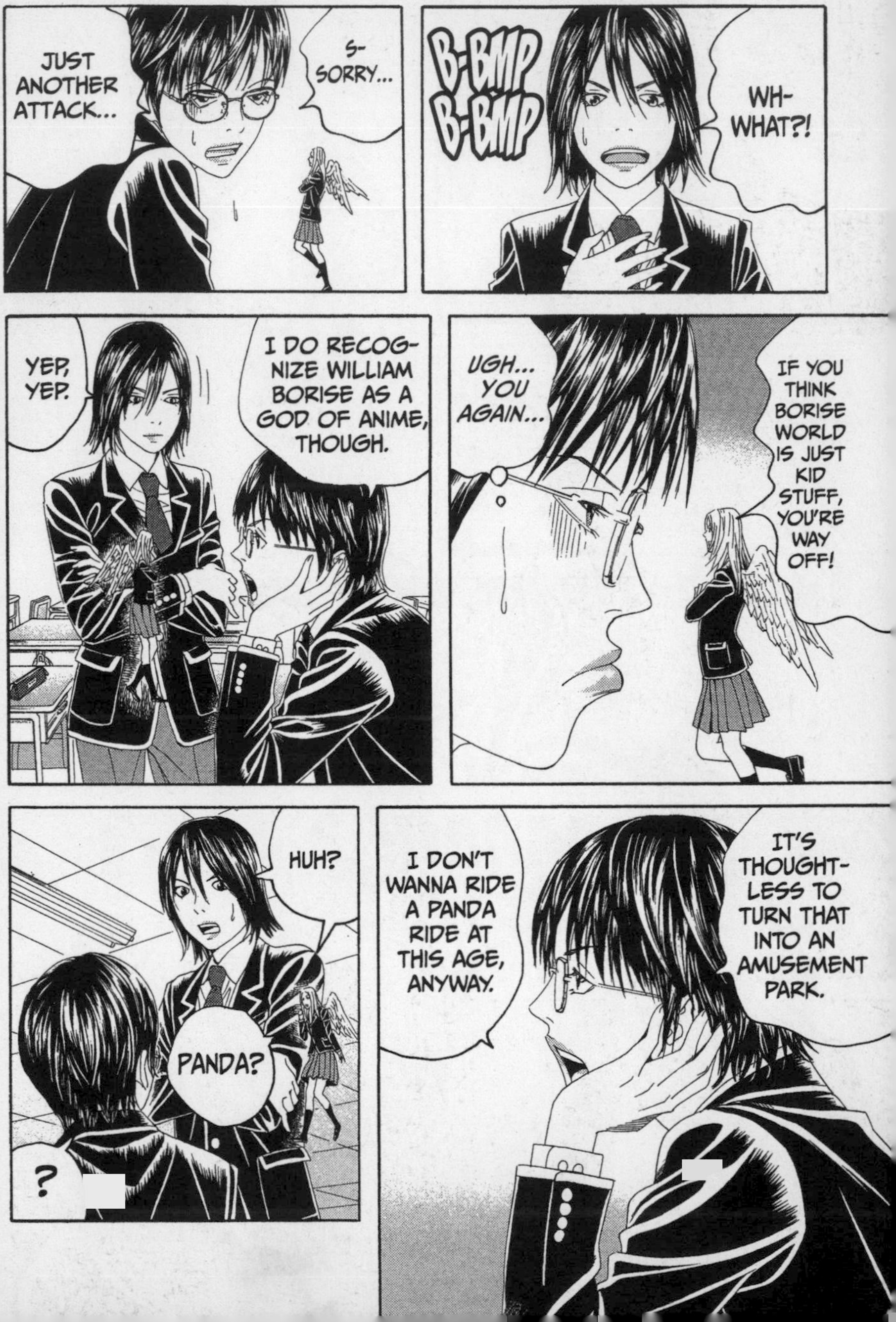
WH-WHAT?!
B-BMP B-BMP
S-SORRY...
JUST ANOTHER ATTACK...
IF YOU THINK BORISE WORLD IS JUST KID STUFF, YOU'RE WAY OFF!
UGH... YOU AGAIN...
I DO RECOG-NIZE WILLIAM BORISE AS A GOD OF ANIME, THOUGH.
YEP, YEP.
IT'S THOUGHT-LESS TO TURN THAT INTO AN AMUSEMENT PARK.
I DON'T WANNA RIDE A PANDA RIDE AT THIS AGE, ANYWAY.
HUH?
PANDA?
?

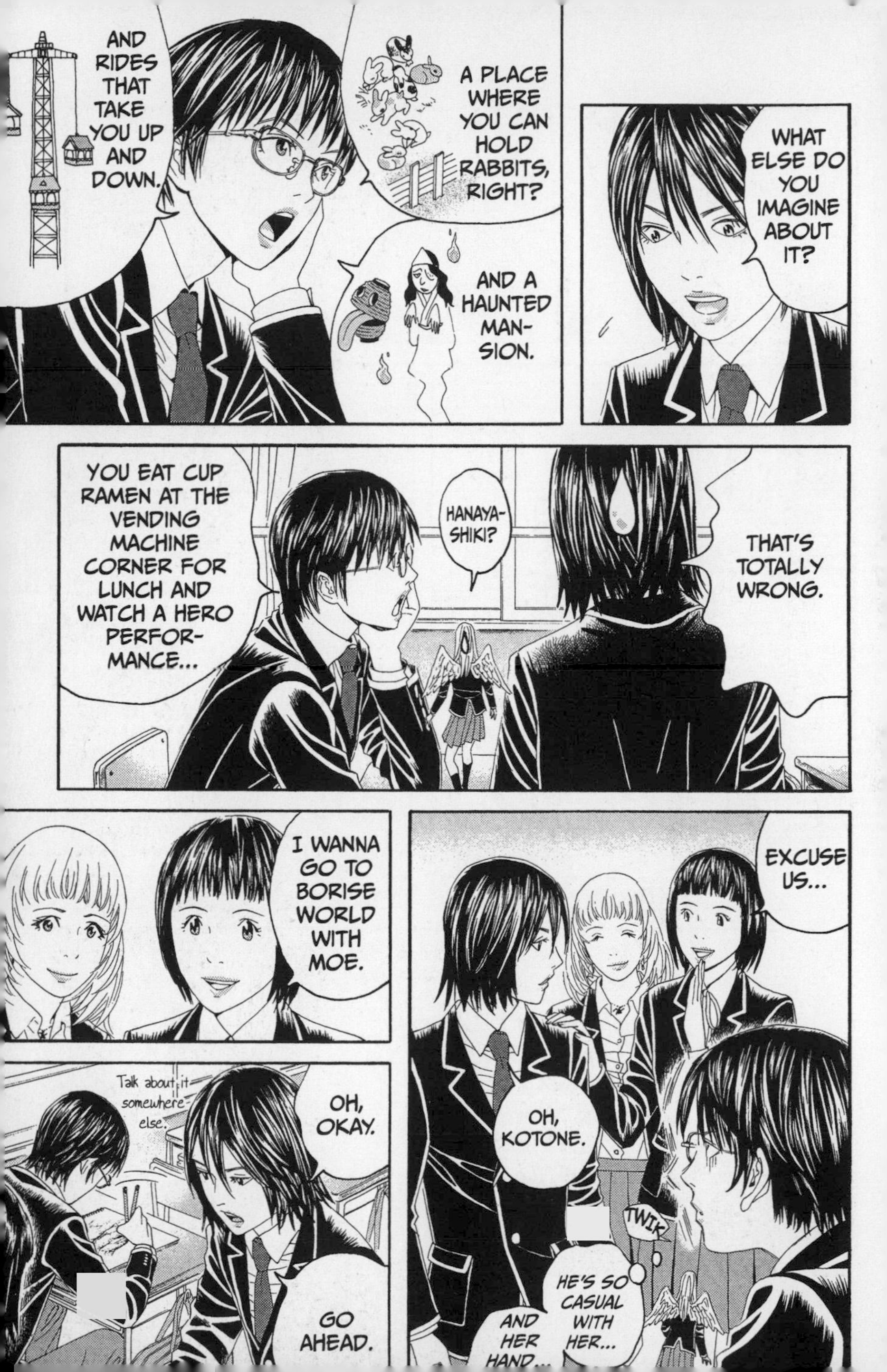
WHAT ELSE DO YOU IMAGINE ABOUT IT?
A PLACE WHERE YOU CAN HOLD RABBITS, RIGHT?
AND A HAUNTED MAN-SION.
AND RIDES THAT TAKE YOU UP AND DOWN.
THAT'S TOTALLY WRONG.
HANAYA-SHIKI?
YOU EAT CUP RAMEN AT THE VENDING MACHINE CORNER FOR LUNCH AND WATCH A HERO PERFOR-MANCE...
EXCUSE US...
OH, KOTONE.
TWIK
HE'S SO CASUAL WITH HER...
AND HER HAND...
I WANNA GO TO BORISE WORLD WITH MOE.
OH, OKAY.
Talk about it somewhere else.
GO AHEAD.

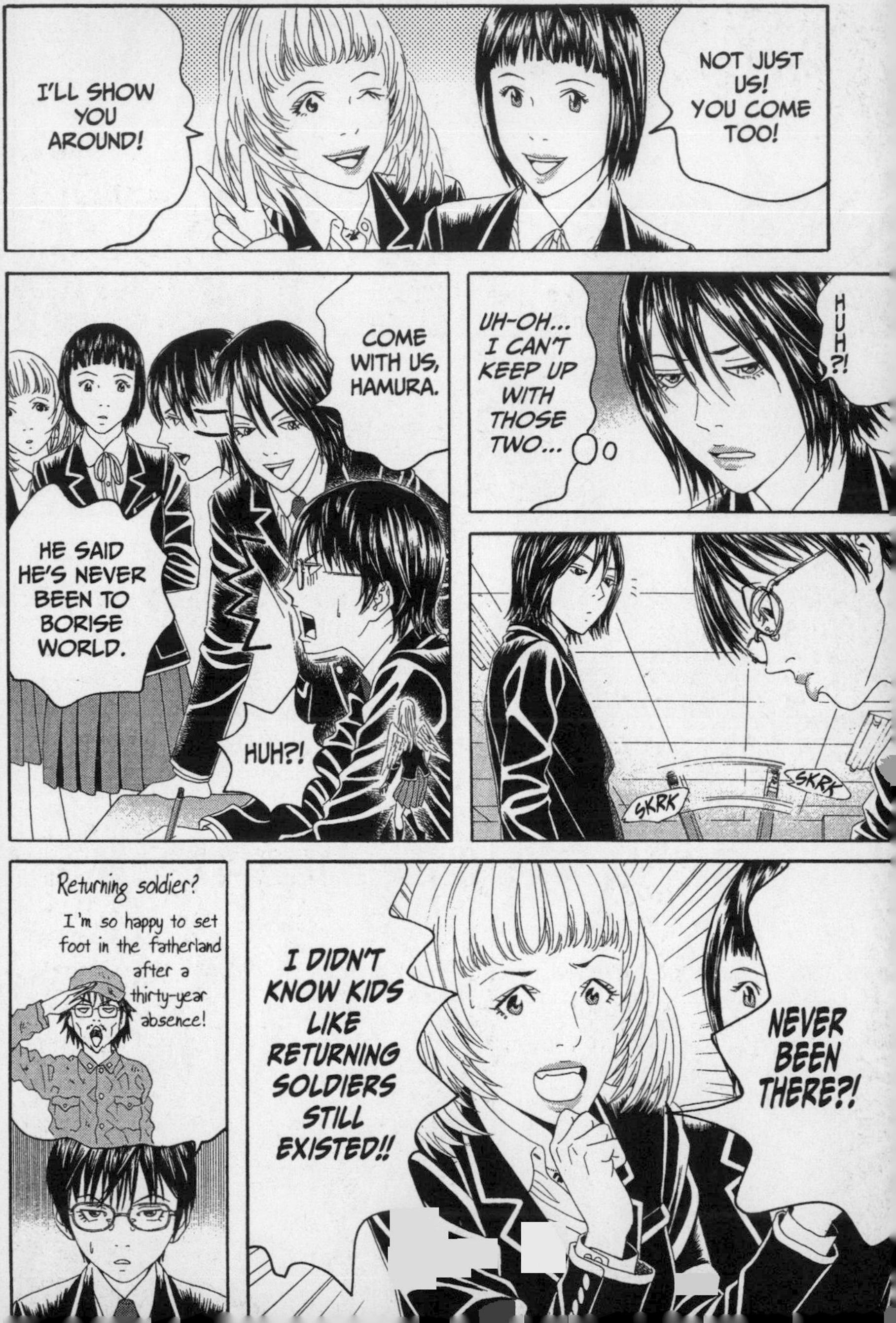
NOT JUST US! YOU COME TOO!
I'LL SHOW YOU AROUND!
HUH?!
UH-OH... I CAN'T KEEP UP WITH THOSE TWO...
SKRK
SKRK
COME WITH US, HAMURA.
HE SAID HE'S NEVER BEEN TO BORISE WORLD.
HUH?!
NEVER BEEN THERE?!
I DIDN'T KNOW KIDS LIKE RETURNING SOLDIERS STILL EXISTED!!
Returning soldier?
I'm so happy to set foot in the fatherland after a thirty-year absence!

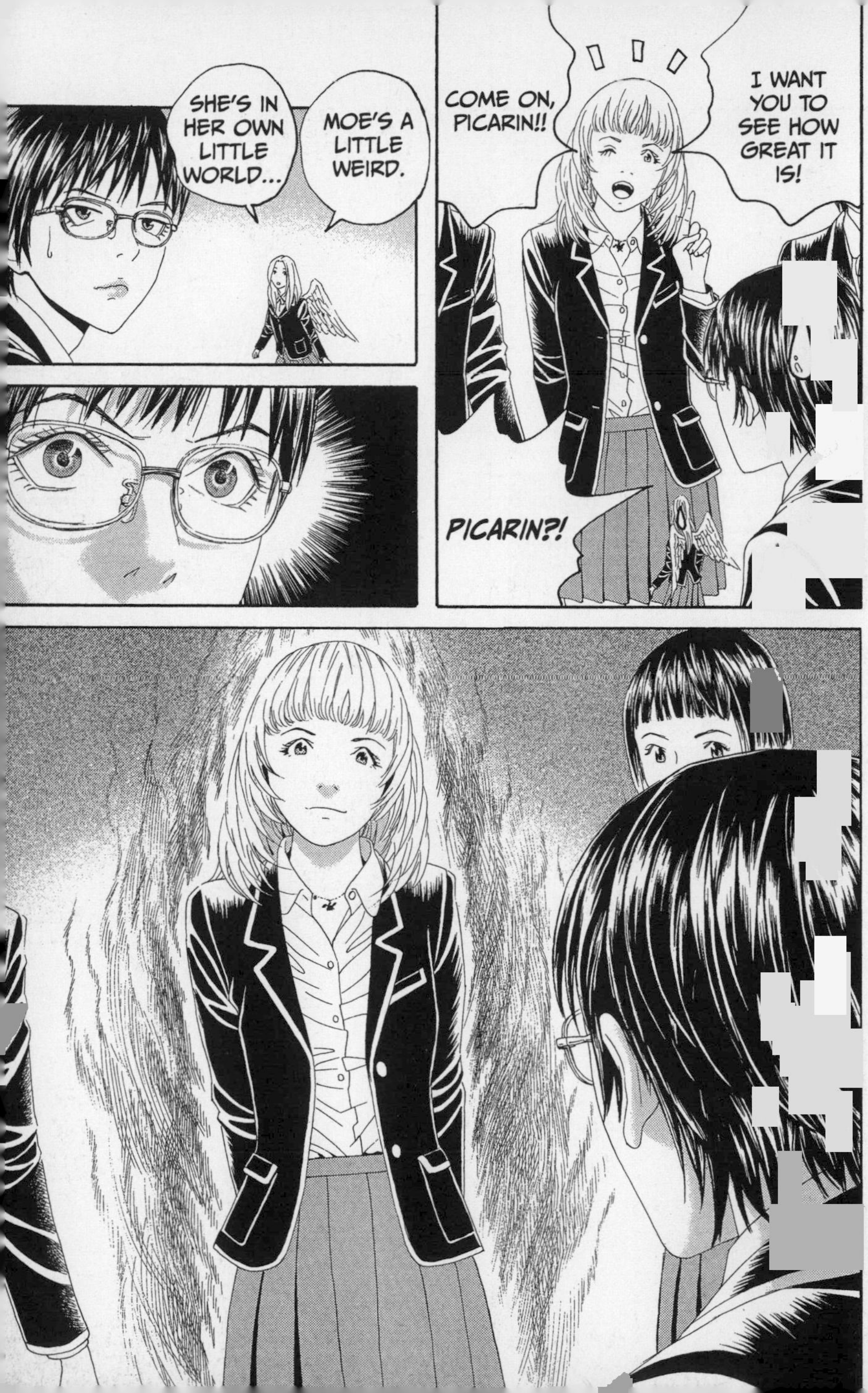
I WANT YOU TO SEE HOW GREAT IT IS!
COME ON, PICARIN!!
PICARIN?!
MOE'S A LITTLE WEIRD.
SHE'S IN HER OWN LITTLE WORLD...

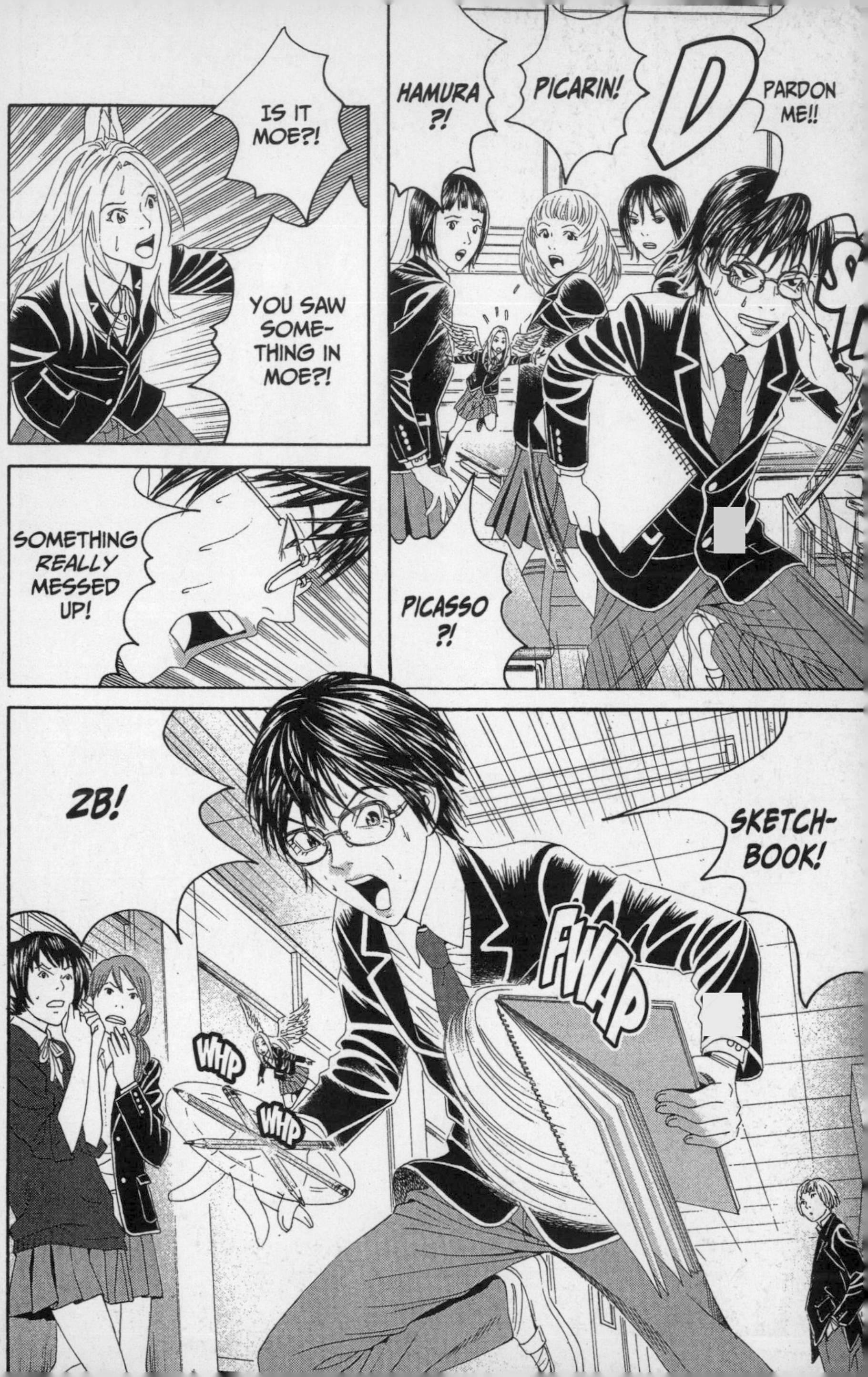
PARDON ME!!
D
PICARIN!
HAMURA ?!
PICASSO ?!
IS IT MOE?!
YOU SAW SOMETHING IN MOE?!
SOMETHING *REALLY* MESSED UP!
SKETCH-BOOK!
FWAP
2B!
WHP
WHP

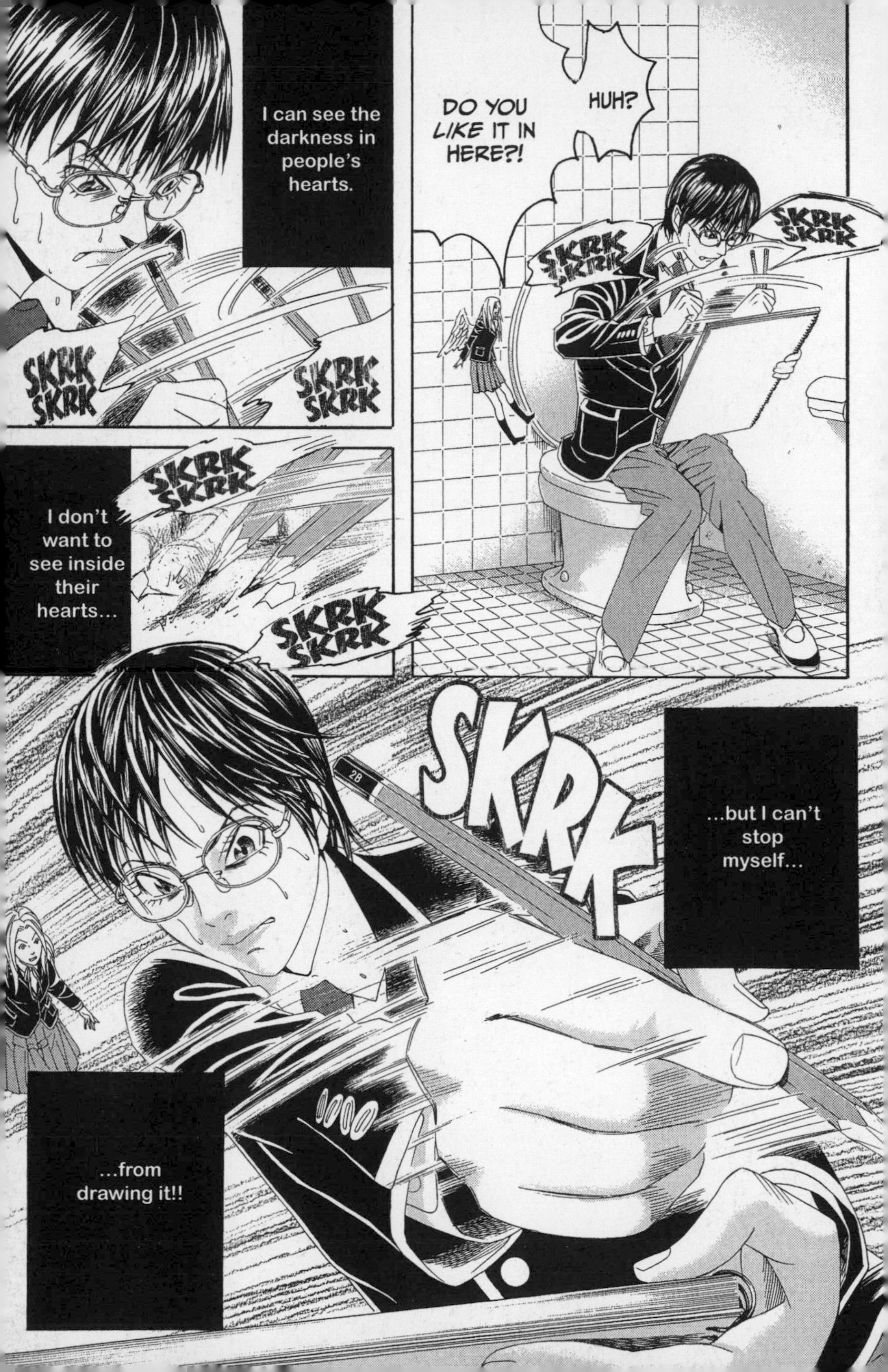
HUH?
DO YOU LIKE IT IN HERE?!
SKRK SKRK
SKRK SKRK
I can see the darkness in people's hearts.
SKRK SKRK
SKRK SKRK
SKRK SKRK
I don't want to see inside their hearts...
SKRK SKRK
...but I can't stop myself...
SKRK
2B
...from drawing it!!

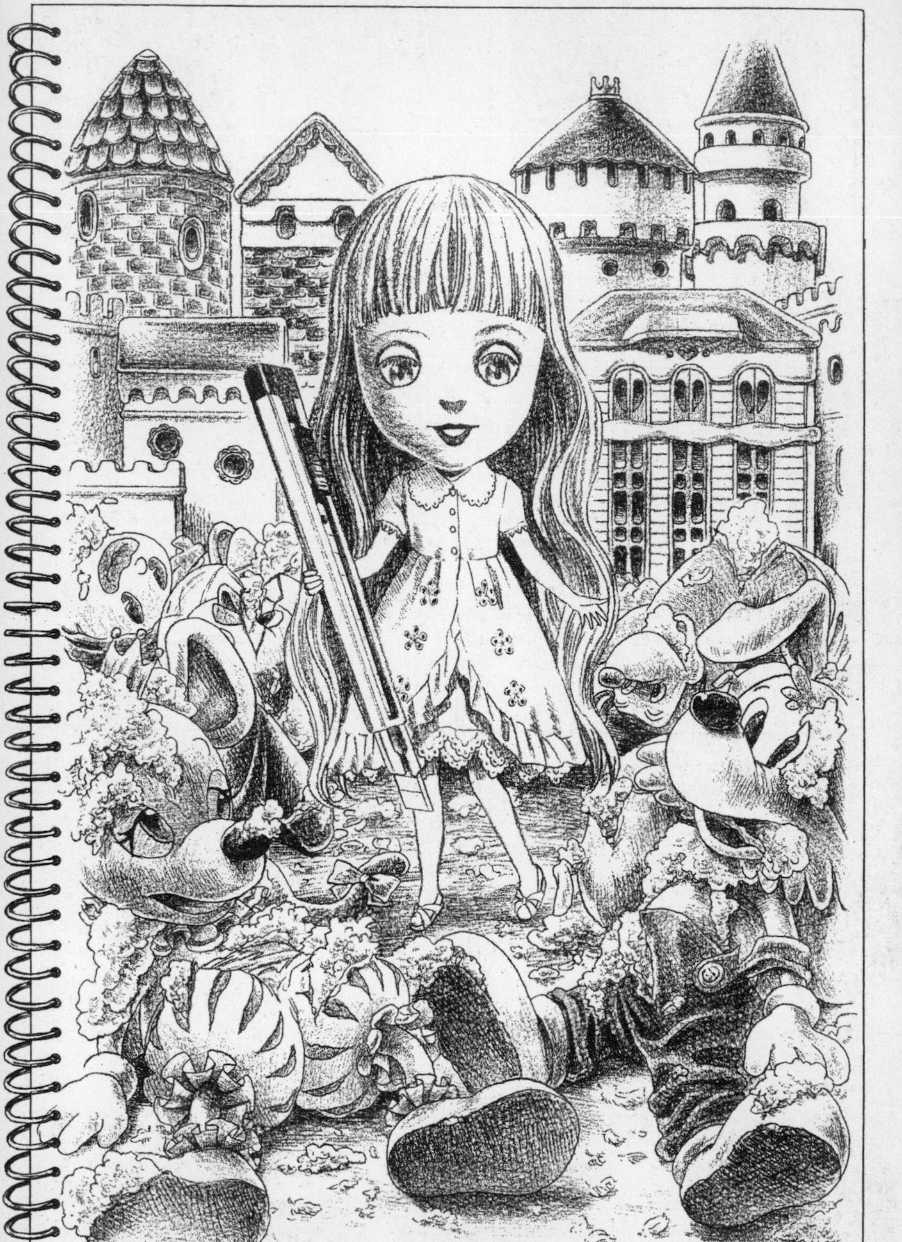

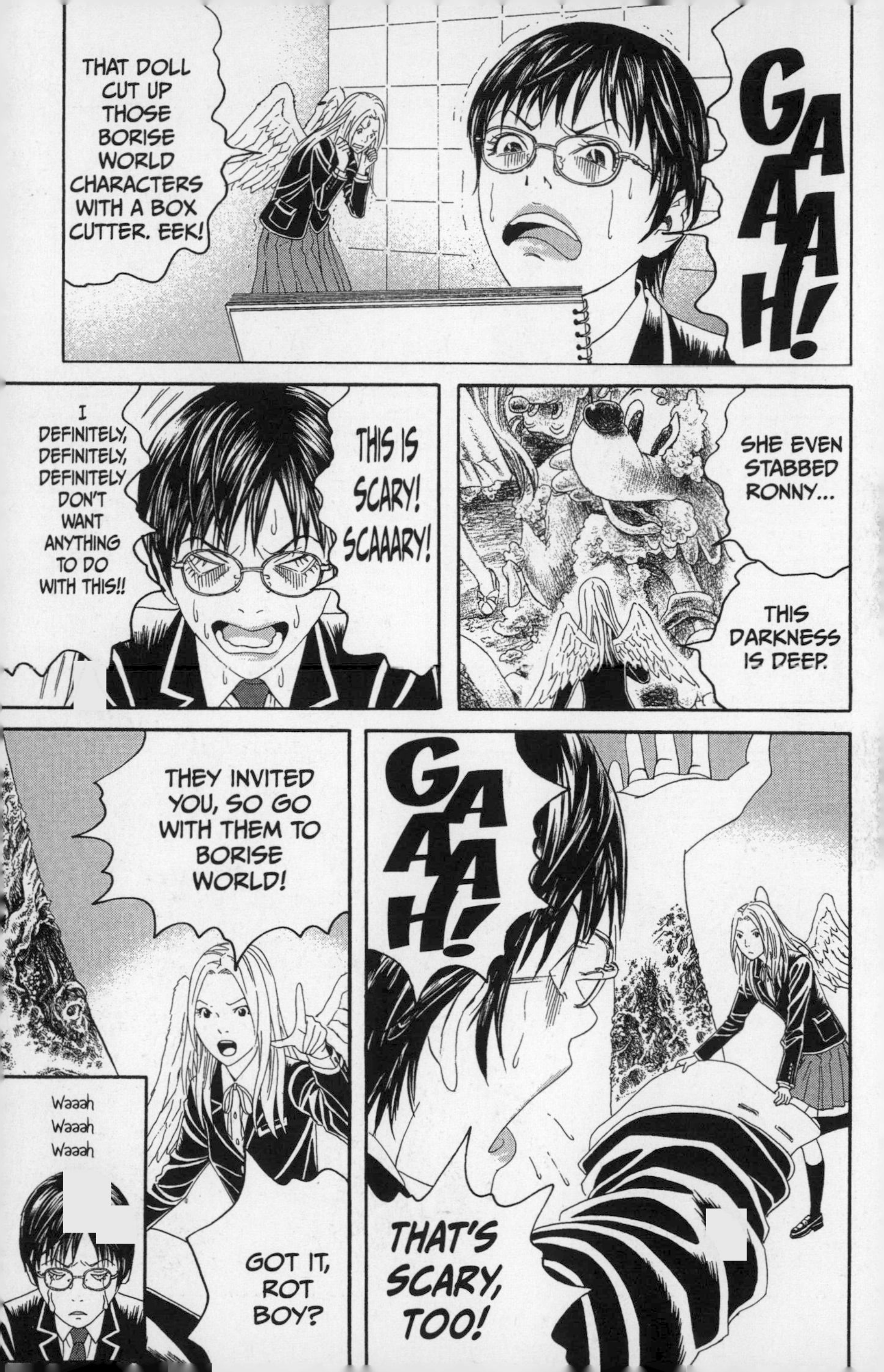
GAAAH!
THAT DOLL CUT UP THOSE BORISE WORLD CHARACTERS WITH A BOX CUTTER. EEK!
SHE EVEN STABBED RONNY...
THIS DARKNESS IS DEEP.
THIS IS SCARY! SCAAARY!
I DEFINITELY, DEFINITELY, DEFINITELY DON'T WANT ANYTHING TO DO WITH THIS!!
GAAAH!
THAT'S SCARY, TOO!
THEY INVITED YOU, SO GO WITH THEM TO BORISE WORLD!
GOT IT, ROT BOY?
Waaah
Waaah
Waaah

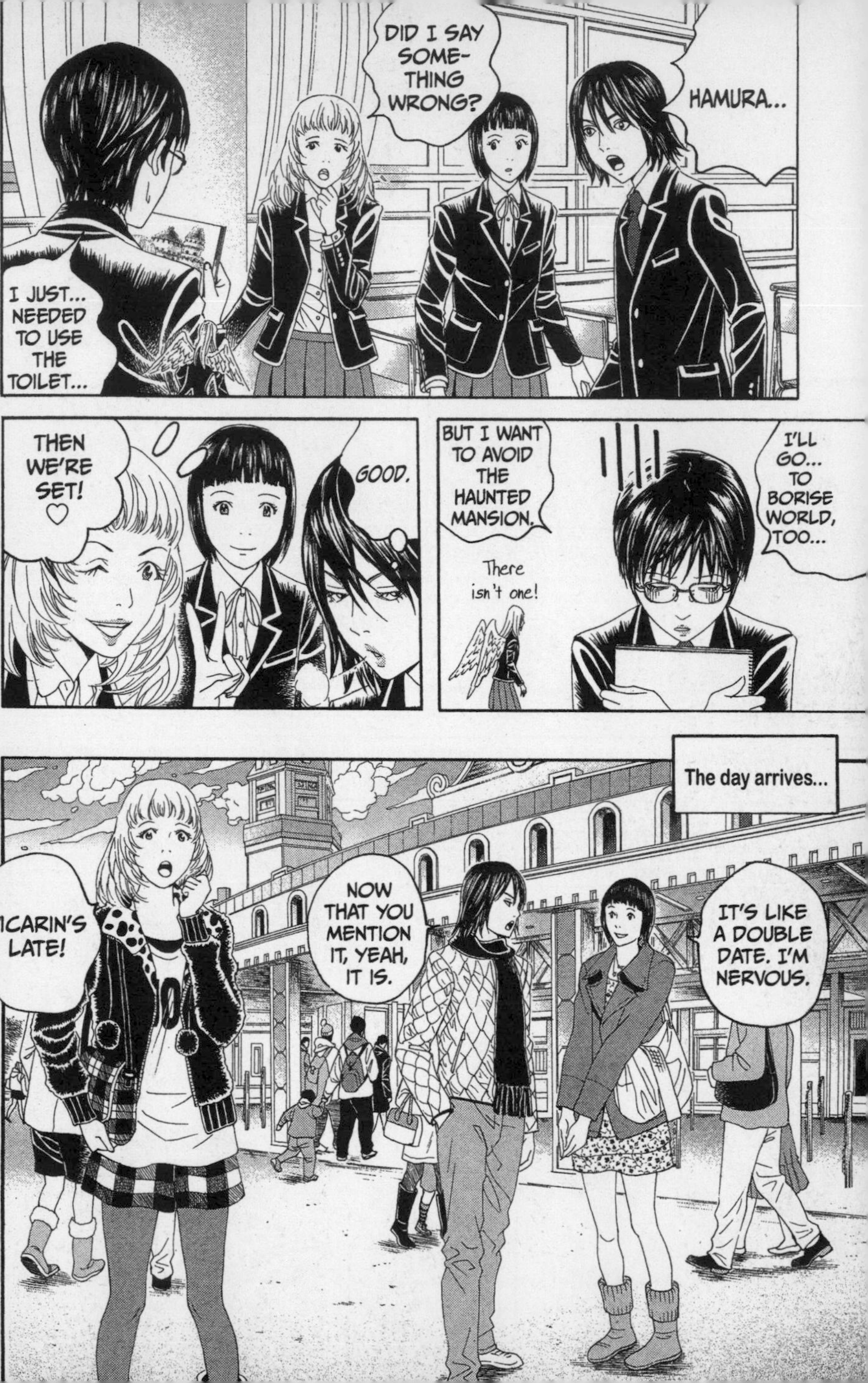
HAMURA...
DID I SAY SOME-THING WRONG?
I JUST... NEEDED TO USE THE TOILET...
I'LL GO... TO BORISE WORLD, TOO...
BUT I WANT TO AVOID THE HAUNTED MANSION.
There isn't one!
GOOD.
THEN WE'RE SET! ♡
The day arrives...
IT'S LIKE A DOUBLE DATE. I'M NERVOUS.
NOW THAT YOU MENTION IT, YEAH, IT IS.
PICARIN'S LATE!

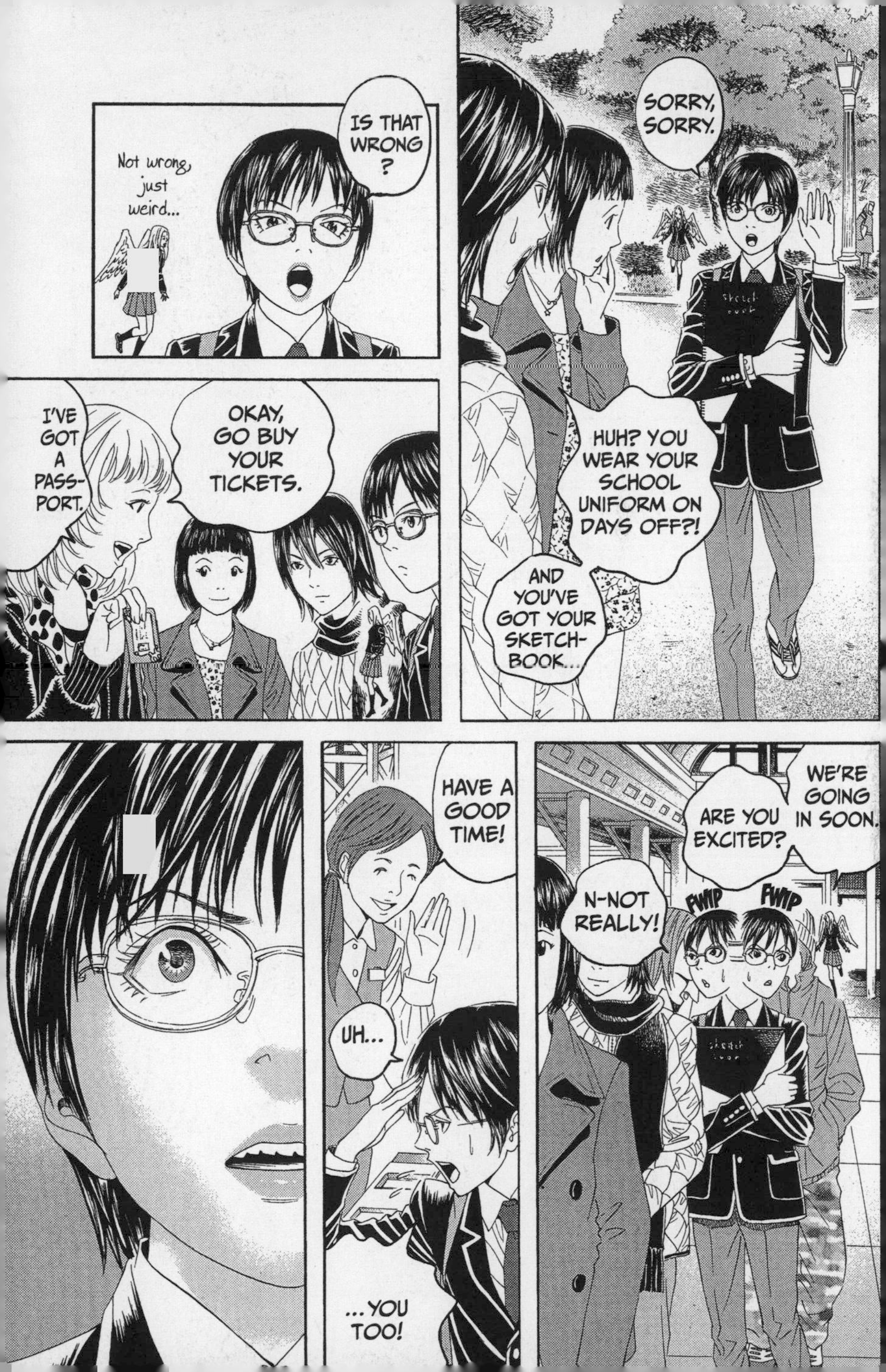
SORRY, SORRY.
HUH? YOU WEAR YOUR SCHOOL UNIFORM ON DAYS OFF?!
AND YOU'VE GOT YOUR SKETCH-BOOK...
IS THAT WRONG?
Not wrong, just weird...
OKAY, GO BUY YOUR TICKETS.
I'VE GOT A PASS-PORT.
WE'RE GOING IN SOON.
ARE YOU EXCITED?
FWIP
FWIP
N-NOT REALLY!
HAVE A GOOD TIME!
UH...
...YOU TOO!

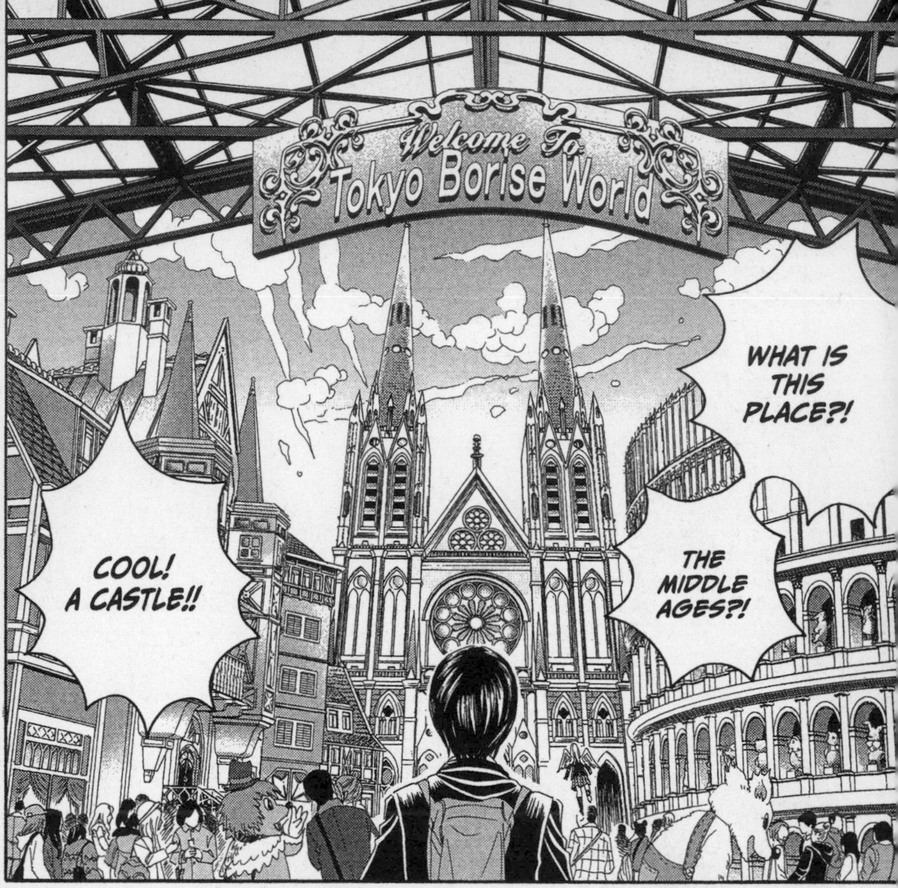
Welcome To
Tokyo Borise World
WHAT IS THIS PLACE?!
THE MIDDLE AGES?!
COOL! A CASTLE!!

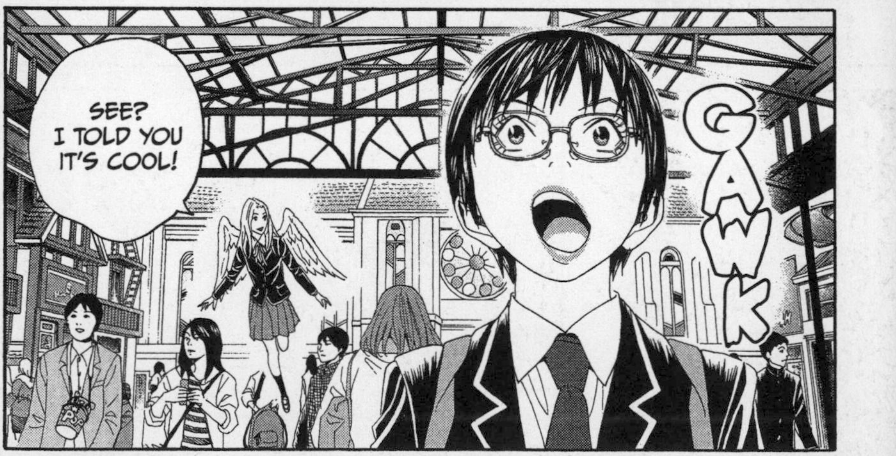
GAWK
SEE? I TOLD YOU IT'S COOL!

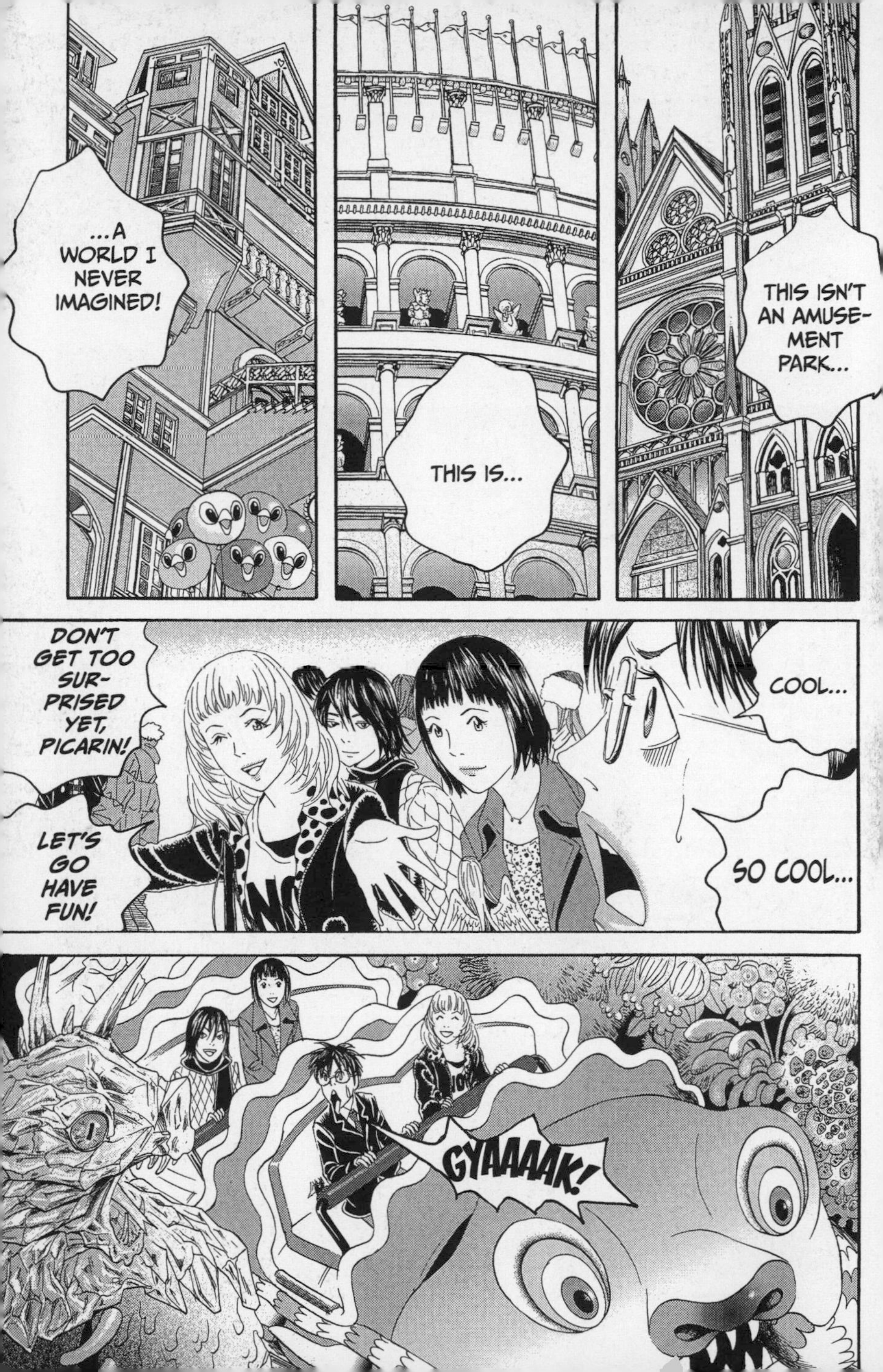
THIS ISN'T AN AMUSEMENT PARK...
THIS IS...
...A WORLD I NEVER IMAGINED!
COOL...
SO COOL...
DON'T GET TOO SURPRISED YET, PICARIN!
LET'S GO HAVE FUN!
GYAAAAK!

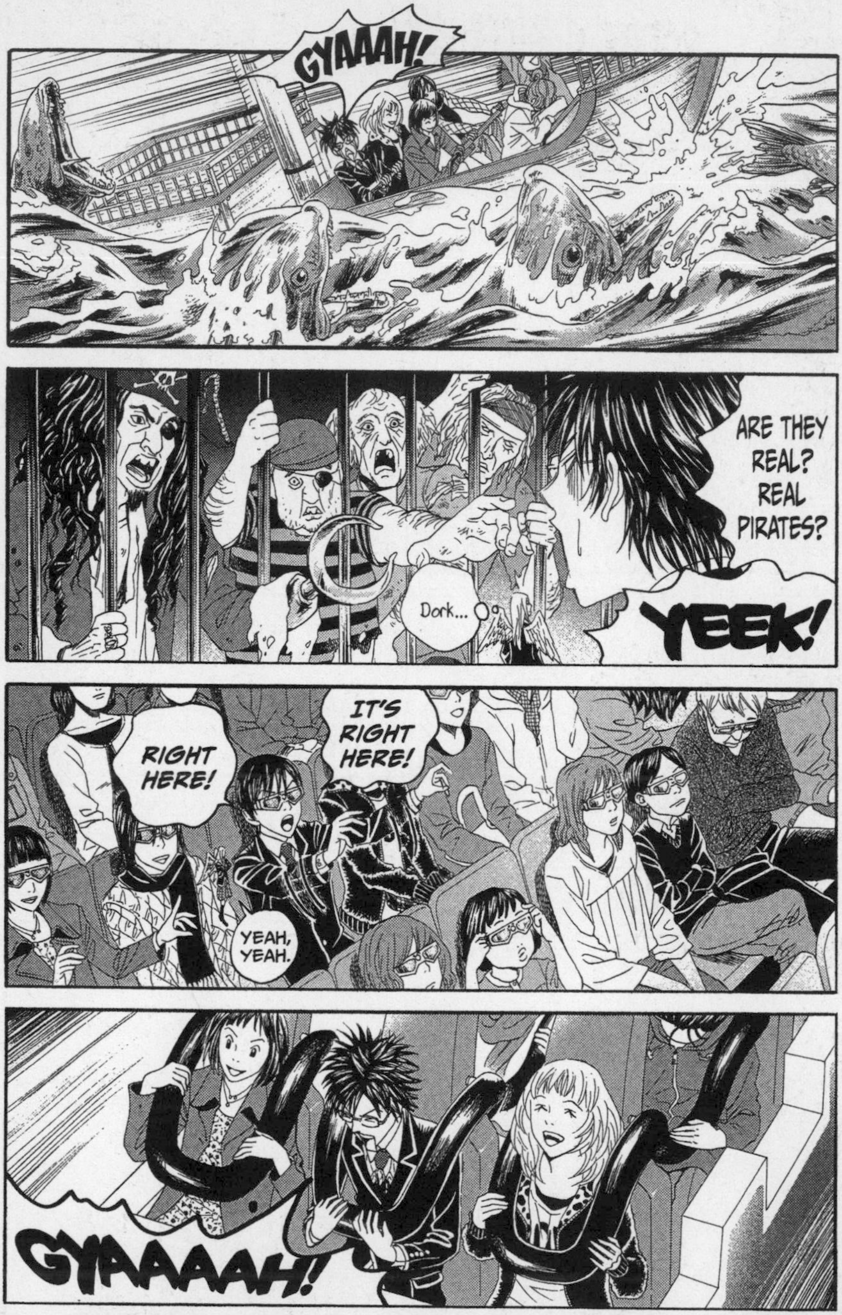
GYAAAH!
ARE THEY REAL? REAL PIRATES?
YEEK!
Dork...
IT'S RIGHT HERE!
RIGHT HERE!
YEAH, YEAH.
GYAAAAH!

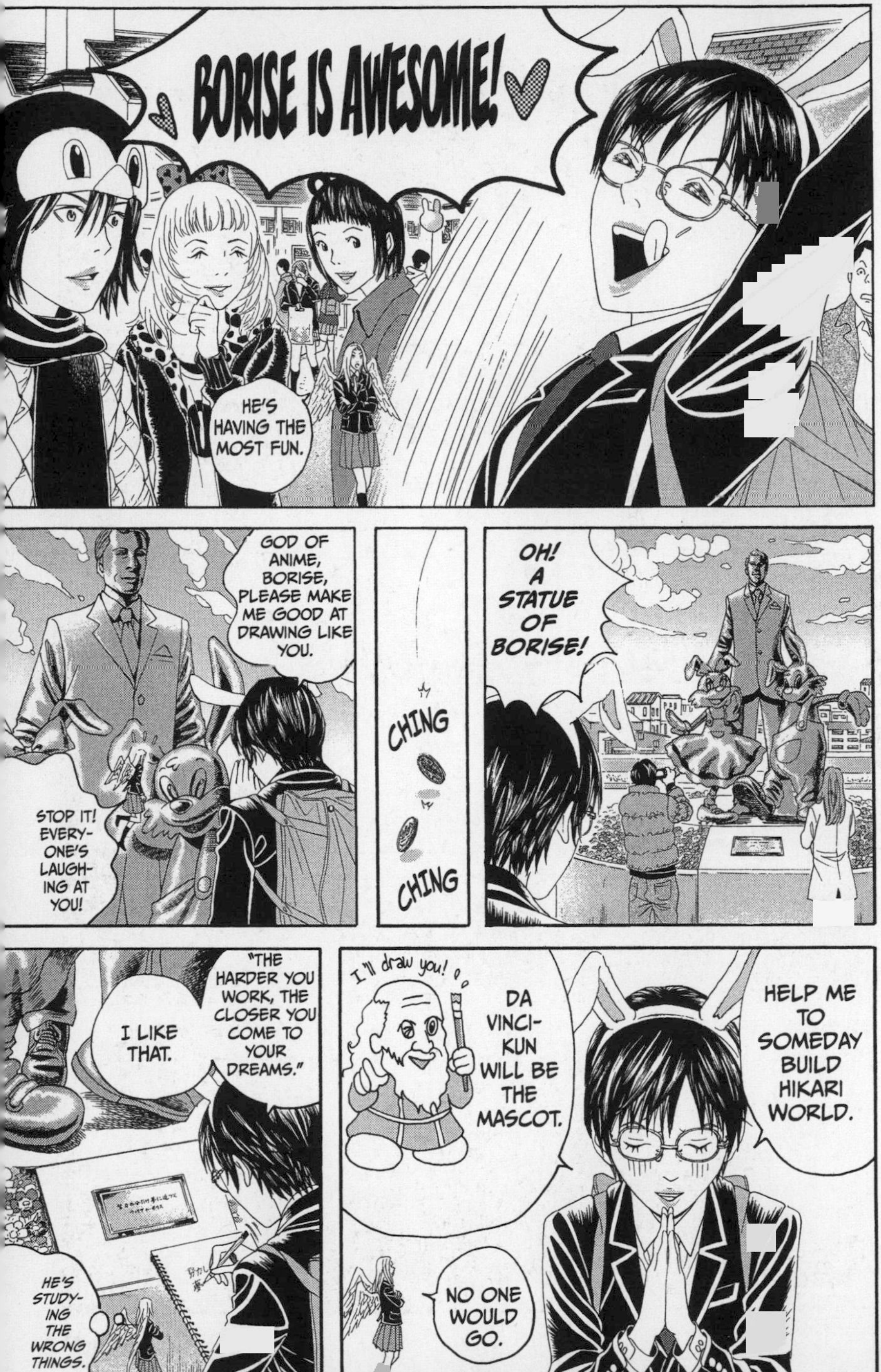
BORISE IS AWESOME!
HE'S HAVING THE MOST FUN.
OH! A STATUE OF BORISE!
CHING
CHING
GOD OF ANIME, BORISE, PLEASE MAKE ME GOOD AT DRAWING LIKE YOU.
STOP IT! EVERYONE'S LAUGHING AT YOU!
HELP ME TO SOMEDAY BUILD HIKARI WORLD.
DA VINCI-KUN WILL BE THE MASCOT.
I'll draw you!
NO ONE WOULD GO.
"THE HARDER YOU WORK, THE CLOSER YOU COME TO YOUR DREAMS."
I LIKE THAT.
HE'S STUDYING THE WRONG THINGS.

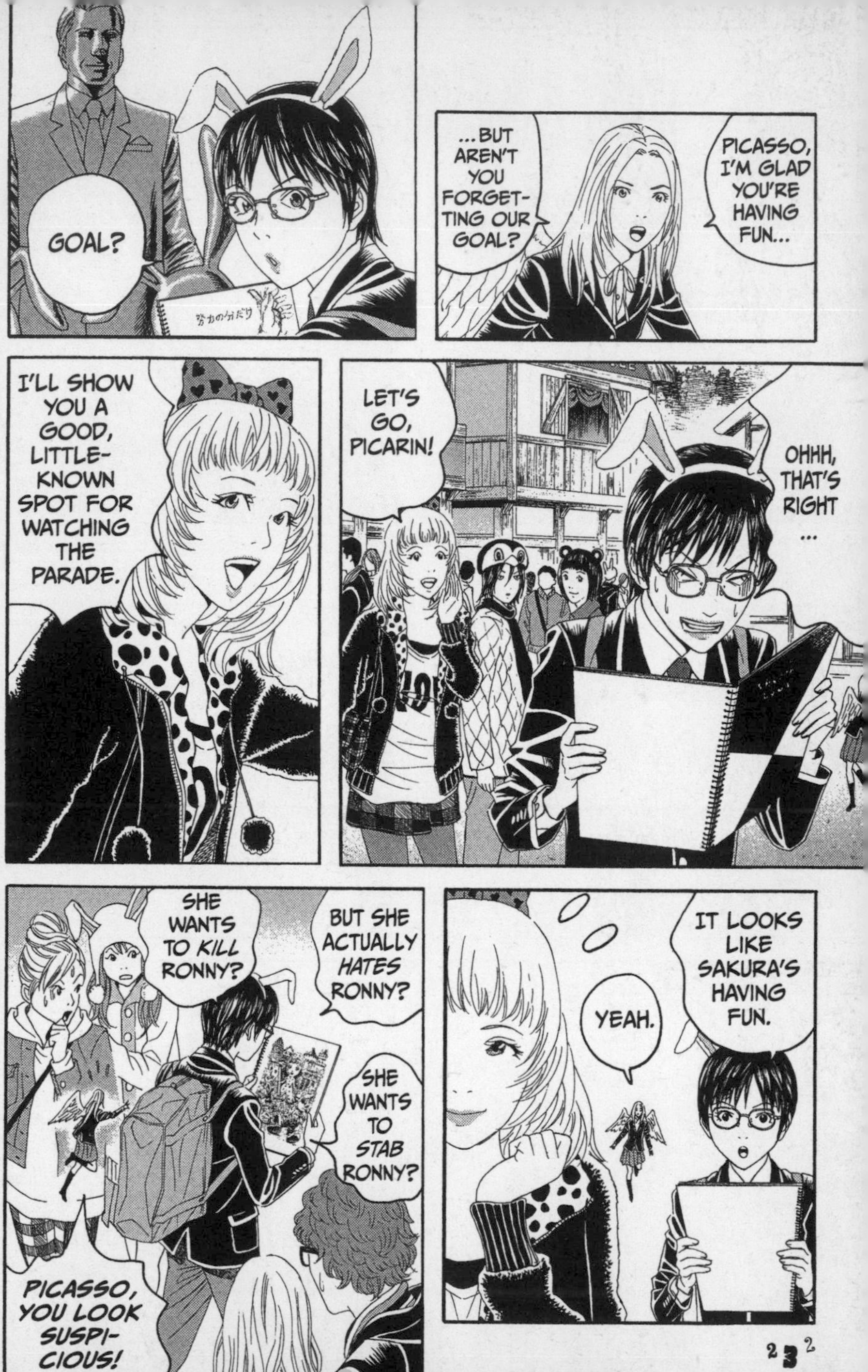
PICASSO, I'M GLAD YOU'RE HAVING FUN...
...BUT AREN'T YOU FORGET-TING OUR GOAL?
GOAL?
OHHH, THAT'S RIGHT ...
LET'S GO, PICARIN!
I'LL SHOW YOU A GOOD, LITTLE-KNOWN SPOT FOR WATCHING THE PARADE.
IT LOOKS LIKE SAKURA'S HAVING FUN.
YEAH.
BUT SHE ACTUALLY *HATES* RONNY?
SHE WANTS TO *KILL* RONNY?
SHE WANTS TO *STAB* RONNY?
PICASSO, YOU LOOK SUSPI-CIOUS!

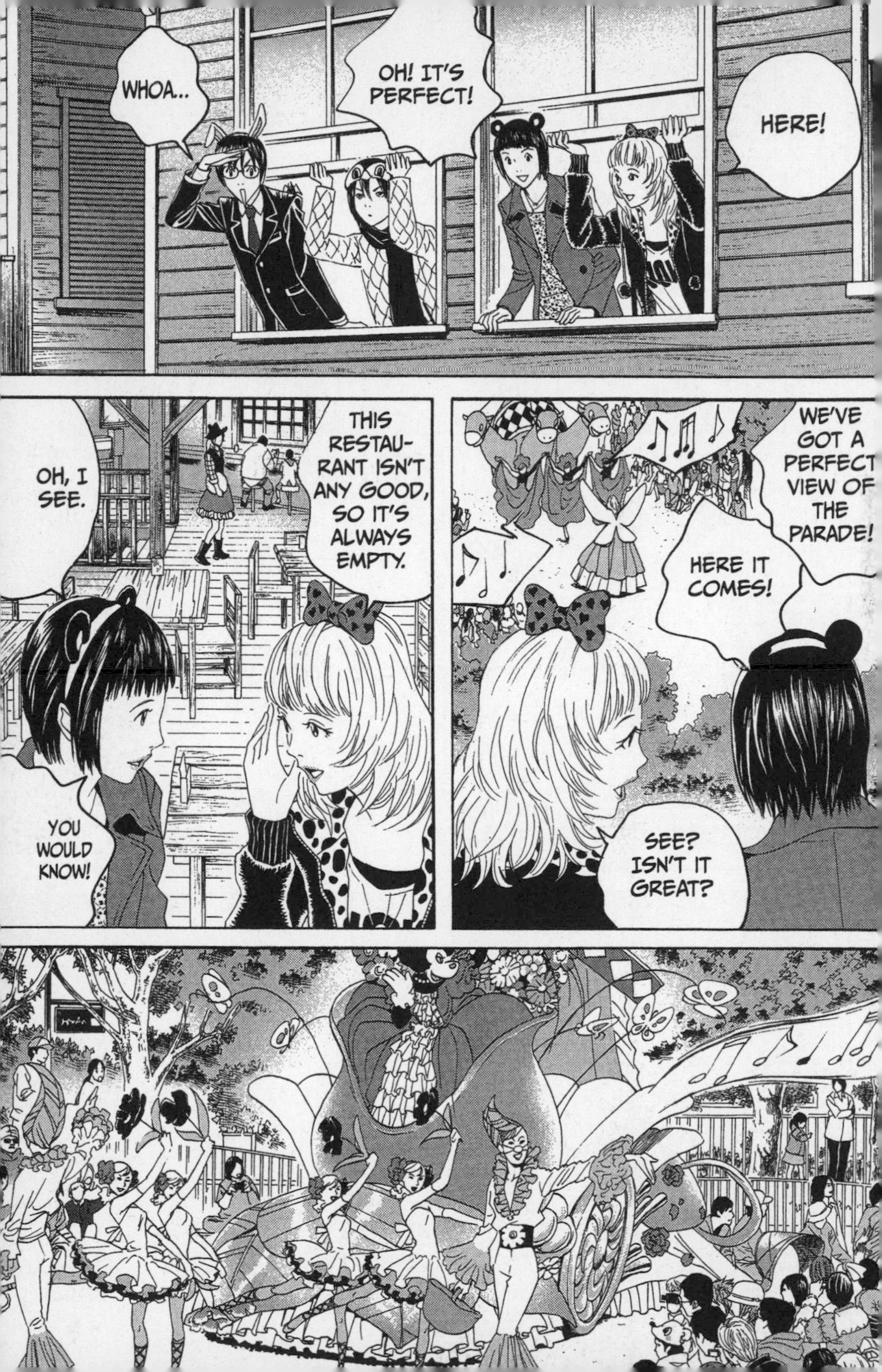
HERE!
OH! IT'S PERFECT!
WHOA...
WE'VE GOT A PERFECT VIEW OF THE PARADE!
HERE IT COMES!
SEE? ISN'T IT GREAT?
THIS RESTAU-RANT ISN'T ANY GOOD, SO IT'S ALWAYS EMPTY.
OH, I SEE.
YOU WOULD KNOW!

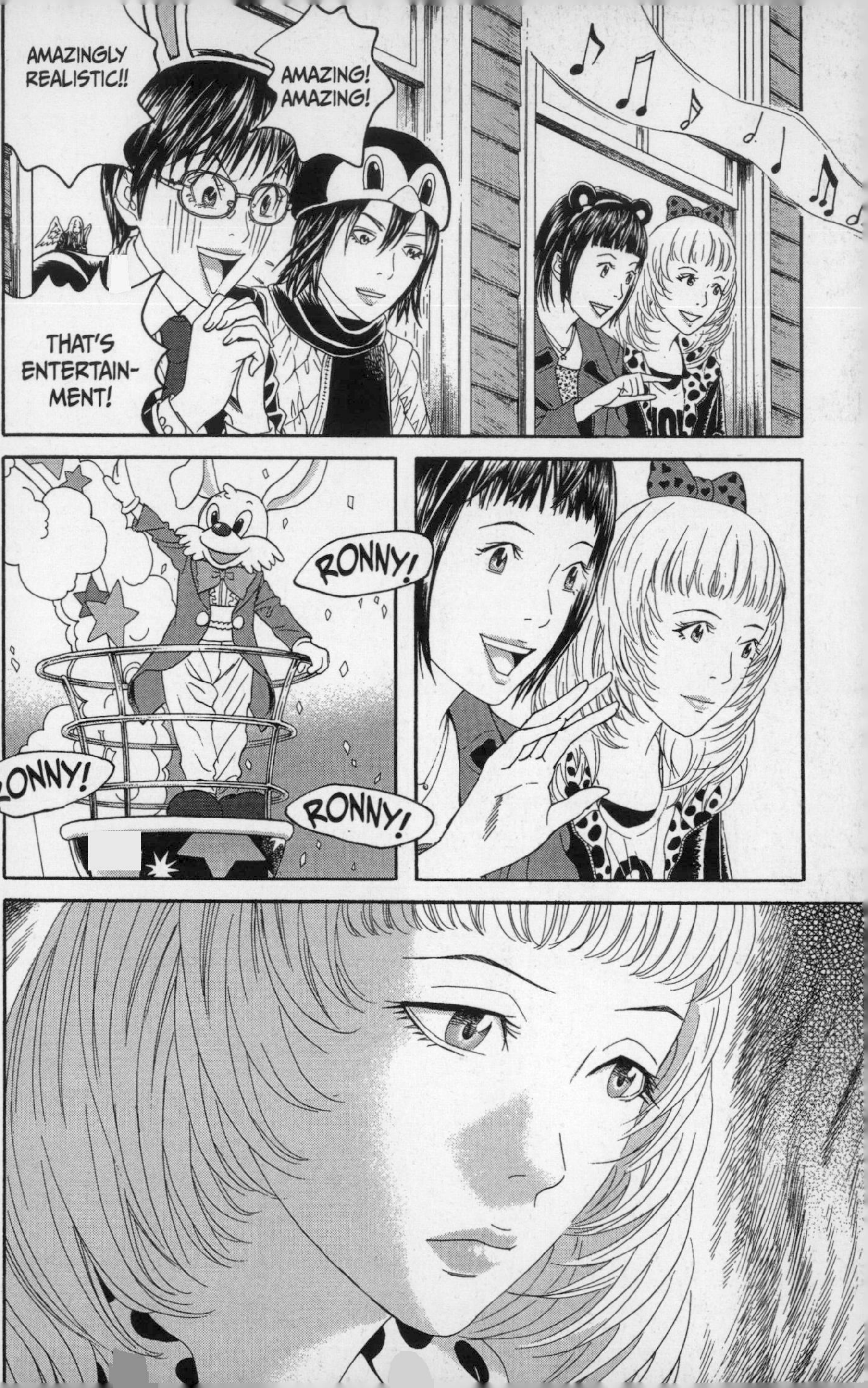
AMAZING! AMAZING!
AMAZINGLY REALISTIC!!
THAT'S ENTERTAIN-MENT!
RONNY!
RONNY!
RONNY!

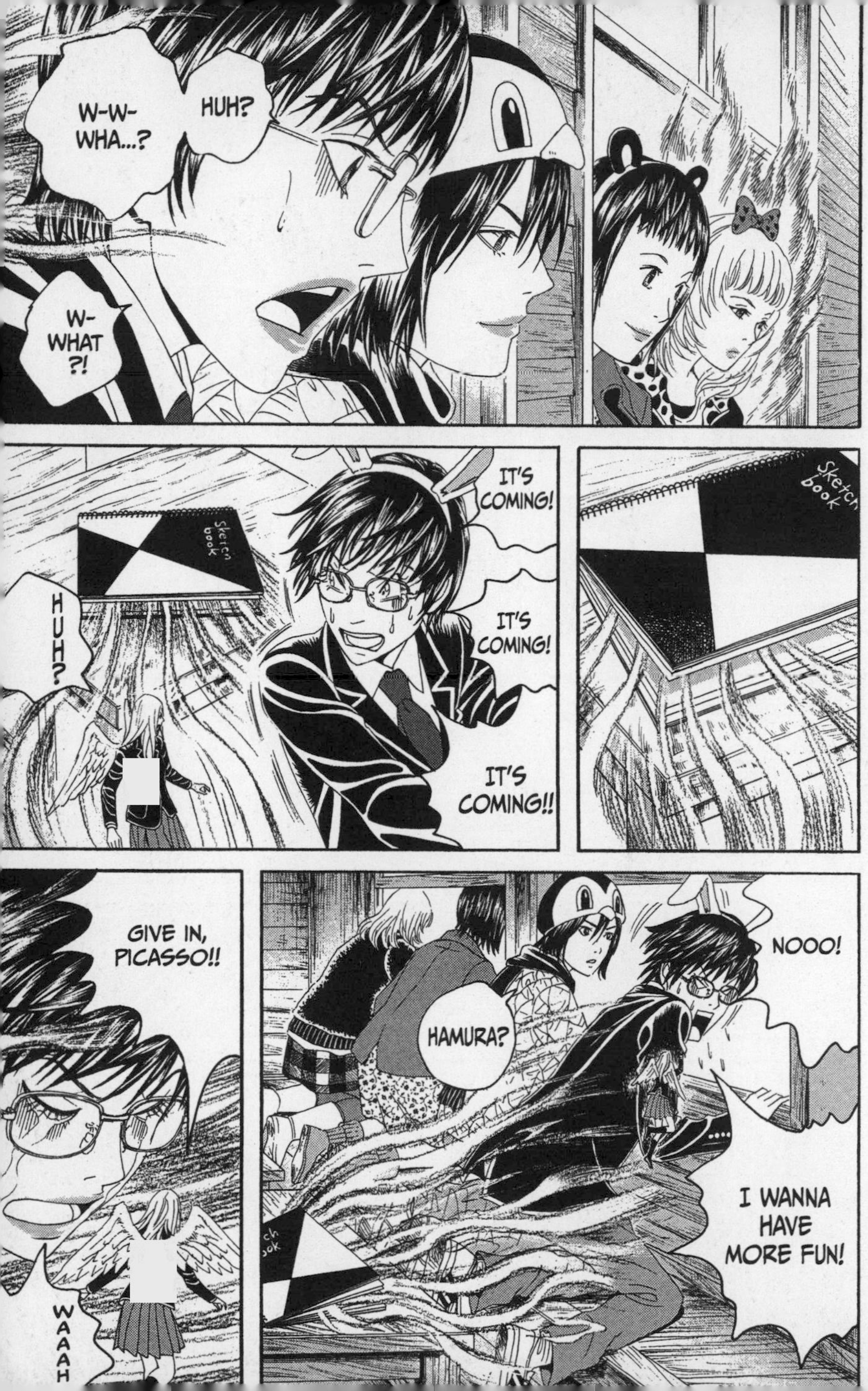
HUH?
W-W- WHA...?
W- WHAT ?!
Sketch book
IT'S COMING!
IT'S COMING!
IT'S COMING!!
HUH?
NOOO!
HAMURA?
I WANNA HAVE MORE FUN!
GIVE IN, PICASSO!!
WAAAAH

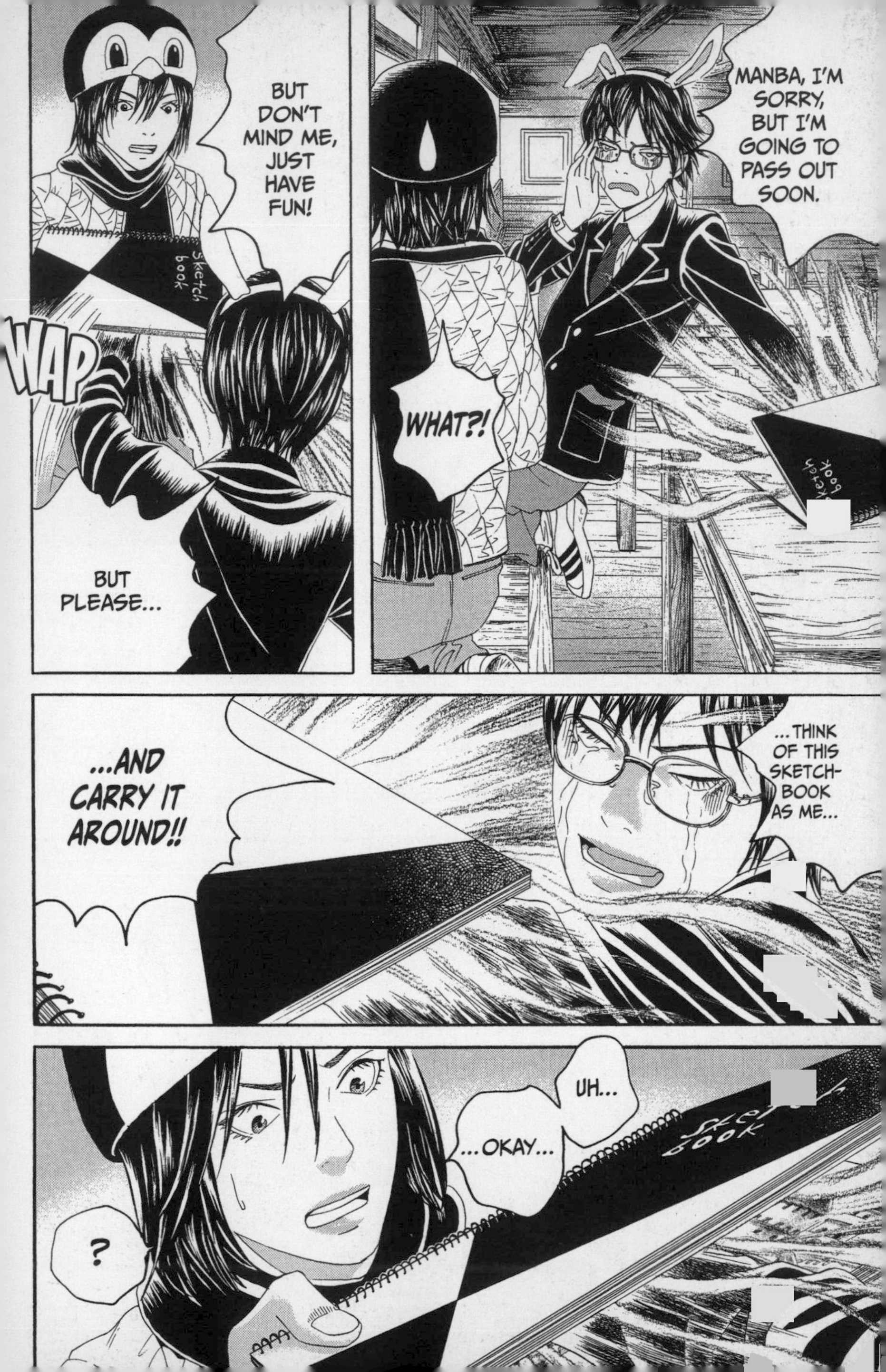
MANBA, I'M SORRY, BUT I'M GOING TO PASS OUT SOON.
WHAT?!
sketch book
BUT DON'T MIND ME, JUST HAVE FUN!
sketch book
WAP
BUT PLEASE...
...THINK OF THIS SKETCH-BOOK AS ME...
...AND CARRY IT AROUND!!
UH...
...OKAY...
sketch book
?

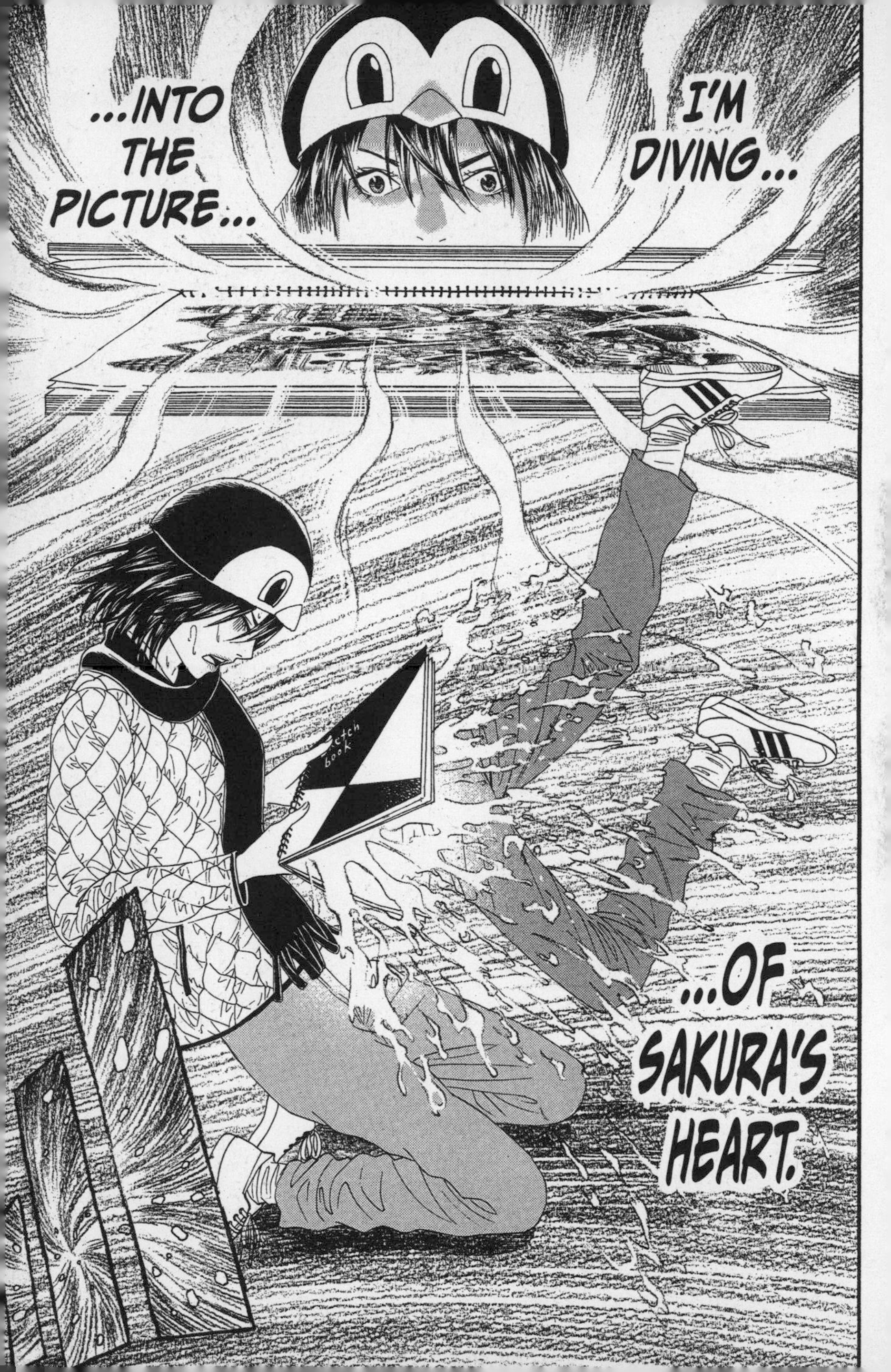
I'M DIVING...
...INTO THE PICTURE...
...OF SAKURA'S HEART.

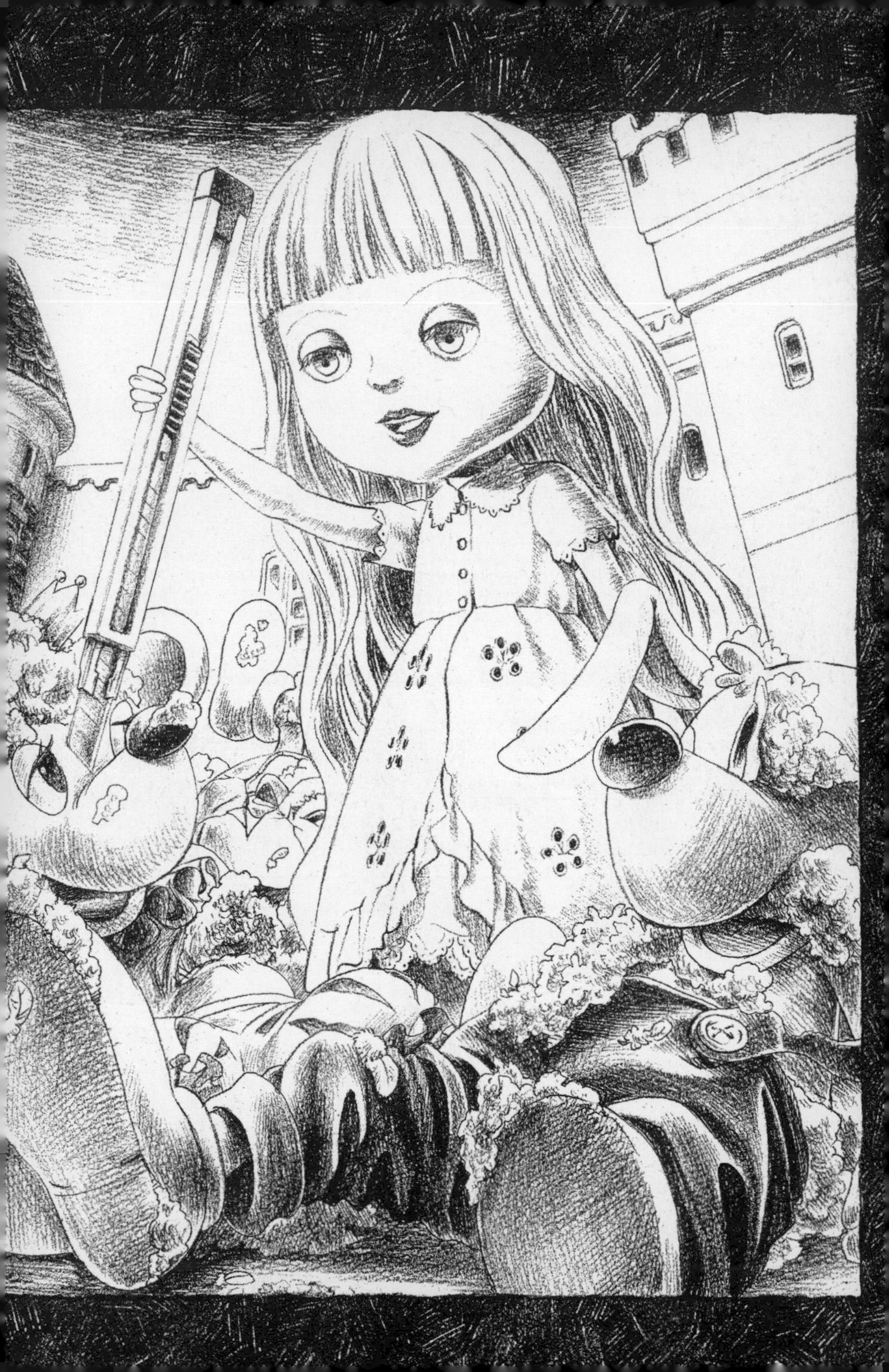

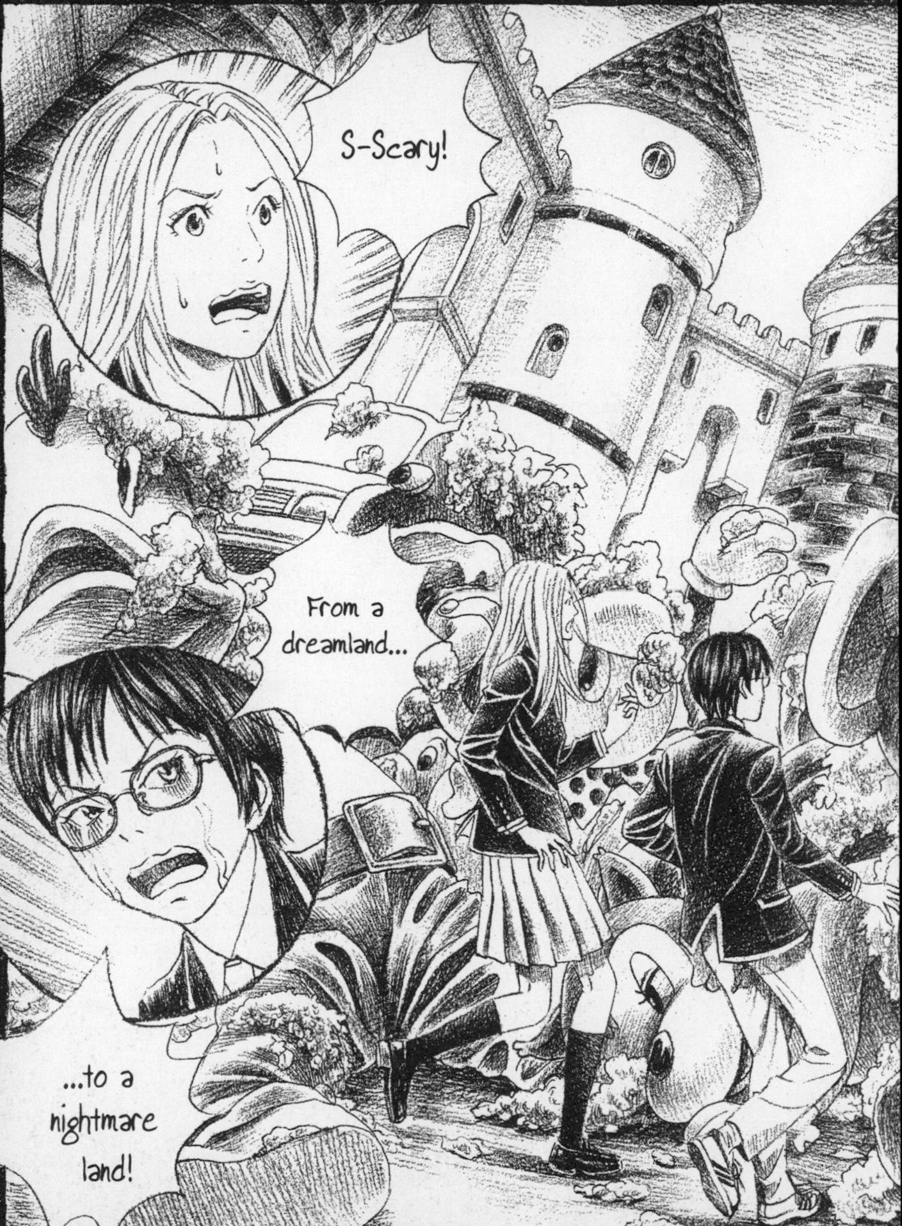
S-Scary!
From a dreamland...
...to a nightmare land!

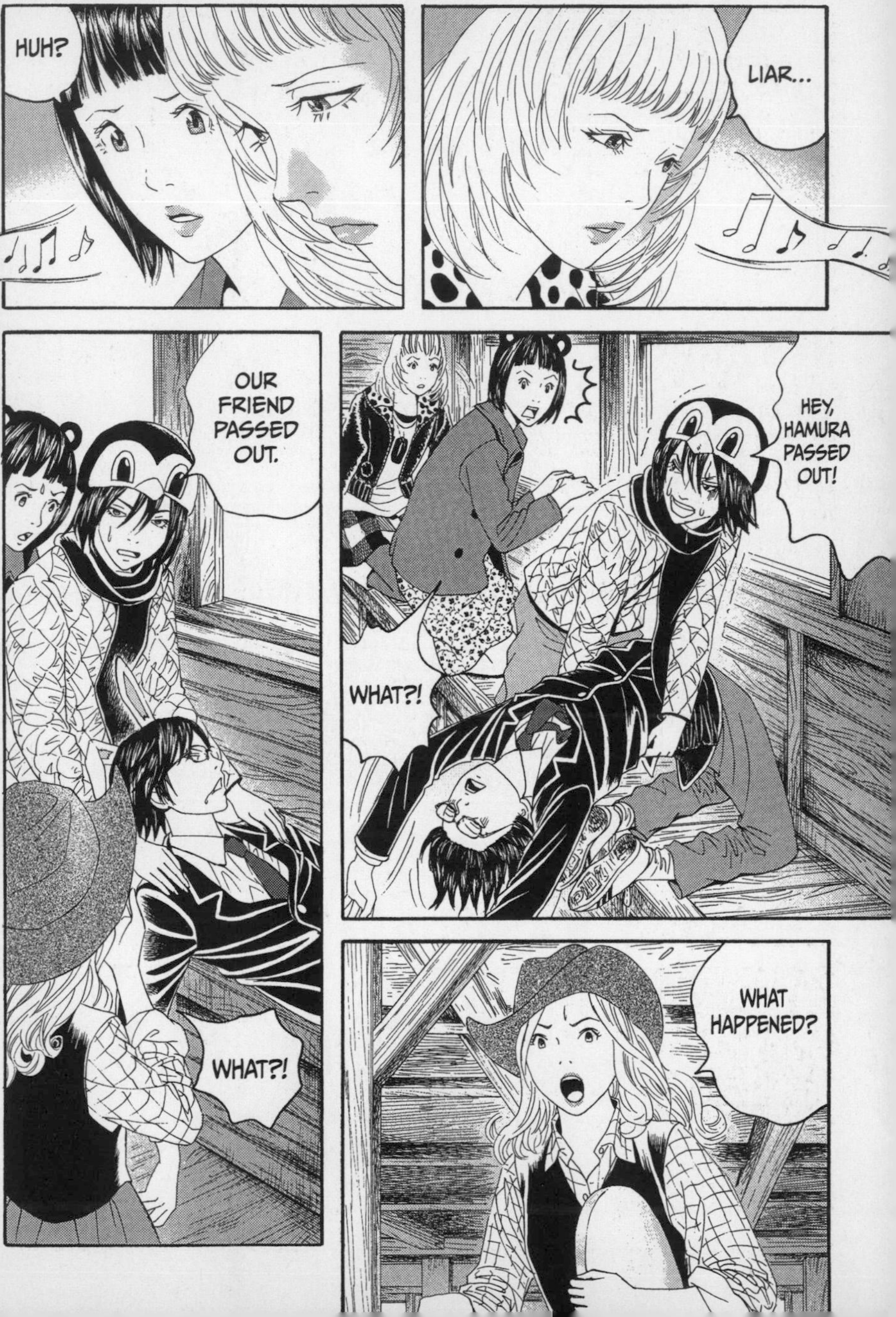
LIAR...
HUH?
HEY, HAMURA PASSED OUT!
WHAT?!
WHAT HAPPENED?
OUR FRIEND PASSED OUT.
WHAT?!

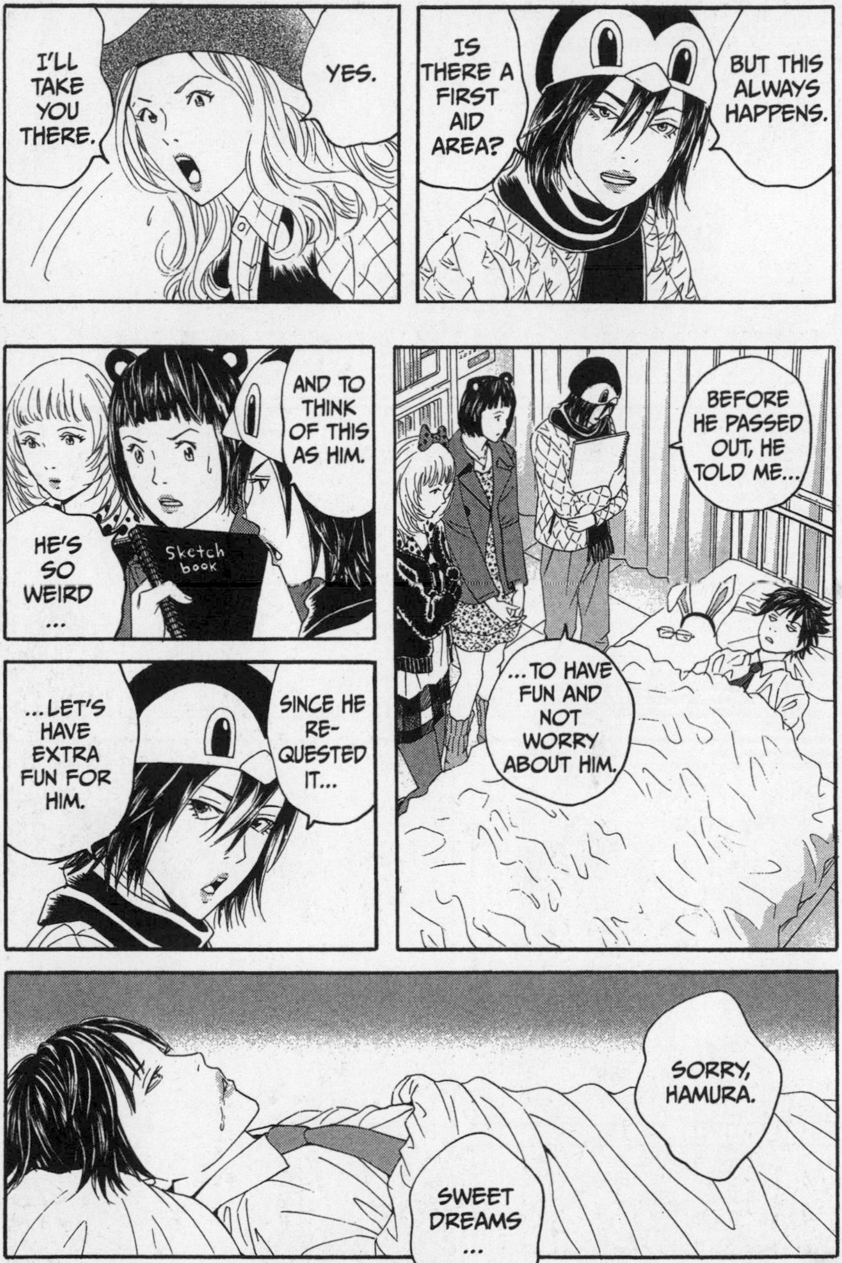
BUT THIS ALWAYS HAPPENS.
IS THERE A FIRST AID AREA?
YES.
I'LL TAKE YOU THERE.
BEFORE HE PASSED OUT, HE TOLD ME...
...TO HAVE FUN AND NOT WORRY ABOUT HIM.
AND TO THINK OF THIS AS HIM.
Sketch book
HE'S SO WEIRD ...
SINCE HE RE-QUESTED IT...
...LET'S HAVE EXTRA FUN FOR HIM.
SORRY, HAMURA.
SWEET DREAMS ...

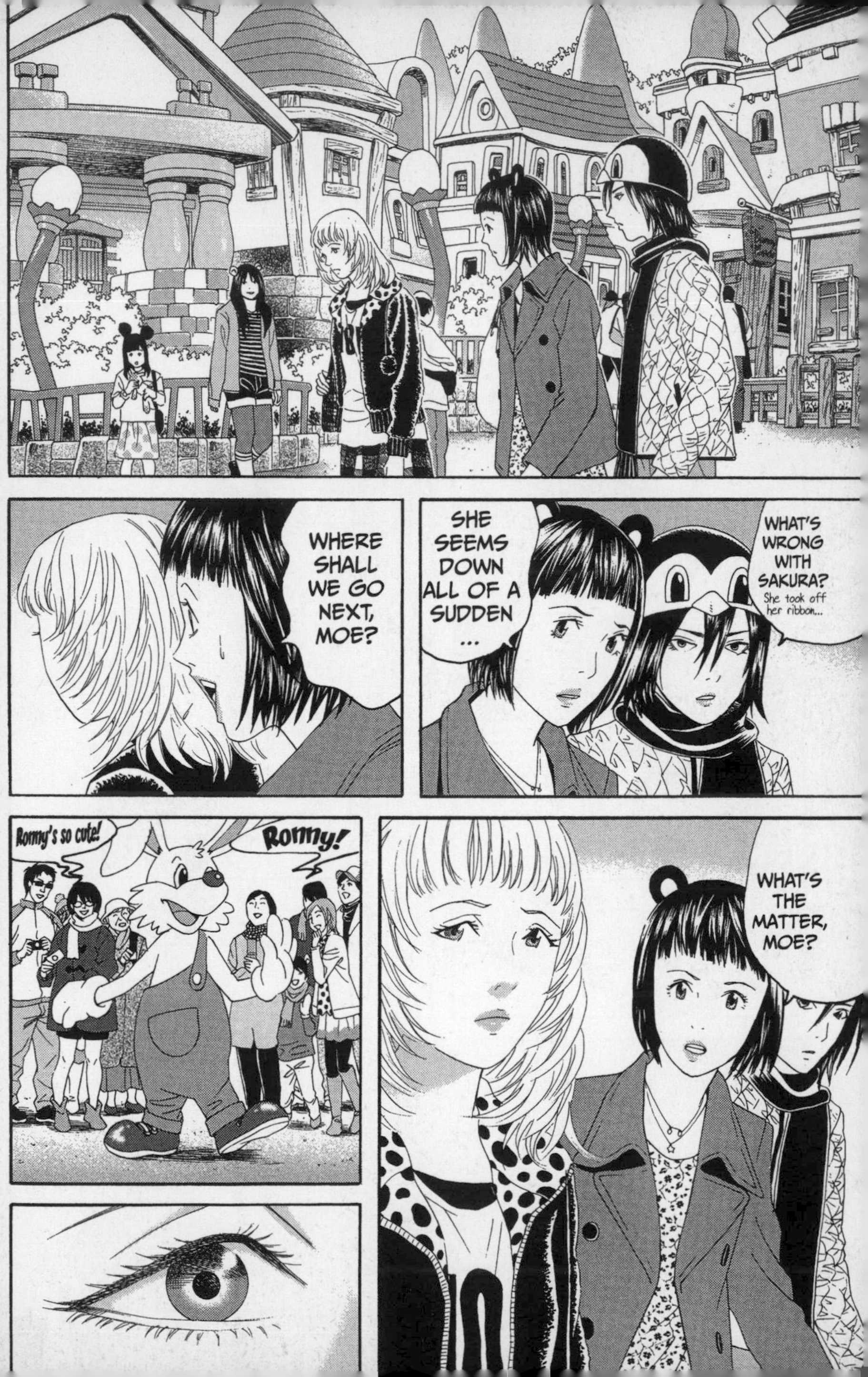
WHAT'S WRONG WITH SAKURA? She took off her ribbon...
SHE SEEMS DOWN ALL OF A SUDDEN ...
WHERE SHALL WE GO NEXT, MOE?
WHAT'S THE MATTER, MOE?
Ronny!
Ronny's so cute!

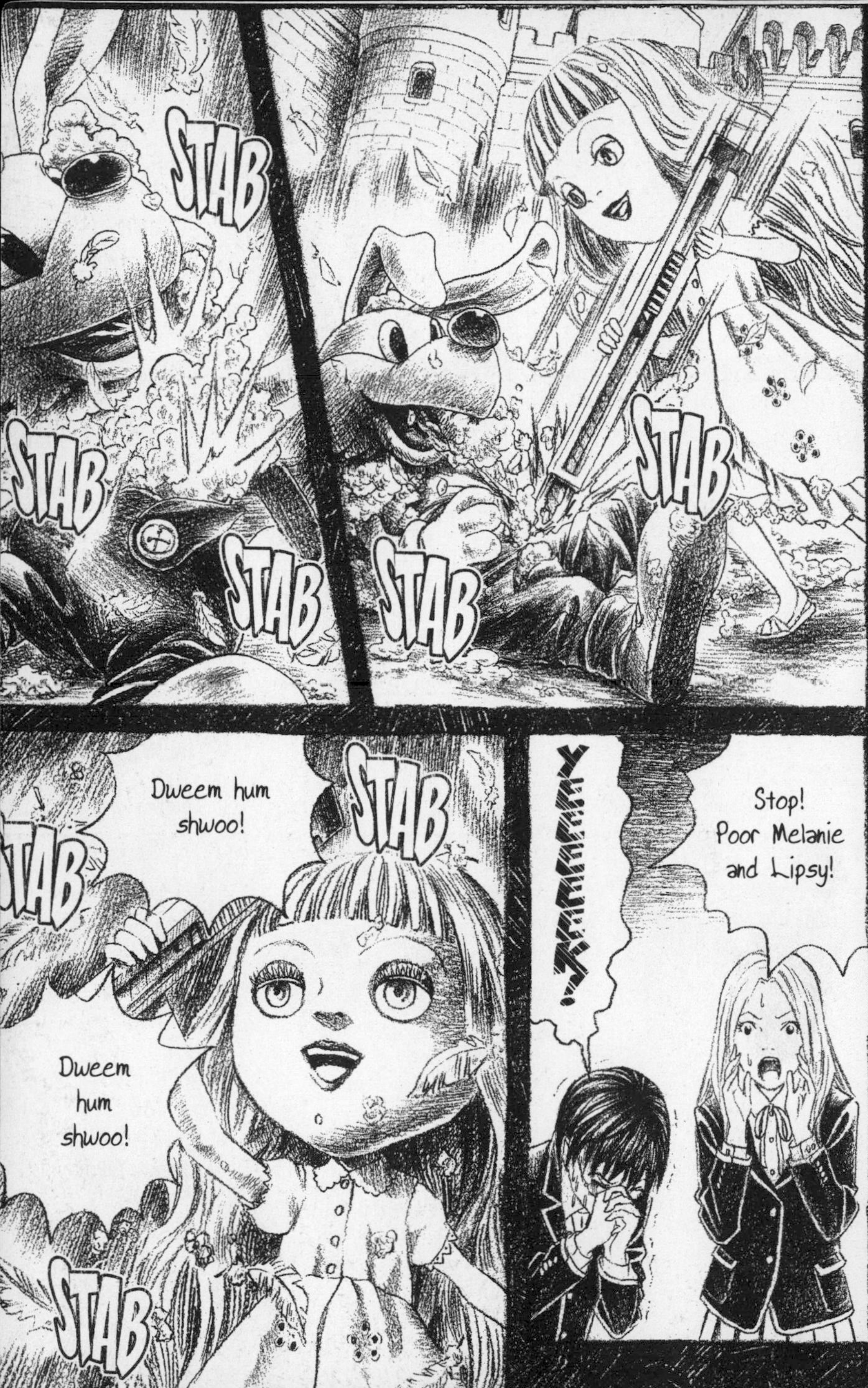

STAB
STAB
STAB
STAB
STAB
YEEEEEEK!
Stop! Poor Melanie and Lipsy!
STAB
Dweem hum shwoo!
STAB
Dweem hum shwoo!
STAB

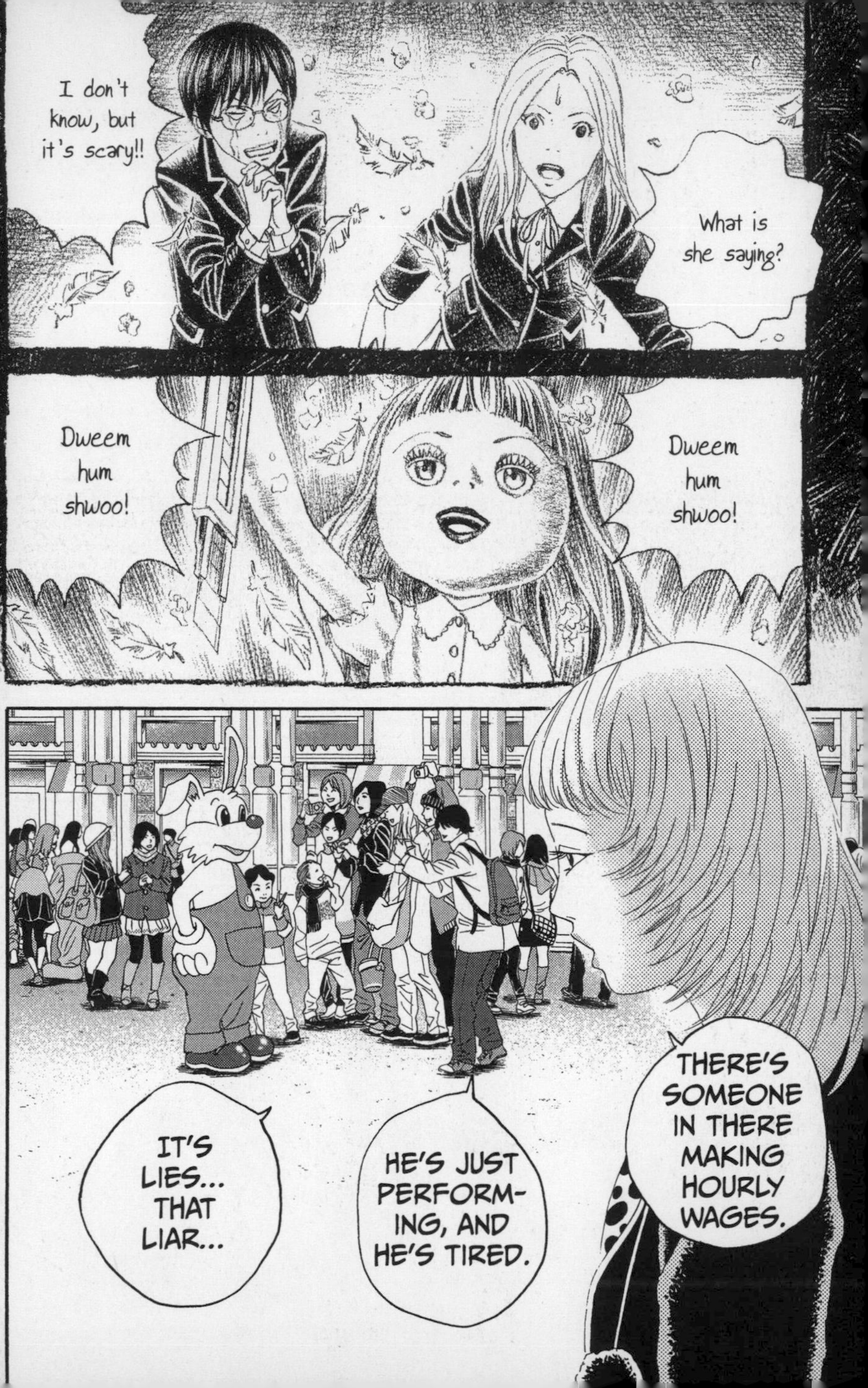

What is she saying?
I don't know, but it's scary!!
Dweem hum shwoo!
Dweem hum shwoo!
THERE'S SOMEONE IN THERE MAKING HOURLY WAGES.
HE'S JUST PERFORM-ING, AND HE'S TIRED.
IT'S LIES... THAT LIAR...

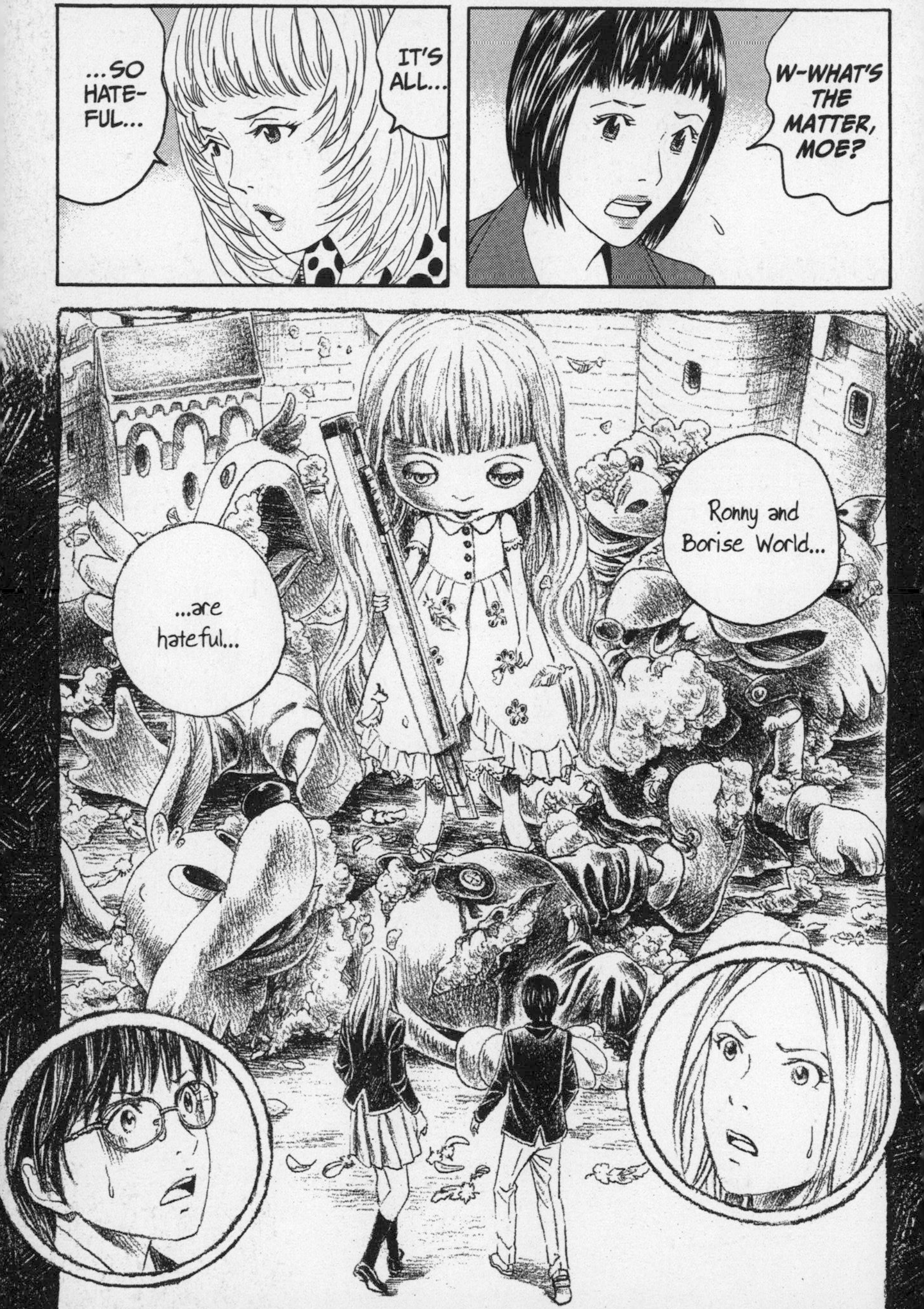
W-WHAT'S THE MATTER, MOE?
IT'S ALL...
...SO HATE-FUL...
Ronny and Borise World...
...are hateful...

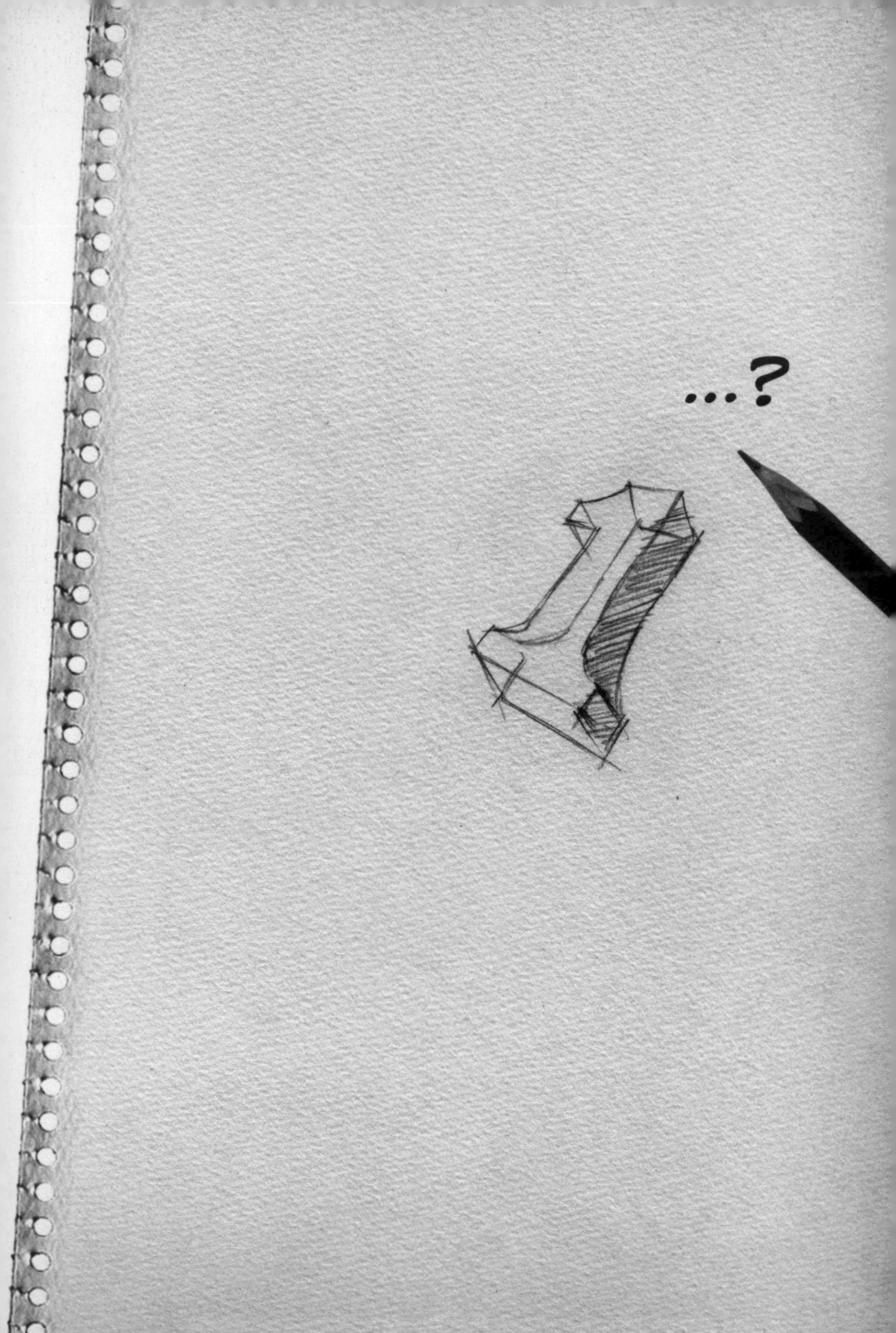
...?

Vision 8: Borise World and Moe (Part I)_Jump SQ, August 2009

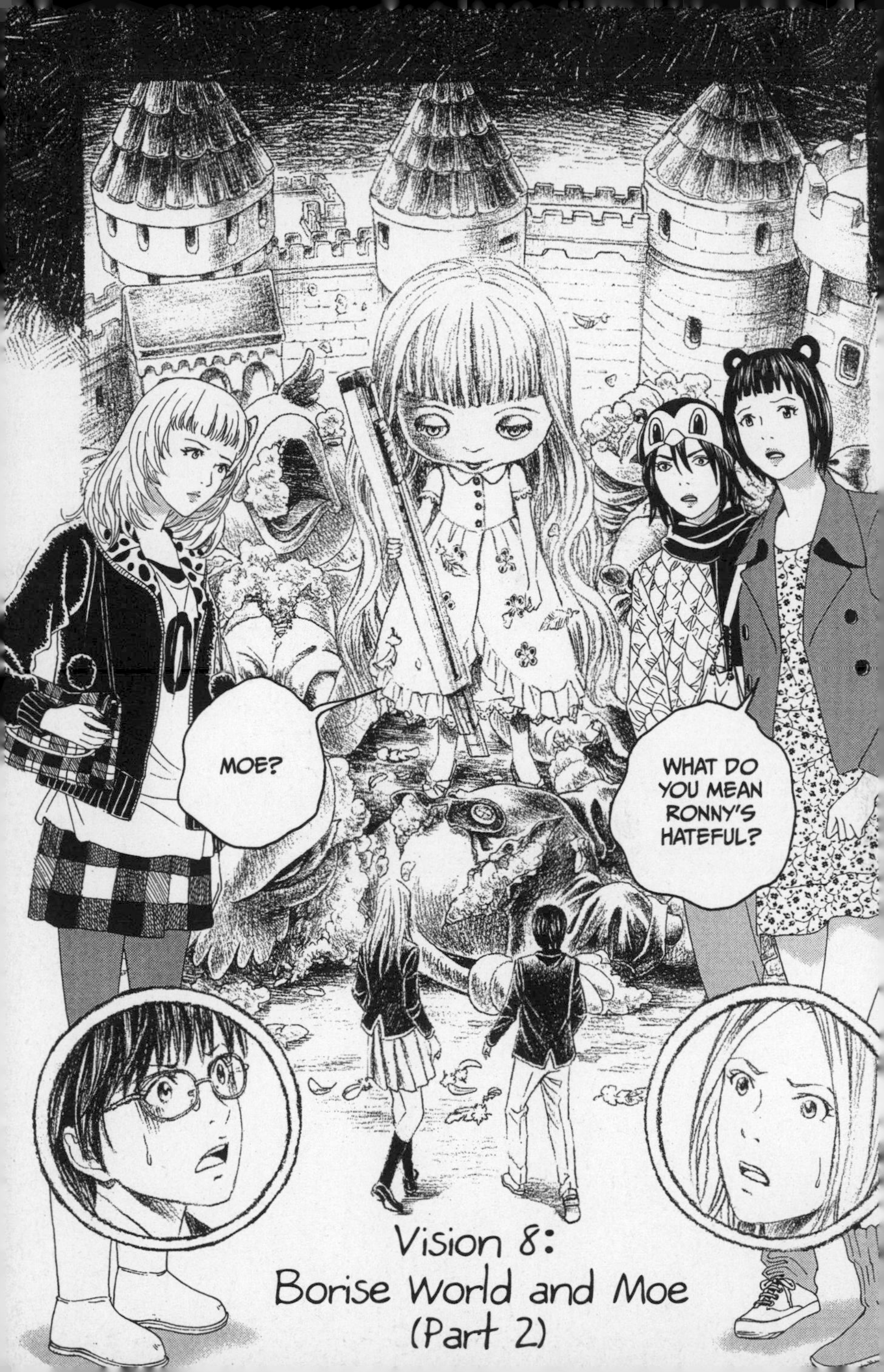
WHAT DO YOU MEAN RONNY'S HATEFUL?
MOE?
Vision 8: Borise World and Moe (Part 2)

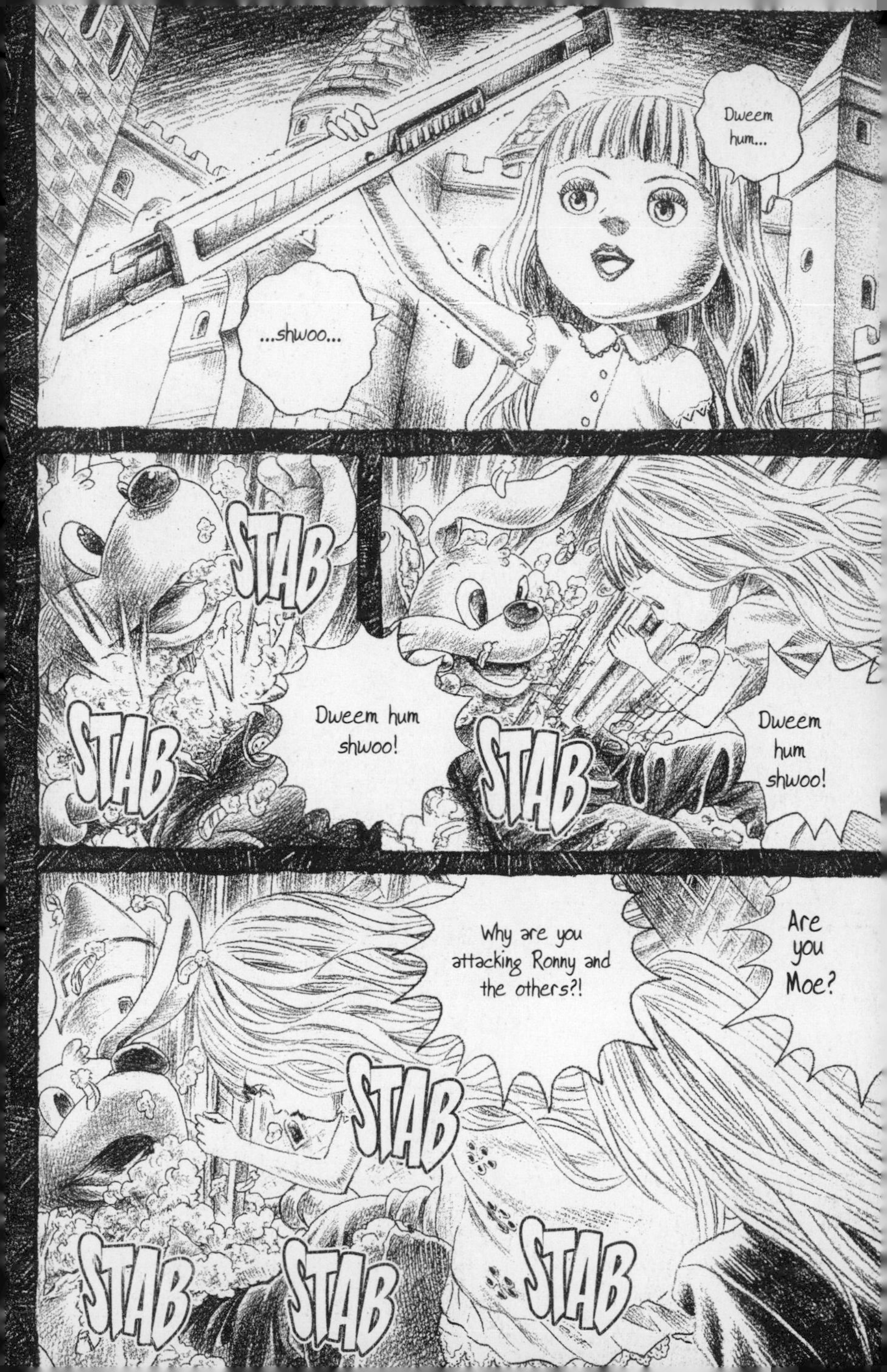
Dweem hum...
...shwoo...
Dweem hum shwoo!
STAB
STAB
Dweem hum shwoo!
STAB
Are you Moe?
Why are you attacking Ronny and the others?!
STAB
STAB
STAB
STAB

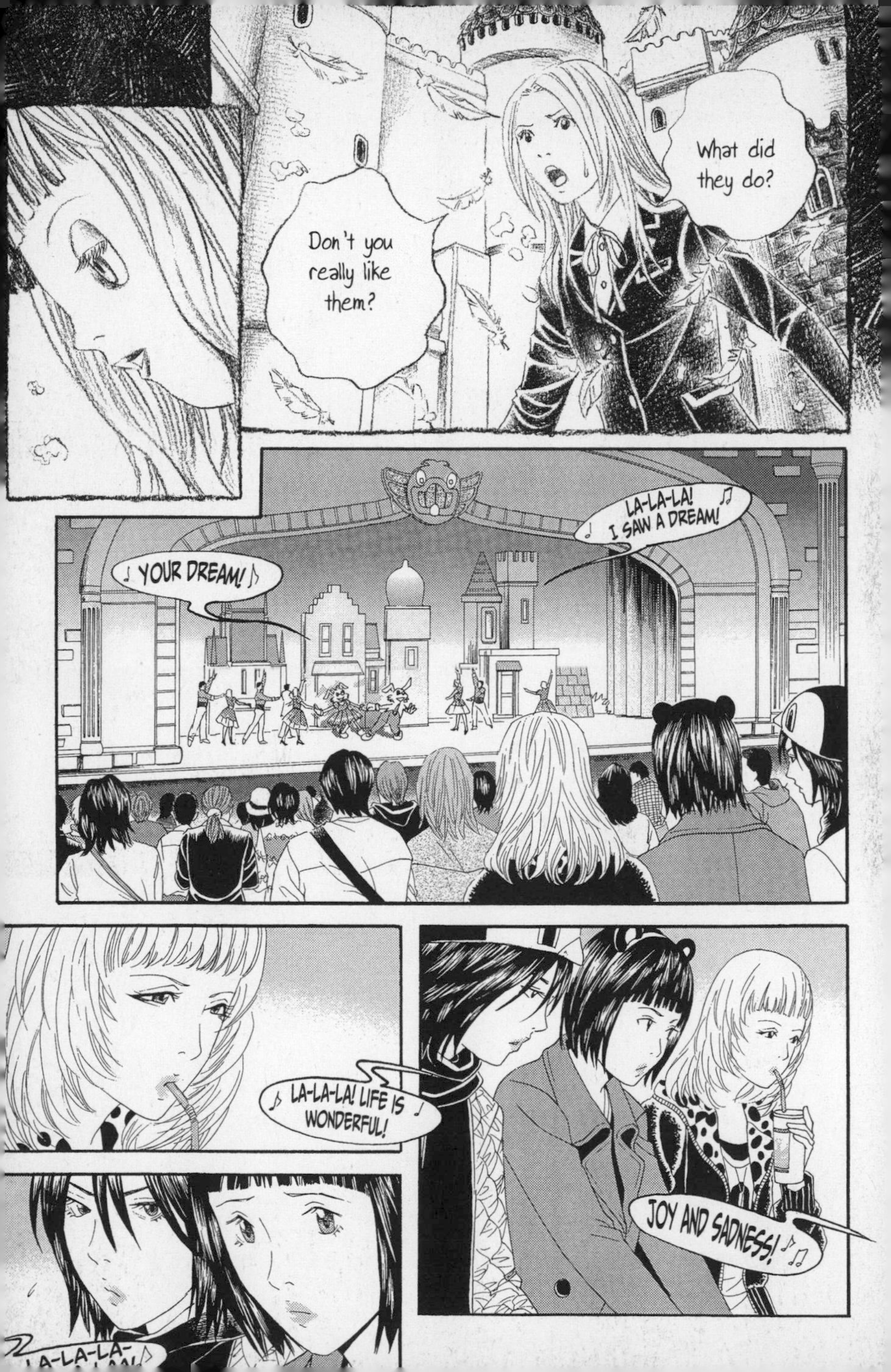
What did they do?
Don't you really like them?
LA-LA-LA! I SAW A DREAM!
YOUR DREAM!
JOY AND SADNESS!
LA-LA-LA! LIFE IS WONDERFUL!
LA-LA-LA-

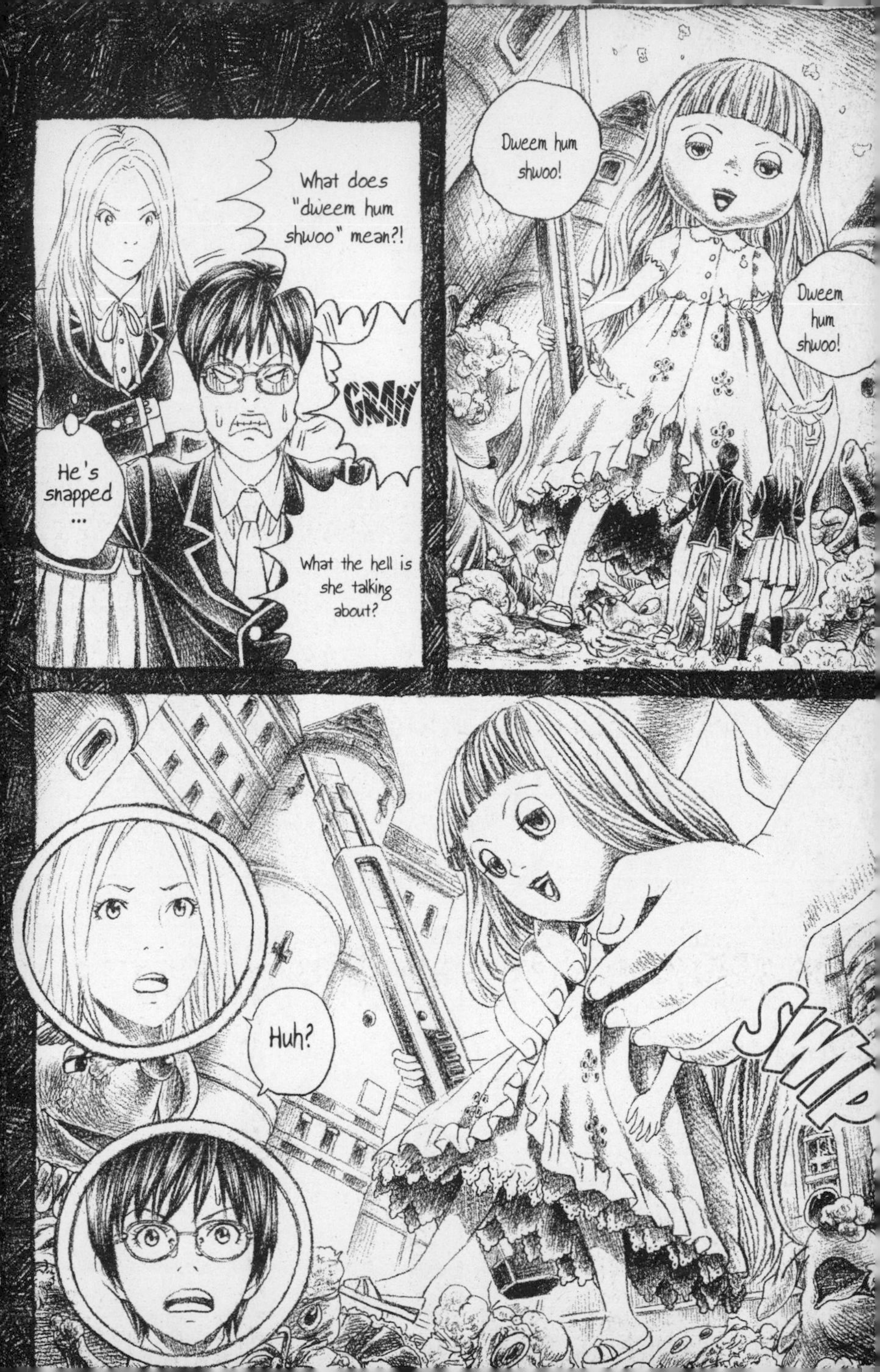
Dweem hum shwoo!
Dweem hum shwoo!
What does "dweem hum shwoo" mean?!
GRAH
He's snapped ...
What the hell is she talking about?
SWIP
Huh?

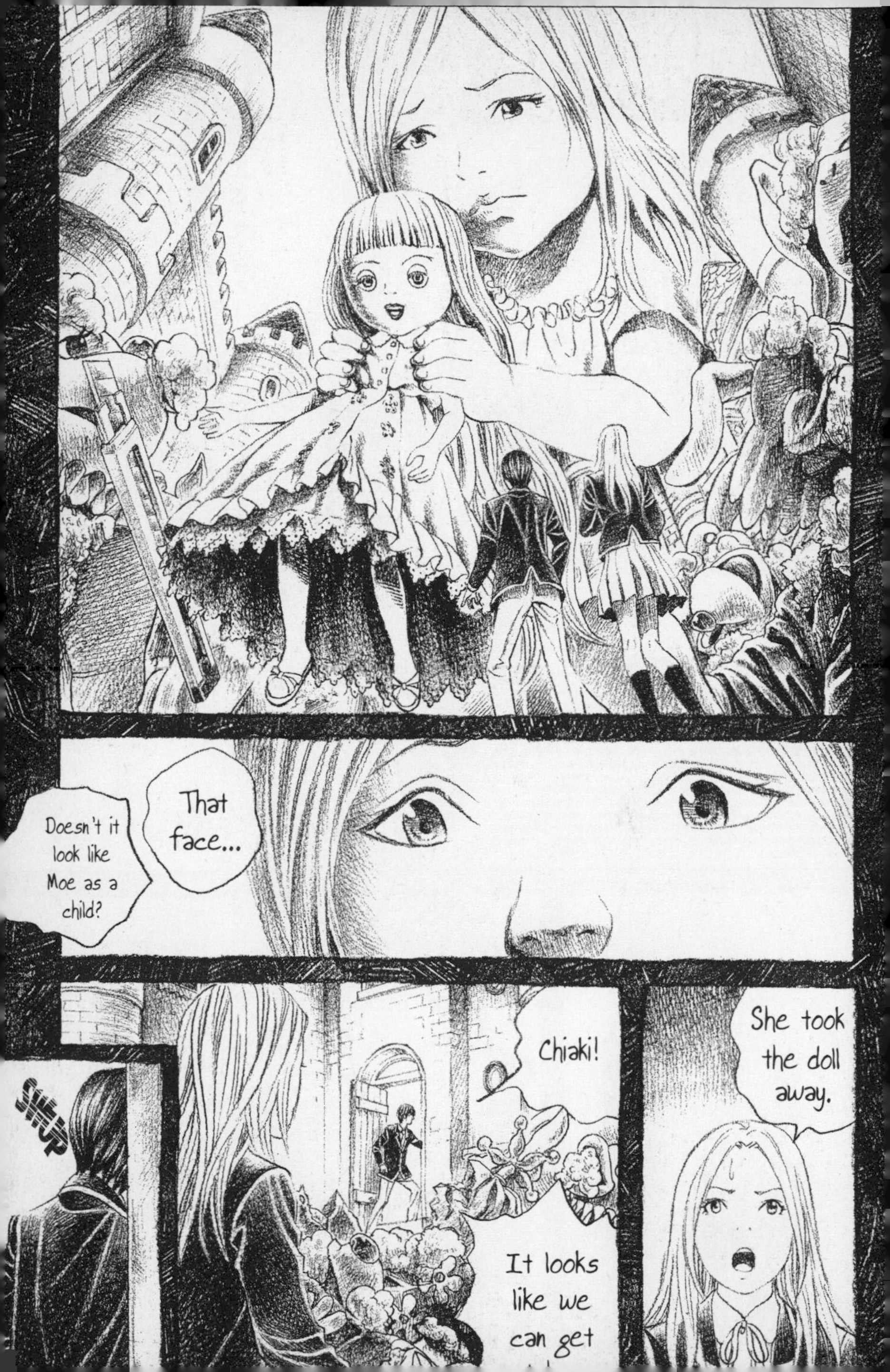
That face...
Doesn't it look like Moe as a child?
She took the doll away.
Chiaki!
It looks like we can get
SHUP

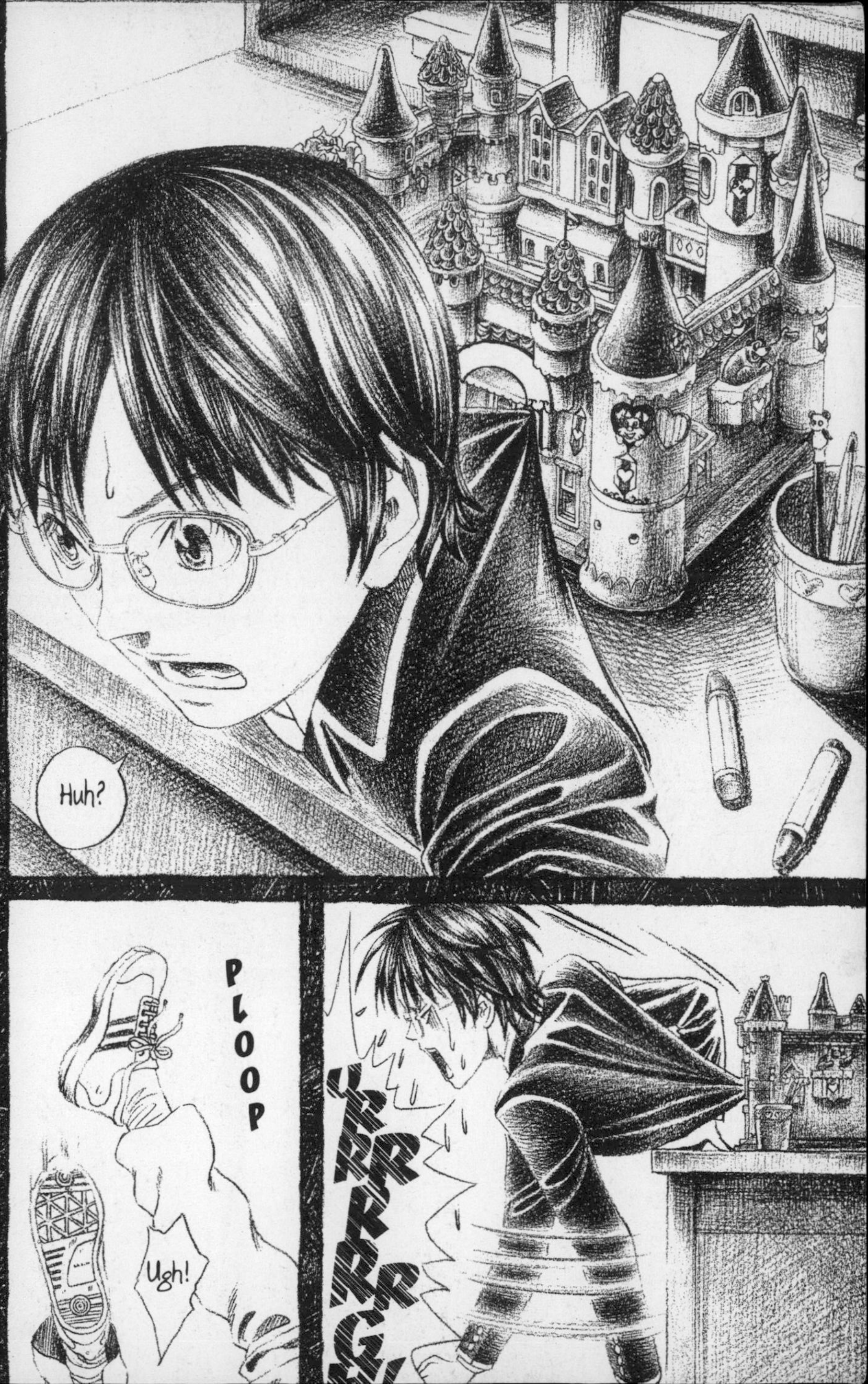
Huh?
URRRRRRG
PLOOP
Ugh!

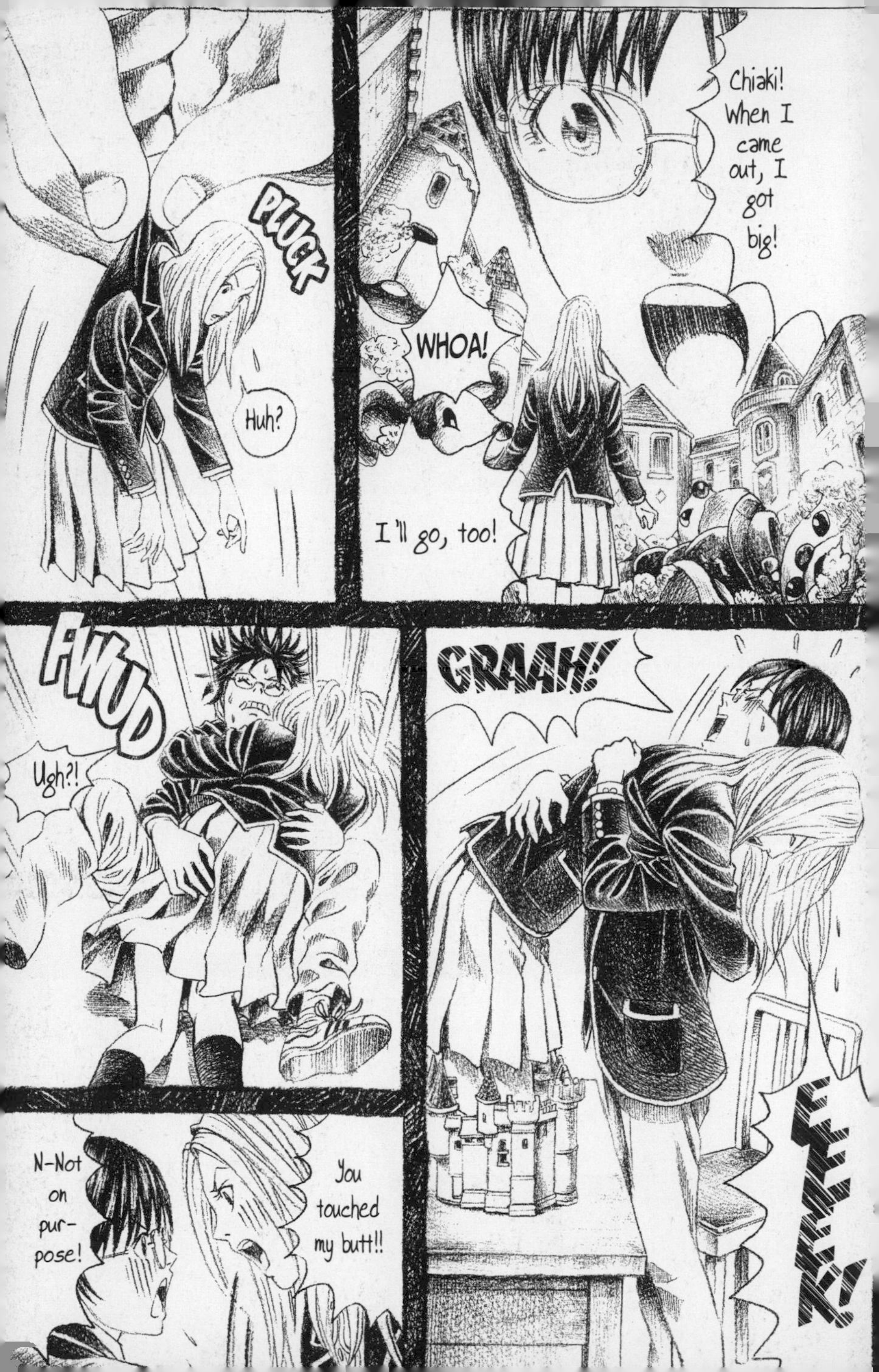
Chiaki! When I came out, I got big!
WHOA!
I'll go, too!
PLUCK
Huh?
GRAAH!
EEEK!
FWUD
Ugh?!
You touched my butt!!
N-Not on purpose!

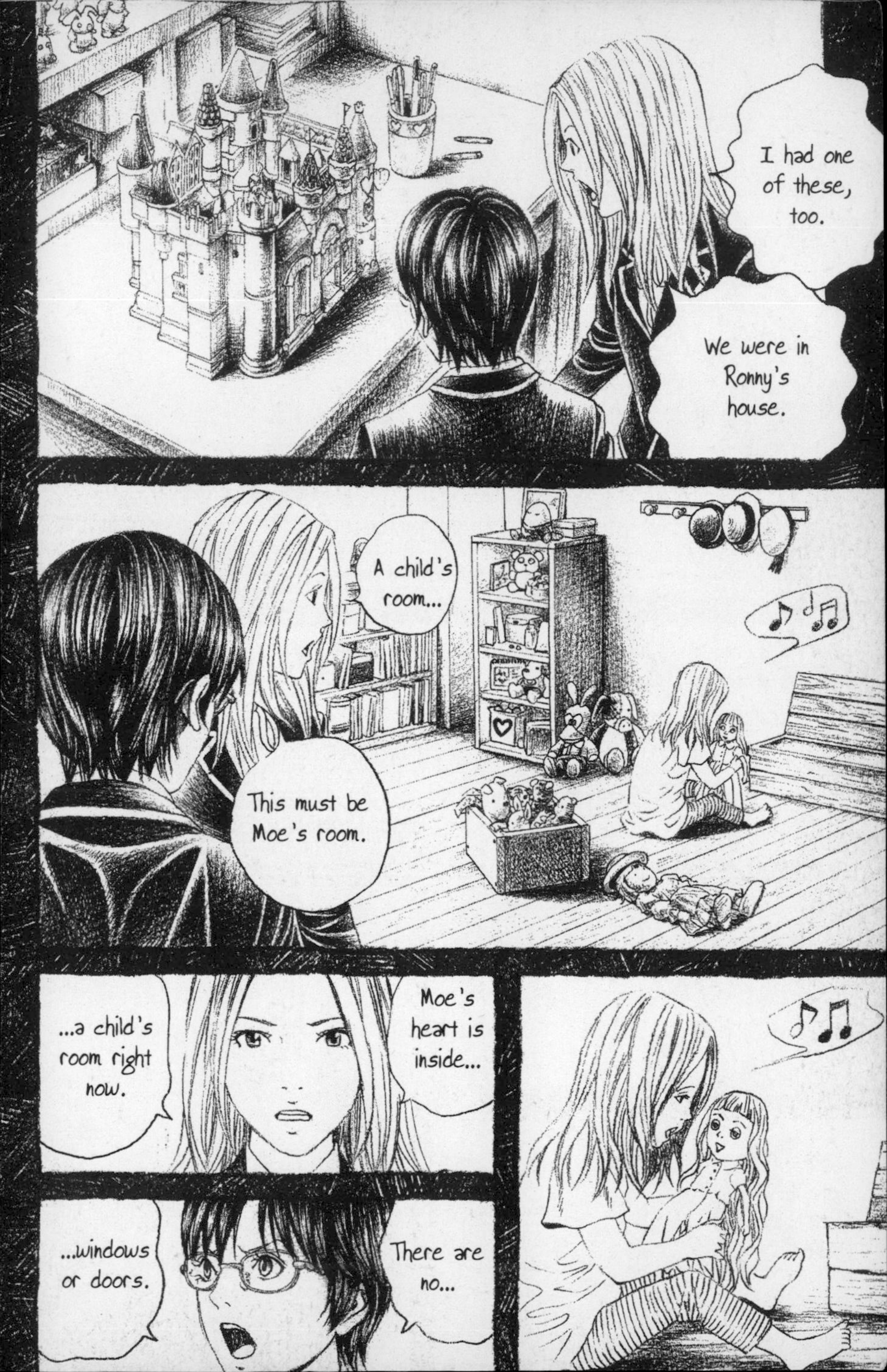
I had one of these, too.
We were in Ronny's house.
A child's room...
This must be Moe's room.
Moe's heart is inside...
...a child's room right now.
There are no...
...windows or doors.

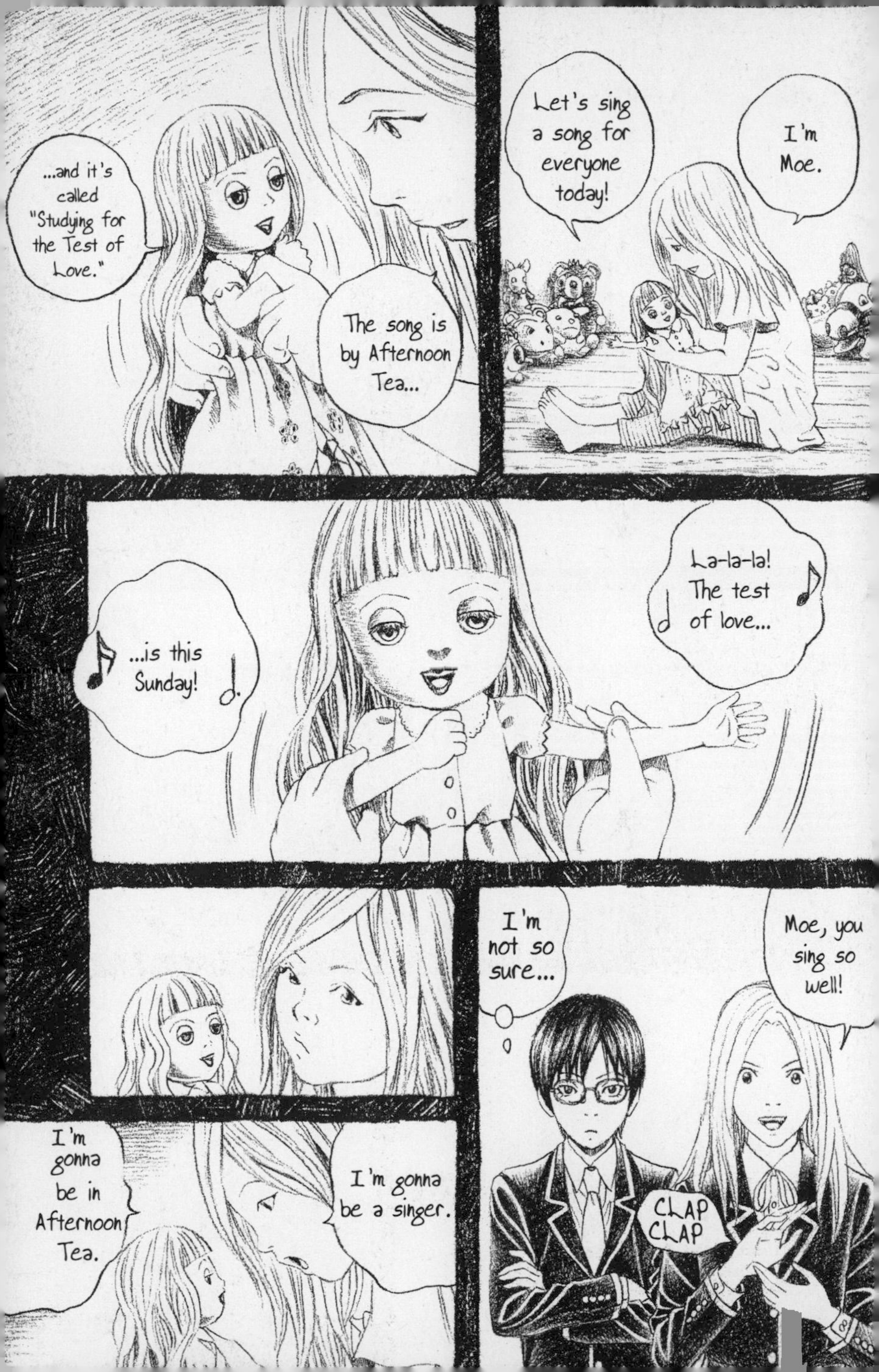
I'm Moe.
Let's sing a song for everyone today!
The song is by Afternoon Tea...
...and it's called "Studying for the Test of Love."
La-la-la! The test of love...
...is this Sunday!
Moe, you sing so well!
I'm not so sure...
CLAP CLAP
I'm gonna be a singer.
I'm gonna be in Afternoon Tea.

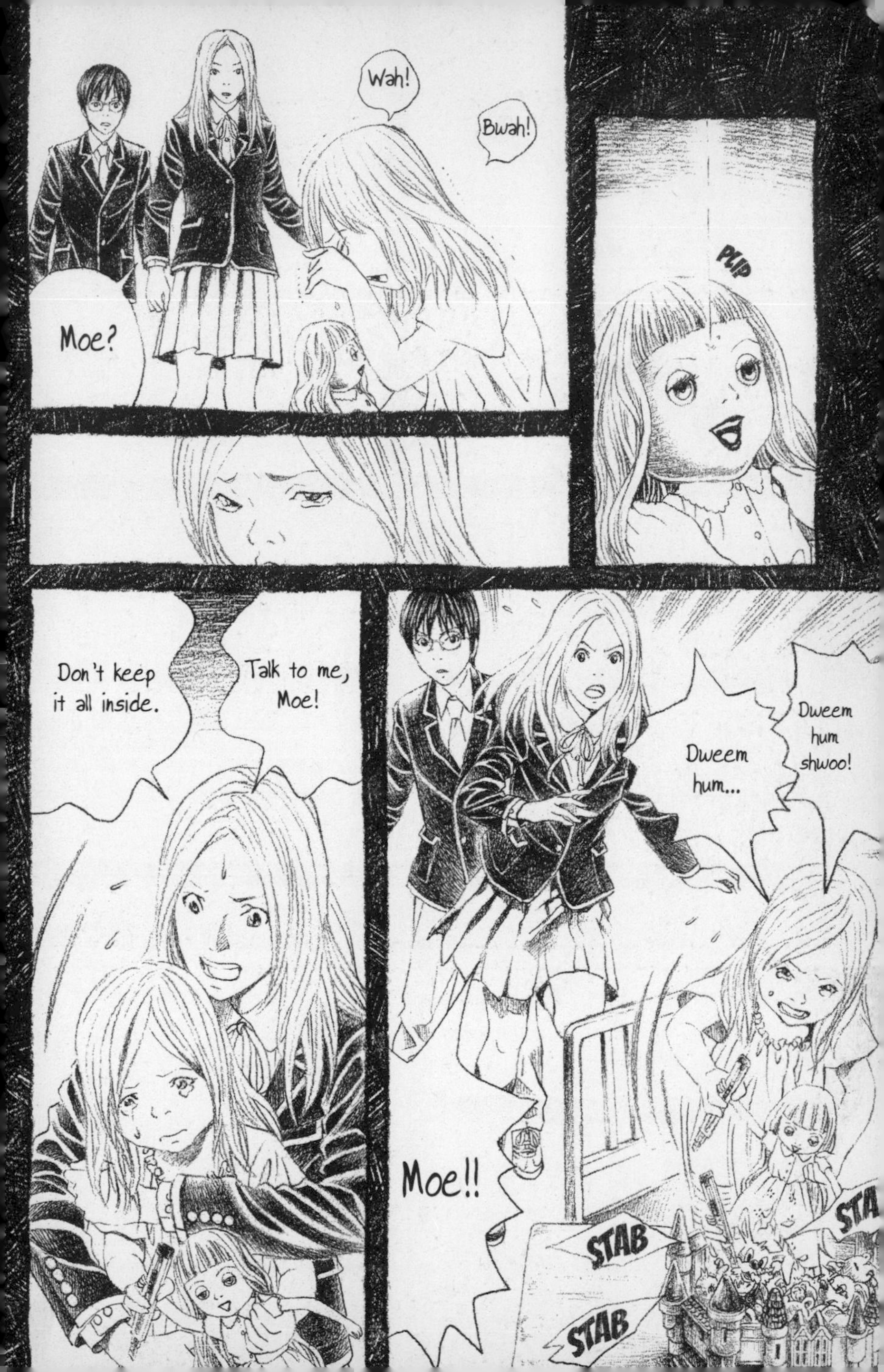
PLIP
Wah!
Bwah!
Moe?
Dweem hum shwoo!
Dweem hum...
STAB
Moe!!
STAB
Talk to me, Moe!
Don't keep it all inside.

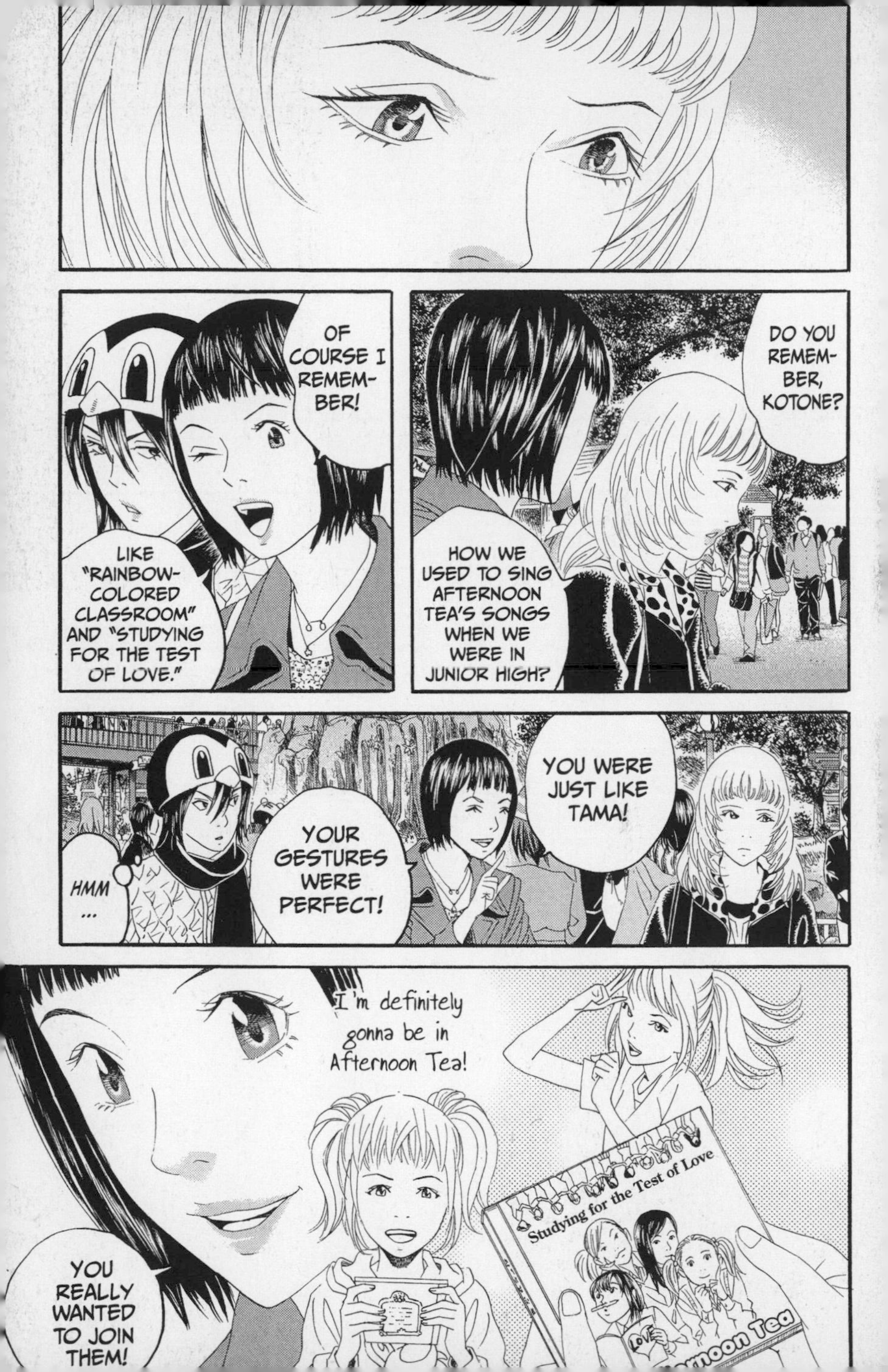
DO YOU REMEMBER, KOTONE?
HOW WE USED TO SING AFTERNOON TEA'S SONGS WHEN WE WERE IN JUNIOR HIGH?
OF COURSE I REMEMBER!
LIKE "RAINBOW-COLORED CLASSROOM" AND "STUDYING FOR THE TEST OF LOVE."
YOU WERE JUST LIKE TAMA!
YOUR GESTURES WERE PERFECT!
HMM ...
I'm definitely gonna be in Afternoon Tea!
Studying for the Test of Love
LOVE
YOU REALLY WANTED TO JOIN THEM!

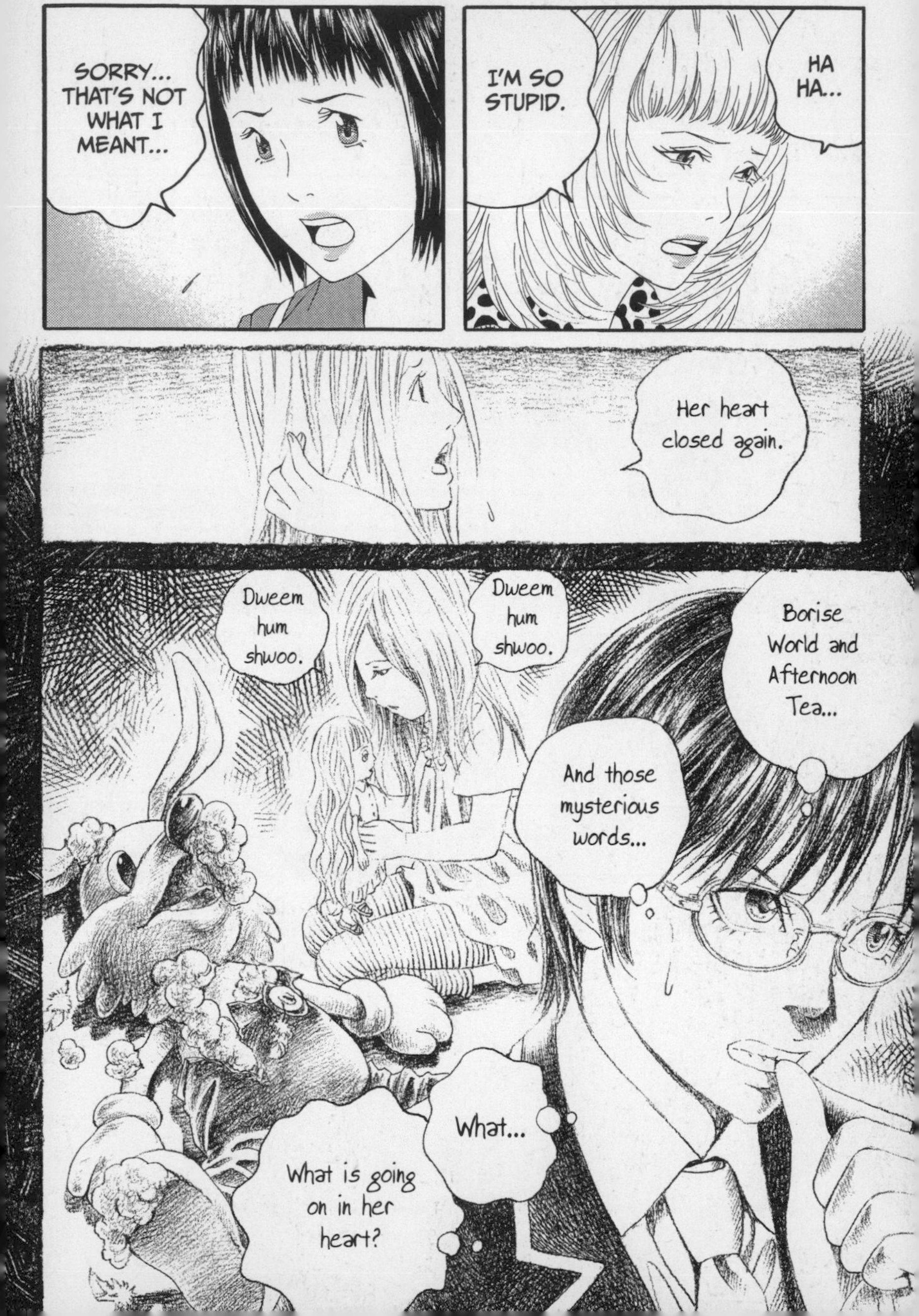

HA HA...
I'M SO STUPID.
SORRY... THAT'S NOT WHAT I MEANT...
Her heart closed again.
Borise World and Afternoon Tea...
And those mysterious words...
Dweem hum shwoo.
Dweem hum shwoo.
What...
What is going on in her heart?

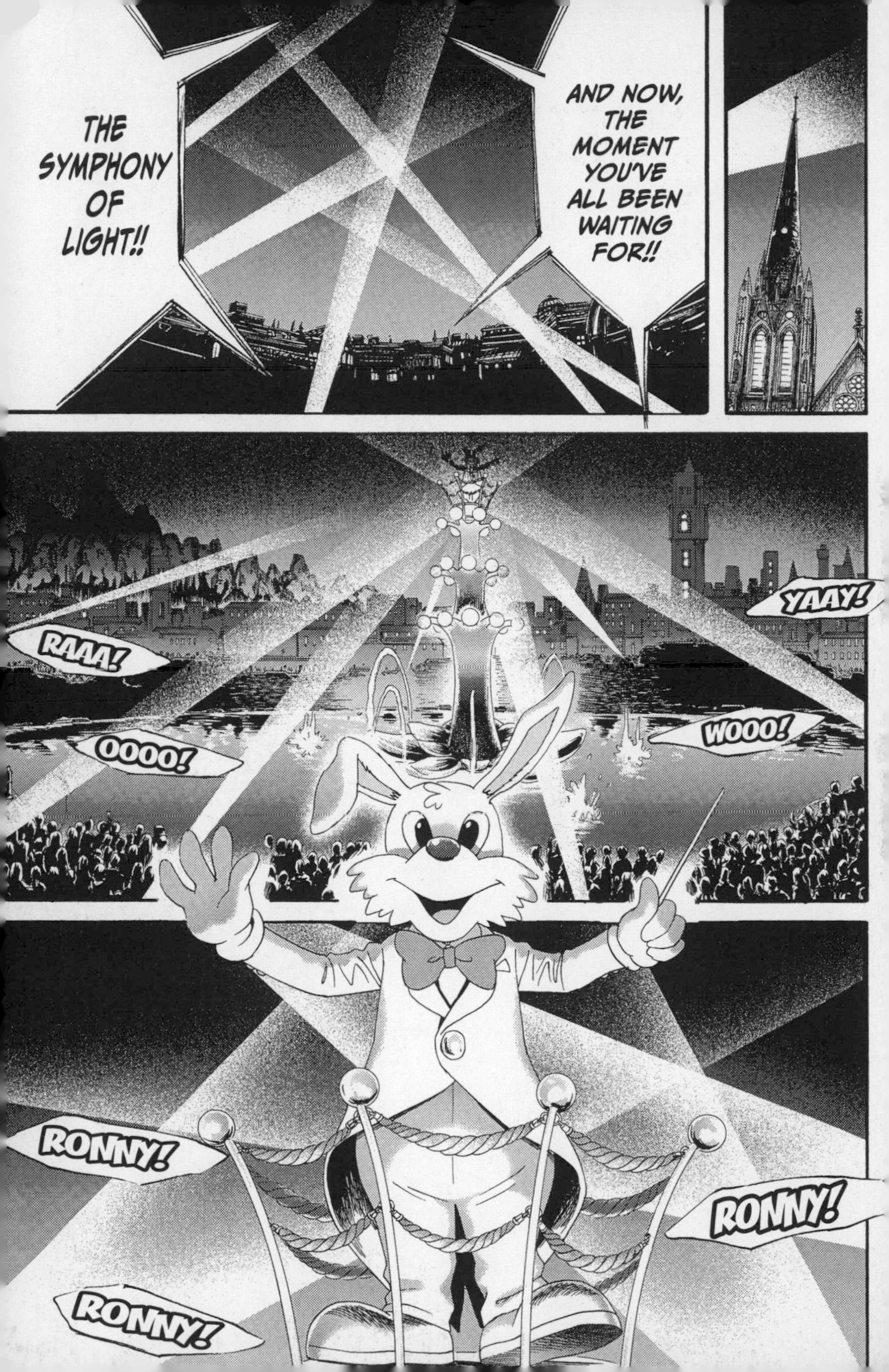
AND NOW, THE MOMENT YOU'VE ALL BEEN WAITING FOR!!
THE SYMPHONY OF LIGHT!!
YAAY!
RAAA!
WOOO!
OOOO!
RONNY!
RONNY!
RONNY!

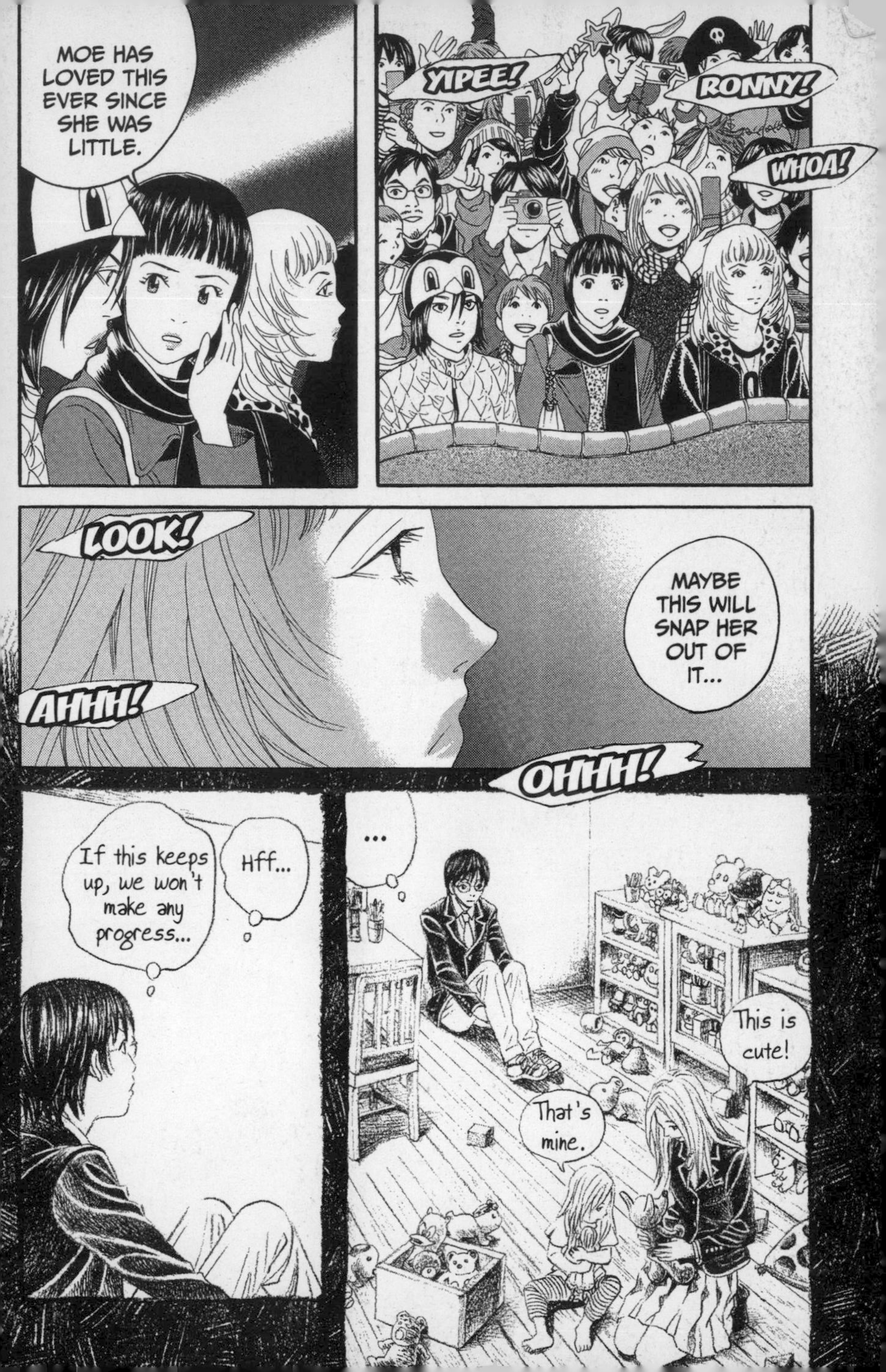
RONNY!
YIPEE!
WHOA!
MOE HAS LOVED THIS EVER SINCE SHE WAS LITTLE.
MAYBE THIS WILL SNAP HER OUT OF IT...
LOOK!
AHHH!
OHHH!
...
This is cute!
That's mine.
Hff...
If this keeps up, we won't make any progress...

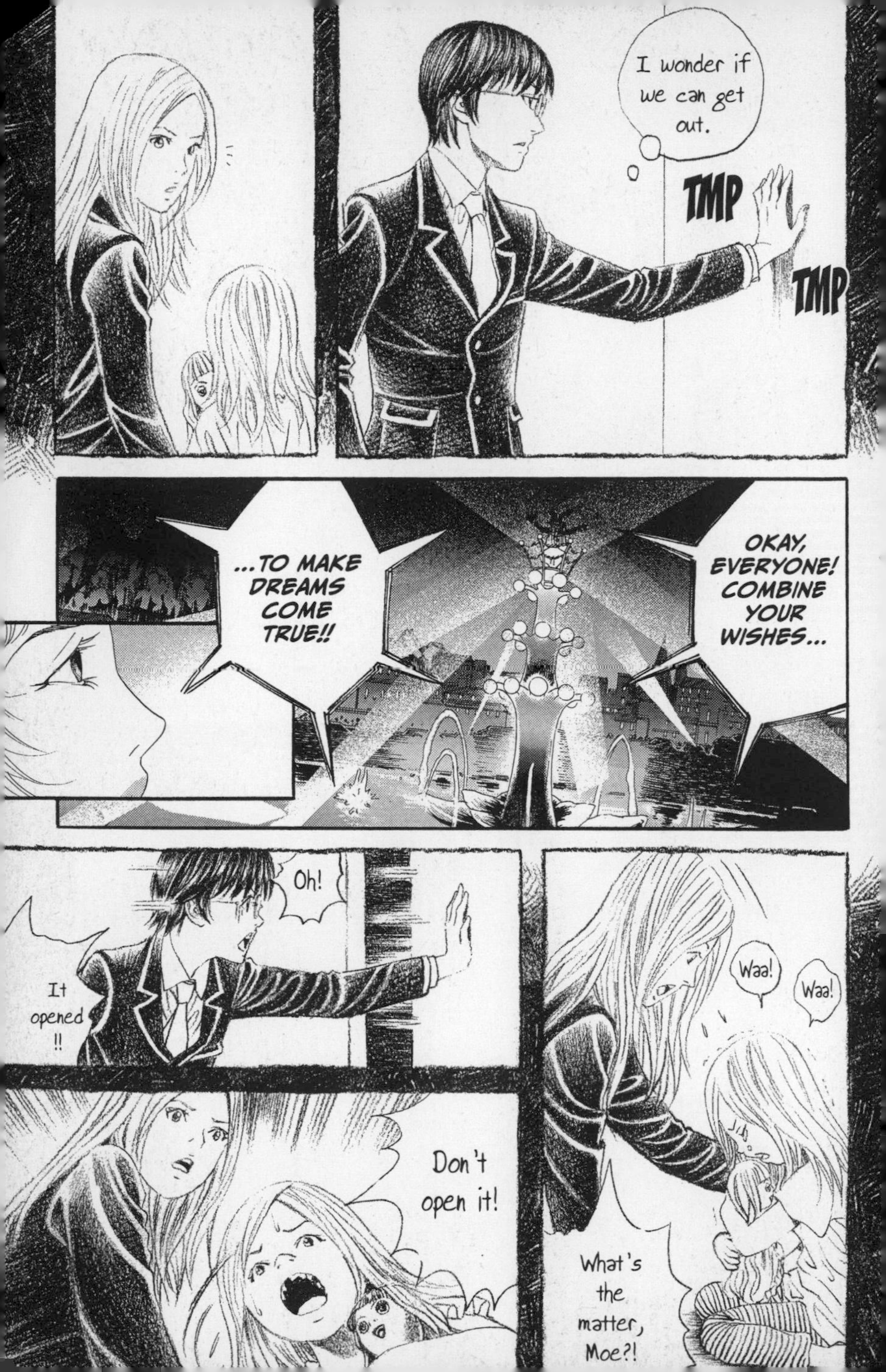
I wonder if we can get out.
TMP
TMP
OKAY, EVERYONE! COMBINE YOUR WISHES...
...TO MAKE DREAMS COME TRUE!!
Waa!
Waa!
What's the matter, Moe?!
Oh!
It opened!!
Don't open it!

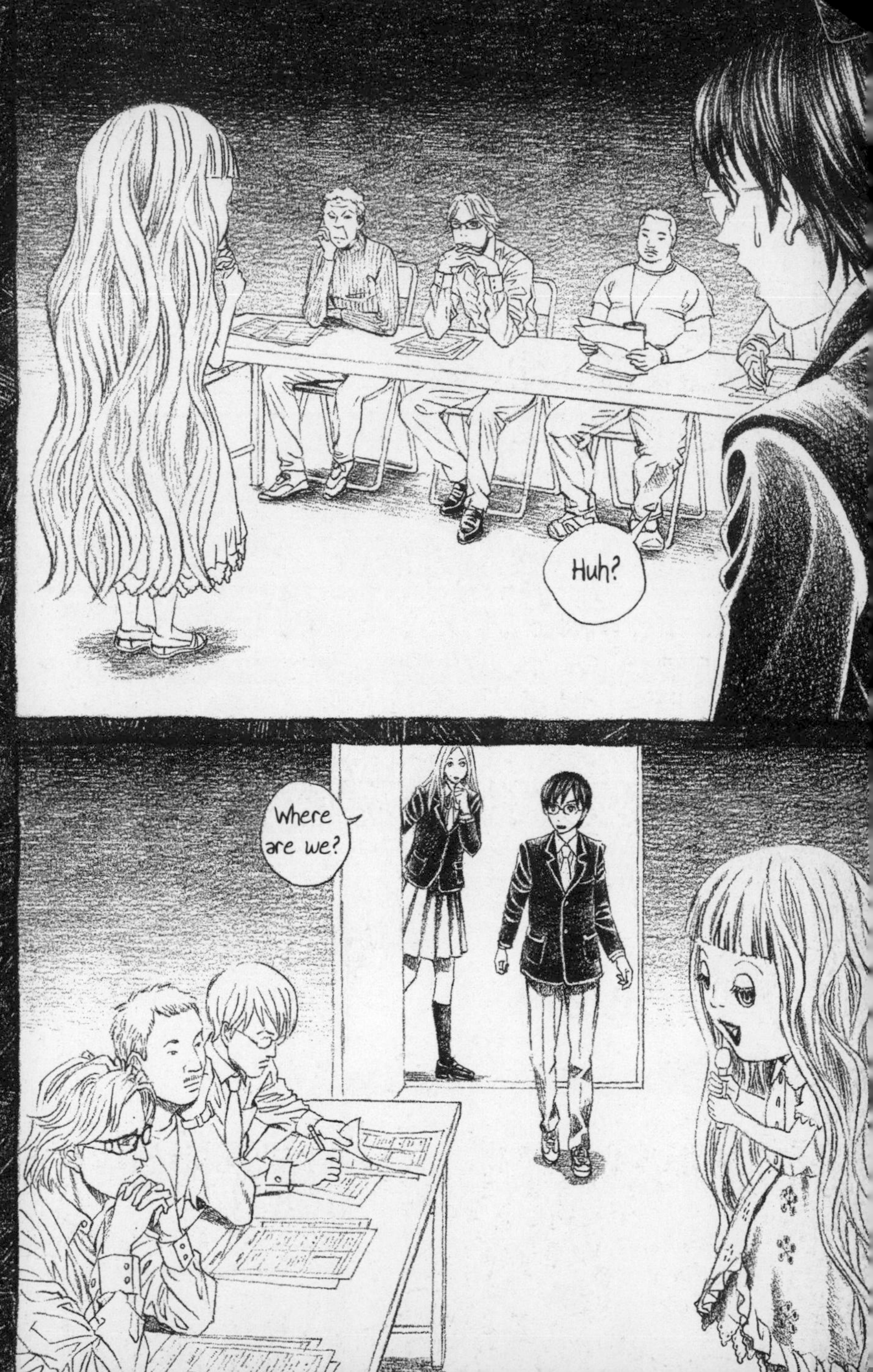
Huh?
Where are we?

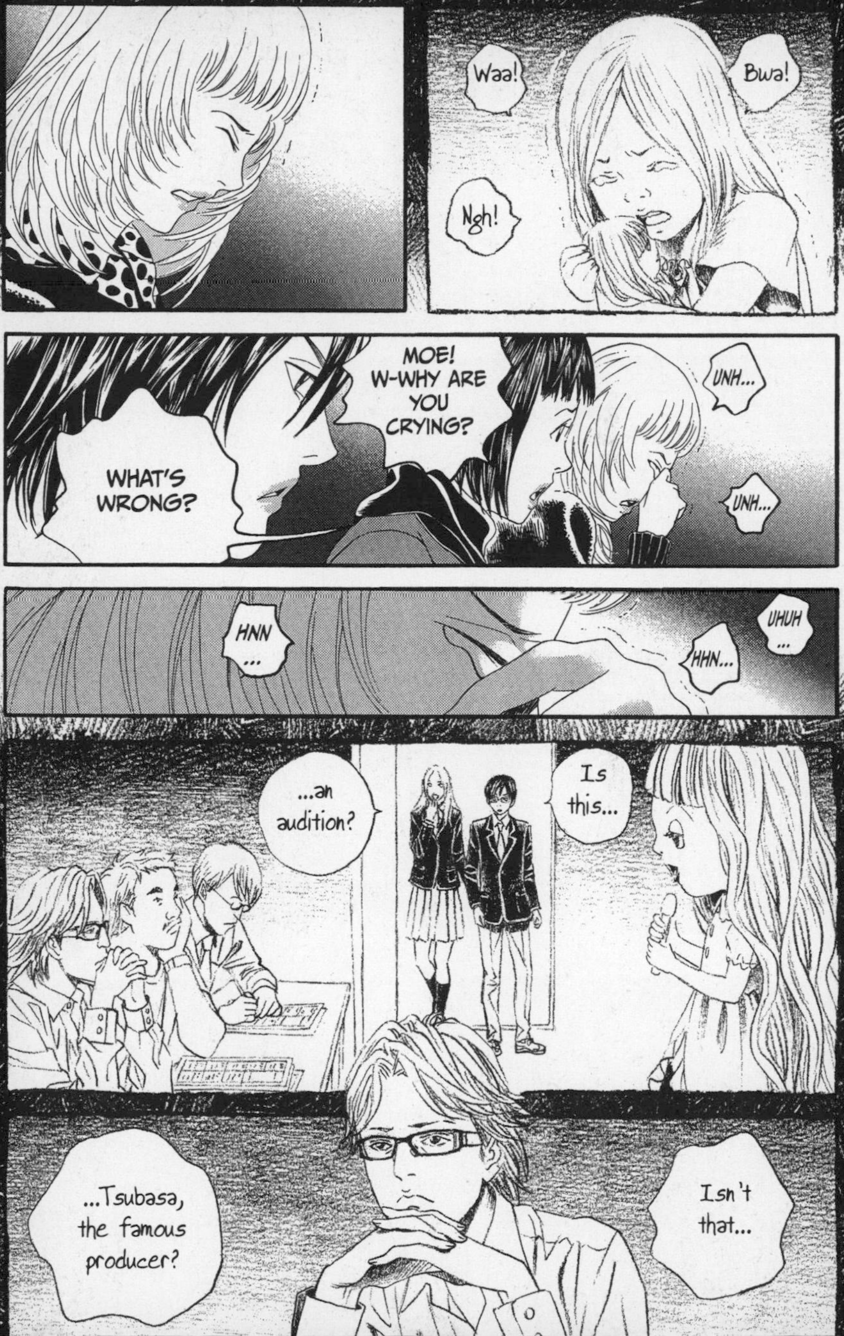
Bwa!
Waa!
Ngh!
UNH...
UNH...
MOE! W-WHY ARE YOU CRYING?
WHAT'S WRONG?
UHUH...
HHN...
HNN...
Is this...
...an audition?
Isn't that...
...Tsubasa, the famous producer?

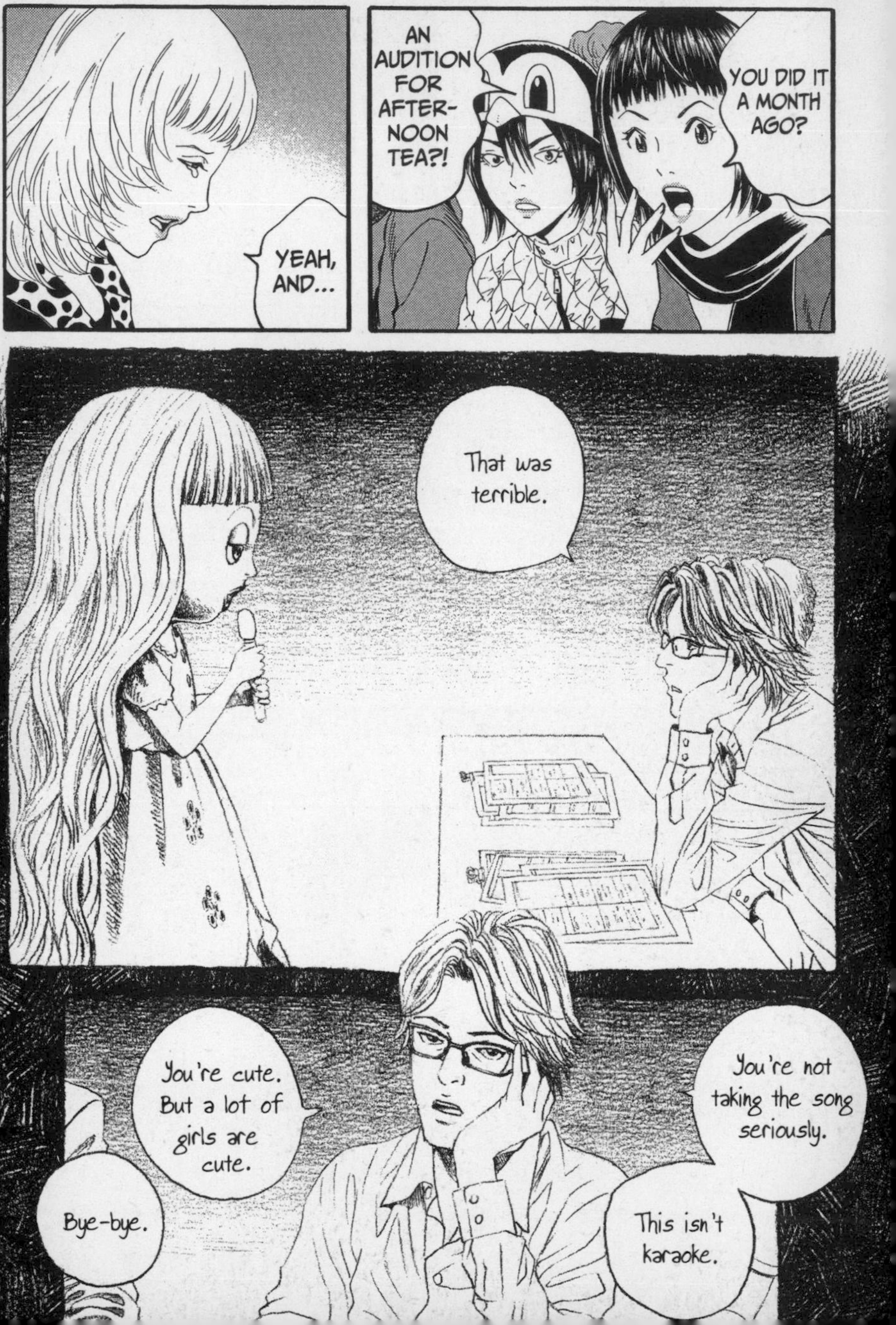
YOU DID IT A MONTH AGO?
AN AUDITION FOR AFTER-NOON TEA?!
YEAH, AND...
That was terrible.
You're not taking the song seriously.
This isn't karaoke.
You're cute. But a lot of girls are cute.
Bye-bye.

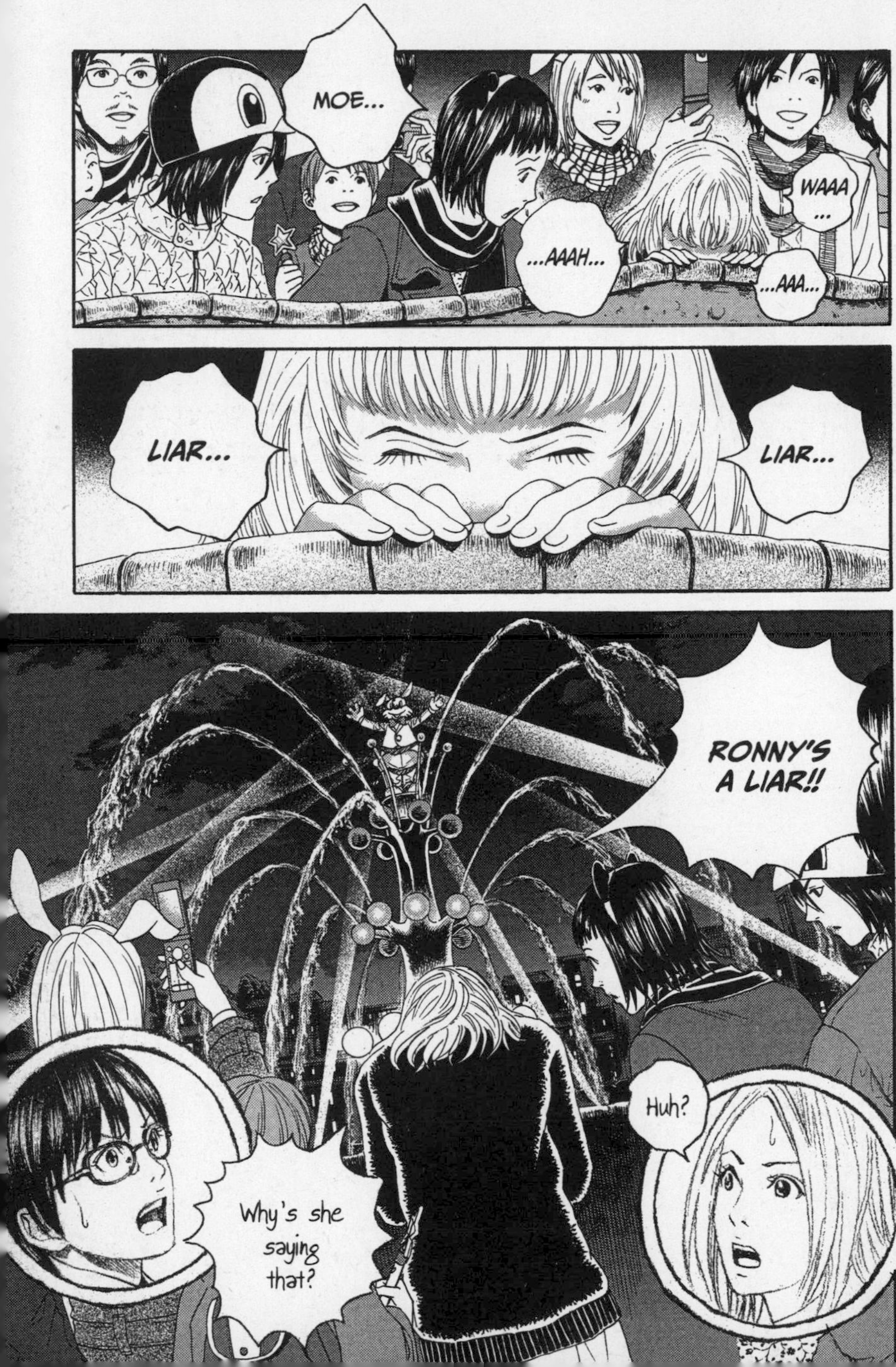
MOE...
WAAA...
...AAAH...
...AAA...
LIAR...
LIAR...
RONNY'S A LIAR!!
Huh?
Why's she saying that?

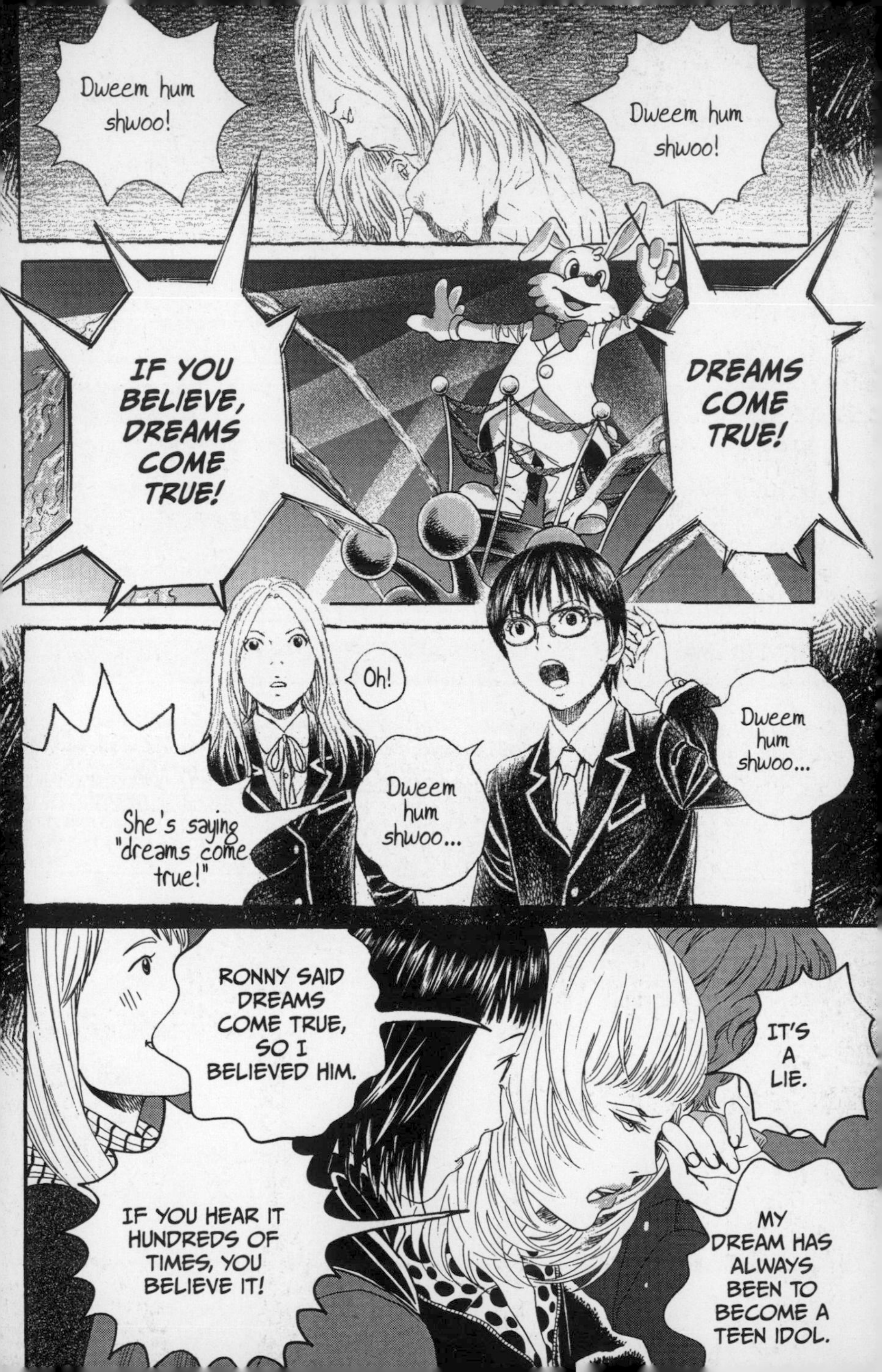
Dweem hum shwoo!
Dweem hum shwoo!
DREAMS COME TRUE!
IF YOU BELIEVE, DREAMS COME TRUE!
Dweem hum shwoo...
Oh!
Dweem hum shwoo...
She's saying "dreams come true!"
IT'S A LIE.
RONNY SAID DREAMS COME TRUE, SO I BELIEVED HIM.
MY DREAM HAS ALWAYS BEEN TO BECOME A TEEN IDOL.
IF YOU HEAR IT HUNDREDS OF TIMES, YOU BELIEVE IT!

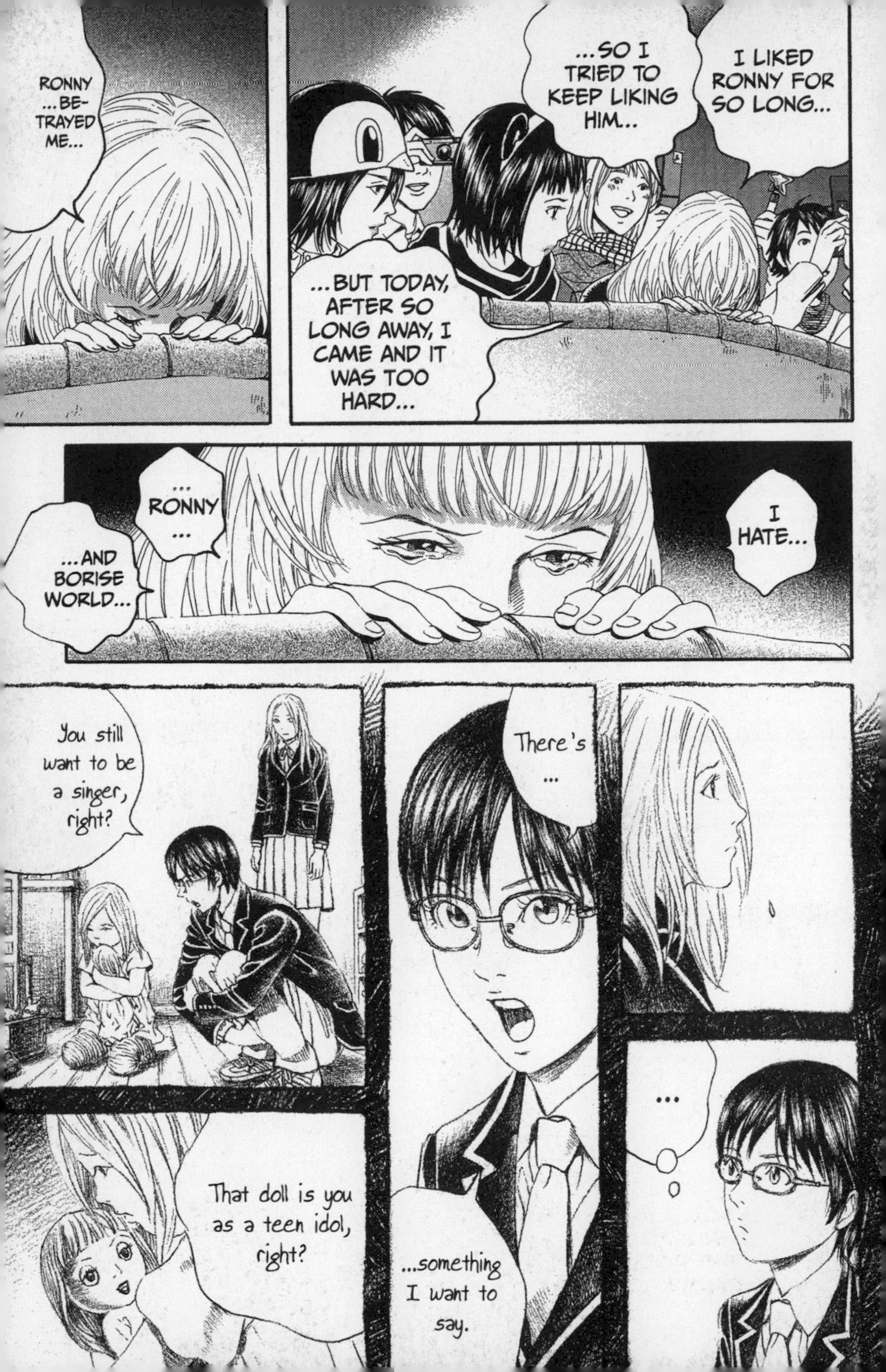
I LIKED RONNY FOR SO LONG...
...SO I TRIED TO KEEP LIKING HIM...
...BUT TODAY, AFTER SO LONG AWAY, I CAME AND IT WAS TOO HARD...
RONNY ...BE-TRAYED ME...
I HATE...
... RONNY ...
...AND BORISE WORLD...
...
There's ...
...something I want to say.
You still want to be a singer, right?
That doll is you as a teen idol, right?

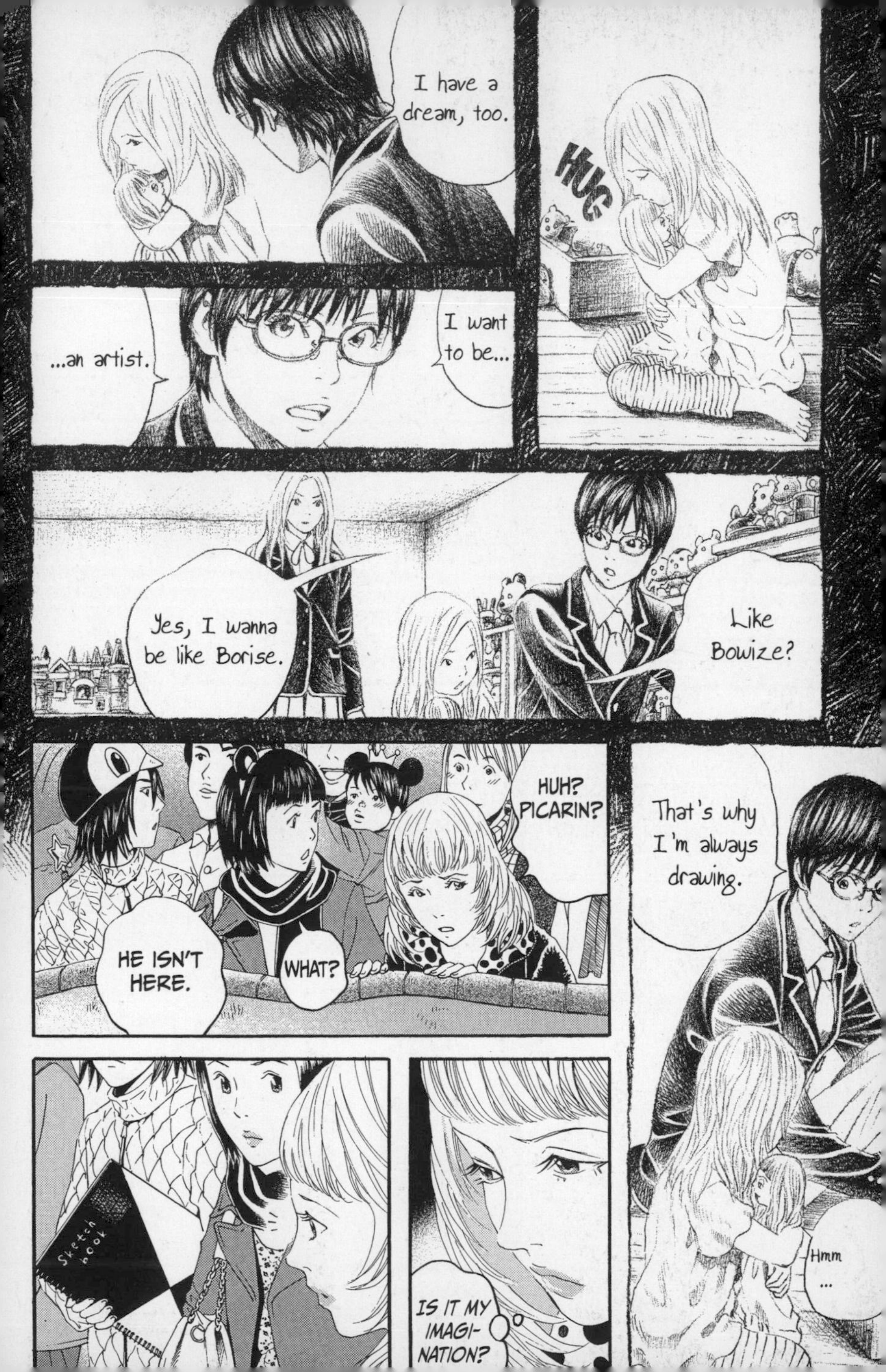
HUG
I have a dream, too.
I want to be...
...an artist.
Like Bowize?
Yes, I wanna be like Borise.
That's why I'm always drawing.
Hmm ...
HUH? PICARIN?
WHAT?
HE ISN'T HERE.
IS IT MY IMAGINATION?
Sketch book

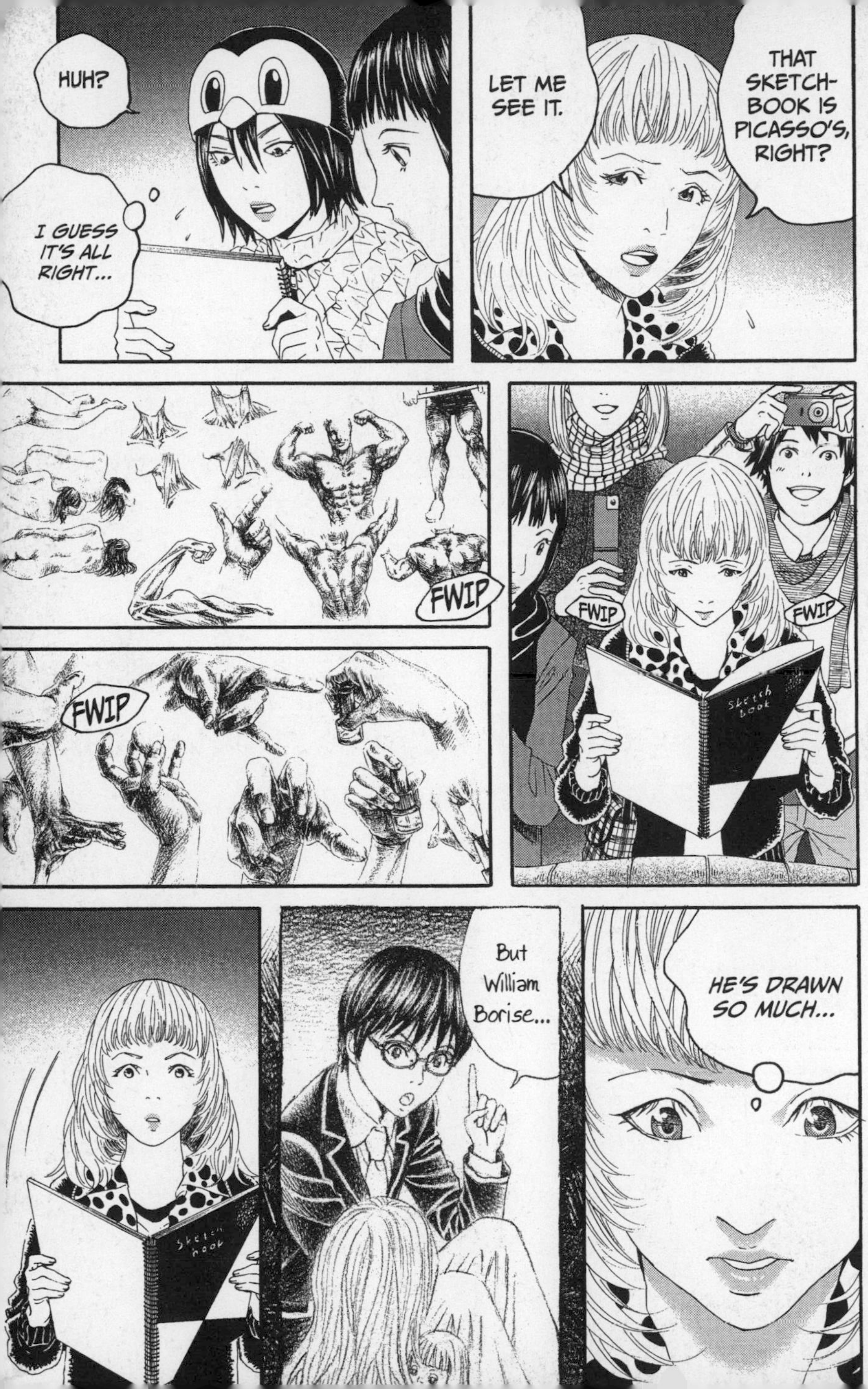
THAT SKETCH-BOOK IS PICASSO'S, RIGHT?
LET ME SEE IT.
HUH?
I GUESS IT'S ALL RIGHT...
FWIP
FWIP
FWIP
FWIP
HE'S DRAWN SO MUCH...
But William Borise...

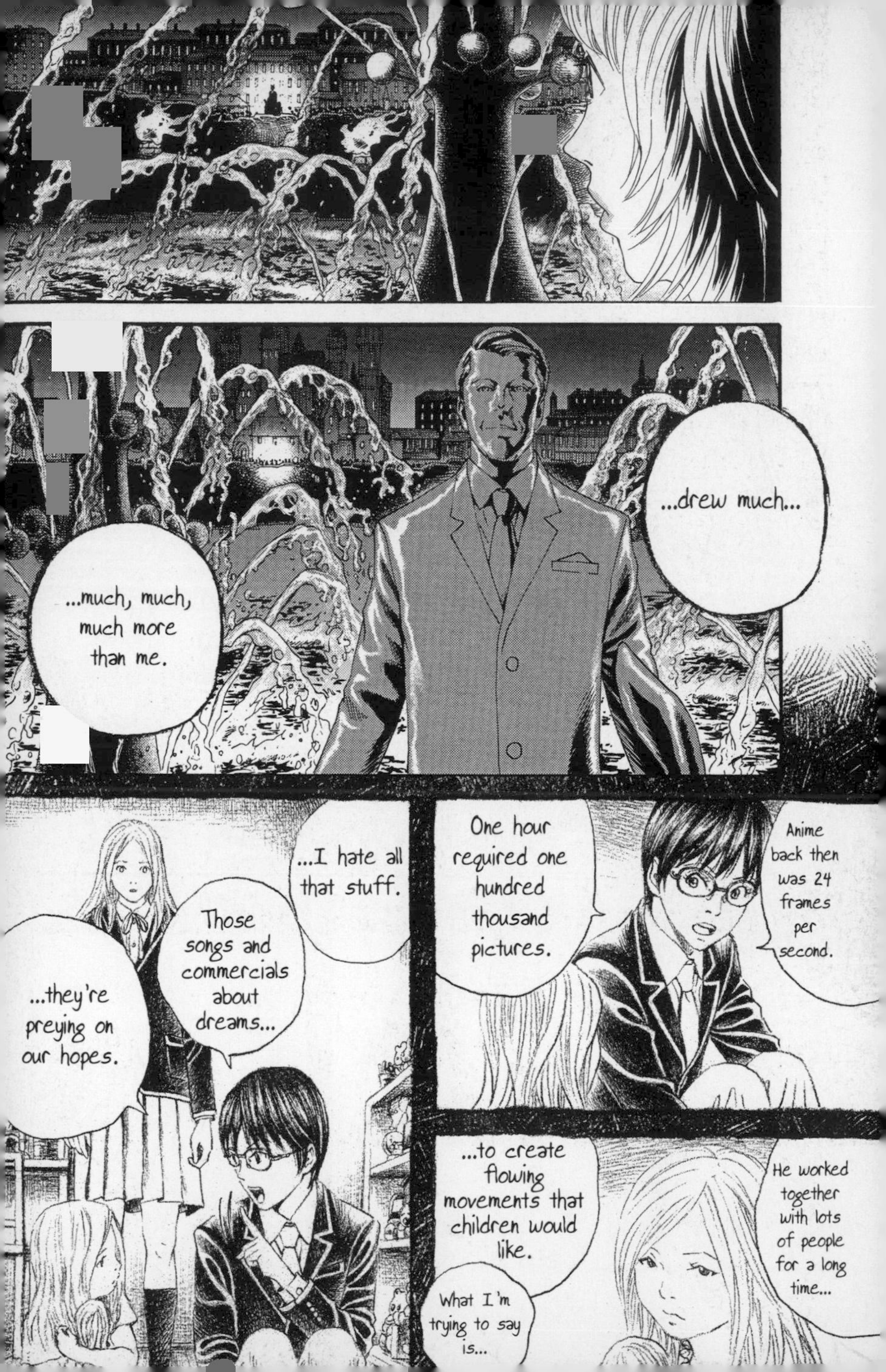
...drew much...
...much, much, much more than me.
Anime back then was 24 frames per second.
One hour required one hundred thousand pictures.
He worked together with lots of people for a long time...
...to create flowing movements that children would like.
What I'm trying to say is...
...I hate all that stuff.
Those songs and commercials about dreams...
...they're preying on our hopes.

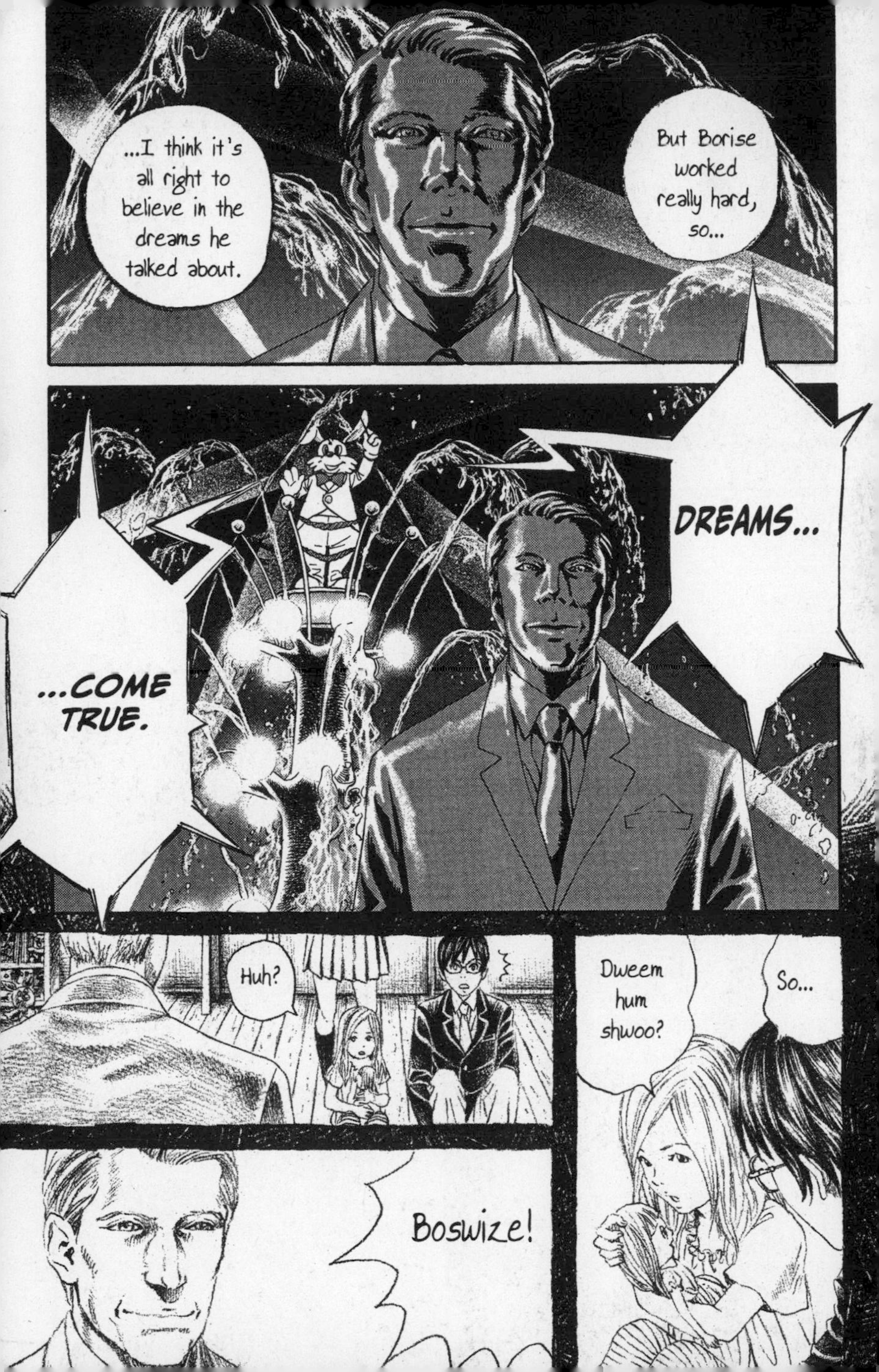
But Borise worked really hard, so...
...I think it's all right to believe in the dreams he talked about.
DREAMS...
...COME TRUE.
So...
Dweem hum shwoo?
Huh?
Boswize!

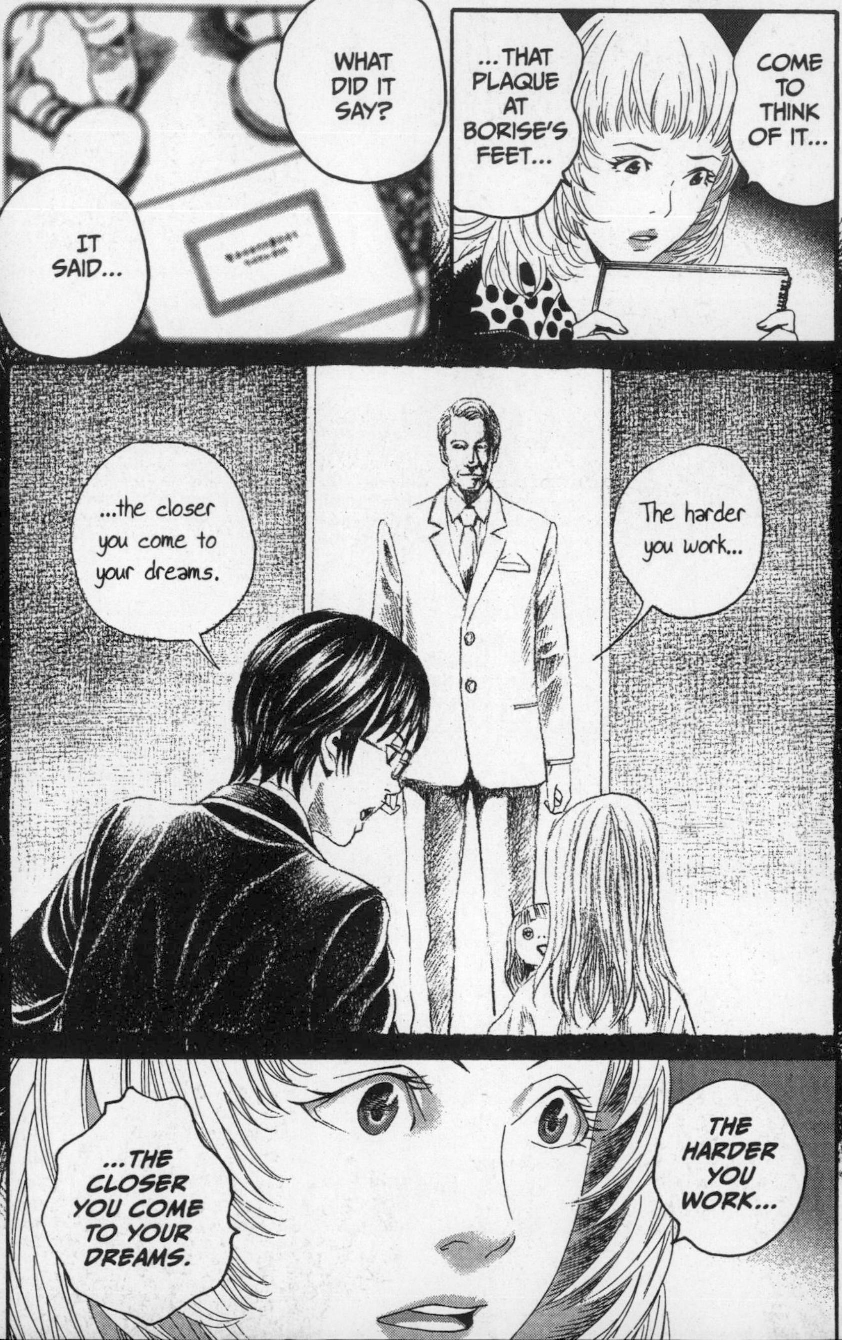
COME TO THINK OF IT...
...THAT PLAQUE AT BORISE'S FEET...
WHAT DID IT SAY?
IT SAID...
The harder you work...
...the closer you come to your dreams.
THE HARDER YOU WORK...
...THE CLOSER YOU COME TO YOUR DREAMS.

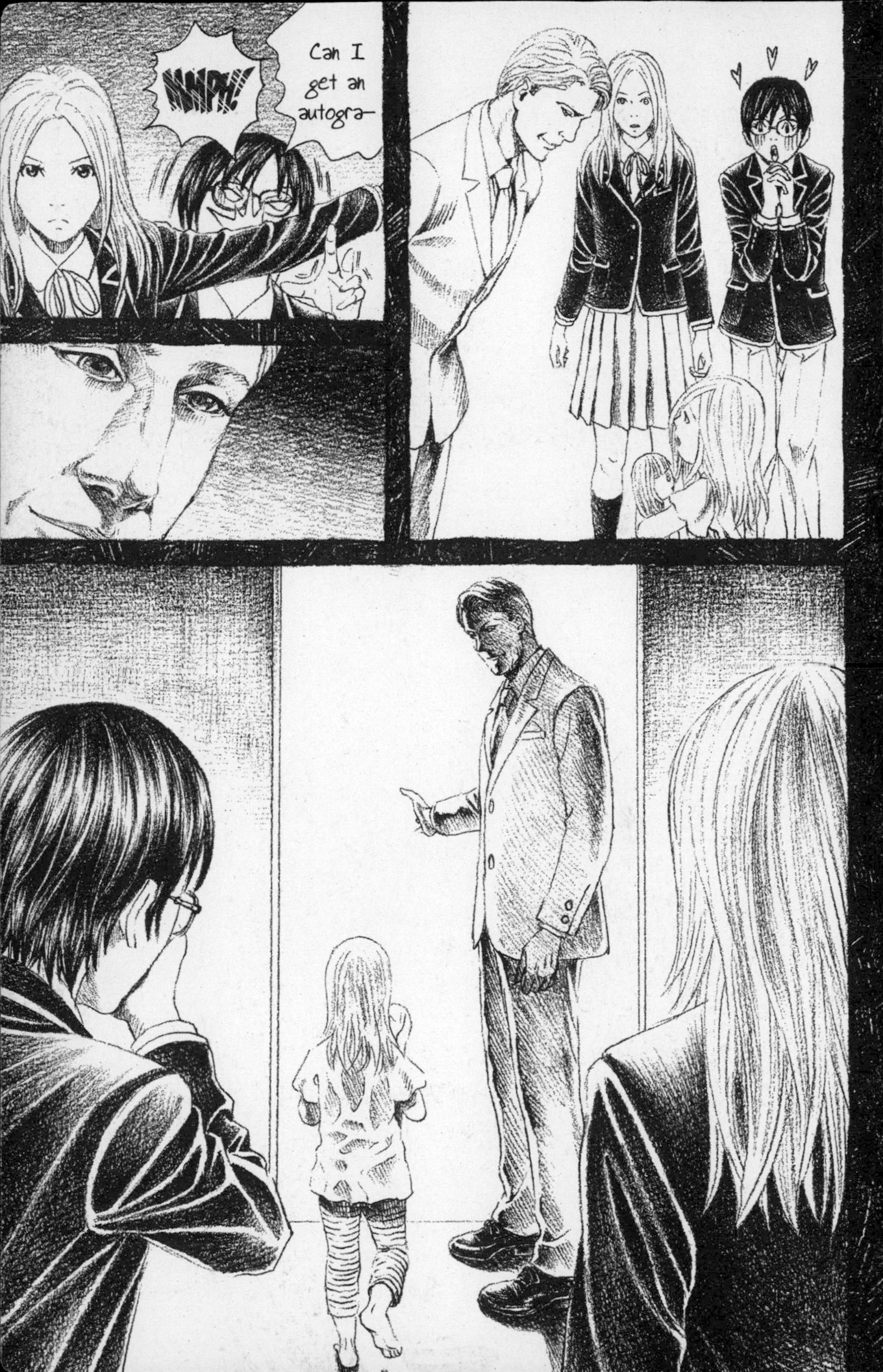
Can I get an autogra—
MMPH!

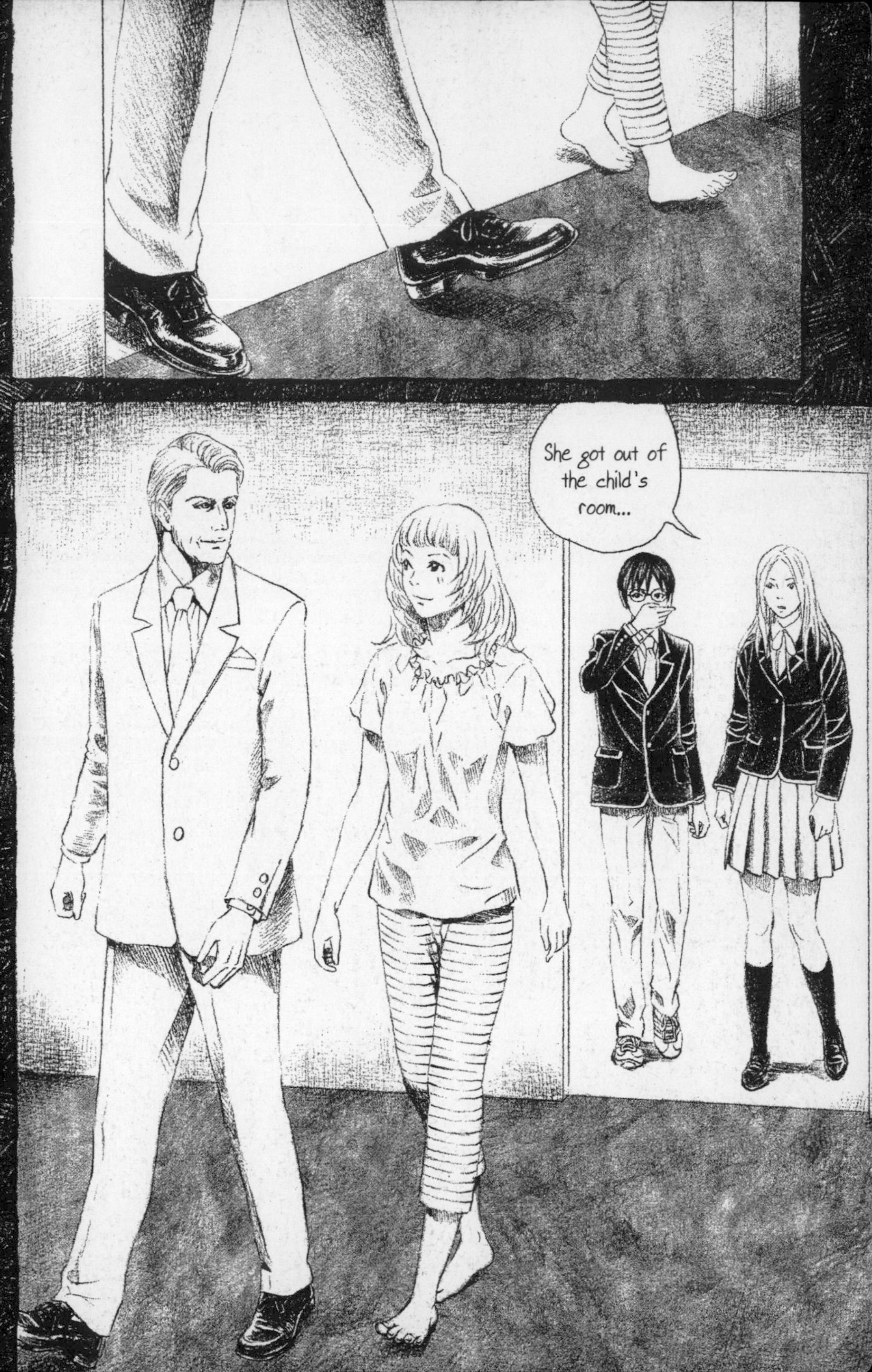
She got out of the child's room...

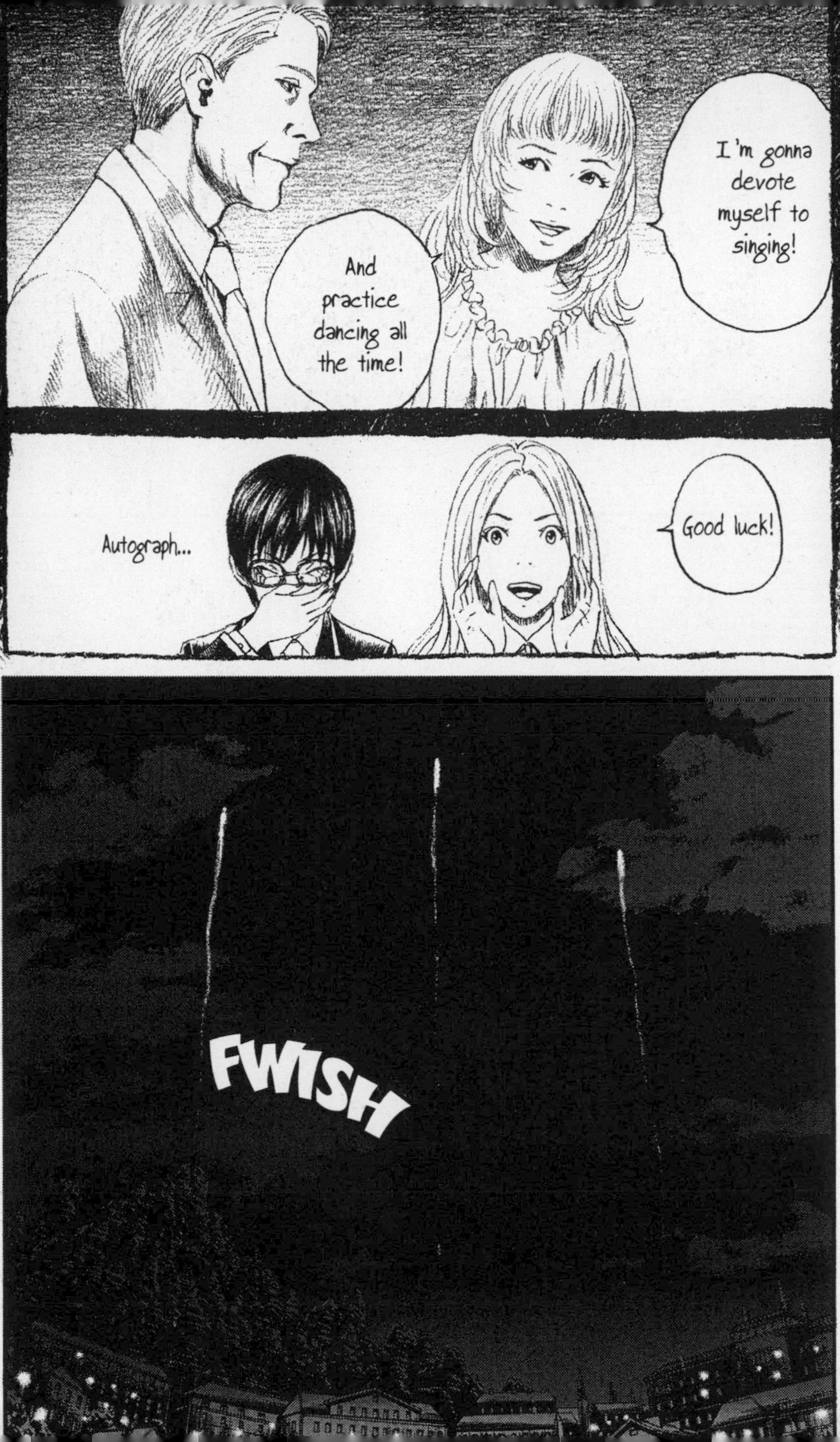
I'm gonna devote myself to singing!
And practice dancing all the time!
Good luck!
Autograph...
FWISH

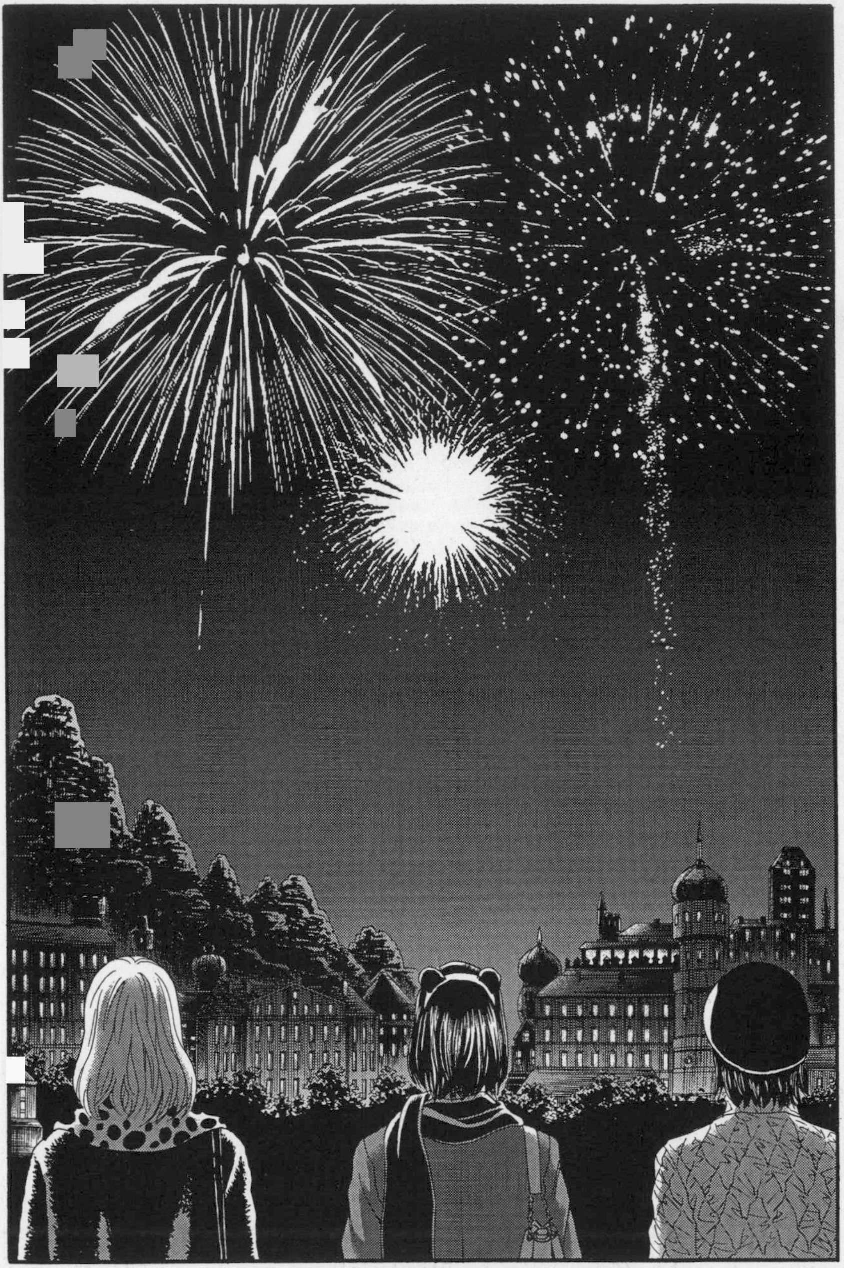

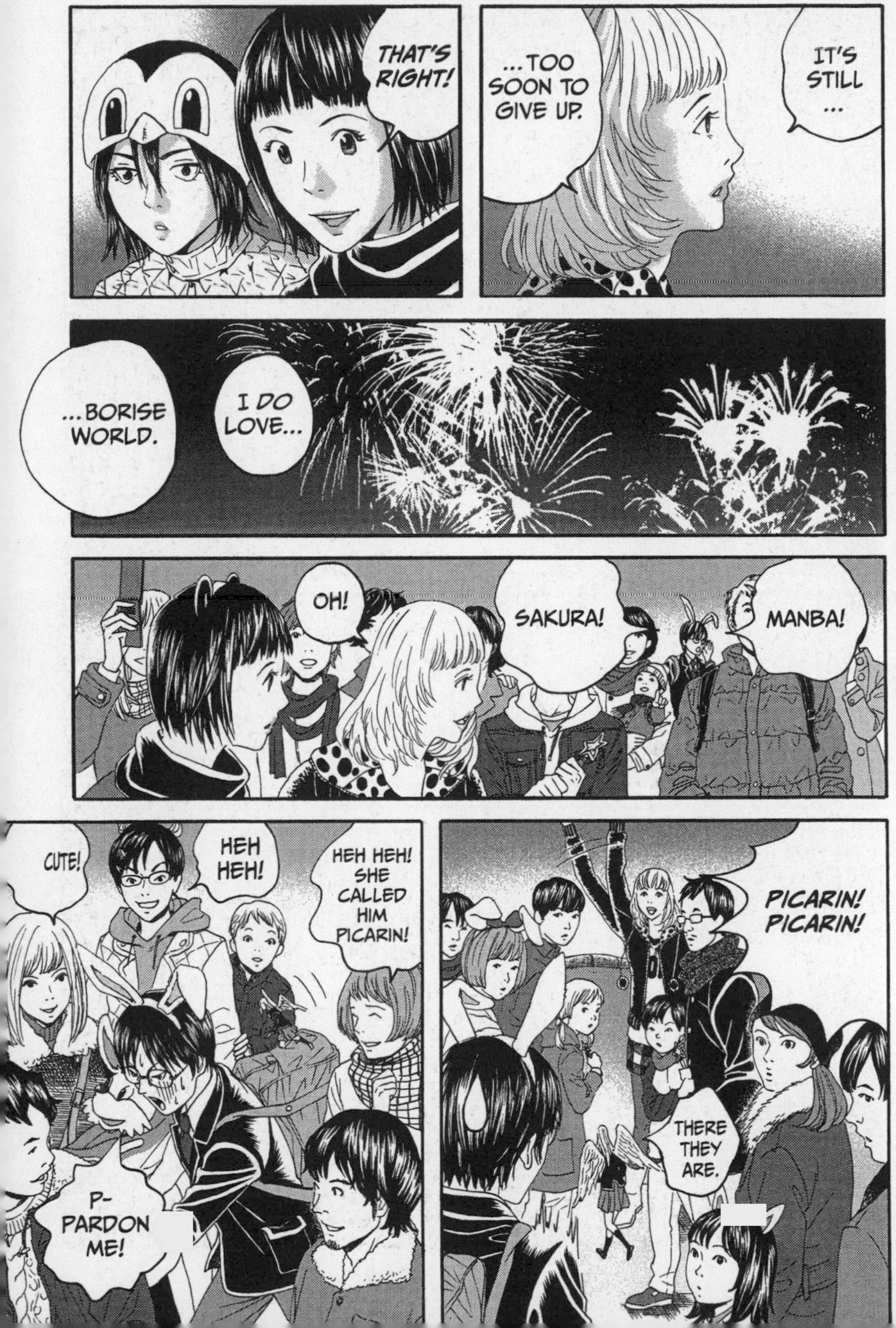
IT'S STILL ...
...TOO SOON TO GIVE UP.
THAT'S RIGHT!
I DO LOVE...
...BORISE WORLD.
MANBA!
SAKURA!
OH!
PICARIN! PICARIN!
THERE THEY ARE.
HEH HEH! SHE CALLED HIM PICARIN!
HEH HEH!
CUTE!
P-PARDON ME!

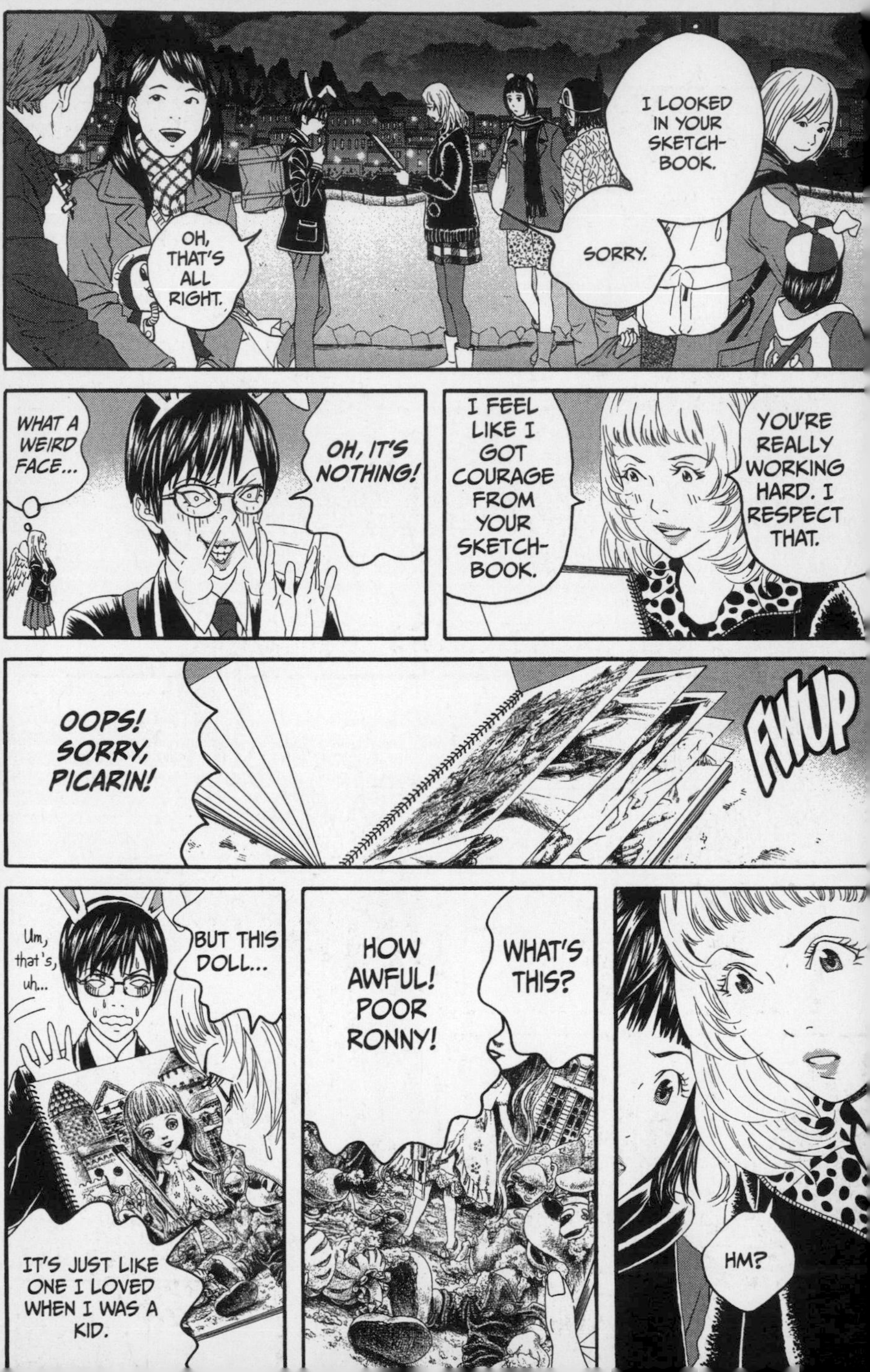
I LOOKED IN YOUR SKETCHBOOK.
SORRY.
OH, THAT'S ALL RIGHT.
YOU'RE REALLY WORKING HARD. I RESPECT THAT.
I FEEL LIKE I GOT COURAGE FROM YOUR SKETCHBOOK.
OH, IT'S NOTHING!
WHAT A WEIRD FACE...
FWUP
OOPS! SORRY, PICARIN!
HM?
WHAT'S THIS?
HOW AWFUL! POOR RONNY!
BUT THIS DOLL...
Um, that's, uh...
IT'S JUST LIKE ONE I LOVED WHEN I WAS A KID.

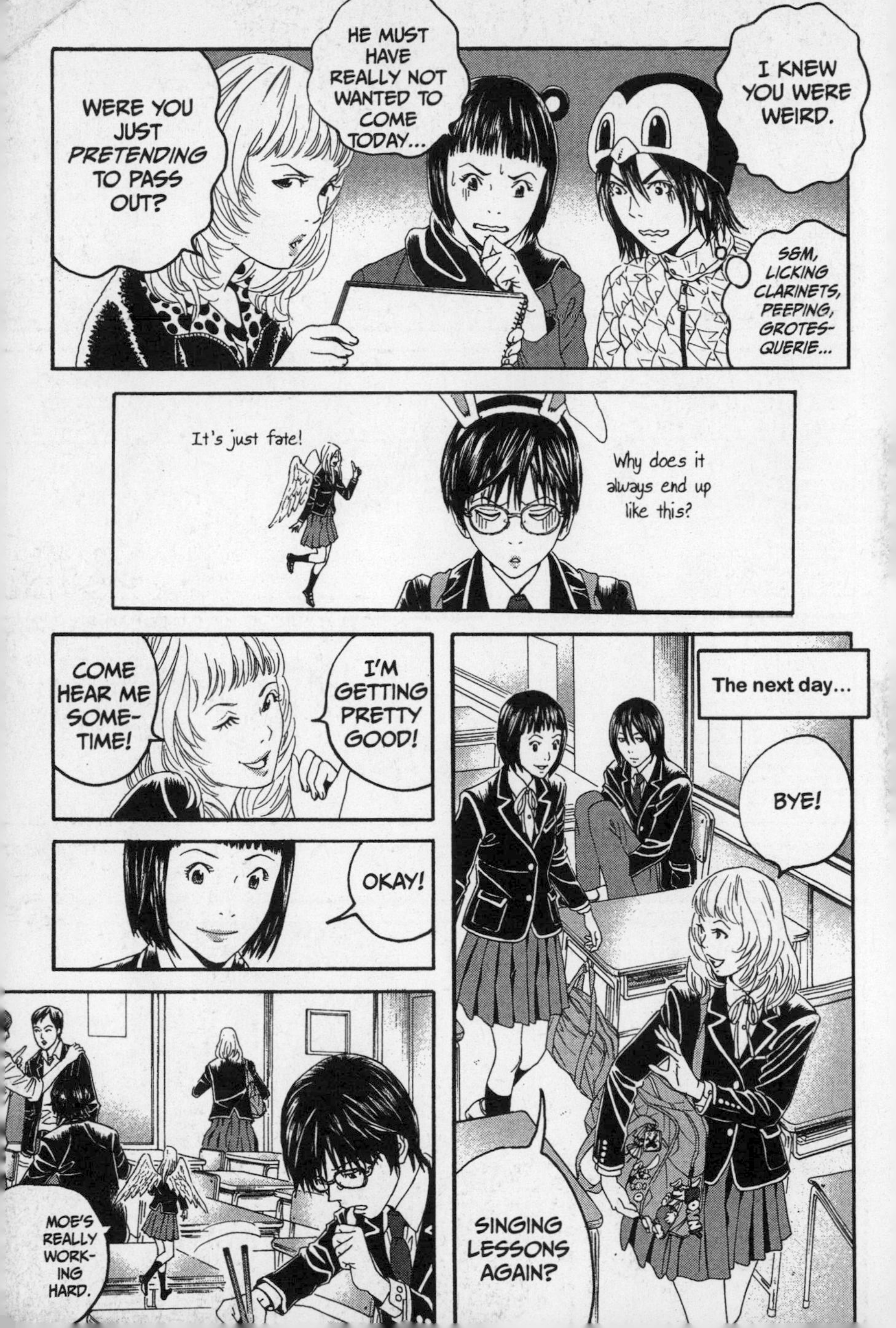
I KNEW YOU WERE WEIRD.
S&M, LICKING CLARINETS, PEEPING, GROTES-QUERIE...
HE MUST HAVE REALLY NOT WANTED TO COME TODAY...
WERE YOU JUST PRETENDING TO PASS OUT?
Why does it always end up like this?
It's just fate!
The next day...
BYE!
SINGING LESSONS AGAIN?
I'M GETTING PRETTY GOOD!
COME HEAR ME SOME-TIME!
OKAY!
MOE'S REALLY WORK-ING HARD.

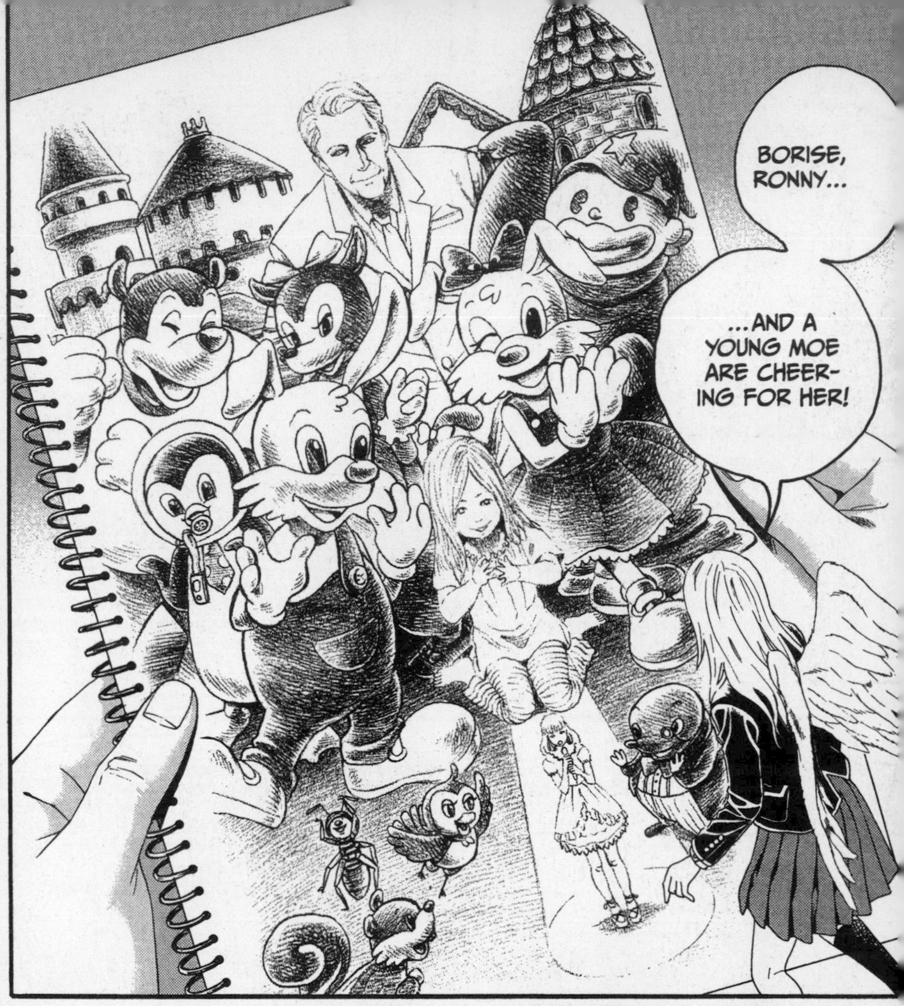
BORISE, RONNY...
...AND A YOUNG MOE ARE CHEER-ING FOR HER!

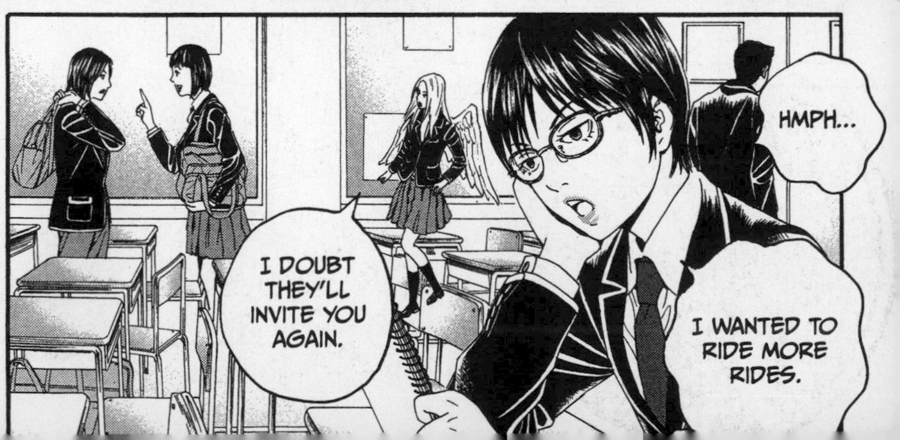
HMPH...
I WANTED TO RIDE MORE RIDES.
I DOUBT THEY'LL INVITE YOU AGAIN.

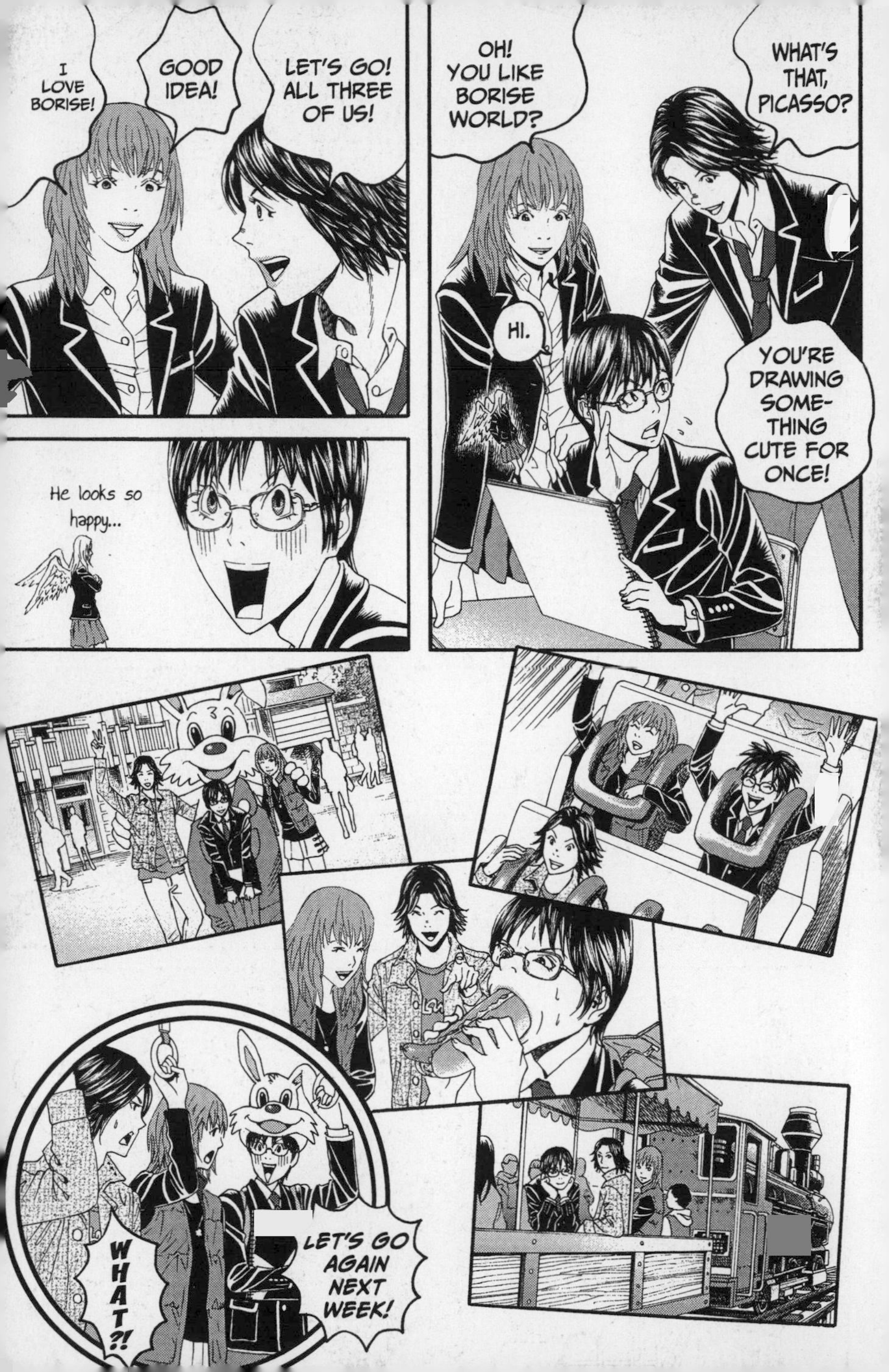
WHAT'S THAT, PICASSO?
OH! YOU LIKE BORISE WORLD?
YOU'RE DRAWING SOME-THING CUTE FOR ONCE!
HI.
LET'S GO! ALL THREE OF US!
GOOD IDEA!
I LOVE BORISE!
He looks so happy...
LET'S GO AGAIN NEXT WEEK!
WHAT?!

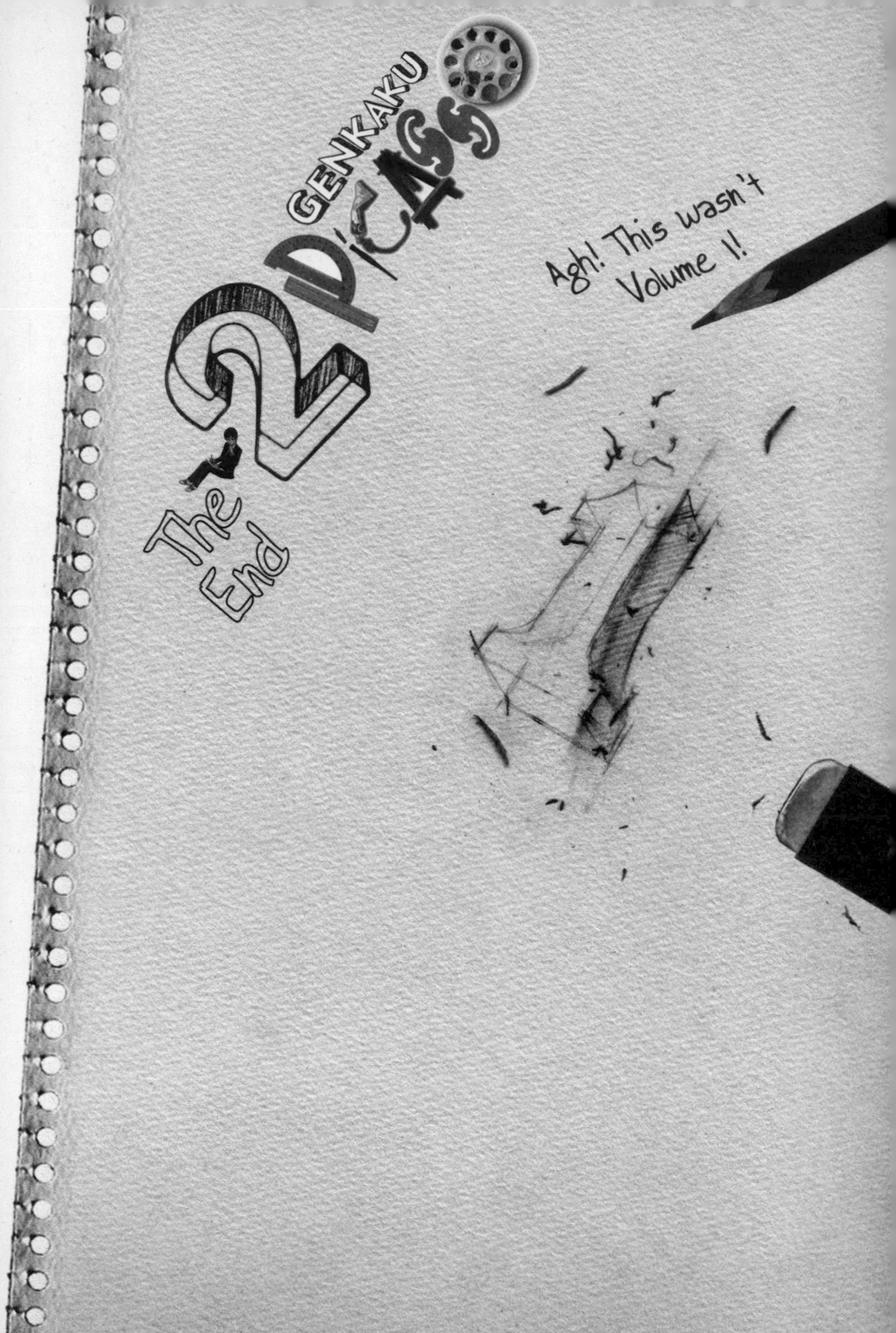
GENKAKU PiCASSO 2
The End
Agh! This wasn't Volume 1!
Borise World and Moe (Part 2)_Jump SQ, September 2009

Picasso's Inquiring Mind

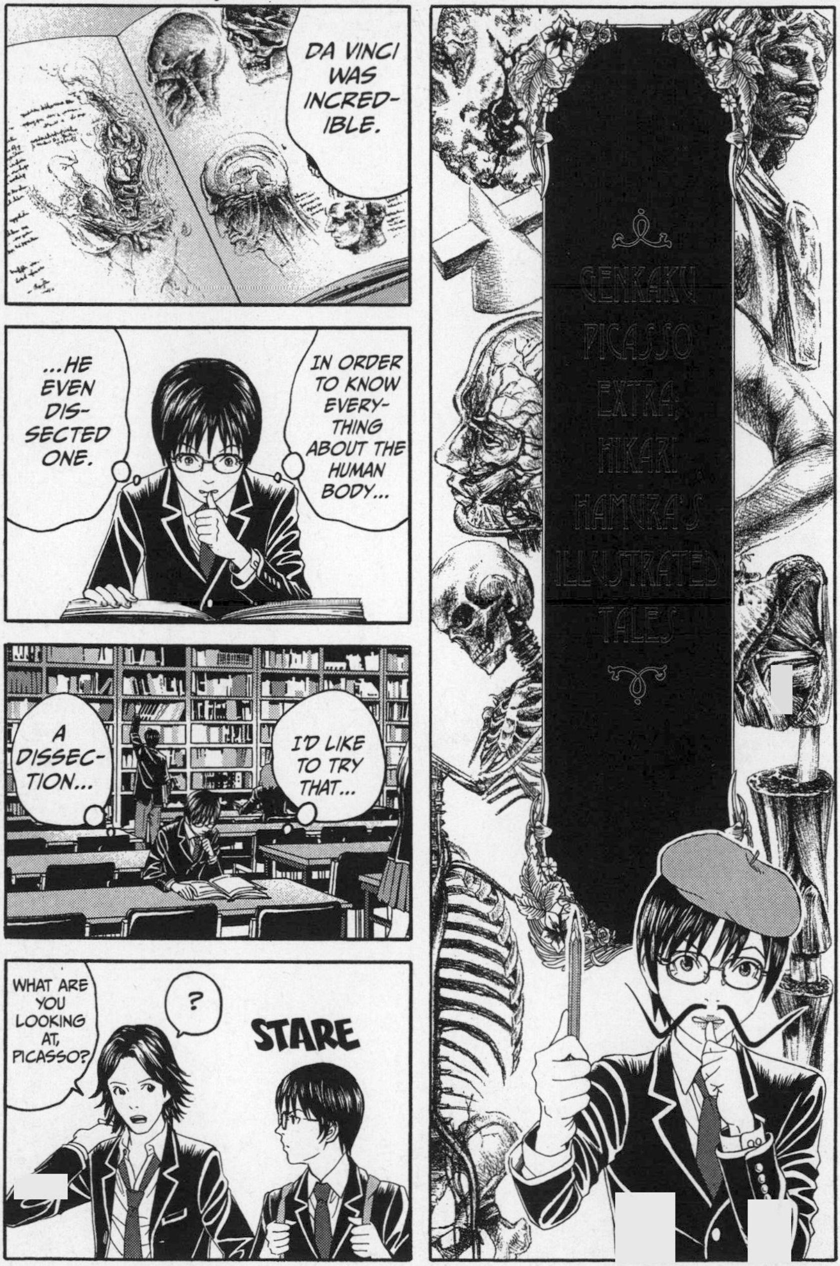

GENKAKU PICASSO EXTRA: HIKARI HAMURA'S ILLUSTRATED TALES
DA VINCI WAS INCREDIBLE.
IN ORDER TO KNOW EVERYTHING ABOUT THE HUMAN BODY...
...HE EVEN DISSECTED ONE.
I'D LIKE TO TRY THAT...
A DISSECTION...
STARE
?
WHAT ARE YOU LOOKING AT, PICASSO?

Picasso Doesn't Like Picasso

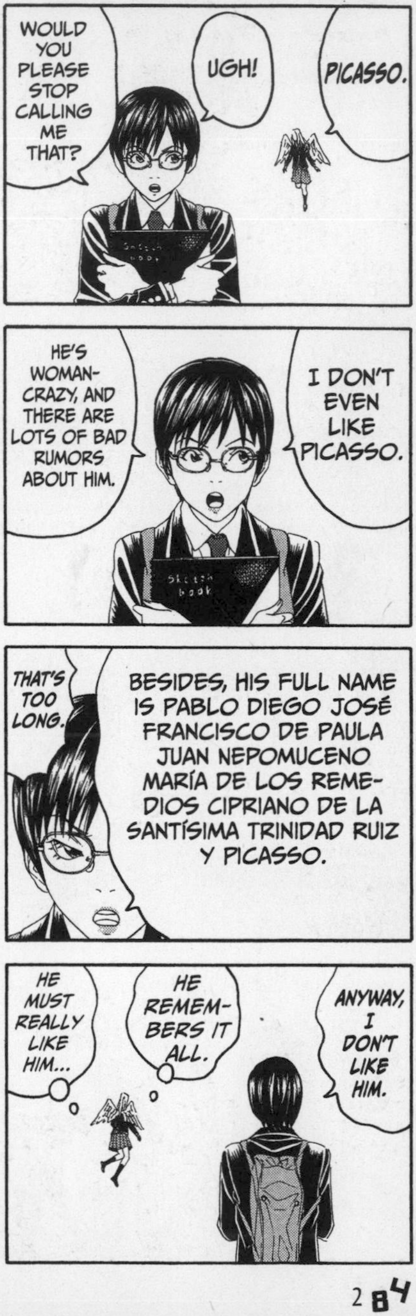
PICASSO.
UGH!
WOULD YOU PLEASE STOP CALLING ME THAT?
I DON'T EVEN LIKE PICASSO.
HE'S WOMAN-CRAZY, AND THERE ARE LOTS OF BAD RUMORS ABOUT HIM.
BESIDES, HIS FULL NAME IS PABLO DIEGO JOSÉ FRANCISCO DE PAULA JUAN NEPOMUCENO MARÍA DE LOS REMEDIOS CIPRIANO DE LA SANTÍSIMA TRINIDAD RUIZ Y PICASSO.
THAT'S TOO LONG.
ANYWAY, I DON'T LIKE HIM.
HE REMEMBERS IT ALL.
HE MUST REALLY LIKE HIM...

Sugiura's Strategy

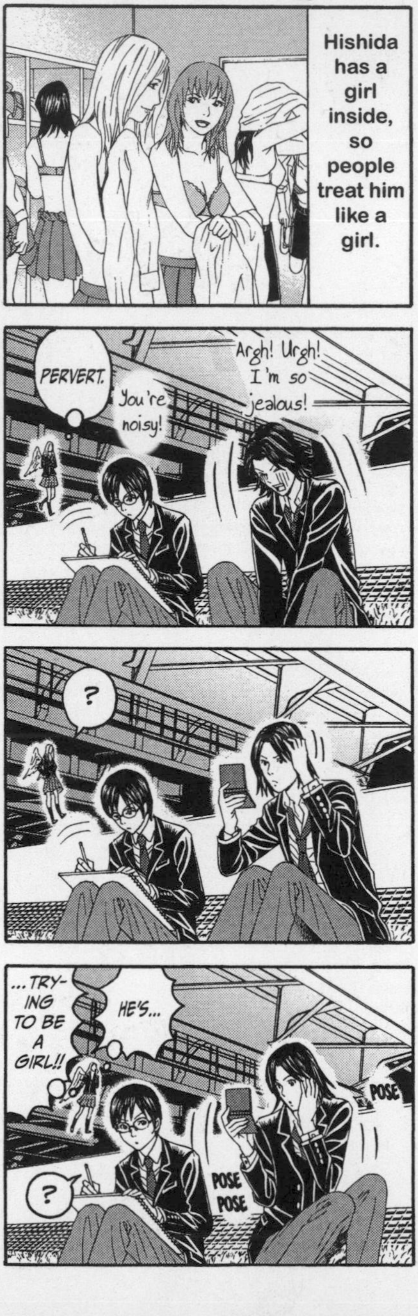
Hishida has a girl inside, so people treat him like a girl.
Argh! Urgh! I'm so jealous!
You're noisy!
PERVERT.
?
HE'S...
...TRYING TO BE A GIRL!!
POSE
POSE POSE
?

Sketch Cafe

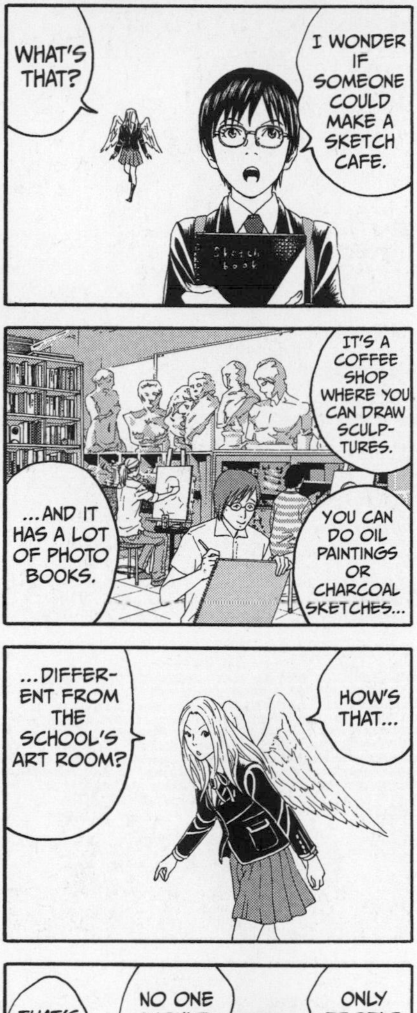
I WONDER IF SOMEONE COULD MAKE A SKETCH CAFE.
WHAT'S THAT?
Sketch book
IT'S A COFFEE SHOP WHERE YOU CAN DRAW SCULPTURES.
YOU CAN DO OIL PAINTINGS OR CHARCOAL SKETCHES...
...AND IT HAS A LOT OF PHOTO BOOKS.
HOW'S THAT...
...DIFFERENT FROM THE SCHOOL'S ART ROOM?
ONLY PEOPLE LIKE ME GO.
NO ONE WOULD LAUGH AT ME.
THAT'S SORT OF SAD...
Sketch book

Kotone's Fantasies

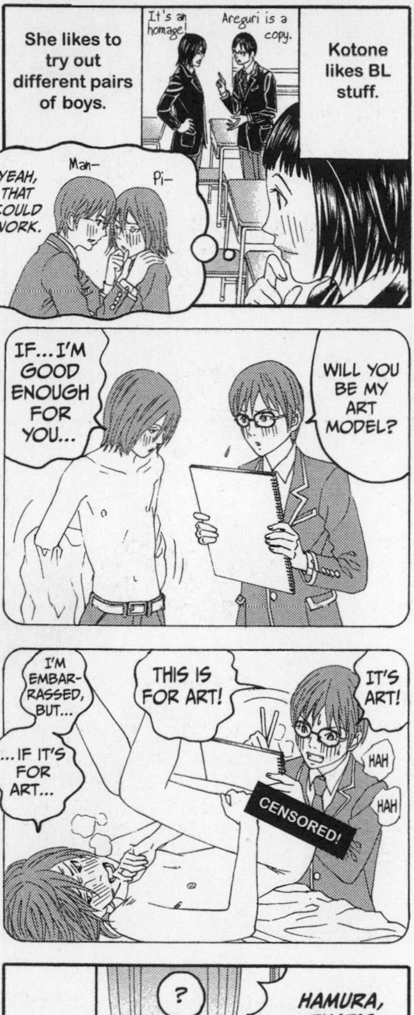
Kotone likes BL stuff.
Areguri is a copy.
It's an homage!
She likes to try out different pairs of boys.
Man-
Pi-
YEAH, THAT COULD WORK.
WILL YOU BE MY ART MODEL?
IF... I'M GOOD ENOUGH FOR YOU...
IT'S ART!
HAH
HAH
THIS IS FOR ART!
CENSORED!
I'M EMBARRASSED, BUT...
...IF IT'S FOR ART...
HAMURA, THAT'S GOING TOO FAR!!
?
Kotone's fantasies often get out of control.

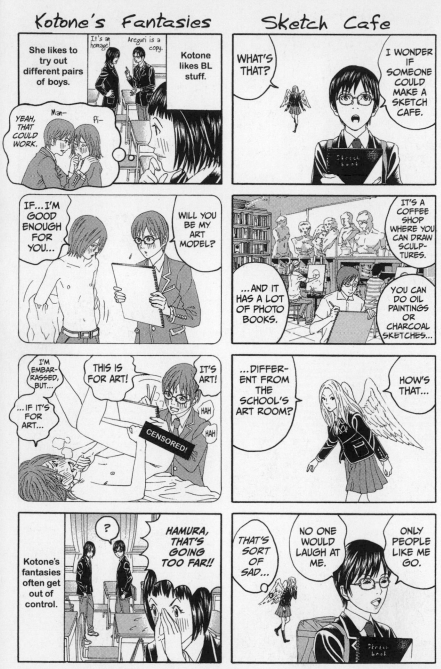

Ota's Hindsight

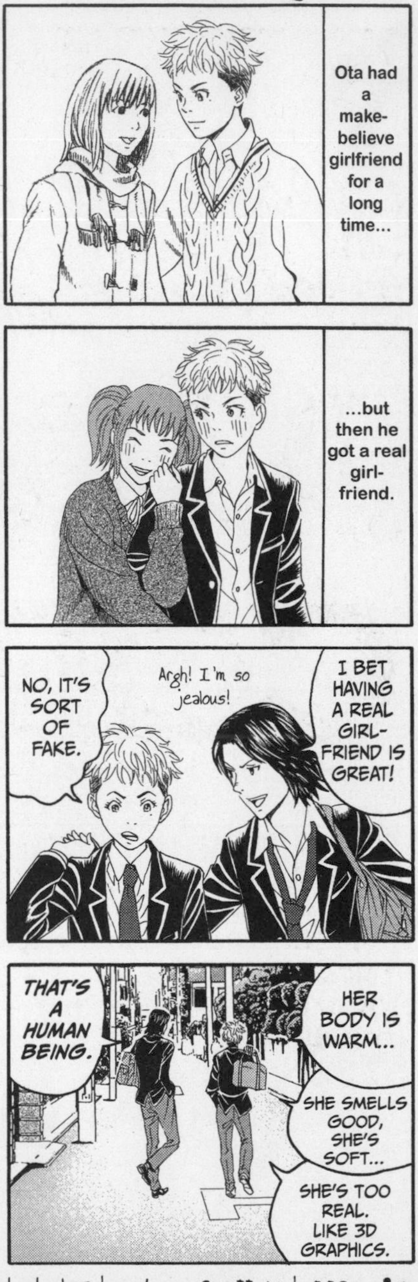
Ota had a make-believe girlfriend for a long time...
...but then he got a real girl-friend.
I BET HAVING A REAL GIRL-FRIEND IS GREAT!
Argh! I'm so jealous!
NO, IT'S SORT OF FAKE.
HER BODY IS WARM...
SHE SMELLS GOOD, SHE'S SOFT...
SHE'S TOO REAL. LIKE 3D GRAPHICS.
THAT'S A HUMAN BEING.

Manba's Observation

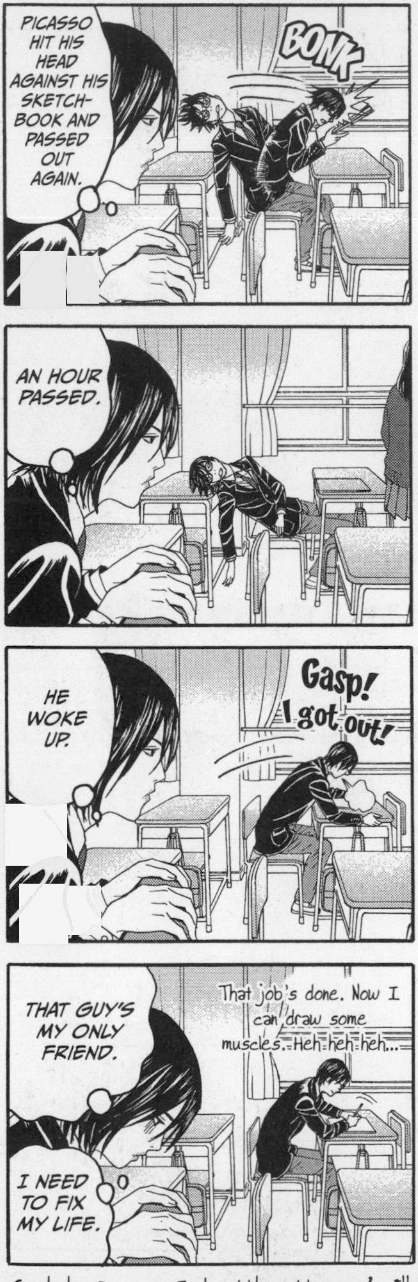
BONK
PICASSO HIT HIS HEAD AGAINST HIS SKETCH-BOOK AND PASSED OUT AGAIN.
AN HOUR PASSED.
Gasp! I got out!
HE WOKE UP.
That job's done. Now I can draw some muscles. Heh heh heh...
THAT GUY'S MY ONLY FRIEND.
I NEED TO FIX MY LIFE.

Genkaku Picasso Extra Hikari Hamura's Illustrated Tales_Jump SQ II, Vol. 003

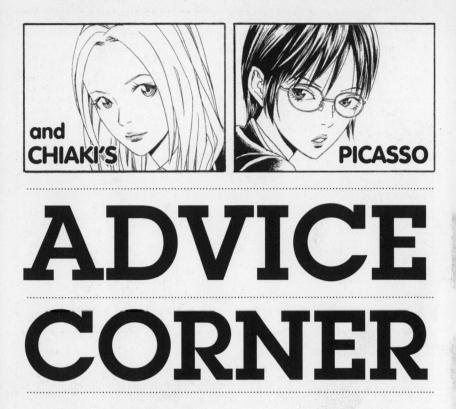

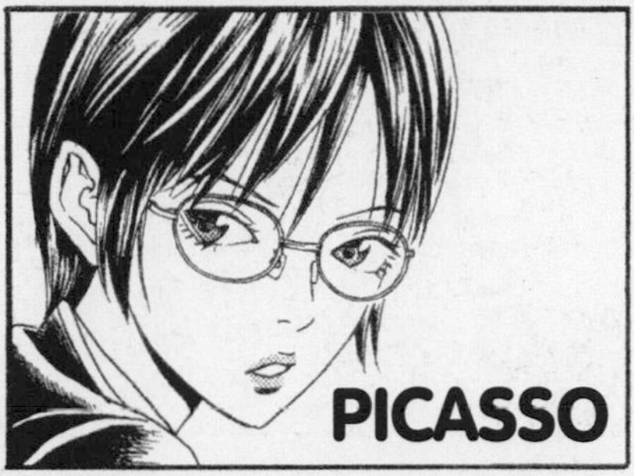
PICASSO

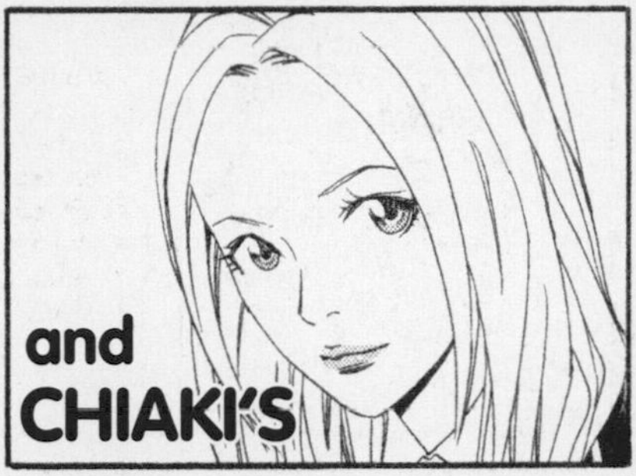
and
CHIAKI'S

ADVICE CORNER

Usamaru Sensei asked readers seeking advice to submit their worries to his blog, *Usagi's One-Man Club*. A lot of people responded! Picasso and Chiaki picked three. Here are their responses.

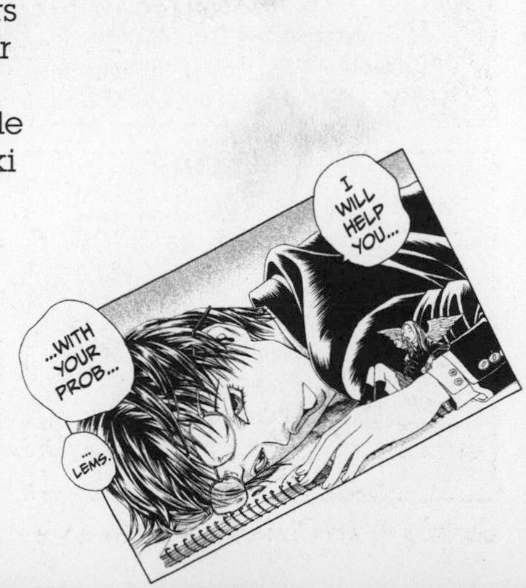
I WILL HELP YOU...
...WITH YOUR PROB...
...LEMS.

PROBLEM 1

Hello, Picasso and Chiaki. I'm always keeping an eye on your exploits, and I'd like to consult you about something. I can never do anything until it becomes absolutely necessary. I say, "Oh, I'll do it tomorrow," and then day after day passes. Life isn't long, and I know this moment will never come twice, but I can't fix myself. Is there anything I can do? The way things are now, I don't move unitl the very last minute, when I'm teetering on the edge. If you tell me I have a weak personality, I won't know what to say. Sorry to bother you with this...but I believe you can give me good advice on how to handle this! Please!!

—Okina

Chiaki: I knew it. What do you think about yourself when you draw up plans but then don't follow them?

Picasso: I hate myself and think maybe I'm worthless...and then I flee to my art.

Chiaki: When plans don't go well, you get down on yourself. I'm pretty good at taking action, but sometimes even when I think, "I gotta do that!" it's hard to find the motivation.

Picasso: Yeah!

Chiaki: So, supposing you have to study English, first take your English textbook and writing utensils, and put them on your desk, and then sit there.

Picasso: And if you still don't feel like doing it?

Chiaki: Just stay there a while.

Picasso: Huh? That's boring!

Chiaki: Yeah, because you're bored, you'll feel like opening up your textbook. The key, though, is not feeling like you need to really tackle it.

Picasso: Our first problem is... Oh, that's pretty easy.

Chiaki: You sure are confident.

Picasso: You just have to draw up a strict plan for each day! I always draw up a detailed plan before exams. Like studying English from five to six in the morning, and then math from eight to ten at night!

Chiaki: Do you really study that much? Even before exams you don't do anything but draw pictures. If you're really studying English from five to six in the morning, your grades should be better.

Picasso: Quiet! I just haven't quite been able to follow my plans!

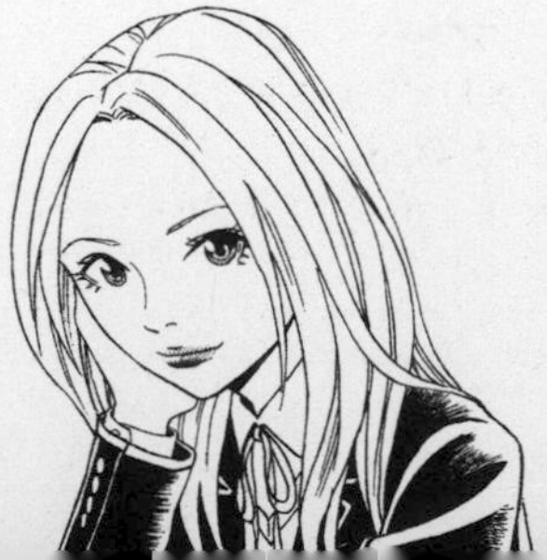

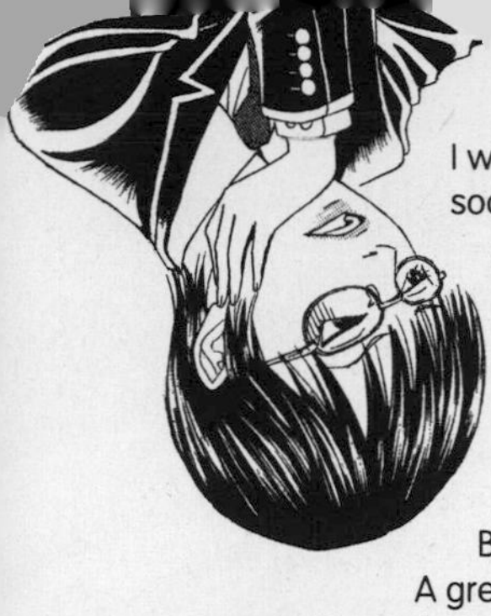

I wish I'd known that sooner!

Chiaki: Yeah. That's why my grades were never worse than yours.

Picasso: Sorry! But that's all right. A great artist doesn't need to study! Which isn't really true, but... [*mutter, mutter*]

Chiaki: Whatever. Even when it comes to things besides studying, just try getting ready to do whatever it is!

Picasso: Why's that?

Chiaki: When you do that, you feel too much pressure and want to quit.

Picasso: Oh, I can understand that.

Chiaki: So you start by just looking up one vocabulary word you don't know, and even though you're not really applying yourself, once you start, the next thing you know, you'll be surprised to find you're getting into it.

Picasso: And once you start getting into it, it isn't so hard to keep going. No fair!

PROBLEM 2

Picasso, please listen to my problem. I am deeply gloomy. I'm just a normal OL (office lady), but when I get home my life is so gloomy I can barely stand it. Have you ever heard of an OL who just sits crouching in a corner of her room, or uses a stethoscope and falls into raptures over the sound of her own heartbeat?! Have you ever heard of a 22-year-old who spends long holidays just doing that and sleeping, but then comes back wearing a satisfied expression as if to say "That was a pretty good holiday!" I sense something similar in falling into raptures while drawing muscles. Picasso, Chiaki, Suigiura (I'm a fan), what should I do to become an active and splendid woman? Please, tell me!

—Ayumi

Picasso: Well, I'm not active, so how should I know?! Besides...she likes Sugiura more than me. We should ask him. He sure is popular.

Chiaki: Uh-oh! Are you bummed out? (*laughs*)

Picasso: N-no! I'm not bummed out!

Picasso: Huh? Isn't that normal? Listening to your heart with a stethoscope is relaxing!

Chiaki: Uh...do you do that at home too?

Picasso: Yeah. Of course. And on my days off, when I'm not drawing, I count the number of stitches in the tatami mat. I'm always saying, "This kind doesn't have very many, heh heh..."

Chiaki: You're the wrong person to ask about this. Ms. Ayumi wants to become active!

active... Well, what about looking for some kind of club, or forming her own, like a stethoscope club or a napping club, and getting together with people who have the same interests?

Chiaki: Oh, that might be good! Talking with people who have the same interests is fun, and you'd have to go out, so it would be active.

Sugiura: Yeah. Even if you didn't talk much, there would still be a sense of connectedness!

Picasso: Then I wanna join a stethoscope club! We can listen to each other's hearts!

Chiaki: You're a perv.

Sugiura: I wanna join a napping club. Wouldn't it be neat if everyone took a nap in Yoyogi Park?

Chiaki: Oh, that's good! When I imagine the stethoscope club, though, I'm not so sure.

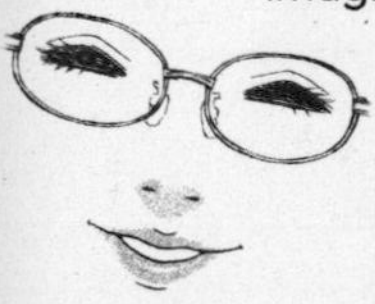

Picasso: Heh heh heh heh. (*imagining*)

Chiaki: Guys like Picasso would show up, so be careful, Ayumi!

Chiaki: Fine then. Let's bring in Sugiura.

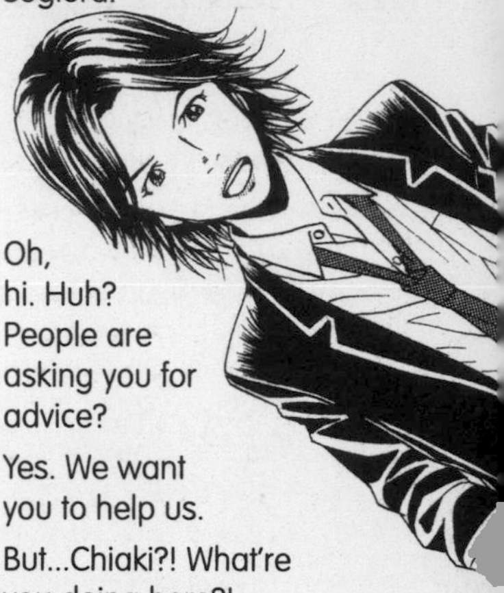

Sugiura: Oh, hi. Huh? People are asking you for advice?

Chiaki: Yes. We want you to help us.

Sugiura: But...Chiaki?! What're you doing here?!

Chiaki: Well, this isn't the main story, so don't worry about little details like that!

Picasso: Th-that's right!

Sugiura: R-really?!

Chiaki: Here, read Ms. Ayumi's problem.

Sugiura: Hmm... It seems like she's satisfied with the way things are. Like she's enjoying herself.

Chiaki: I suppose so.

Sugiura: But she wants to be more

PROBLEM 3

Hello, Picasso and Chiaki! There's someone I like. She's really pretty, so if I tell her how I feel, she'll definitely turn me down. I just date her in my imagination. What should I do?

—Debuzafatto

Chiaki: It's best to hear girls' opinions on this, so Akane and Kotone and I will answer.

Picasso: Huh?! Don't I get to do anything?

Chiaki: Nope. But actually you haven't been any good before now either. (*laughs*)

Picasso: Sorry! Hmph. That's all right. I don't want to help people outside the main story! I'll just draw some muscles.

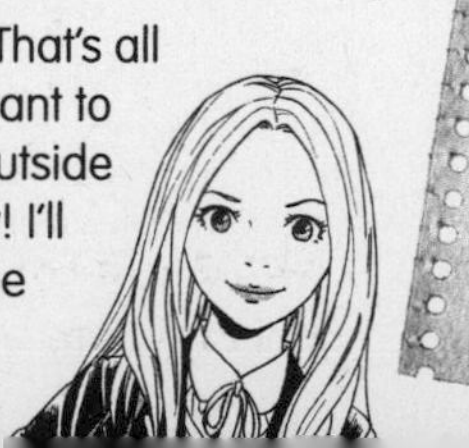

Akane: You're blushing! How cute!

Chiaki: Some girls do just fall for looks, but most girls put more emphasis on personality or attitude than external appearance.

Akane: Like the way Picasso draws every day so he can become an artist. And he may be short, but he can also be very understanding.

Chiaki: I think you may be the only one who thinks Picasso's understanding, but his dedication to art is impressive.

Kotone: Do you think Debuzafatto really isn't cool?

Akane: Come to think of it, he doesn't say.

Chiaki: Yeah, but given his problem... Anyway, whether he's cool or not, you always have a chance if you work on who you are inside. So don't just chase after her, work on yourself as well!

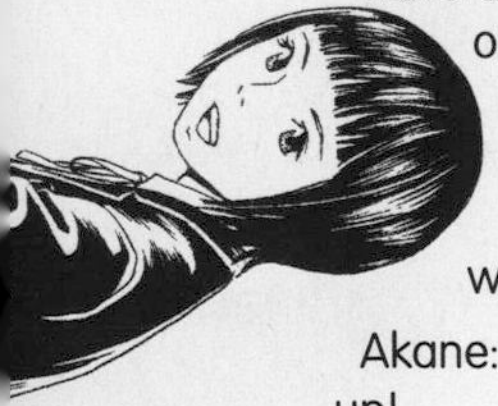

Akane: Nice way to sum it up!

Picasso: Can I come back now?

Chiaki: Now that Picasso's back, goodbye to all our readers! Be polite, Picasso.

Picasso: Bye!

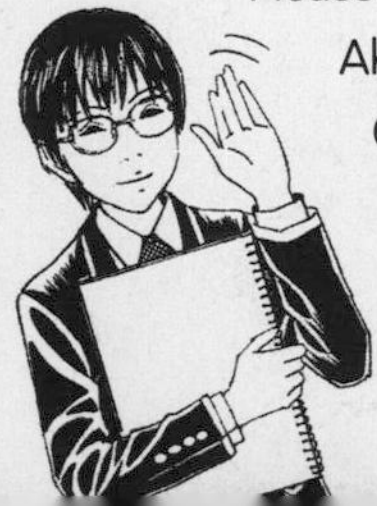

Akane: How cute!

Chiaki & Kotone: I just don't get it...

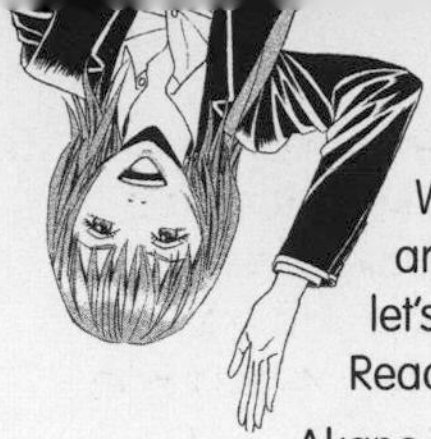

Chiaki: Whatever. While Picasso's playing around with muscles, let's have some girl talk! Ready, Akane? Kotone?

Akane: Sure!

Kotone: Whoa! It's Chiaki!

Chiaki: It's been so long since I saw you two. I never get to talk to you in the main story. This is great!

Akane: I read the problem, but it's not like pretty girls won't go out with anyone who isn't particularly cool, you know.

Kotone: That's right.

Chiaki: You two are examples of that.

Akane: Kotone's cute, but her boyfriend is Manba! Ha ha!

Kotone: That's right.

Chiaki: Yeah, Picasso's a shorty. It's strange how no one likes Sugiura.

Akane: In my work as a model, sometimes I work with male models. A lot of the time, talking to good-looking guys can actually be really boring.

Chiaki: They get a lot of girls just by being cool, so I suppose many of them are just superficial.

Kotone: I don't like guys with bad hygiene, of course, but I'm more impressed by guys who are dedicated to something or truly kind than guys who are just good-looking.

Akane: So Manba must be like that.

Kotone: Um...I guess...

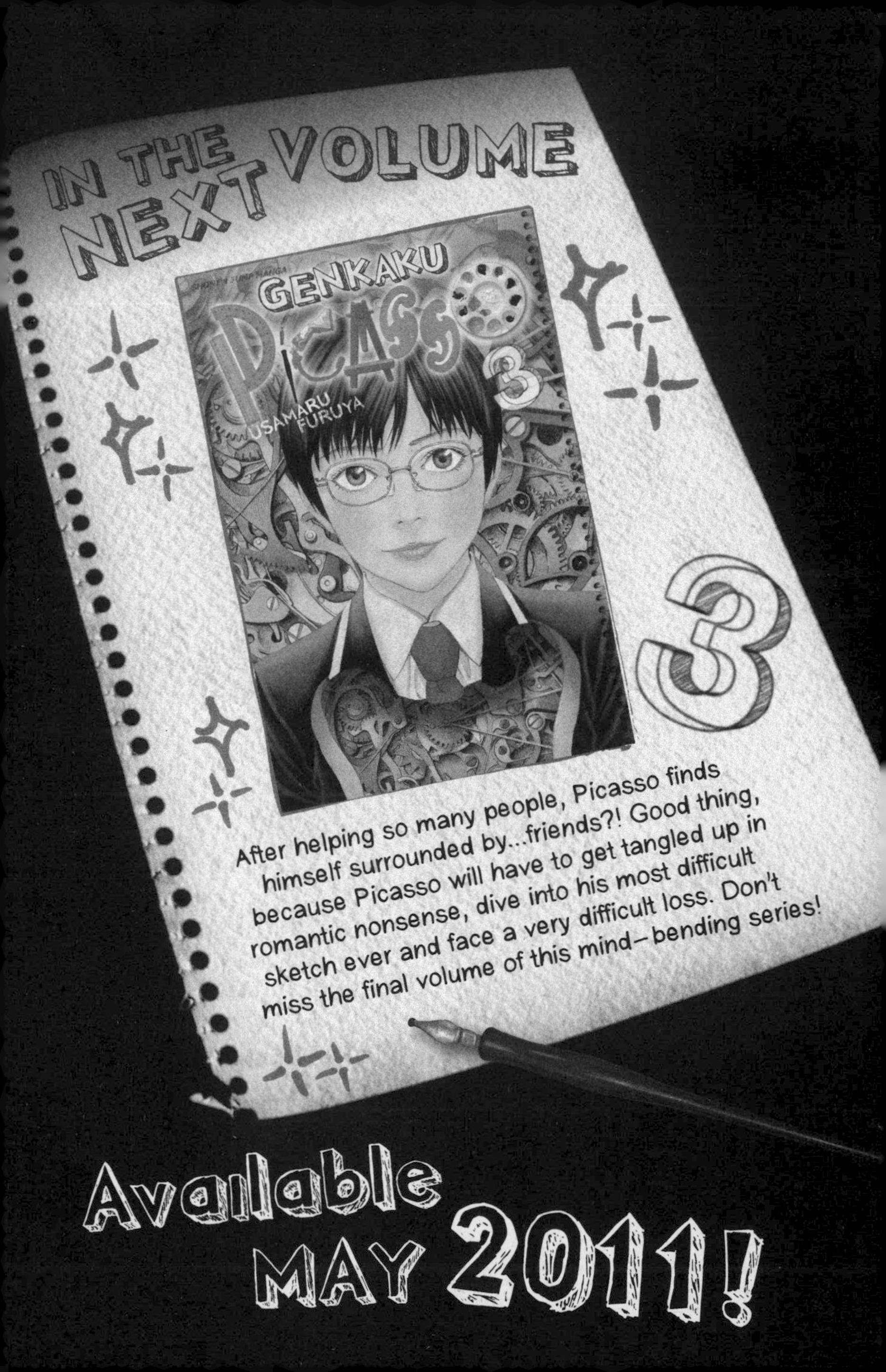
IN THE NEXT VOLUME
GENKAKU
PICASSO
3
USAMARU FURUYA
3
After helping so many people, Picasso finds himself surrounded by...friends?! Good thing, because Picasso will have to get tangled up in romantic nonsense, dive into his most difficult sketch ever and face a very difficult loss. Don't miss the final volume of this mind-bending series!
Available MAY 2011!

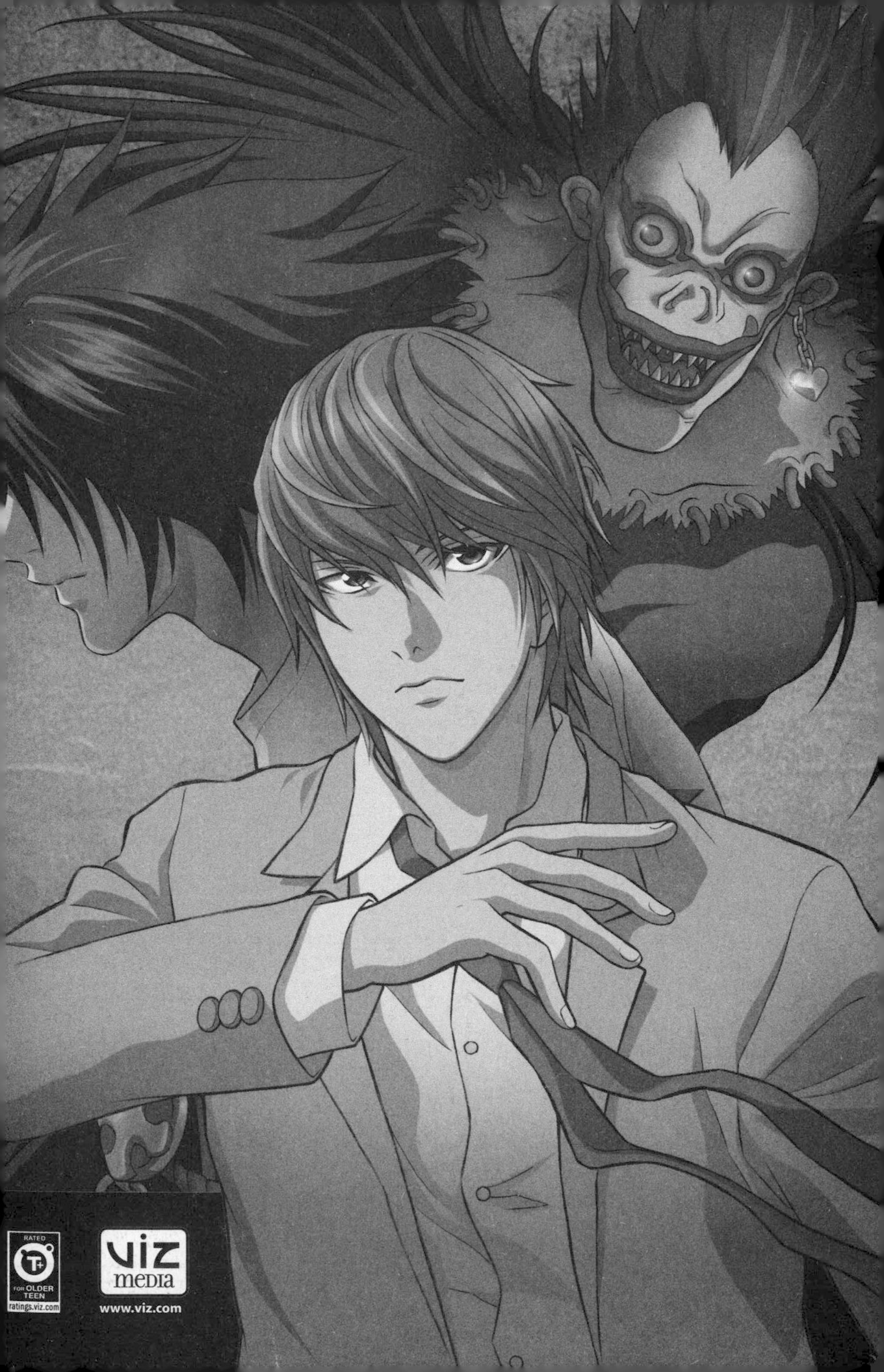
RATED
T+
FOR OLDER TEEN
ratings.viz.com
VIZ media
www.viz.com

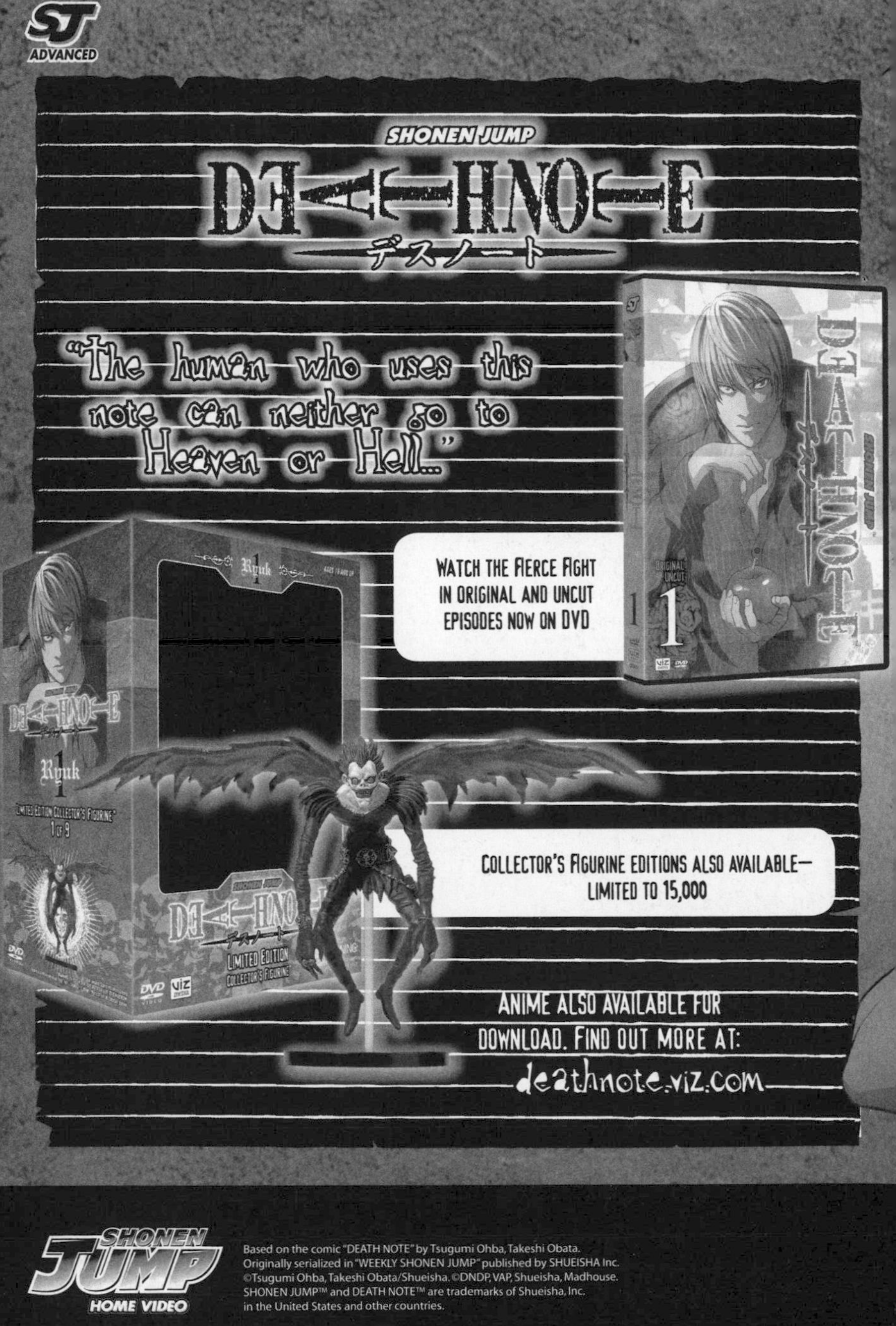
SJ ADVANCED
SHONEN JUMP
DEATH NOTE
デスノート
"The human who uses this note can neither go to Heaven or Hell..."
WATCH THE FIERCE FIGHT IN ORIGINAL AND UNCUT EPISODES NOW ON DVD
ORIGINAL UNCUT
1
Ryuk
LIMITED EDITION COLLECTOR'S FIGURINE
1 OF 9
LIMITED EDITION COLLECTOR'S FIGURINE
COLLECTOR'S FIGURINE EDITIONS ALSO AVAILABLE—LIMITED TO 15,000
ANIME ALSO AVAILABLE FOR DOWNLOAD. FIND OUT MORE AT:
deathnote.viz.com
SHONEN JUMP HOME VIDEO

WRONG WAY

This is the last page!

GENKAKU PICASSO has been printed in the original Japanese format in order to preserve the orientation of the original artwork.

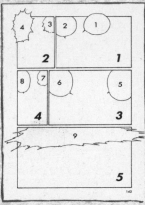

← Follow the action this way.

Please turn it around and begin reading from right to left. Unlike English, Japanese is read right to left, so Japanese comics are read in reverse order from the way English comics are typically read.

Have fun with it!